NE

DICTIONARY

ENGLISH - TAGALOG
TAGALOG - ENGLISH

Contain The All Important Words Phrases And Idioms Of The English Living Language And The New Pilipino Terms

Hinango Sa Mga Wikang Ingles, Kastila, Tagalog - Visaya, Ilongo, Cebuano, Ilocano, Bikol, Pampango At Sa Mga Wikang Pandaigdig.

Prepared By:

Maria Rosario Enriquez
M. Jacobo Enriquez

MARREN PUBLISHING HOUSE, INC.
1157 Quezon Ave., Quezon City

2000 EDITION

NEW HANDY WEBSTER'S DICTIONARY

ENGLISH - TAGALOG
TAGALOG - ENGLISH

PREFACE

The author has compiled in this ENGLISH-TAGALOG TAGALOG-ENGLISH POCKET DICTIONARY hundreds and hundreds of the most common Pilipino words based on fundamental word lists compiled by educators from well-known universities in the Philippines, as well as words taken from the Institute of National Language vocabulary and from many linguists and linguistic sources. This rich vocabulary contains words used in everyday life. It is very practical. The English equivalents have been chosen for their accuracy and simplicity in meaning as used in everyday conversations. Pilipino equivalents which have been derived from Spanish or English words or from the vernaculars, have been incorporated together with their colloquialism to enrich the Pilipino Language of today.

The orthography of Filipino words is in conformity with the rules of the official grammar published by the Institute of National Language of the Department of Education.

At the back of this new vocabulary can be found a list of common everyday terms, scientific and geographic terms, business terms, social and physical science terms, as well as terms and expressions having reference to teaching and government.

The Publisher

CONTENTS:

ABBREVIATONS USED

adj.—Adjective—Pang-uri

adv.—Adverb—Pang-abay

art.—Article—Pantukoy

conj.—Conjunction—Pangatníg

interj.—Interjection—Pandamdám

n.—Noun—Pangngalan

prep.—Preposition—Pang-ukol

pron.—Pronoun—Panghalíp

rw.—Root Word—Salitang Ugat

v.—Verb—Pandiwà

abandon, v. to leave permanently. Pabayaan.

abolish, v. to annul. Rebokahin; alisin; pawiin.

abolition, n. annulment. Pagpawi; pag-aalis.

abominable, adj. detestable. Abominable; kasuklam-suklam.

aborigines, n. first inhabitants. Mga unang tao o mamamayan.

abort, v. to miscarry. Magaborto; makunan.

abortive, adj. unsuccessful. Wala pa sa panahon.

abounding, adj. plentiful. Abundante; sagana.

above, adv. & prep. in a higher place than. Ariba; sa itaas; sa ibabaw.

abrasion, n. a rubbing off. Raspa; gasgas; galos; pagkakatkat.

abrasive, adj. with abrasion. Maligasgas.

abridge, v. to shorten. Paikliin; putulin.

abridgment, n. shortened form. Kontraksiyon; pagpapaikli; pagputol.

abroad, adv. out of the country. Sa labas ng bayan o ng bansa.

abrogate, v. to annul; render valueless. Pawalang-bisa.

abrupt, adj. suddenly terminating. Bigla; madalian.

abscess, n. tumor with pus. Sugat na may nana; tumor.

abscission, n. cutting off. Pagputol; pagkaputol; paghinto.

abscond, v. to hide away. Eskapo; tumalilis; magtanan.

absence, n. state of being away. Di-pagsipot; pagliban; pagkawala; wala.

absent, adj. not present. Ausente; wala; hindi kaharap.

absent-minded, adj. preoccupied. Limut-limot; malilimutin.

absolute, adj. unlimited. Absoluto; walang takda.

absolution, n. pardon. Absolusiyon; pardon; patawad; kapatawaran sa pagkakasala.

absolve, v. to free from. Absuwelto; pawalang-sala.

absorb, v. to swallow; to assimilate. Sipsipin; lagumin.

absorption, n. sucking up; taking in. Pagsipsip; paglagom.

abstain, v. to refrain. Pigilin ang sarili

abstinence, n. self-restraint. Abstinensiya; pagbabawal sa sarili; pagpipigil sa sarili.

abstract, n. a summary of. Ekstrakto; buod; lagom.

absurd, adj. ridiculous; without reason. Baligho; walang katuwiran.

abundance, n. plenty; fullness. Abundansiya; kasaganaan.

abundant, adj. plentiful. Abundante; sagana.

abuse, v. to misuse; to overdo Abusuhin; magmalabis.

abuse, n. ill treatment. Abuso; pagmamalabis.

abysmal, adj. bottomless; without end. Walang hanggan; walang katapusan.

academical, adj. pertaining to an academy. Akademiko; ukol sa kolehiyo o pamantasan.

academic year, n. school year. Taong akademiko; isang taong kurso.

academy, n. a private college or institution. Paaralan; kolehiyo; akademya.

accede, v. to comply with. Sumang-ayon; pumayag.

accelerate, v. to hasten; to speed up. Bilisan; pabilisin.

accentuate, v. to mark with stress. Tuldikan; lagyan ng mga tuldik.

accept, v. to receive. Akseptahin; tanggapin.

acceptance, n. reception. Pagtanggap.

access, n. admission; means of approach. Akseso; daan; paraan ng pagpasok.

accessible, adj. approachable; within reach. Mararaanan; mararating.

accident, n. mishap. Aksidente; sakuna; pangyayaring di-sinasadya.

accidental, adj. by chance. Aksidental; di-sinasadya.

acclaim, v. to applaud. Purihin; bigyang-dangal.

acclamation, n. applause. Aklamasiyon; pabigkas at sabayang paghahalal ng papa.

acclamatory, adj. with approval. Kapuripuri.

acclimated, adj. get used to. Aklimatado; sanay sa klima o panahon.

accommodate, v. to oblige; to do a favor. Akomodado; magbigay; pagbigyan.

accompaniment, n. something added in company. Akompaniyamento; pagsaliw; pagsabay.

accompany, v. to go with. Akompaniyahan; sabayan; saliwan.

accomplice, n. an associate or partner in crime. Kasangkot; kasabuwat; kasapakat.

accomplish, v. to complete. Nakumpleto; gawin; tupdin; tapusin.

accomplishment, n. attainment. Katuparan o pagkatapos ng isang gawain.

accord, n. harmony. Akuwerdo; pagkakasundo; pagkakaisa.

according, adv. in conformance with. Segun; ayon sa; ayon kay.

accost, v. speak to; to hold. Kausapin; pigilin at kausapin.

account, n. computation. Kuwenta; utang.

account, v. to explain. Magkuwenta; isulit.

accountable, adj. answerable. Responsable; may pananagutan.

accountant, n. a bookkeeper. Kontador publiko; akawntan; bukkiper.

accredit, v. attribute to. Bigyang-halaga; pahalagahan.

accrue, v. to increase. Matipon; maragdagan.

accumulate, v. to amass. Akumulado; dumami.

accuracy, n. exactness. Katumpakan; kawastuan.

accurate, adj. correct. Eksakto; wasto; tumpak.

accursed, adj. doomed. Kasumpa-sumpa.

accusable, adj. liable to accusation. Akusable; maaaring pagbintangan; kabintangbintang.

accusation, n. blame; charge. Akusasiyon; bintang.

accuse, v. to blame; to charge. Akusahan; pagbintangan; paratangan.

accustom, v. being familiar with. Nagawi; hiratihin.

ache, n. pain. Dolor; sakit.

achieve, v. to accomplish. Isagawa; tamuhin.

achievement, n. accomplishment. Ang nagawa; layuning natupad.

acid, adj. sour. Maagriyo; maasim.

acidity, n. sourness. Kaasiman.

acknowledge, v. to admit; to accept. Kilalanin; aminin.

acknowledgment, n. recognition. Pagkilala; pag-amin.

acme, n. highest point. Rurok; kaitaasan.
acne, n. pimple. Isang uri ng sakit sa balat; tagihawat.
acolyte, n. a novice. Akolito; sakristan.
acquaint, v. to inform; to familiarize. Ipaalam; ipakilala.
acquaintance, n. a person one know. Konosido; kakilala.
acquaintanceship, n. intimacy; meeting. Konosimyento; pagkikilala.
acquiesce, v. to agree; to consent. Kumumporme; sumang-ayon; pumayag.
acquire, v. to obtain. Matamo; makuha.
acquit, v. to set free. Pawalang-sala.
acrid, adj. bitter; pungent. Mapakla; maaskad.
acrimonious, adj. sarcastic Sarkastiko; nakauuyam; nakatutuya.
acrobat, n. circus performer. Akrobat; sirkero.
across, adv. from side to side; crosswise. Nakahalang; saibayo; sa pagtawid.
act, v. to do; to move. Gumanap; isagawa; gawin; kumilos.
act, n. an exertion of energy or force; deed. Aksiyon; kilos; gawa.
activate, v. to render active. Paganapin; pakilusin; pagalawin.
active, adj. busy. Aktibo; masigla; magaslaw.
acting, n. process of doing. Akting; arte.
activity, n. movement; work. Aktibidades; gawain.
actor, n. one who acts, esp. a male. Aktor; artistang lalaki.
actress, n. a female who acts Artistang babae; aktres.
acumen, n. mental acuteness. Katalasan ng pakiramdam.
acute, adj. intense; penetrating. Matalim; matindi; masidhi.
adage, n. proverb. Adahiyo; kasabihan.
Adam, n. first man on earth. Adan; unang nilikhang lalaki.
adapt, v. to fit; to base on. Iakma; iangkop; ibagay.
add, v. unite in one sum. Sumahin; pagsamahin; dagdagan.
addicted, adj. got used to. Sugapa; may malaking hilig sa.
addition, n. the act or process of adding or uniting. Adisiyon; pagdadagdag; pagsasama-sama.
additional, adj. added. Adisyonal; karagdagan.
addle, adj. confused; muddled. Lito; gulo.
address, v. to speak to. Iukol; kausapin; magsalita.
address, n. direction. Adres; direksiyon; bilang at daan ng tirahan.
adequate, adj. sufficient; enough. Adekuwado; sapat; husto.
adhere, v. to stick fast. Dumikit; sumunod.
adherent, adj. sticky. Madikit.
adhesion, n. a close union. Adhesiyon; pagdikit.
adhesive, adj. tenacious; sticky. Madikit; naninikit.
adieu, interj. goodby; so long. Adiyos; paalam.
adjacent, adj. near; close. Kalapit; kanugnog.
adjective, n. word qualifying. Adhektibo; pang-uri.
adjoin, v. to join; put together. Pagsudlungin; pagkabitin.
adjoining, adj. close to; neighboring. Karatig; kanugnog.

adjourn, v. to suspend; to finish. Tapusin; itindig.

adjudge, v. to sentence. Disisyunan; hatulan.

adjudicate, v. to sentence according to law. Hatulan ayon sa batas.

adjunct, n. an addition to. Isang karagdagang di-lubhang mahalaga.

adjust, v. to conform to. Ibagay; iakma; ayusin.

administer, v. to manage. Administrahan; pangasiwaan.

administration, n. conduct. Pangangasiwa; administrasyon.

admirable, adj. praiseworthy. Admirable; kahanga-hanga.

admiration, n. esteem; approval. Admirasiyon; paghanga.

admire, v. regard with esteem. Hangaan; humanga.

admirer, n. one who admires. Tagahanga.

admission, n. grant entrance. Admisiyon; pagtanggap.

admit, v. allow to enter. Admitihin; tanggapin.

admixture, n. a mixing. Pagkakahalu-halo.

admonition, n. advice; counsel. Konseho; abiso; paalaala.

adopt, v. to take as one's own. Adaptahin; ampunin.

adopter, n. one who adopts. Tagapag-ampon.

adorable, adj. worthy of esteem. Adorable; karapat-dapat sa pagsamba.

adoration, n. esteem; worship. Adorasyon; pagsamba.

adore, v. to worship. Sumamba; sambahin.

adorn, v. to decorate. Adornohan; palamutihan; gayakan.

adornment, n. embellishment. Adorno; gayak; palamuti.

adrift, adj. floating. Lulutang-lutang.

adroit, adj. skillful. Sanay; may kaya; mapanlikha.

adulation, n. flattery. Adulasiyon; labis na papuri.

adult, adj. full grown; mature; legally of age. Adulto; may sapat na gulang.

adulterated, adj. debased; impure. Adulterado; may halo.

adulterer, n. one who commits adultery. Adultero; adultera; nakikiapid.

adultery, n. unfaithfulness to spouse. Adulteriya; pakikigulo; pakikiapid.

advance, v. to move forward. Ipagpauna; sumulong; isulong.

advancement, n. promotion. Pagtaas; pagsulong.

advantage, n. benefit. Bentahe; kabutihan; kalamangan.

advent, n. the coming of. Pagdating.

adventure, n. a remarkable occurrence. Abentura; pakikipagsapalaran.

adventurer, n. one who takes risks. Abenturero; taong nakikipagsapalaran.

adverb, n. modifying word. Pang-abay.

adverbial, adj. pertaining to an adverb. Ukol sa pang-abay.

adversary, n. opponent. Adbersaryo; kalaban; katunggali.

adverse, adj. contrary to; opposite of. Di ka sang-ayon; kasalungat.

advertise, v. to announce publicly. Ianunsiyo; ipabatid sa madla.

advice, n. counsel given; suggestion. Konseho; payo.

advise, v. to counsel. Patalastasan; pagpayuhan.

adviser, n. one who gives counsel. Konsehero; taga-payo.

advocate, v. to plead in favor. Imungkahi; itagubilin.

aerial, adj. of the air; about the air. Ukol sa papawirin.

affable, adj. courteous; gracious. Kaiga-igaya; kawili-wiling kausapin.

affect, v. produce an effect or change. Magkabisa.

affection, n. love; goodwill. Amor; pagmamahal; pag-ibig.

again, adv. once more; repeated. Muli; uli.

against, prep. in an opposite direction. Kontra; nakasandal; laban.

age, n. lifetime of a person. Gulang; idad.

aged, adj. old; very matured. Matanda; magulang.

agency, n. commercial or government office. Ahensiya; sangay.

agenda, n. a list of items to do. Talaan ng mga gawain; programa, adyenda.

agent, n. representative. Kinatawan; representante; ahente.

aggrandize, v. make greater in scope. Magpalawak ng kapangyarihan.

aggravate, v. to make serious. Pabigatin; palubhain.

aggressive, adj. bellicose; first to move. Agresibo; masugid; malakas ang loob.

Agnus Dei, n. a prayer in mass said before the Holy Communion; a medal, or frequently a cake of pax, consecrated by the Pope, stamped with the figure of a lamb supporting the banner of the cross. Kordero ng Diyos; ang panalangin sa misa bago makinabang; mga bilog na pagkit na may larawan ng tupa.

agitate, v. to cause concern. Makabagabag: makabalisa.

agonize, v. to suffer violently Maghirap; magdusa.

agrarian, adj. relating to land. Agraryo; ukol sa lupa.

agree, v. consent. Pumayag; sumang-ayon.

agreement, n. conformity; settlement. Pinagkayarian; kasunduan.

agricultural, adj. pertaining to agriculture. Agrikultural; hinggil sa pagsasaka.

aground, adv. stranded. Barado; sadsad.

ague, n. fever chills. Lagnat na pabugsu-bugso.

ahead, adv. in advance. Sa harap; nauuna.

aid, n. help; support. Katulong; tulong.

aid, v. to help. Tumulong.

ailment, n. sickness. Karamdaman.

aim, n. objective. Puntirya; pakay; layunin.

aimless, adj. without purpose. Walang layunin.

air, n. the earth's atmosphere. Hangin; himpapawid.

air, v. expose to the air. Pahanginan.

aisle, n. a passageway giving access, as in the seats in a church. Maliit na daan; daang nasa pagitan ng hanay ng mga upuan.

ajar, adv. & adj. partly open. Nakapuwang; bukas ng bahagya.

alarm, n. warning of danger. Alarma; pagibik; hudyat.

alarming, adj. calculated to rouse alarm. Nakatatakot; nakababakla.

alcohol, n. distilled liquid. Alkohol.

alcoholic, adj. an addicted drunk; drunkard. Alkoholiko; lasenggo.

alert, adj. ever ready. Listo; laging handa; mabilis.

alias, n. an assumed name. Alyas; balatkayong pangalan.

alibi, n. excuse. Dahilan; alibay.

alien, n. a foreigner. Estranghero; dayuhan.

alight, v. to dismount. Dumapo; manaog; pumanaog; bumaba.

align, v. to form into a line. Humanay; pumila; humilera.

alike, adj. similar. Magkahawig; magkatulad.

alive, adj. existent. Maliksi; buhay.

all, adj. the whole quantity or number of. Todo; lahat.

alleluia, interj. praise ye the Lord. Aleluya; purihin ang Diyos.

all powerful, adj. omnipotent. Makapangyarihan sa lahat.

All-Saints' Day, n. a church festival held on November 1. Araw ng mga Patay.

All-Souls' Day, n. a church festival held on November 2nd, when prayers are offered for the dead. Araw ng mga Kaluluwa; Nob. 2.

allay, v. pacify; calm. Pahupain; payapain.

allegation, n. an assertion or plea. Alegasiyon, paratang.

alleviate, v. make easier; lessen. Pagaanin; lunasan.

alley, n. narrow passage. Maliit na daan; kalyehon

allied, adj. joined together by compact or treaty. Aliyado; magkakampi.

alligator, n. a large lizard-like reptile, similar to the crocodile. Buwaya.

allot, v. to apportion; to set apart. Ilaan; iukol; pagayaw-ayawin.

allow, v. permit. Payagan; pahintulutan.

allowance, n. stated quantity; share or allotment. Rasyon; panggastos.

allude, v. refer casually or indirectly. Tukuyin; banggitin.

alms, n. gifts of charity. Limos.

alone, adj. single; solitary. Solo; nag-iisa.

along, adv. by the side of. Paayon ng; sa buong hinabahaba.

aloof, adv. & adj. withdrawn; unsympathetic. Malayo; walang malasakit.

aloud, adv. audibly. Malakas na tinig.

also, adv. in addition; too. Gayon din; din; rin.

altar, n. communion table. Dambana; altar.

alter, v. to change. Alterahin; baguhin; bumago.

alternate, n. act of turns; substitute. Kapalit; pamalit; sustitusiyon.

alternative, n. a choice. Alternatibo; pagkakataong makapili sa dalawang bagay; mapamimilian; alternatibo.

although, conj. in spite of the fact that; Bagaman; kahit na.

altitude, n. height. Altura; taas.

altogether, adv. entirely. Buo; ganap.

always, adv. throughout; all time. Siyempre; lagi; palagi.

am, v. first person of verb *be* Ay.

amateur, n. a person who does something poorly. Amatyur.

amaze, v. to astonish. Pahangain; gulatin; magtaka.
amazement, n. surprise. Pagkagulat; pagtataka.
ambassador, n. a diplomat. Embahador; sugo.
ambition, n. desire to excel. Ambisiyon; lunggati; hangarin.
ambitious, adj. aspiring. Ambisiyoso; mápaglunggati; mapaghangad.
ambulance, n. a vehicle for carrying the sick or wounded. Ambulansiya.
ambush, v. attack unexpectedly from a hidden position. Tambangan; harangin.
ambush, n. an act of attacking unexpectedly. Ambus; harang.
amend, v. make better. Amendahin; korihen; ituwid; susugan.
amend, n. alteration. Susog.
amenda, n. recompense. Reparasiyon; bayad-pinsala.
amiable, adj. pleasing; friendly. Amable; kaibig-ibig.
amidst, prep. in the middle. Sa gitna ng.
amity, n. friendly relations. Amistad; pagkakaibigan.
ammunition, n. loading for firearms. Munisyon.
among, prep. with or by the whole of. Sa gitna ng; sa hanay.
amount, n. value or sum. Kabuuan; halaga.
amount, v. reach in quantity or degree. Maghahalaga; aabot.
ample, adj. plentiful; sufficient. Sagana.
amplifier, n. a device for increasing the amplitude of electrical impulses. Amplikador; amplipayer.
amplify, v. enlarge. Palawakin; punan.
amputate, v. to cut off. Ampyutahan; putulin!
amputation, n. a cutting off. Amputasiyon; pagputol.
amuse, v. entertain; divert. Aliwin; maglibang.
amusing, adj. entertaining. Nakaaaliw; nakatutuwa; nakalilibang.
amusement, n. a diversion. Dibersiyon; aliwan; libangan.
an, art. a word used before a vowel. Uno; una, isa.
analogy, n. resemblance. Analohiya; relasiyon; pagkakahawig; pagkakaugnay.
analysis, n. determination of causes from results. Pagsusuri; analisis.
analyze, v. solve by analysis. Analisahin; suriin.
anarchist, n. insurrectionist. Anarkista; manggugulo sa bayan.
ancestor, n. a progenitor. Abuwelo; abuwela; ninuno.
anchor, n. an instrument for holding a vessel. Angkla.
anchor, v. fix firmly in place. Pumundo; dumadaong.
anchorite, n. a recluse; a monk. Ermitanyo.
ancient, adj. very old. Antigo; matanda; luma.
and, conj. a word that connects. At.
anecdote, n. short narration. Anekdota.
anemia, n. deficiency in blood. Anemya; kakulangan sa dugo.
anemic, adj. weak; not strong. Anemiko; putlain; kulang sa dugo.
anesthesia, n. drug that induces insensibility. Pampamanhid; anistesiya.
anesthetic, adj. insensitive. Nagpapamanhid.

angel, n. an attendant of God, esp. a messenger. Anghel.

angel, (guardian), n. an angel that guards a person. Anghel na tagatanod.

angelus, n. a solemn devotion in memory of the incarnation. Orasyon.

anger, n. resentment. Galit; poot.

anger, v. excite to anger. Nagproboka; galitin.

angle, n. where two lines meet. Salikop; anggulo.

angrily, adv. in an angry manner. Pagalit; padabog.

angry, adj. feeling of anger; tempestuous. Galit.

anguish, n. great pain. Hapis; dalamhati.

animal, n. living things in the animal kingdom. Animal; hayop.

animate, v. give life to. Pasiglahin; bigyang-buhay.

animated, adj. having life; lively. Animado; maybuhay; buhay; masigla.

ankle, n. the joint connecting the foot with the leg. Bukung-bukong.

annex, n. supplement. Adisiyon; kaugnay; sangay.

annex, v. to attach at the end; affix. Isanib; iugnay.

annihilate, v. to destroy. Lipulin.

annihilation. n. destruction; ruin. Pagkalipol.

anniversary, n. the celebration of such a date. Anibersaryo; kaarawan.

announce, v. give notice. Ipatalastas; ibabala; ipahayag.

announcement, n. declaration; a formal notice. Anunsiyo; patalastas; paunawa.

annoy. v. irk and harass; to molest. Yamutin; buwisitin; gambalain.

annual, adj. occurring or returning once a year. Taunan.

annul, v. to invalidate. Pawalang-saysay; pawalang-bisa.

annunciation, n. the announcement by Gabriel to Mary that She would bear Jesus. Anunsasyon; Ang pagbati ng Arkanghel Gabriel kay Birhen Maria at ang pagbabalita ritong Siya'y magiging Ina ng Diyos.

anomalous, adj. irregular. Anomalo; tiwali.

anomaly, n. irregularity. Anomalya; katiwalian.

anonymous, adj. from an unacknowledged source. Di-kilala.

another, adj. different. Isa pa; iba.

answer, v. make a reply or response. Managot; sumagot; tumugon.

answer, n. a reply or response. Sagot; tugon.

ant, n. a small insect that lives in communities. Guyam; langgam.

antagonism, n. opposition. Antagonismo; oposisyon; pagkakasalungatan; pagkakalaban.

antagonistic, adj. opposed; unfriendly. Salungat; laban.

antagonize, v. striving against. Kalabanin.

antecedent, adj.& n. that goes before. Antisidente; nauna.

ant-hill, n. a little mound formed by ants for their habitation. Punso.

anthrax, n. malignant disease of animals. Antrako; bukol.

anticipate, v. to forestall. Mauna; asahan.

antidote, n. counter-poison.

Pamatay-bisa ng lason.

antique, **adj.** belonging to former times; old-fashioned. Antigo; luma.

antique, n. a relic of antiquity. Bagay na luma o yari nang unang panahon.

antiseptic, n. a substance for combating disease. Antiseptiko.

apart, adv. in pieces. Aparte; bukod; hiwalay.

apartment, n. a single room. Apartment; aksesorya.

ape, n. the gorilla; kind of monkey. Unggoy; bakulaw.

apiece, adv. for each. Por piraso, bawa't isa; ang isa.

apologize, v. make apology. Humingi ng paumanhin.

apology, n. expression of regret for a slight or injury Apolohiya; eskusa; paumanhin.

apostle, n. a disciple of Christ chosen to preach the gospel. Alagad; apostol; isa sa labindalawang apostoles ni Hesus.

Apostles' Creed, n. a brief and authoritative summary of the articles of Christian faith. Ang Kredo; Ang Sumasampalataya.

apostrophe, n. a mark of punctuation indicating an omission. Apostrope; kudlit.

appal, v. to dismay; terrify. Masindak; manlumo; manlambot.

appalling, adj. fearsome. Nakasisindak; nakapanlulumo.

apparatus, n. utensil. Anarato; kasangkapan.

apparent, adj. evident; obvious. Malinaw; maliwanag; di-maikakaila.

apparently, adv. evidently; obviously. Sa malas.

appeal, v. beseech; request. Umapila, maghabol.

appeal, n. a call or entreaty for aid, etc. Apelasiyon; paghahabol.

appear, v. become visible; be known. Magmukha; magpakita; humarap.

appearance, n. aspect; mien. Wangis; pagharap; kaanyuan; pagpapakita.

appease, v. to calm down. Palubagin; payapain.

appendage, n. a subordinate part. Kabit.

appendix, n. a supplement; an addition. Apendise; dagdag sa aklat.

appetite, n. desire for food. Gana.

appetizer, n. a snack to whet the appetite. Pampagana.

applaud, v. to praise. Palakpakan; purihin.

applause, n. approval; praise Aploso; palakpakan.

apple, n. a kind of fruit. Mansanas.

application, n. a request or petition. Aplikasiyon; paghaharap ng kahilingan; pagsasagawa o paglalapat ng isang bagay o simulaing natutuhan.

appoint, v. to assign. Itakda; italaga; hirangin.

apportion, v. to divide equally Paghati-hatiin.

appraise, v. to estimate value. Halagahán; tasahan.

appreciate, v. value fairly. Pasalamatan; pahalagahan.

appreciation, n. esteem; value. Pasasalamat; pagpapahalaga.

apprehend, v. to understand. Maunawaan; mawatasan; intindihin.

apprise, v. to inform. Impormahan; pagbigay-alam; pabatiran.

approach, v. to come near. Lumapit; lapitan.

approach, n. method or means of access; proximity. Daang papunta; paglapit.

appropriate, adj. suitable; applicable. Angkop; bagay.

appropriate, v. allot (money) for a specific use. Ariin; bigyan ng salapi.

appropriation, n. allotment. Apropriyasiyon; kaukulang gastos o bahagi.

April, n. fourth month of the year. Abril.

apron, n. an outer garment worn to protect the clothing. Delantar; tapis; apron.

apt, adj. quick in learning. Marunong; matalino; madaling matuto.

aptitude, n. special fitness; aptness. Talino; hilig; kakayahan.

arbiter, n. arbitrator; judge. Arbitrador; tagapamagitan; tagahatol.

arch, n. curve shaped structure with support. Balantok; arko.

archbishop, n. a bishop who has the supervision of other bishops and also exercises episcopal authority in his own diocese. Arsobispo.

archbishopric, n. the jurisdiction, office, or see of an archbishop. Arsobispado; ang kapangyarihan o tanggapan ng isang arsobispo.

archdiocese, n. territory of an archbishop. Purok na nasasakop ng isang arsobispo.

archeologist, n. one who studies past culture. Arkeologo; isang mag-aaral ng mga bagay-bagay na ukol sa unang panahon.

archer. n. one who uses a bow and arrow. Arkero; mamamana.

archives, n. place where public documents are kept. Arkibo; taguan ng mga kasulatan at katibayang nasusulat.

ardent, adj. zealous; eager. Maapoy; maalab; marubdob.

ardor, n. zeal; enthusiasm. Sigla; sigasig; alab ng damdamin; kataimtiman.

area, n. extent; scope. Sukat; lawak; laki.

argue, v. to dispute. Magmatwid; makipagtalo.

argument, n. debate. Argumento; pakikipagtalo; matuwid.

arid, adj. lacking moisture. Tigang; tuyo.

aright, adv. rightly; correctly. Ng tama; nang wasto.

arise, v. get up; move upward. Bumangon; tumindig.

aristocrat, n. a noble. Aristokrata; kabilang sa angkang mahal.

arithmetic, n. the art of computation; the most elementary branch of mathematics. Palatuusan; aritmetika.

arm, n. the upper limb of the human body, extending from shoulder to hand. Braso; bisig.

arm, n. a weapon. Armas; sandata.

armed, adj. ready with arms. Armado; sandatahan.

armless, adj. without arms; without weapons. Walang sandata; walang bisig.

armor, n. any covering worn for protection against offensive weapons. Armadura; baluti.

armpit, n. the cavity under the shoulder or upper arm. Kilikili.

army, n. a large body of men trained for war on land.

Hukbo; army.

aroma, n. fragrance; a pleasant odor. Aroma; bango; samyo.

around, adv. & prep. on all sides. Sa lahat ng panig; sa paligid.

arouse, v. rouse up. Gisingin; pag-alabin ang damdamin.

arraign, v. to charge before a court. Isakdal.

arrange, v. put in proper order. Aregluhin; ayusin.

arrangement, n. act of arranging. Areglo; pagkakaayos; ayos.

array, n. regular order or arrangement. Pormasiyon; pagkakaayos; pagkakahanay.

arrest, v. to capture; to seize. Arestuhin; hulihin; dakpin.

arrival, n. coming to a place. Pagdating.

arrive, v. to reach a certain point. Dumating.

arrogance, n. assumption. Pagmamataas.

arrogant, adj. aggressively haughty. Arogante; mapagmataas.

arrogate, v. claim unjustly. Sarilinin; kamkamin.

arrow, n. a rodlike missile weapon made to be shot from a bow. Pana; palaso.

arsenal, n. an armory. Arsenal; taguan ng mga sandata.

arson, n. malicious burning of a building. Insendiyo; panununog.

art, n. skillful workmanship. Arte; sining.

artery, n. large blood vessel. Arteria; malaking ugat na dinadaluyan ng dugo.

article, n. any commodity. Artikulo; bagay; paninda.

articulate, adj. expressive. Artikulado; maliwanag; malinaw.

articulate, v. say or speak distinctly with clear separation of syllables. Magsalita nang wasto at malinaw.

artificial, adj. man-made; contrived by human skill; Di-natural; artipisyal; di-likas.

artillery, n. troops servicing mounted guns. Artiliyeria; mga sandatang pandigma.

artist, n. a performer in an art of entertainment. Artista.

artless, adj. ingeneous; naive Natural; likas.

as, conj. in similar manner Kaparis; gaya; tulad.

ascend, v. go upward. Tumaas; pumanhik; umakyat

ascendancy, n. domination; influence. Pagtaas; pag-akyat.

Ascension, n. a rising of Christ into heaven. Asensiyon; ang pag-akyat ni Kristo sa langit.

ascertain, v. to determine. Siguraduhin; tiyakin.

ash, n. the incombustible residue that remains after burning. Senisa; abo.

ashen, adj. pale; of ashes. Abuhin; kulay-abo; maputla.

ashore, adv. to or on land; on shore. Sa pampang; nasa katihan.

Ash Wednesday, n. first day of Lent. Miyerkules de Senisa; Miyerkules ng Abo.

ashy, adj. ash-colored. Maabo.

aside, adv. on or to one side; apart. Bukod; sa isang tabi.

assessor, n. an officer of justice who sits to assist a judge. Asesor; kasangguni ng hukom sa hukuman.

assumption, n. the bodily

taking up into Heaven of the Virgin Mary after her death. Ang pag-aakyat sa kabanal-banalang Birhen Maria sa langit.

asthma, n. a disorder of respiration marked by labored breathing. Asma; hika.

asthmatic, adj. suffering from asthma. Asmatiko; hikain.

astonish, v. amaze. Gitlain; gulatin.

astonishment, n. amazement; wonder. Pagkagulat; sorpresa.

astray, adv. away from the proper path; wandering. Nalilihis; naligaw.

astrology, n. the study of the supposed influence of the heavenly bodies on human affairs. Astrolohiya; panghuhula sa pamamagitan ng lagay ng mga planeta.

astronomy, n. general science of all celestial bodies. Astronomiya; ang agham tungkol sa daigdig at mga buntala.

astuteness, n. cunning; shrewdness. Katalasan ng pag-iisip o ng pakiramdam.

asylum, n. any place of refuge. Ampunan.

at, prep. used in many idiomatic phrases to imply local or relative position, direction of motion or activity, time, order, etc. Sa.

atheism, n. the doctrine that there is no God. Ateismo; pagkawalang-Diyos.

athlete, n. one who engages in exercises of physical agility and strength. Atlet; atleta; manlalaro.

atmosphere, n. the air. Atmospera; ang simoy na nakapaligid sa buong daigdig.

atomic, adj. relating to atoms. Atomiko; nauukol sa atomiko; may uring atomik.

atone, v. make amends for sin or deficiency. Magtika; magsisi.

atonement, n. expiation; reparation. Pagtitika; pagsisisi; pagbabayad sa mga nagawang kasalanan.

atop, adv. on or at the top. Sa ibabaw; sa itaas.

attach, v. fasten; affix. Isama; kumabit; ikabit.

attachment, n. adherence. Pagkakaugnay; pangkabit; mabuting pagtingin.

attack, v. to assault. Atakihin; salakayin; lusubin.

attack, n. assault. Atake; pagsalakay; pagdaluhong.

attain, v. reach or achieve. Makuha; matamo.

attainment, n. acquisition. Kakayahan; natamo; natapos; naabot.

attempt, n. effort put forth. Subukin; tangka.

attend, v. to be present at. Pumunta; dumalo.

attendance, n. the act of attending. Pagdalo; pagpasok.

attendant, n. one who attends another, as for service. Sirbiyente; serbidor; katulong; tagapaglingkod.

attention, n. observant care; notice. Atensiyon; pansin.

attentive, adj. giving attention; courteous. Mapagpunyagi; taimtim sa pakikinig o pagmamasid.

attest, v. bear witness to. Saksihan; magpatunay; patunayan.

attestation, n. testimony. Atestasiyon; pruweba; pagpapatunay; katunayan.

attic, n. a garret. Silid sa ibabaw ng kisame.

attire, n. clothing; apparel.

Bihis; kasuutan.

attitude, n. position. Ayos; palagay.

attorney, n. lawyer; legal agent. Abogado; mananang-gol; atorni.

attract, v. invite or allure. Higupin; akitin; umakit.

attraction, n. allurement. Atraksiyon; pang-akit; atraksiyon.

attractive, adj. alluring. Kahali-halina; kaakit-akit.

attribute, n. inherent quality. Kalidad; katangian.

attribute, v. to ascribe; impute. Isisi; iukol.

audit, v. to examine and certify accounts. Rebisahin; suriin.

auditor, n. hearer; adjuster. Awditor; tagasuri.

auditory, adj. pertaining to the sense or organs of hearing. Awditibo; ukol sa pakikinig.

augar, n. a tool to bore. Barena; pambutas.

augment, v. to increase. Umentuhan; dagdagan; damihan.

August, n. the 8th month of the year. Agosto.

aunt, n. sister of one's father or mother; step-mother. Tiya; kapatid na babae ng ina o ng ama; ale.

austerity, n. severity; rigor. Kawalang luho; pagpapakasakit sa katawan upang matamo ang kagalingan ng kaluluwa.

authentic, adj. genuine. Awtentiko; tunay.

author, n. originator. Awtor; may akda.

authority, n. legal power. Awtoridad; kapangyarihan.

authorize, v. to empower (a person). Bigyan matwid; bigyang-kapangyarihan.

autograph, n. signature. Signatura; sulat kamay na lagda ng isang tao.

automatic, adj. self-acting. Awtomatiko; gumagalaw sa sarili.

autonomy, adj. power or right of self-government. Awtonomiya; karapatang mamahala sa sarili.

autopsy, n. examination after death. Awtopsiya; pagsuri sa bangkay.

avail, v. have force or efficacy. Aprobetsahin; gamitin.

avarice, n. greed of gain. Kasakiman.

Ave Maria, n. Hail Mary; devotional words often repeated in the Roman Catholic Church, Ave Maria; ang Aba Ginoong Maria; ang pagbati sa orasyon.

avenge, v. to take vengeance. Benggahin; ipaghiganti.

avenue, n. a wide street. Abenida; lansangan.

aver, v. affirm with confidence. Paninindigan; patunayan.

averse, adj. reluctant; unwilling. Di-mahilig; salungat.

aviary, n. bird enclosure. Alagaan ng mga ibon.

avid, adj. eager. Sabik.

avoid, v. to evade; shun. Iwasan.

avoidance, n. act of avoiding. Ebasyón; pag-iwas.

avow, v. to declare openly. Ipahayag nang tahasan; aminin.

await, v. to wait for. Hintayin.

awake, adj. to arouse. Pukawin; gising.

away, adv. apart; off. Wala; sa malayo.

awe, n. reverential fear. Mapitagang pagkatakot.

awful, adj. dreadful. Nakasisindak; kalagim-lagim.

awhile, adj. for a short time. Sandali.

awkward, adj. clumsy. Malamya; di-bihasa; nakahihiya.

awl, n. a tool for punching small holes in leather, wood, etc. Lesna; balibol.

awning, n. rooflike covering over a place. Sibi; tolda.

ax, n. a tool for cutting, chopping, etc. Palakol.

axiom, n. self-evident truth. Aksiyoma; simulain o katotohanang kinikilala ng lahat.

axle, n. bar on which a wheel turns. Ehe ng gulong.

azure, adj. sky blue. Bughaw-langit.

B

babble, n. idle talk. Satsatan; usapang walang saysay.

babble, v. to talk indistinctly. Magsatsatan; magdaldalan.

babbler, n. a teller of secrets. Daldalera; daldalero.

baboon, n. any of several large monkeys. Malaking unggoy.

baby, n. infant. Beybi; sanggol.

bachelor, n. an unmarried man. Binata.

back, adv. at, or toward the rear; in return. Atras; sa likod; uli.

back, v. to support, as with authority or money. Itaguyod.

back, n. part of body. Likod.

backpay, n. payment for past dues. Bakpey; habol-bayad.

backbite, v. to speak evil of (the absent). Manirang puri.

backbone, n. the spine. Gulugod.

backer, n. sponsor or supporter. Sustinador; tagapagtaguyod; tagaalalay.

background, n. the parts situated in a rear. Pondo; sanligan.

backstair, n. private stairs; in the back part of the house. Eskalera; hagdan sa likuran; hagdang lihim.

backward, adj. behind in time or progress. Paurong; huli sa panahon; mabagal; walang pag-unlad.

bacon, n. salted and smoked sides and back of a pig. Tosino; inasnang laman ng baboy.

bad, adj. wicked. Malo; masama; nakasisira.

badge, n. mark of distinction. Dibisa; tsapa.

badly, adv. unskillfully. Masama; malubha.

badness, n. want of good qualities, physical or moral. Kasamaan.

baffle, v. to elude; to thwart. Guluhin; lituhin.

bag, n. a sack; wallet; a pouch. Bag; supot; bayong.

baggage, n. luggage. Bagahe; dala-dalahan ng manlalakbay.

bail, n. security given to obtain the temporary release of a prisoner. Piyansa; lagak.

bail, v. to grant or obtain release of a prisoner in jail. Magpiyansa; magbigay ng lagak.

bailable, adj. capable of being admitted to bail. Maaaring pansamantalang palayain sa pamamagitan ng lagak.

bait, n. a lure. Tukso; pain.

bait, v. to torment; to tease. Tuksuhin; painan.

bake, v. to cook by dry heat.

Lutuin sa hurno.

baker, n. one who makes and sells bread, cake, etc. Panadero, magtitinapay.

bakery, n. house for baking. Panaderya, tindahan ng tinapay.

baking, n. the quantity baked at one time. Naluluto sa hurno.

balance, n. instrument for weighing. Balanse; timbangan.

balance, v. to weigh. Timbangin.

bald, adj. without hair. Panot; kalbo.

bale, n. a large bundle or package. Paldo.

bale, v. to pack. Palduhin.

baleful, adj. menacing; malign. Masama; nakakatakot.

balk, v. to disappoint. Tumigil; biguin.

ball, n. round body. Bola.

ballad, n. song; light poem. Balad; awit.

balloon, n. gas airship. Balun; lobo.

balm, n. any of various aromatic resinous substances. Balsamo; pampapawi ng hapdi o ng sakit ng loob.

balmy, adj. mild; fragrant. May uring balsamo; mabango.

bamboo, n. a woody tropical grass. Bambu; kawayan.

ban, v. to forbid; prohibit. Ipagbawal.

banana, n. a tropical fruit. Banana; saging.

banca, n. a boat. Bangka; baroto.

band, n. bandage; a company. Banda; benda o panali; paha; pulutong ng mga tao, mga kawal o mga musikero.

band, v. to unite. Magsamasama; magtipun-tipon; lagyan ng paha o benda.

bandanna, n. a large colored handkerchief. Panyuwelo; bandana; malaking panyong pang-ulo.

banderole, n. a small flag or banner. Banderita; munting watawat.

bandit, n. robber; an outlaw. Mandarambong; manghaharang; tulisan; bandido.

bandmaster, n. the conductor of a band. Musikerong tagapamahala.

bandylegged, adj. having crooked legs. Umpog ang mga tuhod; piki.

bang, v. to strike violently or noisily. Pumutok; lumikha ng ingay; mambugbog nang may ingay; ipinid nang padabog.

bang, n. a loud, sudden, explosive noise. Putok; ingay na likha ng isang palo, hampas o suntok.

banish, v. to exile. Ipatapon.

banishment, n. exile. Distiyero; pagpapatapon.

bank, n. money depository. Bangko; pampang; tabing-ilog o tabing-dagat.

bank, v. to deposit in a bank. Ibangko; maghulog ng salapi sa bangko.

banker, n. a bank officer. Bangkero.

bankrupt, adj. insolvent. Bangkrap; hapay; said ang salapi.

banner, n. a standard or flag. Bandila; watawat; bandera.

banns, pl., n. notice of an intended marriage, displayed or read in a church. Tawag, tatlong ulit na pagpapahayag ng binabalak na kasal, na ginagawa sa simbahan ng bawa't ikakasal.

banquet, n. a feast. Piging;

handaan; bangkete.

banter, n. light ridicule. Biro; tukso.

banter, v. to make fun of. Manukso; biruin.

banyan, n. an East Indian fig tree whose branches set out adventitious roots to the ground. Bantano; puno ng baliti.

baptism, n. a sacrament of Christian Church, signalized by sprinkling with, or immersion in water. Babtismo; binyag.

baptize, v. to immerse in water. Binyagan; magbinyag.

bar, n. a bolt; obstruction. Hadlang; bilihan ng alak; bareta; rehas; tarangka.

barb, n. a sharp point. Tulis ng palaso; tinik.

barbarian, n. a man in a primitive, savage, or uncivilized state. Barbaro; mabalasik; hindi sibilisado.

barbaric, adj. foreign; rude. Mabalasik; di-sibilisado.

barbarism, n. savageness. Barbarismo; kabalasikan.

barbecue, n. animal dressed whole. Asado; inihaw o nilitsong baboy o ano mang hayop.

barbed, adj. having barbs. May mga tinik o tulis.

barber, n. one whose occupation is to give haircuts, shaves, etc. Manggugupit ng buhok· barbero.

bard, n. poet. Poeta; makata; makatang umaawit.

bare, v. to strip; to lay open to view. Alisan ng takip; hubaran; ihayag.

barefooted, adj. feet without stockings or shoes. Walang sapin ang mga paa; nakayapak.

barely, adv. merely. Bahagya na.

bargain, n. a contract. Baratilyo; kontrata; kasunduan; bilihan.

bargain, v. to make an agreement about the transfer of property. Makipagkasunduan; tumawad.

bark, n. the outer rind of a tree, shrub, etc.; the abrupt explosive cry of a dog. Balat ng kahoy; tahol.

barley, n. grain. Sebada.

barn, n. storehouse for hay. Kamalig.

barn yard, n. a yard next to a barn. Bakuran ng bangan; kamalig.

barometer, n. instrument to weigh the atmosphere. Panukat ng init o lamig ng panahon; barometro.

barracks, n. house for soldiers. Kuwartel; himpilan ng mga kawal; baraks.

barrel, n. a sort of cask. Bariles.

barren, adj. unfruitful; sterile. Baog; tigang.

barricade, v. to block with a barrier. Halangan.

barrister, n. a lawyer. Abugado; manananggol.

barter, v. to trade by exchange of commodities. Baratuhin; makipagtawaran; ipagpalit.

basal, adj. relating to base. Saligan; batayan.

base, adj. vile; low. Hamak; duwag; imbi.

base, n. bottom; foundation. Paanan; pondo; patungan; batayan.

base, v. to debase or counterfeit; to make foundation for. Siraan; ibatay.

baseball, n. a game of ball played by two sides of nine

players each, on a diamond connecting four bases. Ang pambansang laro ng Estados Unidos; besbol.

basement, n. lowest story of a building. Baysmen; palapag ng isang malaking gusali na nasa ilalim ng lupa.

bashful, adj. shy; timid. Mahiyain.

bashfulness, n. excessive modesty; timorous shyness. Kakimian; pagkamahiyain.

basilika, n. an oblong building with a nave higher than its aisles. Basilika; simbahan; isang gusaling ang gitna ay nabubukod sa mga tabi sa pamamagitan ng mga poste.

basin, n. a shallow, circular vessel for holding liquids. Palanggana.

basis, n. foundation. Base; batayan.

basketball, n. a game played with a large inflated ball. Basketbol.

basket, n. a container woven of pliable reeds, etc. Basket; buslo; batulang.

bassinet, n. a basket with a hood over one end, used as a cradle. Basinete; kuna.

bastard, n. illegitimate child. Bastardo; anak sa labas.

baste, v. to sew with temporary stitches. Itahing pansamantala; ihilbana.

bastion, n. a projecting portion of fortification. Balwarte.

bat, n. a heavy club or cudgel. Bat; pamalo ng bola.

bath, n. a washing of the body in water. Paligo; paliligo.

bathe, v. immerse or be immersed in liquid for cleansing. Maligo; paliguan.

baton, n. a staff, etc. as a mark of office. Batón; batuta.

battalion, n. a body of troops. Batalyon.

battery, n. a device for producing an electric current for storing electricity. Batirya.

battle, n. a fight; hostile encounter or engagement between opposing forces. Labanan; digmaan.

bawdy, adj. filthy or obscene. Malaswa; mahalay.

bawl, v. to shout out. Sumigaw; magsalita nang pagigil.

bay, n. a recess in a shore; an inlet. Bay; lóok.

bayonet, n. a daggerlike instrument attached at the muzzle of a rifle. Bayoneta.

bead, n. one of a string of small balls of glass, pearl, etc. used as an ornament or in a rosary. Abaloryo; butil ng rosaryo.

beak, n. horny bill of a bird. Tuka.

beach, n. seashore. Baybay; pampang.

beam, n. a bundle of parallel; rays of light. Sepo; sinag.

beaming, adj. bright. Makinang; maliwanag.

bear, v. to carry; to support; to bring forth. Dalhin; tiisin.

bear, n. a fierce animal. Oso.

beard, n. hair on the face of a man, especially on the chin. Balbas.

bearer, n. a carrier. Portador; maydala.

beast, n. an animal. Hayop.

beat, v. to strike repeatedly. Bayuhin; paluin; bugbugin.

beatification, n. the act of the Pope by which he declares a person beatified. Ang pagpapahayag ng Papa na ang isang taong namatay na ay pinagpala ng langit, o pagiging santo.

beatitude, n. blessedness. Pagkapinagpala; pagkamaluwalhati.

beautiful, adj. having beauty. Maalindog; maganda.

beautify, v. to make or become beautiful. Pagandahin.

beauty, n. a pleasing excellence. Alindog; kagandahan.

become, v. to be made. Bumagay; maging.

becoming, adj. attractive; suitable. Desente; akma; bagay; angkop.

bed, n. a piece of furniture on which one sleeps. Tulugan; higaan; kama.

bedbug, n. a small flat, wingless, hemipterous bloodsucking insect that infests houses and especially beds. Surot.

bedeck, v. decorate; hang ornaments on. Adornohan; gayakan; maggayak.

bedspread, n. cover for bed. Kobrekama; takip ng kama.

bedpan, n. a toilet pan for persons confined to bed Tsata.

bee, n. an insect that lives in colonies and gather honey. Bubuyog.

beef, n. flesh of ox or cow. Karne ng baka.

beer, n. an alcoholic beverage made from grain. Bir; serbesa.

beetle, n. an insect having forewings modified as hard, horny structures, useless in flight. Uwang; salagubang.

befit, v. to suit; be appropriate to. Bumagay; babagay.

befitting, adj. suiting; appropriate; proper. Akma; bagay; angkop.

beg, v. to ask as alms; to ask humbly or earnestly. Humingi; magpalimos.

beget, v. to procreate; to produce as an effect. Magbunga; manganak.

beggar, n. one who begs or is poor. Pulubi.

beginning, n. first effort. Prinsipyo; orihen; simulain; simula.

beguile, v. to delude; to deceive. Enganyuhin; ganyakin, amukiin.

behavior, n. conduct. Asal; kilos; ugali.

behead, v. cut off the head of. Pugutan ng ulo.

behind, prep. in the rear; at the back of. Sa likod.

behold, v. to see plainly. Tingnan; masdan.

being, n. existence. Buhay; katauhan; pagiging tao.

belated, adj. coming late or too late. Atrasado; huli; dumating nang huli.

belch, v. to eject wind from the stomach through the mouth. Dumighay.

belfry, n. a tower for a bell. Kampanaryo.

belie, v. to slander; to villify. Pasinungalingan.

belief, n. an accepted opinion. Paniniwala.

believe, v. to exercise faith. Sumampalataya; maniwala.

belittle, v. to make lower in importance. Dustain; hamakin.

bell, n. a hollow metal device giving forth a resonant or tinkling sound when struck. Batingaw; kampana.

belle, n. a reigning beauty. Dilag; isang babaing bata at maganda.

bellow, v. to make a loud, hollow noise; roar. Sumigaw; bumulyaw.

bell-ringer, n. a ringer of churchbell. Tagatugtog ng kampana; kampanero.

belly, n. the abdomen; the stomach. Tiyan.

belong, v. to be a property of. Maging pag-aari; gawing ari; ariin.

belonging, n. possession. Pag-aari; ari.

beloved, n. greatly loved. Kerida; giliw; sinta.

below, prep. & adv. inferior; beneath. Sa ibaba; sa ilalim.

belt, n. a flexible band worn around the waist. Banda; koreya; sinturon.

bemire, v. to soil in mire. Siraang puri; putikan; dumihan.

bemoan, v. to lament. Itangis; ipaghinagpis; maghinagpis.

bench, n. a long seat. Upuan; bangko.

bend, v. to curve. Yumuko; baluktutin.

bend, n. a curve or crook. Liko; kurba.

benediction, n. a blessing. Benidiksiyon; bendisyon; basbas.

benefit, n. advantage. Benepisiyo; kapakanan; kapakinabangan.

benefit, v. to do good; to gain advantage. Makabuti; makinabang.

benign, adj. kind; generous. Mabuting loob; mabait; mapagbigay.

bequeath, v. to hand down. Ipamana.

berate, v. to scold. Kagalitan.

bereave, v. to make desolate through loss (of) especially by death. Alisan; maging malungkot dahil sa pagkawala ng isang tao.

bereavement, n. deprivation, particularly the loss of a friend by death. Pagkawala; pagkaulila; pangungulila.

berth, n. a sleeping compartment. Tutulugan; kamarote.

beset, v. to assail; to harass. Napapaligiran; laging hinaharang.

beside, prep. near; by the side of. Sa tabi.

besmear, v. to smear over; to soil. Dumihan; dungisan.

best, adj. highest degree of excellence. Pinakamagaling; superyor; pinakamahusay; pinakamabuti.

bestow, v. to give. Ibigay; ipagkaloob.

bet, n. a wager; the stake. Taya; pusta.

bet, v. to pledge as a forfeit in support of an opinion. Tumaya; pumusta.

betray, v. to deliver treacherously to an enemy. Magtaksil; ipagkanulo.

betrayal, n. act of betraying. Pagtataksil; pagkakanulo.

better, adj. & adv. superior quality; in a more excellent way. Mabuti kaysa; higit sa.

better, v. to surpass; to improve. Paunlarin; gawing mabuti kaysa; pahigitin.

between, prep. in the middle of. Sa pagitan.

beware, v. to be cautious. Mag-ingat.

bewitch, v. to please extremely; to charm. Maakit; magayuma; gayumahin.

beyond, prep. a distance. Sa kabila ng; sa dako pa roon.

bias, n. an oblique line or direction. Bayas; pagkiling.

bib, v. to drink frequently.

Uminom nang malimit.

bible, n. the collection of sacred writings of Christianity, comprising the Old and New testaments. Banal na kasulatan; Bibliya.

bicker, v. to engage in a petulant quarrel. Mag-away.

bid, v. to order. Ordenahan; utusan.

bier, n. carriage for the dead. Andas; karo ng patay.

big, adj. large in size, extent, degree, etc. Grande; malaki.

bigamy, n. crime of having two wives or husbands at the same time. Bigamya; dalawang asawa.

bill, n. horny beak of a bird; statement of goods purchased; Utang; tuka; kuwenta.

bin, n. a storage compartment. Granero; taguan ng palay.

bind, v. to fasten. Gapusin; pag-isahin; itali.

biology, n. science of life. Biyolohiya.

bird, n. any feather-covered vertebrate animal whose forelimbs form wings. Ibon.

birth, n. the bringing forth of offspring. Nasimiyento; kapanganakan.

birthday, n. the day of one's birth. Kompleanyo; araw ng kapanganakan; kaarawan.

biscuit, n. a kind of bread. Galyetas; biskotso; biskuwit.

bisect, v. to divide into two equal parts, as line. Hatiin sa dalawang magkasinlaking bahagi.

bishop, n. head of a diocese Obispo.

bishopric, n. office of a bishop. Ang tanggapan ng obispo; obispado.

bite, n. the act of biting. Kagat.

bite, v. to seize with the teeth. Kagatin.

bitingly, adv. sarcastically. Nakasasakit; nakatutuya; nakasusugat.

bitter, adj. having an acid taste. Masaklap; mapait.

black, adj. without brightness or color. Maitim.

blackboard, n. a writing board. Pisara.

blacken, v. to make black. Paitimin.

blacksmith, n. one who does iron works. Panday.

bladder, n. bag containing the urine. Pantog.

blade, n. sharp part of a tool. Talim; kutsilyo.

blanch, v. to grow white. Mamuti; mamutla.

blank, adj. without writing. Puwang; blangko; walang sulat.

blanket, n. a covering for beds. Blangket; kumot.

blaspheme, v. to speak evil of. Lumapastangan; magsalita ng laban sa kabutihan o katotohanan.

blasphemy, n. an indignity. Paglapastangan sa Diyos o sa alinmang banal na bagay.

blaze, n. a flame. Puwego; ningas; apoy.

blaze, v. to burst into flame. Magningas; mag-alab.

bleach, v. to make or become white, pale, or colorless. Paputiin; ikula.

bleed, v. to lose blood. Kunan ng dugo; magdugo.

blemish, v. to deface; damage. Mantsahan; dumihan; dungisan.

blemish, n. a defect; a stain. Dungis; dumi; mantsa.

blend, v. to mix. Timplahin; paghaluin; pagsamahin.

blend, n. smooth mixture. Timpla; pagkakahaluhalo; pagsasama-sama.

bless, v. to make holy or happy. Bendisyunan; basbasan.

blessed, adj. consecrated. Benditado; pinagpala; banal.

blessing, n. benediction. Bendisyon; basbas.

blind, adj. lacking or having lost the sense of sight. Bulag.

blind, v. to deprive of sight. Silawin; bulagin.

blink, v. to wink rapidly and repeatedly. Kumurap; pumikit-pikit.

bliss, n. supreme happiness. Kabanalan; kaligayahan.

blister, n. a pustule. Paltos; lintos; paso.

blithe, adj. joyous. Masaya; masigla.

block, n. a solid mass of stone, wood, metal, etc. Bloke; troso; putol na kahoy; hulmahang kahoy.

blood, n. the red fluid that circulates in the arteries and veins. Dugo.

bloody, v. to stain with blood. Mantsahan ng dugo; madugo.

bloom, n. a blossom; flower. Plores; bulaklak ng halaman.

bloom, v. to produce blossoms. Mamulaklak; mamukadkad.

blouse, n. woman's wear. Blusa.

blue, n. the pure hue of clear sky. Asul; bughaw.

bluff, n. one who bluffs. Kayabangan.

blunder, v. to act stupidly. Malito; magkamali.

blunt, adj. dull. Pulpol.

boar, n. the male swine. Ba rakong baboy.

board, v. to enter (a ship train, etc.). Lumulan; sumakay.

board, n. an official body of persons who direct some activity. Lupon; bord.

boarding house, n. a house where board and lodging is furnished. Bording haws; bahay na pinangangaserahan.

boast, v. to speak exaggeratedly about oneself. Magpasikat; magyabang; maghambog.

boastful, adj. given to boasting. Pasikat; hambog; mayabang.

boat, n. small water craft. Bangka; bote.

body, n. the physical structure of an animal. Katawan.

bog, n. a marsh. Latian; kumunoy.

bogus, adj. counterfeit. Palso, di-tunay; huwad.

boil, v. to be agitated by heat. Pakuluin.

bold, adj. brave. Brabo; pangahas; matapang.

bolt, n. sliding rod lock. Tornilyo; tarangka.

bolo, n. big, heavy knife. Itak.

bomb, n. an explosive missile. Bomba.

bomb, v. to hurl bombs at or on. Bombahin.

bond, n. a sealed instrument which guarantees to pay a stated sum by a specified day. Bono; lagak.

bone, n. the hard tissue of which the skeleton is made. Buto.

bonfire, n. fire built in the open for celebration. Siga.

bony, adj. having prominent bones. Butuhán; mabuto; payat.

book, n. a printed work or

sheets bound together. Libro; aklat.

booklet, n. a small book. Buklet.

bookkeeper, n. a keeper of account books. Tenidor de libro; tagatala ng kuwenta.

bookcase, n. a place where books are kept. Aklatan; istante ng aklat.

booth, n. a light structure for shelter, exhibition of wares, etc. Tindahan; puwesto.

boothblack, n. shoeshine boy. Limpiyabota.

border, n. a side or edge. Tabi; gilid; hanggahan.

bore, v. to pierce (a substance) or make (a hole, etc.) with a drill; wear out by dullness. Inisin; bagutin; butasin.

bore, n. a hole made by or as if by boring. Barena; taong nakababagot; pambutas.

bosom, n. the breast. Kalooban; dibdib.

both, conj. equally. Pareho; kapwa.

bottle, n. a vessel for holding liquids, usually of glass. Botelya; bote.

bottom, n. the lowest or deepest part of anything; the base. Ang bahaging pinakamababa ng isang bagay; kalaliman.

bough, n. branch of a tree. Sanga.

bounce, n. a blow or thrust. Talbog.

bound, adj. confined; destined. Naliligid; nalilibot; nakukulong.

boundless, adj. unlimited. Walang hanggan.

bounty, n. generosity. Kabutihang loob; kasaganaan; biyaya.

bow, v. to bend as an act of reverence. Yumukod; paggalang.

bow, n. part of a hunting gear. Busog.

bowels, n. the intestines. Bituka.

bowl, n. a deep dish or basin. Mangkok; tasa.

box, n. a receptacle of wood, metal, cardboard, etc. with a lid. Kaha; kahon.

box, v. to put in a box. Ikahon; ilagay sa kahon.

boxer, n. a pugilist. Bakser; boksingero.

boy, n. a male child. Boy; mutsatso; utusang lalaki; batang lalaki.

boycott, v. to abstain from buying or using. Tikisin; huwag pahalagahan; huwag sundin; iboykoteho.

braid, v. to interlace three strands, as of hair. Magtirintas.

braid, n. a length of braided hair. Tirintas.

brain, n. the organ of thought, consciousness, and body control. Talino; utak.

bran, n. husk of grain. Darak.

branch, n. a limb, as of tree. Sangay; sanga.

brand, n. a trademark to identify a product. Marka; tatak.

brass, n. an alloy of copper and zinc. Tanso; bronse.

brave, adj. courageous. Balyente; pangahás; matapang.

brave, v. to face with courage. Pangahasán; harapin; sagupain.

bravery, n. courage. Balor; katapangan; tapang.

breach, n. a gap or opening. Sira; siwang.

breadth, n. width. Antso; lapad; luwang.

break, v. to crush. Labagin; basagin.
break, n. a gap; a fracture. Pagkakataon; puwang; siwang.
breast, n. the chest. Petso; dibdib.
breath, n. air exhaled and inhaled in respiration. Respirasiyon; paghinga; hininga.
breathe, v. to inhale and exhale air. Huminga.
breeding, n. upbringing. Edukasiyon; pinagkalakhan; pinag-aralan.
breeze, n. a current of air, esp. a light one. Brisas; simoy.
brethren, n. plural of brother. Hermano; mga kapatid; mga kapanalig sa relihiyon.
breviary, n. a book of daily prayers. Aklat ng mga pang-araw-araw na dasal at babasahin ng obispo, pari at diyakono.
bride, n. a newly married woman or about to be married. Nobya; babaing ikakasal.
bridegroom, n. a man newly married, or about to be married. Nobyo.
bridge, n. a structure spanning a river or road. Puwente; tulay.
brief, adj. short; concise. Bribe; maikli.
briefness, n. brevity; conciseness. Kalaguman; kaiklian.
bright, adj. shining. Maliwanag; maningning.
brightness, n. lustre; splendor. Brilyo; kaliwanagan; kaningningan.
brilliant, adj. sparkling; illustrious. Brilyante; maningning.
brim, n. edge; brink. Borde; gilid; labi.
broaden, v. to increase the width of. Laparan; luwangan.
broadcast, v. to send by radio. Isahimpapawid; brodkast.
broken, adj. fractured. Basag.
broom, n. an implement used to sweep dirt. Walis.
brood, v. to think gloomily. Magmuni; mag-isip.
brood, n. the young hatched in one's nest or of one's mother. Inakay.
broth, n. liquid in which meat has been boiled. Kaldo; sabaw.
brother, n. son of same parent. Hermano; kapatid na lalaki.
brother-in-law, n. one's husband's or wife's brother. Bayaw.
brow, n. hairy ridge over eye. Kilay.
brown, adj. of a dark or dusky color, inclining to redness. Moreno; kayumanggi.
brush, n. an instrument consisting of bristles, hair, or the like, set in a handle, used for painting. etc. Brotsa; sipilyo.
brush, v. to sweep, rub, remove, etc., with a brush. Magsipilyo.
brute, adj. savage. Hayop; bruto.
bubble, n. a thin film of liquid holding gas or air. Bula.
bucket, n. a pail. Timba; balde.
bud, n. an undeveloped swelling on a plant that may open into a leaf or flower. Usbong; buko ng isang bulaklak.
build, v. to construct. Magtayo; magtatag.
build, n. bodily figure or

shape. Anyo; estilo; tayo; tindig.

building, n. any architectural structure. Edipisyo; gusali; bilding.

bulky, adj. large, massive. Matambok; makapal.

bull, n. a male cow. Bakang lalaki; toro.

bull (papal), **n.** a formal papal document. Bula; isang opisyal na kasulatan ng Papa, na may tatak.

bullet, n. a small missile to be fired from a firearm. Bala; punglo.

bulwark, n. a wall for defense; fortification. Balwarte; tanggulan.

bunch, n. a cluster. Buwig; bungkos.

bundle, n. a bound parcel. Bungkos; tangkas.

buoy, n. an anchored float to guide navigation. Salbabida; buya.

bureau, n. an executive branch or office of a government. Komoda; kawanihan; buro.

burglar, n. one who breaks into a house with intent to rob. Ladron; magnanakaw.

burial, n. interment. Paglilibing; libing.

burn, n. an injury caused by fire, heat, or radiation. Sunog; paso.

burn, v. to be on fire. Pasuin; sunugin.

burnish, v. to polish by friction. Kuskusin; pakintabin.

burse, n. a purse to hold something valuable. Parisukat na lalagyan ng kalis; pondo o salaping laan sa mga mag-aaral na nangangailangan lalo na para sa mga nag-aaral magpari.

burst, v. to break for internal pressure to explode. Sumabog; bumulalas; pumutok.

burst, n. an explosion. Pagsabog; putok.

bury, v. entomb. Ilibing; ibaon.

bus, n. a large public motor vehicle; Omnibus; bus.

bush, n. a low, woody shrub. Arbusto; mababang halamang may matigas na puno.

business, n. occupation. Negosyo; hanapbuhay; gawain; bisnis.

busy, adj. actively occupied. Okupado; abala; maraming gawain.

but, conj. unless; nevertheless; though. Nguni't; datapuwa't; subali't.

butcher, n. one who slaughters animals for food and dresses meat for market; a retail dealer in meat. Karnisero; magkakarne; mangangatay.

butcher, v. to kill or slaughter for food or for market. Patayin; katayin.

butter, n. a fatty substance made by churning cream. Bater; mantikilya.

button, n. a knot or disk used on clothes as an ornament or as fastener. Buton; butones.

button, v. to fasten with a button or buttons. Isara; butonesan; lagyan ng butones.

buy, v. purchase. Bumili; bilhin.

buyer, n. a purchaser. Tagabili; mamimili.

by, prep. through the action or agency of. Ni; sa pamamagitan.

bygone, adj. past; out-of-date. Pasado; lumipas; nakaraan

bystander, n. a chance looker-on. Miron; manonood.

C

cab, n. a horse-drawn or motor vehicle for public hire. Kotse; taksi.

cabaret, n. restaurant with dancing and singing. Bahay sayawan; kabaret.

cabbage, n. a vegetable plant having edible leaves formed into a thick compact head. Repolyo.

cabin, n. a cottage; hut. Dampa; kamarote.

cabinet, n. a piece of furniture used as a cupboard. Iskaparate; aparador; gabinete.

cable, n. telegraph under seas. Pahatid kawad; kable.

cackle, n. noise of a hen. Pumutak.

cadaver, n. corpse. Kadaber; labi; bangkay.

cadet, n. a young man in training for army service. Kadete.

cajole, v. to flatter. Utuin; amukiin.

cake, n. a sweet food baked from dough. Bibingka; keyk.

calabash, n. any of various gourds or gourd trees. Malaking kalabasa.

calamity, n. a disaster. Kalamidad; sakuna; kasawian.

calculate, v. to compute. Kalkulahin; tantiyahin.

calendar, n. an almanac; Kalendaryo; talaarawan.

calesa, n. horse-drawn carriage. Kalesa; karetela.

caliber, n. bore of gun. Kalibre; kakayahan; katangian.

call, v. to utter loudly. Tawagin.

call, n. a cry or shout. Sigaw; tawag.

callous, adj. unfeeling. Kaloso; walang pakiramdam.

calm, adj. quiet; still. Payapa; mahinahon.

calumny, n. a slander. Kalunya; paninirang-puri.

calvary, n. place of Christ's crucifixion. Kalbaryo; ang pook na pinagpakuan sa krus sa ating P. Hesukristo.

camel, n. a large ruminant quadruped used in Asia and Africa as a beast of burden. Kamelyo.

camera, n. photographic apparatus. Pangkuha ng larawan; kamera; kodak.

camp, n. a place for the erection of temporary shelters. Kampamento; kampo.

camp, v. to live temporarily in tent. Humimpil sa kampo.

campaign, n. the competition by rival political candidates and organizations. Kilusan; kampanya; labanan.

campus, n. the grounds of a college or other school. Bakuran ng kolehiyo; kampus.

can, n. a metal container or receptacle. Lata.

can, v. to have power. Marunong; maaari.

canal, n. an artificial way for navigation, irrigation, etc. Daluyan ng tubig; kanal.

cancel, v. to make void; annul. Kansilahin; kaltasin; alisin; pawalang-bisa.

candelabrum, n. a candlestick. Kandelabra; kandelerong maraming tirikan ng kandila.

candid, adj. fair; frank. Prangko; tapat; matapat.

candidate, n. office or honor seeker. Kandidato; kandidata.

candle, n. a slender piece of tallow, wax, etc. with an embedded wick, burned to give light. Kandila.

candlemass, n. an ecclesiastical festival, Feb. 2, in honor of the presentation of the infant Jesus in the Temple and the purification of the Virgin Mary. Kandilarya; araw ng pangilin dahil sa pagdalisay sa Mahal na Birhen.

canella, n. the cinnamonlike bark of a West Indian tree, used as a condiment and in medicine. Kanela.

cannon, n. mounted gun for firing heavy projectiles. Kanyon.

canon, n. an ecclesiastical rule or law. Batas o tuntuning pansimbahan. Kanon.

canon law, n. a collection of ecclesiastical constitution for the regulation of a church. Mga batas o tuntunin para sa dapat asalin ng mga katoliko.

canopy, n. a suspended covering over a bed, entrance, etc. Kanopi; habong; langit-langitan.

canteen, n. a shop, bar, a recreation hall in a military camp, barracks, etc. Kantin; maliit na tindahang karaniwang kinabibilhan ng alak at mga inuming pampalamig; kantina.

cap, n. a headgear. Gora; kap.

cardinal, adj. principal; of first importance. Mahalaga; pangunahin.

Cardinal, n. a church dignitary ranking next to the Pope. Kardinal.

care, n. solicitude; regard. Pag-iingat; pag-aalaga; pagtingin.

care, v. to be concerned or solicitous. Pag-ingatan; alagaan; mag-alaga.

career, n. a general course of action, especially progress in a lifework. Karera: propesyon.

careful, adj. cautious in one's actions. Maalalay; maingat.

carefulness, n. the state or quality of being careful. Pag-iingat.

careless, adj. heedless; negligent. Bulagsak; pabaya; hindi maingat.

caress, n. an expression of affection, as an embrace, kiss, etc. Himas; pagmamahal.

Carmelite, n. a mendicant friar of a religious order founded in the 12th century. Mga Carmelita; pari o mongha; mga orden ng Carmen.

carnal, adj. not spiritual; sexual. Karnal; ukol sa katawan; malibog.

carnivorous, adj. flesh-eating. Karniboro; mapagkain ng karne; kumakain ng karne.

carpenter, n. a workman who builds houses and does other types of woodwork. Anluwagi; karpintero.

carpentry, n. the art of cutting, framing, and joining timber. Karpinteriya; pagkakarpintero; pag-aanluwagi; ukol sa gawain ng anluwagi.

carriage, n. a wheeled vehicle for conveying persons, usually drawn by horses. Tikas; tindig o tayo; sasakyan; karwahe.

carry, v. to convey from one place to another. Buhatin; dalhin; magdala.

cart, n. a two-wheeled vehicle. Kalesa; kariton.

carton, n. pasteboard box for packing small articles. Kahon; karton.

cartoon, n. a caricature made as a commentary on current events, or to illustrate a joke on narrative. Kartun; karikatura; mga larawang guhit na ang layunin ay magpatawa o manukso.

case, n. instance of the occurrence, existence, etc., of something. Kalagayan; kaso; usapin; kahon.

cash, n. money, esp. money on hand. Kuwaltang nakahanda; salapi; kas.

cashier, n. one who has charge of cash or money as in a bank. Kahero; tagapamahala ng salapi.

casket, n. a small box, esp. for jewels. Ataul; maliit na kahon; kahita.

cassock, n. a long, close-fitting garment worn by clergymen. Sutana.

cast, v. to hurl; throw. Ihulog; ihagis.

cast, n. anything formed in a mold, as a figure in bronze, plaster, etc. Anyo; molde; hulmahan.

caste, n. one of the hereditary social classes among the Hindus. Lahi; kasta.

castille, n. a former kingdom comprising most of Spain. Kastila.

castle, n. a fortified residence of feudal times; a fortress. Kastilyo.

catalogue, n. a list of separate items. Katalogo.

cataract, n. a waterfall, esp. a large one; a disease of the eye, characterized by opacity of the lens. Talon; katarata; panlalabo ng lente ng mata.

catechism, n. an elementary book on the principles of a religion, in the form of questions and answers. Katesismo.

catechist, n. one who teaches catechism. Tagapagturo ng katesismo; katekista.

cathedral, n. the throne or seat of a bishop in the cathedral or episcopal church of his diocese. Ang upuan ng obispo sa pangunahing simbahan ng kanyang diyosesis.

cathedral, n. the principal church in a diocese, that which is specially the church of the bishop. Katedral; ang simbahang kinaroroonan ng upuan ng obispo.

catholic, n. a member of the Universal Christian church. Katoliko.

celebrate, v. to commemorate (a day or event) with festivities, ceremonies, etc. Ipagdiwang; magdiwang.

celebration, n. the act of observing with appropriate rites or ceremonies. Selebrasyon; pagdiriwang.

celibacy, n. the state of being unmarried. Solterya; ang kalagayang nag-iisa o walang asawa.

celibate, adj. unmarried. Walang asawa.

cell, n. one of many like rooms, as in a prison. Munting silid; piitan; selda; kulungan.

cellar, n. a room under a building partly or wholly underground. Kuwarto sa ilalim ng isang gusali; bodega sa silong.

cement, n. any of various adhesive plastic substance. Simyento.

cemetery, n. a burial ground; graveyard. Sementeryo; libingan.

cenacle, n. a room where the Last Supper was held. Senakulo; ang silid na pinagdausan ng Huling Hapunan.

censor, n. an official who examines documents for objectionable information before delivery. Sensor; tagasuri.

censure, v. to reprove; to criticize adversely. Kagalitan; paalalahanan ukol sa di mabuting nagawa.

center, n. the mid-point. Pusod; gitna; sentro.

centimeter, n. one hundredth part of a meter. Sentimetro.

century, n. one hundred years. Senturya; dantaon; siglo.

cereal, n. edible grain or seeds; food, prepared from corn, wheat, etc. Mga butil ng palay, mais at sebada.

cerebral, adj. pertaining to the brain. Serebral; ukol sa utak.

ceremonial, adj. a system of ceremonies, rites, or formalities. Ukol sa seremonya; seremonyal.

ceremony, n. a formal occasion; a rite. Seremonya.

certain, adj. sure to occur; inevitable. Siyerto; tiyak.

certificate of birth, n. a document of attestation pertaining to birth. Papel ng kapanganakan.

certify, v. attest to; to guarantee as certain. Patunayan.

cesspool, n. a pit for the reception of sewage. Hukay ng dumi ng tao na karaniwang kilala sa tawag na poso negro.

chafe, v. to warm by rubbing. Magalit; kiskisin; pag-initin.

chain, n. a connected series of links of metal or other material. Kadena; tanikala.

chair, n. a seat with a back and legs usually for one person. Upuan; silya.

chalet, n. a kind of cottage, low and with wide eaves. Kasita; tsalet.

chalice, n. a drinking cup; a cup for the wine of the Eucharist or Mass. Kalis.

chalk, n. a soft powdery limestone consisting chiefly of fossil shells. Tsok: tisa; yeso.

challenge, v. a call to battle or debate. Probokahin; hamunin.

chamber, n. a room; the meeting hall of a legislative or other assembly. Silid; kapulungan; kamara.

champion, n. one who defends a person or a cause. Kampeon; tagapagtanggol.

chance, n. fate; luck; an opportunity. Pangyayari; pagkakataon; kapalaran.

chancel, n. an enclosed space about the altar of a church. Presbiteryo; bahagi ng simbahang malapit sa altar; harapan ng altar.

change, n. alteration. Pagbabago; pagpapalit.

change, v. to alter. Baguhin; palitan.

changeful, adj. inconstant; uncertain. Papalit-palit; pabagu-bago.

chant, v. to sing religiously. Kumanta; umawit.

chaos, n. very great confusion. Ganap na kaguluhan.

chapel, n. a small church. Kapilya; tsapel.

chaplain, n. a clergyman serving a special group, as a legislature, army, navy, etc. Pari ng mga kawal o marino, kapelyan.

character, n. a trait. Karakter; pagkatao.

charge, v. to put a load in or on; to impose or ask as a price. Atasan; ikarga; ilagay sa kuwenta.

charity, n. benevolence; the quality of sympathetic understanding. Karidad; kabutihang-loob; kawanggawa.

chart, n. a marine map. Tsart; talangguhit; mapa.

chase, v. to pursue; to hurt. Sundan; habulin.

chaste, adj. pure. Puro; dalisay; malinis.

chat, v. to talk familiarly. Dumaldal; satsatan.

chatty, adj. conversational; given to or full of familiar talk. Masatsat; madaldal.

cheap, adj. of little value. Barato; mura.

cheat, v. to deceive. Manloko; mandaya.

cheat, n. a fraud; swindle. Lalang; daya.

check, n. a written order to a bank to pay money. Tseke.

check, v. to restrain or control. Sugpuin; pigilin.

cheese, n. food from milk. Keso.

cheerful, adj. pleasant; arising from good spirits. Masaya.

cheek, n. part of the face. Pisngi.

cherub, n. an angel, often represented as a beautiful winged child. Kerubin; anghel na nasa ikalawang hanay ng mga anghel na malapit sa trono ng Diyos.

chest, n. part of the body. Dibdib.

chess, n. a game for two played on a board of 64 checkered squares. Ahedres; tses.

chew, v. to masticate. Nguyain.

chide, v. to rebuke. Reprobahin; kagalitan.

chief, n. principal; leader. Hepe; tsip; puno; nangungulo.

child, n. a young human offspring. Iho; iha; bata.

chill, v. shiver; make cold. Ginawin; palamigin; ibabad sa yelo.

chilly, adj. producing a sensation of cold. Maginaw; malamig.

chimney, n. a structure usually vertical, containing a passage by which the smoke, gases, etc., of a fire are carried off. Tsiminea.

Chinese, n. a native of China. Insik; intsik.

chin, n. part of the face. Baba.

chinning ring, n. a ring used for exercising. Argolya, tinan.

chip, n. a small fragment, as of wood, or stone. Maliit na piraso; ritaso.

chirp, n. a short, shrill sound made by birds or insects. Huni.

chirp, v. to make or utter with a short, sharp sound, as small birds and certain insects. Humuni.

chisel, n. a tool used by a carpenter. Pait.

chocolate, n. a breakfast drink. Tsokolate.

choice, n. opportunity or right to choose; selection. Pili; hilig; ang pinili.

choir, n. a chorus in a church. Koro.

choke, v. to suffocate. Sakalin; hindi makahinga; mabulunan.

choose, v. to select from two or more. Mabutihin; mamili; pumili; humirang.

chop, v. to cut into pieces. Tilarin; sibakin; tadtarin.

chorus, n. a group of persons singing together. Maramihang tinig; koro.

chrism, n. a consecrated oil used in baptism, confirmation, etc. Krisma; langis na binindisyunan at ginagamit sa kumpil at binyag.

christen, v. to baptize. Bawtisahan; binyagan.

christening, n. baptizing. Babtismo; pagbibinyag.

Christian, n. an adherent of Christianity. Binyagan; kristiyano.

Christmas, n. the festival celebrating the birth of Christ; Dec. 25. Kristmas; Pasko.

church, n. an edifice for public Christian worship. Simbahan; iglesya.

church spire, n. tapering structure erected on a tower of a church. Ang matulis na bubong ng simbahan.

circumcision, n. removal of the foreskin of males. Sirkumsisyon; pagdalisay sa kaluluwa; pagtule.

circumstance, n. incident. Sirkumstansiya; pangyayari; pagkakataon.

cite, v. to quote. Banggitin.

city, n. a large or important town. Siyudad; lunsod.

civilized, adj. educated to social usages; refined. Sibilisado, may kabihasnan; bihasa.

civilly, adv. politely; courteously. Nang magalang.

claim, n. right to demand a thing. Deretso; karapatan.

clam, n. any of several varieties of bivalve mollusks. Halaan.

clan, n. a family or tribe, esp. Scottish. Tribu; angkan; lipi.

clandestine, adj. secret; covert; furtive. Sekreto; lihim.

clash, v. to strike with a resounding or violent collision. Ihampas; ibangga.

clasp, v. to grasp; to embrace. Yakapin; yapusin.

class, n. an order or rank, esp. of persons. Pangkat ng lipunan; klase; uri.

classify, v. sort into group having common character. Klasipikahin; uriin; pag-uriuriin.

claw, n. a sharp, usually curved nail on the foot of an animal. Sipit; kukong matutulis.

clay, n. a species of earth. Putik; luwad.

clean, adj. free from dirt or irrelevant substances. Walang dumi; malinis.

clean, v. to get rid of dirt. Limpyahin; maglinis; linisin.

clear, adj. bright; transparent. Klaro; malinaw; maliwanag.

clearance, n. act of clearing. Klirans; paglinaw; kasulatang nagpapatibay na ang isang tao'y wala nang pananagutan.

clearness, n. the state or quality of being clear. Klaridad; kalinawan; linaw.

clemency, n. mercy. Klemensiya; awa; habag.

clergy, n. the body of men ordained for religious work. Klero; taong tumanggap ng sakramento ng pagpapare; orden ng mga pari.

clerical, adj. pertaining to the clergy or to affairs of the church; pertaining to written records, copies or to office work. Klerikal; ukol sa kawani o klerk; ukol sa mga pari.

clever, adj. talented, bright. Intelihente; matalino; tuso.

cleverness, n. skill; ingenuity. Talento; kakayahan; katalinuhan.

client, n. one who applies to a lawyer for advice or aid; a customer. Kliyente.

cliff, n. the high, steep face of a rocky mass. Bangin; talampas.

climate, n. temperature. Panahon; klima.

climax, n. the culmination of one or more events. Klaymaks; kasukdulan.

climb, v. to ascend with effort. Umakyat; sumampa.

climber, n. one who climbs. Tagaakyat; hagdanan; akyatan.

cling, v. to adhere closely. Manikit; dumikit.

clip, n. a mechanical clasping device, as a paper clip. Klip; pang-ipit.

cloak, n. a loose-fitting, sleeveless outer garment. Kapa.

clock, n. a stationary timepiece. Relos; orasan.

clock-maker, n. one who repairs and fixes clocks. Manggagawa o mangungumpuni ng orasan; relohero.

cloister, n. a monastery or nunnery. Monasteryo; klaustro; ang nakukulong na tirahan ng mga pari o mongha.

close, v. to shut; to end. Tapusin; isara; ipinid.

closet, n. a small room or cabinet for clothing, food, etc. Taguan ng mga gamit; munting silid.

cloth, n. fabric woven from filaments of wool, cotton, etc. Damit; tela.

clothe, v. to dress; to provide with clothing. Bihisan; damtan.

clothes, n. garments for the body; wearing apparel. Ropa; mga damit.

clothier, n. a maker or seller of woolen cloth or clothes. Sastre; mananahi ng mga damit; magdaramit.

cloud, n. white or gray masses of suspended water or ice particles at varying heights above the earth. Alapaap; ulap.

cloudy, adj. overcast with clouds. Maulap.

clown, n. a comedian, especially in a circus. Klawn; payaso.

club, n. a heavy stick, usually thicker at one end than at the other. Samahan; kapisanan; klub.

cluster, n. a bunch. Pulutong; kumpol; buwig.

clutch, v. to hold tightly. Hawakan nang mahigpit.

coach, n. a large, closed, four-wheeled carriage. Kotse.

coadjutor, n. an assistant as of a bishop or prelate. Ang pari o obispong katulong ng ibang pari o obispo; koadhutor

coal, n. a combustible mineral substance. Karbon.

coal-mine, n. a mine or pit in which coal is dug. Mina ng karbon.

coarse, adj. rough; unrefined. Bastos; magaspang.

coast, n. seashore. Baybay-dagat.

coat, n. an outer garment with sleeves, covering the

upper part of the body. Abrigo; amerikana.

coat of arm, n. the heraldic bearings of a person. Armadura; sagisag.

coax, v. to influence by gentle persuasion. Suyuin; udyukan; himukin.

cobbler, n. a man who mends or makes shoes. Manggagawa ng sapatos; sapatero.

cobweb, n. a spider's web. Sapot ng gagamba; bahay gagamba.

cock, n. a rooster. Galyo; tandang; tatyaw.

cocked, adj. turned up. May tapon; napapasakan.

cockroach, n. an insect infesting kitchen, etc. Ipis.

cocoa, n. a chocolate powder Kakaw.

coconut, n. big, round nut with husk. Niyog.

cocoon, n. a silky case in which larvae develop. Bahay-uod; kukún.

cod, n. one of the most important North Atlantic food fishes. Bakalaw.

cod-liver oil, n. oil extracted from the liver of the common cod. Langis ng atay ng bakalaw.

coffee, n. a beverage. Kape.

coffee-pot, n. a covered pot in which the decoction or infusion of coffee is made or in which it is brought upon the table for drinking. Kapiterang lalagyan ng kape.

coffin, n. a burial casket. Ataul; kabaong.

coil, n. series of spirals or rings. Rolyo.

coin, n. stamped metal money. Moneda; barya.

coincide, v. to correspond exactly; to agree. Tumugon; makatulad; masabay; mataon; magkataon; makapareho.

cold, adj. chilling. Maginaw; malamig.

coldness, n. relative absence of heat. Ginaw; lamig.

colic, adj paroxysmal pain in the abdomen or bowels. Koliko; masasakitin ang tiyan.

collaborate, v. to work with another, esp. in writing. Makipagtulungan; kumampi; makiisa.

collaborator, n. an associate in a treacherous act. Kolaboretor.

collapse, n. a sudden failure or falling in. Pagkalugmok; pagguho; paghihimatay.

collapse, v. to break, fall in, or give way. Mapalugmok; himatayin; gumuho.

collar, n. a band or harness worn around the neck. Kolar; kuwelyo.

colleague, n. an associate. Kompanyero; kasama.

collect, v. to gather together Kulektahin; tipunin; singilin.

collection, n. the act or practice of collecting or of gathering. Kuleksiyon; natipon; nasingil.

college, n. an institution of higher learning. Kolehiyo; paaralan.

collide, v. come into violent contact; to crash. Bumangga; mabangga.

collier, n. coal miner. Karbonero; minero ng karbon.

colliery, n. a coal mine. Mina ng karbon.

collision, n. crash. Kolisiyon; banggaan

colonel, n. an officer ranking in most armies below a brigadier general; Koronel.

colony, n. a settlement. Pulutong; kuyog; kolonya.

color, n. a pigment; a dye. Kolor; kulay.

colossal, adj. of giant size. Malaking-malaki.

column, n. a pillar. Hanay; malaking haligi; kolumna.

comb, n. a toothed piece of bone, metal, etc. for arranging the hair. Payneta; suklay.

comb, v. to dress the hair, etc. with a comb. Magsuklay.

combat, n. a fight; a battle. Kombat; pakikihamok; paghahamok.

combine, v. to join. Pag-isahin; pagsamahin.

combustion, n. burning. Kombustiyon; pagkasunog; pagdiringas.

come, v. to approach. Lumapit; dumating.

come across, v. to see by chance. Makita; matagpuan.

come into, v. to acquire by bequest or inheritance. Entra; pumasok.

come out, v. to remove from within. Lumabas.

come up, v. to ascend. Pumanhik; umakyat.

comedian, n. a comic person. Mapagpatawa; komiko; komedyante.

comedy, n. a comic play. Katatawanan; komedya.

comet, n. a tailed star. Kometa.

comfort, v. to console. Aliwin.

comfortable, adj. affording ease; well off. Komodo; maginhawa.

comical, adj. exciting mirth. Komiko; nakakatawa.

comma, n. a punctuation mark indicating a brief or minor pause. Koma; kuwit.

command, v. to order. Manduhan; mag-utos; utusan.

commanding, adj. imposing. Nakaaakit ng pagsunod; makapangyarihan.

commemorate, v. celebrate. Gunitain; alalahanin.

commence, v. to begin. Umpisahan; simulan.

commencement, n. beginning; first existence. Umpisa; simula.

commend, v. to speak of. Purihin; irekomenda; bigyan ng mabuting patunay.

comment, n. remark. Pansin; puna.

commerce, n. trade. Komersiyo; kalakal.

commiserate, v. to pity; to condole with. Makiramay; makidalamhati.

commit, v. to do, to give in trust. Ipasok; iadya; gawin; gumawa; mangako.

common, adj. general; familiar. Pambalana; pangkaraniwan.

commotion, n. disturbance. Komusiyon; kaguluhan.

commune, v. to have intercourse with. Makipag-unawaan; makipag-usap.

communicate, v. to impart knowledge of; make known. Makipag-ugnay; makipag-alam; makipagtalastasan.

communication, n. means of sending messages, orders, etc. Kumunikasiyon; pakikipag-alam; pakikipag-usap.

communion, n. reception of the Eucharist. Komunyon; pakikinabang.

community, n. a society of people. Kumunidad; bayan; purok.

compact, n. an agreement; a treaty. Pakto; kasunduan.

companion, n. one who accompanies or associates with another. Kompanyero; kasama.

company, n. an assemblage. Kompanya; samahan.

compare, v. to note the resemblance and differences of. Ikumpara; ihambing.

comparison, n. similitude. Kumparisiyon; paghahambing.

compass, n. an instrument for showing direction; boundary; range. Aguhon; kompas.

compel, v. to urge; to force. Pilitin.

compensate, v. to pay for; recompense. Bayaran; gantimpalaan.

compensation, n. an equivalent for services, debt, loss, suffering, etc.; a set off. Kumpensasiyon; gantimpala; bayad.

compete, v. contend with another. Makipaglaban; makipagpaligsahan; makipagunahan.

competition, n. rivalry. Kumpetensiya; paligsahan.

compile, v. to put together in one book or work. Pagsamasamahin; tipunin.

complain, v. to express pain; resentment, etc. Magsumbong; magreklamo; dumaing; magdulog ng karaingan.

complement, n. fullness. Komplemento; kapupunan.

complete, adj. whole; absolute. Kompleto; buo; husto.

completeness, n. the state of being complete. Kahustuhan; kabuuan.

complexion, n. color of skin. Kumpleksiyon; kutis.

compliance, n. obedience. Pagsunod; pagkamasunurin.

complicate, v. to render intricate or involved. Palubhain; guluhin.

compliment, n. praise. Sumunod: sumang-ayon.

compose, v. to make up. Bumuo; lumikha; kumatha.

composer, n. a writer of music; an author. Maykatha; maylikha; kompositor.

composition, n. a production. Komposisyon; akda; katha.

composure, n. tranquility. Kompustura; kahinahunan.

compound, n. something formed by combining parts. Kompuwesto; pagkakahaluhalo ng maraming bagay sa isang kabuuan.

comprehend, v. to understand; to know. Maintindihan; mawatasan; maunawaan.

compress, v. to press together. Siksikin; pipiin.

compromise, n. a settlement of differences by mutual concessions. Kompromiso; kasunduan; unawaan.

compromise, v. to adjust by mutual concessions. Makipagkasunduan; makipagunawaan.

compulsion, n. strong irrational impulse. Kumpulsiyon; pamimilit.

compulsory, adj. compelling; obligatory. Obligatoryo; sapilitan.

comrade, n. a close friend. Komrada; kasama.

conceal, v. to hide. Ilihim; itago.

concede, v. to admit as true. Sumang-ayon.

conceit, n. vanity. Amorpropiyo; pagpapahalaga; paghahambog sa sarili.

conceited, adj. vain. Labis magpahalaga sa sarili.

conceive, v. to have an idea. Isipin; balakin.

concentrate, v. to focus. Magkonsentra; magtining; ibuhos ang buong pag-iisip.

concern, v. to relate to. Pakialam; mabahala; pag-aalala.

concert, n. musical harmony. Tugmaan; serenata; konsiyerto.

concession, n. a boon. Konsesiyon; pagbibigay; kagandahang-loob.

conciliate, v. to gain goodwill. Makipagkasundo; makipag-unawaan.

concise, adj. brief. Tuwiran; maikli; maigsi.

conclave, n. the meeting of the cardinals for election of a Pope. Pagpupulong ng mga Kardinal upang maghalal ng Papa.

conclusion, n. a result or outcome. Konklusiyon; wakas; katapusan.

conclude, v. to end; to decide. Magkonklusiyon; tapusin; ipalagay.

concoct, v. to devise; to contrive, as a plot. Gumawa; lumikha; umimbento.

concourse, n. assemblage. Konkurso; isang pagtitipon; sangandaan.

concrete, adj. actual; real. Kongkreto; nakikita't nahihipo.

concur, v. to agree. Pumayag; sumang-ayon.

concussion, n. shock. Konkasyon; panginginig; pagkasindak dahil sa banggaan.

condemn, v. to express strong disapproval of; to pronounce guilty. Parusahan; isumpa.

condense, v. to make dense; to reduce to liquid or solid Palaputin; buuin; paikliin.

condescend, v. to stoop; to deign. Sumang-ayon o sumuko nang may katigasang-loob.

condition, n. a state of being. Kondisiyon; kalagayan; ayos.

condole, v. to sympathize. Makidalamhati; makiramay.

conduce, v. to lead or contribute. Panggalingan; makatulong.

conduct, n. behavior. Kunduk-ta; kilos; asal.

confectionery, n. candy. Matamis; mga kendi.

confer, v. to bestow. Isang-'guni; ipagkaloob.

confess, v. to admit one's sin's to a priest to obtain absolution. Magkumpisiyon; ikumpisal; mangumpisal.

confession, n. an avowal. Kumpesiyon; pangungumpisal.

confidant, n. bosom friend. Kompidante; katapatang-loob.

confidence, n. reliance. Kompidensiya; kompiyansa; pagtitiwala.

confident, adj. sure of oneself; bold. Nakasisiguro; nakatitiyak; tiwala.

confine, v. to imprison. Ikulong; ipiit.

confine, n. boundary. Kulungan; hanggahan; piitan.

confirm, v. to verify. Kumpermahan; patunayan.

confirmation, n. the ceremony of confirming, reassurance. Kumpirmasiyon; kumpil.

confiscate, v. to forfeit. Kumpiskahin; ilitin; samsamin.

conflagration, n. a great fire Insendiyo; sunog.

conflict. n. a fight or struggle Konplikto; pagtatalo; pagkakasalungatan.

conform, v. to comply. Kumumporme; umayon; umalinsunod.
confound, v. to perplex. Malito, lituhin.
confraternity, n. brotherhood. Konpradiya; konpraternidad; hermanidad; samahan; kapatiran.
confront, v. to face. Konprontahin; iharap; harapin.
confuse, v. to jumble; mix up. Ipagkamali; guluhin; lituhin.
congeal, v. to freeze; stiffen. Tumigas; mamuo; makurta.
congestion, n. rush of blood. Kongestiyon; pagsisiksikan.
congratulate, v. to felicitate. Batiin.
congratulatory, adj. containing or expressing congratulation. Kongratulatoryo; nagsasaad ng pagbati.
congregate, v. to assemble. Tipunin; pagsama-samahin.
congregation, n. audience; assemblage. Kongregasiyon; pagtitipon.
congress, n. conference; assembly; lawmaker. Batasan; kapulungan; kongreso.
conjugal, adj. matrimonial. Matrimonyal; pangmag-asawa.
conjugate, v. to inflect (a verb). Banghayin.
connect, v. to join. Ikunekta; idugtong; ikabit.
connection, n. relation. Kuneksiyon; mga kinakapitan; mga taong tumutulong; kaugnayan.
conquer, v. to subdue. Talunin; gahisin; lupigin; sakupin.
conqueror, n. victor. Kongkistador; mananakop.
conquest, n. triumph. Pananakop; panlulupig.
conscience, n. knowledge of right and wrong. Budhi; konsiyensiya.
conscientious, adj. scrupulous. Matapat; maingat at matiyaga.
conscious, adj. aware of one's existence, feelings and thoughts. May pakiramdam; nagkakamalay.
consciousness, n. knowledge. Pakiramdam; malay; pagkamalay; kamalayan.
conscript, n. one pressed into military or naval service. Konskripsiyon; sapilitang pagsusundalo.
consecutive, adj. following or succeeding one another in regular order. Saksesibo; sunud-sunod.
consent, v. to agree. Pahintulutan; sumang-ayon; pumayag.
consequence, n. a result. Kahalagahan; bunga; kinalabasan.
conservative, n. moderate. Makaluma; mahinahon; konserbatibo.
consider, v. to deem to be; to think. Kunsiderahin; isaalang-alang; ayunan.
considerate, adj. thoughtful of others. Indulhente; mapagbigay; mapag-alang-alang.
considering, adj. & prep. having regard to; taking into account. Itinuturing; isinasaalang-alang.
consign, v. to entrust. Italaga; ipagkatiwala sa iba; ibahin.
consignment, n. the act of consigning. Konsignasiyon; paghahabilin; pagtitiwala sa iba.
consecration, n. dedication of service and worship of God Konsegrasyon; pag-aalay sa

Diyos.

consist, v. to be composed of. Buuin; binubuo.

consistent, adj. compatible; firm. Konsistente; di-pabagu-bago.

consolation, n. comfort; solace. Konsolasiyon; pag-aliw; kaaliwan.

console, v. to comfort. Aliwin.

consolidate, v. to unite firmly in one body. Pag-isahin; pagsama-samahin; buuin.

consolidation, n. the act of forming a firm compact mass, body, or system. Konsolidasyon; pagsasama-sama; pagbubuo.

consort, n. a partner; an intimate associate. Abay; konsorte.

conspicuous, adj. easy to be seen. Madaling makita; kapuna-puna; kapansin-pansin.

conspiracy, n. a plot. Kunsperasiyon; pakana; sapakatan; sabwatan.

constant, adj. firm. Konstante; tapat; walang pagbabago.

constipation, n. condition of the bowels marked by difficult evacuation. Kunstipasiyon; di-pagdumi; tibi.

construe, v. to interpret. Ipaliwanag; bigyan ng kahulugan.

consul, n. a diplomatic officer chiefly concerned with trade. Konsul.

consulate, n. office of consul. Tanggapan ng konsul; konsulado.

consult, v. to seek an opinion. Ikunsulta, sumangguni.

consume, v. to spend; use up. Ubusin; gamitin.

consumption, n. the using up of goods and services. Konsumo; pag-ubos; paggamit.

consumptive, adj. wasteful; destructive. Bulagsak; ubus-ubos.

contain, v. to include or embody. Mapaglalagyan; naglalaman.

contaminate, v. to pollute. Mahawa; hawahan.

contamination, n. pollution; defilement; taint. Kontaminasiyon; pagkakahawa.

contemplate, v. to view or reflect upon attentively. Kuntemplahin; isipin; balakin.

contemplation, n. reflection. Kontemplasiyon; meditasiyon; pagninilay-nilay.

contemporary, adj. existing or occuring at the same time. Kontemporero; kapanahon.

contempt, n. act of despising; scorn. Dispresyuhin; paghamak.

content, adj. pleased. Kontento; nasisiyahan.

contents, n. subject matter, as of a book. Nilalaman.

contest, v. tc compete or vie for. Kontestahin; tutulan; labanan.

continual, adj. uninterrupted. Walang hinto; patuloy; walang patid.

continue, v. to keep on with. Ipagpatuloy; ituloy; dugtungan.

contraband, n. smuggled goods. Kontrabando; labag na kalakal; ismagel.

contraction, n. shortening; shrinkage. Abrebiyatura, paikli.

contradict, v. to oppose. Pabulaanan; salungatin; sumalungat.

contribute, v. to pay a share. Magkontribusiyon; umabuloy.

contrition, **n.** sincere penitence. Pagtitika; pagsisisi.

contrive, v. to devise. Umimbento; gawan ng paraan.

control, v. .to exercise power over. Kontrolin; supilin; mapigil; pigilin.

convalescence, n. recovery. Konbalensiya; pagpapalakas pagkatapos magkasakit.

convenient, adj. favorable. Kumbiniyente; walang sagabal; maluwag; magaan.

convent, n. a monastery or nunnery. Monasteryo; kumbento.

converge, v. to meet in a point. Magsalikop; magsalubong.

converse, v. talk informally. Mag-usap.

convert, n. a converted person esp. as to religion. Kumbertido; ang taong inakit o pinapaniwala.

convert, v. to persuade to change policy, religion, etc. Kumbertihin; akitin; palipatin mula sa isang pananampalataya.

convince, v. to persuade (a person) to believe. Kumbinsihin; papaniwala.

conviction, n. strong belief. Kumbiksiyon; pananalig; paniniwala.

cook, v. to prepare food. Mangusina; lutuin; magluto.

cool, adj. calm; moderate; cold. Presko; mahinahon; malamig.

cool-headed, adj. having a temper not easily excited. Malamig ang ulo.

cooperate, v. to work together toward a common goal. Makiisa; tumulong.

cooperation, n. activity shared for mutual benefit. Kooperasiyon; pakikiisa; pagtulong.

copius, adj. ample. Abundante; sagana.

copper, n. a malleable ductile metallic element. Tanso.

copy, n. a reproduction or imitation of an original. Salin; sipi; kopya.

copy, v. to imitate. Gayahin; sipiin; sumipi; kopyahin.

cord, v. to bind or fasten with cords. Talian ng lubid.

cordial, adj. hearty. Kordiyal; taos-puso.

core, n. inner part; pith. Kalagitnaan; ubod; kaibuturan.

cork, n. a stopper. Kórk; tapon.

corner, n. the meeting place of two converging lines or surfaces. Kanto; sulok; panulukan.

corona, n. a crown; halo. Halo; kornisa; pabilog na sinag; ang buhok na nasa paligid ng ulo ng pari.

coroner, n. the presiding officer at an inquest into a cause of death. Koroner; ang taong sumisiyasat sa bangkay upang mabatid ang sanhi ng pagkamatay.

corpse, n. a dead body. Kadaber; bangkay.

corpulent, adj. fat; obese. Kurpulento; mataba.

correct, adj. accurate; free from error. Korekto; tumpak; wasto.

correct, v. to rectify; to exact. Kurehin; iwasto; itumpak.

corridor, n. a narrow passageway. Daang makitid; pasilyo; koridor.

corroborate, v. to confirm. Patunayan.

corrode, v. to rust. Kalawangin.

corrugated, adj. wrinkled. Kanalado; kulu-kulubot.

corrupt, adj. guilty of dishonesty. Kuruptu; masama; nasusuhulan.
cost, n. charge; expense. Presyo; halaga.
costly, adj. expensive. Kustoso; mahal.
costume, n. dress for stage wear; Trahe; kasuutan; bihis.
cosy, adj. snug; comfortable. Komodo; maginhawa.
cotton, n. a soft white fibrous mass from a plant. Algodon; bulak.
cough, v. to expel air from the lungs with effort and noise. Umubo.
counsel, n. advice. Konseho; tagapayo.
count, n. the act of reckoning; a nobleman. Kuwenta; bilang; konde.
count, v. name numbers in order. Bumilang.
counterfeit, adj. false; forged. Konterpit; huwad.
countess, n. a woman having the rank of a count or earl in her own right. Kondesa.
country, n. a region. Bukid; bansa; bayan.
couple, n. a pair. Dalawa; pareha.
coupon, n. interest certificate. Kupon.
courage, n. valor; daring. Lakas ng loob; tapang.
courageous, adj. brave; valiant. Balyente; matapang.
course, n. a systematic series of studies. Kurso; karera.
court, n. legal tribunal. Hukuman; korte.
courteous, adj. polite. Mapitagan; magalang.
courtesy, n. civility; excellence of manner. Kortesya; paggalang.
courtship, n. act of wooing. Pagligaw.
cousin, n. child of mother's or father's sister or brother. Primo; prima; pinsan.
cover, n. anything which veils or conceals. Kubiyerta; takip.
cover, v. to put something over or upon. Damtán; takpan.
coverlet, n. a bedspread. Sobrekama; kobrekama.
covet, v. to desire eagerly. Hangarin; pagnasaan.
cow, n. female of the ox. Baka.
coward, adj. lacking courage; timid. Kubarde; duwag.
crab, n. a shellfish. Alimasag; alimango.
crack, n. narrow fissure. Lamat; putok; siwang; biyak.
crack, v. to break without complete separation of parts. Pumutok; siwangan; biyakin.
craft, n. art; skill. Arte; sining.
cramp, n. a sudden painful contraction of a muscle. Kalambre; pulikat.
cramp, v. hinder from free action. Kalambrihin; pulikatin.
crash, v. to smash; shatter. Ilagpak; ibagok; ibangga.
crave, v. to long for. Hangarin; nasain; pagnasaan.
crayon, n. for coloring. Krayola; koloring.
crawl, v. to advance slowly or feebly. Umusad; gumapang.
crazy, adj. insane. Loko; sira; baliw.
creak, v. to make a squeaking noise. Krik; umalit-it.
cream, n. the rich, oily part of milk, Gata ng gatas; krema.
crease, n. mark of fold. Tupi; pileges.

crease, v. to make a fold or furrow. Itupi; lagyan ng pileges.
create, v. to make. Lumalang; lumikha; gumawa.
creation, n. formation. Likha.
creator, n. one who creates or makes; God. Kreador; Poong lumikha.
creature, n. any being. Nilikha; nilalang.
credible, adj. worthy of belief. Mapaniniwalaan.
credit, n. borrowing power. Kredito; utang.
credo, n. the Apostle's Creed; any creed. Kredo; paniniwala; pananampalataya.
creed, n. religious belief. Panuntunan; paniniwala; pananampalataya.
creep, v. to crawl. Gumapang.
crew, n. a ship's company. Tripulante; mga tauhan ng bapor.
crime, n. an offense punishable by law. Sala; krimen; kasalanan.
criminal, n. a person guilty of wrongdoing. Kriminal; salarin.
crimson, n. a deep-red color. Krimson; mapulang-mapula.
cripple, n. a lame person. Paralitiko; lumpo.
crisis, n. a decisive stage in the course of anything. Krisis.
critic, n. one who censures or finds fault. Mamumuna; kritiko; tagapansin.
criticize, v. to make judgment as to merits and faults. Sensurahin; mamintas; magbigay ng pansin.
crooked, adj. bent; curled. Kurbado; baluktot.
cross, n. a symbol of Christian religion; two intersecting stakes, bars, or lines. Paghihirap; kurus; krus.
cross, v. to make the sign of the cross on or over; to intersect. Bumagtas; nagkurus; tumawid.
crowd, n. a throng. Pulutong ng mga tao.
crown, n. a monarch's jeweled headdress. Putong; korona.
crozier, n. a bishop's crook. Tungkod ng obispo.
crucifix, n. cross of our Lord. Krusipiho.
crude, adj. unrefined; unpolished. Krudo; magaspang.
cruel, adj. pitiless. Tampalasan, malupit; mabagsik.
cruise, n. an ocean trip for pleasure. Biyahe; paglalakbay-dagat.
crumb, n. a small fragment, esp. of bread. Maliliit na piraso; mumo.
crush, v. to break into bits. Pipiin; ligisin; durugin.
crutch, n. a prop under arm used by a lame person. Krats; tungkod ng pilay; muleta.
cucumber, n. a trailing plant. Katmon; pipino.
cult, n. a particular system of religious worship. Kulto; paraan ng pananampalataya.
cultivate, v. to foster. Bungkalin; linangin; patubuin; alagaan.
cunning, adj. ingenious; sly. Magdaraya; tuso.
curia, n. the Roman See in its temporal aspect, including the pope, cardinals, etc. Kuria; hukuman ng Papa.
cup, n. a bowl-shaped vessel. Kalis; tasa; kopa.
cupboard, n. a place for storing dishes. Paminggalan.
curable, adj. that may be

cured. Maaaring gamutin.

curate, n. a minister. Kura; pari.

cure, v. to heal. Gamutin.

curious, adj. inquisitive. Kurioso; mausisa.

curl, v. to form into ringlet. Magkulot; kulutin.

current, n. a moving stream of water, air, electricity, etc. Agos; kuryente.

curse, n. a profane oath. Tungayaw; sumpa.

curtain, n. fabric hung to adorn or conceal, as at windows, a stage. Tabing; kurtina.

curve, n. bend. Kurba; liko.

cushion, n. a pillow. Kutson; almuhadon.

custard, n. a cooked dessert of eggs and milk. Matamis; letse-plan.

custom, n. usual habit or practice. Kustumbre; ugali; gawi.

customer, n. a patron; a client. Parukyano; suki.

customary, adj. usual; habitual. Akustumbrado; kinaugalian; kinagisnan.

custom-house, n. a government office at a seaport for collecting custom duties, clearing vessels. Kostum; adwana.

cut, n. style. Korte; tabas.

cut, v. gash; shape, as a garment. Kortehin; putulin; tabasin.

cutlet, n. a thin slice of meat. Kustilyas; tsuleta.

cutting, n. a piece cut off. Retaso; pinagtabasan.

cynic, n. a sneering fault-finder. Siniko; mapag-alinlangan.

cynosure, n. attractive point. Tampulan; tudlaan ng pansin.

D

dabble, v. splash or play in water. Wisikan; wiligan ng tubig.

daddy, n. a pet name for father. Itay; papa; tatay.

daft, adj. foolish; silly. Tonto; luko-luko; sintu-sinto.

dagger, n. a poniard. Patalim; punyal.

dahlia, n. a flower. Dalya.

daily, adj. & n. newspaper everyday. Diyaryo; pang-araw-araw.

dainty, adj. of delicate beauty; fastidious. Maselan; mayumi at kasiya-siya.

dairy, n. a milk-farm. Letserya; gatasan.

dale, n. a small valley. Libis: lambak.

dalmatic, n. the vestment used by the deacon at mass, and worn also by bishops over the chasuble. Dalmatika; kasuutang banal ng mga diyakono.

damage, n. injury; loss. Danyos; pinsala; sira.

damaging, adj. injuring. Perhuwisyo; nakasisira.

dame, n. a lady. Dalaga; dama; abay na babae.

damn, v. to curse. Isumpa; sumpain.

damnation, n. condemnation. Kodemnasiyon; pagsumpa.

damning, adj. detestable. Kasumpa-sumpa.

damp, adj. moist. Malagihay; mahalumigmig; basa-basa.

damsel, n. a maiden; a girl. Senyorita; dalaga.

dance, n. a succession of ordered steps and movements to music. Dansa; sayaw.

dance, v. to move the body and feet rhythmically to music. Bumayle; sumayaw: magsayaw.

dancer, n. one who dances. Baylerina; mananayaw.
danger, n. risk; peril. Peligro; panganib.
dangerous, adj. hazardous. Peligroso; mapanganib.
dangle, v. to hang loose. Ibitin; ilawit.
dapper, adj. neat; trim. Bonita; bonito; maganda; malinis; makinis.
dare, v. to venture; to defy. Hamunin; mangahas.
daring, n. boldness. Walang takot; malakas ang loob; matapang.
dark, adj. obscure. Maitim; madilim.
darkness, n. obscurity. Kadiliman; karimlan; dilim.
darling, n. dearly beloved. Giliw; irog; ang minamahal.
date, n. a certain day Takda; petsa.
daughter, n. a female child or person in relation to her parents. Iha; anak na babae.
daughter-in-law, n. a son's wife. Manugang na babae
dawn, n. break of day. Bukang-liwayway; simula ng ano mang bagay; madaling-araw.
day, n. twenty-four hours; the interval of light between two successive nights. Panahon; araw.
daylight, n. sunlight. Liwanag ng araw.
dazzle, v. to surprise with display. Silawin sa matinding liwanag.
deacon, n. a cleric or layman who assists a minister. Diyakono.
deaconess, n. female deacon. Diyakonesa.
dead, adj. destitute of life. Muwerto; patay.
deaden, v. to make vapid. Bawasan o pahinain; patayin ang damdamin; alisan ng pakiramdam.
deadly, adj. fatal; malignant. Destruktibo; mortal; nakamamatay.
deaf, adj. unable to hear. Bingi.
deafness, n. want of hearing. Sordera; kabingihan.
deal, n. a stroke of business. Trato; kasunduan.
dean, n. an ecclesiastical dignitary ranking next to the bishop. Dekano; sa simbahang katoliko, ang pangulong pari na kasunod ng obispo.
dear, adj. beloved. Kerido; minamahal.
death, n. cessation of life. Muwerte; kamatayan.
debark, v. to disembark. Dumisembarko; umahon sa bapor.
debase, v. to degrade. Hamakin.
debate, n. a discussion. Diskusiyon; pagtatalo.
debt, n. that which is owed. Utang.
debtor, n. one who owes something. Ang may-utang.
debut, n. a first public appearance. Debu; pagpapakilala sa lipunan.
decay, n. deterioration. Pagkasira; pagkabulok.
decay, v. to deteriorate; decompose. Masira; mabulok.
deceit, n. a fraud. Enganyo; daya; kadayaan.
deceitful, adj. fraudulent. Enganiyoso; enganiyosa; mandaraya; manlilinlang.
deceive, v. to delude. Dayain; mandaya.
December, n. the 12th month of the year containing 31 days. Disyembre.

decent, **adj.** respectable. Desente; kagalang-galang.
deception, **n.** misrepresentation. Desepsiyon; pagdaraya.
decide, **v.** to make up one's mind. Magdisisyon; pagpasiyahan; magpasiya; hatulan.
decision, **n.** determination. Desisyon; pasiya; kapasiyahan.
deck, **n.** the floor of a ship. Kubyerta.
declare, **v.** to assert. Magdeklara; ipahayag; magsalita.
declination, **n.** a bending, sloping, or moving downward. Deklinasiyon; paghilig.
decline, **v.** to refuse. Tanggihan; manghina.
decompose, **v.** to separate into constituent parts. Magkahiwa-hiwalay; mabulok.
decorate, **v.** to ornament. Dekorahan; palamutihan.
decrease, **v.** to become less; to reduce. Bawasan; liitan.
decrease, **n.** a reduction. Paghina; pagbabawas.
decree, **n.** edict. Dikrito; utos.
decretal, **n.** a Papal decree. Liham ng Papa na may lamang kapasiyahan.
dedicate, **v.** to devote. Italaga; ihandog; ialay.
deduct, **v.** take from. Awasin; bawasan.
deed, **n.** an act. Akto; gawa; gawain.
deem, **v.** to judge; to think. Husgahan; ipasiya; pasiyahan.
deep, **adj.** profound. Propundo; malalim.
deepen, **v.** to make deeper. Palalimin; laliman.
deer, **n.** a ruminant mammal the male of which bears deciduous horns or antlers. Usa.
deface, **v.** to disfigure. Dispigurahin; papangitin.
defalcate, **v.** to embezzle. Lustayin; dispalkuhin.
defalcation, **n.** a fraudulent deficiency in money matters. Dispalko; paglustay.
defame, **v.** to slander. Siraan; manirang-puri.
defamation, **n.** calumny. Depamasiyon; paninirang-puri.
default, **v.** to fail to fulfill an obligation. Pumaltos; huwag tumupad; magpabaya.
defeat, **n.** a setback; a loss. Pagkatalo.
defeat, **v.** to conquer or overcome in a battle or contest. Talunin.
defect, **n.** an imperfection. Depekto; kasiraan; kapintasan.
defective, **adj.** faulty; imperfect. Depektoso; maysira; may kapintasan.
defense, **n.** a safeguard. Depensa; pagtatanggol.
defend, **v.** to uphold; vindicate. Ipagdepender; ipagtanggol.
defender, **n.** a vindication, either by arms or by arguments. Depensor; tagapagtanggol.
defensive, **adj.** protective. Depensibo; nakalaang magtanggol.
defer, **v.** to delay; to postpone. Ipagpaliban.
deference, **n.** respect. Deperensiya; pagsasaalang-alang.
deficiency, **n.** shortage. Palta; kakulangan.
defile, **v.** to soil; sully. Siraan; dumhan.
define, **v.** to describe. Depinahin; bigyang-katuturan; tu-

ringan.

definable, adj. capable or having the limits ascertained, fixed and determined. Mabibigyan katuturan: maaaring tiyakin.

definite, adj. & n. fixed; exact: Depenito· tiyak.

definite, adj. fixed; exact; Depenito; tiyak.

deformed, adj. disfigured. May pinsala.

defraud, v. to cheat; dupe. Deprode; dayain; linlangin.

defray, v. to pay. Magbayad.

deft, adj. dextrous; skillful. May kakayahan.

defunct, adj. dead. Dipunto; nasira; nawala.

defy, v. to challenge. Probokahin; suwayin; hamunin.

degrade, v. to debase. Despresiyuhin; hamakin; kutyain.

degree, n. a step; rank. Grado; antas.

deity, n. a god or goddess. Diyedad; diyus-diyusan.

dejected, adj. sad; depressed. Malungkot; matamlay.

delay, n. a putting off. Pagkaantala; pagkabalam.

delegate, n. an emissary; a deputy. Delegado; kinatawan.

delete, v. take out; erase. Burahin; alisin.

deliberate, adj. careful; intentional. Sinadya; maingat.

deliberation, n. careful consideration. Deliberasiyon; pagtitimbang-timbang.

delicate, adj. fragile; exquisite. Maselan; delikado; marikit.

delightful, adj. charming; highly pleasing. Kalugudlugod; puspos ng aliw.

deliver, v. to give or hand over. Iintrega; ipagkaloob; ibigay; dalhin; iligtas.

delivery, n. act or manner of giving or sending forth. Paghahatid; pagkakaloob; pagbibigay.

demolish, v. to ruin; to destroy. Wasakin; gibain.

demon, n. a devil. Satanas; demonyo.

demonstrate, v. to describe or explain. Itanghal; ipakita; ituro.

demoralize, v. to dishearten. Siraan ng loob.

demur, v. to object. Mag-atubili.

demure, adj. affectedly modest Modesto; mabini.

denial, n. a disavowal. Pagtanggi; pagtatuwa.

denominate, v. to name; to designate. Hirangin; italaga.

denounce, v. to blame or brand publicly. Tuligsain; ihayag ang pagkukulang.

dense, adj. thick; compact. Siksik; makapal.

dent, n. a notch. Yupi.

dentist, n. a tooth-doctor. Dentista.

denunciation, n. open and vehement condemnation. Pagtatatwa; pagsusuplong; pagpaparatang.

deny, v. to refuse to admit the truth of. Pabulaanan; itatuwa.

depart, v. to move from. Umalis; lumisan.

department, n. a distinct part of anything arranged in division. Departamento; kagawaran.

departure, n. a going away. Pag-alis; paglisan.

depend, v. to rely upon. Dumepende; umasa.

dependent, n. contingent; subordinate. Dependiyente; alaga; taong umaasa sa tulong ng kapwa.

depose, v. to dethrone. Deponer; alisin.
deposit, v. to place for safekeeping. Magdeposito; maglagak.
depravity, n. a vitiated state. Korupsiyon; kasamaan.
depress. v. to weaken; sadden. Pahinain; patamlayin; palungkutin.
deprive, v. to divest. Pagkaitan; alisan.
depth, n. deepness. Katindihan; lalim.
depthless, adj. shallow. Superpisyal; mababaw.
descend, v. to move downward. Manaog; bumaba.
descent, n. downfall. Pagpanaog; pagbaba.
describe, v. to explain. Isalaysay; ilarawan.
description, n. representation. Deskripsiyon; paglalarawan.
desert, n. a wilderness. Disyerto; hindi tinatahanan.
desert, v. to forsake. Pabayaan; layasan; iwan.
deserving, adj. meritorious. Meritoryo; karapat-dapat.
desiccate, v. to dry up. Patuyuin; tuyuin.
designate, v. to point out. Hirangin; italaga; piliin.
desirable, adj. pleasing, excellent or fine. Kanais-nais; mainam.
desire, n. a wish; craving. Pagnanasa; paghahangad; pagnanais.
desirous, adj. wishful. Naghahangad; nagnanais.
desk, n. a table for writing, reading or study. Eskritoryo; pupitre; hapag-sulatan.
desolate, adj. lonely. Malungkot.
despair, n. without hope. Desesperasiya; kawalang-pag-asa.
desperate, adj. hopeless; wild. Desperado; walang pag-asa.
despedida, n. a farewell act. Despedida; pamamaalam.
despise, v. disdain. Despresiyuhin; hamakin; libakin.
dessert, n. a sweet served as the last course of a meal. Matamis; himagas.
destination, n. the predetermined end of a journey. Destinasiyon; hantungan.
destiny, n. fate; fortune. Destino; kapalaran.
destitute, adj. indigent; extremely poor. Mahirap.
destitution, n. poverty. Destitusiyon; kahirapan.
destroy, v. to ruin. Sirain; wasakin.
detach, v. to separate. Isepara; ihiwalay.
detail, v. to particularize. Idetalye; isa-isahin.
detain, v. to hold back. Detenahin; pigilin; abalahin.
detective, n. secret police. Sekreta.
deter, v. to discourage. Impedehin; abalahin; pigilin.
determine, v. to resolve. Lutasin; tiyakin; pagpasiyahan.
detest, v. to loathe. Kapootán; kamuhian.
detract, v. to take from. Alisan; siraang-puri.
devastate, v. lay waste; pillage. Pinsalain; sirain; iguho.
develop, v. to improve. Palakihin; debelopin; paunlarin; linangin.
device, n. an invention or contrivance. Aparato; pakana; balak; pamamaraan; gamit.
devil, n. supreme evil spirit. Demonyo.
devote, v. consecrate or dedi-

cate. Italaga; iukol; ialay.

devotion, n. worship. Debosiyon; pagsambang taos; tapat na pananalig.

dew, n. moisture. Sereno; hamog.

diabetes, n. a disease commonly due to the inability of the body to use sugar. Isang uri ng sakit sa bato; diyabetes.

diagnosis, n. recognition of a disease by its symptoms. Diyagnosis; pagsusuri.

dialogue, n. conversation between two or more persons. Diyalogo; usapan.

diarrhea, n. abnormal frequent evacuation of the bowels. Pagtatae; iti.

diary, n. a daily record. Dayari; talaarawan.

dictate, v. to order; command. Diktahan; magdikta.

dictator, n. an absolute ruler. Diktador; taong mapagdikta.

dictionary, n. a book giving information on a particular subject, under alphabetically arranged headings. Diksiyunaryo; talatinigan.

die, v. to cease to live. Tumigil; mamatay.

diet, n. food and drink regularly consumed. Pagpigil sa pagkain nang marami; diyeta.

differ, v. to disagree. Umiba; di-sumang-ayon.

difference, n. distinction. Diperensiya; pagkakaiba.

different, adj. unlike. Diperente; iba.

diffident, adj. distrustful. Diskumpiyado; walang tiwala.

difficult, adj. not easy; hard. Malalim; mahirap.

diffuse, v. to spread. Ikalat; isabog.

diffused, adj. widely spread or scattered. Sabog; kalat.

dig, v. to excavate. Kumutkot; humukay.

digest, v. to assimilate. Lagumin; tunawin.

digestible, adj. capable of being digested. Maaaring tunawin.

digger, n. a person or an animal who digs. Kabador; manghuhukay.

dignified, adj. stately; noble. Marangal; kagalang-galang.

dignity, n. decorum. Dignidad; kadakilaan ng anyo at kilos; pagiging kagalang-galang.

digrees, v. to turn aside. Lumayo; humiwalay.

dike, n. an embarkment for restraining the water of the sea or a river. Saplad; dike; pilapil.

dilapidate, v. to reduce to or fall into ruin or decay. Wasakin; sirain; iguho.

dilapidation, n. ruin. Pagkawasak; pagkasira; pagkaguho.

dilate, v. to expand. Palaparin; palakihin; palawakin.

dilemma, n. a quandary. Dilema; pagkagulo; pagkalito.

diligent, adj. assiduous. Dilihente; matiyaga.

dilute, v. weaken by an admixture of water and other liquid. Pahinain; haluan; bantuan.

dim, adj. not bright. Obskuro; madilim.

dimension, n. size; extent. Medida; sukat.

dimidiate, v. to divide into half. Pagdalawahin; hatiin sa dalawang bahagi.

diminish, v. to reduce; lessen. Kaltasan; liitan; bawasan.

diminutive, adj. very small;

tiny. Diminitibo; maliit.

dimly, adv. in an obscure manner. Na malabo; madilim.

dimple, n. natural hollow in some soft part of the body, as in the cheek. Dimpol; biloy.

din, n. loud sound. Ingay.

dine, v. to eat. Kumain.

dingy, adj. dirty. Marumi.

dining-room, n. a room to dine in. Komedor; silid-kainan.

dinner, n. principal meal in the evening. Komida; pagkain; hapunan.

diocese, n. bishop's circuit. Diosis; purok na nasasakupan ng obispo.

dip, n. a short swim; a sloping downward. Sisid; pagkakalubog; bahagyang hukay.

diplomat, n. one employed or skilled in diplomacy. Taong marunong makibagay; diplomatiko.

direct, adj. straightforward; open; sincere. Direkto; tiyak.

direction, n. guidance. Direksiyon; patutunguhan.

dirge, n. funeral music. Punebre; awit ukol sa namatay.

direful, adj. dreadful. Katakut-takot; nakababakla.

dirt, n. filth. Sukal; dumi; basura.

dirty, adj. unclean; soiled. Malaswa; marumi.

disable, v. incapacitate. Baldahin; alisan ng kaya; alisan ng lakas.

disadvantage, n. unfavorable circumstance. Kagahulan; walang kapakinabangan.

disadvantageous, adj. unfavorable to success or prosperity. Disbentahoso; di-pakikinabangan.

disaffirm, v. to deny; to contradict. Kontrahin; pabulaanan.

disagree, v. to be in opposition. Di-magkaisa; sumalungat; di-umayon.

disappear, v. vanish. Magtago; mawala; maglaho.

disappoint, v. to frustrate. Mabigo.

disapproval, n. unfavorable opinion. Disaprobasiyon; di-pagsang-ayon.

disarm, v. to deprive of weapons. Alisan ng sandata.

disarrange, v. to disturb. Wala sa lugar; guluhin.

disaster, n. a misfortune. Disastre; sakuna; kapahamakan.

disband, v. to break up. Buwagin; maghiwa-hiwalay; malansag.

disbelieve, v. to reject as untrue. Di-paniwalaan.

discern, v. to perceive. Makita; maintindihan.

discipline, n. obedience to rules. Kaayusan; disiplina.

disclaim, v. to disavow. Pabulaanan; itatuwa.

disclose, v. to reveal. Ipaalam; ibunyag; ihayag.

discomfiture, n. frustration; utter defeat. Pagkabigo; pagkatalo.

discomfort, n. uneasiness. Pagkabalisa; kawalan ng kaginhawahan.

disconnect, v. to detach. Putulin; alisin sa pagkakakabit; tanggalin.

discord, n. difference of opinions. Hidwaan; di-pagkakasundo.

discount, n. deduction. Diskuwento; rebaha; bawas.

discourage, v. to hinder; dissuade. Pigiiin; mawalan ng loob; manghina ang loob.

discourse, n. talk; conversation. Diskurso; pagsasalita.

discourteous, adj. lacking courtesy; rude. Bastos; walang galang.

discover, v. to find out. Diskubrihin; tuklasin.

discreet, adj. prudent. Maingat; mahinahon.

discretional, n. subject or left to one's discretion. Diskresiyonal; nasa pagpapasiya.

discriminate, v. distinguish. Itangi; piliin.

discussion, n. debate. Diskusiyon; pagtatalo.

disdainful, adj. scornful. Mapang-aba; mapangmata; mapanghamak.

disease, n. malady. Karamdaman; sakit.

disembark, v. to land. Umahon sa bapor.

disembarkation, n. the act of disembarking. Pag-ahon sa bapor.

disengage, v. to extricate. Kumalas; makipagtalusira; humiwalay.

disfavor, n. displeasure; disesteem. Dispabor; pag-ayaw; di-pagsang-ayon.

disfigure, v. to mar beauty. Dispigurahin; papangitin.

disfigurement, n. deformity. Dispigurasiyon; pagpapapangit.

disgrace, n. dishonor. Desgrasiya; kawalang-dangal; kahihiyan.

disgraceful, adj. shameful; dishonorable. Kahiya-hiya; nakasisirang-puri.

disguise, n. artificial or assumed language or appearance intended to deceive. Pagtatago; balatkayo.

disguise, v. to change appearance. Magtago; magbalatkayo.

disgustful, adj. exciting the feeling of disgust. Nakayayamot; nakamumuhi.

dish, n. a receptacle or vessel esp. for food. Plato; pinggan.

dishonest, adj. fraudulent. Ditapat; di-mapagkakatiwalaan.

dishonor, n. ignominy; shame. Kahihiyan; kawalang-puri; kawalang-dangal.

disinfect, v. to kill germs. Disinpektahin; lagyan ng gamot para di mahawa.

disinherit, v. to deprive of inheritance. Alisan ng mana.

dislike, n. aversion; regard with displeasure. Abersiyon; pag-ayaw; pagkamuhi; pagkasuya.

dismal, adj. gloomy. Nakapanlulumo; malungkot.

dismiss, v. to cause to go; reject. Despidihin; paalisin.

disobedient, adj. neglecting or refusing to obey. Disobediyente; ayaw sumunod; matigas ang ulo.

disorderly, adj. contrary to law; irregular. Gusot; magulo.

disown, v. to refuse to own. Ayaw kilalanin; itakwil.

disnel, v. to drive off or away. Itaboy; alisin; iwaksi.

dispensation, n. dealing out; suspension of a rule or law. Dispensasyon; pahintulot.

dispense, v. to deal out; to distribute. Ibigay; isagawa; ipamudmod.

disperse, v. to scatter. Ikalat; paghiwa-hiwalayin.

displace, v. put out of place; replace. Palitan; iwaglit; alisin sa lugar.

display, v. to show; to exhibit. Idispley; itanghal; ihalayhay; ipakita.

displease, v. to provoke. Pagalitin; di-masiyahan.
disquieting, adj. disturbing the mind. Nakababahala; nagdudulot ng alalahanin.
disregard, n. neglect. Pagwawalang-halaga; pagwawalang-bahala.
disreputable, adj. of low character. Walang karangalan.
disrespect, n. irreverence; affront. Ireberensiya; kawalang-galang.
disrobe, v. to undress. Magalis ng damit; maghubad.
dissatisfied, adj. to be ill-pleased; discontented. Diskontento; di-nasisiyahan.
dissolve, v. to melt. Tunawin.
distance, n. interval of space. Distansiya; agwat; layo.
dissimilar, adj. unlike. Di-pareho; magkaiba.
dissipate, v. indulge in vicious life pleasures. Aksayahin; magmalabis; magumon.
distinguish, v. to discriminate. Destinggihin; kilanlin ang kaibahan.
distinguished, adj. eminent. Tanyag; makatatawag ng pansin; katangi-tangi.
distribute, v. to apportion. Ikalat; ipamahagi.
district, n. a section of a city or state. Distrito; purok.
distrust, v. to regard with doubt. Pag-alinlanganan; maghinala; di-magtiwala.
disturb, v. ruffle. Abalahin; guluhin; ligaligin.
diver, n. one who dives. Manlalangoy; maninisid.
diverge, v. to deviate. Lumayo; umiba; humiwalay.
divert, v. to amuse. Ibaling; libangin; baguhin.
divide, v. to apportion. Dibayd; hatiin.
division, n. a partition. Dibisiyon; paghahati; paghahati-hati.
divorce, n. a legal dissolution of the marriage bond. Diborsiyo; pakikipaghiwalay sa asawa.
doctor, n. a physician. Mediko; manggagamot.
doctrine, n. a principle or body of principles. Doktrina; katipunan ng mga tuntunin ng isang katotohanan o paniniwala.
dog, n. a domesticated carnivore bred in a great many varieties. Aso.
doll, n. a toy baby for children. Manyika; manika.
dominate, v. to rule. Duminahin; maghari; makapangyari.
Dominican, n. a member of the St. Dominic order. Dominiko; paring kasapi sa kapatiran ni Sto. Domingo.
donkey, n. the ass. Asno; buriko.
door, n. a barrier that swings or hinges or slides for opening or closing a passageway. Puwerta; bukasan; pinto.
doormat, n. a piece of rug at the door used for wiping the shoes, slippers, etc. Pamahiran ng paa.
doubt, v. to be uncertain about. Magduda; mag-alinlangan.
doubtful, adj. hesitant; uncertain. Alinlangan; nakawawalang-tiwala.
doubtless, adv. certainly. Walang duda; walang alinlangan.
down, adv. to or in a lower position or condition. Pababa; sa ibaba.
dowry, n. the estate that a bride brings to her husband. Dote; bigay-kaya.

doze, v. to sleep lightly. Bahagyang tulog; umidlip.

dozen, n. a group of 12 units or things. Labindalawa; dosena.

drain, v. to empty or exhaust gradually. Limasin; alisan ng tubig; patuyuin.

drake, n. a male duck. Patong lalaki.

draper, n. a dealer in clothes. Mangangalakal ng tela.

drastic, adj. violent. Drastiko; marahas.

draw, v. to make a picture or draft of. Idrowing; magdibuho; gumuhit ng larawan.

dream, v. indulge in reverie. Mangarap; managinip.

dress, n. clothing; attire. Bestido; damit.

dress, v. to put clothes on. Magbihis.

dresser, n. a table with mirror. Tokador.

dressmaker, n. a seamstress. Kusturera; mananahi.

drink, v. to swallow liquid. Uminom.

drinker, n. a drunkard. Buratso; lasenggo; manginginom.

drip, v. to fall into drops. Pumatak; tumulo.

driver, n. one who drives. Drayber; tsuper.

drop, v. to fall. Ihulog; ibagsak.

drown, v. to die in water. Lunurin; malunod.

drowsy, adj. sleepy. Mabigat ang katawan; inaantok.

drum, n. a musical instrument consisting of a hollow frame covered on the top by a tightly stretched membrane which is beaten with sticks in playing. Dram; tambol.

drunk, adj. intoxicated. Lasing; lango.

dry, adj. without moisture. Tuyot; tuyo.

duel, n. a single combat. Duwelo; disapyo.

duet, n. music for two. Duweto; dalawahang-tinig

dull, adj. stupid. Torpe; mapurol ang ulo; di-makintab; mapurol.

dumb, adj. speechless. Walang kibo; pipi.

durable, adj. lasting. Durable; matibay.

dusk, n. twilight. Takip-silim; agaw-dilim

dust, n. fine bits of earth. Lupa; alikabok.

duty, n. moral obligation. Tungkulin.

dwarf, n. a very small being. Bulilit; unano; maliit na tao; duwende.

dwarfish, adj. below the common stature or size. Pandak; maliit; parang unano.

dwell, v. to abide. Tumira; tumahan.

dwelling, n. habitation. Habitasiyon; tahanan.

dwindle, v. to shrink. Maubos; mawalang unti-unti.

dye, v. to stain; to color. Kulayan; magtina.

dying, adj. losing life. Mamamatay; naghihingalo.

dysentery, n. a disease of the large intestine, characterized by diarrhetic discharge of blood mucus from the bowels. Iti; pagtatae; disintirya.

dyspepsia, n. indigestion. Dispepsiya; di-pagkatunaw ng kinain.

dysurin, n. difficulty in discharging the urine, attended with pain and a sensation of heat. Disurya; hirap ng pag-ihi.

E

each, adj. every group or series considered as one. Kada; bawa't.

each, pron. every one individuality. Isa; bawa't isa.

eager, adj. keenly desirous. Ardiyente; sabik; masigasig.

eagerly, adj. in a zealous or enthusiastic manner. Nang buong pananabik; nang buong sigasig.

eagle, n. a large bird of prey. Agila.

ear, n. organ of hearing. Pandinig; tainga.

early, adv. occurring near the beginning. Temprano; maaga.

earn, v. to gain by labor; to merit. Gumana; kumita.

earnest, adj. sincere; diligent. Marubdob; taimtim; masigasig.

earth, n. the world. Daigdig; lupa.

earring, n. a ring or other ornament worn in or on the lobe of the ear. Abete; hikaw.

earthquake, n. a tremor of the earth. Lindol.

ease, n. comfort. Ginhawa; kadalian; kagaanan.

easily, adv. in an easy manner. Madali.

easy, adj. without exertion. Maluwag; madali.

east, s. toward rising sun. Oriente; silangan.

Easter, n. a church festival commemorating the Resurrection of Christ. Pasko ng Pagkabuhay.

easterly, adj. towards the east. Oriental; pasilangan.

eat, v. to consume food. Kumain.

eatable, adj. edible. Puwedeng kanin; makakain.

ebb, v. to recede. Umurong; bumaba; kumati.

ecclesiastical, adj. pertaining to the clergy or the church Eklesiyastiko; nauukol sa simbahan.

echo, v. repeat or imitate. Umalingawngaw; ulitin; gagarin.

echo, n. sound reflected. Eko. alingawngaw.

eclipse, n. obscuration. Paglalaho; eklipse.

economical, adj. frugal, thrifty. Ekonomiko; matipid.

economize, v. manage frugally. Mag-ekonomiya; magtipid.

ecstacy, n. excessive joy. Kasiyahan; kaluwalhatian.

eddy, n. a contrary current. Ipu-ipo; alimpuyo.

edge, n. the border. Bingit; tabi; gilid; dulo.

edible, adj. fit to be eaten. Nakakain; maaaring kanin

edifice, n. a building. Edipisiyo; gusali.

educate, v. to instruct. Pagaralin; turuan.

education, n. instruction. Edukasiyon; pagtuturo; pinagaralan.

eel, n. a snake-like fish. Palós; igat.

effect, n. result. Epekto; resulta; bunga; kinahinatnan.

effective, adj. efficacious. Mabuti; magaling; mabisa; mainam.

effort, n. exertion. Sikap; pagpupunyagi.

egg, n. the roundish reproductive body produced by the female, esp. by the domestic hen. Huwebo; itlog.

eggplant, n. a vegetable plant. Talong.

eight, n. a cardinal number

seven plus one. Otso; walo.

eighteen, n. & adj. a cardinal number, ten plus eight. Disiotso; labingwalo.

eighteenth, adj. next in order after the seventeenth. Ikalabingwalo.

eighty, n. & adj. fourscore. Otsenta; walumpu.

ejaculation, n. a prayer consisting of a few words. Sambitla; maikling panalangin.

elaborate, adj. intricate. Maringal; marangya; labis sa gayak.

elbow, n. joint of arm angle. Kodo; siko

electrician, n. one who installs, operates or repairs electric devices. Elektrisista.

elegant, adj. refined. Elegante; maayos at maganda; makisig.

elephant, n. any of the large mammals of Africa and India, with long prehensile trunk and long tusks of ivory. Elepante.

elementary, adj. primary. Pangunguna; panimula; elementarya.

elevate, v. to raise; to lift up. Angatin; itaas; dakilain.

elevation, n. exaltation. Elebasiyon; pagtataas; ang pagtataas ng ostiya at alak sa Misa.

elicit, v. to draw out; evoke. Makamit; makuha; matamo.

eligible, adj. qualified. Elihible; karapat-dapat.

eliminate, v. remove. Huwag isama; alisin.

elite, n. select body. Selekta; ang mga pinili; mga tanyag.

eloquence, n. speaking well. Elokuwensiya; kahusayan sa pagsasalita o sa pagtatalumpati.

eloquent, adj. having the power of fluent, forcible speech. Elokuwente; mahusay magsalita o magtalumpati.

elope, v. to run away. Tumakas; magtanan.

else, adj. besides. Otro; pa; iba.

elsewhere, adj. in another place. Sa ibang dako; sa ibang lunan.

elusive, adj. hard to grasp or catch. Mahirap hulihin; mailap.

elves, n. mischievous fairies. Mga duwende.

emaciated, adj. thin; wasted. Payat.

emanate, v. to issue from. Manggaling; magmula sa.

emancipator, n. one who liberates or frees. Libertador; tagapagligtas.

embalm, v. to preserve from decay. Gamutin; embalsamuhin.

embargo, n. a prohibition on vessels leaving port. Pagilit; imbargo.

embark, v. to go on ship. Maglayag; pagsakay; paglulan.

embarrass, v. to perplex. Hiyain; mapahiya; mapasubo sa kahihiyan.

embassy, n. the official headquarters of an ambassador. Embahada; tanggapan ng embahador.

embezzle, v. to appropriate fraudulently to one's own use, as money or property. Lustayin ang salapi ng iba.

embezzler, n. one who embezzles. Istapador; manlulustay.

emblem, n. a symbol of a quality, class of persons, etc. Emblema; sagisag.

embrace, v. hug. Yakapin; yapusin.

embracer, n. one who embraces. Abrasador.

embroidery, n. needlework. Burda.

emerald, n. precious stone. Esmeralda.

emerge, v. to appear. Lumitaw; lumabas; sumipot.

emergency, n. pressing necessity. Emerhensiya; di-inaasahang sakuna o pangyayari.

emigrate, v. leaving one's own country to live in another. Dumayo; mangibang-lupain.

eminence, n. loftiness; fame. Kabantugan; eminensiya; kadakilaan; pamagat ng paggalang na iniuukol sa mga kardinal.

eminent, adj. noteworthy. Prominente; kilala; tanyag.

emissary, n. person sent on a mission. Emisaryo; sugo.

emit, v. to send forth. Ihinga; ilabas.

emotion, n. agitation. Emosyon; damdamin.

emperor, n. a monarch. Emperador.

emphasize, v. stress. Aksentuhan; bigyang-diin.

emphatic, adj. marked; striking; expressive. Impatiko; may diin.

empire, n. a realm. Kaharian; imperyo.

employ, v. to hire. Ipasok; pagawin; pagtrabahuhin.

employee, n. one hired. Empleyado; kawani; namamasukan.

employer, n. one who employs. Ang may pagawa; amo; ang pinaglilingkuran.

employment, n. occupation. Empleo; hanapbuhay; gawain; trabaho.

empower, v. to authorize. Tulutan; bigyan ng kapangyarihan.

emptiness, n. vacuity. Basyo; kawalan ng laman.

empty, adj. void; unfurnished. Basyo; walang laman.

emulate, v. to vie with. Tularan; gawing huwaran; parisan.

emulation, n. ambition to equal or excel. Emulasiyon; pagparis; paggaya.

enable, v. to furnish with power or means. Bigyang-kakayahan; itulot.

enact, v. to decree. Ipag-utos; gawing batas; isagawa; ganapin ang papel.

enamour, v. to inflame with love. Ibigin; mahalin.

enchant, v. bewitch. Maakit; mabighani; gayumahin.

enchantment, n. incantation. Engkanto; pagkagayuma.

enclose, v. to put in. Kulungin; bakuran.

encounter, v. to meet in a hostile manner. Makatagpo; sagupain; bakahin.

encourage, v. to give hope, courage or confidence to. Pasiglahin; palakasin ang loob; bigyan ng pag-asa.

encroach, v. to trespass. Samantalahin; sumakop sa di nasasakupan; gampanan ang tungkuling di dapat gampanan.

encyclical, n. circular from the pope to the bishops. Liham ng Papa sa mga obispo.

endowment, n. that which is given or bestowed. Kaloob; dote; halagang inilalaan para sa simbahan o para sa ano mang kilusan.

endure, v. to bear; to sustain. Aguwantahin; batahin; pagtiisan.

enemy, n. a foe; adversary. Kagalit; kaaway.

energy, n. power; vigor. Kakayahan; lakas.

enforce, v. to compel. Pagtibayin; ipasunod; ipagawa.

engorge, v. to swallow with greediness. Kainin ng buong kasibaan; lamunin.

engrave, v. to imprint; to cut in. Itanim sa alaala; iukit.

engulf, v. to swallow up in; submerge. Paligiran; kulungin; lulunin.

enjoin, v. to command. Manduhán; utusan; himukin sa paggawa.

enjoy, v. to delight in. Ikagalak; magtamasa ng kaligayahan.

enlarge, v. to increase; extend. Luwangan; palakihin; palawakin.

enlist, v. to enroll for military or naval service. Itala; ilista; mangalap ng mga kawal.

enliven, v. to make vigorous, active, or gay. Pasayahin; pasiglahin.

ennoble, v. to dignify. Dakilain; itanghal.

enormous, adj. excessive. Labis; malaking-malaki.

enough, adj. sufficient. Bastante; tama na; sapat.

enrichment, n. act of enriching. Pagpapayaman.

enrobe, v. to attire. Magbihis.

en route, adv. on the way. Sa ruta; sa daan; patungo.

enshrine, v. to keep sacred. Idambana.

enslave, v. to make slave of. Alipinin.

ensue, v. to follow. Sumunod.

entangle, v. to make confused or disordered. Masilo at magkagulo-gulo.

enter, v. come into. Umentra; pumasok; sumali.

entertain, v. to amuse. Pakiharapang mabuti; libangin.

entertainment, n. something affording diversion or amusement. Dibersiyon; libangan.

enthrone, v. place on throne. Iluklok sa trono.

enthusiasm, n. ardent zeal. Sigasig; kasiglahan.

entice, v. to allure; to incite. Akitin; gayumahin; himukin.

entire, adj. whole; complete. Entero; buo.

entirely, adv. wholly; fully. Ganap; lubos.

entitle, v. to give a right or claim. Pamagatan; magbigay ng karapatan.

entomb, v. put into a tomb. Ilibing; ilagay sa nitso.

entrap, v. ensnare; catch in a trap. Siluin; hulihin sa patibong.

entreat, v. to beseech; to implore. Pamanhikan; makiusap; sumamo.

entrust, v. to invest with a responsibility. Ipagkaloob; ipagkatiwala.

entry, n. entrance. Entrada; pasukan; lahok.

envelope, n. a cover for a letter. Enbelop; sobre.

envious, adj. full of or expressing envy. Mapangimbulo; mainggitin.

environment, n. the aggregate of surrounding, things or condition. Ang kondisyon o mga sitwasyon sa paligid, sa kabahayan, sa kapitbahay, sa pook; paligid.

envoy, n. minister from one government to another. Sugo.

epic, adj. heroic poem. Epiko; nauukol sa mga tula o awit ng kabayanihan.

epidemic, n. temporary prevalence of a disease in a community. Laganap na sakit; salot; epidemya.

epidermis, n. the outermost skin membrane, integument, or layer of an organic body. Epidermis; anit; pang-ibabaw ng balat; balok.

epilogue, n. a conclusion. Epilogo; pangwakas ng isang talumpati o tulang dramatiko.

Epiphany, n. a Christian festival, Jan. 6. Epipanya; pista ng tatlong hari.

episcopacy, n. the office of a bishop. Episkopado; ang pamahalaan ng obispo.

epitaph, n. words on tomb. Epitapyo; limbag o sulat sa lapida.

equably, adv. in a uniform manner. Igwalmente; magkatulad; magkapantay.

exchange, v. give and receive reciprocally. Ikambiyo; palitan; ipagpalit.

exclude, v. to shut or keep out. Alisin; ibukod; huwag isama.

excommunication, n. exclusion from church. Ikskumunikasiyon; parusa ng simbahan; pag-aalis sa karapatan ng isang tao sa pagtanggap ng sakramento at biyaya.

excursion, n. a short trip for a special purpose. Eskursiyon; maikling paglalakbay sa ibang pook para maglibang o matuto.

excuse, n. pardon; apology. Kapatawaran; paumanhin; dahilan.

execute, v. to perform; Ipatupad; isagawa; gawin.

exercise, n. bodily or mental exertion esp. for training or development. Paggamit; ehersisyo; pagsasanay.

exodus, n. second book of the Old Testament. Eskodo; ang pangalawang aklat ng Matandang-Tipan.

explode, v. to burst. Sumabog; eksplosyon; pumutok; paputok; paputukin.

explosion, n. a violent outburst. Pagsabog; putok; pagputok.

expose, v. lay open to danger, harm, etc. Ilantad; ibunyag; isiwalat; ihayag; ilagay sa panganib.

express, v. to declare. Magpakilala; ipahayag.

expression, n. mode of speech. Ekspresyon; pananalita; pahayag.

expulsion, n. expelling. Ekspulsyon; pag-aalis; pagtitiwalag.

extend, v. to stretch out. Paabutin; palawigin; pahabain.

exterior, n. surface or part outside. Eksteryor; labas.

exterminate, v. destroy utterly. Puksain; lipulin.

external, adj. located outside or apart; outer. Eksternal; panlabas.

extinct, adj. dead. Lipol na; patay na; di na matatagpuan.

extinguish, v. to put out, as a fire. Lipulin; sawatain; alisin ang ningas; patayin.

extra, adj. additional. Ekstra; labis; karagdagan; di-kabilang.

extract, n. a substance or preparation obtained by distillation or other chemical means. Ekstrakto; sipi; katas.

extract, v. draw out; select. Bunutin; katasin; pigain.

extraordinary, adj. beyond the regular or usual order. Ekstra ordinaryo; pambihira; di-pangkaraniwan.

extravagant, adj. wasteful of money. Mapag-aksaya; marangya; labis gumasta.

extreme unction, n. a sacrament in which dying person is anointed with oil by a priest for the health of his soul and body. Ang pagpapahid ng Santo Oleo sa isang taong malapit nang mamatay o nasa panganib.

extricate, v. to release. Lumusot; kumalas; lumagpas; umalis; alisin.

equal, adj. evenly balanced. Ikwal, kapantay; kasinguri.

equalize, v. to make equal. Gawing pareho; pagpantayin; gawing magkauri o magkatulad.

equanimity, n. placidity; evenness of temper. Serenidad; kahinahunan.

equidistant, adj. equally distant. Ekwidistante; magkasinlayo.

equivalent, adj. of equal value. Kaparis; kapareho; katumbas.

era, n. an epoch; a period. Kapanahunan; panahon.

erect, adj. upright. Deretso; tuwid.

erelong, adv. soon. Di nalaunan; di-nagtagal.

erode, v. wear away slowly. Agnasin; ukain.

err, v. to mistake. Magkamali; magkasala.

errand, n. a message. Sadya; iniutos na gawain.

erroneous, adj. incorrect; false. Di-tama; mali; diwasto.

eructate, v. to belch. Bumuga; dumighay; dumuwal.

escape, v. to flee. Umiwas; magtanan; tumakas.

especial, adj. exceptional; special. Espesyal; tangi.

espouse, v. to betroth; to defend; Ipagtanggol; itaguyod.

essence, v. intrinsic nature. Diwa; pabango; esensiya; buod; ang ibig sabihin.

eternal, adj. everlasting. Eterno; walang kamatayan; walang hanggan; magpakailanman.

eucharist, n. sacrament of the Last Supper; Holy Communion: Sakramento sa Huling Hapunan; eukaristiya; ang Sakramentong dugo at katawan ni Kristo.

evacuate, v. to vacate. Magibakweyt; lumikas; magtungo sa ibang pook.

evacuation, n. the act of evacuating. Ibakweysyon; paglikas.

evaporate, v. to disappear. Maglaho; mawala; sumingaw.

evasion, n. subterfuge. Ebasyón; pag-iwas.

eve, n. the night or the day before a festival. Bisperas.

evening, n. close of the day. Gabi.

event, n. occurrence. Bunga; labanan; pangyayari.

evidence, n. testimony; proof. Ebedensiya; katibayan.

evil, adj. wickedness; immoral. Imorál; mali; masama.

exact, adj. accurate; correct. Eksakto; hustung-husto; tiyak.

exalt, v. to elevate in power, honor, etc. Purihin; dakilain; itaas.

examination, n. a testing. Iksamen; pagsusuri; pagsusulit.
excel, v. to surpass. Daigin; higtan; lagpasan.
except, v. to leave out. Huwag ibilang; itangi; huwag isama.
excessive, adj. beyond the usual limit or degree. Iksesibo; labis-labis.
eye, n. the organ of vision. Paningin; mata.
eyebrow, n. the ridge above the eye. Kilay.
eyeglasses, n. a pair of lenses worn to correct vision. Antipara; salamin sa mata.
eyelash, n. one of the hairs at the edge of the eyelid. Pestanya; pilikmata.
eyelid, n. the movable skin over the eyeball. Parpado; talukap ng mata.
eyesight, n. the faculty of seeing. Bista; paningin.
eyry, n. place where birds of prey build nests. Pugad ng ibong mandaragit.

F

fable, n. a feigned story. Kuwentong di-totoo; pabula.
fabric, n. framework; cloth. Tela; kayo.
facade, n. the front of building. Pasada; harapan ng isang gusali.
face, n. the front part of the head from the forehead to the chin. Kara; mukha.
face, v. to look toward; to front toward; Harapin; iharap.
facilitate, v. to make easy. Padaliin.
fact, n. truth; reality. Katunayan; katotohanan.
faction, n. a clique. Lupon; pangkat.
factious, adj. inclined to act for party purposes. Magkalaban; may tanda ng pagkakapangkat-pangkat.
factory, n. a building for manufacturing. Pagawaan; pabrika.
faculty, n. an ability. Kahusayan; likas na kakayahang umunawa ng mga bagay-bagay.
fad, n. a passing style or interest. Moda; kaugalian o pamamaraang namamalagi sa loob ng maikling panahon lamang; uso.
fade, v. to lose color; wither. Maglaho; mawala nang unti-unti; kumupas.
faded, adj. withered. Lipas; kupas.
fail, v. short. Mabigo; di-makatupad; mahulog.
failure, n. insufficiency. Pagkukulang; di-pagtupad; pagkahulog.
faint, adj. feeble; weak. Nanghina; nahihilo; malabo.
fair, n. an exhibition and sale of articles to raise money often for some charitable purpose. Perya.
fair, adj. beautiful. Mainam; maganda; makatarungan.
fairness, n. impartiality. Hustisya; katarungan.
fairy, n. one of a class of supernatural beings, having magical powers for good or evil in human affairs. Diwata; duwende; lambana; engkantada.
faith, n. belief. Paniniwala; pananalig; pananampalataya.
faithful, adj. true; loyal. Matimtiman; tapat; matapat.
faithless, adj. false to a promise or obligation. Di-tapat; taksil.
fall, n. descent. Pagbaba; pag-

bagsak; pagkahulog.

fall, v. to descend rapidly. Malaglag; mabuwal; mahulog; bumagsak.

fallacious, adj. misleading. Nakalilito; di-totoo; nakalilinlang.

fallacy, n. a false idea. Linlang; pagkalinlang.

fall asleep, v. to become dormant. Maidlip; makatulog.

false, adj. untrue; wrong. Mali; huwad; di-tunay; ditotoo.

falsehood, n. an untruth. Kadayaan; kasinungalingan.

fame, n. common estimation. Kabalitaan; katanyagan; kabantugan.

famed, adj. famous. Popular; tanyag; bantog.

familiar, n. intimate. Tagapaglingkod sa tahanan ng obispo o papa; kilala; malapit.

family, n. kindred. Pamilya; mag-anak.

famine, n. extreme and general scarcity of food. Kagutuman; taggutom.

famish, v. to starve. Magutom; mamatay sa gutom.

famous, adj. renowned. Kilala; tanyag; bantog.

fan, s. a device for stirring the air either mechanically or manually. Bentilador; pamaypay; abaniko.

fanatic, adj. wild enthusiast. Sukdulan sa sigasig; panatiko.

fancy, n. imagination. Kapritso; imahinasyon; hilig na kumukupas; guniguni.

fanon, n. napkin used by the priest at mass; an ornament attached to a priest's left arm. Isa sa mga palawit ng mitra ng obispo, abad, o papa.

far, adj. at or to a great distance. Lubha; malayo.

farce, n. a ludicrous drama. Parsa; isang dula o duladulaang labis at di-karaniwan ang mga pangyayari.

fare, n. price of passage. Pasahe; upa sa sasakyan.

farm, n. a tract of land on which crops, animals, etc. are raised. Bukirin; bukid.

farmer, n. one who farms professionally. Agrikultor; taga-bukid; magsasaka.

farther, adj. more distant. Higit ang kalayuan; malayu-layo.

fascinating, adj. charming; enchanting. Kabigha-bighani; kaakit-akit.

fashion, n. prevailing mode, esp. of dress. Moda.

fast, n. voluntary abstinence from food. Di-pagkain; ayuno.

fast, adj. quick. Rapido; mabilis; matulin.

fast, v. to abstain from food. Magkulasyon; magdiyeta; mag-ayuno.

fasten,, v. to attach firmly. Itali; ikabit.

fastidious, adj. hard to please. Pastidiyoso; mahirap masiyahan.

fasting, n. abstaining oneself from food. Abstinensiya; pag-aayuno; pagkukulasyon.

fat, adj. fleshy; plump. Sagana; mataba.

fatal, n. causing death or ruin. Mortal; nakamamatay.

fate, n. destiny; lot. Destino; tadhana; kapalaran.

father, n. a male parent. Padre; ama; tatay.

fatigue, n. weariness from bodily or mental exertion. Pagod; hapo.

fatness, n. plumpness. Katabaan.
fatten, v. to make fat; fertile. Pabulasin; patabain.
faucet, n. water connection. Gripo.
fault, n. a defect; mistake. Kasalanan; kapintasan; kamalian.
faultless, adj. free from fault. Perpekto; walang kapintasan.
favor, n. kindness. Tangkilik; tulong; pabór; utang na loob.
favorite, n. a person or thing regarded with special preference. Itinatangi; ang minamahal; paborito.
fear, n. terror; anxiety. Sindak; takot; pangamba.
fearless, adj. brave. Matapang; walang takot.
feast, n. a sumptuous meal. Handaan; kainan; pista.
feat, n. a noteworthy deed. Kabutihan; gawaing katangi-tangi.
feather, n. plume of a bird. Plumahe; balahibo ng ibon o manok.
feature, n. a prominent or conspicuous part. Pigura; porma; kaanyuan.
February, n. the second month of the year. Pebrero.
fee, n. reward; pay. Butáw; upa; kabayaran; bayad.
feeble, adj. weak; sickly. Masasakitin; mahina.
feed, v. to nourish. Busugin; pakanin.
feel, v. to perceive or examine by touch. Hipuin; damdamin.
feeling, n. emotion; sense of touch. Kamalayan; damdamin; damdam.
feet, n. the terminal parts of the leg of a man or animal. Talampakan; mga paa.
feign, v. to pretend. Magdahilan; magkunwari.
felicitate, v. congratulate. Batiin; handugan ng bati.
felicity, n. happiness; bliss. Pelisidad; kaligayahan.
feline, adj. cat-like. Parang pusa; ugaling pusa.
fell, v. strike down by a blow or out. Mahulog; bumagsak.
fellow, n. a comrade. Kauri; kasamahan.
felon, n. one guilty of crime. May kasalanan; kriminal.
female, n. a sex that bears young. Pemenino; kababaihan; babae.
fence, n. an enclosing barrier. Halang; bakod.
fence, v. to enclose or separate by barrier. Halangán; paderan; bakuran.
ferial, adj. pertaining to holidays or days in which business is not transacted. Ukol sa mga araw sa loob ng sanlinggo maliban sa araw ng linggo.
ferment, v. to agitate; excite. Ligaligin; paasimin; lumikha ng gulo.
fern, n. a plant. Pakô; eletso; isang uri ng halaman.
ferocious, adj. savage; fierce. Mabagsik; mabangis; mabalasik.
ferocity, n. fierceness. Kabagsikan; kabangisan.
ferry, n. passage across a river. Balsa; tawiran.
fertile, adj. productive. Malusog; mataba; mayaman.
fertilizer, n. a substance that enriches the soil, esp. manure. Abono; pataba.
fervour, n. heat. Pusók; alab; ningas.
festive, adj. joyous. Alegre; masaya.
fetch, v. to go and bring. Sunduin; kunin.

fetid, adj. having an offensive odor. Mabahô; mabantot.

fetters, n. shackles. Kadena; gapos; tanikala.

feud, n. a deadly quarrel. Pagkakagalit; alitan.

fever, n. a disease marked by weakness and high temperature. Lagnat.

few, adj. not many. Karampót; unti; ilan.

fiancee, n. a girl to whom a man is engaged. Nobya; Ang katipang babae.

fickle, adj. changeable. Kabilanin; salawahan; pabagubago.

fictitious, adj. pretended. Dilikas; di-tunay; kinatha.

fiddle, n. a violin. Biyolin.

fidelity, n. faithfulness. Pedilidád; katapatan.

fidget, n. restless or uneasy movements. Balisa; kumilos nang tila di-mapalagay.

field, n. a tract of cleared land for cultivation, pasture, etc. Larangan; kampo; malawak na lupaing walang bahay; bukid.

fiend, n. a deadly enemy. Halimaw; demonyo.

fierce, adj. savage; violent. Mabalasik; mabangis.

fiery, adj. full of fire; hot. Mainit; maalab; mainit na tulad ng apoy.

fifteen, adj. the cardinal number between fourteen and sixteen. Kinse; labinlima.

fifty, adj. the cardinal number between forty-nine and fifty-one. Singkuwenta; limampu.

fight, n. a battle; combat. Away; babag; labanan.

fight, v. to engage in combat. Makipag-away; lumaban; makipaglaban.

figure, n. a representation. Pigura; ayos; anyo; larawan; bilang.

file, n. tool for cutting and smoothing. Salansan; hanay; pila; kikil.

file, v. to reduce, smooth, cut or remove with a file. Kikilin.

filial, adj. pertaining to or appropriate to a son or daughter. Karapatan sa magulang.

fill, v. to make full. Lagyan; punuin.

filler, n. a utensil for conveying a liquid into a bottle, cask, etc. Imbudo; pamuno.

filly, n. a young mare. Kabayong babae na may mga apat at kalahating taong gulang.

film, n. a motion picture. Pilm; pelikula.

filter, n. strainer. Panala; salaan.

filter, v. to remove by a filter. Salain.

filth, n. foul matter. Baho; basura; dumi.

fin, n. a membranous winglike projection from the body of a fish. Aleta; palikpik.

final, adj. ultimate; last. Wakas; katapusan; huli.

find, n. a valuable discovery. Hanap; isang bagay na napulot o natagpuan.

fine, adj. consisting of minute particles. Manipis; pino.

finger, n. any of the five terminal members of the hand. Daliri.

finish, v. to end. Tapusin; wakasan.

fire, n. a burning or combustion. Sunog; apoy.

firefly, n. a small beetle that emits light. Alitaptap.

firemen, n. men employed to extinguish or prevent fires. Bumbero; mamamatay-sunog.

firewood, n. wood for fuel. Kahoy na panggatong.
firm, adj. steady; solid. Matigas; pirmi; matatag.
first, adj. preceding all others. Primero; una.
firstly, adj. in the first place. Kauna-unahan; unang-una.
fish, n. a completely aquatic vertebrate, usually with scales and fins. Peskado; isda.
fish, v. try to catch fish. Mangisda.
fisherman, n. one who catches fish. Mangingisda; peskador.
fishing, s. the art or practice of catching fish. Pangingisda.
fist, n. the hand clenched. Suntok; kamao.
fit, n. convulsion. Atake; dismaya; sumpong.
five, adj. cardinal number between four and six. Singko; lima.
fix, n. to establish firmly or immovably. Itakda; ayusin; itatag.
fixed, adj. definitely and permanently placed. Piho; matatag.
flabby, adj. flaccid. Malambot; luyloy.
flag, n. a banner. Bandera; watawat; bandila.
flagellant, n. one who whips himself in religious discipline. Plahelante; mga taong nagpaparusa sa kanilang sarili kung mahal na araw; mga nagpepenitensiya.
flagrant, adj. overly outrageous. Mahalay; kapansin-pansin; hayagan.
flame, n. burning gas or vapor. Liyab; alab; ningas.
flannel, n. soft cloth. Pranela.
flare, v. to blaze with a sudden burst of flame. Mag-apoy; magsiklab; mag-alab; magningas.
flare, v. to blaze with a sudden burst of flame. Magapoy; magsiklab; mag-alab; magningas.
flash, n. a sudden, brief outburst of flame or light. Iglap; sinag na biglang kumislap; kislap.
flat, adj. level or even. Pantay; patag.
flatten, v. to make or become flat. Pantayin; patagin.
flatter, v. to compliment or praise insincerely. Utuin; purihin nang labis.
flattery, n. adulation. Adulasyon; pagpuri ng labis.
flavour, n. taste of a thing. Sabor; linamnam; lasa.
flax, n. a blue-flowered plant grown for its fiber used for making linen, and its seeds, for linseed oil. Lino.
flea, n. a small leaping, bloodsucking insect. Pulgas.
flee, v. escape. Magtanan; umalis; tumakas.
flesh, n. meat; mankind. Karne; laman.
flight, n. fleeing; [illegible] departure. Lipad; pagtakas; pag-alis.
fling, v. to cast; hurl. Ipukól; ihagis; iwaksi.
flirt, v. play being in love, not seriously. Makipagharutan; mang-akit.
float, v. be bouyed up by water or air. Maanod; lumutang.
floating, adj. buoyant. Inaanod; nakalutang.
flood, n. an inundation. Dilubyo; baha.
floor, n. bottom of a room. Suwelo; sahig; lapag.
florist, n. flower grower. Plorista; magbubulaklak.
flour, n. finely ground grain.

Harina.

flourish, v. thrive; prosper. Managana; mamulaklak; lumago.

flow, v. to move along in a stream. Dumaloy; umagos.

flower, n. blossom of plant. Bulaklak.

flush tank, n. part of the sewage bowl. Tangke ng kasilyas o palikuran.

fly, n. any of certain two-winged insects esp. the housefly. Langaw.

fly, v. to move more or less horizontally through the air. Maglakbay sa himpapawid; lumipad.

foam, n. froth; spume. Bula.

focus, n. a central point. Pokus, gitna, sentro.

fold, n. a pleat. Tiklop; pileges.

fold, v. to bend (paper, etc.) over or upon itself. Ilupi; tiklupin.

follow, v. to come or go after; pursue. Subaybayan; sundan; sumunod.

follower, n. one that follows. Alagad; tagasunod.

folly, n. foolishness. Kaululan; kahibangan.

fond, adj. liking; tender. Mawilihin; magiliw; mahilig.

font, n. a baptismal basin. Benditahang gamit sa pagbibinyag; bukal.

food, n. anything that nourishes or sustains. Komida; pagkain.

fool, n. a silly or stupid person. Tonto; ulol; ungas; ugok.

foot, n. the terminal part of the leg of a man or animal. Talampakan; paa.

for, prep. in order to obtain. Sa lugar na; para o dahil sa.

forbear, v. to be patient. Magtiyaga; magtiis.

forbearance, n. patient endurance. Pasensiya; pagtitiis.

forbid, v. to prohibit. Huwag payagan; ipagbawal.

force, n. strength; vigor. Kapangyarihan; lakas.

forcibly, adv. in a forced manner; constrainedly. Nang ubos lakas; nang sapilitan; sa pamamagitan ng lakas.

fore, adj. at or near the front. Pang-unahan; una; unáhan.

forecast, n. a prediction. Prediksiyon; hula.

forefinger, n. the finger next the thumb. Hintuturo.

forego, v. to abstain from. Pabayaan; ipagpaliban; huwag gawain.

forehead, n. the front of the head between the eyes and the scalp. Noo.

foreigner, n. an alien. Estranghero; banyaga; dayuhan.

foresight, n. provision for the future. Probisyon; pangangalaga sa hinaharap; paglalaan sa hinaharap.

forest, n. a large area covered with a dense growth of trees. Kakahuyan; gubat.

forfeit, n. fine for offense. Likom; multa.

forgery, n. counterfeiting. Palsipikasyon ng lagda; panghuhuwad.

forget, v. to lose memory of. Limutin; kalimutan.

forgive, v. to pardon. Patawarin

forgiveness, n. willingness to forgive. Patawad; kapatawaran.

fork, n. a pronged tool for digging, lifting, etc. or for handling food at table. Panduro; tinidor.

forlorn, adj. forsaken. Pinabayaan; malungkot; nangulila.

form, n. external shape; structure. Porma; anyo.

former, adj. preceding in time. Ang nauuna; dati; una.

formulate, v. to state definitely or systematically. Bumalangkas; bumuo.

forsake, v. renounce; abandon. Pabayaan; iwan; limutin.

fort, n. a fortified place. Kuta; muog; tanggulan.

forthcoming, adj. approaching time. Lilitaw; darating.

fortify, v. to strengthen or protect against attack. Kutaan; lagyan ng tanggulan.

fortitude, n. the power to endure pain, hardship, etc. Tapang; lakas at tining ng loob.

fortunate, adj. lucky; successful. Matagumpay; mapalad.

fortune, n. chance; luck. Kayamanan; kapalaran.

forty, n. & adj. a cardinal number ten times four. Kuwarenta; apatnapu.

forward, adv. ahead. Sa harapan; sa unahan.

found, v. discovered. Nakita; natagpuan; napulot.

foundling, n. a child found without a parent or any one to take care of it. Batang pulot.

fountain, n. a spring; a source of water. Pontanya; sibol; bukal.

four, n. & adj. a cardinal number between three and five. Kuwatro; apat.

fourteen, n. & adj. a cardinal number, ten plus four. Katorse; labing-apat.

fourteenth, adj. next after thirteenth. Ikalabing-apat.

fowl, n. an edible bird. Mga ibon o angkan ng ibon.

fraction, n. part of a unit. Kapilas; kaputol; bahagi.

fracture, n. break; breach or split. Linsad; bali ng buto.

fragile, adj. brittle. Marupok; mahina; babasagin.

fragment, n. part broken. Bahagi; piraso; pinagtabasan; isang maliit na pilas.

fragrance, n. a sweet odor Pragansiya; halimuyak; bango.

fragrant, adj. having a pleasant odor. Mabusilak; mabango.

frail, adj. bodily structure. Mahina; marupok.

Franciscan, n. a member of the order of St. Francis of Assisi. Pransiskano; ang orden ni San Francisco.

frank, adj. open; sincere. Prangka; tapat.

frankincense, n. a gum resin burned as incense. Insenso.

frankness, n. the state or quality of being outspoken or unreserved in speech. Pagkahayag; pagkamatapat; katapatan.

fraternity, n. brotherhood. Praternidad; kapatiran; samahan.

fraud, n. deceit. Laláng; huwad; panlilinlang.

freckle, n. a light-brown spot on the skin. Pekas.

free, adj. enjoying personal liberty. Malaya; ligtas; walang bayad; libre.

freedom, n. civil or personal liberty. Libertad; kalayaan.

freeze, v. to become rigid because of loss of heat. Maging yelo; mamuo dahil sa lamig.

frenzy, n. distraction. Kaululan; pagkaulol.

frequent, adj. habitual. Madalas; malimit.

fresh, adj. cool; refreshing. Presko; bagung-bago; sariwa.

freshness, n. the condition or quality of being fresh. Kapreskuhan; kasariwaan.

friar, n. a member of certain Roman Catholic religious orders. Pari; prayle.

friction, n. act of rubbing. Priksyon; kiskis.

Friday, n. the sixth day of the week. Biyernes.

friend, n. a confidant. Amigo; amiga; kaibigan.

fried, adj. cooked in lard. Prito.

fright, n. sudden fear or terror. Sindak; takot.

frightful, adj. terrible. Nakasisindak; katakut-takot; nakakatakot.

frigid, adj. cold; dull. Matamlay; malamig.

frigidity, n. coldness. Katamlayan; kalamigan; ginaw.

frill, n. a ruffle. Maliliit na pileges ng damit.

fritter, n. a small fried butter cake; pancake. Pritilya; pinirito; isang maliit na piraso.

frivolity, n. insignificance. Kahangalan; kilos, bagay o hangad na walang kabuluhan.

frock, n. a dress or gown. Blusa; kasuutan ng bata o ng babae.

frog, n. tailless amphibian with great leaping and swimming ability. Palaka.

frolic, n. fun; merrymaking. Paglalaro; katuwaan; pagkalibang.

from, prep. away. Galing sa; sa; mula; buhat.

frond, n. a finely divided leaf, often large, properly applied to the ferns and some of the palms. Dahon.

front, adj. the foremost part of surface of anything. Delentera; harapan.

frontal, n. a front covering of the altar. Prontero; panakip sa harapan ng altar

frosty, adj. very cold. Malamig.

froth, n. spume; foam. Espuma; bula.

frown, n. stern, angry look. Kunot ng noo; simangot.

frowning, adj. scowling. Pangungunot ng noo; nakasimangot.

frozen, adj. congealed by cold. Manigas; malamig; namuo sa lamig.

frugal. adj. thrifty. Ekonomiko· matipid.

fruit, n. any natural, useful yield of a plant. Bunga; bungangkahoy.

fruiterer, n. a container for fruits. Lalagyan ng bungangkahoy; prutera.

fruitful, adj. abounding in fruits; productive. Mabunga; masagana.

frustrate, v. balk; thwart. Hadlangan; mabigo; biguin.

fry, n. a dish of something fried. Pritada; ano mang bagay na pinirito.

frying pan, n. a skillet. Pirituhan; kawali.

fuel, n. a combustible matter used to maintain fire. Panggatong.

fuel, v. to furnish with or take on fuel. Gatungan; lagyan ng panggatong.

fulfill, v. to accomplish. Gampanan; tapusin; buuin; gawin; tuparin.

fulgent, adj. shining; dazzling. Nakasisilaw; maningning.

full, adj. filled to capacity. Ganap; puno; lipos.

fumble, v. manage awkwardly. Kumapa-kapa; kumilos nang di-tiyak.

fumigate, v. treat with fumes

to disinfect or to destroy pests. Paasuhán; pausukan; suubin.

fun, n. merry amusement. Dibersiyón; biro; katuwaan; paglilibang.

function, n. proper action by which any person, organ, office, structure, etc. fulfills its purpose or duty. Gawa; gamit; kagamitan; tungkulin.

fund, n. a stock or supply, esp. of money, set apart for a purpose. Imbak; laang salapi; pondo; pananalapi.

funeral, n. burial rites. Paglilibing; libing.

fungus, n. any of a group of non-green plants, including the molds, toadtools. rusts, etc. Amag.

funnel, n. pipe or passage Imbudo.

funny, adj. comical. Komika; nakakatawa.

fur, n. the soft, fine hair of certain animals. Balahibo.

furious, adj. mad; frantic. Napopoot; galit na galit.

furnace, n. large stove. Hurno; pugon; apuyan.

furnish, v. to supply; to equip. Dulutan; lagyan ng kasangkapan; bigyan.

furniture, n. the tables, chairs, beds, cabinets, etc. required in a house, office, or the like. Muwebles; mga kasangkapan sa bahay.

furor, n. great excitement. Sumpong; kaguluhan.

furrow, n. a long trench. Ang pinagdaraanan ng araro; tudling.

further, adv. to a greater extent; moreover. Nang kaunti pa; sa dako pa roon; sa malayu-layo.

fury, n. madness; rage. Matinding galit.

fuse, n. a ribbon, tube or the like, filled or saturated with combustible matter, for igniting an explosive. Piyús; mitsa; lambal.

fusion, n. blending. Pagsasanib; paghahalu-halo; pagsasama-sama.

fuss, n. needless or useless bustle. Pagkabahala sa maliliit na bagay; kilos na di kailangan at nakagagambala.

futile, adj. useless. Hindi matagumpay; walang saysay; walang bunga.

future, adj. yet to come or happen. Panghinaharap; hinaharap.

future, n. time to come. Ang hinaharap; ang kinabukasan.

G

gabble, v. to talk rapidly and unintelligently. Dumaldal; sumatsat.

gag, v. to stop up the mouth to prevent speech. Busalán; tapalan ang bibig.

gaiety, n. liveliness. Katuwaan; kasayahan.

gain, v. earn by effort. Magtubo; magananansiya; makinabang.

gait, n. manner of walking. Lakad; paraan ng paglakad.

gala, n. a festival. Gala; pista.

gall, n. bile. Apdo; pait.

gallant, adj. brave; honorable. Marangal; galante; magalang.

gallery, n. a covered passage. Palko; galerya.

gallon, n. four quarts. Galon.

gallop, n. a rapid, springing gait, esp. of a horse. Takbong may lukso; mabilis na takbo.

gamble, v. risk money on a game of chance. Pumusta; magsugal.

gambler, n. one who gambles. Tahur; sugarol; manunugal.

game, n. a play. Sugal; huwego; laro.

gaming-house, n. a gambling house. Bahay-sugalan.

gander, n. the male goose. Gansang lalaki.

gang, n. a company of persons acting or going about together. Gang; barkada; pangkat.

gaol, n. a jail. Karsel; piitan; bilangguan.

gap, n. an opening. Paso: patlang; puwang.

gape, v. open the mouth wide. Ibuka; maghikab; mapanganga.

garb, n. attire. Bestido; trahe; kasuotan.

garbage, n. refuse. Sukal; basura; dumi.

garden, n. a plot of ground where flowers, fruits, or vegetables are grown. Hardin; taniman; halamanan.

gardener, n. one whose occupation is to keep a garden. Maghahalaman; tagapagalaga ng halamanan; hardinero.

gargle, n. liquid for rinsing the throat. Mumog; pagmumumog.

garland, n. a wreath of flowers or leaves. Garlân; kuwintas (na bulaklak).

garlic, n. a bulb with a strong onionlike flavor, used in cooking. Bawang.

garment, n. any article of clothing. Bestido; baro; damit; kasuutan.

garnish, v. to adorn with something colorful. Palamutihan; ayusan; gayakan.

garrison, n. a fort, castle, or fortified town furnished with troops. Garisón; himpilan ng mga kawal.

garter, n. stocking fastener. Ligas; garter.

gas, n. noxious fumes. Petrolyo; gaas.

gash, n. a long, deep wound or cut. Kalmot; hiwa; laslas.

gasp, v. to labor for breath painfully. Humingal; huminga-hinga.

gastric, adj. pertaining to the stomach. Gastriko; ukol sa sikmura.

gate, n. an opening for passage into an inclosure. Pintuan; tarangkahan.

gather, n. assemble. Mamulot; tipunin; mag-umpukan.

gauge, v. measure; estimate. Sukatin; tantiyahin.

gay, adj. merry. Alegre; masaya; kaaya-aya.

gaze, v. to look steadily or intently. Tumingin; tumitig.

gazelle, n. a small, graceful antelope. Gasela; batang usa.

gazette, n. a newspaper. Gaseta; pahayagan.

gelatin, n. an animal jelly. Helatina; dikya.

gem, n. a precious stone. Mahalagang bato; hiyas.

gender, n. in grammar, the classification of feminine, masculine, and neuter. Kasarian.

general, adj. universal. Laganap; panlahat; kalahatan. panlahat; kalahatan

generate, v. produce; form. Magdulot; pagmulan; panggalingan.

generation, n. each ancestor in a line of descent. Henerasyón; salin-lahi.

generosity, n. readiness or liberality in giving. Kabutihang-loob; pagkabuiang-gugo; pagkamapagbigay

genial, **adj.** cheerful. Mabuting makiharap; masaya.

genius, **n.** exceptional mental and creative power. Pantas; henyo.

genteel, **adj.** affectedly refined. Hentil; may mabuting katauhan; magalang; maginoo.

gentle, **adj.** soft; mild. Suwabe; mahinhin; mabini; malumay; banayad.

gentleman, **n.** an honorable man of fine feelings. Kabalyero; maginoo.

genuflection, **n.** bending of the knee as in adoration. Ang pagluhod ng kanang tuhod bilang pagsamba at paggalang sa Diyos na nasa Sakramentong Banal.

genuine, **adj.** real. Lantay; likas; tunay.

geography, **n.** the science that deals with the earth, its peoples, climate, nature, etc. Karunungan sa mga lupain; heograpiya; balat-lupa.

germ, **n.** a microbe. Payak na sangkap ng buhay; mikrobyo

gesticulate, **v.** to make gestures, esp. when speaking excitedly. Kumumpas.

gesture, **n.** a movement of the body, head, arm, hands, or face expressive of an idea. Kumpas; kilos.

get, **v.** to obtain, gain, or acquire. Matamo; makuha; kunin.

ghastly, **adj.** very pale. Kakila-kilabot; maputla.

ghost, **n.** a spectre; a spirit. Pantasma; multo.

giant, **n.** an imaginary being of superhuman size. Malaking tao; higante.

giddiness, **n.** the state of being giddy. Pagkalulà; pagkaliyo; pagkahilo.

giddy, **adj.** dizzy. Nalululà; naliliyo; nahihilo.

gift, **n.** a present. Regalo; handog.

gigantic, **adj.** huge. Lubhang malaki; malaking-malaki.

gills, **n.** respiratory organs of fish. Hasang.

gin, **n.** a liquor. Gin; hinebra; alak.

ginger, **n.** an aromatic root. Luya.

girdle, **n.** a belt. Bigkis; sinturon.

girl, **n.** a young woman or female child. Ninya; batang babae.

give, **v.** to bestow. Magkaloob; maghandog; ibigay, bigyan.

glad, **adj.** joyful. Maligaya; natutuwa; masaya.

gladness, **n.** the state or quality of being glad. Kasayahan; katuwaan.

glance, **n.** glimpse. Sulyap.

glaring, **adj.** shining dazzlingly. Nakasisilaw; kapansin-pansin.

glass, **n.** an article, as a mirror, tumbler, etc. Baso; salamin; bubog.

glitter, **v.** to shine. Kumislap; kuminang.

globe, **n.** the earth. Sansinukob; globo; daigdig.

gloom, **n.** melancholy. Kapanglawan; dilim; kadiliman; kalungkutan.

gloomy, **adj.** dusky or dark; dismal. Malamlam; madilim; malungkot.

glorious, **adj.** delightful; full of glory. Gloryoso; ilustre; maluwalhati; kagalang-galang.

glory, **n.** exalted honor. Luwalhati; glorya; langit.

glove, n. a covering for the hand, with a separate sheath on each finger. Glab; guwantes.

glow, n. luminosity. Baga; liyab; sinag; ningning; kislap.

glue, n. a sticky substance. Glu; kola; pandikit.

gluttony, n. excess in eating or drinking. Katakawan; kasibaan.

go, v. to move or proceed. Umalis; lakad; paroon.

goal, n. any object of ambition or desire. Hantungan; layunin.

goat, n. a ruminant animal. Kambing.

God, n. Supreme Being, creator and master of all. Bathala; Diyos; Maykapal.

God's sake, interj. because of God. Alang-alang sa Diyos.

godfather, n. a man who sponsors a child at baptism. Padrino; ninong.

godmother, n. a woman who sponsors a child at baptism. Madrina; ninang.

goggles, n. spectacles. Antipara; salamin sa mata

gold, n. a precious yellow metal highly malleable and ductile. Oro; ginto.

golden, adj. made of gold. Mala-ginto; ginintuan.

golf, n. a game played on an extensive course, in which the object is to drive a ball into a series of holes in the fewest number of strokes. Golp; isang uri ng larong ginagamitan ng bola at pamalo ng bola.

golgotha, n. calvary. Golgota; ang bundok ng kalbaryo na pinagpakuan kay Kristo.

good, adj. well-behaved. Magaling; mabuti.

good afternoon, interj. a kind wish between persons meeting or parting at afternoon. Magandang hapon.

goodbye, interj. a farewell wish. Adyos; paalam.

Good Friday, n. the Friday before Easter, observed as the anniversary of the crucifixion of Jesus. Biyernes Santo.

good morning, interj. a kind wish between persons meeting or parting at morning. Magandang umaga.

goose, n. a large web-footed bird, esp. the female, similar to the duck. Gansa.

gorgeous, adj. magnificent. Kahanga-hanga; maganda; kaakit-akit; maningning.

gorilla, n. the largest known manlike ape. Gorilya; mabangis at malaking unggoy.

gory, adj. bloody. Madugo.

gospel, n. record of Christ's life and teachings. Ebanghelyo; banal na kasulatan.

gossip, n. trifling talks, esp. of other persons. Satsatan; tsismis.

gout, n. a painful inflammation of the joints, esp. of the great toe. Rayuma.

govern, v. to rule by right of authority. Pangasiwaan; pamahalaan; mamahala.

government, n. the administration. Pamahalaan; gobyerno.

governor, n. executive head of a province. Gobernador; punong-lalawigan.

gown, n. a woman's dress or robe. Bestido; damit ng babae.

grab, v. to seize suddenly and eagerly. Dukutin; sunggaban; agawin.

grace, n. favor or goodwill. Grasyá; pabor; biyaya; utang na loob.

graceful, adj. characterized by grace; elegant. Grasyosa; mabikas; kaaya-aya.

graduation, n. ceremony of conferring decrees or diploma. Gradwasyon.

grail, (Holy) n. a cup which according to medieval legend was used by Jesus at the Last Supper, and in which Joseph of Arimathea received the last drops of Jesus' blood at the Cross. Kalis; ang banal na kopang ginamit ni Hesus sa Huling Hapunan.

grain, n. a seed. Buto; butil.

grammar, n. speech or writing in accordance with standard usage. Gramatiká; balarila.

granary, n. house for grain. Granero; imbakan ng palay o mga butil na ani; kamalig.

grand, adj. majestic. Maringal; malaki.

grandchild, n. a child of one's son or daughter. Apo.

grandfather, n. a forefather. Agwelo; lolo; nunong lalaki.

grandmother, n. an ancestress. Agwela; lola; nunong babae.

grant, v. to give. Pahintulután; ipagkaloob; ibigay.

grantee, n. the recipient of a grant. Donataryo; ang tumanggap ng biyaya o ng ipinagkaloob.

grapple, v. lay fast hold of. Makipagbuno; hawakan nang mahigpit.

grasp, v. seize and hold. Sunggaban; pigilan nang buong higpit.

grass, n. green herbage sending up spikelike shoots or blades. Herba; damo.

grasshopper, n. a large jumping insect. Lukton; tipaklong; balang.

grassy, adj. covered with grass. Madamo.

grate, n. frame of bars. Réhas.

grateful, adj. thankful. Nagpapasalamat; tumatanaw ng utang na loob.

gratification, n. satisfaction. Gratipikasyon; kasiyahan.

gratitude, n. thankfulness. Pagtanaw ng utang na loob; pasasalamat.

grave, adj. earnest; somber. Malubha; maselan; taimtim; di-tumatawa.

gravel, n. fragments of rock larger than sand. Bato; graba.

graveyard, n. cemetery. Sementeryo; libingan.

gravy, n. sauce from meat. Salsa.

gray, adj. black and white blend; also, grey. Kulay abo; abuhin.

graze, v. feed on grass, etc. as cattle. Daplisan; pagalain sa damuhan; manginain.

grease, n. animal fat. Grasa; sebo.

greasy, adj. oily; smeared grease. Marumi; magrasa; masebo.

great, adj. notable. Malaki; dakila; kahanga-hanga.

greed, n. inordinate or rapacious desire, esp. for wealth. Borasidád; katakawan; kasakiman.

greedy, adj. very eager for wealth. Timawa; masiba; sakim.

green, adj. a mixture of blue and yellow. Berde; luntian.

greet, v. to address, with some form of salutation. Tanggapin; batiin; salubungin.

greeting, n. salutation. Salutasyon; pagbati.

grief, n. sorrow. Hapis; kalungkutan.

grievance, n. a cause of complaint. Karaingan; hinakdal; hinanakit.

grieve, v. mourn. Mamighati; ikalungkot; damdamin.

grim, adj. frightful. Mabalasik; malagim; nakatatakot.

grimace, n. a twisting of the face, expressive of pain, disgust, etc. Ngiwi; simangot.

grime, n. deeply ingrained dirt. Libag; banil; dusing; dumi.

grin, n. a broad smile that shows the teeth. Ngisi.

grind, v. pulverize. Dikdikin; gilingin.

grindstone, n. a rotating abrasive wheel. Hasaan; gigilingan.

gritty, adj. sandy; plucky. Nakapangingilo; maligasgas.

grope, v. to feel one's way. Apuhapin; kumapa.

ground, n. land; soil. Saligan; lupa.

group, n. a cluster. Grupo; lupon; pulutong.

grow, v. to increase in size, power, etc. Sumupling; tumubo; lumaki.

growl, v. to utter a deep guttural sound of anger or hostility. Umungol.

guarantee, v. to make oneself answerable for. Garantiyahán; sagutan.

guard, n. a sentry. Sentri; taliba; bantay.

guard, v. to protect. Guwardiyahan; bantayan.

guardian angel, n. an angel guarding an individual. Anghel na tagatanod.

guardian, n. a trustee, warden, or keeper. Tagapanga laga; tagatanod; tagakupkop.

guess, n. opinion without certainty. Palagay; haka; tantiya; hula; hinuha.

guess, v. to surmise. Hulaan.

guest, n. a visitor; Kumbidado; panauhin; bisita.

guffaw, n. loud laughter. Halakhak; malakas na tawang nakakahawa.

guidance, n. direction; management. Direksiyon; pagakay; pamamatnubay; pagtuwid.

guide, n. directional marker. Giya; tagaturo ng landas; patnubay.

guilt, n. the fact of having violated law or right. Kasalanan.

guilty, adj. justly chargeable with guilt or offense. May kasalanan.

guitar, n. a six-stringed musical instrument plucked with the fingers. Kudyapi; gitara.

gun, n. any of various portable firearms. Iskopeta; sandata; baril.

gunshot, n. a shot fired from a gun. Putok ng baril.

gutter, n. a channel for carrying off water, as at the eaves of a roof or at a roadside. Kanal; bambang; alulod.

gymnastics, n. the practice or art of gymnastic exercises. Himnastiko; ang sining ng pag-eehersisyo sa katawan.

gypsy, n. a member of a vagabond, dark-skinned race. Hitano; hitana.

gyrate, v. rotate. Umiikot.

H

habeas corpus, n. a writ demanding that a prisoner be given an immediate hearing or else be released. Habeyás korpus; isang kautusang nagpapahintulot na ang isang bilanggo ay magkaroon ng karapatang litisin sa harap ng hukuman.

haberdasher, n. a dealer in accessory articles for men. Tagapagbili ng mga kasuutang panlalaki.

habit, n. a custom or usage. Kustumbre; abito; ugali; kinagawian.

habitable, adj. capable of being lived in. Maaaring tirahan.

habitation, n. a dwelling. Habitasyón; tirahan.

haggard, adj. wild-looking, as from terror, suffering, or fatigue. Payat; hapo; nangangalumata.

haggle, v. bargain in a petty manner. Tumawad; makipagtawaran.

hair, n. any fine, filamentous outgrowth. Balahibo; buhok.

hairbrush, n. instrument consisting of bristles for the hair. Brutsa sa buhok; sipilyo ng buhok.

hairpin, n. a slender U-shaped piece of wire, shell, etc. used by women to fasten the hair. Agohilya; pangipit sa buhok.

hairy, adj. having much hair. Mabuhok; mabalahibo.

hale, adj. healthy. Mabuti ang katawan; malusog.

half, adj. one of the two equal parts. Medya; bahagi; kalahati.

half-breed, n. a person of mixed races. Mestiso; mestisa.

hall, n. a large room for public assemblies. Gusali; bulwagan; salas.

hallow, v. regard as sacred. Igalang; sambahin.

hallucination, n. delusion. Kathang-isip; guni-guni; alusinasyon.

halo, n. a circle of light around the head, as of a saint. Halo; sinag na pabilog.

halt, v. stop. Pumara; tumigil; patigilin.

halve, v. divide into two equal parts. Hatiin sa dalawa.

ham, n. the buttock of a hog. Hamon.

hamlet, n. a small village. Poblasyón; maliit na nayon.

hammer, n. an instrument for driving nails, beating metal, etc. comprising a heavy solid head set on a handle. Pamukpok; martilyo.

hammer, v. beat, drive etc. with or as with a hammer. Martilyuhin; pukpukin ng martilyo

hammock, n. a swinging bed. Duyan; hamaka.

hamper, n. a large basket. Tiklis; buslong malalim para sa iba't ibang gamit.

hamper, v. to hinder. Pigilin; hadlangan.

hand, n. the terminal part of the arm, consisting of the palm and five fingers. Mano; kamay.

hand, v. to deliver or pass with the hand. Iabot; ibigay.

handbill, n. a small printed bill or announcement. Kartel· paskin.

handbook, n. a guidebook for travelers. Aklat-patnubay; manwal.

handful, n. as much or as many as the hand can contain. Kaunti; isang dakot; isang kamay na puno.

handkerchief, n. a small piece of cloth for wiping the nose, etc. Panyuwelo; panyo; panyolito.

handle, n. a part of a thing which is to be grasped by the hand in using or moving it. Tanganán; puluhan; hawakán; tangkay.

handle, v. touch, manipulate, manage or control with the hands. Hawakan.

handrail, n. bar of wood or metal used as support. Gabay.

handsome, adj. comely; having a pleasing aspect. Mabikas; maganda.

handwriting, n. writing done by hand. Iskritura; sulat-kamay.

handy, adj. accessible. Laging handa; madaling hawakan; madaling dalhin.

hang, v. to suspend. Bitayin; isabit; ibitin.

happen, v. to chance; occur. Magkataon; mangyari.

happily, adv. in a happy manner. Sa kabutihang palad; sa paraang maligaya.

happiness, n. felicity. Kaligayahan; kasayahan.

happy, adj. pleased; satisfied. Maligaya; masaya.

harangue, v. to deliver a speech. Magtalumpati; manuligsa; tuligsain.

harbor, n. a portion of a body of water along the shore providing shelter for ships. Pondohan; kanlungan ng mga sasakyang-dagat.

hard, adj. tough; difficult. Mahigpit; matigas; mahirap.

harden, v. make or become harder. Tumigas.

hard-hearted, adj. pitiless. Walang awa; walang puso; matigas ang kalooban.

hardly, adv. with difficulty. Hindi gaano; bahagya na; may kahirapan.

hardship, n. severe labor. Paghihirap; kahirapan; sagabal.

hardware, n. store where wares made of metal, as tools, cutlery, etc. are sold. Mga kasangkapang yari sa bakal; tindahan ng mga kagamitang tulad ńg turnilyo, pako, yero, atbp.

hardy, adj. strong; enduring. Malusog; matigas; may laban.

harlequin, n. a clown. Payaso; arlekin.

harm, n. physical or moral injury. Kasamaan; panganib; pinsala.

harmful, adj. injurious. Nakasasama; nakapipinsala.

harmless, adj. unable to harm. Inosente; walang malay; di-mapanganib.

harp, n. a musical instrument with strings played by plucking. Alpa.

harsh, adj. severe in character or effect. Mabalasik; malupit; marahas; tampalasan.

harvest, n. a crop or yield. Gapas; ani.

harvester, n. a reaper. Tagagapas; tagaani.

hash, n. minced meat. Pikadilyo; pira-pirasong karneng iginisa o nilutong may pira-pirasong patatas.

haste, n. swiftness. Kabilisan; pagmamadali; kabiglaan.

hasten, v. to hurry. Biglain; padaliin; pabilisin.

hastily, adv. in a hasty manner. Biglaan; buong pagmamadali.

hat, n. a shaped covering for the head. Sambalilo; sumbrero.

hatch, v. produce from eggs. Pisain (ang itlog ng manok o ibon).

hatchet, n. a small ax. Palataw; maliit na palakol.

hate, n. strong dislike. Pagkapoot; pagkamuhi; pagkagalit.

hate, v. to dislike. Kapootan; kamuhian; kayamutan.

hatred, n. enmity; ill-will. Poot; muhi; galit.

haughty, adj. arrogant. Palalo; mapagmataas.

haunt, n. a place of frequent resort. Pook na malimit dalawin; tigilan; lungga.

haunt, v. to visit frequently. Dalawing malimit; gambalain.

have, v. to possess. Mayroon; magkaroon.

havoc, n. devastation. Pinsala; kapahamakan; kasiraan.

hawk, n. a raptorial bird, allied to eagles and falcons. Palkon; lawin.

hay, n. plants, as grass, cut and cured for fodder. Ginikan; dayami.

haystack, n. a stack of hay with a conical or ridged top. Mandala.

hazard, n. risk. Sagabal; peligro; mapanganib.

haze, n. obscurity. Pagkalito; labo; panlalabo ng isipan.

he, pron. third person, singular; masculine. Siya (lalaki).

head, n. the uppermost part of the human body, above the neck. Puno; ulo.

headache, n. pain located in the head. Sakit ng ulo.

headquarters, n. principal or main office. Kuwartel Heneral; himpilang pangkalahatan.

headstrong, adj. stubborn. Hangál; matigas ang ulo.

heal, v. to cure. Lunasan; pagalingin; gamutin.

healing, adj. curing. Makalunas; nakagagaling.

health, n. soundness of body condition. Katayuan ng katawan; kalusugan.

healthy, adj. in good condition. Walang sakit; malusog.

heap, n. a collection of things laid together, esp. in a raised pile. Tambak; bunton.

hear, v. perceive by ear. Dinggin; pakinggan; makinig.

hearing, n. the ability to perceive by ear. Pakikinig; pandinig.

hearsay, n. rumor. Satsat; tsismis; bulung-bulungan.

hearse, n. carriage for dead. Andas; karo ng patay

heart, n. the principal organ that causes blood to circulate in the body. Puso.

hearth, n. place for fire. Apuyan; tahanan.

heat, n. warmth. Subo; init.

heat, v. to make hot. Painitin; iinit.

heaven, n. the abode of God and the blessed. Kalangitan; langit.

heavenly, adj. blissful. Banal; makalangit.

heaviness, n. massiveness. Kabigatan; bigat.

heel, n. the back part of the foot. Takong; sakong.

height, n. stature. Altura; taas.

heir, n. one who inherits property from another. Eredero; tagapagmana.

helicopter, n. an airplane which is lifted in the air by a horizontal propeller. Helikopter.

hell, n. the abode or state of the wicked after death. Impiyerno.

help, v. to aid or save. Damayan; tumulong.

helpful, adj. useful. Maalalay;

matulungin; kapaki-pakinabang.

helpless, adj. desperate. Inutil; taong walang magawa para sa sarili.

her, pron. the objective case of she. Kanya (babae).

herb, n. an annual plant whose stem does not become woody, often used for medicine, flavoring, etc. Halamang-damo; munting halamang may malambot at matubig na puno.

herd, n. a number of animals together. Pulutong; kawan.

here, adv. in, or toward this place. Dini; dito.

hereafter, adv. in the future. Pagkaraan nito; sa hinaharap; mula ngayon.

heretic, n. a professed believer who maintains religious opinions contrary to those accepted by his church. Erehe; ang naniniwala sa maling doktrina o pananampalataya.

hermitage, n. a dwelling of a hermit. Ermita.

hermit, n. one who has retired to a solitary place, esp. for a life of religious seclusion. Ermitanyo.

hero, n. a man admired for his courage, fortitude, prowess, nobility, etc. Bida; bayani.

heroine, n. a female hero. Bayaning babae.

hers, pron. a form of the possessive **her**. Sa kanya.

hesitate, v. pause. Matigilan; mag-alinlangan; mag-atubili.

hide, n. the skin of an animal, raw or dressed. Kuwero; balat ng hayop; katad.

hide, v. keep out of view. Ilihim; itago; magtago.

hideous, adj. frightful in appearance or character. Kasindak-sindak; nakatatakot; masamang anyo.

hierarchy, n. a body of persons organized by rank, in church or government. Pamahalaan ng mga pari; ang iba't ibang antas ng tungkulin ng mga pari; herarkiya.

high, adj. tall. Matayog; mataas.

highest, adj. tallest. Pinakamatayog; pinakamataas.

High Mass, n. a Mass celebrated according to the complete rite by a priest or prelate attended by a deacon and subdeacon, parts of the Mass being chanted or sung by the ministers and parts by the choir. Misa mayor.

highness, n. state of being high. Altura; kataasan.

hill, n. a conspicuous natural elevation of the earth's surface. Burol.

hilt, n. handle of a sword. Puluhan; tatangnan ng espada.

hinder, v. to impede. Hadlangan; lagyan ng sagabal; pigilin.

hindrance, n. an obstacle. Hadlang; sagabal.

hinge, n. the joint on which a door, shuttle, lid, or the like, moves. Bisagra.

hinge, v. turn or depend on. Masalalay; lagyan ng bisagra; ikabit.

hint, n. a covert suggestion or implication. Suhestiyón; iparamdam; mungkahing di-tuwiran.

hip, n. the haunch. Kadera; pigi.

hire, v. to rent. Alkilahin; upahan.

hit, n. a blow, impact, or collision. Hampas; suntok; palo; tama.

hit, v. to strike. Hampasin; patamaan; paluin.

hitch, v. to fasten. Isingkaw; ikabit; kumabit.

hither, adv. to this place. Dito; dine.

hithermost, adj. nearest on this side. Pinakamalapit.

hitherto, adv. up to this time. Magmula ngayon; hanggang ngayon.

hive, n. house for bees. Bahay ng pukyutan.

hives, n. a skin disease. Mga pantal.

hoard, v. to accumulate (food, money, etc.) for preservation or future use. Itago; mag-impok; magtipon.

hoard, n. a stock or store laid by for preservation or future use. Ipon; inimpok; kayamanang nakatago.

hoars, adj. gruff, husky vocal tone. Walang boses; namamalat.

hoax, n. a mischievous deception. Lalang; linlang; daya; biro.

hobble, v. to walk lamely. Umika-ika; lumakad nang papilay.

hobby, n. an occupation pursued for recreation. Libangan; paboritong gawain ng isang tao.

hoe, n. a blade fixed on a long handle, for cultivating earth, cutting weeds, etc. Asada; asarol.

hog, n. swine. Baboy.

hogsty, n. a pen or inclosure for hogs. Kulungan ng baboy; alagaan ng baboy; banlat.

hoist, v. to raise or lift up. Ialsa; itaas.

hold, v. to have or keep in the hand. Pigilin; hawakan; maglaman; maglulan.

holder, n. something to hold a thing. Tagatangan; hawakan; sisidlan.

holdupper, n. one who uses force in order to rob a person. Holdaper.

hole, n. an opening; an aperture. Butas.

holiday, n. religious festival. Pista; araw na pangilin.

holiness, n. state or character of being sacred or devout. Kabanalan.

hollow, adj. excavated; empty. Humpak; malundo; hungkag; walang laman.

holy, adj. perfectly pure. Santo; banal; madasalin.

Holy Communion, n. the Eucharist. Eukaristiya; komunyon.

Holy Father, n. the Pope. Banal na Ama; Santo Papa.

Holy water, n. a sacred or blessed water used in the church. Agwa bendita.

Holy Week, n. the week preceding Easter Sunday. Semana Santa; linggo ng mga Mahal na Araw.

homage, n. respect or reverence; tribute. Reberensiya; pagsamba; paggalang.

home, n. the house, etc, where one resides. Bahay; tahanan.

homely, adj. domestic; ugly. Pangit; simple; magiliwing tumigil sa tahanan.

homesickness, n. longing for home. Nostalhia; pangungulila sa tahanan o sa tinubuan.

honest, adj. truthful. Malinis; hindi mapag-imbot; tapat; mapagkakatiwalaan.

honey, n. a sweet fluid produced by bees from the nectar of flowers. Pulot-pukyutan.

honeymoon, n. a trip by a newly-married couple. Pulot-gata; hanimun

honor, n. dignity. Kapurihan; karangalan; dangal.

honorable, adj. noble or distinguished. Kapuri-puri; marangal.

hood, n. a covering for the head often attached to a cloak, etc. Takip ng ulo; pamindong na pakapa ng damit ng isang babae.

hoof, n. the horny covering of the foot of certain animals, as the ox, horse, etc. Kuko ng kabayo o ng ano mang hayop na kauri nito.

hook, n. a curved or angular piece of metal or the like, used to catch, hold, or sustain something. Kawil; kalawit.

hoop, n. a circular band; circular ring of wood or metal rolled by children. Pagulong; bilog; isang bagay na tila singsing.

hoop, v. to bind with a hoop. Singsingan; lagyan ng bilog o ng bagay na bilog.

hoot, v. to shout, esp. in derision. Sumutsot nang patuya o pauyam.

hop, n. a short leap; esp. on one foot. Kandirit; paglundag-lundag.

hop, v. to leap, esp. only one foot. Kumandirit; lumundag-lundag.

hope, n. confidence in a future event. Pag-asa.

hope, v. expect or look forward to, with desire and confidence. Asahan; umasa.

hopeful, adj. full of hope. Puno ng pag-asa; umaasa.

hopeless, adj. affording no hope. Desperado; walang pag-asa.

horde, n. a multitude. Lipon; kawan.

horizon, n. the circular line where the sky, earth and seas appear to meet. Guhittagpuan.

horizontal, adj. on the level. Horisontál; pahiga; pahanay sa lupa.

horn, n. a spikelike growth on the head, as of cattle. Pansuwag; sungay.

hornbill, n. any of the large tropical Old World birds characterized by a very large bill surmounted by a horny protuberance. Kalaw.

horned, adj. made of horn. Sungayan.

hornet, n. a kind of wasp. Putakti.

hornpipe, n. an English clarinet; a lively dance, tune. Klarinete; patunog na mahaba; patunog na hinihipan.

horrid, adj. dreadful. Kasindak--sindak.

horrify, v. shock intensely. Biglain; sindakin; takutin.

horror, n. excessive fear. Pagkasuklam; matinding pagkatakot.

Hosanna, interj. praise to God. Hosana; sambitla ng pagpuri sa Diyos.

horse, n. a stallion. Kabayo.

hospital, n. an institution for care and treatment of the sick and injured. Ospital; pagamutan.

host, n. one who entertains another esp. in his own house; the bread consecrated in the Eucharist. Punong abala; ostiya; ang mayhanda; ang maybahay na lalaki.

hostess, n. a female host. Ang babaing may handa; ang maybahay na babae.

hot, adj. having or giving the

sensation of heat. Maapoy; mapusok; mainit.

hot-headed, adj. of fiery temper. Madaling magalit; mainit ang ulo.

hotel, n. a public house that furnishes lodging, food, etc. to travelers or other guests. Bahay-tuluyan; otel.

hound, n. any of various hunting dogs. Asong ginagamit sa pangangaso; asong bundok.

hour, n. measure of time equal to 60 minutes or one twenty-fourth of a solar day. Oras.

hourly, adv. every hour; frequently. Tuwing isang oras; oras-oras; bawa't oras.

house, n. a dwelling. Kapulungan; bahay; tahanan.

household, n. those occupying a house together. Sambahayan; bahay; ang mag-anak; kasambahay.

housekeeper, n. a woman who does or directs the work of a household. Taong-bahay; ang namamahala sa bahay.

housemaid, n. a female servant employed in general work in a household. Katulong na babae; utusang babae.

how, adv. by what means. Gaano; paano.

however, adv. in whatever manner. Paano man; gayon man.

howl, n. the cry of a dog, wolf, etc. Palahaw; alulong; ungal.

howl, v. to utter a loud, prolonged mournful cry, as that of a wolf. Umalulong; umungal.

huddle, v. crowd together. Magsiksikan; mag-umpukumpok; maggitgitan.

hue, n. a color. Kolór; kulay.

hug, n. a close embrace. Yapos; yakap.

hug, v. to embrace. Yapusin; yakapin.

huge, adj. very large. Malaki; malawak.

hull, n. the shell, husk, etc. of a nut, fruit, or grain. Balat.

hull, v. to remove the hull of. Balatan; alisan ng balat.

human, adj. being a man. Tao; makatao.

humble, adj. meek and modest in manner. Mababang-loob; mapagkumbaba; mababa.

humid, adj. moist; damp. Mahalumigmig; basa-basa.

humiliate, v. subject to shame or disgrace. Ilagay sa kahihiyan; hamakin; hiyain.

humility, n. humbleness. Humilidad; kababaang-loob.

humorous, adj. funny. Masaya; komiko; nakakatawa.

hump, n. a protuberance or swelling, esp. a natural or morbid curvature of the back. Umbok; tambok; kakubaan; pagkahukot.

I

I, pron. the personal pronoun, first person. Ako.

ice, n. solid form of water, produced by freezing. Yelo.

ice, v. to cool with ice; freeze. Lagyan ng yelo; ibabad sa yelo.

ice cream, n. a frozen confection. Sorbetes.

iconology, n. the doctrine of images or emblematical representations. Ikonolohiya; ang sining ng paglalarawan ng mga kabutihan, kasamaan, at ibang bagay na nauukol sa ugali at kalikasan sa pamamagitan ng bantayog, larawan o mga sagisag.

idea, n. conception; thought. Balak; ideya; palagay; kuro-kuro.

ideal, adj. constituting a standard of perfection. Huwaran; walang kapintasan; uliran.

identical, adj. just the same. Kapareho; magkatulad na magkatulad; iyon din.

identify, v. to recognize. Suriin; kilanlin.

idiot, s. an utterly foolish person. Tanga; sintu-sinto; hangal.

idle, adj. doing nothing; inactive. Batugan; bulakbol; walang gawa; tamad.

idle, v. to pass time in idleness. Magbulakbol.

idol, n. an object of worship. Diyus-diyusan; idolo; tao o bagay na minamahal nang labis.

idolatry, n. worship of idols. Labis na pagmamahal; idolatriya; pagsamba sa mga idolo.

if, conj. in case that. Kung; pangatnig na pasubali.

ignite, v. kindle; take fire. Sindihan; pagkiskisin; apuyan.

ignoble, adj. of low character Mababa ang pagkatao; imbi.

ignorance, n. lack of knowledge. Ignoransya; kawalang-muwang; kamangmangan.

ignorant, adj. illiterate; uninformed. Ignorante; mulala; walang muwang; mangmang.

ill, adj. sick; unwell. Malubha; masama; may sakit.

illegal, adj. unauthorized. Ilegál; labag sa batas; mali.

illegitimate, adj. unlawful. Di-ipinahihintulot; labag sa batas.

illimitable, adj. limitless; boundless. Walang katapusan; walang hanggan.

illiterate, adj. showing lack of culture. Ignorante; mangmang.

illness, n. sickness. Karamdaman; sakit.

illuminate, v. to light up. Ilawan; liwanagan; tanglawan.

illumination, n. a supply of light. Iluminasyón; liwanag; tanglaw.

illusion, n. a mistaken perception or belief. Ilusyón; pangarap; malikmata.

illusive, adj. deceptive. Mapanlinlang; mailap.

illustrate, v. to make clear as with examples. Ilarawan; ihalimbawa; larawang-guhit.

illustration, n. explanation. Ilustrasyón; halimbawa; larawang guhit.

image, n. statue; picture. Gunita; imahen; larawan.

imaginary, adj. fanciful. Hindi totoo; likha ng pag-iisip.

imagination, n. conception. Imahinasyon; likhang-isip; guni-guni.

imagine, v. to think; conceive. Ipalagay; ihaka; isipin; akalain.

imbecile, adj. infirm; mentally feeble. Mapurol; sira-sira; mahinang pag-iisip; sintusinto.

imbibe, v. to drink; absorb. Sipsipin; inumin.

imitate, v. simulate. Tularan; gagarin; parisan; gayahin.

imitation, n. a copy, likeness, or counterfeit. Imitasyón; bagay na ipinaris sa iba; paggaya.

Immaculate Conception, n. the unique privilege by which the Virgin Mary was conceived in her mother's womb without the stain of original sin, thru the anticipated merits of

Jesus Christ. Imakulada Consepsiyon; dalisay na pagdadalang-tao.

immediately, adv. directly; instantly. Kaagad-agad; agad; sa sandaling ito.

immense, adj. very great; vast. Malapad; malawak; malaki.

immensity, n. infinity. Kalaparan; kawalang hanggan ng laki o lawak.

immigrate, v. to settle in a new country. Mandayuhan; magtungo at tumira sa ibang lupain.

imminent, adj. impending. Darating; malapit.

impart, v. to grant; bestow; make known. Bahaginan; magbigay; ipahayag; ipabatid.

impartial, adj. just; fair. Imparsyal; pareho.

impatient, adj. hasty. Balisa; walang tiyaga; naiinip.

impede, v. to hinder. Hadlangan; lagyan ng sagabal; abalahin.

impediment, n. hindrance. Hadlang; sagabal.

impel, v. to urge on. Itaboy; hikayatin; udyukan.

impenitence, n. obduracy. Impenitensya; katigasan ng damdamin; kawalan ng pagsisisi sa nagawang sala.

imperceptible, adj. very slight, gradual, or subtle. Hindi maramdaman; hindi makita; hindi mahalata.

imperfect, adj. faulty; defective. Di-ganap; di-lubos; may kapintasan.

imperil, v. to endanger. Isapanganib; ilagay sa panganib.

imperishable, adj. everlasting. Walang kamatayan; walang pagkasira.

impertinence, n. rudeness. Impertinensiya; kawalang-galang.

impertinent, adj. intrusive or presumptuous. Pangahas; walang galang; bastos.

implicate, v. to be involved or concerned with. Isama; isangkot; iramay.

implore, v. beseech; to supplicate. Pamanhikan; ipakiusap; idalangin.

imply, v. to denote. Ipahiwatig; ipakahulugan.

import, v. bring in, as wares from a foreign country. Umangkat; bumili ng kalakal sa ibang bansa.

important, adj. significant. Importante; mahalaga.

impose, v. to lay on. Magpataw; iatang; ipapasan.

imposing, adj. impressive. Maringal; nakatatawag ng pansin.

imposition, n. the laying on of something as a burden, obligation, etc. Imposisyón; pagpapataw; pagpapatong; sa simbahang Katolika, ang pagpapatong ng kamay ng pari sa ulo o balikat ng isang binibinyagan, kinukumpilan o binabasbasan.

impossible, adj. that cannot be done or effected. Imposible; di-maaari; mahirap mangyari.

imprimatur, n. an official license to publish. Imprimatur; salitang Latin na nangangahulugang "maaaring limbagin"; pagbibigay ng pahintulot na limbagin ang isang aklat.

imprison, v. to put into prison. Ikulong; ipiit; ibilanggo.

improbable, adj. not likely to be true or to happen. Di-mangyayari; mahirap mangyari.

improve, v. to better; increase

in value or utility. Pabutihin; paunlarin.

impulsive, adj. impetuous; violent. Mapusok; pabigla-biglá.

impure, adj. mixed with something else. Marumi; di dalisay; mayhalo.

in, prep. inward; on the inside. Sa; nasa sa loob.

inability, n. incapacity. Kawalang magagawa: di-kakayahan.

inaccessible, adj. may not be reached. Di naraanan.

inactive, adj. idle. Nakahinto; walang gawa.

inadequate, adj. insufficient. Di-sapat; kulang.

inanimate, adj. not alive; quiescent. Walang buhay; walang galaw.

inapplicable, adj. unsuited. Di-tama; di-maaaring iangkop o ilapat.

inappropriate, adj. unsuitable. Di-angkop; di-dapat; di-bagay.

inarticulate, adj. indistinct. Di-makapagsalita; di-makapangusap; pipi.

inattention, n. heedlessness. Di-pakikinig; di-pagpansin.

inattentive, adj. heedless. Di-nakikinig.

inaudible, adj. not heard. Di-marinig; mahina.

inaugurate, v. to make a formal beginning of. Pasinayaan; ipagdiwang.

inauguration, n. the act of inaugurating or the ceremonies connected with such an act. Inagurasyón; pasinaya; pagdiriwang.

inauspicious, adj. unlucky. Di-mapalad; di-kapansin-pansin.

inborn, adj. natural. Katutubo sa sarili; taglay mula pagiging tao: likas.

incalculable, adj. beyond calculation. Di-makalkulá; di-matantiya; di-mabilang.

incanable, adj. unable. Walang kaya

incapacity, n. inability. Inkapasidad; di-kakayahan.

incarcerate, v. put or hold in prison. Ikulong; ibilanggo.

incarnation, n. existence in bodily form. Inkarnasyón; pagkakatawang-tao; ang pagiging isa ng Diyos at ng tao sa katawan ni Kristo.

incase, v. to cover; enclose. Ikahón; ipaloob sa kahon.

incautious, adj. unwary. Bulagsak; walang ingat; pabaya.

incendiary, n. house burner. Manunulsol; manununog.

incense, n. an aromatic material or the perfume it produces when burned. Insenso; kamanyang; pansuob.

incentive, n. motive; spur. Hangarin; pampasigla; pangudyok.

incessant, adj. unceasing. Insesante; walang tigil.

inch, n. a unit of length, one twelfth of a foot. Pulgada; dali.

incident, n. a casual happening. Insidente; pangyayari.

incinerate, v. burn to ashes. Insinerahin; sunugin.

incise, v. to cut into. Hiwain.

incite, v. to urge or stimulate; stir up. Upatan; sulsulan; udyukan; pag-initin.

inclement, adj. unmerciful; severe or harsh. Walang awa; masama; mabagsik.

inclination, n. bent, liking, or preference. Inklinasyón; hilig.

incline, v. to bend; to lean. Kumiling; humilig; yumuko.

inclose, v. to shed in. Paligiran; kulungin; palibutan.

include, v. take in; be composed of. Ilakip; isama; ibilang.

incognito, adv. & adj. unknown. Walang liwanag; di kilala.

incoherence, n. not logical. Inkoherensiya; kalabuan; kawalan ng linaw.

incoherent, adj. rambling and unintelligible. Inkoherente; malabo; di-malinaw.

income, n. revenue; profit. Sahod; kita.

incompetence, n. not fit; not suitable. Inkompetensiya; kawalan ng kaya.

incompetent, adj. incapable. Di-marunong; walang kaya.

incomplete, adj. unfinished. Di-husto; di-tapos; di-yari; kulang.

incomprehensible, adj. incapable of being understood. Di-maintindihan; di-maunawaan.

inconceivable, adj. incapable of being conceived or thought of. Di-maaaring isipin; di-malirip; di-mawari.

inconsiderate, adj. imprudent. Walang pakundangan; walang habas; walang alang-alang.

inconsistent, adj. contradictory. Inkonsistente; paiba-iba; salawahan.

inconvenient, adj. inopportune; disadvantageous or troublesome. Masuliranin; nakaaabala; nakagagambala.

incorporate, v. unite in a society, corporation, etc. Gawing korporasyón; isama; isama sa karamihan

incorrect, adj. erroneous; inexact. Di-tama; mali; di-tumpak.

increase, n. growth. Umento; dagdag.

increase, v. augment. Umentuhan; dagdagan; damihan.

incredible, adj. impossible to be believed. Di-kapani-paniwala, mahirap paniwalaan.

incredulity, n. a refusal of belief. Inkredulidád; di-paniniwala; alinlangan.

incriminate, v. to involve in an accusation. Paratangan; iramay; isangkot.

incubator, n. a heated apparatus for hatching eggs, nurturing babies, etc. Inkubeytor; pisaan ng itlog.

incur, v. encounter as an experience. Mangyari; gawin; pasukan.

incurable, adj. beyond the power of skill and medicine. Walang paggaling; di-mapagagaling; walang lunas.

indecency, n. immodesty. Kalaswaan; kahalayan.

indeed, adv. in fact; in truth. Talaga nga; tunay; oo nga.

indefensible, adj. incapable of being defended, vindicated or justified. Indepensible; hindi maipagtatanggol.

indefinite, adj. without fixed or specific limit. Malabo; di-tiyak; walang hanggan.

indelible, adj. incapable of being deleted or obliterated. Di-napapawi; di-mabubura.

indemnity, n. paid for a loss. Indemnidad; kabayaran o lagak laban sa pagkawala o pagkasira.

indention, n. an indenting, as of a line. Pasok; pagkabaku-bako; yupi; palugit.

independence, n. self-reliance. Kasarinlán; kalayaan.

indescribable, adj. incapable of being described. Di-makilala; di-mailarawan.

indeterminable, adj. not to be determined or ended. Indeterminable; hindi matiyak.

india-rubber, n. a soft variety of rubber. Goma.

Indian, n. the aboriginal race of America. Indiyan.

indicate, v. point out. Ipakita; tandaan.

indication, n. sign; token. Indikasyón; tanda.

indict, v. to accuse; to impeach. Akusahán; paratangan.

indictment, n. a charge. Akusasyón; paratang.

indifference, n. unconcern. Kawalang halaga; kawalang bahala.

indigence, n. want. Pangangailangan; karalitaan; kahirapan.

indigent, adj. poor; needy. Pobre: maralita; mahirap.

indigestible adj. hard to digest or assimilate. Di-matunaw; mahirap tunawin.

indignant, adj. feeling or showing anger, esp. righteous anger. Poot; galit.

indigo, n. a blue dye. Indigo; tina; matingkad na bughaw.

indirect, adj. deviating from a course. Paliguy-ligoy; dituwiran.

indiscreet, adj. injudicious; inconsiderate. Padalus-dalos; di-maingat; walang lihim.

indiscriminate, adj. not carefully selected. Malabo; walang pili; walang linaw.

indispensable, adj. absolutely necessary or requisite. Indispensable; kailangan; di-maitatakwil.

indisputable, adj. incontrovertible; incontestable. Di-matututulan; di-mapag-aalinlanganan; di-mapangangatwiranan.

indissoluble, adj. firm; stable. Pirme; walang bago; tiyak na nananatili.

indistinct, adj. not clear; obscure to the mind. Di-maliwanag; malabo.

individual, adj. of one person. Hiwalay; solo; sarili; nag-iisa.

indivisible, adj. incapable of being divided. Di-mahahati.

indolence, n. laziness. Indolensiya; katamaran.

indoors, adv. in or into a house or building. Sa loob ng bahay.

indorse, v. to sanction. Ilipat.

induce, v. lead by persuasion or influence. Himukin; ganyakin; sulsulan.

induct, v. to install; introduce, esp. formally, as into a place, office, etc. Ilagay sa katungkulan; italaga.

indulge, v. to yield; to satisfy. Magpakalabis; palayawin; mamalagi.

industrious, adj. hard-working; diligent. Masipag.

industry, n. manufacturing trade. Sipag; industriya.

ineffectual, adj. powerless or impotent. Walang kaukulan; walang bisa.

inefficient, adj. incompetent. Di-sanay; walang kaya.

inelegant, adj. wanting in elegance. Magaslaw; di mahinhin; magaspang.

ineligible, adj. not worthy to be chosen or preferred. Di karapatdapat.

inert, adj. having no inherent power to move or act. Walang kilos; di-gumagalaw.

inertia, n. inactivity. Inersiya; di-pagkilos; di-gumagalaw.

inestimable, adj. invaluable. Inestimable; di-mahalagahan.

inexact, adj. not precisely correct or true. Di-husto; di-tiyak.

inexpensive, adj. cheap; of low price. Barato; mura.

inexperienced, adj. want of experience. Walang karanasan.

inexplicable, adj. incapable of being explained or interpreted. Di-maipaliwanag.

infallible, adj. perfectly reliable; incapable of erring or falling into error. Siyerto; di-magkakamali; tiyak.

infamous, adj. notoriously evil; shamefully bad. May masamang pangalan; kasumpa-sumpa.

infamy, n. public disgrace. Inpamya; kawalang puri.

infant, n. a baby or young child. Bata; sanggol.

infanticide, n. the killing of an infant. Pagpatay sa sanggol.

infatuation, n. state of being inspired with a foolish passion. Inpatuwasyón; pagkahaling; maapoy nguni't pansamantalang pag-ibig.

infect, v. to taint. Salinan; hawahan; mahawahan ng sakit o mikrobyo.

infectious, adj. contagious. Kumakalat; nakahahawa.

infer, v. to deduce. Akalain; ipalagay; halawin.

inferior, adj. lower in rank or grade. Marupok; mababang uri.

infernal, adj. devilish; hellish. Mala-impiyerno; tila impiyerno.

infertile, adj. not fruitful or productive. Esteril; baog.

infidel, n. an unbeliever. Pagano; ang hindi naniniwala.

infidelity. n. unfaithfulness. Pagpapabaya; di-pagtatapat; kataksilan.

infirm, adj. weak; not in good health. Mabuway; mahina ang katawan; may sakit.

infirmity, n. illness; weakness. Sakit; kahinaan.

inflame, v. excite highly; set on fire; to set a flame or a fire. Pukawin; palalain; pag-alabin; sindihan; pagdingasin.

inflammable, adj. combustible. Madaling magsiklab; madaling magdingas.

inflate, v. to swell or puff out. Papintugin; palakihin.

inflation, n. the state of being inflated. Implasyón; pagpintog; paglaki.

inflexible, adj. rigid; inexorable. Matigas; di-mababaluktot; di-mababago; di-mababali.

inform, v. to make known to. Isumbong; ipagbigay-alam; ipabatid; ibalita.

information, n. knowledge concerning some facts or circumstances. Inpormasyón; balita; kaalaman; nalalaman.

informer, n. one who gives information. Inpormer; espiya.

infrequent, adj. seldom occuring. Madalang; di-malimit.

infuriate, v. make angry. Inisin; pagalitin.

ingenius, adj. witty. Bihasa; maparaan; matalino; tuso.

ingot, n. a bar of metal. Bara ng metal; lingote.

ingratitude, n. unthankfulness. Kawalan ng utang na loob.

ingredient, n. component part. Lahok; sangkap.

inhabit, v. to live in. Tirahan.

inhabitable, adj. may be lived in. Habitable; maaaring tirahan.

inhabitant, n. a resident. Ang nananahanan; ang nakatira.

inhale, v. draw into the lungs; breathe in. Langhapin; huminga nang papasok.

inherit, v. to succeed to; to acquire by gift or succession. Manahin; magmana.

inhibition, n. the checking, restraining or blocking of metal process physiological reaction, etc. Inhibisyón; pagpigil sa sarili; pansariling mga saloobin.

initial, adj. placed at the beginning. Inisiyál; unang titik ng pangalan.

injection, n. the act of injecting; something injected. Iniksiyon.

injure, v. do harm to; hurt. Pinsalain; saktan; siraan.

injunction, n. a command, order or admonition. Indyangsiyon.

ink, n. a fluid used for writing or printing. Tinta.

inland, adj. pertaining to or situated in the interior part of a country or region. Dalatan; loob ng isang bansa.

inmate, n. a fellow lodger. Preso; ang nakatira sa bahay-ampunan; pasyente; bilanggo.

inn, n. a tavern. Posada; bahay-tuluyan.

inner, adj. situated in or further within. Interyor; dakong loob.

innocence, n. purity. Kalinisan; kawalang-malay.

inquire, v. to ask about. Magtanong; mag-usisa.

inquiry, n. search for truth. Pagsisiyasat; pagtatanong.

insane, adj. mad; distracted. Ulol; baliw.

insect, n. any member of a class of tiny winged invertebrates. Insekto; kulisap.

insecure, adj. not secure. Di-tiwasay; di-matatag.

insensible, adj. unfeeling. Walang pakiramdam; walang katuturan.

inseparable, adj. always together; not to be parted. Inseperable; laging magkasama; di-mapaghihiwalay.

insert, v. to put in; place inside or among. Isingit; ipaloob.

inside, adv. in or into the inner part; within the space. Interyor; sa loob.

insignificant, adj. without importance. Insignipikante; walang halaga.

insincere, adj. false; deceptive. Di-tapat; di-lubos ang pakikisama o niloloob.

insinuate, v. to hint; to imply shyly. Iparamdam; ipahiwatig.

insist, v. to persist in. Igiit; ipilit.

insolence, n. imprudence. Kabastusán; pag-uyam.

insolent, adj. contemptuously rude; disrespectful, or insulting. Bastos; mapanguyam; mapagmataas.

insomnia, v. sleeplessness. Insomniya; di-pagkakatulog.

inspect, v. to examine. Inspeksiyunin; siyasatin.

inspector, n. one who inspects; a title of various executive or supervisory officers. Inspektor; tagasiyasat.

inspiration, n. an inspiring or animating action or influence. Inspirasyon; pamukaw-sigla.

inspire, v. to enliven. Pagbaguhing loob; bigyan ng pampasigla.

instability, n. want of firmness. Instabilidad; kawalan ng tatag; kabuwayan.

instantaneous, adj immediate. Dagli; biglaan; madaling-madali; agad-agad.

instead, adv. in place of. Sa lugar ng; sa halip.

instinct, n. inner prompting. Likas na simbuyo; katutubong hilig.

instruct, v. to teach; to direct. Atasan; ituro; itagubilin.

instructive, adj. serving to teach. Nakapagtuturo.

instrument, n. tool, implement, or apparatus. Instrumento; kasangkapan; gamit.

insufficient, adj. inadequate to any need, use or purpose. Kapós; di-sapat; kulang.

insult, n. abuse by word or action. Insulto; paghamak; pag-uyam.

insure, v. to secure. Tiyakin; isiguro; isa-katibayan.

intact, adj. entire; remaining uninjured. Walang kulang; buo; di-magalaw.

integrity, n. honesty. Integridad; katapatan; kabutihan ng pagkatao.

intellect, n. understanding. Talino; karunungan; katalasan ng isip.

intelligible, adj. comprehensible. Maiintindihan; nauunawaan.

intend, v. to mean. Sadyain; balakin; isaisip na gagawin.

intense, adj. strained; ardent. Maalab; marubdob.

intention, n. purpose; aim. Intensiyon; saloobin; balak na isagawa.

inter, v. to bury. Ibaón; ilibing.

intercession, n. mediation. Intersesyon; pakikialam; pamamagitan.

interesting, adj. attracting attention. Kawili wili; nakapananabik; nakagigising ng sigla.

interfere, v. to interpose. Humadlang; makialam.

interim, n. the meantime. Pansamantala; pagitan; panahong namagitan.

interloper, n. one who unwarrantably intrudes or thrusts himself into a business, position or matter. Intremetido; taong nanghihimasok.

intermediate, adj. intervening. Panggitna; intermedya.

interminable, adj. endless. Walang katapusan:

intermingle, v. to mingle, one with another. Makihalubilo.

interpose, v. place between; to mediate. Makialam; mangabala; sumingit; gumiit.

interpret, v. to explain. Ipakahulugan; ipaliwanag.

interrogate, v. to question. mag-usisa.

interrupt, v. to hinder; to intrude upon the action or speech of. Hadlangan; mang-abala; gambalain.

interval, n. intervening time. Patlang; pagitan.

intervene, v, to come between. Makialam; mamagitan.

interview, n. a questioning. Interbyu; panayam.

intestine, n. the lower part of the alimentary tract. Bituka.

intimate, adj. familiar. Intimo; matalik.

intimidate, v. scare. Takutin; pagbalaan.

intolerable, adj. insufferable. Di-mapapayagan; di-mapagtitiisan.

intoxicate, v. make drunk. Pukawin ng labis; malasing.
intoxication, n. drunkenness. Intoksikasyón; pagkalasing; kalasingan.
intrepid, adj. fearless; bold. Walang gulat; matapang; malakas ang loob.
intricate, adj. complex. Mahirap intindihin; masalimuot.
introduce, v. make known. Iharap; ipakilala.
introduction, n. a formal presentation of one person to another and others. Introduksiyón; pagpapakilala.
introit, n. a piece sung or chanted while the priest proceeds to the altar to celebrate mass. Ang panalanging binibigkas pagpanhik ng pari sa altar pagkatapos ng mga dasal sa simulang misa.
intrusion, n. unwarrantable entrance. Pagpasok ng walang pahintulot; panghihimasok.
inundate, v. flood. Bumaha.
invade, v. to enter hastily. Pakialaman; salakayin; lusubin.
invader, n. one who invades. Manlulusob.
invalid, adj. disabled; infirm. Walang saysay; may sakit.
invasion, n. incursion. Paglusob; pagsalakay
invent, v. to contrive. Umimbento; tumuklas.
invention, n. an original creation. Imbento; pagtuklas.
inventory, n. a list of goods. Imbentaryo; talaan ng mga bagay-bagay.
invert, v. turn upside down. Itaob; saliwain; baligtarin; pagtaliwasin.
invest, v. put (money) to profitable use. Gumugol; mamuhunan; maglagay ng puhunan.
investigate, v. search into. Imbestigahan; siyasatin.
investiture, n. formal bestowal of a right. Paggagawad ng tungkulin; pagtatalaga sa katungkulan.
invigorate, v. to strengthen. Pasiglahin; palakasin; bigyan ng lakas.
inviolate, adj. not desecrated. Walang maibibintang.
invisible, adj. not perceptible by the eye. Inbisibol; di-nakikita; nakatago.
invitation, n. solicitation. Imbitasyon; paanyaya.
invite, v. request the presence of. Imbitahin; anyayahan; kumbidahin.
invoke. v. implore; call for. Pamanhikan; tawagin; banggitin; isaalang-alang.
involuntary, adj. unintentional. Inbolontaryo; di-kinukusa; di-sinasadya.
involve, v. implicate. Ihalo; masangkot; isangkot.
invulnerable, adj. uninjurable. Inbulnerable; di-tinatablan; di-masasaktan.
inward, adv. toward the inside or interior. Interno; sa loob; paloob; papasok.
irate, adj. angry. Galit.
ire, n. anger; rage. Galit.
irksome, adj. tedious. Nakasusuya; nakaiinis.
irony, n. sarcasm. Kabaligtaran; panunuya; panguuyam.
irradicate, v. to erase; remove; Alisin; burahin.
irregular, adj. without symmetry or formal arrangement, etc. Di-pantay; di-tuwid; laban sa kinikilalang tumpak
irregularity. n. variable; abnormal. Di-kapantayan; katiwalian; di-kaayusan.

irrelevant, adj. not applicable or pertinent. Walang kinalaman; di-ugnay; walang kaugnayan.

irremovability, n. the quality or state of being irremovable. Imobilidad; ang karapatang hinahawakan ng mga pari upang di maalis sa tungkulin, maliban sa sanhing binabanggit sa batas ng Iglesya.

irresponsible, adj. not responsible or accountable. Iresponsable; walang pananagutan.

irritate, v. vex; annoy. Inisin; yamutin; galitin.

irritation, n. provocation. Iritasyón; pagkainis; pagkayamot; pagkagalit.

island, n. land entirely surrounded by water. Isla; pulo.

islet, n. a small island. Maliit na pulo.

isolate, v. detach; separate. Ihiwalay; ibukod; papagisahin.

issue, v. send out. Bigyan; umalis; lumabas.

itch, n. an itching skin disease. Kati; galis.

itchy, adj. infected with or having the sensation as if suffering from itch. Magalis; makati.

itemize, v. to state or list by items. Isa-isahin; iturong isa-isa ang mga bagay.

itinerant, adj. traveling from place to place. Itenerante; palakbay-lakbay.

itinerary, n. a plan of travel esp. a proposed route. Itineraryo; giya; talaan ng mga pook na paglalakbayan.

itself, pron. emphatic or reflexive form of it. Iyon din; ang sarili; ang kanyang sarili.

ivory, n. elephant's tusks. Garing; pangil ng elepante.

ivy, n. a climbing plant. Isang uri ng halamang baging.

J

jab, n. a sharp thrust. Dunggol; dyab.

jab, v. to poke; strike suddenly and sharply. Dunggulin.

jackal, n. a wild dog of Asia and Africa. Tsakal; hayop na kamukha ng aso.

jacket, n. a short coat. Dyaket; damit na maikling karaniwa'y hanggang baywang lamang.

jade, n. a green mineral prized for jewelry. Isang uri ng esmeralda.

jade, n. an inferior or wornout horse. Masamang babae; kabayong walang saysay.

jag, n. a sharp notch or tooth. Ngipin; tulis.

jag, v. cut so as to form notches or teeth. Lagyan ng mga ngipin; lagyan ng mga tulis.

jagged, adj. having sharp projections; uneven; notched. May mga ngipin; bakubako

jail, n. a prison. Karsel; piitan.

jam, n. sugar-cooked fruit. Dyam; bungangkahoy na minatamis.

jam, v. to crowd so as to hinder motion or extrication. Barahan; magsiksikan; magkagulo.

jangle, n. a harsh or metallic sound. Ingay na nakasasakit ng tainga; pagtatalo.

janitor, n. the caretaker of a building. Diyanitor; utusan sa mga kolehiyo o paaralan.

January, n. the first month of the year. Enero.

Japanese, adj. native of Japan. Hapones.

jar, n. a wide-mouthed vessel; a harsh impact. Tapayan; gusi; yumanig; ibangga; mag-ingat nang walang tuto.

jaundice, n. a disease that causes a yellowish tinge in the skin. Isang uri ng sakit na ang maykatawan ay naninilaw.

jaunt, n. short trip for pleasure. Ekskursiyon; isang pang-aliw na paglalakbay.

jaunty, adj. sprightly. Garboso; masigla.

Javanese, adj. a native, or the language of Java. Habanes; ukol sa pulo ng Haba.

jaw, n. either of the two bony structures that form the mouth. Mandibula; panga.

jealous, adj. suspicious fears or envious resentment; suspicious or fearful rivalry, as in love. Seloso; panibughuin; mapanaghiliin.

jeer, v. scoff at; derive: mock. Uyamin; tuyain.

jelly, n. prepared fruits. Gulaman; haleya.

jellyfish, n. a marine invertebrate. Medusa; dikya.

jerk, v. to pull suddenly. Umalog; batakin nang pabigla.

Jerusalem, n. a holy city in Palestine where Jesus suffered and died. Herusalem, isang lunsod sa Palestina na pinagdusahan at kinamatayan ni Kristo.

jest, n. joke; fun. Pagkutya; biro; pagpapatawa.

jester, n. one who jests. Tagapagpatawa; mambibiro.

Jesuit, n. member of Society of Jesus. Heswita; ang kapatirang kilala sa tawag na kapatiran ni Hesus na ang daglat ay "S. J."

Jesus, n. born 6 B.C. and crucified A.D. 29, the founder of the Christian religion. Hesus, ang pangalang ang kahulugan ay "Ang Panginoon ay Kaligtasan" si Hesus ay tunay na Diyos na ang kapangyarihan ay tulad ng Diyos Ama at Diyos Espiritu Santo.

Jew, n. descendant of Ancient Hebrews; Israelite. Hudyo.

jewel, n. a precious stone. Alahas; hiyas.

jeweler, n. one who makes or deals in jewelry. Alahero; mag-aalahas.

jilt, v. to deceive in love. Dayain; itakwil ang kasuyo.

job, n. one's profession, trade, or employment. Empleyo; gawain.

join, v. put together, combine; unite. Pagsamahin; pagkabitin; pagdugtungin.

joint, adj. junction; shared by different individuals. Dugtong; buko; sugpungan.

joke, n. a jest. Siste; biro; tukso.

jolly, adj. gay; merry; cheerful. Mapagpatawa; masaya.

jolt, n. shake; a sudden jerk. Uga; alog; pag-alog.

journey, n. travel; tour. Biyahe; paglalakbay.

jovial, adj. gay; cheerful. Mapagpatawa; masaya

joy, n. bliss; delight. Galak; kaligayahan; tuwa.

jubilee, n. season of festivity. Anibersaryo; panahon ng kasayahan at pagdiriwang.

judge, n. arbitrator; magistrate. Huwes; hukom.

judge, v. to bear and determine authoritatively as a

controversy. Husgahan; hukuman; hatulan.

judgment, n. decision; opinion. Paghuhukom; hatol; paghatol.

judicious, adj. prudent; wise. Matino; maingat; matalino.

jug, n. a vessel for holding liquids; pitcher. Pitsel; salong.

juice, n. sap of anything. Dyus; katas.

juiceless, adj. without any juice. Walang katas; tuyo.

juicy, adj. full of juice. Makatas.

July, n. the seventh month of the year. Hulyo.

jump, n. a leap. Lukso; lundag; talon.

jump, v. spring from the ground or from any support. Lumukso; lumundag; tumalon.

junction, n. union; joining. Pagsasama; salikop; sugpungan.

June, n. the sixth month of the year. Hunyo.

jungle, n. dense thicket; a wilderness. Gubat.

junior, adj. one younger than another. Dyunior; bata; bata kaysa.

junket, n. a picnic; an excursion. Bangkete; piknik; handaan; paglalakbay na gugol ng bayan.

jurisdiction, n. legal power. Pamamahala; nasasakupan; sakop; pook na nasa ilalim ng kapangyarihan ng simbahan.

just, adj. upright; fair-minded. Tama; husto; makatarungan.

justice, n. equity; conformity to moral principles or law Hustisya; katarungan.

justification, n. vindication. Pagbibigay-matwid; pagbibigay-katarungan.

justify, v. to prove to be just or conformable to justice, reason, or law. Alisan ng pala; bigyan ng katarungan.

justly, adv. in a just manner. Sa paraang makatarungan: nang buong katarungan.

jut, n. a projection. Ungos; tulis; usli.

juvenile, adj. young; youthful. Pambata; bata; ukol sa bata.

juxtaposition, n. nearness. Pagkakalapit-lapit; pagkakatabi; pagkakaagapay.

K

kale, n. a variety of cabbage with curled or wrinkled leaves. Isang uri ng repolyong may mga dahong kulot.

Kanaka, n. a native of Hawaii. Kanaka; tubo sa Haway.

keel, n. a central longitudinal part from which a frame is built upwards, as on a ship. Kilya; ang pangunahing bahaging pahaba ng isang bapor.

keen, adj. having a sharp edge or point; intense in feeling. Matindi; matalas; matalim.

keenness, n. acuteness; eagerness. Katalasan; kataliman.

keep, v. maintain possession or custody of. Humawak; itago; itinggal; pag-ingatan.

keeper, n. one who guards, watches, or takes care of something or someone. Tagapag-alaga; tagapagtago; bantay.

keepsake, n. a souvenir or memento. Regalo; kaloob; handog; alaala

ken, n. range of sight or knowledge. Bista; abot-tanaw.

kennel, n. a house for dogs. Bahay o kulungan ng aso.

kettle, n. a covered vessel for the heating of liquids or for cooking. Lutuan; kaldero.

key, n. an instrument for opening and closing a lock, valve, circuit, etc. Susi.

kick, n. a blow with the foot. Tadyak; sipa.

kick, v. to strike with the foot. Tadyakan; sipain; paalisin.

kickback, n. a response, usually vigorous. Kikbak; suhol.

kid, n. young of a goat. Batang kambing.

kidnap, n. unlawful snatch or seizure. Kidnap; dukot.

kidney, n. urinary gland. Bato.

kill, v. put to death. Wakasan; patayin.

kin, n. one's relatives collectively. Parientes; kamaganak.

kind, adj. benevolent; considerate. Magiliw; mabait.

kindly, adj. agreeable; considerate. Kaiga-igaya; magiliw.

king, n. a male sovereign; a monarch. Hari.

kingdom, n. dominion of king. Kaharian.

kingfisher, n. a diving bird. Kasaykasay; piskador.

kiss, n. a gentle touch or contact. Halik.

kitchen, n. cooking room. Silid-lutuan; kusina.

kite, n. a light contrivance held captive by a long cord, designed to be supported in air by the wind. Sapi-sapi; guryon; saranggola.

kitten, n. a young cat. Maliit na pusa; kuting.

knack, n. special ability or skill. Kabihasaan; kasanayan; samut-samot.

knave, n. rascal; scoundrel. Taong mapagkunwari at magdaraya.

knead, v. work into a mass. Masahin; magmasa; gumawa ng masa.

kneel, v. rest on the knee. Luhod; lumuhod.

knife, n. a tool for cutting. Panaksak; kutsilyo; lanseta.

knight, n. medieval mounted soldier of noble birth. Kabalyero; ang mandirigmang nakakabayo noong Edad Medya.

knit, v. to make fabric by interlooping a single strand of yarn on needles. Maggantsilyo; magniting; pag-isahin.

knock, n. the act of striking noisily. Tuktok; suntok; buntal; katok.

knock, v. to hit; strike. Paluin; pabagsakin; manuntok; mambuntal; kumatok.

knocker, n. a device for rapping at a door. Pangkatok.

knocking, n. the act of rapping; striking at. Tuktok; pagkatok.

knoll, n. little round hill. Burol na pabilog.

knot, n. an interlacement of loops. Bukó; buhol.

know, v. have knowledge or information of. Maunawaan; makilala; malaman; mabatid.

knowledge, n. awareness; cognizance. Kabatiran; kaalaman; karunungan.

knuckle, n. a joint of the finger. Buko ng daliri.

koran, n. the sacred book of the Mohammedans. Koran; banal na kasulatan ng mga Mohametanos.

L

labarum, n. the standard adopted by Constantine the Great after his conversion to Christianity. Ang estandarte ng krus na dala ni Constantino sa kanyang mga pagsalakay; isang tungkod na may bandilang nakakabit bilang sagisag ng mga kristiyano.

label, n. a mark or title of identification. Etiketa; tanda; pilas ng papel na may pangalan ng tinatandaan.

label, v. to attach or affix a mark to indicate nature of a thing. Lagyan ng etiketa; tandaan; lagyan ng tanda.

labial, adj. relating to the lips. Ukol sa mga labi.

labor, n. hard work; a task. Trabaho; gawain.

labor, v. work at persistently. Magtrabaho; gumawa.

laborious, adj. diligent; assiduous. Matiyaga; magawain; mahirap.

lace, n. plaited cord. Engkahe; puntas; laso.

lack, n. want; need. Kawalan; kakulangan.

lad, n. a boy or youth. Binatilyo; batang lalaki.

ladder, n. frame with steps. Panhikan; hagdan.

ladle, n. utensil for dipping. Kutsaron; sandok; panandok.

lady-like. adj. like a lady in any respect. Tulad ng isang babaing kagalang-galang.

lady-love, n. a female sweetheart. Katipan; nobya, babaing minamahal.

lag, v. move slowly; hang back. Magpaiwan; magpahuli.

lair, n. wild beast's couch. Guwarida; kuweba ng hayop.

lake, n. a large body of water surrounded by land. Dagatdagatan; look; lawa.

lamb, n. a young sheep. Kordero; tupa.

lame, adj. limping. Maliit ang isang paa; pilay.

lameness, n. the condition of being lame. Pagkapilay.

lament, n. an expression of grief. Panaghoy; panangis; panambitan.

lament, v. to mourn; grieve. Manangis.

lamentation, n. wailing; an expression of sorrow ... mentasyón; panangis; panambitan.

lamp, n. a vessel for burning an illuminant. Ilawan; lampara; gasera.

lance, n. a weapon comprising spear with a metal head. Sibat; lanseta.

land, n. a region or country the surface of the earth, esp. the dry parts. Bayan; lupa.

land, v. arrive at a place or condition. Bumaba; dumaong; umahon sa katihan.

landed, adj. having estate in land. Hasendado; may lupa; may-ari ng lupa.

landlady, n. a mistress of an inn or of a lodging-house. Propitarya; kasera.

landlord, n. an owner of rented land, building, etc Propiyetaryo; kasero.

landscape, n. a view or picture of rural scenery. Larawan ng tanawin· ang ba hagi ng tanawing nakikita.

landmark, n. a conspicuous object serving to bound or identify a place. Muhon; hanggahan; tanda ng hanggahan.

lane, n. a narrow passage; a rural road or path. Daanan; makipot na landas.

language, n. human speech. Lenguahe; pananalita; wika.

languid, adj. spiritless; weak. Hapo; mahina.

lank, adj. meagerly slim. Payat na mataas.

lantern, n. an inclosed lamp. Lanterna; parol.

lap, n. platform formed by the thighs when one sits. Kandungan.

lap, v. lick up (a liquid) with the tongue. Himurin; dilaan.

lapel, n. a fold in the front of a coat below the collar. Solapa.

lapidate, v. to throw stones. Batuhin.

lapse, n. the passing by away, as of time. Paglipas.

lard, n. fat of swine melted. Mantika.

large, adj. great in size, amount, number, degree, etc. Malawak; malaki.

lass, n. girl; young woman. Tinedyer; dalagita.

lassitude, n. weariness. Kahapuan; katamaran; kawalan ng ganang kumilos.

last, v. endure; continue to exist or progress. Magtagal; magpatuloy ng pagkabuhay.

latch, v. fastening for doors. Isarado; lagyan ng aldaba.

late, adj. coming after the proper time. Nakaraan; huli; tanghali na.

lather, n. a soap foam. Bula ng sabon.

latria, n. the highest kind of worship, or that paid to God, distinguished by Roman Catholics from dulia, or the inferior worship paid to saints. Ang pinakamataas na anyo ng pagsambang maaaring ialay.

latter, adj. last of two mentioned. Huli; nahuhuli.

laugh, v. to show mirth. Tumawa.

laughter, n. merriment. Halakhak; pagtawa.

launch, n. a large open boat. Lantsa.

laundress, n. washerwoman. Labandera; tagalabang babae.

laundry, n. washing-room. Labanderiya; londri; labahan.

laurel, n. the bay tree; a wreath of laurel leaves, as an emblem of honor. Kapurihan; laurel; karangalan.

lavish, v. expend or bestow in generous amount. Masagana; buntunan.

law, n. a rule of action. Batas.

lawn, n. grass-plot. Damuhan.

lawyer, n. a legal counselor. Manananggol; abugado; abugada.

lay, v. put in a condition, situation, or position. Ihiga; ilagay; ilapag ang isang bagay.

lazy, adj. indolent; sluggish. Batugan; tamad.

lead, n. a soft, heavy metal. Tingga.

lead, v. guide by the hand. Ihatid; akayin; manguna.

leader, n. one who or that which leads; a chief director. Lider; hepe; patnugot; taga-akay; pinuno.

leaf, n. a flat green blade growing from a stem of a plant; a page. Dahon; pahina.

league, n. confederacy; alliance. Kapisanan; liga; samahan.

leak, n. oozing out. Tulo; butas.

lean, adj. thin. Maliit; payat.

lean, v. rest against or rely on something. Sumandig; sumandal; humilig.

leap, n. a jump or bound. Lukso; talon; lundag.

leap, v. to jump over or across. Lumukso; tumalon; lumundag.

learn, v. to get knowledge of. Malaman; matutuhan.

learning, n. systematic knowledge. Kaalaman; karunungan; pagkatuto.

lease, v. grant or obtain the use of (land, buildings, etc.) at a fixed rental. Paupahan.

least, adj. smallest. Pinakakaunti; pinakamaliit; pinakamababa.

leather, n. a dressed hide. Kuwero; katad.

leave, n. permission. Permiso; pahintulot.

leave, v. go away from. Umaiis; iwanan.

lectern, n. a desk or stand on which the large books used in the services of the Roman Catholic and other churches are placed. Atril; patungan ng aklat o papel na tinutunghayan samantalang nakaupo o nakatayo.

lectionary, n. a book containing portions of scriptures to be read for particular days. Lisyonaryo; aklat na naglalaman ng mga aral na binabasa sa mga banal na panunungkulan.

lecture, n. a discourse to an audience. Talumpati; panayam; pangaral.

ledge, n. a rim. Tabi; gilid.

leech, n. a blood-sucking worm. Linta.

left, adj. opposite to right. Kaliwa.

leg, n. one of the limbs that support and move the human or animal body. Pata; binti.

legacy, n. bequest by a will. Mana; pamana.

legal, adj. authorized by law. Legal; ayon sa batas.

legate, n. an ambassador. Embahador; kinatawan; sugo ng Papa sa isang layunin.

legend, n. a widely accepted but unverified story. Leyenda; alamat.

legitimation, n. the act of making or rendering legitimate. Lehitimasyon; ang pagkilala sa isang anak sa labas, ayon sa batas.

leisure, n. spare time. oras na malaya; panahon ng paglilibang at pagpapahingalay.

lemonade, n. a beverage of sweetened lemon juice and water. Limonada.

lend, v. grant temporarily. Pautangin; pahiramin.

lender, n. one who lends. Ang nagpautang; ang nagpapahiram.

lengthy, adj. very long. Largo; mahaba.

lenient, adj. merciful. Maawain; maluwag; mapagbigay.

lent, n. fast of forty days; an annual period of fasting and penitence in Christian ritual. Mahal na Araw; kuwaresma.

less, adj. not so large, so much, or so important. Kulang; kakaunti kaysa.

lesson, n. a session of instruction. Aral; liksyon; aralin.

let, n. allow; permit. Hayaan; pahintulutan.

letter, n. one of the characters in writing or printing. Letra; titik.

letter-box, n. a box for receiving letters; a post-office box. Buson.

lettuce, n. a plant with large green leaves, used in salad. Litsugas.

level, adj. being in a horizontal plane; having a smooth, even surface. Nibél; patag; pantay.

liability, n. state of being liable or responsible. Responsibilidad; sagutin.

liar, n. one who tells a lie. Bulaan; sinungaling.

libel, n. defamation of a person in writing. Libelo; paninirang-puri sa pamamagitan ng isang lathala.

liberty, n. freedom. Libertad; kalayaan.

library, n. a room or a building where a collection of books, manuscripts, etc. is available. Bibliotika; silid-aklatan.

licentiate, n. one licensed to exercise a profession. Lisensiyado; ang karangalang ipinagkakaloob ng mga pamantasan sa mga pag-aaral.

lick, v. pass the tongue over. Talunin; dilaan; himurin.

lid, n. a movable cover. Tuntong; takip.

lie, **n.** a falsehood. Kabulaanan; kasinungalingan.

life, n. a condition or course of living. Pamumuhay; buhay.

lifeless, adj. dead; inanimate. Patay; walang buhay.

lifelike, adj. true to life; like a living person. Natural; parang buhay.

lift, v. raise; elevate. Iangat; itaas; buhatin.

ligament, n. a band of tissue connecting bodily parts. Ligamento; mga lamad na nagdurugtong sa mga buto.

light, n. illumination. Ilaw; liwanag; linaw.

lighten, v. make or become light. Gaanan; pagaanin.

lightning, n. sudden flash of light by the discharge of atmospheric electricity. Lintik; kidlat.

like, adj. similar; analogous. Kapareho; tulad; gaya.

likely, adj. probably destined to happen or be. Malamang; maaaring mangyari.

lily, n. any of various bulbous plants with showy bell or horn-shaped flowers. Liryo.

limbo, n. a region where unbaptized souls of children reside after death. Limbo; pook na tinutunguhan ng mga kaluluwa ng mga sanggol na nangamatay nang hindi binyagan.

lime, n. a greenish-yellow citrus fruit. Apog; dayap.

line, n. a straight mark of little breadth. Linya; guhit.

lineage, n. race; genealogy. Pinagmulan; lahi.

linen, n. thread, yarn, or cloth made from flax. De ilo; linen; linso.

linger, v. remain beyond a usual or appointed time. Umali-aligid; magpaumat-umat.

lining; n. an inner covering. Aporo; tutop.

link, n. something that connects; a loop. Kawil; pang-ugnay.

lion, n. a large ferocious cat of Africa and Asia. Leon.

lioness, n. a female lion. Leong babae.

lip, n. either of the two fleshy parts forming the opening of the mouth. Labi.

liquid, adj. fluid. Likido; tunaw.

list, n. a record of number of items. Listahan; talaan.

listen, v. to hear. Pakinggan; makinig.

listener, n. one who listens. Tagapakinig; taong nakikinig.

litany, n. a ceremonial prayer with responses. Litanya; panalangin ng mga sunud-sunod na kahilingan.

literature, n. artistic writings. Literatura; panitikan.

lithe, adj. pliant; flexible. Nababaluktot; malambot.

litigation, n. a lawsuit. Litigasyón; usapin.

litter, n. a number of young brought forth at one birth. Kamada.

little, adj. small in size, amount, number, degree or duration. Maliit; kaunti.

liturgy, n. ritual of prayer. Liturhiya; ang mga pagdarasal, pagmimisa, sakramento at iba pang gawaing ginagampanan sa Simbahan ayon sa mga tuntunin at batas ng Iglesya.

live, adj. having life; alive. Bibo; buhay.

livelihood, n. an occupation that furnishes means of support. Kabuhayan; ikinabubuhay.

lively, adj. brisk; vigorous. Masaya; masigla; maliksi.

liver, n. the vital organ that secretes bile. Atay.

lizard, n. a small four-legged reptile with a long scaly body. Butiki.

load, n. a burden. Karga; pasanin; dala.

loan, n. something lent; the act of lending. Pautang; pahiram; utang.

lobster, n. an edible marine crustacean. Ulang.

local, adj. limited to a place. Lokál; pampook.

locality, n. a place; community; section. Lokalidad; lunan; pook.

locate, v. discover or describe the place or locality of. Hanapin; matagpuan; makita.

lock, n. a device that fastens and prevents the opening, detachment, movement, etc. of a door. Seradura; aldaba; kandado.

locked, adj. fastened by a lock or locks. Sarado; nakaaldaba; nakasusi.

lodge, n. a temporary habitation; meeting place of members of a society. Bahay-panuluyan; bahay-bantayan; munting bahay; bahagi ng isang kapisanang lihim.

lodger, n. one living in hired quarters. Panauhin; nangungupahan.

lodging, n. temporary abode; quarters hired for residence. Habitasyón; tirahan; mga silid na inuupahan.

log, n. a bulky piece of timber. Troso; puno ng kahoy na inalisan ng mga sanga't ugat.

logic, n. the science of correct reasoning. Lohika; katwiran; katumpakan.

loiter, v. to linger idly; waste time. Magpalabuy-laboy; magpaumat-umat; mag-aksaya ng panahon.

loiterer, n. one who loiters. Haragan; tamad; bulakbol.

lone, adj. solitary; being alone. Solitaryo; solo; nag-iisa.

loneliness, n. in a lonely state. Kalungkutan; pag-iisa; pangungulila.

long, adj. having great extent in time or space. Largo;

mahaba.

long, v. feel a strong desire. Naisin ng buong taimtim; nasain nang buong pananabik.

longanimity, n. long-suffering; forbearance. Pagtitiis; katatagan sa pagtatamo o paggawa ng kabutihan kahit sa gitna ng mga katiwalian.

longing, n. earnest desire. Pagnanasa nang buong pananabik.

look, v. exercise the power of vision. Hanapin; tingnan; isaalang-alang.

look, n. outward appearance or aspect. Tingin; kaanyuan.

loose, adj. unbind; release. Tanggal; maluwag; kalag.

loosen, v. make or become loose or loosen. Pakawalan; paluwagin; kalagin.

loot, n. booty seized in war; plunder; spoils. Lut; mga bagay na sinamsam ng isang hukbong nagtagumpay; mga ninakaw.

lopsided, adj. heavier on or leaning to, one side. Tagilid na tagilid.

Lord, n. God; Jesus Christ; Panginoon; hari; Diyos.

lose, v. miss and not know where to find. Maligaw; mawala.

loss, n. failure to hold, keep, or preserve. Kawalan; pagkawala; pangulugi.

lost, adj. no longer possessed; wasted. Nasira; nawala.

lot, n. a distinct portion or parcel, esp. of land. Pitak ng lupa; lote.

loth, adj. unwilling; loath. Nasusuklam; nasusuya; walang hangad.

lottery, n. game of chance. Pagpapalabunot; loterya.

loud, adj. strongly audible; noisy. Maingay; malakas.

louse, n. a small blood-sucking insect. Kuto.

lovable, adj. worthy to be loved. Kaakit-akit; kaibig-ibig.

love, n. an object of affection. Amor; pag-ibig.

lovely, adj. beautiful; delightful. Kaibig-ibig; maganda.

loveless, adj. void of love. Walang pag-ibig.

loveliness, n. great beauty. Kariktan; kagandahan.

loving, adj. fond; affectionate. Mapagmahal; magiliw.

low, adj. below a usual or standard level; deep. Mahina; mahaba.

lower, adj. deeper; more inferior. Mababa-baba; mababa kaysa.

lowest, adj. deepest; much inferior. Pinakamabababa.

lowly, adj. humble. Mababang loob; mapagkumbaba; hamak; mababa.

low mass, n. said without music and by one priest. Misa risada.

loyal, adj. faithful. Tapat.

loyalty, n. fidelity. Katapatan.

lubricate, v. make smooth. Grasahan; langisan; lagyan ng pampadulas.

luck, n. good fortune. Suwerte; kapalaran.

lucky, adj. fortunate. Masuwerte; mapalad.

lucrative, adj. profitable. Lukratibo; kapaki-pakinabang.

luggage, n. baggage; trunks, valises, etc. Abastos; mga dala-dalahan ng isang manlalakbay.

lukewarm, adj. tepid; moderately warm. Malahininga; maligamgam.

lull, n. a period of temporary

quiet or rest. Pansandaliang katahimikan.

lumber, n. timber sawed and split for use. Kahoy; troso; tabla.

luminary, n. that which diffuses light; one who enlightens mankind. Tampok; bituing namumukod.

luminous, adj. shining. Maningning; maliwanag.

lump, n. mass of solid material without regular shape; knob; swelling. Masa; tambok; bukol.

lunatic, n. a crazy person. Sira-sira; baliw.

lunch, n. a midday meal. Pananghalian; tanghalian.

lung, n. organ of respiration. Pulmon; baga.

lure, v. to entice or attract. Akitin; yayain sa isang patibong; himukin.

lurk, v. lie in wait; to remain secretly. Manubok; mangubli; mag-abang.

luscious, adj. delicious. Matamis; kalugod-lugod; masarap.

lust, n. passionate or lewd desire. Kahibuan; kalibugan; nasa.

lustful, adj. sensual. Mayamo; malibog.

lusty, adj. vigorous; strong. Masigla; malakas.

luxuriant, adj. being in great abundance; plentiful. Marami; makapal; sagana; malago.

luxury, n. an extravagant indulgence. Karangyaan; luho; mga mamahaling gamit na di lubhang kailangan.

lye, n. solution of potash. Lihiya.

lying, adj. uttering falsehood. Bulaan; sinungaling.

lynch, v. punishment without law. Patayin ng walang paglilitis; parusahan ng marami nang hindi na hinihintay ang hatol ng batas.

lyre, n. a stringed musical instrument of ancient Greece. Lira.

lyric, n. a lyric poem or song. Tulang liriko.

lyrist, n. a poet who writes lyrics. Makatang liriko.

M

macaroni, n. thin tubes of dried wheat paste used as food. Makaroni.

machine, n. any device that transfers or converts energy from one form to another, esp. for manufacturing. Makinarya; makina.

machinery, n. machines or parts of machines collectively. Makinarya.

mad, adj. enraged; of unsound mind. Loko; ulol; baliw.

madman, n. an insane person. Loko; baliw na lalaki.

madness, n. lunacy; insanity. Kaululan; kabaliwan.

Madonna, n. The Virgin Mary. Madona; katumbas ng ginang; pangalawang iniangkop sa ilang larawan ng Birhen.

Magdalene, n. a reformed prostitute. Magdalena; pangalang iniangkop sa mga babaing nagsisisi.

maggot, n. the larva of an insect; a worm. Uod.

magi, n. priests, in ancient Persia; the "Three Wise Men". Tatlong Hari; mga haring mago ng Silangan.

magic, n. witchcraft; pretended art of producing effects by supernatural forces. Salamangka; mahiya; engkanto.

magistrate, n. a minor judge or judicial officer. Hukom;

mahistrado.

magnanimity, n. nobility or dignity of soul. Magnanimidad; kagandahang-loob.

magnet, n. a loadstone. Magneto; balani.

magnificent, adj. pompous; grand. Maringal; dakila; kahanga-hanga.

magnify, v. to make great or greater. Palabisan; palakihin.

maid, n. a girl; an unmarried woman. Babaing walang asawa; dalaga.

mail, n. letters or packages sent by post. Sulat; koreo; baluti.

maim, v. to cripple; to wound. Putulin; durugin; lumpuhin.

main, adj. principal; chief. Prinsipal; pangunahin; pinakabuod.

maintain, v. preserve; keep in condition. Pamalagiin; itaguyod; kupkupin.

maize, n. Indian corn. Mais.

majestic, adj. magnificent. Maringal; kagalang-galang; kapita-pitagan.

majesty, n. grandeur. Kamaharlikaan; kamahalan.

major, adj. greater in importance, quantity, or extent. Pangunahin; nakararami.

major, n. an officer ranking next above a captain. Medyor.

majority, n. more than half. Kalamangan; ang nakararami.

make, n. construction; nature; brand. Uri; modelo; tatak; anyo; yari.

make, v. bring into being; form. Iutos; gumawa.

make-believe, adj. pretended. Kunwari.

maker, n. one who makes; manufacturer. Manggagawa.

malady, n. a disease. Sakit; karamdaman.

male, adj. masculine. Maskulino; lalaki; ukol sa lalaki.

malediction, n. a curse; evil speaking. Maldiksiyon; paghahangad ng masama sa kapwa.

male-teacher, n. a masculine teacher. Maestro; gurong lalaki.

malice, n. spite; rancor; a hostile act. Malisya; masamang hangarin.

malleability, n. capable of being shaped or extended. Paglalagay sa anumang hugis; kalambutan at kakunatan; kadaliang hubugin.

mallet, n. wooden hammer. Maso; pamukpok.

maltreat, v. to treat ill. Maltratuhin; apihin.

man, n. adult male person. Mamà; tao; lalaki.

manacle, n. chain for the hands. Manilya; posas.

manage, v. to govern; to direct or control. Maisagawa; pamahalaan pangasiwaan.

management, n. board of managers; directing; controlling; administration. Pamamahala.

manager, n. one who directs any operations. Manedyer; administrador; tagapamahala.

mandate, n. command. Orden; utos; kautusan.

mangle, v. to cut or slash; to disfigure. Gutayin; lumpuhin; durugin.

mania, n. a form of insanity, marked by great excitement. Sumpong; pagkahibang; kahibangan; pagkahaling.

manifest, v. demonstrate; give evidence. Ihayag; ipakita; ipahalata.

manifestation, n. a showing; display; demonstration. Manipestasyon; pagpapakita; katotohanang nakikita; bagay o kilos na namamalas.

manifold, adj. many; numerous, Iba-iba ang uri; maraming-marami.

mantum, n. cape of the Pope. Kapa ng Papa.

manual, n. a handbook; a book of instruction. Manuál; aklat ng panuto; patnubay.

manufacture, n. the making of goods, by hand or machinery. Pagyari; produkto.

manufacturer, n. one who manufactures. Pabrikante; tagagawa.

manure, n. any substance, chiefly stable refuse, used to fertilize land. Abono; dumi ng hayop.

manuscript, n. a book or document written by hand. Manuskrito; sinulat; katha.

many, adj. various; numerous. Marami.

map, n. a drawing of all or a part of the earth's surface, or the heavens. Mapa.

mar, v. to injure; to spoil. Papangitin; siraan; dungisan.

marble, n. hard crystalline limestone, used in sculpture and architecture. Marmol.

march, n. advance or progress from one place to another. Pagsulong; martsa.

march, v. proceed on foot. Lumakad; magmartsa.

marchioness, n. marquis' wife. Asawa ng markes; markesa.

mare, n. female of a horse. Kabayong babae.

margin, n. border; edge Marhen; gilid; palugit.

marine, adj. pertaining to the sea, or navigation; nautical. Pandagat; marino; ukol sa dagat.

mark, v. to brand; observe. Markahan; tandaan.

marker, n. anything used as a mark. Pantatak; pananda.

market, n. an assemblage of people or a place for buying and getting. Tiyangge; palengke; pamilihan.

marriage, n. wedlock. Matrimonyo; kasal.

marriageable, adj. of an age suitable for marriage. May layang magpakasal; maaaring pakasal.

married, adj. conjugal. Kasal na; may asawa.

marrow, n. substance in bones. Modula; utak ng buto.

marry, v. join in wedlock. Ikasal; pakasal.

marsh, n. a swamp; a watery tract. Latian; putikan; sapang maputik.

marshal, n. a high officer in an army. Mariskal ng hukbo.

martyr, n. one persecuted in defense of a belief or cause. Martir.

martyrdom, n. the state of being a martyr. Pagiging martir.

martyrology, n. a history or account of martyrs with their sufferings. Martirolohiyo; aklat na naglalaman ng talaan at talambuhay ng mga martir at mga santo.

marvel, n. prodigy; wonder. Bagay na kahanga-hanga; kababalaghan.

marvel, v. wonder at; be moved by wonder. Mamangha; humanga.

marvelous, adj. wonderful; extra-ordinary. Kataka-taka; kahanga-hanga.

masculine, adj. male; manly. Maskulino; lalaki; ukol sa lalaki.

mash, v. to crush; to make into a mash. Pipiin; lamasin.

mask, v. to disguise or conceal. Itago; magmaskara; magbalatkayo.

masquerade, n. a disguise; a false pretense. Balatkayo.

mass, n. a lump; the bulk. Masa; bunton; bulto.

mass, n. the services of the Eucharist in the Roman Catholic and Greek churches. the Roman Catholic communion service. Misa.

massacre, v. the indiscriminate, wholesale killing of humans. Maramihang pagpatay; patayin nang walang habag.

massage, n. rubbing of muscles and joints. Masahe.

massive, adj. bulky; heavy. Malaki't makapal; mabigat.

master, n. a chief; an instructor. Pinuno; guro; panginoon; amo.

masterly, adv. skillful. Bihasa; nang buong kaya.

mat, n. a piece of fabric woven of straw, etc. used on the floor or table. Banig.

mat, v. to cover or lay with mats. Latagan; maglatag ng banig.

match, n. a chemically tipped piece of wood, etc. Posporo.

match, v. correspond; sulit; harmonize. Pagbagayin; ilapat; iagpang.

match-box, n. a box of matches. Kahon ng posporo.

matches, adj. having no equal. Walang kapantay; walang katulad.

mate, n. a companion; a husband or wife. Kapares; kasama; asawa; konsorte.

material, n. substance; raw matter to be developed. Sangkap; gamit; kagamitan.

materialism, n. the belief that nothing exists except matter. Materyialismo.

maternal, adj. pertaining to a mother. Ukol sa ina; sa panig ng ina.

mathematics, n. the science of numbers in all their relations and applications. Pagtutuos; matematika.

matins, n. morning worship. Mga panalangin o pagsamba sa umaga.

matrimony, n. the ceremony or sacrament of marriage. Matrimonyo; kasal.

matrix, n. the womb. Matris; bahay-bata.

matron, n. married woman. Matrona; babaing may asawa; ina.

matted, adj. roughly tangled. Lubid-lubid.

matter, n. the substance of which physical objects consist. Bagay.

mattress, n. a cloth case filled with padding, used as or on a bed. Kutson.

mature, adj. complete in natural growth, fully developed. Sapat sa gulang; magulang.

maul, v. to beat harshly. Gulpihin; bugbugin.

Maundy Thursday, n. the Thursday before Good Friday, on which the Sovereign of England distributes alms to a certain number of poor persons at Whitehall. Huwebes Santo,

maxim, n. an axiom. Tuntunin o asal; kasabihan; kawikaan.

maximum, n. the great quantity or amount possible. Pinakamalaki; sukdulan.

May, n. the fifth month of

the year. Mayo.

maybe, adv. perhaps. Baka sakali; marahil.

mayonnaise, n. a kind of salad dressing. Mayonesa.

mayor, n. chief municipal or city officer. Alkalde; meyor; punung-bayan.

maze, n. a labyrinth; a confusing path. Liku-likong landas; pampalito; kaguluhan.

me, pron. the person speaking. Akó.

meadow, n. grass land. Pastulan; parang.

mealtime, n. the usual time of eating meals. Oras ng pagkain.

mean, adj. vile; base; inferior in quality. Marumi; imbi; mababa; hamak.

meander, v. wander aimlessly; pursue a winding course. Magpaliku-liko.

meaning, n. significance; purpose. Kahulugan; ang ibig sabihin.

meaningless, adj. having no significance. Di-importante; walang saysay; walang kahulugan.

meanness, n. want of dignity or rank; want of spirit or honor. Kaimbihan.

meanwhile, adv. meantime; in the interval. Habang; samantala.

measles, n. an infectious eruptive disease, chiefly in children. Tigdas.

measure, n. any standard of comparison, estimation, or judgment. Medida; sukat; sukatan.

measure, v. estimate; ascertain the extent of. Takalin; sukatin.

measured, adj. uniform; regular. Pantay-pantay; pare-pareho.

meat, n. the flesh of animals used for food. Karne; laman.

mechanic, n. a skilled worker with tools. Mekaniko.

medal, n. a coinlike piece of metal inscribed to commemorate an event. Medalya.

meddle, v. to interpose; to intrude upon another's affair. Manghimasok; makialam.

meddler, n. a busybody. Pakialamera.

median, n. the middle. Panggitna; gitna.

mediator, n. one who mediates between parties at variance for the purpose of reconciling them. Tagapamagitan.

Mediatrix, n. Virgin Mary; a female mediator. Ang Birhen Maria; tagapamagitan.

mediation, n. interposition; intervention; intercession. Medyasión; pamamagitan.

medical, adj. pertaining to medicine. Ukol sa gamot o sa panggagamot.

medicine, n. a substance for treating a disease; a remedy. Lunas; remedyo; gamot.

mediocre, adj. of average quality. Kainaman.

meditate, v. to think; to intend. Nilay-nilayin; magisip-isip.

medium, n. middle place. Gitna; tagapamagitan.

meek, adj. soft; mild; gentle. Mahinahon; maamo; mapakumbaba.

meet, adj. suitable; proper. Angkop; karapat-dapat.

meet, v. to come to; encounter. Magharap; tagpuin; salubungin.

meeting, n. a coming together; an assembly. Miting; pagtatagpo; pulong.

melancholy, adj. gloomy; depressed in spirits. Mapanglaw· malungkot; hapis.

melee, n. hand-to-hand fight among a number of fighters. Labu-labo.

melon, n. a large fruit with juicy flesh inside a rind. Milon.

melt, v. to dissolve. Malusaw; tunawin; matunaw.

member, n. a part of any aggregate or whole. Miyembro; kaanib; kasapi.

memoir, n. a record of facts. Talaan ng mga alaala.

memoria, n. preservative of memory; a container of the martyr's relics. Memorya; lalagyan ng mga relikya ng mga martir na kung minsan ay dinadala sa prusisyon; tanda ng alaala.

memory, n. remembrance; reminiscence. Gunita; isip; pag-iisip; alaala.

men, n. male persons. Mga lalaki; kalalakihan.

menace, n. a threat. Banta; panganib.

mend, v. to patch; to repair; improve. Ayusin; kumpunihin.

mendicant, n. a beggar. Pulubi.

menology, n. calendar of saints and martyrs with their feasts. Kalendaryong may mga pangalan ng mga martir at mga kompesor.

mental, adj. intellectual. Pangkaisipan; ukol sa pag-iisip.

mention, n. a brief reference. Pagbanggit; banggit.

mention, v. refer to briefly or incidentally. Banggitin.

mentor, n. a wise and trusted adviser. Taga-payo.

merchandise, n. commodities brought and sold. Paninda; kalakal.

merchant, n. a trader. Mangangalakal.

merciful, adj. compassionate. Mahabagin; maawain.

merciless, adj. pitiless. Walang habag; walang awa.

mercury, n. quicksilver. Asoge.

mercy, n. tenderness. Awa; habag.

mere, adj. nothing else than; only. Lamang.

merge, v. to consolidate; unite. Ipisan; isama; isanib.

merit, n. worthiness; due reward. Katangian; kakayahan.

mermaid, n. sea nymph. Sirena.

merrily, adv. in a joyful manner. Nang masaya; nang buong kasayahan.

merry, adj. gay; jovial. Tuwang-tuwa; masaya.

mess, n. a confused condition or situation. Gusot; kaguluhan; mga sabog o kalat.

Messiah, n. Jesus Christ; a savior. Ang Mesiyas; si Kristo.

message, n. an errand; a verbal or written communication. Mensahe; pahatid.

messenger, n. one sent. Sugo.

metaphysics, n. the philosophy of mind. Metapisika; ang agham na tumatalakay sa mga suliranin ng mga bagay na nananatili sa ibabaw ng lupa, ng kalikasan at sanhi ng mga iyon.

mezzanine, n. a low story between two higher stories of building. Entresuwelo.

mice, n. small rodents (pl. of mouse). Mga daga.

microbe, n. a germ; a bacterium. Mikrobyo.

middle, n. in the center. Gitna.

midnight, n. 12 o'clock at night. Hatinggabi.

midwife, n. a nurse at childbirth. Hilot; komadrona.

might, n. power; strength. Lakas; kapangyarihan.

mightily, adv. powerfully; greatly. Nang buong lakas.

migrate, v. to change one's place of abode. Magtungo sa ibang lupain; mangibang-bayan.

migration, n. a moving from one place to another. Pandarayuhan.

mild, adj. gentle. Mahinahon; kaigihan.

mildew, n. a white fungus coating on fabrics or leather due to exposure to moisture. Tagulamin.

military, adj. pertaining to the army, a soldier, or affairs of war. Militar; ukol sa hukbong katihan.

milk, n. a lacteal fluid. Gatas.

milkman, n. a man that sells milk or carries milk to market. Maggagatas.

mill, n. any of various machines for grinding, or otherwise working materials into proper form. Kiskisan; gilingan.

millennium, n. the 1,000 years of Christ's reign on earth. Isang libong taon; ayon sa Bagong Tipan, ang panahong ipaghahari ni Kristo sa daigdig.

millimeter, n. the thousandth part of a meter. Milimetro.

millier, n. one who makes headgear for women. Mananahi; modista.

million, n. one thousand times. 1,000. Milyón; angaw.

millionaire, s. a person with a million dollars. Milyonaryo.

mimic, v. imitate for sport. Imitahin; gayahin; tularan.

mince, v. to chop up into very small pieces. Tadtarin.

mind, n. intellect; sanity. Pag-iisip; isip.

mindful, adj. attentive. Nag-iisip; maingat; maalaala; maasikaso.

mine, pron. belongs to me; possessive form of I. Akin.

mine, n. a deposit of mineral ores or coal, or the excavation made for removing them. Mina; minahan.

mine, v. extract ores, etc. lay explosive mines. Lagyan ng pasabog; magmina; gumawa sa minahan.

mingle, v. mix; blend. Makihalo; makisama.

miniature, adj. on a small scale. Maliit; munti.

minimize, v. to reduce. Bawasan.

minister, n. clergyman; priest. Ministro; pari; alagad ng simbahan.

mint, n. place where money is made. Gawaan ng salapi.

miracle, n. supernatural event. Milagro; himala; kababalaghan.

mirage, n. optical illusion. Malikmata.

mire, n. slush. Lusak; pusali.

mirror, n. looking-glass. Espeho; salamin.

mirth, n. merriment. Katuwaan; kasayahan.

misapprehend, v. to misunderstand. Hindi maunawaan.

misappropriate, v. take or use dishonestly. Lustayin.

misbehave, v. behave badly. Mag masamang asal; kumilos nang di mabuti.

misbelieve, n. erroneous belief; false religion. Maling paniniwala; di-paniniwala.

miscalculate, v. reckon incorrectly. Mamali ng taya;

tantiyahin nang mali.

miscarry, v. to fall of the intended effect; to bring forth child before the proper time. Mabigo; pagkamalang dalhin ang isang bagay; makunan.

miscellaneous, adj. various. Samut-samot; sari-sari; bala-balaki.

mischance, n. bad luck. Masamang kapalaran.

mischief, n. harm; injury. Kapinsalaan; sama; sira; gawang di-mabuti.

misclaim, n. an erroneous claim. Maling pag-angkin.

misconduct, n. improper conduct or behavior. Masamang gawi; masamang kilos.

misdeed, n. an improper action. Masamang gawa; gawaing di-mabuti.

miser, n. covetous person. Taong labis ang kakuriputan.

miserable, adj. unhappy. Malungkot.

miserere, n. the name given to the 50th psalm in the vulgate, corresponding to the 51st Psalm in the English version, beginning 'Miserere mei. Domine' (Pity me, O Lord). Miserere; ang simula ng dasal ng pagsisisi na nagsisimula sa gayong salita.

misery, n. wretchedness. Karukhaan; kahapisan; kalungkutan.

misfortune, n. calamity; bad luck. Disgrasya; kasamaang-palad.

misgiving, n. a doubt; hesitation. Duda; alinlangan.

misgovernment, n. bad administration or management of public or private affairs. Masamang pamamahala.

misguide, v. to direct to a wrong purpose or end. Imali ng daan.

mishap, n. ill luck. Disgrasya; masamang palad.

misinform, v. give incorrect information to. Magbigay ng maling balita.

misinterpret, v. to interpret wrongly. Ipakahulugan nang pamali.

misjudge, v. to have an unjust opinion (of). Husgahan ng mali; humatol nang di-tumpak.

mislay, v. to lay in a wrong place. Ilagay ang isang bagay sa di niya lunan.

mislead, v. to lead astray. Iligaw.

misleading, adj. causing error. Nakakalinlang.

misprint, n. a typographical error. Maling limbag.

mispronounce, v. to pronounce incorrectly. Bigkasin nang di-wasto.

misquotation, n. an erroneous quotation. Maling banggit.

misquote, v. quote incorrectly. Banggitin nang mali.

misread, v. to read amiss. Basahin nang mali.

misrepresent, v. to represent falsely. Magbigay ng maling kuro; magpanggap nang di-wasto.

miss, n. a girl; unmarried woman, Binibini; dalaga.

missal, n. the Roman Catholic mass-book; a prayer book. Aklat ng misa; misal.

missing, adj. wanting; lost. Nawawala.

mission, n. a charge to go and perform a specific service and duty. Misyón; layunin; ang pook na pinagdadalhan sa isang pari na napapailalim sa kanyang pamamahala.

misspell, v. spell incorrectly. Baybayin nang mali.

mistake, n. error, ill judge. Mali; kamalian.

mister, (Mr.) n. a conventional title for man, usually written Mr. Mister, Ginoo.

mistress, n. woman in control. Senyora; panginoong babae.

Mrs., n. a title before the surname of a married woman. Ginang.

mistrust, n. suspicion. Paghihinala; di pagtitiwala.

misunderstand, v. to understand incorrectly. Di-maintindihan; unawain nang di-tumpak.

mitigate, v. to make mild Palamigin.

mitre, n. episcopal crown. Mitra; isang uri ng sumbrerong mataas at matulis na isinusuot ng mga arsobispo at obispo sa mga pagkakataong pormal

mix, v. to blend; to unite. Timplahin; ihalo; isama

mix-up, n. a confusion. Kaguluhan.

mixed, adj. blended by mixing; indiscriminate. Magulo; halu-halo; sama-sama.

mixer, n. a person who gets along well with others. Taong magaling makisama.

moan, v. to lament; grieve. Managhoy; dumaing.

mob, n. a crowd; disorderly assemblage of persons. Ang pulutong ng mga taong nagkakagulo.

mobile, adj. easily moved. Mobil; gumagalaw; lumalakad.

mock, v. to deride; jeer. Kutyain; uyamin; tuyain.

mode, n. style; fashion. Kalakaran; moda.

model, n. a standard for imitation or comparison. Modelo; huwaran.

moderate, adj. temperate. Mahinahon; katamtaman.

modern, adj. pertaining to or characteristic of present or recent times. Moderno; makabago.

modest, adj. decent; manifesting humility; propriety, and restraint. Di-mapagmataas; di-hambog; mahinhin.

modesty, n. decency. Katimpian; kahinhinan; di-kagaslawan.

moist, adj. damp; slightly wet Mahalumigmig; basa-basa.

moisten, v. to make moist or damp. Basain.

moisture, n. a slight wetness. Halumigmig.

molar, n. a tooth with a broad surface for grinding. Bagang.

moment, n. short space of time. Sandali; saglit.

monastery, n. a convent; the premises occupied by monks. Monasteryo; tirahan ng mga mongha o monghe.

Monday, n. the second day of the week. Lunes.

money, n. medium of exchange. Kuwarta; salapi; pera.

monk, n. religious recluse. Monghe; pari.

monkey, n. an ape; baboon. Unggoy; tsonggo.

monopolize, v. to have or get exclusive possession or control of. Sarilihin.

monstrance, n. in the Roman Catholic Church the transparent or glassfaced shrine in which the consecrated host is presented for the people. Ang banal na lalagyan ng Santisimo Sakramento na itinataas upang sambahin o dinadala sa mga prusisyon.

monument, n. a memorial

structure or statue. Monumento; bantayog.

mood, n. state of mind. Kundisyon; sumpong; kalagayan ng pag-iisip.

moody, adj. likely to have changes of mood. Sumpungin.

moon, n. the heavenly body that revolves around the earth monthly and shines by the sun's reflected light; earth's satellite. Buwan.

morality, n. the practice of moral duties; ethics; virtue. Moralidad; ,kaasalang naaayon sa mabuting pamantayan.

moral philosophy, n. ethics. Pilosopiya moral.

morals, n. principles or habits with respect to right or wrong conduct. Kustumbre; kaugalian.

morbid, adj. diseased; mentally unhealthy. Di-malusog; masakitin; mahina.

more, adj. in greater number or measure. Lalong marami; higit.

morganatic, adj. referring to a marriage between a man of high rank and a woman of less rank. Morganatiko; tawag sa pag-aasawang ang babae ay may mababang kabuhayan kaysa lalaki.

morning, n. the period between midnight and noon or dawn and noon. Umaga.

morose, adj. gloomy; sullen. Nalulumbay.

morrow, n. the next day after this. Bukas; ang araw na susunod.

morsel, n. mouthful; a bite. Kapiraso; subo.

mortal, adj. & n. subject to death. May kamatayan mortal; makatao.

mortal sin, n. a grave and serious sin. Kasalanang mortal.

mortar, n. a bowl or device in which substances are pounded. Almires; lusong.

mortification, n. humiliation or slight vexation. Pagpaparusa sa sarili.

mostly, adv. chiefly; mainly. Karaniwan; karamihan.

moth, n. a nocturnal insect resembling the butterfly. Gamugamo.

mother, n. a female parent. Nanay; ina.

mother country, n. a country which has sent out colonies, in relation to the colonies. Inang-bayan.

Mother-Superior, n. the head of a female religious community. Madre superyora.

mother-in-law, n. the mother of one's wife or husband. Biyenang babae.

motion, n. a movement; gesture. Mungkahi; galaw; kilos.

motionless, adj. at rest. Di-kumikilos; walang galaw.

motivate, v. to provide with a motive; to induce; incite. Ibuyo.

motley, adj. of various colors. Iba-iba; halu-halo; sari-sari.

motto, n. a maxim; a phrase or word expressive of one's guiding principle. Kasabihan; salawikain.

mould, n. earth; soil; a form. Molde; hulmahan.

mountain, n. a lofty, natural elevation of the earth's surface. Bundok.

mountainous, adj. abounding in mountains. Mabundok.

mourn, v. to grieve. Ipagdalamhati; maghinagpis; ipagluksa.

mournful, adj. sad; sorrowful; gloomy. Malungkot; nakahahapis.

mouse, n. a small rodent. Daga.

mousetrap, n. a trap for catching mice. Patibong ng daga.

moustache, n. hair on the upper lip. Bigote.

mouth, n. the opening through or in which an animal takes food, masticates and gives vocal utterance. Bibig; bunganga̕.

mouthful, n. the amount the mouth can easily hold. Sansubo.

move, v. to change position; advance. Lumakad; kumilos; gumalaw.

movement, n. the act or manner of moving. Kilos; galaw.

movie, n. a motion picture. Sine; pelikula.

mow, v. to cut grass. Gapasin; putulin; tabasan.

much, adj. & adv. abundant; greatly. Malaki; marami.

mud, n. wet, soft earth; mire. Putik.

muddle, n. confused state. Gulo; kaguluhan.

mulberry, n. a tree or its berrylike, collective fruit. Puno ng moras.

mull, v. heat, sweeten and spice as wine or ale. Nuynuyin; painitin; patamisin at rikaduhan upang maging inumin, gaya ng alak, atb.

multiply, v. to increase the number or quantity. Multiplikahin; paramihin.

multitude, n. populace. Karamihan; pulutong; maraming tao.

mumble, v. speak indistinctly. Bumulong-bulong.

mumps, n. an inflammation and swelling of the salivary gland. Beke.

munch, v. to chew vigorously and steadily. Ngumata.

mundane, adj. of this world. Makamundo; makalupa.

murmur, n. a low noise. Aliw-iw; bulong; anas; anasan.

museum, s. a building for an exhibit of art, science, etc. Museo.

mushroom, n. spongy plant. Kabute; taingang-daga.

music, n. harmony; melody. Tugtugin; musika.

musician, n. one skilled in music. Musiko; manunugtog.

mustard, n. a plant; its seed made into a paste and used as a condiment or medicinally. Mustasa.

musty, adj. mouldy; antiquated. Maamag.

mute, n. one incapable of speech. Pipi.

mutilate, v. maim or disfigure esp. by depriving of a limb. Gutayin; durugin.

mutiny, an open rebellion. Pag-aalsa; paghihimagsik.

mutter, v. to murmur. Umungol; bumulong.

my. pron. belonging to me. Ko; akin.

myself, pron. an intensifier of *me* or *I*; a reflexive substitute for *me*. Ako; sarili ko.

mysterious, adj. obscure; puzzling. Misteryoso; mahiwaga.

mystery, n. an enigma or puzzle. Misteryo; hiwaga.

mystic, n. one who believes in, or practices, mysticism. Mistiko; ang taong tuwirang tumatanggap ng makalangit na inspirasyon.

myth, n. a legend. Alamat; katakataka.

N

nab, v. seize suddenly; arrest. Sunggabán; dakpin; hulihin.

nag, n. constant scolding or urging. Paulit-ulit na panyayamot; pag-ukilkil nang pag-ukilkil.

nail, n. the horny covering at the end of a finger or toe; a slender pointed piece of metal, used to hold things together, esp. wood. Kuko; pako.

naked, adj. unclothed; nude. Hubô; hubad; walang takip.

name, n. a descriptive word or title. Ngalan; pangalan.

name, v. mention; specify. Turan; pangalan; banggitin ang pangalan; banggitin.

nap, v. take a short sleep. Umidlip.

nape, n. the back of the neck. Batok.

napkin, n. a mouth cloth at table. Serbilyeta.

narrate, v. to relate; tell. Ikuwento; isalaysay.

narrow, adj. small width; not broad. Makipot; makitid.

narrow-minded, adj. lacking breadth of view or sympathy. Makitid ang isip.

narrowness, n. illiberality; want of enlarged views. Kakiputan; kakitiran.

nasty, adj. dirty; filthy. Mahalay; marumi; nakasusuklam.

natal, n. pertaining to one's birth. Nauukol sa pagsilang; ukol sa kapanganakan.

nation, n. a race of people having a common descent, language and culture. Bayan; bansa; nasyon.

nationalism, n. a patriotic feeling or effort. Pagka-makabayan.

nativity, n. birth. Pagsilang; ang kapanganakan.

natural, adj. formed by nature; not artificial. Natural; likas.

nature, n. the material universe. Katangian; kalikasan.

naught, adj. nothing. Pagkawala; wala; Masama.

naughty, adj. disobedient; bad; wicked. Salbahe; pilyo; matigas ang ulo.

nausea, adj. loathing. Nauseya; hilo; alibadbad.

nautical, adj. pertaining to ships, seamen, or navigation. Notiko; ukol sa paglalakbay-dagat.

navel, n. umbilicus. Pusod.

navigate, v. to steer or manage a ship. Umugit; pilotohan; timunan.

navigator, n. one who sails the seas. Maglalayag.

Nazarene, n. an inhabitant of Nazareth; a name given to Christ and the early converts to Christianity. Nasareno; tubo sa Nasaret, Palestina; tawag kay Kristo dahil sa paninirahan Niya sa Nasaret.

near, prep. & adv. close to; almost. Malapit; kalapit.

nearby, adv. close at hand. Kalapit; malapit.

nearly, adv. closely; almost. Halos; kamuntik na.

neat, adj. adroit; clean; tidy. Malinis at maayos.

necessary, adj. required; essential. Nesesaryo; kailangan.

necessitate, v. compel. Kailanganin.

necessity, n. the state or fact of being inevitable or necessary. Nesesidad; pangangailangan.

neck, n. the slender part of

the body between the head and shoulders. Kuwelyo, leeg.

necklace, n. neck ornament. Kuwintas.

necrology, n. death register. Nekrolohiya; talaan ng mga namatay na.

necktie, n. band worn around a collar. Kurbata.

nectar, n. delicious beverage. Nektar; matamis at malinamnam na inumin.

need, n. want; necessity or lack. Nesesidad; pangangailangan.

needful, adj. necessary. Nangangailangan.

needle, n. sewing tool. Karayom.

needless, adj. unnecessary. Superplo; inutil; di-kailangan.

needs, n. of necessity; necessarily. Kagamitan; kailangan.

nefarious, adj. very wicked. Napakasama.

negate, v. to deny. Tumanggi.

negative, adj. expressing denial or refusal. Negatibo; salungat.

neglect, n. lack of attention or care. Kapabayaan; neglihensiya.

neglect, v. disregard; leave uncared for. Pabayaan.

negligence, n. carelessness; forgetfulness. Kapabayaan; kawalang-ingat.

negligent, adj. guilty of or characterized by neglect, esp. of duty. Walang-ingat; pabaya.

negotiator, n. one that negotiates. Tagapamagitan.

negress, n. a female negro. Negra.

negro, n. a member of the darkest-skinned, or black race. Negro.

neigh, n. the sound that a horse makes. Halinghing.

neighbor, n. one who lives near by. Kapitbahay; kalapit.

neophyte, n. a novice. Baguhan; ang bagong binyag sa tunay na pananampalataya.

nephew, n. son of a brother or a sister. Pamangking lalaki.

nerve, n. physical force. Lakas-loob; nerbiyos; mga ugat.

nervous, adj. easily agitated; high-strung. Matakutin; nerbiyoso; madaling matakot.

nest, n. a place used by or made by birds, insects, turtles etc. for laying eggs and hatching young. Pugad.

net, n. a contrivance made of coarse string tied in meshes, for catching fish, birds, etc. Lambat; tubò.

net, v. capture, as with a net; earn as clear profit. Hulihin sa lambat; kunin o makuha ang linis na kita.

nettle, adj. to sting; to irritate. Suyain; inisin; yamutin.

neurotic, n. a person who is too nervous. Nerbiyoso.

neutral, adj. adhering to neither side. Walang kinikilingan; walang pinapanigan.

never, adv. at no time. Hindi kailanman.

never-ending, adj. without end. Walang-hanggan; walang katapusan.

nevertheless, adv. in spite of that; yet. Kahit na; maski na; gayon man.

new, adj. recently made, discovered. Bago; makabago; moderno.

New Testament, n. the new canonical book of the sacred scriptures. Bagong Tipan.

Bagong Testamento.

news, n. tiding esp. of recent public events; the reports published in newspaper. Balita; ulat.

newspaper, n. a printed publication giving chiefly news. Pahayagan; peryodiko; diyaryo.

New Year's Day, n. January 1st. Bagong Taon.

next, adj. nearest. Kasunod; pinakamalapit.

nib, n. the point of anything, esp. of a pen; a bird's beak. Tuka (ng ibon); tulis.

nib, v. to furnish with a nib; to mend the nib of, as a pen. Tulisan.

nibble, n. a small bite. Manginain; pagkagat nang unti-unti.

nice, adj. exact; neat; delicate. Mainam; maganda; wastô.

nickname, n. a name given in familiarity or derision. Palayaw; bansâg.

nicotine, n. a poison contained in the leaves of tobacco. Nikotina.

niece. n. daughter of a sister or brother. Pamangking babae.

nigger, n. a negro. Negro; negra.

nigh, prep. near. Malapit.

night, n. the time from sunset to sunrise; darkness. Gabi.

nightfall, n. the coming of night Takipsilim; dapit-hapon.

nightgown. n. a dress worn in bed. Naitgawn; damit na pantulog.

nightly, adj. done by night; happening in the night. Panggabi.

nightly, adv. by night; every night. Tuwing gabi; sa lahat ng gabi; gabi-gabi.

nightmare, n. a horrid dream; a terrifying dream. Nakatatakot na panaginip; bangungot.

nil, n. nothing. Wala.

nimble, adj. quick; active. Bibo; mabilis at masigla.

nimbus, n. in art, a bright cloud or a halo around the head of a divine or saintly person. Ang bilog na sinag o liwanag na ipinaliligid sa ulo ng santo.

nine, n. & adj. the cardinal number between eight and ten. Nuwebe; siyam.

ninety, n. & adj. nine times ten. Nubenta; siyamnapu.

ninth, adj. first after eight. Ika-siyam.

nip, v. to pinch; bite. Kagatin o putulin ng ngipin; kurutin; sipitin; sugpuin.

nipa, n. an East Indian palm. Puno ng sasa.

nippers, n. the large claws of a crab or lobster. Panipit; sipit ng alimango at mga kauri nito.

nipple, n. small projection through which a baby animal gets its mother's milk. Utong.

no, adv. a word of denial, refusal, or dissent. Wala; hindi.

noble, adj. exalted; of high birth rank, or title. Dakila; mabunyi.

nobleness, n. nobility; magnificence. Kadakilaan.

nobly, adv. splendidly; magnificently. Nang buong kadakilaan.

nobody, pron. not anyone. Walang sino man.

nocturn, n. night. Gabi.

nod, n. a short, quick inclination of the head, as in a greeting. Pagtangô; tango.

nod, v. to incline the head assent. Tumango.

node, n. a knot; knob. Hati; buko; buhol.

noise, n. outcry; clamor. Ingay; gulo.

noiseless, adj. without sound. Walang ingay.

noisy, adj. full of, or making, loud sounds. Maingay; magulo.

nomad, n. a wanderer. Palaboy; layás.

nominal, adj. existing in name only; so-called. Sa pangalan lamang at di sa katotohanan.

nominate, v. to name; propose for an elective office. Italaga; magharap; magpasok.

nomination, n. naming. Pagtatalaga; pagmumungkahi ng pangalan para sa isang tungkulin.

nonchalance, n. cool; unconcern; indifference. Kalamigan ng loob.

none, pron. no one; not one. Wala.

normal, adj. of the usual standard. Karaniwan.

north, n. the point of the compass on the right of the person facing the setting sun. Hilaga.

northeast, n. & adj. midway between north and east. Hilagang-silangan.

nose, n. the organ of smell. Ilong.

nosebleed, n. bleeding from the nose. Pagdugo ng ilong; balinguyngoy.

nostril, n. an external opening of the nose. Butas ng ilong.

not, adv. no; a word expressing denial, refusal, or negation. Hindi; wala.

notable, adj. remarkable. Tanyag; kilala; bantog.

notably, adv. in a notable manner. Kapansin-pansin.

notary, n. a law officer. Notaryo; taong may kapahintulutang patotohanan ang mga kasulatan; kasunduan, atb.

notch, n. a nick; cut. Bingot.

note, n. a short letter; notice; due bill. Tandâ; nota; tala.

note, v. observe carefully; make a record of. Pansinin.

notebook, n. a book of or for notes. Notbuk; kuwaderno.

noted, adj. eminent. Kilala; tanyag; bantog.

noteworthy, adj. notable. Kapuri-puri; kapansin-pansin; kagalang-galang.

nothing, n. absence of everything. Wala.

notice, n. remark; observation; attention. Paunawa; pansin; balita.

notice, v. perceive; observe; remark upon. Mapuna; pansinin.

notify, v. to make known; inform. Pagsabihan; ipaalam; balitaan.

notion, n. thought; opinion. Hakà; warì; palagay.

notoriety, n. state of being notorious or widely known. Kabansagan sa gawang dimabuti.

nought, adj. nothing. Wala.

noun, n. a word denoting a person, place, or thing. Pangngalan.

nourish, v. to support by food. Alagaan; pakanin; palusugin.

nourishing, adj. promoting growth; nutritious. Pampalusog; nakapagpapalusog.

nourishment, n. food. Pagkain.

novel, adj. new and striking. Bago.

novel, n. fictitious narrative.

Kathambuhay; nobela.

novelty, n. new or unusual thing or experience. Bagong bagay o karanasan.

November, n. the eleventh month of the year. Nobyembre.

novena, n. a religious period of nine days Nobena; pagsisiyam.

novice, n. a beginner. Baguhan; nobisyada.

now, adv. at present; in this age. Ngayon.

nowadays, adv. at the present day. Sa panahong ito.

nowhere, adv. not anywhere. Wala saanman.

nude, adj. bare; naked. Walang saplot; hubô; hubad.

nudge, n. a touch with the elbow. Siko; pagsiko upang tawagin ang pansin; bunggô.

nugget, n. lump. Tipak.

nuisance, n. an annoying or obnoxious person or thing. Iyong nakasasagabal o nakayayamot.

nullify, v. to make void. Pawalang halaga; pawalan ng saysay.

numb, adj. motionless; insensible. Namamanhid; Walang pakiramdam.

number, n. the sum or an aggregation of persons or things. Bilang; dami; numero.

numberless, adj. countless. Di-mabilang.

numbness, n. lack of feeling or movement. Pamamanhid.

numerable, adj. that maybe numbered or counted. Mabibilang.

numerous, adj. a great many; in great number. Marami; makapal.

nun, n. a woman living under religious vows in a convent. Mongha.

nunnery, n. a building where nuns live. Kumbento.

nuncio, n. a Papal envoy. Kinatawan ng Papa sa pamahalaan ng ibang bansa.

nuptial, adj. pertaining to marriage or a wedding ceremony. Ukol sa kasal; nupsiyal.

nurse, n. a woman in charge of young children; one who cares for the sick. Nars.

nurse, v. to cherish; to take care of. Alagaan; mag-alaga.

nurture, n. food; education. Pagpapalaki; pagtuturo.

nut, n. the kernel itself. Nuwes.

nutrition, n. food; nourishment. Pagkain.

O

oaf, n. a simpleton or blackhead; a lout. Sintu-sinto; batang may mahinang pag-iisip; tunggák.

oar, n. a long pole with a flat end used in rowing. Gaod.

oak, n. a valuable hardwood tree, whose fruit is the acorn. Isang uri ng matigas na punongkahoy.

oar, n. flat pole to propel boats. Gaod; sagwan.

oar, v. to row. Gumaod; sumagwan.

oat, n. a cereal plant or its seeds, used for food, esp. for horses. Abena.

oath, n. solemn declaration with God as witness. Sumpa; panunumpa.

oatmeal, n. crushed and hulled oats; oat porridge. Harina ng abena; owtmil.

obedience, n. submission. Pagkamasunurin.

obedient, adj. submissive to authority: willing to obey. Masunurin.

obeisance, n. deference or homage. Paggalang; saludo.

obese, adj. fat; corpulent. Obeso; mataba.

obesity, n. excessive corpulency. Katabaan,

obey, v. to submit to; comply with the command of. Sumunod; makinig.

object, n. aim; end; motive. Bagay; pakay; layon

object, v. offer opposition; feel or state disapproval; to oppose. Tumutol; tutulan; tumanggi.

objective, n. opposition; disapproval. Hantungan; layunin; pagtutol.

oblation, n. a religious offering. Paggalang; pagdakila at pagpapakasakit.

oblige, v. to compel. Pilitin; pagbigyan; tumupad sa tungkulin; mapilitan.

obliging, adj. helpful; friendly. Masunurin; mapagbigay; magalang.

oblique, adj. slanting. Pahilis.

obliterate, v. to remove all traces of; to destroy. Palisin; burahin; pawiin.

oblivion, n. forgetfulness. Paglimot.

oblivious, adj. not mindful. Hindi alintana.

oblong, adj. longer than broad and with sides parallel. Taluhaba.

obnoxious, adj. offensive; odious. Nakayayamot; nakasusuklam; nakaiinis.

obscence, adj. lewd; immodest. Mahalay.

obscure, adj. not clear; uncertain. Malabo.

observance, n. attention. Pagsunod; pagmamasid.

observatory, n. a building for observing stars and other heavenly bodies. Obserbatoryo.

observe, v. watch: take note of; perceive. Matyagan; masdan; sundin; obserbahan.

observer, n. a spectator. Tagamasid; tagapagbantay; tagasunod.

obsolete, adj. out of use: out of date. Di na gamit; lipas.

obstacle, n. an obstruction; hindrance. Sagabal; hadlang; balakid.

obstetrician, n. a medical and surgical specialist in childbirth. Dalubhasa sa pagpapaanak.

obstinacy, n. stubbornness. Katigasan ng ulo.

obstinate, adj. stubborn. Matigas ang ulo.

obstract, v. to block up. Hadlangan; lagyan ng balakid; harangin.

obtain, v. to gain; acquire. Makamit; kunin; makuha.

obtainable, adj. capable of being obtained. Makukuha; maaaring makuha.

obviate, v. to remove; make unnecessary. Alisan ng hadlang.

obvious, adj. easily seen. Nakikita; nahahalata; maliwanag.

occasion, n. opportunity. Panahon; pangyayari; pagkakataon.

occasion, v. to cause incidentally; to produce; to induce. Magbigay ng pagkakataon; udyukan.

occasional, adj. casual; incidental. Pana-panahon; paminsan-minsan.

occult, adj. mysterious. Mahiwaga.

occupation, n. business; employment. Tungkulin; trabaho.

occupy, v. employ; inhabit. Akupahan; tigilan; tirhan.
occur, v. to happen. Mangyari; maalala; pangyarihin.
occurrence, n. an incident; a happening. Pangyayari; pagdating.
octagon, n. plane figure of eight sides and angles. Oktagon; ang bagay na may walong gilid.
October, n. tenth month of the year. Oktubre.
octopus, n. devilfish; a sea mollusk with eight sucking arms. Oktupus; pugita.
ocular, adj. of the eye; visual. Tungkol sa mata.
odd, adj. peculiar; not even. Gansál; kaiba sa karaniwan; di-mahahati sa dalawa nang walang labis; di-pangkaraniwan; kaiba.
oddity, n. singularity. Kalokohan; kaibhan; pagkakaiba.
ode, n. a poem full of noble feeling expressed with dignity. Oda.
odious, adj. deserving of hate; repugnant. Nakayayamot; nakasusuklam.
odor, n. smell. Amoy.
of, prep. from; belonging to; concerning. Kay; sa; ni; ng.
offend, v. to annoy; to displease; annoyance; an affront. Pagalitin; saktan ang damdamin; pagsugat sa damdamin.
offer, n. proposal; present. Operta; oper; handog; alay; alok; dulutan.
offer, v. present or put forward for acceptance; to suggest; propose. Ihandog; ialay.
offering, n. giving something as an act of worship. Paghahandog; pag-aalay.
office, n. position of trust; official employment. Upisina; tungkulin; tanggapan.
officiate, v. to discharge duties of an office. Mangasiwa; tumupad sa tungkulin; mamahala.
often, adv. frequently. Malimit; madalas.
oil, n. an unctuous substance. Asete; langis.
oil-shop, n. shop where oil is available. Aseterya; tindahan ng langis.
Oil (Holy), n. blessed or consecrated oil. Santo Oleo; Banal na Langis.
oily, adj. like oil. Malangis.
ointment, n. a balm for healing or beautifying the skin. Isang uri ng malagkit at malangis na panlunas sa balat; ungguwento.
old, adj. aged; worn out. Matanda; dati; malaon.
Old Testament, n. the collection of biblical books comprising the Scriptures of "The Old Covenant." Lumang Testamento; Matandang Tipan.
old-timer, n. a person who has long been a resident, worker, member. Datihan.
olive, v. fruit used as relish. Oliba.
omelet, n. fried beaten egg. Tortilyang itlog; binating itlog na pinirito.
omen, n. a sign or event prophetic of the future; prognostic. Babalâ.
omission, n. slight; neglect. Pagkakaalis; pagkakalaktaw; pag-iwan; pagkakaligta.
omit, v. to leave out. Kaligtaan; iwan; alisin.
omnipotence, n. complete power; unlimited power. Walang hanggang kapangyarihan.
omnipresence, n. the faculty

or power of being present in every place at the same time. Pagkakaparoon sa lahat ng dako.

omniscience, n. the faculty of knowing everything. Kaalaman sa lahat ng bagay; karunungan ng Diyos.

on, prep. above and in contact with. Sa; sa ibabaw.

once, adv. one time; formerly. Dati; noon; minsan.

oncoming, adj. approaching. Nalalapit; darating.

one, adj. single unit; the same. Isa; uno.

onion, n. a plant with a pungent edible bulk. Sibuyas.

on looker, n. a spectator. Espektador; manonood; tagamasid.

only, adj. single; sole. Solo; tangi.

onslaught, n. an attack. Mabangis na paglusob; asalto.

ontology, n. the branch of meta-physics that investigates the nature of being and of the first principles, or categories involved. Ontolohiya; sangay ng metapisika na nagsusuri sa pagkabuhay o pagiging buhay.

onward, adj. forward; on. Pasulong; paunlad.

ooze, v. to pass out through small openings. Dumaloy; tumagas.

opal, n. a precious stone. Opalo.

opaque, adj. not clear; dark, obscure. Makapal; di-tinatagusan ng liwanag.

open, adj. permitting passage through. Abyerta; bukas.

opening, n. a breach; an open space. Puwang; butas; simula; bukasan; lagusan.

opera, n. a play that is mostly sung. Opera.

operation, n. action; act or manner of operating Operasyon; pagpapalakad; paggawa; pagtistis.

opinion, n. view; conclusion. Opinyon; palagay; kuru-kuro.

opinionated, adj. conceited; obstinate in one's opinion. Mapagmagaling; matigas ang ulo.

opium, n. a narcotic drug derived from the poppy. Opyo; apyan.

opponent, n. an antagonist; adversary. Katunggali; kalaban.

opportune, adj. seasonable. Naáangkop; napapanahon.

opportunity, n. a favorable occasion or time. Pagkakataon; oportunidad.

oppose, v. to resist; object to. Salungatin; labanan.

opposite, adj. facing; adverse. Kabila; katapat; salungat.

opposition, n. resistance. Tagasalungat; pagsalungat.

oppress, v. crush; subdue; treat tyranically. Tikisin; apihin.

optician, n. one skilled in optics; maker or dealer in optical instruments. Optiko; manggagawa ng salamin sa mata.

optimism, n. hopefulness. Optimismo; pag-asa sa mabuting ibubunga.

option, n. choice. Pagpili; karapatang pumili.

optional, adj. left to one's choice. Hindi ubligado.

opulence, n. wealth. Kayamanan; kasaganaan.

opulent, adj. wealthy. Mayaman; sagana.

or, conj. a connective between words, clauses, terms, etc. indicating an alternative or explanation. O; ni.

oracle, n. in ancient times, an answer given by a god. Orakulo.

oral, adj. spoken; delivered by mouth. Berbal; pasalita; pabigkas.

orange, n. the round, juicy. deep yellow citrus fruit of an evergreen tree. Kahel; dalandan.

oration, n. rhetorical speech. Orasyon; talumpati.

orator, n. eloquent speaker. Orador; mananalumpati.

orb, n. round body; sphere. Ruweda; bilog; gulong.

orbed, adj. round; circular. Mabilog.

orbit, n. path of a star; a regular circuit, esp. of a planet. Ang pabilog na daang nilalandas ng isang planeta sa kanyang pagkilos; landas.

orchard, n. a fruit garden; a grove of fruit trees. Taniman ng mga punungkahoy.

orchestra, n. musical band. Orkesta.

orchids, n. tropical plants with brilliant flowers. Orkidyas; mga dapo.

ordain, v. to appoint; decree; enact. Iatas; itakda; ordenahán; iutos.

order, n. a rule; a command. Orden; kalagayan; kaayusan; uri; utos.

order, v. to direct. Ayusin; utusan; iutos.

orderliness, n. an orderly condition. Kaayusan.

orderly, adj. systematic. Maayos.

ordinal, n. noting order. Panunuran; magkapanunod.

ordinary, adj. common; usual. Ordinaryo; pangkaraniwan.

ordination, n. conferring of Holy Orders. Ordinasyon; ang paggagawad ng pagkapari.

organ, n. a large musical instrument played by releasing compressed air through pipes. Sangkáp; tagapamanság; organo; isang uri ng pantugtog na may hangin; bahagi ng katawang tumutupad ng sariling tungkulin.

orgy, n. a wild drunken revel. Lasingan.

origin, n. source; beginning. Pinagmulán; simula.

original sin, n. the first sin of Adam namely the eating of the forbidden fruit. Kasalanang orihinal; kasalanang minana kay Eba.

ornate, adj. adorned. Mapalamuti; maadorno.

orphan, n. one without parents. Ulila.

orphanage, n. a house for orphans. Bahay-ampunan.

oscillate, v. to vibrate; vacillate. Umuguy-ugoy.

osculation, n. a kiss. Halik.

ossicle, n. a small bone. Maliit na buto.

ostiary, n. one ordered to the four minor orders; a porter. Bantay; tanod-pinto.

ostracize, v. to exclude, banish or exile. Itakwil.

other, pron. a different person or thing. Iba.

ought, v. should; be bound, or obliged or sure (to). Nararapat; kailangang tupdin.

our, pron. possessive form of *we*. Atin; amin.

Our Father, n. God. Ama Namin.

ours, pron. form of *our* used predicatively. Amin; atin.

ourselves, pron. us; no others. Ating sarili.

oust, v. to push out; drive out. Magpalayas, palayasin.

out, adv. away from or not in

a place, position, state, etc. Paalis; lipas; sa labas.

outbid, v. to outdo in bidding. Tawaran nang higit sa mga katunggali, talunin sa tawaran; mahigtan.

outbreak, n. a sudden eruption. Pagsisimula; gulo pagputok; pagsiklab; paghihimagsik.

outburst, n. an outbreak of emotion. Pagbulalás; putok.

outcome, n. result; consequence. Bunga; resulta.

outdated, adj. out-of-date; old-fashioned. Lipas na sa moda.

outdo, v. surpass. Higtan; malampasan.

outer, v. farther out; external. Panlabas; sa dakong labas.

outfit, n. equipment for a special purpose, trade, etc. Kasangkapan; kagamitan.

outgoing, adj. vacating; retiring. Paalis; paalis sa isang tungkulin.

outgrow, v. became too large or knowing for. Maunahan sa paglaki; lumagpas sa paglaki.

outgrowth, n. an offshoot; a result. Tubo; kinahinatnan.

outing, n. a pleasure trip. Maikling pagliliwaliw; paglabas; pamamasyal; paglilibang.

outlandish, adj. unfamiliar; bizarre. Kakaiba; banyaga; di-pangkaraniwan ang anyo o kilos.

outlaw, n. a haunted criminal. Bandido; mandarambong; manghaharang; manliligalig.

outlay, n. expenditure, as of money, effort, etc. Gugol; takdang gastahin.

outlet, n. a means of exit or escape. Lagusan; labasan; butas na labasan.

outline, n. exterior line; a rough draft as of a speech; plan; a summary. Disenyo; balangkas.

outlive, v. to live longer than. Mabuhay nang higit sa takdang taning.

out-of-doors, adv. in the open air. Sa labas ng bahay.

outlook, n. a view or scene from a place; the prospect for the future. Bista; paningin; pangitain.

outlying, adj. remote. Liblib; malayo.

outpost, n. a place for a guard or a small number of soldiers. Himpilan.

output, n. the amount produced. Ang dami ng nayayari.

outrage, n. cruel or wanton violence. Matinding galit.

outrageous, adj. flagrantly contrary. Nakagagalit.

outright, adv. all at once; openly. Ganap; tahasan; agad; walang pasubali.

outrun, v. to outstrip in running; to exceed. Maunahan sa pagtakbo.

outside, n. external part. Labas.

outsider, n. one not belonging to a particular set. Tagalabas.

outskirt, n. a border; the outlying district, as of a city. Sa dakong labas ng isang bayan.

outspoken, adj. frank; not reserved. Tapat kung magsalita.

outstanding, adj. wellknown; prominent. Tanyag; bantog.

outweigh, v. exceed in weight or importance. Mahigtan; malagpasan sa kabutihan.

outwit, v. surpass in intelligence. Malamangan sa pag-iisip; daigin sa pag-iisip.

oval, adj. shaped like an egg; elliptical. Biluhaba; habilóg.

ovary, n. female organ in which egg cells are formed. Ubaryo; bahay-bata.

ovation, n. popular homage. Pagpupuri at paghanga; pagbubunyi.

oven, n. cavity to bake in. Hurnuhan; hurno.

over, prep. above; higher than. Sa ibabaw; sa itaas; sa kabila; mahigit sa.

overbearing, adj. insolent; haughty; arrogant. Malupit; mahigpit; mapagmataas; mapanupil.

overboard, adv. off a ship into the water. Sa labas ng sasakyang dagat; sa dagat.

overburden, v. to load with too great weight. Bigyan ng labis na pasanin.

overcast, v. darkened, esp. by clouds; to overcloud. Padilimin; tabingan.

overcautious, adj. too cautious. Labis na maingat.

overcloud, v. to become clouded over. Mag-ulap; mangulimlim.

overcoat, n. a heavy coat worn over the regular coat. Oberkot; gaban; abrigo.

overcome, v. to surmount; to be victorious. Talunin; daigin; pagtagumpayan.

overconfidence, n. too great or excessive confidence. Labis na pagtitiwala.

overdo, v. to do or carry to excess; to exaggerate. Gawin ang higit na kailangan; labisan.

overdose, n. too big a dose. Labis na dosis.

overdress, v. be too ostentatiously attired. Magbihis nang lagpas sa talagang dapat.

overflow, v. run over the edge or boundary (of). Bumaha; umagos nang labis; umapaw.

overgrown, adj. grown too big. Sobra ang laki.

overhang, v. project beyond. Yumungyong.

overhead, adv. above. Sa ibabaw ng ulo; sa itaas.

overhear, v. hear without the speaker's knowledge. Maulinigan; marinig nang di sinasadya.

overjoyed, adj. exceedingly glad. Tuwang-tuwa; labis na katuwaan.

overlap, v. to cover and extend beyond. Magsanib.

overload, to load too heavily. Magkarga nang labis.

overlook, v. fail to notice; ignore. Makaligtaan.

overmuch, adj. too much; exceeding what is necessary or proper. Labis-labis; lagpaslagpasan.

overnight, adv. during the night. Nang magdamag.

overpay, v. to pay in excess. Bayaran ng labis.

overpower, v. subdue; overwhelm. Matalo; madaig; mapipilan.

override, v. to act in spite of. Magpawalang-halaga.

overrun, v. swarm over in great numbers. Lusubin; salakayin.

overseer, n. a supervisor; superintendent. Superintende; tagapamahala; katiwala.

overshadow, v. darken, as by casting a shadow on. Matakpan ng anino; malililiman; marimlan.

oversight, n. a failure to notice or think. Pagkalingat; di pagkapansin.

overskirt, n. a skirt worn over.

Sayang pang-ibabaw.

oversleep, v. sleep too late. Makatulog nang lagpas sa takdang panahon.

overspread, v. to spread or scatter over. Ikalat; itakip; isabog.

overtake, v. catch up with. Abutin; abutan.

overthrow, v. defeat; force out of power, as a government. Alisin sa luklukan; ibagsak; talunin.

overtime, n. extra time. Obertaym; higit na oras; lamay.

owner, n. one who owns; proprietor. May-ari.

oyster, n. an edible salt water bivalve mollusk. Talaba.

P

pabular, adj. pertaining to food or pabulum. Nakapagpapalusog; nagpapalakas.

pabulum, n. food. Pagkain; pampalusog; pampalakas.

pace, n. measure by steps; a single step or its distance. Hakbang; bilis o sukat ng paghakbang.

pacific, adj. peaceable; conciliatory. Pasipiko; payapa; tahimik.

pacifier, n. one who pacifies; a simulated nipple for a baby. Tagapamayapa; pampatahimik.

pacify, v. to appease; calm. Payapain; patahimikin.

package, n. a bundle of goods; a small wrapped bundle. Balutan.

packet, n. a small pack. Pakete.

pact, n. an agreement. Pakto; kasunduan.

paddle, n. a short oar. Sagwan.

paddle, v. to row; to propel (canoe). Sumagwan.

paddy, n. ricefield. Palayan.

padlock, n. pendent lock. Kandado.

padlock. v. to fasten with or as with a padlock. Ikandado; lagyan ng kandado.

pagan, adj. not Christian. Pagano; hindi Kristiyano; hindi binyagan.

page, n. one side of a printed leaf of a book, etc. Dahon; pahina.

pageant, n. pompous show. Palabas; marangyang pagtatanghal.

pagoda, n. a temple. Templong marami ang palapag.

pail, n. a bucket. Balde; timba.

pain, n. a physical hurt. Sakit; hapdi; kirot.

painful. adj. giving or accompanied by pain. Makirot; mahapdi; masakit.

paint, n. pigment; coloring matter. Pintura.

paint, v. to apply paint (to). Pintahan.

painter, n. a person who paints pictures; an artist. Pintor.

pair, n. two of a sort. Pares; pareha.

palace, n. a stately house. Palasyo.

palatine, n. court dignitary. Palatino; tungkol sa mga kaloob na tungkulin sa Korte ng Papa.

pale, adj. not ruddy; pallid. Maputla; di maliwanag.

Palestine, n. a former country in SW Asia, now divided into Israel and Arab Palestine. Palestina, ang banal na bayan.

pall, n. covering for a coffin. Takip ng ataul; lambóng.

pallium, n. an ecclesiastical or other pall; the mantle of a mollusk. Palyo; kasuotang ipinagkaloob ng Papa sa arsobispo; ito'y makitid na bandang lanang puti na may palawit sa likod at harap.

Palm Sunday, n. the Sunday before Easter. Linggo ng Palaspas.

palpitate, v. to beat very rapidly. Tumibok ng mabilis.

pamper, v. to indulge too much. Palayawin.

pamphlet, n. a booklet with paper cover. Pamplet; munting aklat.

pan, n. a dish for cooking and other household uses. Kawali.

panacea, n. cure all; remedy for all diseases. Panlunas sa lahat.

panel, n. square in door. Bahagi ng dingding; parihabang pilas ng tabla.

panic, n. sudden fright. Matinding pagkatakot.

pant, n. a gasp; act of fast breathing. Palpitasyon; hingal; pulso.

pantomime, n. representation in gesture. Pantomima; piping palabas.

pantry, n. a small room for storing food and dishes. Paminggalan.

pants, n. trousers. Pantalong largo o korto; salawal.

papacy, n. papal authority. Ang panunungkulan ng Papa.

paper, n. substance to write on. Sulatán; papel.

papers, n. credentials, bank notes, bills of exchange. Dokumento; mga kasulatan.

parable, n. a fable; a fictitious story pointing a moral. Parabula; patalinghagang kuwento.

parade, n. military or other march: pompous display. Parada.

paradise, n. place of bliss. Paraiso; langit.

paragon, n. a model of excellence or perfection. Uliran; huwaran.

paragraph, n. a distinct section of written matter. Parapo; talataan.

parallel, adj. lying side by side: as lines, but never meeting. Paralelo: magkahanay; magkatulad; magkaagapay.

paralysis, n. loss of motion; complete or partial loss of power to feel or move. Pagkawala ng pakiramdam; paralisis.

paralyze, v. affect with paralysis; render helpless or ineffective. Maparalisis; dimakakilos; mawalan ng lakas.

paramour, n. a lover. Ang iniibig; kaagulo; kalaguyò.

pardon, n. forgiveness; excuse. Kapatawaran; paumanhin.

pare, v. to cut, trim or shave off the outer part of. Balatan; talupan.

parent, n. father or mother. Magulang; ama o ina; pinagmulan.

parish, n. the district under a clergyman's care. Parokya.

parishioner, n. a member of a church congregation. Kasapi sa parokya.

parking, n. a place used to put or leave anything for a time. Parking, himpilan.

part, n. a section. Parte; bahagi.

part, v. divide into sections; separate; hold apart. Partihin; paghatiin; paghiwalayin.

partake, v. to eat or drink some. Sumalo; makisalo.

particular., adj. not general;

apart from others: unusual. Partikular; tangi: tiyak.

parting, n. separation; a division. Separasyon; paghihiwalay.

partly, adv. in some measure or degree. Pabahagi.

partner, n. one who is associated with another, as in business, marriage, dancing, etc. Kasosyo; kasama.

part-time, adj. for part of the usual time. Pansamantala.

party, n. a group gathered together for some purpose, as for amusement or entertainment. Reunyon; lapian; isang pagtitipon.

pass, n. a narrow road or a defile between two mountains. Pasilyo; munting daan.

pass, v. to go by. Dumaan.

passable, adj. that may be proceeded through or over. Madaraanan.

passage, n. a hall or way through a building; passage way. Pasilyo; daanan.

passably, adv. tolerably; moderately. Nang kainaman.

passenger, n. a traveler on some form of conveyance. Pasahero; taong lulan ng sasakyan.

passion, n. any kind of feeling or emotion, as hope, fear, joy; grieve. anger, love, desire, especially when of compelling force. Pasyon; masimbuyóng damdamin; poót: pag-ibig; ang huling paghihirap at kamatayang dinanas ng ating Manananakop.

passionate, adj. easily moved to anger. Matindi; maalab; mapusok.

passive, adj. unresisting; not acting, but acted upon; Malamig ang loob; walang kibo.

Passover, n. Jewish festival. Pasko ng mga Ebreo.

passport, n. permit. Pasaporte; katibayan ng karapatang makapaglakbay.

password, n. a secret word that allows a person who says it to pass a guard. Hudyat; senyas.

paste, n. an adhesive substance usually containing starch. Pasta; pandikit; masa.

pastime, n. amusement; diversion. Libangan; aliwan.

pastor, n. clergyman. Pastor; pari.

pastoral, n. a letter or circular addressed by a bishop to the clergy and people of his diocese. Isang liham ng obispo sa kanyang mga nasasakupan para sa kanilang kagalingan.

pasture, n. grassland for grazing cattle. Madamóng bukid o burol; pastulan.

pat, v. tap or stroke gently with the hand. Tapikin.

patch, n. a piece of cloth or metal, used to cover a hole or worn place. Tagpi.

patch, v. mend with a patch. Tagpian.

paten, n. the plate for the bread in the celebration of the Eucharist. Ang pinggang metal na pinagsasalalayan ng ostiya kung nagmimisa.

patent, n. an official document granting a privilege, especially a temporary monopoly to an inventor. Patente; karapatang bigay sa isang imbentor o manunulat sa takdang taning na panahon.

Pater Noster, n. Lord's Prayer. Ama Namin.

path, n. a footway; any road. Landas.

pathetic, adj. exciting pity; full of pathos. Kaawaawa; kahabag-habag.

patience, n. calm endurance. Pasensiya; tiyaga; paumanhin.

patient, n. a person who is being treated by a doctor. Pasyente; ang maysakit.

patriarch, n. a father or ruler of a tribe. Patriarka; ayon sa Bibliya, ang ama ng isang mag-anak o ang puno ng isang lipi o lahi.

patrimony, n. inherited estate. Patrimonyo; ari-arian; mana.

patriot, n. a person who loves and loyally supports his country. Bayani; taong makabayan.

patriotic, adj. inspired by the love of one's country. Patriyotiko; makabayan.

patriotism, n. love and loyal support of one's country. Kabayanihan.

patrol, n. guard. Patrulya; bantay.

patron, n. a supporter; a guardian saint; a regular customer of shop. Tagatangkilik; tagapagtanggol; suki.

patronize, v. to favor (shop, restaurant, etc.) with one's trade. Tangkilikin.

pattern, n. an example; a model to be copied; ideal. Huwaran; halimbawa.

pauper, n. a very poor person, usually supported by the community. Pobre; pulubi.

pause, n. an interval of silence or inaction, Sandaling pagtigil; sandali ng katahimikan.

pause, v. stop; hesitate; linger for a time. Tumigil o humintong sandali; maghintay.

pave, v. cover with bricks or cement. Latagan ng bató o aspalto; patagin; ihanda para sa isang bagay.

pavement, n. the surface of streets, sidewalks, made of concrete. Palitada; simento; aspalto.

paw, n. the foot of a beast with nails or claws. Matutulis na kuko; mga paa o kamay ng hayop na may matutulis na kuko.

pawn, n. a pledge. Prenda; sangla.

pawn, v. deposit as security for a loan. Isangla.

pawnbroker, n. a person licensed to lend money on pledged property. Prendero; ang tumatanggap ng mga sangla.

pawnshop, n. the shop of a pawnbroker. Bahay-sanglaan.

pay, n. wages, salary; employment for gain. Bayad; sahod.

pay, v. compensate (a person) for services rendered or goods supplied. Magbayad; bayaran; mag-ukol.

paymaster, n. a person whose job is to pay wages. Pagador; tagapagsuweldo.

payment, n. the act of paying; that which is paid. Kabayaran; bayad.

pea, n. the round edible green seed of a leguminous vine. Gisantes; sitsaro; patani.

peace, n. tranquility; quietness. Kapayapaan; katahimikan.

peacefulness, n. the state or quality of being peaceful. Kapayapaan; katahimikan.

peach, n. a round juicy fruit with a fuzzy, red-tinged skin. Milokoton.

peacock, n. a large bird with beautiful feathers and tail. Pabo real.

peak, n. pointed hilltop; the highest point. Tugatog; kaitaasan; taluktok.

peal, n. the loud ringing of a bell or of thunder, laughter, etc. Dagundong; dupikal ng batingaw.

peanut, n. a seed like a nut used for food. Mani.

pear, n. the juicy fruit of a tree related to the apple. Peras.

pearl, n. a hard lustrous body found in the shells of certain mollusks and valued as a gem. Perlas.

peasant, n. rural laborer. Magsasaka; pangkaraniwang taga-nayon.

pebble, n. small round stone. Bato.

peck, v. strike or pick up with, or as with the beak. Tukain.

peculiar, adj. particular; odd; queer. Naiiba sa karaniwan; di-karaniwan; kakatuwa.

pedagogue, n. a teacher. Guro.

pecunitary, adj. monetary. Ukol sa salapi.

pedantic, adj. pertaining to a pedant or to pedantry. Mapagparangalan ng karunungan; hambog.

peddle, v. to carry from place to place and sell. Maglako; ilako.

peddler, n. one who peddles, a hawker. Manlalako; tagapaglako.

pedestrian, n. foot traveler. Pedestriyan; taong naglalakad.

pediatrics, n. the medical care and treatment of children. Pedyatriks; sangay ng panggagamot na ukol sa mga sakit ng mga bata.

peek, v. to look quickly and shyly. Sumulyap; sulyapan.

peel, n. the rind. Balat ng bungangkahoy.

peel, v. to strip the rind, skin, or bark from. Balatan; talupan; alisan ng balat.

peep, v. look shyly or furtively. Sumilip; silipin.

peeper, n. a prying or spying person. Maninilip; tagasilip.

peer, n. a person of equal civil rank or standing; an equal before the law. Kapantay; kauri; isang dugong mahal sa Inglatera.

peerless, adj. having no peer or equal; matchless. Walang kapantay o katulad

peevish, adj. fretful, irritable. Suyâ; inis; yamot; bugnutin.

peg, n. a tapering pin of wood or metal. Isang pakong yari sa kahoy.

pelf, n. money; riches. Dinero; Salapi; kayamanan.

pelt, n. animal skin. Balat; katad; pelyeho.

pellet, n. a little ball of dough or lead. Bolita; munting bola; bola.

pen, n. an instrument for writing with ink. Pluma; panulat ng tinta.

penalty, n. p[illegible] [illegible]aparusahan; parusa; multa.

penance, n. suffering for sin. Penitensiya; pagsisisi.

pencil, n. tool to mark. Lapis; gamit sa pagsulat.

pendant, n. anything hanging. Palamuting nakasabit na tulad ng agnos.

pending, adj. waiting to be decided or settled. Nakabitin; hinihintay.

pendulum, n. oscillating body. Penduló; isang bagay o nakasabit sa isang tiyak na lunan at duruyan-duyan.

penetrate, v. to enter into. Tumalab; tumagos; pumasok; maunawaan.
penetration, n. a piercing. Penetrasyon; pagtagos; pagpasok; pag-unawa.
peninsula, n. land almost surrounded by water. Peninsula; tangway; bahagi ng lupang halos naliligid ng tubig.
penitence, n. sorrow for sin. Penitensiya; pagsisisi.
penitent, adj. contrite; repentant. Penitente; nagsisisi.
penitentiary, n. a prison. Penitensiyaryo; bilibid; parusahan; bilangguan.
penknife, n. a small knife. Kartapluma; lanseta.
pen name, n. a name used by a writer instead of his real name. Sagisag-panulat.
pennant, n. a small flag. Munting watawat.
penniless, adj. moneyless. Pobre; maralita; mahirap; walang salapi.
pension, n. a regular payment for past services. Pensiyon.
pensioner, n. a dependent, one who is pensioned. Taong tumatanggap ng pensiyon; pensiyonado.
pensive, adj. thoughtful; reflective. Palaisip.
pentagon, n. five angled figure. Pentagono; hugis na may limang gilid.
Pentecost, n. a Christian festival; Whitsunday. Pagdiriwang ng mga Hudyo na idinaraos tuwing ika-50 at ika-51 araw pagkatapos ng Pasko.
penury, n. poverty. Penurya; karalitaan.
peon, n. a day laborer. Piyon; katulong.
people, n. the whole of a particular body or group of persons. Mga tao.
pep, n. vigor; energy. Sigla; lakas.
pepper, n. a pungent spice. Paminta; sili.
peptic, adj. pertaining to digestion. Ukol sa panunaw.
per, prep. by means of; through. Bawa't isa; sa pamamagitan.
perambulator, n. baby carriage. Munting karwahe ng mga sanggol.
perceivable, adj. perceptible. Perseptible; makikita.
percent, n. hundreths. Porsiyento; bahagdan.
perception, n. the act or faculty of perceiving. Persepsiyon; kakayahang makakita o makaunawa.
perch, n. any of various edible fishes; a roost for birds. Isang uri ng isda; tuntungan; hapunan; mataas na luklukan.
perfect, adj. having no faults. Walang mali; tamang lahat.
perfection, n. being perfect. Kasakdalan; kawalan ng kapintasan.
perfume, n. a volatile sweet-smelling liquid. Pabango.
perhaps, adv. possibly; it may be. Marahil.
peril, n. danger; hazard. Peligro; panganib.
perilous, adj. full of danger. Peligroso; mapanganib.
perimeter, n. the outer boundary of a surface or figure. Buong gilid; paikot.
period, n. portion of time. Tanging-panahon; tuldok.
perish, v. to be destroyed; die. Mamatay.
perishable, adj. mortal; easily spoiled, as goods. Maaaring mamatay; nabubulok.
perjure, v. make false oath. Isumpa ang kasinungali-

ngan.

perjury, n. the willful giving of false testimony under oath. Pagsumpa ng kasinungalingan.

permanence, n. continuance: fixedness. Pagkapalagian.

permanent, adj. lasting or intending to last indefinitely. Permanente; palagian.

permeate, v. pass through; penetrate. Maglagos; tumagos.

permission, n. authorization; allowance, license or liberty granted. Permiso; pahintulot.

permit, v. allow; give formal consent to; make possible. Payagan; tulutan; pahintulutan.

pernicious, adj. very hurtful; ruinous. Nakamamatay; masama; makasisirang puri.

perpendicular, adj. upright; standing straightup. Patayo; patirik.

perpetual, adj. continual; everlasting; Panghabang panahon; walang katapusan; lagi.

perpetual adoration, n. the act of everlasting adoration. Pagsambang walang katapusan o panghabang panahon.

perplex, v. to embarrass; make confused or bewildered; puzzle. Mag-alinlangan; malito; dulutan ng alinlangan.

perplexed, adj. puzzled; intricate. Nalilito; nag-aalinlangan.

persecute, v. to harass persistently. Pahirapan; apihin; usigin.

persecution, n. torment. Paguusig; pang-aapi.

perseverance, n. constancy. Tiyaga; pagtitiyaga.

persevere, v. persist in anything undertaken. Magtiyaga.

persist, v. continue firm. Magpumilit; magtagal.

person, n. a human being. Persona; tao; panauhan.

personable, adj. having a pleasant appearance. Kaakit-akit; maganda.

personnel, n. persons employed in any work, business or service. Mga tauhan.

perspire, v. excrete waste fluids through the pores; sweat. Magpawis; pawisan.

pestilence, n. a deadly epidemic disease. Pestilensiya; peste; salot.

pet, n. an animal or bird that is cherished; a favorite. Paborito; itinatangi; mahal; alagang hayop.

petal, n. flower leaf. Petal; talulot.

petition, n. a request; an earnest entreaty. Petisyon: luhog; pamanhik.

petticoat, n. a woman s underskirt. Nagwas; saya.

petty, adj. small; trivial. Maliit; di-mahalaga; hamak.

petulant, adj. fretful; capricious. Yamot; mainit ang ulo; bugnutin.

pew, n. seat in church. Upuan sa simbahan; bangkong may sandalan.

phantom, n. an apparition; specter. Nakatatakot na pangitain; di-tunay.

Pharisees, n. Jewish sect; those who follow the letter, not the spirit of the (religious) law. Mga Pariseyo, ang mga Hudyong noong panahon ni Kristo ay ayaw makialam o makihalubilo sa mga hentil.

pharmacy, n. drug store. Parmasya; bilihan ng gamot.

phenomenal, adj. extra-ordinary. Hindi pangkaraniwan.

philanthropic, adj. charitable; benevolent. Mapagkawang-gawa.

philanthropist, n. a person who loves mankind and works for its welfare. Pilantropo; taong mapagkawang-gawa.

philosopher, n. man versed in philosophy. Pilosopo.

philosophy, n. principles of human knowledge. Pilosopiya.

photograph, n. a picture. Potograpiya; larawan; retrato.

phrase, n. a group of words. Parirala.

physician, n. a doctor. Mediko; manggagamot.

pick, v. to choose. Piliin; damputin; pitasin; anihin.

picket, n. a small body of troops sent out to scout, guard, etc. Munting pulutong ng mga bantay o kawal.

pickle, n. food preserved in brine or vinegar solution. Atsara; buro; kilawin.

piece, n. fragment; a part or portion. Piyesa; piraso; bahagi.

pier, n. a structure extending into the water, and used as a landing place. Piyer; pantalan; daungan.

pierce, v. to penetrate; make a hole in. Butasin; patagusin.

piercer, n. an instrument that pierces. Pambutas.

piety, n. reverence for God; devoutness. Kabanalan; kaloobang ukol sa Diyos.

pig, n. hog, especially a young one. Baboy; biik.

pigeon, n. a bird. Kalapati.

pigment, n. basis of paint; coloring matter. Pigmento; kulay.

pigsty, n. sty or pen for pigs. Kulungan ng baboy.

pike, n. a pole sharpened at one end. Tulos; istaka.

pile, n. heap; mass. Bunton; salansan.

piles, n. hemorrhoids. Almoranas.

pilfer, v. steal in small amounts. Nakawin nang unti-unti; umitin.

pilgrim, n. one who travels, especially to a holy place as an act of devotion. Manlalakbay sa banal na lunan; peregrino.

pilgrimage, n. a journey. Paglalakbay sa banal na lupain; peregrinasiyon.

pill, n. a small tablet of medicine. Pildoras.

pillar, n. a column. Haliging malaki; tukod.

pillow, n. a soft cushion to rest the head upon. Almohadon; unan.

pillow-case, n. a cover for a pillow. Punda ng unan.

pilot, n. a steerman. Piloto; abyador.

pimple, n. a blotch. Tagihawat.

pin, n. a pointed piece, especially of thin wire, to join or attach things. Alpiler; aspile; panduro.

pin, v. hold fast. Iaspile; tiyakin o ilagay sa palagiang lunan ang isang bagay; duruin.

pincers, n. tool for pulling. Sipit; panipit.

pinch, n. a squeeze; a nip. Kurot; kaunti.

pinch, v. nip or squeeze between two surfaces. Kurutin; pilipitin.

pine, v. grieve; long (for); languish. Mangulila; manabik.

pineapple, n. a tropical plant

or its sweet fruit. Pinya.
pinnacle, high peak or point. Tuktok; karurukan.
pious, adj. religious. Banal; relihiyoso.
pipe, n. a long tube for covering a fluid. Pipa; tubo; pito.
piquant, adj. sharp; pungent. Matalim; matulis o nakasasakit sa damdamin.
pistol, n. small hand-gun. Pistola; baril.
pit, n. a hole in the ground. Hoyo; hukay; butas na malalim.
pitch, v. to throw. Ihagis.
pitchdark, adj. completely dark. Madilim na madilim.
pitchfork, n. a tool for lifting hay. Kalaykay.
pitcher, n. a container with a lip at one side and a handle at the other.
piteous, adj. sad; arousing pity. Kahabag-habag; nakakaawa.
pitfall, n. a trap. Patibong; bitag.
pity, n. compassion. Habag; awa.
placard, n. a posted bill. Kartel; kartelon; paskil.
placate, v. pacify; conciliate. Payapain; amuin.
place, n. region; locality; spot. Lugar; lunan.
placid, adj. gentle; quiet. Payapa; tahimik.
plagiarism, n. taking and using as one's own the ideas, writings, of another. Pamanlahiyo.
plague, n. a pestilential epidemic disease. Peste; salot.
plain, adj. flat; level; unobstruced. Liso; simple; walang palamuti; payak; patag.
plain, n. an extent of level country. Kapatagan.
plain-clothes man, n. a detective. Sekreta; tiktik.
plainly, adv. in a plain manner. Malinaw.
plan, n. a formulated scheme for getting something done. Plano; proyekto; balak.
planet, n. one of the heavenly bodies that move around the sun. Planeta.
plant, n. a seedling or cutting. Pananim; halaman; tanim.
plant, v. put in the ground to cultivate. Magtanim; ilagay; itatag.
plaster, v. to spread something on; apply plaster to. Iplaster; tapalan; dikitan.
plaster, n. a remedy spread on cloth and applied to the body; wall coating. Implasto; tapal.
plate, n. shallow dish. Plato; pinggan.
platform, n. a raised flooring. Plataporma· mataas na tuntungan; entablado.
platter, n. a flat dish. Bandehado.
play, n. amusement; diversion: fun; game. Huwego: laro.
play, v. engage in a game. Maglaro.
player, n. a performer in a game, play, etc. Manlalaro
playground, n. a piece of ground for play. Palaruan.
plea, n. an entreaty; pretext. Panawagan; pakiusap.
plead, v. to implore; persuade; beg. Mangatwiran; lumuhog; makiusap.
pleasant, adj. cheerful. Kasiya-siya; nakakawili.
pleasantry, n. gayety. Palitan ng nakakawiling mga salita; tudyuhan.
please, v. to delight; to gratify. Masiyahan; ikalugod; dulutan ng kasiyahan.
pleasing, adj. attractive;

agreeable. Nakalulugod; nakasisiya.

pleasure, n. delight: enjoyment. Kagustuhan; kasiyahan.

pleat, n. a fold, as of cloth. Pileges.

plebeian, adj. low social rank; pertaining to the common people. Plebeyo; pangkaraniwan.

pledge, n. a pawn; security Prenda; sangla: pangako.

plenary, adj. full; complete. Lubos; ganap.

plentiful, adj. ample; fruitful. Sagana; marami.

plenty, n. abundance. Kasaganaan.

pliable, adj. easily bent; flexible. Nababaluktot; malambot.

plot, n. a small piece of ground. Munting lagay ng lupa; kapirasong lupa.

plough, n. an implement that furrows and turns over the soil; agricultural tool. Araro.

plough, v. till with a plow; move, or push through. Mag-araro; araruhin.

pluck, v. to pull. Bunutin; pitasin.

pluck, n. spirit; courage. Tapang; lakas ng loob.

plug, n. a stopper. Tapon; panakip-butas.

plug, v. to stop or fill with or as with a plug. Tapunan; pasakan.

plumage, n. the feathers of a bird. Balahibo; plumahe.

plumber, n. a worker on water pipes, bathroom fixture, steam fitting. Plumero; manggagawa ng gripo, palikuran; tubero.

plump, adj. fat; well-rounded. Mataba; mabilog.

plunder, n. pillage; booty. Pinagnakawan; pinag-umitan; dambungin; pandarambong.

plunder, v. rob; take by force. Agawin o nakawin ang ariarian ng mga tinalo sa digmaan.

plural, adj. containing or designating more than one. Pangngalang pangmarami.

plus, prep. added to. Idinagdag; isinama.

pneumonia, n. a disease in which the lungs are inflamed. Pulmonya.

pocket, n. small pouch inserted in clothing. Bolsilyo; bulsa.

pocket, v. put in a pocket. Ilagay sa bulsa; ipamulsa.

poem, n. a composition in verse. Tula.

poet, n. one who writes poems or is capable of lofty artistic expression. Makata; manunulà.

point, n. a sharp or tapering end. Dulong matulis; tulis.

poison, v. give poison to; a substance that causes injury or death upon ingestion, contact, or injection. Lasunin; lason.

police, n. civil officer. Pulis; pulisya.

policy, n. a plan of action; way of management. Patakaran; palakad.

polish, v. make smooth and glassy, as by rubbing. Pakintabin; pakinisin.

polite, adj. showing good manners toward others. Magalang; mapitagan.

politics, n. the science and art of government. Pulitika.

poloshirt, n. a man's clothing. Polosirt.

pollute, v. to defile; make impure. Parumihin; hawahan.

polygamy, n. system allowing a man more than one living **wife**. Poligamya; pagkakaroon ng higit sa isang asawang babae.

pomp, n. stately or splendid display. Karingalán· karangyaan.

pond, n. a pool of water; a body of standing water smaller than a lake. Sapasapaan; munting sapa.

ponder, v. to consider; to think. Limiin; isipin; pagaralan.

pontiff, n. a high priest; the Pope. Ang Papa.

pontifical, n. a book containing rites and ceremonies ecclesiastical in nature. Pontipikal; aklat ng mga seremonyas ng simbahang Katolika.

pool, n. a small pond. Hukay na tinitigilan ng tubig; munting balon.

poor, adj. having little or nothing in the way of wealth, gcods, or means of subsistence. Pobre; maralita; mahirap.

Pope, n. the bishop of Rome as head of the Roman Catholic Church. Papa.

popgun, n. a toy gun. Baril-barilan.

popular, adj. suited to many; generally liked, Popular; tanyag; kilala.

population, n. whole people; total number of inhabitants of a place. Ang tiyak na bilang ng mga naninirahan sa isang pook.

porch, n. a veranda. Portiko; beranda.

pork, n. flesh of swine. Karne ng baboy.

port, n. a harbor. Piyer; daungan ng mga sasakyang-tubig.

portable, adj. capable of being carried or moved. Bitbitin.

porter, n. a door-keeper. Portero; tanod-pinto; bantay-pinto.

portion, n. allotment; a share. Parte; bahagi.

portrait, n. one's likeness; a picture of a person especially one done in oils. Retrato; larawan.

pose, n. position of the body. Tindig; anyo; tikas.

position, n. situation. Pusisyon; lagay.

positive, adj. confident; definite. Positibo; tiyak.

possess, v. to have; to own. Angkinin; magkaroon; ariin.

possession, n. the state of having and controlling something owned. Pag-aari.

possible, adj. may be done. Posible; maaari.

post, n. an upright timber or stake; an assignment; the mail. Poste; puwesto; koreo; haligi; tungkulin.

postage, n. amount paid on anything sent by mail. Bayad sa koreo.

postcommunion, n. prayer said after the Holy Communion. Ang dasal pagkatapos ng pakikinabang.

postage stamp, n. a stamp showing prepayment of postage. Selyo sa liham.

post-haste, adv. with speed. Lubhang mabilis; madali; mabilis.

posthumous, adj. born after one's father's death; published after the author's death. Postumus; nangyari pagkatapos na mamatay ang isang tao.

postman, n. man who carries mail for the government. Kartero; taga-hatid sulat.

postulant, n. a candidate for

a novitiate. Postulante; ang isang naghahangad pumasok sa monasteryo na nagdaraan sa isang pagsubok bago maging nobisyada.

posture, n. bodily position; carriage. Pustura; tindig.

postwar, adj. after the war. Pagkatapos ng digmaan.

pot, n. a round deep vessel, as for cooking. Palayok.

potato, n. a plant or its important edible tuber. Patatas; papas.

pouch, n. a small bag or sack; a marsupium. Bolsilyo; supot.

poultice, n. a soft, warm mass applied to a sore spot. Kataplasma; tapal.

pounce, v. to fall upon or seize. Dakmain; sakmalin.

pound, v. beat; crush. Dikdikin; bayuhin.

pour, v. flow; send forth. Ibuhos.

poverty, n. condition of being poor with respect to money, goods, or means of subsistence. Kahirapan; karalitaan.

powder, n. a mixture of fine, dry particles, as pulverized talc used as a cosmetic. Pulbos.

powder, v. sprinkle with or as with powder; reduce to powder. Durugin; bayuhin; magpulbos.

power, n. force; strength. Potensiya; lakas; kapangyarihan.

powerful, adj. having or exerting great power or force. Makapangyarihan, malakas; mabisa.

practice, n. habit; usage; frequent performance. Kinaugalian; pagsasanay; kinagawian; paraan.

praise, n. compliments; applause. Paghanga; papuri. reward. Bigay-pala; premyo.

praiseworthy, adj. laudable; commendable. Kahangahanga; kapuri-puri.

prawn, n. an edible shrimplike crustacean. Ulang.

pray, v. ask God's grace; petition for. Magdasal; mangaral.

prayer, n. a supplication to God; a religious service; entreaty. Orasyon; dasal; dalangin.

prayer book, n. a book or forms for prayers. Debosiyonaryo; aklat-dasalan.

preach, v. to proclaim; teach; to deliver (a sermon). Magturo; magsermon; mangaral.

preacher, n. a clergyman; anyone who preaches. Predikador; pari; taga-sermon.

preaching, n. the act of delivering a sermon. Pangaral; sermon.

preamble, n. an introduction to a speech or writing. Paunang salita.

precarious, adj. uncertain; insecure. Peligroso; mabuway; di-tiyak; mapanganib.

precaution, n. previous care. Pag-iingat.

precious, adj. of great value. Mahalaga; mahal.

precipice, n. a cliff. Tangwa.

precipitate, v. cause to happen suddenly or too soon. Maging sanhi; magbunsod; pangyarihin agad; iumang; isubo.

precise, adj. exact; strict; definite; accurate. Tiyak; tumpak; tamang-tama.

preclude, v. to shut out; prevent. Huwag isama; humadlang.

preconceive, v. to conceive beforehand. Balakin nang

una.

predecessor, n. one who preceded another; an ancestor. Ang sinundan; ang nauna.

predestination, n. the doctrine of foreordination; fate; destiny. Katalagahan ng Diyos.

predicament, n. critical condition. Gipit na kalagayan.

predict, v. to foretell. Hulaan.

prediction, n. prophecy; foretelling. Hula.

predominant, adj. superior. Namamayani; namamaibabaw.

preface, n. an introduction. Paunang salita; prepasiyo.

prefer, v. to regard more. Naisin ng higit kaysa; itangi; piliin.

preference, n. choice. Ang gusto; ang pinili.

prefect, n. an administrative head. Ang pinuno ng isang Kapatirang Romano na karaniwa'y isang kardenal.

prejudice, n. previous bias. Paunang hatol.

prelate, n. a high ecclesiastical dignitary; an archbishop. Karaniwang tawag sa isang pari.

preliminary, adj. & n. introductory; a preparatory step. Pauna; paghahanda.

premature, adj. happening too early. Wala pa sa panahon.

premeditate, v. to intend; think about and contrive beforehand. Balakin.

premise, n. a previous statement from which something is inferred or concluded. Hakà; palagay; kinatatayuan o kinalalagyan.

premium, n. a bounty; a prize; Bigay-pala; premyo; gantimpala.

preparation, n. making ready. Paghahanda.

prepare, v. to make ready. Ihanda; maghanda.

preposition, n. a word that shows certain relations between other words. Pangukol.

presbyter, n. an elder or a person somewhat advanced in age, who had authority in the early Christian Church; a priest. Isang taong na kakaalam sa simbahan; pari.

prescribe, v. to order. Iutos.

prescription, n. a medical recipe. Hatol; tuntunin; reseta.

present, adj. being or occurring at this time. Kaharap; kasalukuyan.

presentation, n. introduction. Paghaharap; pagpapakilala.

preserve, v. to keep from decay. Pangalagaan; panatilihin; itinggal; imbakin.

preserver, n. one who saves. Tagapangalaga, taga-imbak.

preside, v. to watch over. Mangulo.

president, n. chief officer. Presidente; panguio.

press, n. the practice and industry of printing or publishing. Imprenta; limbagan; pahayagan.

pressure, n. the continued action of a weight or force. Bigat; puwersa; presyon.

prestige, n. reputation. Kabantugan.

presume, v. take for granted; assume. Sapantahain; ipalagay.

presumption, n. something believed on inconclusive evidence. Sapantaha; akala; palagay.

pretence, n. assumption; false profession; pretext. Pagpapakunwari.

pretty, adj. pleasing; attractive. Kaakit-akit; maganda.

prevail, v. be victorious; to overcome. Magwagi; umiral; manaig; mahimok.

prevalent, adj. of wide use or occurrence; widespread. Namamayani; kalat.

prevent, v. to hinder; impede. Hadlangan; pigilin.

prevention, n. hindrance. Hadlang; pagpigil.

previous, adj. coming or occurring before something else. Nakaraan; nauna; sinundan.

prey, n. an animal hunted or seized for food. Hayop na sisilain; biktima.

price, n. value set. Halaga; presyo.

priceless, adj. invaluable. Walang halaga.

prick, v. to pierce with something sharp or pointed. Duruin; sundutin ng matulis na bagay.

prickle, n. a small thornlike projection. Subyáng; tinik.

pride, n. vanity; self-respect. Sariling pagpapahalaga; pagmamalaki; kayabangan.

priest, n. an ecclesiastic. Alagad ng simbahan; pari; saserdote.

priesthood, n. office of priest. Pagpapari.

prim, adj. formal; demure. Maayos na maayos; ayos at makinis.

prim, v. to be affectedly nice; formal; neat; demure. Gumayak nang maayos.

primarily, adv. first in order. Pangunahin; una sa lahat.

primary, adj. first. Primarya; mahalaga sa lahat.

prime, adj. & n. early; first rate. Kabataan; kalakasan; pinakamataas.

primer, n. the first book in reading. Panimulang aklat sa pagbasa.

primitive, adj. early; original; simple. Kauna-unahan; una; ukol sa unang panahon; makaluma.

prince, n. a king's son. Prinsipe; anak na lalaki ng hari.

princess, n. a king's daughter. Prinsesa; anak na babae ng isang hari.

principal, adj. a head; chief. Pinakamahalaga; pangunahin.

principle, n. a rule of science explaining how things act. Alituntunin; prinsipyo; simulain.

print, n. impress by types; a mark made by impression. Limbag; limbagin; marka; impresiyon.

print, v. impress; form an imitation of types. Limbagin; markahan.

printing press, n. a press for the printing of books. Limbagan; palimbagan.

prior, n. a male superior in a religious order or house. Priyor; tagapamahala sa isang malayang monasteryo.

prior, adj. former; preceding in time, order, or importance. Maaga; bago dumating; nauna; una.

prioress, n. a female prior. Ang pinuno o tagapamahala ng mga madre o mongha.

priority, n. being earlier in time. Kaunahan.

prison, n. a jail. Karsel; bilangguan; piitan; kulungan.

prisoner, n. a captive. Bilanggo.

private, adj. common soldier; belonging to some particular person or persons. Lihim; pribado; pansarili.

privilege, n. a special advantage enjoyed by a person. Tanging karapatan.

prize, n. a reward given as a symbol of superiority. Premyo; gantimpala; prais.

pro, adv. for the affirmative. Maka; ayon; sang-ayon sa.

probability, n. likelihood. Bagay na maaaring maganap o mangyari.

probably, adv. likely. Kaipalà; maaari; mangyayari.

problem, n. question to solve, a difficult or perplexing matter. Problema; suliranin.

procathedral, n. a church used as a cathedral. Pansamantalang katedral ng isang obispo.

procedure, n. method of doing things. Paraan; kaparaanan.

proceed, v. to go forward. Magpatuloy; magmulâ.

proceeding, n. a measure or step taken. Paraan; pamamaraan; hakbang.

process, n. course; progress. Takbo; kasalukuyang ginagawa; paraan.

procession, n. a formal or ceremonious parade of persons, animals vehicles or other things. Prusisyon; pila.

proclaim. v. to announce. Iproklama; magpatalastas; ipahayag.

procrastination, n. the act of putting things off till later. Pagpapaliban.

procurator, n. among the ancient Romans, any of various imperial officers with fiscal or administrative powers. Ahente; tagakuha o tagabili.

procure, v. to obtain; contrive and effect. Magtamó; hanapin; kunin.

prodigal, adj. profuse; lavish; wasteful; bountiful. Alibugha; mapagbulagsak; bulastog; lagalag.

prodigious, adj. enormous. Dikaraniwan; kahanga-hanga; napakalaki.

prodigy, n. a marvel; a wonder. Kababalaghan

produce, v. to bring forth. Ilabas; magbunga; gumawa; umani.

product, n. a result; an effect. Bagay na ginawa; ani; produkto; bunga; yari.

profane, adj. irreligious; irreverent. Walang galang; dibanal; bastos; lapastangan.

profanity, n. irreverence. Kàwalang galang; salita o kilos na laban sa kabanalan.

profess, v. to avow; declare openly. Ipahalata; ipahayag; ipabatid sa madla; paalam.

profession, n. an avowal; a vocation esp. in a branch of science. Propesyon; katungkulan; hanapbuhay.

proffer, v. to offer; tender. Ialok; ialay; ihandog.

proficiency, n. ability. Kakayahan.

proficient, adj. thoroughly qualified; skilled. Sanay; mahusay; dalubhasa.

profile, n. side-face; a contour. Tabas o anyo.

profit, n. advantage; benefit. Pakinabang; tubo; napalâ.

profitable, adj. bringing gain. Kapaki-pakinabang.

profound, adj. deep; thorough. Malalim.

profuse, adj. copious; abundant. Sagana; marami.

program, n. a printed list of events, performers, etc. in any public entertainment. Programa; palatuntunan.

progress, n. advancement. Progreso; kaunlaran; pagunlad.

prohibit, v. to forbid. Ipagbawal.

project, n. a plan. Plano; balak; panukala.

prolific, adj. fruitful. Mabunga; maraming nagagawa.

prologue, n. introduction. Pambungad; paunang salita o paliwanag.

promenade, n. a walk; a stroll for pleasure. Pamamasyal.

prominent, adj. standing out; distinguished. Bantog; tanyag; kilala.

promise, n. one's pledge to another that one will or will not do something. Pangako.

promontory, n. headland; high land jutting into the sea. Tangos; mataas na lupang nakausli sa dagat o baybayin.

promote, v. to raise in rank or importance. Itaas; iasenso.

promotion, n. encouragement; growth or improvement. Pagtataas; pagtataguyod; promosiyon.

prompt. adj quick: ready; on time. Maagap; maliksi; husto sa oras.

promulgation, n. publication; open declaration. Pagpapahayag; pagbabalita.

prone, adj. bending forward; lying face downward. Nakahilig; nakadapa.

pronoun, n. a word used to represent a noun previously stated or understood. Panghalip.

pronounce, v. to speak distinctly. Bigkasin; ipahayag.

pronounced, adj. strongly marked; decided. Maliwanag; tiyak.

pronunciation, n. proper speaking; the uttering of words; esp. with correct sounds and accents. Pagbigkas; bigkas.

proof, n. evidence sufficient to establish a thing as true. Pruweba; patunay; patotoo; katibayan.

prop, n. a support. Suhay; tukod.

prop, v. support or keep from falling, as by placing something under or against. Suhayan; tukuran.

propaganda, n. ideas disseminated to support a doctrine. Propaganda; paglalathala.

propagate, v. to spread; disseminate. Magpalaganap; magparami; ikalat; palaganapin.

propel, v. to drive forward. Ibunsod; itulak; palakarin.

proper, adj. appropriate. Nararapat; tama; tumpak; ayos; angkop; dapat.

property, n. that which one owns; possession. Ari-arian; katangian.

prophecy, n. a foretelling. Pagsasabi ng mangyayari; hula.

prophet, n. one who foretells future events. Manghuhulà; propeta; tagasabi ng mangyayari.

propinquity, n. nearness. Proksimidad; kalapitan.

proportion, n. a ratio; just or proper share. Kaugnayan; pagkakabagay-bagay; proporsiyon.

proportionate, adj. proportional; having due proportion or relation. Kaigihan; katamtaman; nababagay.

proposal, n. a plan. Panukala; balak.

propose, v. to offer; to suggest. Imungkahi; ipanukala; balakin.

propound, v. offer for consideration, as a question. Magharap; imungkahi; ipanukala.

proprietor, n. an owner. May-ari; propiyetaryo.

propriety, n. fitness; rightness. Karapatan; kaayusan; kaangkupan; kawastuan.

prose, n. ordinary language. Prosa; tuluyan.

prosecution, n. the process of exhibiting formal charges against an offender before a legal tribunal. Paglilitis; pagsasagawa.

proselyte, n. a convert from one creed, sect, or party to another. Taong nahimok lumipat sa ibang pananampalataya.

prospect, n. a view; expectation; a possible buyer, client, etc. Isang inaasahang suki; tanawin; pag-asa; hinaharap.

prosper, v. to thrive; succeed. Yumaman; magtagumpay; umunlad; sumagana.

prosperity, n. success; a period of economic well-being. Prosperidad; paglago; pagtatagumpay; kasaganaan.

prosperous, adj. successful. Mayaman; matagumpay; sagana.

prostitute, n. lewd for hire; a harlot. Puta; kalapating mababa ang lipad; babaing nagbibili ng laman; masamang babae.

prostrate, v. lying flat. Magpatirapa; dumapa; ihulog o ibagsak nang padapa; pagurin.

protect, v. to defend. Ipagsanggalang; ipagtanggol; kupkupin.

protection, n. the act or effect of protecting; that which keeps safe. Proteksiyon; pagtatanggol; pagkukupkop.

protector, n. a defender. Tagapagsanggalang; tagapagtanggol; tagakupkop.

protest, v. to oppose. Di-umayon; tumutol.

Protestant, n. Christian denomination (1) that differs from the church of Rome, and that sprang from the Reformation. (2) A Christian Church not Roman or Orthodox Catholic. Protestante; pananampalatayang salungat sa simbahang Katolika.

promartyr, n. the first martyr. Ang unang martir sa alin mang bansa.

protract, v. to prolong. Tumagal; patagalin.

protrude, v. to project. Umusli.

proud, adj. haughty; arrogant. Suberbiyo; Arogante; mapagmataas.

prove, v. make certain, by producing evidence; probate. Patunayan.

proverb, n. an adage. Proberbiyo; salawikain; kasabihan.

proverbial, adj. well-known. Kilala; bantog.

provide, v. to procure beforehand. Magdulot; maghanda; maglaan; itadhana; sustentuhan; bigyan.

providence, n. God's care; foresight. Katalagahan ng Maykapal; kapalaran.

province, n. an administrative division of a country. Probinsiya; lalawigan.

provision, n. store, supplies, as of food; providing. Probisyon; mga pagkaing binili o tinipon; rasyon.

provisional, adj. conditional; temporary. Pansamantala.

provoke, v. to irritate; stir up. Probokahin; galitin.

provost, n. chief dignitary of a cathedral. Ang namumuno sa kapulungan ng mga pari.

prowess, n. bravery; daring. Tapang; lakas ng loob; kagitingan.

prowl, v. to rove for prey. Umali-aligid; maglibot; lumabuy-laboy upang humanap ng masisila.

proximate, adj. nearest. Malapit; kalapit.

proxy, n. a substitute. Kahalili; kapalit na pansamantala; kinatawan; proksi.

prudent, adj. wise; discreet. Matalino at maingat.

prune, v. to trim off something superflous esp. branches. Alisan ng mga bahaging walang kaukulan; putulan: bawasan.

pry, v. peer; peep. Sumilip; manubok; maniktik.

psalmody, n. singing psalms. Pag-awit ng mga dasal o banal na imno; ang musika para sa tinurang pag-awit.

pseudo, adj. feigned; sham. Huwad; di-tunay.

pseudonym, n. pen name. Seudonim; sagisag; pangalan sa panulat.

psychiatrist, n. a doctor who treats mental diseases. Espesyalista sa sakit sa isip.

public, adj. known to all. Publiko; hayag; kalat.

publish, v. to make known; proclaim. Ipalimbag; ihayag; ilathala.

pudicity, n. modesty; chastity. Pagpigil sa sarili upang di magkasala; kalinisang-puri.

puff, v. emit a puff; breathe hard. Magbugá; humitit; papintugin; lagyan ng hangin para pumintog.

pugnacious, adj. quarrelsome. Palaawáy; mapanghamok; mapang-away.

pug nose, n. a short, tip-tilted nose. Ilong na sarat.

pull, v. draw with force toward one; tug. Hilahin; batakin.

pulp, n. the soft fleshy part of any fruit. Laman; lamukot.

pulpit, n. church rostrum. Pulpito.

pulse, n. throbbing of blood in an artery. Pulso; pintig.

pulverize, v. reduce to ashes. Pulbusin; durugin; gawing pulbos.

pump, n. a machine for moving, or compressing, liquids or gases. Bomba.

punch, n. a mixed beverage. Isang uri ng inuming binubuo ng tubig; katas ng limon at asukal.

punch, v. to strike, as with the fist; poke; prod. Buntalin; suntukin.

punctual, adj. prompt. exact. Husto sa oras; Maagap.

punctuate, v. to divide into sentences by points. Bantasan.

punctuation, n. the use of periods, commas, and other marks to help make the meaning clear. Palabantasan.

puncture, v. prick; make a small hole in. Butasin.

punish, v. inflict a penalty on (a person) or for (an offense) Kastiguhin; parusahan.

punishable, adj. liable to punishment; capable of being punished. Dapat parusahan; maaaring parusahan.

punishment, n. chastisement. Kastigo; parusa.

puppet, **n.** a child's doll; a doll moved by wires. Tautauhan; Manika.

puppy, **n.** a young dog. Tuta.

purchase, **v.** to buy. Bumili; bilhin.

pure, **adj.** clean; genuine. Puro; dalisay.

purgative, **n.** cathartic. Purga.

purgatory, **n.** a place where penitent souls are purified. Purgatoryo.

purge, **v.** cleanse from impurities, bodily or spiritual. Linisin; alisan; purgahin.

purification, **n.** purifying. Paglilinis; pagdalisay.

purify, **n.** chastity; state of being pure. Kalinisan; kadalisayan.

purpose, **n.** intention; aim. Hangarin; layunin; tunguhin; gawain.

purposely, **adv.** deliberately; intentionally. Kusa; sadya.

purse, **n.** any small receptacle for carrying money. Lukbutan; pitaka.

pursue, **v.** to chase; follow. Tugisin; maghanap; ipagpatuloy; ituloy.

pursuit, **n.** an occupation. Pagpapatuloy; paghabol; gawin.

pus, **n.** the matter of a sore. Nana.

push, **v.** to advance or extend by effort; force one's way Itulak.

push-over, **n.** something very easy to do. Bagay na madaling gawin.

put, **v.** set, lay, or cause to be in any place, position, or condition. Ilapag; ilagay.

putative, **adj.** supposed. Karaniwang ipinalalagay na gayon; ipinalalagay.

putrid, **adj.** rotten; foul. Mabaho; bulok.

putty, **n.** a soft, daughty cement for filling cracks, etc. Masilya.

puzzle, **n.** a perplexing problem. Mahirap na suliranin; palaisipan.

pygmy, **n.** dwarf. Unano.

pyjamas, **n.** garments to sleep in. Padyama.

python, **n.** a large snake that crushes its prey. Sawa.

pyx, **n.** a covered vessel used in the Roman Catholic Church for holding the consecrated host. Ang munting sisidlang nag-iingat sa ostiya.

Q

quack, **n.** the cry of a duck; a false pretender to medical skill. Kakak ng pato; taong mapagpanggap; taong magdaraya; albularyo.

quack, **v.** to make a noise as a duck. Kumakak na tulad ng pato; magpanggap; mandaya.

quackery, **n.** deceptive practice. Pagpapanggap; pagdaraya.

quadrate, **adj.** even. Kuwadrado; parisu..at.

quadruped, **n.** a four-footed animal. Hayop na may apat na paa.

quadruple, **adj.** four times. Apat-apat; apatan.

quaff, **v.** drink freely. Uminom ng malakas; tumungga.

quaint, **adj.** pleasingly odd or unusual. Katangi-tangi; kaiba; di-karaniwan.

quail, **n.** a small game bird. Pugo.

quake, **n.** a shaking or tremulous agitation, esp. an earthquake. Pangangatog; lindol; pagyanig.

quake, **v.** tremble; shake; shudder. Mangatog; lumindol; yumanig.

qualification, n. fitness. Kakayahan; katangian.
qualify, v. fill requirements for a place or occupation. Maging dapat; magkaroon ng mga katangiang kinakailangan.
quality, n. characteristic. Katangian; kagalingan; uri.
qualm, n. a twinge of conscience. Pagkabalisa; alinlangan; pagkatigatig.
quandary, n. a state of doubt. Pag-aalinlangan.
quantity, n. amount; bulk; weight. Dami.
quarantine, n. prohibition of intercourse. Kuwarentina; pagbubukod; paghihiwalay sa karamihan.
quarrel, n. an angry dispute. Alitan; away; pakikipagkagalit.
quarrelsome, adj. easily provoked. Palaaway.
quarry, n. a mine of stone. Tibagan ng bato.
quart, n. 4th part of gallon. Isang kapat ng isang galon.
quarter, n. a 4th part; a section. Sangkapat; pansamantalang tirahan.
quarter, v. divide into four equal parts. Hatiin sa apat.
quarterly, adv. once in a quarter of a year. Minsan tuwing tatlong buwan; tuwing sangkapat na taon.
quartette, n. a group of four. Pangkát ng apat; apatan.
quash, v. subdue; annul. Sugpuin; pawalang-bisa; pigilin; supilin.
quasi, adj. & adv. a prefix meaning *as it*. Di tunay; wari bang; tila baga.
quaver, v. to shake; tremble. Manginig; mangatal.
quay, n. a dock for landing and loading a ship's cargo. Muwelye; daungan; pantalan.
queen, n. a king's wife. Reyna; asawa ng hari.
queer, adj. odd; strange. Katuwa; kaiba.
quell, v. to subdue; to quiet. Gapiin; sugpuin; supilin.
quench, v. to extinguish. Patigilin; pawiin.
quenchable, adj. extinguishable. Maaaring pawiin.
querulous, adj. complaining; fretful. Bugnutin; paladaing; mareklamo.
query, n. a question; an inquiry. Tanong.
quest, n. a search. Paghahanap.
question, n. an interrogation. Tanong; panukala; suliranin.
question, v. to ask; inquire of. Tanungin; magtanong; pagalinlanganan.
questionable, adj. suspicious. Mapag-alinlanganan; kahina-hinala.
queue, n. hair braided and worn pigtail; a waiting line. Tirintas; pila; hilera.
quick, adj. fast; speedy. Mabilis; madali.
quicken, v. make or become faster or more active. Dalidaliin; buhayin; pabilisin; bilisan; dalian.
quickly, adv. swiftly; rapidly; Nang buong bilis; agad; madali.
quickness, n. rapidness. Kabilisan.
quicksand, n. a bog. Kumunoy.
quicksilver, n. mercury. Asoge.
quiet, adj. still; calm; silent. Payapa; tahimik; mayumi.
quiet, v. to calm; pacify. Payapain; patahimikin.
quietly, adv. silently. Matahimik.

quill, n. a pen made from a feather. Pakpak na panulat.
quinine, n. powdered Peruvian bark. Kinina.
quinsy, n. severe inflammation of the throat and tonsils accompanied by swelling and pus. Pamamaga ng tonsil.
quintet, n. a group of five. Limahang tinig; limahang instrumento ng musika.
quintuple, adj. fivefold. Limalima; limahan.
quip, n. a witty remark. Biro.
quirk, n. a quick turn. Kapritso; sumpong; biglang balik.
quirt, n. a short riding whip. Latigo; kumpas.
quit, v. to leave; cease. Umayaw; huminto; iwan; itigil.
quite, adv. completely; wholly. Ganap; halos; buo; lahat.
quiver, v. to shake. Manginig.
quivering, adj. trembling. Nanginginig.
quiz, n. an enigma; puzzle. Tanong; pagsusulit; iksamen.
quiz, v. to question. Tanungin; usisain; bigyan ng pagsusulit.
quondam, adj. former; in time past. Tungkol sa panahong lumipas; dati.
quorum, n. required number of members to conduct business in any society. Korum.
quota, n. a share. Kaparte; bahaging ukol; takda; kuwota.
quotable, n. citable. Maaaring banggitin o sipiin.
quotation, n. citation. Ang bahaging binanggit; binabanggit o inuulit; sipi.
quote, v. to cite. Banggitin; sipiin.

R

Rabbi, n. a Jewish clergyman; expounder of the law. Pantas ng mga Hudyo; kapirasong telang itim na ikinakabit sa kuwelyo ng mga pari.
rabbit, n. a small rodent related to the hare. Kuneho.
rabble, n. a disorderly crowd; mob. Kaguluhan; pulutong ng mga manggugulo.
rabid, adj. furious. Marahas; masugid; panatiko.
rabies, n. an infectious disease; hydrophobia. Sakit na nagmumula sa kagat ng aso; haydropobya.
race, n. a family, division of people, tribe or nation; a contest or effort to reach a goal first. Lipi; labanan; lahi; karera.
race, v. engage in a contest of speed. Makipagkarera.
racket, n. din; hurly-burly. Raketa; kaguluhan; raket.
radiant, adj. shining. Maaliwalas; maningning; makinang.
radiate, v. to emit rays. Magbigay ng sinag; magsabog ng ningning; magningning.
radical, adj. natural to; inherent. Katutubo; likas.
radish, n. the crisp, pungent root of a garden plant. Labanos.
raffle, n. a sort of lottery. Ripa.
raffle, v. to dispose of by raffle. Pagripahan.
raft, n. floating wooden framework. Balsa.
rag, n. a torn or waste piece of cloth. Basahan.
rage, n. anger. Matinding galit.
ragged, adj. shaggy. Magaspang; gulanit; tila basahan.
raid, n. invasion. Paglusob; pagsalakay.
raid, v. attack; rob. Lumusob; sumalakay.

rail, n. a bar passing from one support to another, as for a barrier. Barandilya; gabay; riles.

railroad, n. a common carrier operating trains over permanent tracks of rails; the tracks. Daang-bakal; perokaril.

raiment, n. vesture; dress. Damit; kasuotan.

rain, n. water falling in drops from the clouds. Ulan.

rain, v. produce water falling in drops. Umulan.

rainbow, n. an arc of prismatic colors. Bahaghari; revnbo.

raincoat, n. coat for protection from rain. Kapote.

rain-water, n. water fallen as rain. Tubig-ulan.

rainy, adj. constantly or often raining. Maulan.

raise, v. to lift; to erect. Itindig; itaas.

raisin, n. a dried grape. Pasas; ubas na pinatuyo.

rajah, n. a Malayan ruler. Raha.

rake, n. a long-handled toothed implement for scrapping loose materials together. Pangalaykay; kalaykay pangkalahig.

rake, v. gather or smooth with or as with a rake. Kalahigin; kalaykayin.

rally, v. to bring together. Pagtipun-tipunin.

rally, n. mass meeting. Raly.

ram, v. to strike against. Bungguin; bayuhin.

ramble, n. a sauntering walk. Pamamasyal na walang tiyak na patutunguhan.

ramble, v. roam or wander about. Gumala-gala; mamasyal nang walang tiyak na tunguhin.

rampant, adj. exuberant. Namamayaning ganap; palasak.

rampart, n. a bulwark. Tanggulan; balwarte.

ranch, n. a very large farm. Rantso.

rancid, adj. having a rank, tainted smell or taste. Maanta.

range, n. a row. Hilera; hanay.

ranger, n. a person employed to guard a tract of forest. Tanod-gubat.

rank, n. a class; order; standing; relative position. Uri; taas ng tungkulin; ranggo.

ransack, v. to search thoroughly. Halughugin.

ransom, n. price paid for a release. Tubos; panubos.

rap, n. a quick, smart, or light blow. Katok; tuktok.

rap, v. to strike esp. with a quick, smart, or light sharp blow. Kumatok.

rapid, adj. quick; swift. Mabilis.

rapidity, n. celerity. Kabilisan.

rapture, n. ecstasy. Lubos na kagalakan; kaligayahan.

rare, adj. scarce. Pambihira; madalang.

rarely, adv. scarcely. Bihira; madalang.

rascal, n. a scoundrel; rogue. Pilyo; saragate; salbahe.

rashness, n. hastiness. Pagkapabigla-bigla.

rasping, adj. harsh. Nakasasakit ng tainga; magaspang.

rat, n. a rodent similar to the mouse but larger. Daga.

rate, n. charge; degree. Halaga; paraan; uri.

rate, v. to estimate. Halagahan; ituring; ipalagay.

rather, adv. more properly. Higit na mabuti; lalong mabuti.

ratify, v. to confirm. Sang-

ayunan; pagtibayin.
ration, n. allowance, especially of a necessity. Rasyon; kaukulang parte.
rational, adj. reasonable. Makatwiran.
rattan, n. East Indian cane. Ratan; yantok.
rattle, v. make or cause to make a rapid succession of clicking sounds. Yamutin; galitin; guluhin; kalampagin; kalantugin; dumaldal.
ravage, v. devastate; pillage. Pinsalain; wasakin; pagnakawan; dambungin; huthutin.
rave, v. to be furious. Magalit na mabuti; magtungayaw na tulad ng isang baliw.
ravel, v. to become frayed out or separated into threads. Makalas; matastas.
raven, n. a large black bird like the crow. Uwak.
ravenously, adv. voraciously. Nang buong katakawan; nang buong kasibaan.
ravine, n. a deep hollow. Mababa't malalim na hukay na gawa ng tubig; bangin.
ravish, v. rape. Punuin ng kasiyahan; itangay; gahasain.
raw, adj. uncooked. Hilaw; baguhan.
ray, n. a line of light. Sinag; banaag.
raze, v. level to the ground. Ibagsak; ihapay sa lupa; burahin.
razor, n. a tool with a sharp blade to shave with. Labaha; pang-ahit.
reach, v. attain; arrive at. Dukwangin; abutin; kunin
react, v. to act in response. Gumanti.
read, v. to peruse; learn. Bumasa.
readable, adj. worth reading. Nababasa.
readily, adv. willingly; easily. Agad; kaagad; kara-karaka.
readiness, n. being ready. Kagapan; kahandaan.
readjust, v. to arrange again. Ayusing muli.
real, adj. true; genuine. Tunay; totoo.
reality, n. fact; truth. Katotohanan.
realm, n. a kingdom; an empire. Kaharian.
ream, n. 20 quires of paper. Resma; paldo ng papel.
reap, v. cut grain; harvest. Gumapas; umani.
reaper, n. one who reaps. Mang-aani; manggagapas.
re-appear, v. to appear again. Bumalik; lumitaw na muli.
rear, v. to make grow; bring up. Palakihin; alagaan.
reason, n. motive. Katwiran; matwid; rasón; dahilan.
reasonable, adj. just. Makatwiran; makatarungan.
rebel, n. one who resists authority. Manghihimagsik; rebelde.
rebellion, n. insurrection. Himagsikan; paghihimagsik.
rebound, v. to bound back from force of impact. Bumalik; tumalbog; sumikad.
rebuild, v. to build again. Itayong muli.
rebuke, v. to chide; reprimand. Sisihin; pagwikaan; kagalitan; sumbatan.
recall, v. call back. Alalahanin; pabalikin; bawiin
recapitulate, v. reiterate. Lagumin; pagbalikan; ibigay ang buod.
recede, v. to retreat. Umurong; kumati.
receipt, n. acknowledgment. Resibo.
receive, v. accept; get. Tanggapin.
recent, adj. new; fresh; mo-

dern. Di pa natatagalan; bago; di pa nalalaunan.

reception, n. a receiving; entertainment. Pagtanggap; salu-salo.

recess, n. intermission. Rises; retiro; sandaling pamamahinga.

recidivism, n. relapse into crime by a convicted criminal. Pagkakamali o pagkakasalang muli.

reciprocal, adj. mutual. Tumanggap at gumanti; gantihan.

recipe, n. directions for preparing something to eat. Resipe; paraan ng pagluluto.

recite, v. to rehearse. Bumigkas; magsabi.

reclaim, v. to take back. Bawiin; kuning muli.

recline, v. lean or lie back. Humingâ; humilig; sumandal; magpahinga.

recluse, n. solitary; a hermit. Taong namumuhay nang tahimik at nag-iisa; ermitanyo.

recognition, n. acknowledgment; being known. Pagkakilala; pag-amin.

recognize, v. know again. Makilala; aminin; kilalanin.

recoil, v. to rebound. Umurong; manliit; sumikad.

recollect, v. to remember. Gunitain; alalahanin; pagbalikan sa isip.

recollection, n. memory; remembrance. Gunita; alaala.

recommend, v. to commend to another. Itagubilin; ipayo; irekomenda; ipakilala ang kabutihan.

recommendation, n. a credential. Tagubilin; rekomendasyon; pagpapakilala sa kabutihan; tagubilin.

reconciliation, n. restoring of harmony. Pakikipagkasundong muli.

reconstruction, n. building again or anew. Magpanibagong tatag.

record, n. a thing written or kept. Tala; ulat.

recover, v. to get back something lost. Bawiin.

recreation. n. diversion from toil. Libangan; aliwan.

rector, n. parish minister. Rektor; paring nangungulo sa isang kolehiyo o seminaryo.

red, adj. a warm bright color; the color of fresh blood. Pula; mapula.

redeem, v. to buy back; rescue. Mailigtas; tubusin; matubos.

Redeemer, n. Saviour; Jesus Christ. Ang Manunubos; si Kristo.

redemption, n. deliverance. Pagtubos; katubusan; kaligtasan.

red-handed, adj. caught in the very act of crime or of some fault. Huli sa akto.

redouble, v. to become greatly or repeatedly increased. Pag-ibayuhin; gawing dalawang ulit; doblehin.

redress, n. indemnification. Lunas; pagtutuwid sa mali.

reduce, v. diminish in size, quantity, or value. Bawasan; liitan.

refer, v. to submit for consideration and decision. Tumukoy; isangguni; sumangguni.

referee, n. a judge of play in games and sports. Tagahatol; reperi.

reference, n. consultation; the act of referring. Pagbanggit; sanggunian; pagtukoy.

refine, v. to purify. Gawing pino; pinuhin; dalisayin;

pakinisin.

reflect, v. to think; bring about. Dili-dilihin; isip-isipin; ibalik.

reflection, n. a thought. Pag didili-d i l i; **pag-iisip-isip; pagmumuni-muni.**

reflux, v. a flowing back. Paagusing muli; ibalik ang agos.

reform, v. to correct. **Pagbuti**hin; pagbabago.

reformation, n. act of reforming. Pagbabago; pagpapakabuti.

reformatory, n. an institution for young offenders. Repormatoryo; piitan o paaralan para sa mga batang lumabag sa batas.

refract, v. bend abruptly. Iliko; ilihis.

refrain, v. to forbear; to hold oneself back. Pigilin; piitin; magpigil.

refresh, v. to reanimate; to reinvigorate by rest or food. Magpahinga; magpalakas; magpalamig; papanariwain.

refresher, n. one that refreshes. Pampalamig; pampasariwa; pampalakas.

refreshment, n. that which refreshes, especially food or drink. Paminindal; pampalamig.

refrigerator, n. something that keeps things cool. Repridyeretor; palamigan.

refuge, n. a shelter or protection from danger or distress; an asylum. Kublihan; kanlungan; ampunan.

refugee, n. a person who flees for refuge or safety. Takas.

refulgent, adj. bright; shining. Maningning; makinang.

refund, v. to repay; to reimburse. Isauli; ibalik.

refusal, n. a denial; option. Pagkakaila; pagtanggi; pag-ayaw.

refuse, v. to deny; say no. Magkaila; tumanggi; umayaw.

refute, v. to disprove. Pawalang-saysay; patunayang ditotoo; pasinungalingan.

regain, v. to recover. **Makuhang muli; mapanumbalik; mabawi.**

regal, adj. royal; kingly. **Maringal; parang hari; makahari;** regal.

regale, n. entertainment; a feast. **Karapatang panghari; karapatan ng isang haring tanggapin ang kita ng isang nasasakupan ng obispong walang namamahala.**

regard, n. respect; concern. Konsiderasyon; **paggalang; respeto.**

regard, v. look upon; consider. **Igalang; ituring; pag-alangalangan.**

regarding, prep. concerning; about. **Tungkol sa; hinggil sa.**

regardless, adj. careless; **heedless; indifferent. Sa kabila ng; walang ingat.**

regatta, n. a boat race **especially of yachts. Regata; karera ng mga bangka; paligsahan sa pagsagwan.**

regeneration, n. new birth. **Panibagong buhay; muling pagsilang; pagpapakabuting muli.**

regent, n. one who governs **when the legitimate ruler cannot. Rehente; ang namumuno sa isang kaharian kung ang hari ay wala may sakit o dili kaya'y bata pa.**

regime, n. a system of government or rule. Pamunuan.

regimen, n. course of diet; a **system of regulation or remedy. Wastong pag-aayaw-**

ayaw ng pagkain upang mapanumbalik ang kalusugan.

Regina Coeli, n. Blessed Virgin Mary. Reyna ng Kalangitan; ang Birhen Maria.

region, n. a district, section, a country. Rehiyon; pook.

regional, adj. sectional. Rehiyonal; pampook; pandanay.

register, n. a list; record. Rehistro; talaan.

register, v. to enroll. Magparehistro.

registrar, n. record-keeper. Taga-sulat; taga-ingat ng talaan; tagatala.

regress, v. passage back; return. Bumalik; magbalik.

regression, n. the act of passing back or returning. Pag babalik.

regret, n. sorrow, remorse, grief. Lungkot; hinayang panghihinayang na may halong lungkot; sumbat ng budhi.

regret, v. to lament; be distressed on account of. Ikinahihinayang; ikinalulungkot; ikinalulumbay.

regular, adj. normal. Katamtaman; lagi; pangkaraniwan; maayos.

regulate, v. to adjust; direct or govern by rule. Pangasiwaan; ayusin; isaayos.

regulation, n. a governing direction; a precept. Palakad; tuntunin; kautusan.

rehabilitate, v. to restore to a good condition. Isaayos; baguhin.

rehabilitation, n. restoring to former standing. Pagpapanibagong-buhay.

rehearsal, n. practice. Pagsasanay; ensayo.

rehearse, v. to practice for a public performance. Sanayin; magsanay; mag-ensayo.

reign, n. sovereignty; royal or supreme power. Soberanya; pamumuno; pamamahala; paghahari.

reign, v. to rule; to prevail. Mamahala; maghari; mamuno.

reimburse, v. to repay; refund. Mag-abono; magdagdag sa takdang gastos.

rein, n. a bridle strap. Renda.

rein, v. to restrain. Pigilan; rendahin.

reinforce, v. to strengthen with new force or materials. Palakasin; patibayin.

reinstate, v. to put back. Ibalik sa tungkuling inalisan o pinag-alisan.

reiterate, v. to repeat. Ulitin.

reject, v. to refuse; cut off. Ayawan; tanggihan.

rejoice, v. to be glad. Magsaya; magalak; matuwa.

rejoin, v. to join again. Sumamang muli; makisamang muli.

rejuvenate, v. make young again; youthful. Pabatain; gawing bata; papasariwain; pagbaguhin.

relapse, n. a falling back into a former bad state, either of health or of morals. Pagkabinat; binat.

relate. v. tell; narrate. Ikuwento; isalaysay; iugnay.

related, adj. connected. Kaugnay; konektado.

relation, n. kindred; kinship. Kaugnayan; kamag-anak.

relax, v. slacken; ease. Magpahinga; magluwag.

relay, v. to take and carry farther. Ihatid.

release, v. to set free. Palayain; pakawalan; palabasin.

relegate, v. to remand; consign. Iukol; itakda.

relent, v. feel compassion; yield. Maawa; mahabag; umayon.

relentless, adj. pitiless. Walang awa; matigas.
relevant, adj. applicable; pertinent. Nararapat; pertinente; kaugnay; angkop.
reliable, adj. trustworthy. Mapagkakatiwalaan; maaasahan.
relic, n. a souvenir; a memento held in religious veneration. Alaala; banal na bagay na may himalang nagawa; Relikya.
relict, n. a widow. Balong babae; biyuda.
relief, n. alleviation; comfort. Tulong; ginhawa; lugod.
relieve, v. to ease; succor. Maibsan; mapaginhawa; halinhan.
religion, n. belief in God or gods. Relihiyon; pananampalataya.
religious. adj. pious; devout. Madasalin; relihiyoso; banal; masugid manampalataya.
reliquary. n. depository for relics. Relikaryo; lalagyan ng mga relikya.
relish, n. taste; liking. Lasa; sarap.
relish. v. be pleased with, especially eat with pleasure. Masarapan. Magustuhan.
reluctance, n. unwillingness; hesitation. Atubili; pagbabantulot.
reluctant, adj. unwilling. Atubili; bantulot.
rely, v. to trust: depend. Umasa; magtiwala.
remain, v. to stay. Maiwan; manatili.
remainder, n. what is left; a surplus. Naiwan; tira; natira; labi.
remains, n. corpse; relics. Bangkay; ang mga labi ng taong namatay; kadaber.
remark, v. note in the mind; express by way of comment. Punahin; banggitin; sabihin; pansinin.
remarkable, adj. extraordinary; worthy of notice. Kapuna-puna; katangi-tangi; kapansin-pansin; di-karaniwan.
remedial, adj. curing. Panlunas; nakagagaling.
remedy, n. a cure. Lunas; remedyo.
remedy, v. to cure; heal. Lunasan; gamutin.
remember, v. retain in the mind; recollect. Alalahanin; tandaan.
remembrance, n. a memento. Pagkatanda; alaala.
remind, v. to put in mind. Ipaalaala.
reminisce, v. to talk or think about past experiences or events. Gunitain; alalahanin.
remit, v. pardon; forgive. Ipadala ang salapi; patawarin; pawalang sala.
remnant, n. a fragment; a remainder of a bolt of cloth or ribbon. Labi; retaso; tira.
remodel. v. to make over; convert. Baguhin; ibahin.
remorse, n. self-accusatory regret. Pagsisisi; pagkabalisa; pagtitika.
remote, adj. distant; far away. Malayo.
removal, n. a removing. Paglilipat; pag-aalis; pagtanggal.
remove, v. move; to banish. Ilipat; alisin; tanggalin.
rend, v. tear apart violently. Punitin; wasakin.
render, v. afford for use or benefit. Gawin; ibigay; isagawa.
rendezvous, n. meeting place. Tagpuan.
renew, v. to make new; to re-

peat. Baguhin; sariwain; ulitin; magpanibagong simula.

renounce, **v.** reject; give up. Itanggi; itakwil; itatuwa.

renovate, **v.** to make new or as if new again. Baguhin; ayusin; gawing bago; kumpunihin.

renowned, **adj.** famous; well-known. Kilalang-kilala; tanyag; bantog.

rent, **v.** to pay for the use of property. Alkilahin; upahan.

renunciation, **n.** rejection. Pagtatakwil; pagtatatuwa; pagkakaila.

repair, **n.** the act of restoring to good condition. Kumpuni; pagkumpuni.

repair, **v.** to fix; make amends for. Kumpunihin.

reparation, **n.** restoration; restitution. Pagbabayad sa nagawang pagkakasala; bayad-pinsala; reparasyon.

repartee, **n.** a witty reply. Mabirong sagot; pakli.

repay, **v.** to pay back. Bayaran; gantihan; magbigay ng gantimpala.

repeat, **v.** do or say again. Ulitin; gawin o sabihing muli.

repel, **v.** drive back; resist. Paurungin; hadlangan; pigilin.

repent, **v.** regret; feel sorry. Magtika; magsisi.

repentance, **n.** sorrow for sin. Pagtitika; pagsisisi.

repentant, **adj.** repenting; expressing repentance. Nagsisisi; nagtitika.

repercussion, **n.** the reaction to, or result of, an action. Bunga ng pangyayari; alingawngaw; ganti.

repetition, **n.** the act or result of repeating. Repetisiyon; pag-uulit.

replace, **v.** to fill or take the place of. Halinhan; palitan.

replete, **adj.** completely filled. Punong-puno; sagana.

reply, **n.** response, answer. Tugon; sagot.

reply, **v.** say in answer; respond. Sumagot; sagutin; tumugon.

report, **n.** a statement of facts or figures ascertained by investigation. Report; notisiya; ulat; balita.

report, **v.** give an account of. Mag-ulat; iulat; ibalita; sabihin.

reporter, **n.** a person who gathers news for a newspaper. Reporter; mamamahayag.

repose, **v.** be at rest; be tranquil. Magpahinga; magtiwala.

repository, **n.** place of deposit; a place where things are situated or stored. Repositoryo; tinggalan; imbakan.

represent, **v.** to act for; describe. Katawanin; ipakilala; ilarawan.

representation, **n.** the act of representing. Pagkatawan.

representative, **n.** one authorized to act for another or others. Kinatawan; representante.

reprieve, **n.** a respite. Pansamantalang pagtigil ng sakit; pagpigil sa isang parusa; pagliliban.

reprimand, **v.** to chide; reprove severely. Pagsabihan; pagbalaan; kagalitan.

reprint, **v.** to print again. Muling limbagin.

reprobation, **n.** condemnation. Ang kalagayan ng mga di-nakikiisa sa Diyos.

repugnant, **adj.** highly distasteful Nakasusuklam; nakapopoot.

repulsive, adj. repelling; offensive. Nakapandidiri; nakaiinis.

reputable, adj. of good repute; respectable. Kagalang-galang.

reputation, n. good name; fame. Karangalan; puri; dangal; mabuting pangalan.

request, n. a petition; demand. Kahilingan; petisiyon; pakiusap.

request, v. to ask; express desire for. Humiling; makiusap.

requiem, n. hymn for dead. Misa para sa mga patay.

require, v. to demand; ask or claim, as by right. Humingi; humiling; ipagawa nang sapilitan.

requisite, adj. necessary; indispensable. Kailangan; nesesaryo.

rescue, v. to free from evil or danger. Iligtas; palayain; sagipin.

research, n. inquiry; study or investigation of facts. Pananaliksik; pagsisiyasat.

research, v. to investigate carefully. Manaliksik; magsiyasat;

resemblance, n. a likeness; a similarity in appearance. Pagkakatulad; pagkakamukhâ; makahawig; makamukhà.

resent, v. consider to be an injury or an affront. Ikagalit; tutulan.

resentment, n. the feeling of indignation. Poot; pagdaramdam; hinanakit.

reservation, n. something reserved; a withholding. Reserbasyón; paglalaan; pagpipigil.

reserve, v. retain or set apart for future or special use. Ireserba; itago; ilaan; itaan.

reserved, adj. reticent; self-restrained. Mahinahon; matimpi.

reservoir, n. a supply stored for future use; a place of storage. Imbakan; deposito.

reside, v. to live; to dwell in. Tumira; manirahan.

residence, n. a place of abode; a dwelling. Tirahan; tahanan.

resident, n. one who dwells in a certain place. Ang taong naninirahan; nananahanan.

residential, adj. fitted for homes or residences. Pamahayan.

residue, n. that which is left over; remainder. Latak; tira.

resign, v. to give up. Magbitiw sa gawain o tungkulin; magdimite.

resignation, n. a giving up. Resignasyon; pagbibitiw sa tungkulin.

resist, v. to oppose; act against. Lumaban; tumanggi; pigilan.

resoluble, adj. capable of being melted or dissolved. Natutunaw; maaaring tunawin.

resolute, adj. firm; steady. Nakahanda; buo sa loob.

resolution. n. determination; firmness. Resolusyon; kapasiyahan.

resolve, v. to determine; decide. Pagpasyahan; ipasiya.

resonance, n. an echoing. Taginting; tunog; alingawngaw.

resonant, adj. resounding. Mataginting; matunog; maalingawngaw.

resort, n. a place frequented by the general public. Kublihan; bakasyunan; pook na malimit pagbakasyunan.

resource, n. any source of aid or support. Pinagkukunan; takbuhan; paraan; kakayahan.

resourceful, adj. clever in finding and utilizing resources. Marunong; mapamaraan; maraming mapagkukunan.

respect, n. high esteem. Pagpipitagan; paggalang.

respect, v. treat with special consideration or high regard. Pagpitaganan; irespeto; igalang; gumalang.

respectable, adj. worthy of esteem; highly regarded. Kagalang-galang.

respectively, adv. as regards each one in the order mentioned. Alinsunod sa pagkakasunod-sunod.

respiration, n. breathing. Paghinga; respirasyon.

respirator, n. a device to produce involuntary breathing. Kasangkapang inilalagay sa ilong at bibig para makahinga ang maysakit.

respire. v. breathe. Huminga.

respite. n. delay; an interval of rest or relief; a postponement. Palugit; pagtigil.

resplendent, adj. brilliant; splendid. Maliwanag; maningning; makinang.

respond. v. to reply. Sumagot; sagutin; tumugon.

responsibility, n. the state of being responsible. Katungkulan; pananagutan

responsory, n. a response; an antiphonary. Ang mga dasal na isinasagot; responsoryo.

rest, n. a state of quiet or peace. Pagpapahinga; pahinga; labî.

rest, v. be tranquil; take repose. Magpahinga; huminto.

restaurant, n. a place to buy and eat a meal. Restauran; karihan.

restitution, n. the act of making amends; restoration. Pagbabayad sa pinsala; bayad-pinsala; restitusyon.

restoration, n. renewal; repair. Pagbabalik; panunumbalik; pagkakauli.

restrain, v. hold back; check. Pigilin.

restrict, v. to limit. Pasubalian; lagyan ng hangganan o wakas.

restricted, adj. limited; kept within limits. Natatakdaan; limitado.

result, n. consequence. Wakas; bunga; kinahinatnan; resulta.

resume, v. to begin again. Ipagpatuloy.

resurrection. n. rising from the death. Pagkabuhay na mag-uli; panunumbalik; resureksiyon.

retail, v. to sell in small quantities; Itingî; ipagbili nang tingian.

retailer, n. a retail merchant or dealer. Magtitingi.

retain, v. to keep; hold. Bimbinin; pigilin; itanim sa isip.

retaliate, v. return like for like, esp. evil for evil. Gumanti; maghiganti.

retch, v. to make efforts to vomit. Dumuwal.

retention, n. custody; the act or result of retaining. Pagpiit; pagpigil; pagpapanatili; retensiyon.

retire, v. to draw back; go to bed. Magpahinga; umurong; magretiro.

retirement, n. state of being retired; privacy; solitude. Pagpapahinga; retiro.

retort, v. to reply quickly or

sharply. Ipakli.

retract, v. to recant; to take back. Bawiin; kuning muli.

retreat, v. the act of withdrawing. Umurong; umatras.

retrieve, v. to recover; regain. Makuhang muli; mabawi.

retrograde, adj. going backward. Paurong; tumbalik.

retrospect, n. view of the past. Paggunita sa nakaraan o sa lumipas.

retrospective, adj. looking back. Tungkol sa panahong lumipas; retrospektibo.

return, n. the act of returning; recurrence; repayment. Pagbabalik; tubo; ganansiya.

return, v. to come back; retort. Bumalik; ibalik; tumugon.

reunion, n. a coming together again. Muling pagtitipontipon.

reveal, n. to make known. Ihayag; ipakita; ibunyag.

revelation, n. act of revealing; a surprise. Pagpapakita; pagbubunyag; paghahayag.

revelry, n. noisy jollity. Pagtitipong maingay at magulo; harana.

revenge, n. retaliation of wrongs. Paghihiganti; bengansa.

revengeful, adj. seeking vengeance. Mapaghiganti; bengatibo.

reverence, n. veneration. Paggalang; reberensiya.

reverend, adj. deserving of respect; title given to the clergy. Kagalang-galang; reberendo.

reverent, adj. submissive. Mapitagan; magalang.

reverse, n. invert; opposite; contrary. Taliwas; baligtad; kontraryo.

reversible, adj. finished on both sides so that either can be used as the right side. Kabilaan.

revert, v. return. Isauli; ibalik; bumalik.

review, n. a going over anything again. Muling pagsusuri; pagbabalik-aral; repaso.

revise, v. make changes or corrections in. Palitan; baguhin.

revision, n. the act or work of revising. Pagwawasto; pagbabago; rebisyon.

revival, n. act of reviving: religious awakening. Muling pagkabuhay; renasimyento.

revive, v. return to life. Buhaying muli; pasiglahing muli.

revoke, v. annul by taking back. Baguhin; bawiin; kuning muli.

revolt, n. an uprising against government or authority. Paghihimagsik; rebolusiyon; paglaban.

revolting, adj. repulsive. Nakaiinis; nakasusuklam.

revolution, n. rebellion. Himagsikan: rebolusiyon.

revolve, v. to turn around; rotate. Uminog; umikot.

revolver, n. a pistol. Pistola; rebolber; baril.

reward, n. a return made for something done. Ganti; gantimpala.

rewrite, v. to write again. Isulat na muli.

rheumatism, n. inflammation of joints and muscles. Rayuma.

rhyme, n. poetry; agreement in the terminal sounds of words or verses. Tugma.

rib, n. one of the series of curved bones enclosing the chest of man and animals. Tadyang.

ribbon, n. a narrow strip of fabric, as silk. Liston; sintas; laso.

rice, n. valuable food grain. Kanin; bigas; palay.

ricefield, n. a field where rice is planted and grown. Palayan.

rich, adj. wealthy; abundantly supplied. Sagana; mayaman.

rid, v. free from anything superflous or objectionable. Paalisin; itaboy; palayasin.

riddle, n. an enigma; a puzzling question. Palaisipan; bugtong.

ride, v. be carried. Sumakay; lumulan.

ridicule, v. to make fun of. Kutyain; uyamin; tuyain; libakin.

rift, v. to burst open; to split. Hatiin; halitin; sirain.

right, adj. fit; proper; true. Tama; kanan; matuwid; wasto.

rigid, adj. stiff; inflexible. Matigas; di-mababali.

rigor, n. strictness; severity. Kahigpitan; kabagsikan.

rim, n. edge; border. Tabingtabi; gilid; labi.

rind, n. bark; husk; thick skin. Balat; banakal.

ring, n. a circle; an ornamental band for the finger. Bilog; singsing; anilyo.

ring, v. sound loudly and clearly. Patunugin.

rinse, v. wash lightly with fresh water. Magbanlaw; banlawan.

riot, n. a mob; violence. Pagkakaingay; gulo; kaguluhan.

rip, v. to tear or cut open or off. Punitin; sirain; lapain.

ripe, adj. ready for harvest. Hinog.

ripen, v. to become or make ripe. Mahinog.

ripple, n. small wave. Munting alon.

rise, n. ascent; emergence; increase. Pag-alsa; pagtaas; pag-akyat.

rise, v. move upward. Tumindig; umalsa; magbangon; tumaas; umakyat.

risk, n. hazard; danger; peril. Panganib; peligro.

risky, adj. dangerous; hazardous. Mapanganib; peligroso.

rite, n. ceremony. Ang seremonya ukol sa relihiyon.

ritual, n. a form or system of rites. Seremonya; ritual.

rival, n. an opponent; one who is in pursuit of the same object or thing. Kalaban; kaaway; kaagaw.

rival, v. stand in competition with. Makipagpaligsahan. makipag-agaw.

river, n. a large stream of water flowing throughout the year. Ilog.

riverside, n. the bank of a river. Tabing-ilog; pangpang.

rivulet, n. a small stream or brook. Munting sapa; batis.

road, n. a public way for passage or travel. Lansangan; karsada; daan.

roam, v. to wander; ramble. Lumaboy; gumala.

roar, n. the strong loud cry of a beast; a loud cry of a person in distress; pain, anger. Sigaw; ungol.

roar, v. make a full, deep sound, as of wind, waves, or a crowd. Sumigaw; umungol.

roast, v. cook before an open fire or in an oven. Litsunin; ihaw.

rob, v. deprive of something by force. Nakawan.

robber, n. a thief; one who robs. Magnanakaw; tulisan.

robe, n. a gown or a long, loose

outer garment, sometimes symbolizing honor or authority. Balabal; kasuotan; damit.

robust, adj. strong; healthy. Malakas; malusog.

rock, n. stone. Bato.

roe, n. fish eggs. Itlog ng isda.

roll, n. something wound into a cylinder. Ikot; talaan; bilot; rolyo.

rolling, adj. revolving; undulating. Pagulong-gulong; bilut-bilot.

Roman Catholic, n. a member of the Christian Church of which the Pope or Bishop of Rome, is the Pontiff. Katolika Romana.

romance, n. a love affair. Pag-ibig; romansa.

romantic, adj. appealing to fancy and imagination. Romantiko.

Rome, n. the capital of Italy Roma; kabisera ng Italya.

roof, n. the external upper covering of a house, building or car. Bubong; bubungan.

room, n. extent of space, great or small. Silid; kuwarto.

roost, v. perch, as a bird. Humapon sa hapunán.

rooster, n. a male domestic fowl. Tandang; tatyaw.

root, n. the part of a plant that grows downward into the soil; a source, origin, or cause, Ugat; pinanggalingan.

rope, n. a thick strong cord made of several strands twisted together. Lubid; kordon.

rosary, n. a string of beads used in counting prayers. Rosaryo; mga butil ng dasalan.

rose, n. a thorny shrub bearing flowers in various colors. Rosas.

roster, n. a list giving eacn person's name and duties. Talaan; listahan.

rostrum, n. platform for public speaking. Plataporma; entablado.

rotten, adj. putrid. Bulok; si ra

rough, adj. rude; harsh; uneven. Magaspang; baku-bako.

round, adj. having the slope, or approximately the shape of a circle. cylinder, or sphere. Bilog; mabilog.

roundabout, adj. indirect. Pasikut-sikot; paligoy-ligoy.

route, n. a course of travel; a way; road. Daan; ruta.

row, n. a series of persons or things in a straight line. Pila; hanay; linya; hilera.

rowdy, adj. disreputable; rough. Magulo; maharót; may magaspang na ugali.

royal, adj. pertaining or related to a king or queen. Marangal; ukol sa hari; makahari.

rub. v. apply pressure and friction over a surface. Haplusin; kuskusin; kiskisin.

rubber, n. elastic stuff. Goma.

rubbish, n. trash; waste materials. Basura; dumi; tira.

ruby, n. a precious stone, red in color. Rubi.

rudder, n. steering gear. Timon.

rude, adj. rough; coarse; harsh. Bastos; magaspang.

rudeness, n. the state or quality of being rude. Kagaspangan; kabastusan.

rug, n. a heavy floor covering. Alpombra.

ruin, n. destruction. Pagkakagiba; pagkasira; guho.

ruin, v. to demolish; to perish. Iguho; sirain.

ruinous, adj. tending to **ruin.** Nakapipinsala; nakasisira.

rule, v. govern; control. Pagharian; maghari; sakupin; guhitan; mamahala.

ruler, n. governor. Tagapamahala; punungbayan; puno; hari.

rummage, v. to search in a disorderly way. Halungkatin.

rumor, n. hearsay; an unconfirmed but widely circulated story. Balitang hindi pa tiyak ang katotohanan; bulung-bulungan; higing; tsismis.

rump, n. the hind part of an animal, Pigi.

run, n. flow; course. Takbo.

run, v. make haste; rush. Tumakbo; takbo.

running, adj. moving swiftly or rapidly. Tumatakbo

rupture, n. a breach of peace. Putok; sira; gahak; gahi.

rupture, v. break; burst. Sirain; gahakin; punitin.

rural, adj. pertaining to the country or country life. Pambukid; ukol sa bukid; rurál.

ruse, n. trick; stratagem. Lalang; patibong; enganyo.

rush, v. move or drive forward with violent haste. Pabilisin; padaliin; ipagtabuyan; magmadali.

rust, n. a coating on metal caused by damp air. Kalawang.

rust, v. to contract or gather rust. Kalawangin.

rustle, n. a low rattle or sound. Alatiit; tunog ng papel na ginagalaw.

rustler, n. a cattle thief. Magnanakaw ng baka o kalabaw.

rusty, adj. covered with rust. Kalawangin; kinakalawang.

ruthless, adj. cruel; pitiless. Walang-awa; malupit; walang habag.

S

sabbath, n. day of rest. Sunday. Ang ikapitong araw ng sanlinggo na iniuukol ng mga Hudyo sa pamamahinga.

saber, n. an arc-edged, curved sword. Matalas at baluktot na ispada; sable.

sabotage, n. the damage done maliciously and usually against an enemy. Sabotahe.

sable, n. & adj. a kind of weasel like mammal yielding dark, glossy fur. **Isang** uri ng munting hayop na may makapal at makintab na balahibo; ang mabalahibong balat ng hayop na ito; maitim.

sack, n. a bag especially a large one. Sako; supot.

sacrament, n. a religious rite. Sakramento; Eukaristiya; banal na panunumpa sa isang tungkulin.

sacred, adj. holy; divine. Banal; natatalaga sa Diyos.

Sacred Heart, n. Divine Heart of Jesus; a symbol of the Divine Love of Jesus to mankind. Banal na Puso.

sacrifice, n. an offering, as to God or a deity. Pagpapakasakit; handog; sakripisyo.

sacrifice, v. to offer to a god. Magpakasakit; magsakripisyo.

sacrilege, n. profanation of something sacred. Paglapastangan sa mga banal na bagay; sakrilehiyo.

sacristan, n. sexton. Sakristan; ang namamahala sa sakristiya.

sacristy, n. vestry-room. Sakristiya; bihisan ng pari bago magmisa.

sad, adj. sorrowful. Malungkot; nakalulunos.
sadden, v. to make sad. Palungkutin.
sadness, n. being sad. Kapighatian; kalungkutan.
safe, adj. secure from harm. Tiwasay; ligtas.
safeguard, n. a defense; a means of security or protection. Pananggalang; tanggulan.
safely, adv. in a safe manner. Ligtas.
safety, n. security. Katiwasayan; kaligtasan.
sage, adj. a wise man. Matalino; marunong; dalubhasà.
sail, n. extent of canvas. Layag.
sail, v. move along in or as in a vessel. Maglayag.
sailor, n. seaman; mariner. **Mandaragat**; marino.
saint, n. holy or sanctified person. Banal; santo; santa.
sake, n. motive; account. Adhika; kapakanan.
salable, adj. marketable. Maaaring mabili; maipagbibili.
salad, n. a dish of uncooked green herbs, fruit and vegetables. Ensalada.
salary, n. wages; compensation for work. Sahod; suweldo.
sale, n. an act of selling; vent. Pinagbilhan; pagbibili; benta.
salient, adj. leaping; bounding; Nangingibabaw; nangunguna.
saline, adj. consisting of salt. Maalat.
saliva, n. a fluid secreted in the mouth. Laway.
sallow, adj. sickly; yellow; pale. Masasaktin; maputla.
salmon, n. a marine and freshwater food fish. Salmon.
salon, n. a large room for receiving or entertaining. Salas; bulwagan.
salt, n. a mineral sodium chloride, found in deposits, and used as a seasoning. Asin.
salt, v. season or preserve with salt. Asnan; lagyan ng asin.
saltpeter, n. a salty, white mineral used in preserving. Salitre.
salty, adj. full of salt. **Maalat.**
salvage, n. reward for saving goods; the property saved from danger of loss. **Mga** bagay na nailigtas pagkatapos ng isang sakuna; **karapatan** sa mga bagay na nailigtas.
salvation, n. redemption. Kaligtasan; salbasyon.
salve, n. a healing ointment. Tapal; panapal; implasto.
salvo, n. a discharge of artillery. Pagpupugay ng **hukbong**-katihan o **hukbong**-dagat.
Samaritan, n. a native or inhabitant of Samaria. Taga-Samaria; Samaritano.
same, adj. identical; alike; similar. Iyon din; katulad; pareho.
sample, n. a representative specimen. Halimbawa; sampol; muwestra.
sanction, n. authorization. Pormal na pagpapatibay.
sanctity, n. saintliness; sacredness. Kabanalan.
sanctuary, n. a holy place. Santuwaryo; bahagi ng simbahang nasasakop o nakukulong ng barandilya.
sand, n. granular particles of decomposed rocks. Buhangin.
sandal, n. sort of slipper strapped to the foot. San-

dalyas.

sandpaper, n. a strong paper with a layer of sand glued on it. Papel de liha

sandwich, n. two slices of bread with some kind of filling between them. Sanwits; amparadados.

sandy, adj. of or like sand. Mabuhangin.

sane, adj. sound in mind. Matinô; maliwanag ang isip.

sanguine, adj. red, hopeful. Pulang tila dugo; maalab; may tiwala sa sarili.

sanitary, adj. hygienic. Malinis; sanitaryo.

sap, n. the fluid that circulates in a plant. Dagta.

sappy, adj. full of sap or vitality. Madagta.

sarcasm, n. keen reproach; bitter irony. Pang-uyam; parunggit.

sardine, n. a small fish allied to the herring, often canned in oil. Sardinas.

satan, n. the devil. Satanas; demonyo.

satin, n. soft shining silk. Sedang makintab at malambot; satin.

satisfaction, n. gratification. Kasiyahan; Satispaksiyon.

saturate, v. to soak fully. Mabasang mabuti; mababad.

satisfy, v. to gratify completely; convince. Masiyahan; mabigyan ng kasiyahan; busugin.

Saturday, n. the 7th day of the week. Sabado.

sauce, n. a condiment, a relish or appetizer. Sawsawan; sarsa.

saucer, n. a shallow dish in which a cup is placed. Sowser; platito.

saucy, adj. insolent; rude. Bastos; may magaspang na ugali.

sausage, n. ground meat, seasoned and enclosed in prepared animal intestine. Langgonisa; soriso.

savage, adj. wild; untamed; an uncivilized person. Mabangis; mailap.

save, v. preserve from danger, injury, or loss. Iligtas; magtipid; mag-ipon; mag-impok.

savings, n. money saved. Ang naimpok.

savior, n. one who saves or rescues. Tagapagligtas.

savory, adj. tasty; agreeable. Malinamnam; malasa; masarap.

saw, n. a cutting tool with a thin blade having teeth. Lagari.

saw, v. cut with; use a saw. Lagariin.

say, v. to state; speak; tell. Sabihin; bigkasin.

saying, n. a proverbial expression. Pagsasalita; kawikaan; kasabihan.

scab. n. crust over a sore. Langib

scabbard, n. a sword-sheath. Suksukan ng ispada; baina.

scaffold, n. a raised, temporary platform for support. Bibitayan; kadalso.

scald. v. to burn with hot liquid. Mapaso; mabanlian.

scale, n. a weighing machine; a measure; one part of the thin layer covering fish and snakes. Timbangan; kaliskis.

scale. v. weigh; deprive of scales. Kaliskisan; timbangin.

scalp, n. the integument of the upper part of the head. Anit.

scaly, adj. covered with, or like scales. Makaliskis.

scan, v. to look at closely; examine with care. Masdang

mabuti.

scandal, n. disgrace; offense; iskandalo; alingasngas.

scandalous, adj. disgraceful. Magulo, maalingasngas.

scanty, adj. small; narrow. Karampot; kaunti; katiting.

scapular, n. a kind of badge, consisting of two small squares of brown stuff, of the same colour as the carmelite habit, connected by two lengths of tape, and worn in honour of the Virgin Mary. Kalmen; eskapularyo.

scar, n. a cicatrix. Peklat; pilat.

scar, v. to mark with a scar; to wound. Sugatan; lagyan ng pilat; pilatan.

scarce, adj. insufficient; not abundant; not plentiful. Bihira; madalang; kakaunti; bahagya.

scarcely, adv. barely. Babahagya pa.

scarcity, n. short supply. Kakulangan; kadahupan; kakapusan.

scare, v. to frighten. Sindakin; takutin; matakot.

scarlet, adj. bright red color. Matingkad na pula; iskarlata.

scat, intj. go away. Supi; suu; pandamdam na pambulas.

scathe, v. to injure; criticize severely. Murahin; saktan· siraan.

scatter, v. to disperse; dispose. Ikalat; isabog.

scavenger, n. public collector of ashes and garbage. Basurero; tagawalis.

scene, n. view; part of a play. Eksena; tanawin; larawan; tagpuan; tagpo.

scenery, n. landscape. Bista; tanawin.

scent, v. smell; perfume. Amuyin; pabanguhin.

scentless, adj. inodorous; destitute of smell. Walang amoy.

scepter, n. a symbol of royal power or authority. Setro.

schedule, n. a statement of contents, details. Skediyul; talaan ng mga gagawin o patutunguhan; itineraryo.

scheme, n. a plan; a design. Balak; plano.

scholar, n. man of learning. Mag-aaral; marunong; pantas; iskolar.

school, n. an educational establishment. Paaralan; iskuwelahan.

schoolroom, n. a room for teaching. Silid-aralan.

schoolmistress, n. female who governs and teaches in a school. Gurong babae; maestra.

science, n. a branch of knowledge. Agham; siyensiya.

scion, n. a descendant. Anak; supling; tagapagmana.

scissors, n. a cutting instrument consisting of two pivoted blades. Gunting.

scold, v. to chide; find fault. Murahin; pagsalitaan; kagalitan.

scope, n. intellectual range; outlook. Sakop ng tingin o kilos.

scorch, v. burn superficially. Pasuin; sunugin.

score, v. to make, record or write an account. Guhitan; tandaan; mag-eskor.

score, n. a record. Eskor, guhitan; talaan.

scorn, v. disdain; reject. Hamakin; uyamin.

scorpion, n. a venomous arachnid. Alakdan; iskorpiyon.

scoundrel, n. a rascal; an unprincipled man. Sanggano; masamang tao.

scour, v. to purge; cleanse of dirt. Kuskusin; gusgusin; linisin.

scourge, v. to whip. Paluin; hampasin; bugbugin.

scout, v. reconnoiter; ridicule. Subukan; matyagan; tiktikan; manmanan.

scowl, n. angry. Simangot.

scowl, v. look gloomy, severe, or angry. Sumimangot.

scramble, v. struggle for possession. Kumilos nang mabilis at magulo; gumapang; iskrambol.

scrape, v. shave the surface of. Kudkurin; kaskasin; kayurin.

scratch, n. a slight mark produced by something sharp. Kalmót; galos; kamot.

scratch, v. mark or wound slightly. Kalmutin; galusan; kamutin.

scrawl, v. to write or draw clumsily. Sumulat nang pakahig; kahigin.

scream, n. loud shrill cry. Tili.

scream, v. utter a sharp, piercing outcry; emit a shrill sound. Tumili.

screen, n. a shelter sieve; sheet upon which moving pictures are thrown. Pansalà; tabing.

screen, v. sift; protect; con ceal. Salain; uriing mabuti; tabingan.

screw, n. a nail-like device having an external thread, that turns in a nut or is driven into wood. Tornilyo.

screwdriver, n. a tool for turning screws. Pamihit ng tornilyo; disturnilyador; iskrudrayber.

scribble, v. to write carelessly or hastily. Sumulat nang padalus-dalos o padaskol.

script, n. handwriting. Sulatkamay.

scribe, n. a public writer; penman. Taga-talâ; eskribiyente; tagasulat.

Scripture, n. the Bible; any sacred writing. Banal na Aklat; Bibliya.

scrub, v. cleanse by rubbing hard. Lampasuhin; kuskusin.

scrutiny, n. examination. Masusing pagmamasid.

sculptor, n. carver of stone. Manlililok; iskultor.

scum, n. thin layer that rises to the top of a liquid. Iskoma; linab.

sea, n. salt water on the earth's surface. Dagat.

seafarer, n. mariner; sailor. Manlalayag; marinero; magdaragat.

seal, v. authenticate, close, or secure, with a seal; close. Tatákan; isara; lagyan ng selyo; ipinid.

seam, n. suture of two edges; the line formed by joining two edges especially in sewing. Tahi; daan ng makina; dugtong.

seamstress, n. woman who earns her living by sewing. Mananahi; modista; kosturera.

search, v. to try to find by looking. Hanapin.

seashore, n. the land along the sea. Baybayin; tabingdagat.

season, n. a period of the year characterized by particular conditions of weather, temperature. Panahon.

seat, n. a place or thing to sit on. Luklukan; upuan; silya.

seaweed, n. a name given generally to any plant growing in the sea but more particularly to members of the order algae. Liya; halamang-tubig.

second, adj. the next after the first order, time or value; the ordinal of two; subordinate. Segundo; pangalawa: ikalawa.

second-class, adj. of or belonging to the class next after the first. Segunda klase; pangalawang-uri.

secret, n. something not revealed. Lihim; sekreto.

secretary, n. a recording or corresponding officer. Kalihim; sekretaryo.

secure, v. free from danger. Patatagin; ikuha; ilagay sa panatag o ligtas na katayuan; ipinid.

sedative, n. medicine that lessens pain or excitement. Gamot na pampakalma.

seduce, v. entice to evil. Himukin sa masama; rahuyuin.

see, v. perceive by the eye. Makakita; maunawaan; alamin; tingnan.

seed, n. the fertilized and natural ovule of a plant. Semilya; binhi; buto.

seek, v. go in search or quest of. Sikaping matamo; magsikap; hanapin.

seem, v. to appear to be. Magmukha; mag-anyo.

seize, v. take legal or forcible possesion of. Sunggaban; samsamin; Bihira.

select, v. to choose. Piliin; humirang.

self, n. one's own. Sarili.

selfish, adj. ungenerous. Sakim; makasarili; maramot.

sell, v. transfer to another for money; engage in selling. Magbili; ipagbili; itinda.

seller, n. one who sells. Tagapagtinda; tindera.

semblance, n. likeness. Pagkakawangis; pagkakawangki.

semicolon, n. a mark of punctuation (;) which separates major sentence elements more distinctly than the commas. Tuldukuwit.

seminar, n. a meeting on orientation of objectives. Seminar; miting; pag-aaral; pulong.

seminary, n. a school for the ministry or for young women. Seminaryo.

semivowel, n. a half vowel; a sound partaking of the nature of both a vowel and a consonant. Malapatinig.

senate, n. a legislative assembly, a body of senators. Mataas na kapulungan; senado.

senator, n. member of a senate. Senador; mambabatas.

send, v. cause to go; dispatch. Ipadala; magpadala.

senile, adj. pertaining to or characterizing old age. Matanda; mahina; ulyanin.

senior, adj. older. Nakatatanda.

sensation, n. excited feeling. Pandama; pakiramdam; kagulat-gulat.

sense, n. intellect; meaning. Pandama; diwa; kahulugan; pag-iisip; sentido.

sensible, adj. wise; reasonable. Matalino; may katwiran.

sensitive, adj. easily affected. Maramdamin.

sensuality, n. unrestrained self-gratification. Kamunduhan.

sentence, n. judgment; a group of words constituting a complete statement. Hatol; pangungusap; parusa.

sentence, v. to doom to punishment. Parusahan; hatulan.

sentiment, n. a mixture of

thought and feeling. Damdamin.

sentinel, n. soldier on guard. Bantay.

separate, adj. divided; apart. Di-magkakabit; hiwalay.

separate, v. to divide; disjoin. Ihiwalay; ibukod.

separation, n. a place, line or point of parting. Paghihiwalay; separasyon.

septic, adj. causing infection. Nakakahawa.

seraph, n. an angel of high order. Anghel na kinakatawan ng ulo ng batang may pakpak.

serene, adj. calm; placid. Payapa; tahimik; mahinahon.

series, n. things alike in a row. Serye; hanay; hilera.

sermon, n. religious discourse. Sermon; pangaral.

serve, v. attend or wait upon; work for; aid. Magsilbi; chain; maglingkod; paglingkuran.

service, n. office; duty. Paglilingkod; serbisyo.

serviceable, adj. useful. Maaaring maglingkod; mapaglingkod; magagamit; mahalaga.

service, adj. slavish; mean. Mapangayupapà; aba.

session, n. meeting. Pulong; pagtitipon ng mga kasapi ng isang kapisanan.

set, v. put in a certain place or position; fix; adjust. Itama; magtakda; iayos; ihanda; ilagay.

setback, n. a check to progress. Hadlang; balakid; sagabal.

settle, v. fix in position or condition; establish. Iayos; ilagay sa tiyak na lunan; ayusin; lutasin; manirahan.

seven, adj. & n. the cardinal number between 6 and 8. Pito; Siyete.

Seven Dolors, n. Seven Sorrows of Our Lady. Pitong sakit; Siyete Dolores.

seventeen, adj. & n. the cardinal number seven plus ten. Labimpito; disesiyete.

seventy, adj. & n. the cardinal number seven times ten. Pitumpu; sitenta.

sever, v. to divide; to disjoin. Putulin; sirain; ihiwalay.

several, adj. diverse, being more than two or three, but not many. Ilan; iba-iba.

severe, adj. serious or earnest; harsh; harshly extreme. Mahigpit; malubhà; mabigat; mabalasik.

severity, n. harshness. Balasik; bagsik; kabalasikan.

sew, v. to join by stitches. Manulsi; manahi; itahi.

sewage, n. the waste matter that passes through sewers. Dumi sa imburnal.

sex, n. the anatomical and physiological distinction between male and female. Kasarian.

sexton, n. officer of a church; minor official. Sakristan.

shabby, adj. much worn. Gamit na gamit na.

shack, n. a roughly built hut. Kubo; dampa.

shadow, n. a reflected image. Kadiliman; anino.

shady, adj. out of sunlight. Malilim.

shake, v. to move violently; cause to vibrate or tremble. Ugain; alugin; yugyugin.

shallow, adj. not deep; superficial. Mababaw.

sham, adj. trickery; counterfeit; pretended. Huwad; ditunay; kunwari.

shame, n. consciousness of guilt; disgrace or dishonor. Kahihiyan; hiya.

shame, v. make ashamed; disgrace. Mahiyâ; hiyain.
shameful, adj. disgraceful. Kahiya-hiya; nakahihiya.
shameless, adj. overbold; conscicnceless. Walang hiya.
shamelessly, adv. impudently. Buong kawalang-hiyaan.
shampoo, n. a preparation used for cleaning the hair. Siyampu; gugo.
shape, n. form; outward contour. Kalagayan; porma; anyo; hubog; hugis.
shape, v. to adjust; take form. Hubugin; lagyan ng hugis.
share, n. portion; an alloted part. Bahagì; kahati; kaparti.
share, v. partake; give a portion to others. Partihan; ipamahagi; hatiin; humati.
shark, n. a large and ferocious marine fish. Pating.
sharp, adj. having a fine cutting edge or point. Matalas; matalim; maaskad.
sharpen, v. make or become sharp. Tasahán; patalasin; ihasa.
sharpness, n. keenness of edge or point; pungency. Kataliman; katalasan; kaaskaran.
shatter, v. break into piece. Sirain; iwasak; iguho; durugin.
shawl, n. a loose covering for the shoulders. Balabal; alampay.
she, pron., the third person, singular form, nominative. Siya.
shears, n. large scissors. Malaking gunting.
sheath, n. a scabbard; a case. Kaluban; baina; suksukan ng ispada o itak.
shed, n. a rude structure for shelter or storage. Habong; silungan.
shed, v. throw off, molt, or cause to flow off. Tumulo; ibuhos; alisin.
sheen, n. brightness; splendor. Ningning; kintab; kinang.
sheepish, adj. bashful. Mahiyaing labis; kimi.
sheer, adj. very thin. Napakanipis.
sheet, n. thin bed cover; a broad flat, very thin piece of anything. Sapin (sa kama, atb.); pilyego ng papel; piraso.
shelf, n. a horizontal plank for supporting objects. Pitak ng aparador; istante.
shell, n. a hard outer case of covering. Tabiki; matigas na balat ng bungangkahoy; kartutso.
sew, v. to join by stitches.
shelter, n. a roofed place; a place for refuge or safety. Silungan; tanggulan; **kanlungan**; tirahan.
shepherd, n. a sheep herder; a pastor. Tagapag-alaga ng tupa; pastol.
sherbet, n. frozen fruit-flavored mixture containing milk. Sorbetes.
sherry, n. amber-colored wine of southern Spain. Alak ng Jerez.
shield, n. a broad plate of defensive armor. Kalasag; panalag; pananggol.
shield, v. protect; screen. Ipagsanggalang; ipagtanggol; salagin.
shift, n. a change; a turning. Paglipat; pagpapalit..
shift, v. to change. Pagpapalit; lumipat; magbago.
shimmer, n. a tremulous gleam or glistening. **Liwanag** na aandap-andap; **kisap**.
shimmer, v. to glisten. **Kumislap**; umandap-andap.
shin, n. leg below the **knee**.

Harapan ng binti; lulod.

shine, v. to cause to gleam. Magliwanag; sumikat; magningning.

shining, adj. gleaming; radiant; bright. Marikit; makinang; maningning.

ship, n. a large vessel, usually seagoing. Bapor; sasakyangdagat.

shipment, n. a quantity of goods shipped. Kargamento; kargada ng bapor.

shipwreck, n. destruction or loss of a ship. Pagkawasak ng bapor.

shiver, n. shake from cold or fear. Pangangatog; panginginig.

shock, n. sudden agitation; a violent collision. Pagyanig; putok; banggaan; pagkabangga; pagkabigla.

shock, v. affect with a shock; surprise; outrage; horrify. Matakot; alugin; banggain; biglain.

shocking, adj. causing great surprise or horror. Nakapangingilabot.

shoe, n. a covering for the human foot. Sapatos.

shoemaker, n. one who makes or repairs shoes. Sapatero; manggagawa ng sapatos.

shoot, v. to discharge a gun; hit, wound, or kill with a missile from a weapon. Patamaan; barilin.

shooting star, n. a meteor. Bulalakaw.

shop. n. a store; workroom; factory. Talyer; gawaan; tindahan.

shopkeeper, n. a tradesman. Tindero; tindera; may-ari ng tindahan o pagawaan.

shore, n. coast. Pampang; tabing-dagat; baybay-dagat; aplaya.

short, adj. not long; brief; concise. Maigsi; maliit; kulang; maikli.

shortage, n. lack; too small an amount. Kakulangan; kakapusan.

shortcoming, n. failing. Pagkukulang; kapintasan.

shorten, v. to contract; make shorter. Iklian; paikliin.

shorthand, n. a system of taking notes; stenography. Iklilat; takigrapiya; esteno.

shortly, adv. soon; in a short or brief time or manner. Di-malalaunan; sa loob ng madaling panahon.

shorts, n. loose trousers worn by men in sports. Korto; putot.

shoulder, n. joint which connects the arm to the body. Balikat.

shout, n. vehement outcry. Sigaw.

shout, v. to cry out; laugh noisily. Sumigaw.

shove, v. to push. Itulak.

shovel, n. a long-handed implement with a broad scoop. Pala.

show, n. a theatrical performance. Pagtatanghal; palabas.

show, v. allow to be seen; exhibit; indicate. Magpalabas; ipakita; ituro.

shower, n. light rainfall; bestowal of gift. Ambon; siyawer.

shower, v. wet copiously; rain a little. Paulanán; umambon; ibuhos.

shred, n. a fragment; a particle. Gutay; piraso; bahagi; pilas.

shrew, n. a bad tempered, quarrelsome woman. Palaaway na babae.

shrewd, adj. cunning; sensible; astute. Tuso.

shriek, v. to cry in anguish.

Tumili.

shrimp, n. an edible, long-tailed crustacean. Hipon.

shrine, n. a sacred place. Banal na lugar.

shrink, v. to contract; diminish. Umikli; umurong.

shrivel, v. draw in wrinkles. Matuyô; malanta; mangulubot.

shroud, v. cover. Ikubli; lambungan; takpan; balutin ang patay na ililibing.

shrub, n. a bush. Palumpóng; munting halamang may matigas na puno.

shrug, v. drawn up shoulders. Magkibit ng balikat.

shudder, v. to quake; tremble. Mangatog; manginig.

shuffle, v. mix; move with scraping feet. Balasahin ang baraha; isalisod ang paa.

shun, v. to avoid; refrain from. Layuan; iwasan.

shut, v. close; bring together. Sarhan; ipinid; magsara.

shy, v. start back in fear. Tumabi; umiwas.

sick, adj. ill; not well. Maysakit.

sickening, adj. causing nausea or disgust. Nakasusuka; nakasusuklam.

sickness, n. disease; illness. Karamdaman; sakit.

side, n. a terminal surface or line. Gilid; tabi; tagiliran.

side altar, n. altar situated at the side. Altar sa tabi.

sidewalk, n. place to walk at the side of a street. Bangketa.

sideways, adv. laterally. Patabi; patagilid.

siege, n. a prolonged surrounding of a place by an enemy. Bangkulong; kubkob.

sieve, n. vessel for sifting. Bistay; salaan.

sift, v. to separate large pieces from small by shaking in a sieve. Bistayin; salain.

sigh, n. a single deep involuntary respiration. Buntunghininga.

sight, n. sense of seeing. Pangmasid; paningin; bista.

sight, v. get sight of. Tingnán; matanaw; makita.

sightless, adj. blind. Bulag.

sign, n. a mark or symbol. Senyas; karatula; bakas; tanda; pananda.

sign, v. write one's signature. Lumagda.

signal, n. a sign carrying a message often in code. Hudyat; palatandaan.

signature, n. a name signed. Lagda; pirma.

signboard, n. a board having a notice. Karatula.

significance, n. the real or implied meaning. Halaga; kahulugan.

signify, v. mean; suggest. Maging tanda; mangahulugan; ipahalata; ipamalas.

silence, n. absence of sound or noise. Katahimikan.

silent, adj. perfectly quiet. Tahimik.

silk, n. a fine, soft fiber, produced by the silkworm. Sutla; seda.

silver, n. a precious metallic chemical element, no. 47, symbol, Ag. Pilak; plata.

silver, v. to cover superficially with a coat of silver; to give a silvery sheen or silver-like luster to. Ilubog sa pilak; gawing tila pilak.

silverware, n. table utensils. Kubyertos.

similar, adj. resembling. Katulad; kahawig.

simple, adj. plain; not elaborate. Magaan; simple; payak.

simultaneous, adj. exsisting,

done, or happening at the same time. Sabay-sabay.

sin, n. a transgression of the law of God; a serious fault. Kasalanan; sala.

sin, v. commit a sin. Magkasala.

since, adv. subsequently; from then till now. Sapul pa; simula; mula; buhat.

sincere, adj. free from pretense or deceit. Matapat; taos-puso.

sincerity, n. freedom from pretense or deceit. Katapatan.

sing, v. utter musical sounds. Umawit; kumanta.

singer, n. one who sings; a skilled or professional vocalist. Manganganta; mang-aawit.

single, adj. one individual; pertaining to one person or thing. Solo; pang-isahan; nag-iisa.

single, v. select individually. Itangi; piliin.

singly, adv. separately; individually. Isa-isa.

singular, adj. unusual; eccentric. Pambihira; kaiba; di-pangkaraniwan.

sink, v. to penetrate; submerge. Ibaba; ilubog.

sip, v. to drink little by little. Higupin; sipsipin.

sir, n. a respectful term of address to a man. Senyor; ginoo.

sister, n. a female relative having the same parents as another. Kapatid na babae.

sister of charity, n. a sister working for charitable purposes. Madre ng kawanggawa.

sit, v. be seated. Maupo; umupo; limliman.

situation, n. a position. Tayo; lagay; puwesto.

six, adj. & n. the cardinal number between five and seven. Anim.

sixth, adj. one of six equal parts. Ikaanim; pang-anim.

size, n. volume; extent; a standard measure for clothes, etc. Saklaw; dami; laki.

sizzling, v. to make a hissing sound as when fat is frying or burning. Sumagitsit.

skeptical, adj. doubting; incredulous. Mapag-alinlangan.

sketch, v. delineate or describe roughly. Ilarawan; iguhit.

skilled, adj. knowing; proficient. Bihasa; sanay.

skim, v. lift or scrape off the top of (a liquid). Bawasan; alisan ng kulo; hapawin.

skin, n. the outer covering of the body. Balat; upak.

skin, v. remove the skin from; peel. Balatan; alisan ng balat.

skip, v. jump lightly; bounce; pass over something. Laktawan; lumukso; talikdan; kumandirit.

skirt, n. a garment or part of it hanging down from the waist. Palda; saya.

skull, n. the cranium. Bao ng ulo; bungo.

sky, n. the surrounding space as seen from the earth. Himpapawid; langit.

slack, adj. lax; loose. Mabagal; mahina; maluwag; pabaya.

slacken, v. to relax; to loosen. Bumagal; bawahan; luwagan; ipagpaliban.

slander, n. aspersion; defamation by utterance. Paninirang-puri.

slang, n. words, phrases, etc. not accepted as good language usage. Pabalbal na salita.

slate, n. a fine-grained rock, easily split; a plate of this rock as for writing upon. Pisara.

slaughter, **v.** to kill. Katayin; patayin.

slave, n. a person who is the property of another. Busabos; alipin.

sleep, n. the natural state of bodily rest, marked by suspension of consciousness. Tulog; pagtulog.

sleep, v. go to sleep. Matulog.

sleepless, adj. wakeful; having no rest; without sleep. Walang tulog.

sleeve, n. the part of a garment that covers the arm. Manggas.

sleight, n. an artful feat, esp. of conjuring. Kasanayan; katusuhan.

slender, **adj.** thin; small; slight. Balingkinitan; payat; maliit.

slice, n. a thin bread piece. Hiwa; putol.

slice, v. to cut into thin pieces. Hiwain; putulin.

slide, n. an act of sliding. Dulas; pagdulas; paragos na ginagamit sa pagpapadulas.

slide. **v.** to slip over. Magpadausdos; magpadulas; dumulas.

slight, v. disdain; ignore. Hamakin; di-pansinin; pawalang-halaga.

slim, adj. slender; thin. Balingkinitan; maliit; payat.

slime, n. a glutinous substance. Putik na malagkit; burak; lansa.

slimy, **adj.** covered with slime. Malagkit; maburak; malansa.

slip, n. an act of slipping. Pagdulas; paglaktaw.

slip, n. chemise. Kamison.

slipper, n. a thin, low shoe. Tsinelas.

slippery, adj. glib; smooth. Madulas.

slit, n. a long, narrow, straight cut. Hiwa; biyak; laslas.

slit, v. make a long narrow cut in. Hiwain; biyakin; laslasin.

slogan, n. a word or phrase used like a war cry by any party, class or business. Salawikain; pamansag.

sloppy, adj. not neat. Burara; hindi maingat.

sloth, n. laziness; indolence. Katamaran.

slovenly, adj. negligent of personal neatness. Salaula; pabaya; marusing; marumi.

slow, adj. late; dull. Makupad; marahan; mabagal.

slumber, **v.** to sleep lightly. Umidlip; matulog.

sly, adj. cunning; shrewd. Pilyo; tuso.

small, adj. little; petty. Maliit; munti.

smallpox, n. an acute contagious disease often leaving pockmarks on its survivors. Bulutong.

smart, adj. clever; keen; neat; fashionable; groomed. Matalino; makirot; makisig.

smash, v. break into pieces. Wasakin; durugin; basagin.

smear, v. to blot; to stain. Dumhan; dungisan; bahiran.

smear, n. stain; a blot or blotch. Dumi; dungis; mantsa.

smell, n. odor; scent; aroma. Amoy.

smell, v. perceive thru the nose; inhale the odor of. Langhapin; amuyin.

smelt, v. to melt or fuse. Tunawin.

smile, v. assume or express by a smile. Ngumiti.

smoke, **n.** the visible vapor given off by a burning

substance. Asó; usok.
smoke, v. to give off or emit smoke. Humitit; pausukan; manigarilyo o manabako.
smooth, adj. even; glossy. Makinis; pantay; pulido; pino.
smooth, v. make smooth, calm; mollify. Pakinisin; payapain.
smother, v. suffocate. Sagkaan ang paghinga; inisin.
smudge, v. stain; blacken. Sigan; pausukan.
smuggle, v. import in fraud; transport (goods) secretly, esp. to avoid payment of duties. Ipasok nang labag sa batas; ismagel.
snail, n. a mollusk with a spiral shell. Suso; kuhol.
snake, n. any of an order of reptiles with elongated, tubular, limbless bodies; serpent. Ulupong; ahas.
snap, v. to bite at; break suddenly. Sakmalin; wasakin; patunugin ang mga daliri; mabilis na kunan ng larawan.
snare, v. catch; entangle. Umangan; siluin; hulihin sa pamamagitan ng patibong.
snarl, v. to growl sharply and show one's teeth. Angilan; umungol.
snatch, v. to grab hastily. Hablutin; agawin; daklutin.
sneeze, n. emission of air thru the nose and mouth. Bahin; pagbabahin.
sneeze, v. make a sneeze. Bumahin; magbahin.
sniff, v. draw in air audibly. Suminghot.
snip, v. to clip; cut off with one light stroke. Gupitin.
snob, n. one who unduly esteems social position. Taong mapangmata, taong mapagmataas.
snore, n. a noisy breathing in sleep. Paghihilik; hilik.
snout, n. nose of a beast. Nguso.
snow, n. flakes of water crystal. Niyebe; yelo.
snow-white, adj. white as snow; very white. Simputi ng yelo.
snowy, adj. abounding with snow; covered with snow. Maniyebe; mayelo.
snub, n. a check; a rebuke. Paghamak; pagmata.
snub, v. to slight designly. Pagmalakhan; hamakin; matahin.
snub-nosed, adj. turned up at the tip. Sarat; pango.
snuff, n. pulverized tobacco; sniff; that part of a candle wick which has been charred by the flame. Tulo ng kandila; mitsa; pulbos ng tabako.
snuff, v. extinguish, as a candle; to smell. Langhapin; amuyin; singhutin; hipan.
snug, adj. comfortable; cozy. Maginhawa; nasa kasiya-siyang kalagayan.
so, adv. in that way; in the same way. Paganyan; totoo; talaga.
soak, v. to saturate thoroughly; to be permeated by a liquid. Basaing mabuti; ibabad.
soap, n. a substance used for cleansing. Sabon.
soap, v. cover or treat with soap. Sabunin.
soapy, adj. containing soap; flattering. Masabon; mabula.
soar, v. to fly aloft. Pumailanglang; tumaas; lumipad nang pataas.
sob, n. a convulsive catching of the breath in weeping. Hibik; hikbi.

sob, v. to weep convulsively. Humikbi.

sober, adj. temperate; serious; sedate. Mahinahon; matino; di-nagbibiro.

sobriety, n. temperance. Kahinahunan; katinuan.

social, adj. companionable. Sosyal; panlipunan; mahilig sa lipunan.

society, n. fellowship; an association; companionship. Sosyiedad; samahan; lipunan; kapisanan.

sock, n. a short stocking. Kalsetin; medyas na maikli.

sod, n. the upper layer of grassy land. Kipil ng lupang may damo.

soft, adj. mild; delicate, melodious, etc. Malambot; malata; malamlam; mahinay.

softball, n. a game of ball. Sopbol.

soften, v. make or become softer. Palambutin; palatain.

softness, n. mildness; gentleness. Kalambutan; kahinayán.

soil, n. the portion of the earth's surface in which plants grow. Lupa.

soil, v. stain; defile; make dirty or foul. Batikan; dumhan, dungisan.

sojourn, v. to stay for a time. Tumigil na pansamantala.

soldier, n. a warrior. Sundalo; kawal.

sole, adj. single; only. Itangi; nag-iisa.

solemn, adj. sober in manner or aspect; gravely impressive. Magalang; kapitapitagan; pormal; taimtim; dakila.

solicit, v. to importune; seek to obtain; request. Maghanap; mangilak; hingin; hilingin.

solid, adj. compact; undivided. Matatag; nagkakaisa; buo.

solidify, v. make or become solid. Buuin; mamuo.

solitary, n. living alone. Taong nag-iisa; ermitanyo.

soluble, adj. that can be desolved. Maaaring matunaw.

solution, n. an explanation or answer. Solusyon; paraan ng paglutas; kalutasan.

solve, v. to clear up. Lutasin; sagutin.

sombre, adj. dark; gloomy. Madilim; malungkot.

some, adj. more or less; certain. Kaunti; ilan; mangilan-ngilan.

somehow, adv. in some way; in an unspecified way. Sa paano mang paraan; paano't paano man; kahit paano.

somersault, n. the act of turning heads over head. Sirko; pagbaligtad.

something, n. an unspecified thing; a portion. Isang bagay; ano man.

sometimes, adv. at some indefinite time. Kung minsan; paminsan-minsan.

somewhere, adv. in at, or to some unspecified place. Saan man.

son, n. a male child. Anak na lalaki.

song, n. a short poem set to music. Awit; kanta.

son-in-law, n. the husband of one's daughter. Manugang na lalaki.

sonorous, adj. full and rich in sound. Mataginting; matunog.

soon, adv. in a short time; early; before long. Sa lalong madaling panahon; agad; madali; di-nalaunan.

soot, n. condensed smoke. Agiw.

soothe, v. to calm; allay. Payapain, aliwin.

sorcerer, n. a conjurer. Mangkukulam.

sorcery, n. enchantment; magic; witchcraft. Panggagaway; kulam; pangungulam.

sordid, adj. vile; base; gross. Marumi; imbi; nakaririmarim; nakasusuklam; nakayayamot.

sore, adj. painful. Makirot; masakit.

soreness, n. painfulness. Pangingirot; pananakit.

sorrow, n. grief; sadness. Dalamhati; sakit; kalungkutan.

sorry, adj. grieved; sorrowful. Nagdaramdam; nalulungkot.

soul, n. the spiritual part of a man. Kaluluwa.

sound, n. anything audible. Ingay; tunog; ugong.

sound, adj. in good condition; healthy; reliable. Malusog; walang pinsala; matino.

soup, n. strong broth. Sabaw; sopas.

sour, adj. acid; tart. Maasim.

source, n. the place from which anything comes or is obtained. Pinagmumulan; pinagkukunan.

south, n. the point of the compass opposite the north. Timog.

sow, n. a female hog. Inahing baboy.

sow, v. to scatter as seed. Itanim; ikalat; ihasik.

space, n. enough room; extension. Patlang; pagitan; puwang; lunang walang laman.

spacious, adj. roomy; wide. Maluwang; malawak.

spade, n. small shovel. Ispada; pala.

span; n. hand's breadth; a space of time. Agwat; dangkal; iglap; maikling panahon.

spank, n. a slap. Sampal; hampas; palo sa puwit.

spank, v. slap with open hands. Sampalin; hampasin; paluin sa puwit.

spare, v. to forgive; show mercy. Patawarin; kaawaan.

spark, n. a particle of fire. Kislap; alipato.

spark, v. produce or issue as sparks. Kumislap; kumisap.

sparkle, v. to send out little spark. Pumilansik; kuminang.

sparse, adj. thinly scattered; scanty. Madalang; kaunti; bahagya.

speak, v. utter words; talk. Magsalita; sabihin.

speaker, n. one who speaks; an orator. Mananalumpati; ang taong nagsasalita.

spear, n. long pointed weapon. Sibat.

special, adj. particular; distinctive. Espesyal; di-karaniwan; tangi.

specially, adv. particularly. Lalo na.

specific, adj. definite. Tiyak; partikular.

speckle, n. a mark of small spots. Mantsa; bahid.

spectacles, n. eyeglasses. Salamin sa mata.

spectator, n. a looker on. Manonood; tagamasid.

spectre, n. an apparition. Multo.

speculate, v. make a risky investment. Makipagsapalaran.

speech, n. the act of speaking; a public talk. Pagsasalita; talumpati.

speechless, adj. unable to speak. Di-makapagsalita; dimakapangusap.

speed, n. rapidity of motion or performance. Katulinan; bilis; kabilisan.

speedy, adj. quick; swift; rapid. Matulin; mabilis.

spelling, n. the act of one who spells; orthography. pagbaybay.

spend, v. to expend; to pay or give out (money, etc.). Gumugol; gumasta.

spendthrift, n. a prodigal. Gastador; bulagsak; walang taros gumasta.

sphere, n. globe; orb; circuit. Globo; mundo; bilog.

spice, n. a seasoning; something that adds flavor or interest. Pampalasa; pampagana.

spider, n. an eight-legged arachnid esp. one that spins a web. Gagamba.

spider's web, n. habitation of a spider. Bahay ng gagamba; sapot ng gagamba.

spill, v. cause or allow to run or fall out. Itapon; iligwak.

spin, v. draw out and twist into threads, as wool, etc. Magsinulid.

spine, n. the backbone. Tinik; gulugod.

spinster, n. unmarried woman. Matandang dalaga.

spiny, adj. thorny; Matinik.

spiral, adj. winding like a screw. Paikid; pilipit.

spirit, n. the soul. Espiritu; diwa; kaluluwa.

spit, v. eject saliva from the mouth. Dumura.

spiteful, adj. malicious. Mapaghiganti.

splash, n. the act or sound of splashing. Pagsaboy ng tubig; kalabog sa tubig

splash, v. spatter, as with water or mud. Sabuyan ng tubig; kumalabog sa tubig.

splendid, adj. magnificent. Kahanga-hanga; mahusay; kapuri-puri.

splendour, n. magnificence. Dingal; ningning.

splint, n. a thin piece of wood, etc. used to immobilize a fractured bone. Balangkat; lapat.

splinter, n. a thin sharp piece of wood. Salubsob; subyang.

split, n. a crack; a division. Biyak; hiwa; hati.

split, v. divide; disunite. Tilarin; biyakin; hiwain; hatiin.

spoils, n. plunder; booty. Ang mga sinamsam; ang mga bagay na naiilit sa mga kaaway.

spokesman, n. one who speaks for others. Espoksman; tagapagsalita.

sponsor, n. a godfather or godmother. Esponsor; ninong o ninang.

spontaneous, adj. voluntary instinctive. Kusa at bigla.

spoon, n. a utensil consisting of a concave bowl and a handle. Kutsara.

sport, n. diversion. Palakasan; libangan; laro.

spot, n. a stain; a blemish; place. Batik; dungis; pook o lunan.

spotless, adj. free from stain or impurity. Malinis; walang bahid-dungis.

spouse, n. husband or wife. Asawa; kabyak ng puso.

sprain, n. a violent straining of muscles and ligaments. Dislokasyon; pilay.

spray, v. scatter or supply as a spray. Wisikan; wiligan; iwilig.

spread, n. an expanse. Pagpapalaganap; pagkakalat; paglalatag.

spree, n. a lively frolic. Katuwaan; pagsasaya.

sprig, n. a shoot, twig or small bunch. Supang; supling.

spring, n. the vernal season, in

North America approximately March 21 to June 21. Tagsibol.

sprinkle, v. scatter in drops or particles. Wisikan; wiligan; diligin.

sprinkling, n. a small scattered amount. Dilig; iwilig.

sprout, n. a fresh outgrowth from a plant or tree. Supling.

sprout, v. to germinate; begin to grow; put forth shoots. Tumubò; magsupling; sumupling.

spry, adj. nimble; active; lively. Maliksi; listo; masigla; mabilis.

spume, n. foam; froth. Bula; espuma.

spurious, adj. counterfeit. Huwad; di-tunay; may halo.

spurn, v. reject with disdain. Tanggihan nang may paghamak.

sputter, v. to speak hastily. Ibuga; lumikha ng ingay na pabuga-buga.

spy, n. a secret agent in enemy territory. Ispiya; maniniktik.

spy, v. observe secretly. Tanuran ng lihim; maniktik; manubok; mag-ispiya.

squabble, n. a petty quarrel. pagtatalo; pag-aaway.

squabble, v. bicker; to scuffle. Magbangayan; mag-away; magtalo.

squalid, adj. foul; filthy; dirty. Marumi.

squalor, n. coarseness; filthy. Karukhaan at panlilimahid; karumihan; kabahuan.

squander, v. spend wastefully. Lustayin; aksayahin.

square, adj. exact at right angles. Kuwadrado; parisukat.

squat, v. to sit on the heels. Tumingkayad; lumupagi.

squatter, n. a person who settles on another's land without right. Iskuwater.

squeeze, v. exert pressure upon. Pigain.

stab, n. the thrust of a pointed weapon. Saksak.

stab, v. pierce with or thrust with, a pointed weapon. Saksakin.

stable, adj. fixed; steady. Panatag; matatag.

stable, n. house for horses and cattle. Kuwadra.

stag, n. a male or red deer. Usang lalaki.

stage, n. a raised platform. Entablado; plataporma; tanghalan.

stage, v. exhibit on a stage. Magpalabas; itanghal.

stagger, v. to falter; move unsteadily. Manlupaypay; lumakad nang pasuray-suray.

stagnant, adj. not running or flowing. Hindi umaagos; tigil.

stain, n. a blot; a taint. Mantsa; dumi.

stainless, adj. unblemish; free from spots or stains. Malinis; walang dungis.

stair, n. a series of steps. Baitang; hagdan.

stale, adj. old; tasteless; trite. Bilasa; panis; luma; laon.

stalk, n. stem of a plant. Tangkay.

stall, n. part of a stable where a horse or cow is kept and fed; a booth; a seat or pew. Kakanan ng hayop; puwesto sa palengke; bahagi ng isang kuwadra.

stall, v. to keep in a stall. Mag-atubili; huminto; pigilin; lagyan ng sagabal para mahinto; ilagay sa kuwadra.

stallion, n. a male horse kept for breeding. Kabayong lalaking hindi kapon.

stalwart, adj. strong and brave. Matipuno; malusog; malakas.

stamina, n. vital strength. Lakas.

stammer, v. falter in speech; speak or utter with involuntary breaks and repetitions. Mautal; magsalita nang pautal-utal.

stammering, adj. stuttering. Utal; nauutal.

stamp, n. a piece of adhesive paper, as postage. Selyo.

stamp, v. affix a stamp on. Selyuhan; lagyan ng selyo.

stampede, n. concerted, panic-striken rush. Takbuhan dahil sa matinding sindak.

stanch, adj. sound; firm; trustworthy. Matapat; masugid.

stand, n. a determined position; a structure. platform, or piece of furniture. Puwesto; paninindigan.

stand, v. be upon the feet. Tumayo; tumindig.

standard, n. a flag or emblem; a criterion. Uliran; parisan; bandila; watawat; pamantayan.

stanza, n. a verse of a poem; group of lines of poetry. Estropa; saknong.

star, n. a body in space, esp. one outside the solar system. Tala; bituin.

starch, n. stiffening substance. Gawgaw; almirol.

starch, v. stiffen with starch. Almirulan.

stare, v, to look intently. Tumitig.

stark, adj. rigid; sheer. Ganap; matigas.

starlike, adj. resembling a star. Tulad ng bituin.

start, n. a beginning; outset. Umpisa; simula; sapulan.

start, v. to begin or enter upon an action, etc. Umpisahan; simulan; sapulan.

startle, v. surprise; alarm; shock. Takutin; gulatin; magulat.

starvation, n. a suffering extremely from want of food. Pagkamatay sa gutom.

starve, v. perish with hunger. Gutumin; mamatay sa gutom.

state, n. mode or form of existence. Estado; kalagayan.

state, v. declare; to tell. Isalaysay; ipahayag; sabihin.

statement, n. something stated; account; report. Ulat; pahayag.

station, n. an assigned place or position; standing. Istasyon; katayuan; himpilan; kalagayan sa buhay.

stationary, adj. fixed. Hindi tumitinag; hindi nag-iiba; walang pagbabago.

statistics, n. numerical facts about things or people. Estadistika.

status, n. state; condition; position. Kalagayan; katayuan.

status quo, n. the existing state or affairs. Ang kasalukuyang lagay.

stay, v. remain; hold out. Tumigil.

steady, adj. firm; regular; uniform. Walang galaw; matatag; palagian.

steal, v. to take by theft. Magnakaw.

stealth, n. a secret act. Kilos na palihim o patago.

steam. n. vapor of water. Usok ng kumukulong tubig; singaw.

steel, n. iron with carbon. Asero.

steep, adj. precipitous. Matarik.

steer, v. direct and govern;

guide. Palakarin; pilotohan; patnubayan; pamahalaan; akayin.

stellar, adj. relating to stars. Ukol sa mga bituin.

stem, n. the main body of a plant, the supporting stalk. Tangkay.

stenography, n. a method of rapid writing in symbols. Takigrapiya; istenograpiko

step, n. gait; pace. Baitang; hakbang; lumakad.

step, walk; go; dance. Lumakad; humakbang.

stepfather, n. a mother's second or subsequent husband. Padrasto; asawang kauli ng ina.

stepmother, n. a father's second or subsequent wife. Madrasta; asawang kauli ng ama.

stern, adj. severe in look; harsh. Mahigpit; mabalasik.

stew, v. boil or seethe slowly. Ilaga.

stick, n. a piece of wood, etc. generally small and slender. Palito; patpat; kaputol na kahoy.

stick, v. to adhere. Dumikit; mamalagi; huwag humiwalay.

stiff, adj. rigid; inflexible. Pormal; matigas.

still, adj. motionless; tranquil; silent. Walang ingay; tahimik; walang kilos.

stimulant, n. something that excites, stir or stimulates. Pampasigla.

sting, v. pain by pricking. Tusukin; duruin.

stir, v. agitate; move briskly. Pagalawin; haluin; kumilos.

stitch, n. in sewing, knitting, etc., one whole movement of the needle. Sulsi; tahi.

stock, n. a reserve supply; the shares of a corporation. Natatago; inimbak; katawan.

stocking, n. a knitted covering for the foot and lower leg. Medyas (ng babae).

stole, n. an ecclesiastical vestment. Estola (ng pari); makitid na bandanang inilalagay sa leeg ng pari.

stomach, n. organ in which food is digested. Sikmura; tiyan.

stone, n. a piece of rock. Bato.

stoop, n. a stooping movement or position. Yuko; yukod; baba.

stop, v. cease from; discontinue. Huminto; tumigil.

storage, n. act of storing goods. Pag-iimbak.

store, n. place where goods are stored or kept for sale. Tindahan; almasen.

storm, n. an atmospheric disturbance, with high wind, rain, or snow, etc. Bagyo.

story, n. a tale; narrative. Kuwento; kasaysayan.

stoup, n. vessel for liquids; a basin for holy water. Lalagyan ng agwa bendita sa simbahan.

stove, n. a heater; an apparatus for furnishing heat or for cooking. Apuyan; pugon; kalan.

stowaway, n. one who hides on a ship to get free passage. Taong nagtatago sa loob ng sasakyang-dagat o sa tren para di umupa.

strabismus, n. a squinting. Kadulingan.

straggle, v. wander away; astray. Lumaboy; lumakad-lakad.

straggler, n. a wanderer. Palaboy; bagamundo.

straight, adj. upright; without bend or deviation. Tuloy-tuloy; tuwid.

straightforward, adj. direct; honest; open. Tuwirán; tapat.

strain, n. a violent effort. Pilitin; pagkakahigpitan; pagkapuwersa.

strait, adj. narrow; confined; strict. Makipot; masikip; makitid.

strait, n. a narrow passage; a position of difficulty or need. Makipot na daanan ng tubig; kipot.

strange, adj. foreign; unusual. Kakatwâ; banyaga; kataka-taka; di-karaniwan,

stranger, n. a foreigner; a newcomer. Di-kilala; banyaga; taga-ibang bayan; estranghero.

strangle, v. to choke. Sakalin.

strap, n. a narrow strip of leather, etc. Sintas; korea; tirante; panali.

straw, n. stock of grain. Istro; ginikan; dayami.

stray, adj. wandering; isolated; casual. Ligaw.

stray, v. wander; deviate. Maglibot; maligaw.

streak, n. a long mark; a line. Bakas; guhit; sinag.

stream, n. a running water. Batis; agos; sapa.

stream, v. to flow in a stream. Tumakbo; dumaloy; umagos.

street, n. a road; a passageway for vehicles and pedestrians in a town or city. Daan; kalye.

strength, n. power; force; vigor. Kalakasán; puwersa; lakas.

strengthen, v. make strong. Palakasin.

strenuous, adj. active; ardent; energetic. Nakahahapo; nakapapagod.

stress, n. pressure; force. Tindi.

stretch, n. an extent of distance, area or time. Unat; panahon; haba; pagbatak.

stretch, v. extend too far. Hatakin; batakin; pahabain.

stretcher, n. a litter; a device for stretching. Kamilya; lonang may mahabang kahoy sa magkabilang tabi na ginagamit na pambuhat sa mga maysakit.

strict, adj. precise; exact; severe. Estrikto; mahigpit.

stride, n. a long step or its distance. Malaking hakbang.

stride, v. walk with long steps. Lumakad nang malalaki ang hakbang.

strife, n. contention; conflict; discord. Labanan; pagtatalo; alitan.

strike, n. a refusal by employees to work; a suitable pitch not hit. Istrayk; welga; pag-aklas; hampas.

string, n. a slender rope; a line; thread; cord, or thong. Panali; bagting; tali; pisi.

string, v. to make a string of. Kuwerdasan; talian; itali ng pisi.

stringency, n. strictness. Kabagsikan; kahigpitan.

stringent, adj. tense; vigorous. Istrikto; mahigpit; mabagsik.

strip, n. a narrow piece as of cloth. Paha; mahaba't makitid na piraso ng damit, katad o ano mang bagay.

strip, v. to take away; deprive of clothing. Tanggalin; maghubad; hubaran; alisan.

stripe, n. a streak or band of a different color or nature. Markang mahaba; guhit.

stripling, n. a youth. Binatilyo.

strive, v. make strenuous effort. Magpunyagi; magpilit; pagpilitan; magsikap.

stroke, n. a blow. Atake; hampas; pukpok; tugtog.
stroll, n. a walk for pleasure. Pamamasyal.
stroll, v. to wander; walk leisurely. Mamasyal.
strong, adj. vigorous; powerful. Matibay; matatag; malakas.
structure, n. the mode of construction or organization. Kayarian; pagkayari; balangkas.
struggle, n. a forcible effort to attain something. Pagpupunyagi; sigasig; pagsisikap.
struggle, v. labor or contend urgently or strenuously. Makipaglaban; magsumigasig; magsikap.
stub, n. a stump; a short remaining piece. Upós; pinagputulan ng punungkahoy na natitira sa lupa; tuod.
stubborn, adj. obstinate; tough. Matigas ang ulo.
stud, n. a buttonlike fastener; an upright support. Butones; pamako o pakong malapad ang ulo.
student, n. one who is engaged in study, as at a college. Mag-aaral; estudyante.
studio, n. workroom of a painter, sculptor, etc. Istudyo; talyer.
studious, adj. thoughtfully attentive to studies. Pala-aral; masipag mag-aral.
stuff, v. to pack or cram full. Siksikan; palamnan; punuin; tapalan.
stumble, v. trip in walking. Matisod; matapilok; marapa.
stump, n. the part of a tree after the main trunk falls off. Bahagi ng punungkahoy na natitira sa lupa pagkaputol ng katawan; tuod.
stun, v. deprive of consciousness by a glow, etc. Lituhin; mabaghan; mawalan ng malay.
stupefaction, n. insensibility. Kagulumihanan; pagkalito; matinding pagkagulat.
stupefy, v. shock; deprive of sensibility. Mabaghan; malito; mabigla; mawalan ng pakiramdam.
stupid, adj. dull, senseless. Tunggak; ungas; mapurol ang isip; istupido.
stupidity, n. dullness. Kahangalan; kaungasan.
stupor, n. lethargy; insensibility. Kawalan ng pandamdam; kawalang malay.
sturdy, adj. strong; robust; unyielding. Matipuno· malakas; malusog.
stutter, n. a hesitation in speaking. Pagkautal.
sty, n. hog pen; any filthy place. Kulungan; maraming bahay.
style, n. manner; prevalent fashion. Estilo, uso; paraan; moda.
stylish, adj. showy; modish. Sunod sa moda; pustoryoso.
suave, adj. gracious. Mapitagan; pinong kumilos; banayad; magalang.
subdivide, v. to divide again. Hatiin sa maliliit na bahagi o pulutong.
subdue, v. overcome by force; conquer. Lupigin; gapihin; supilin.
subject, n. a theme; topic. Pinag-aaralan; paksa; sakop.
subjective, adj. introspective. Nasa kapasiyahan.
sublimate, v. elevate; turn into, or place with more wholesome activities or interests. Itanghal; ibukod sa karamihan; itangi; dakilain.
sublimation, n. exaltation.

Pagtatanghal; pagtataas; pagtatangi; pagdakila.

sublime, adj. grand; noble. Matayog; marangal; mataas; tangi; dakila.

submerge, v. put under water. Ilubog.

submission, n. compliance. Pagsuko; pagsunod; pagpapailalim sa kapasiyahan.

submissive, adj. yielding; obedient. Mababa ang loob; masunurin.

submit, v. to yield. Sumuko; pahinuhod; sumunod; magpailalim sa kapasiyahan.

subordinate, adj. in a lower order or rank; of inferior importance. Nasa mababang antas; Ipailalim; ipangalawa.

subpoena, n. an official written order commanding a person to appear in a law court. Subpena; Utos sa paghaharap sa hukuman.

subscribe, v. to obtain a subscription to a magazine, newspaper, etc.; consent. Suskribe; magpadala ng pahayagan o magasin; umayon; pumanig.

subsequent, adj. succeeding. Subsekuwente; kasunod; sumusunod.

subsequently, adj. afterwards; later on. Nang sumunod: pagkatapos.

subservient, adj. servile; subordinate. Sunud-sunuran; mababa; palasunod.

subside, v. to sink lower. Tumila; humupa; tumigil; kumati; bumaba.

subsidy, n. a grant or contribution of money, esp. made by a government. Tulong na salapi ng pamahalaan.

subsist, v. to continue; exist. Manatili; magpatuloy; mabuhay.

subsistence, n. means of keeping alive. Pantawid-buhay.

substance, n. essential part; subject matter. Diwa; kalamnan; sustansiya.

substantiate, v. to prove; establish by evidence. Bigyang katibayan; patunayan.

substitute, n. a person or thing serving in place of another. Kapalit; pansamantalang kahalili.

substitute, v. to exchange. Palitan; halinhan nang pansamantala; kapalit.

subterfuge, n. trick; evasion. Panlansi; dahilan; pag-iwas; daya; lalang.

subterranean, adj. under earth. Subteranyo; sa ilalim ng lupa.

subtle, adj. artful; crafty; delicate. Pino; sutil; maparaan; tuso; maselan.

subtract, v. to deduct. Restahin; bawasan; alisan.

suburb, n. the outskirts; a district outside of, but adjoining a city. Karatig; arabal; pook sa labas ng lunsod.

subversion, n. overthrow. Pagbabagsak.

subway, n. an underground passage. Daan sa ilalim ng lupa.

succeed, v. to prosper. Magwagi; magtagumpay.

success, n. prosperity. Pagwawagi: tagumpay.

successful, adj. prosperous. Maunlad; matagumpay.

successive, adj. follow in order. Magkasunod; sunud-sunod.

succinct, adj. short; concise. Tuwiran; maikli; maigsi.

succor, n. help. Saklolo; tulong.

suck, v. absorb. Ut-utin; sipsipin; susuhin,

sudden, **adj.** happening or done unexpectedly; abrupt. Agad-agad; bigla; kagyat.

suds, n. bubbles and foam on soapy water. Bula ng sabon.

sue, v. institute process in law against. Ihabla; idemanda; isakdal.

suffer, v. fell or undergo pain. Magtiis; magdusa.

suffocate, v. smother; kill by impeding respiration. Sakalin; mainis; di-makahinga.

suffrage, n. a right to vote. Karapatang bumoto.

sugar, n. sweet substance obtained from sugar cane, beets, etc. Matamis; asukal.

suggest, v. to bring a thought; to show in an indirect way. Imungkahi; ipahiwatig.

suicide. n. self murder. Pagpapakamatay.

suit, n. a petition or appeal; a courtship. Petisyon; demanda; pakiusap; pagligaw; sakdal; kasuutan.

sullen, adj. gloomy; solitary. Masama ang loob; di-nasisiyahan.

summer, n. the warmest season of the year. Tag-araw; tag-init.

sun, n. the central body of the solar system. Araw.

Sunday, n. the first day of the week. Domingo; Linggo.

sunlight, n. the light of the sun; sunshine. Liwanag ng araw

sunrise, n. the ascent of the sun above the horizon in the morning; also, sun-up. Pagsikat ng araw.

sunset, n. the going down of the sun. Paglubog ng araw.

superable, adj. surmountable. Mapagtatagumpayan; maaaring madaig.

superb, adj. grand; magnificent. Kahanga-hanga; magaling; suberbiyo.

superimpose, v. to put on top of something else. Ipatong; ipaibabaw.

superstition, n. credulity. Superstisyon; pamahiin.

supper, n. the evening meal. Pagkain sa gabi; hapunan.

supple, adj. pliant; yielding. Malambot; nababaluktot.

supplement, n. an addition. Suplemento; dagdag.

supplicate, v. to beg humbly and earnestly. Magsumamo; magmakaawa.

supply, n. the quantity available; a store or stock. Panustos; imbak; probisyon; mga pagkain at kagamitang kailangan.

supply, v. to furnish; provide. Dulutan; suplay; bigyan ng mga kailangan.

suppose, v. to consider as possible. Ipalagay.

suppress, v. restrain; repress. Sugpuin; supilin; impitin; sansalain; pigilin.

supremacy, n. highest power. Pangingibabaw; paghahari; pamamayani.

supreme, adj. highest. Kataastaasan; nangingibabaw; pinakamataas.

surcharge, n. an extra charge. Labis na kargada; labis na singil.

sure, adj. certain. Sigurado; siyerto; tiyak.

surely, adv. certainly. Siyang tunay; tiyak na tiyak.

surface, n. upper or exterior part. Kalatagan; ibabaw; ang panlabas ng alin mang bagay.

surfeit, n. excess, esp. in eating or drinking. Impatso; di-pagkatunaw; labis na kabusugan.

surgeon, n. a practitioner of

surgery. Siruhano; maninistis.

surliness, n. moroseness; sourness. Kasungitan.

surmise, n. a guess. Hula; haka; palagay.

surmountable, adj. conquerable. Magagawa; malulutas; mapagtitiisan; mapagtatagumpayan.

surname, n. family name. Pangalang angkan; ngalang angkan; apelyido.

surpass, v. to exceed; Daigin; higitan; lagpasan.

surplice, n. a white, loose-fitting robe or vestment of a clergyman. Puting damit na maikli na ginagamit ng pari sa ibabaw ng kanyang abito.

surplus, n. excess. Labis.

surprise, n. wonder; astonishment. Sorpresa; bagay o pangyayaring di-inaakala.

surrender, v. to yield. Sumurender; sumuko; ibigay.

surround, v. to encompass. Kubkubin; paligiran.

survey, v. to view; scrutinize. Suriin; sukatin; siyasatin; tingnan.

survey, n. a general view; a statistical study. Pagkasukat; pagtingin; pagsisiyasat.

survive, v. to live longer than; remain alive after. Makaligtas.

suspect, v. to mistrust; doubt. Paghinalaan; maghinala.

suspect, n. a person suspected of a crime. Pinaghihinalaan; suspek.

suspend, v. to delay. Ibitin; binbinin; pigilin.

suspension, n. the act of delaying, stopping, or interrupting for a time. Suspensiyon; pagkatigil; pagpigil; pagbalam.

suspicion, n. the state of mind of one who suspects. Hinala; sapantaha.

sustain, v. to hold up; support. Dalhin; alalayan.

swain, n. a young man who lives in the country; a lover. Binatang bukid; manliligaw; mangingibig.

swallow, n. any of various long-winged, graceful birds. Langay-langayan.

swallow, v. to take into the stomach. Lunukin; tanggapin; lulunin.

swamp, n. wet, soft land. Latian.

swan, n. a large, white swimming bird with a gracefully curved neck. Sisne.

sway, v. to swing or cause to swing back and forth. Umuga; umugoy.

swear, v. declare by oath. Sumumpa; manumpa.

sweat, n. perspiration. Pawis.

sweep, v. brush over with a broom. Palisin; magwalis; walisin.

sweepstakes, n. a prize won in a race or contest. Suwipisteks.

sweet, adj. having the taste of sugar or honey. Dulse; matamis.

sweeten, v. to make sweet to taste. Patamisin; lagyan ng matamis.

sweetheart, n. lover. Mangingibig; kasintahan.

swell, n. an increase; a bulge. Lumaki; maga; mamintog.

swerve, v. to turn or cause to turn aside. Lumihis.

swift, adj. quick. Mabilis; matulin.

swiftly, adv. rapidly. Nang buong bilis.

swiftness, n. rapidity. Tulin; bilis.

swim, v. to move along in water by movements of the limbs, fins, tail, etc. Lumangoy; sumisid.

swimmer, n. one who swims. Maninisid; manlalangoy.

swindle, v. to defraud; cheat. Estapa; manlinlang; manggantso; manuba.

swoon, n. faint. Desmaya; paghihimatay.

swoop, v. fall on and seize. Dagitin.

sword, n. a weapon with a long edged blade. Sable; ispada.

syllable, n. the smallest separately articulated element in human utterance. Pantig.

syllabus, n. a compendium; an abstract. Lagom; buod.

symbol, n. type; emblem. Tanda; sagisag; simbolo.

symmetrical, adj. shapely. Simetriko; timbang

symmetry, n. excellence of proportion. Pagkakatugunan; wastong pagkakatimbang ng mga bahagi.

sympathetic, adj. Nakikiisa; nakikiramay; nakauunawa.

sympathy, n. fellow feeling; compassion. Simpatiya; pagsang-ayon; pagkaunawa; pagdamay.

symptom, n. an indication or a sign, esp. of a particular disease. Sintomas; palatandaan.

synagogue, n. Jewish church. Sinagoga; simbahan ng mga Hudyo.

syncope, n. an omission. Pagbabawas; pagkakaltas; maykaltas.

synonym, n. word of same meaning. Sinonimo; singkahulugan.

synonymous, adj. identical. Kaparis; katulad; kagaya; kasingkahulugan.

synopsis, n. summary; review. Buod; lagom.

syrup, n. a sweet, thick liquid. Pulot; arnibal.

system, n. method; scheme. Paraan; ayos.

systematic, adj. Sistematiko; maparaan; maayos.

systole, n. the normal contraction of the heart. Sistole; ang pagpintig na paliit ng puso at pag-agos ng dugo sa mga ugat.

T

tabernacle, n. place or house of worship. Tabernakulo; sambahan ng mga Hudyo; templo.

table, n. flat, smooth board or boards with legs. Mesa o hapag; talaan; talahanayan.

table, v. to place on a table; to postpone discussions of. Ilagay sa ibabaw ng hapag; huwag pahalagahan ang isang balak o pakiusap.

tablecloth, n. cloth, usually of linen, for covering a table before dishes are set for meals. Pantakip sa mesa; mantel.

tablespoon, n. a spoon holding one-half fluid ounce. Kutsara.

tablet, n. a pill; a flat surface; writing pad. Kuwadernong tiklupin; tableta.

tabloid, n. a newspaper that has many pictures and gives the news in short articles. Tabloid.

taboo, v. to prohibit. Ipagbawal.

tabor, n. a small drum. Munting tambol.

tacit, adj. silent. Di-ipinahahayag; tahimik; pahiwatig.

taciturn, adj. silent; reserved in speech. Walang imik; dipalakibo

tack, n. a small, short nail with a large head. Tatsuwela; pakong may malapad na ulo.

tack, v. to nail with tacks, attach, esp. temporarily. Idugtong; ipako; ikabit.

tact, n. nice discernment. Kasanayan sa pagsasabi at paggawâ ng wastong mga bagay; kasanayang makibagay.

tactile, adj. tangible; pertaining to the sense of touch. Nahihipo; nasasalat; nakukuha.

tadpole, n. the aquatic larva or immature form of frogs and toads. Kiti-kiti; munting palaka; uluulo.

tail, n. the posterior extremity of an animal, esp. a projecting appendage. Hulihan; buntot.

tailor, n. maker of clothes. Sastre; mananahi ng mga kasuutan ng lalaki.

taint, n. contamination. Mantsa; bahid; hawa; dungis.

taint, v. to infect; corrupt. Bahiran; mantsahan; mahahawa; hawahan; dungisan.

take, v. get by one's own action. Kanin o inumin; kunin.

tale, n. a story. Kuwento; istorya.

talent, n. an inborn ability. Talino; dunong.

talented, adj. having superior capacities. Matalino; marunong.

talisman, n. an inscribed amulet or charm. Talisman; anting-anting; galing.

talk, n. speech; conversation. Talumpati; usapan; satsatan.

talk, v. to speak. Mag-usap; magsalita; sumatsat

talkative, adj. loquacious. Madaldal; masatsat.

tall, adj. high; lofty. Matayog; matangkad; mataas.

tallow, n. an animal fat. Sebo; taba.

tally, v. make to fit, accord. Tumugon; bilangin; pagtamain; pagparehuhin.

tame, adj. docile; domesticated. Mabait; domestiko; maaamo.

tame, v. to subdue; make tame. Supilin; paamuin.

tamper, v. to meddle; meddle improperly. Makialam.

tan, n. yellowish brown. Moreno; kulaykatad; kayumanggi.

tangle, n. a mass of tangled fibers; a confused jumble. Buhól; gusot; gulo.

tangle. v. to complicate; unite confusedly. Buhul-buhulin; gusutin; guluhin.

tank, n. a cistern; a reservoir. Tangke.

tantalize. v. to torment with the sight of something desired but out of reach. Takawin; hibuin; ipakita ang isang bagay na ibig saka ilayo; tuksuhin.

tap, n. a gentle blow. Tuktok; kalabit; tapik; munting gripo.

tap, v. strike lightly. Tuktukin; kalabitin; tapikin; kunin ang̃ dagta ng isang puno sa pamamagitan ng pag̃hiwa nito.

tape, n. narrow cloth band. Teyp; plaster; sintas; tiras; makitid at mahahabang piraso ng damit o metal.

tapering, adj. gradually diminishing toward a point; becoming smaller in diameter toward one end. Patulis; malaki sa ibaba.

tapestry, n. woven hangings; a woven fabric reproducing

elaborate designs, often pictorial. Damit na binurdahan nang matambok.

tar, n. any of various dark, viscid products obtained from organic substances as wood, coal, etc. Alkitran.

tardy, adj. late. Mabagal; huli.

target, n. mark for rifle and artillery practice. Ang pinatatamaan; tudlaan.

tariff, n. duty on imports. Taripa; buwis sa luwas at angkat.

tarnish, v. to sully; to soil. Papusyawin; mapakla.

task, n. a work to be done; piece of work. Gawain; trabaho; tungkulin.

tassel, n. pendent ornament. Borlas; palawit.

taste, n. the sense by which flavor or savor is perceived, operating through organs in the mouth. Tikim; lasa.

tasteless, adj. having no taste; insipid. Walang lasa.

tasty, adj. palatable. Masarap; malasa.

taunt, n. a bitter or sarcastic reproach. Pagkutya; pagtuya; pag-uyam.

taunt, v. to ridicule; provoke. Kutyain; tuyain; uyamin.

taut, adj. tightly drawn; tense. Mahigpit; matigas; batak na batak.

tavern, n. a house in which liquor is sold to be drunk on the premises; hotel. Karihan; munting otel; bahaytuluyan; taberna.

tawdry, adj. in bad taste; gaudy. Masagwa.

tax, n. assessment; Taks; buwis.

taxidermy, n. art of preserving skins. Taksiderma; ang sining ng paggamot at paglimbak sa mga patay na hayop para magmukhang buhay.

taxpayer, n. one who pays a tax. Takspeyer; mambubuwis.

tea, n. an ornamental plant whose dried leaves, infused with hot water, make a beverage. Tsa.

teach, v. to instruct. Turuan; ituro; magturo.

teacher, n. a person who teaches in school. Guro; maestro; titser.

teachable, adj. capable of being taught. Maaaring turuan.

team, n. a number of persons associated in some joint action. Koponan; pangkat; tim.

tear, n. water from the eyes. Luha; punit; sira.

tease, v. to vex; chaff with good-humored jests. Biruin; guluhin; tuksuhin.

teaspoon, n. a small spoon used in drinking tea. Kutsarita.

tedious, adj. long and tiresome. Matagal at nakapapagod; nakababagot.

teeter, v. move unsteadily. Manimbang; mag-alanganin sa tayo.

teething, n. dentition. Pagngingipin.

teetotal, adj. absolute; whole. Intero; buo; kabuuan.

telegram, n. a message sent by telegraph. Pahatid-kawad; telegrama.

telegraph, n. an apparatus and system for transmitting code messages by electric currents in wires. Telegrapo.

telephone, n. an apparatus and system for transmitting speech and sounds by electric currents in wires.

Telepono.

tell, v. make known; express in words. Isalaysay; sabihin.

temper, n. disposition; mood. Temperamento; kainitan o kalamigan ng ulo; timpla.

temper, v. to moderate. Subhan; gawing kaigihan; timplahin.

temperance, n. moderation, esp. in the use of intoxicating liquors. Kahinahunan; kabutihan; pagpipigil.

temperate, adj. moderate. Katamtaman.

temperature, n. degree of heat or cold. Temperatura; init o lamig.

tempest, n. a violent wind, usually attended with rain, hail or snow. Sigwa; bagyo.

tempestous, adj. stormy. Marahas; binabagyo.

temple, n. place of worship. Simbahan; templo; dalanginan.

temporary, adj. lasting for a time only. Temporaryo; pansamantala.

tempt, v. to entice to evil. Akitin; tuksuhin; hibuin.

temptation, n. allurement; inducing. Tukso.

ten, adj. & n. cardinal number between nine and eleven. Diyes; sampu.

tenable, adj. defensible. Mapanindigan; maaaring ipagtanggol o itaguyod.

tenacious, adj. adhesive or sticky; highly retentive. Mahigpit kumapit; mapilit.

tenancy, n. tenure; period of occupancy as tenant. Pangungupahan; pag-upa; pansamantalang pag-aari.

tenant, n. one who holds property by lease or rent. Ang bumubuwis; nangungupahan.

tend, v. to be inclined or disposed. Magsilbi; dumako; humilig sa isang tiyak na paninindigan o lunan; alagaan.

tendency, n. inclination; leaning. Pagkahilig; gawi; ugali.

tender, adj. soft; kind. Murà; mabait; maselan; malambot; maawain.

tender, v. offer; present for acceptance. Magharap; idulog; ihandog.

tenement, n. a habitation. Bahay; tirahan.

tenet, n. an opinion; principle, or doctrine held to be true. Doktrina; paniwala; simulain.

tenfold, adj. 10 times as much. Sampung ibayo.

tense, adj. stiff. Banát; pigil; naninigas.

tension, n. a stretched condition. Kaigtingan; pagkabanat.

tent, n. a portable shelter of cloth, skins, etc. supported by one or more poles. Tolda.

tenth, adj. first after the ninth. Pansampu; ikasampu.

terminate, v. to bring to an end. Tigilan; tapusin; wakasan.

termination, n. conclusion. Terminasyon; katapusan; wakas.

termite, n. a white ant. Anay.

terrible, adj. dreadful. Kasindak-sindak; katakut-takot.

terrify, v. to frighten. Sindakin; takutin; matakot.

territory, n. a tract of land; a region or district. Teritoryo; purok; sakop; lupain.

terror, n. great fear. Malaking takot; sindak.

terrorize, v. dominate by intimidation. Sindakin; dulutan ng matinding takot.

test, n. a critical trial. Eksamen; pagsubok; pagsusulit.

testament, n. a will. Testamento; habilin.

testify, v. witness; certify. Sumaksi; tumestigo; magpatunay.

testimony, n. evidence. Patunay; katunayan; katibayan.

text, n. subject of discourse. Paksa; nilalaman; teksto.

texture, n. structure. Hipo; kinis o gaspang.

than, conj. a particle used to introduce the second member of a comparison. Kaysa.

thank, v. express gratitude. Pasalamatan; magpasalamat.

thanks, n. an expression of gratitude. Salamat.

that, adj. used to point out some one person or thing or idea. Iyan; iyon.

thatch, n. straw, rushes, or the like, used to cover roofs or stack. Atip na pawid o kugon.

thaw, n. the act or process of melting. Matunaw; tunawin.

the, art. used before a noun or pronoun to particularize it, indicate an individual, mark a generic term, emphasize pre-eminence, etc. Ang; ang mga.

the Nuncio, n. an ambassador of the first rank (not a cardinal) representing the Pope at the seat of a foreign government. Ang Nunsiyo; ang sugo ng Papa.

theatre, n. a play house. Teatro; dulaan.

thee, pron. you; thou. Ikaw.

theft, n. act of stealing. Pagnanakaw.

their, pron. belongs to them. Nila; kanila.

theme, n. a subject; topic. Paksa; tema.

then, adv. at that time. Noon; pagkatapos; saka.

theology, n. science of divinity. Teolohiyá; ang agham ng mga katotohanan sa pananampalataya.

theory, n. an explanation based on thought. Paliwanag; palagay; teoriya.

thence, adv. from that place. Mula roon.

there, adv. in that place. Diyan; doon.

thereafter, adv. accordingly; after that. Pagkatapos noon; mula noon.

therefore, adv. consequently. Kaya; samakatwid.

thermometer, n. an instrument to measure temperature. Termometro; panukat ng init at lamig.

they, pron. nominative, plural of he, she and it. Sila.

thick, adj. dense. Malapot; masinsin; makapal.

thicken, v. make or become thick. Kapalán; gawing makapal.

thief, n. one who commits larceny or robbery. Magnanakaw.

thigh, n. part of the leg between the hip and the knee in man. Pigî; hita.

thimble, n. a covering for finger while sewing. Didal.

thin, adj. slight; slim. Manipis; payat.

thing, n. a material object without life. Bagay.

think, v. form a mental concept of. Ipalagay; isipin; mag-isip.

thirst, n. want of drink. Uhaw.

thirsty, adj. feeling thirst. Nauuhaw.

thirteen, adj. & n. three plus ten. Trese; labintatlo.

thirty, adj. & n. three times

ten. Trenta; tatlumpu.
this, pron. a demonstrative term indicating a person or thing immediately present, nearby, nearer than another, or previously referred to Ito.
thorn, n a prickly spine. Tinik.
thorough, adj. complete or perfect. Puspusan; masusi; ganap.
thou, pron. you. Ikaw.
though, conj. although; if. Kahit na; bagaman.
thought, n. act of thinking. Kuro-kuro; haka; isip; pagiisip.
thoughtful, adj. considerate. Maalalahanin; mapag-isip.
thoughtless, adj. careless; inconsiderate. Walang isip; walang ingat.
thousand, adj. & n. ten times one hundred. Libo; mil.
thrash, v. to beat or whip thoroughly. Paluin; giikin; bugbugin.
thread, n. fiber; filament. Hibla; sinulid.
threadbare, adj. worn-out; tattered. Gulanit; sira-sira.
threat, n. an indication of impending danger or evil. Banta; pananakot; bala; pagbabala.
three, adj.& n. cardinal number between 2 and 4. Tres; tatlo.
thresh. v. to separate the grain or seeds from wheat, rice. Giikin; himayin.
thrift, n. frugality. Pagtitipid; katipiran.
thrifty, adj. frugal; sparing. Ekonomiko; matipid.
thrive, v. to flourish; prosper. Tumubo; mamuhay ng masagana; umunlad; mabuhay.
throat, n. passage through the neck. Lalamunan.
throb, n. a rapid or strong beat. Mabilis o malakas na tibok.
throne, n. seat of a king. Luklukang-hari; trono.
throughout, adv. in every part (of). Sa bawa't panig; sa lahat; sa buong.
thrust, v. to push with force. Tarakan; ulusin; saksak; isuksok.
thud, n. a dull sound. Lagpak; galabog.
thumb, n. the short, thick inner finger of the human hand, next to the forefinger. Hinlalaki.
thunder, n. the loud atmospheric noise that often follows lightning. Kulog.
thunderstorm, n. a storm accompanied with thunder. Bagyong may kulog.
Thursday, n. the 5th day of the week. Huwebes.
thwart, v. to frustrate. Biguin; salungatin.
tiara, n. an ornament worn on the head by women; a diadem worn by the Pope. Tiyara; sumbrero ng Papa na nagpapakilala ng kanyang pagiging ulo ng Simbahang Katoliko.
ticking, n. sound of a clock. Pagtunog; tiktak.
ticket, n. a slip of paper entitling one to admission, service, etc. Bilyete; tiket.
tickle, v. to cause to laugh; touch so as to produce a tinkling sensation. Kilitiin.
ticklish, adj. easily tickled. Makilitiin; nakakikiliti.
tidbit, n. a very pleasing bit of food, news, etc. Kapirasong masarap na pagkain o magandang balita.
tide, n. the ebb and flow of the sea. Agos; paglaki at pagkati ng tubig sa ilog.

tie, n. a necktie; cravat. Kurbata.;

tiger, n. a large carnivorous feline of Asia. Tigre.

tight, adj. firmly or closely fixed in place. Banát; masikip; mahigpit.

tigress, n. a female tiger. Tigreng babae.

till, conj. until. Hanggang sa.

timber, n. building wood. Troso; kahoy; tabla.

time, n. an epoch, era, period, or season. Tiyempo; panahon.

timely, adj. seasonable. Napapanahon.

timepiece, n. a clock or watch. Orasán; relos.

timetable, n. a schedule of time of planned occurrences, esp. a railroad schedule. Itenereraryo; talaan ng oras.

timid, adj. shy; fearful. Mahiyain; kimi.

timidity, n. want of courage. Pagkamahiyain; kakimian.

timorous, adj. full of fear. Temoroso; nag-aalaala; natatakot.

tin, n. a container made of tin plate; sheet iron or steel coated with tin. Lata.

tincture, n. solution of medicine. Tintura.

tingle, v. have a prickling or stinging sensation. Umugong ang tainga.

tiny, adj. very small. Munti; maliit.

tip, n. end; point; hint. Dulo; pabuya; abiso; tip; tulis; pabagsak; pasabi.

tipsy, adj. drunk; intoxicated. Lango; lasing.

tiptoe, n. a walk on the tips of the toes. Lakad na patiyad.

tiresome, adj. tedious; Nakasasawa; nakababagot.

title, n. name; claim of right. Titulo; pamagat.

toad, n. a terrestial member of the frog family. Palaka.

toast, n. sliced bread browned by heat. Inihaw na tinapay; tinapay na tostado.

toastmaster, n. a person who presides at a program. Tagapagkilala; tosmaster.

tobacco, n. a plant whose large leaves, containing nicotine, are prepared for smoking and chewing. Tabako.

today, adv. this day; now. Sa araw na ito; ngayon.

toe, n. part of the foot. Daliri ng paa.

together, adv. with each other; into contact. Samasama; magkasama.

toil, n. labor; drudgery; a laborious task. Paggawa; pagpapakahirap.

toil, v. work hard; labor. Gumawa; magpakahirap.

toiler, n. a laborer. Trabahador; manggagawa.

toilet, n. a water closet, bathroom, or dressing room. Kasilyás; palikuran.

token, n. a sign; note. Senyal; alaala; tanda; palatandaan.

tolerance, n. endurance. Pagpaparaya; pagbabata; pagtitiis.

tolerate, v. to bear with patience; permit. Batahin; tiisin; magparaya.

toll, n. a tax or fee for a particular service. Tol; butaw; buwis na ibinabayad ng mga manlalakbay o ng mga sasakyan sa kanilang dinaraanan.

tomato, n. a plant bearing a pulpy fruit, usually red. Kamatis.

tomb, n. a grave. Libingan.

tombstone, n. a sepulchral stone. Lapida.

tomorrow, adv. the day after this day. Bukas.

tone, n. a sound; quality of sound. Tunog; tono.

tongs, n. a fire utensil; an instrument for grasping and lifting something. Sipit.

tong, n. forced contribution. Tong; lagay; suhol.

tongue, n. organ of speech and of taste. Dila.

tonight, adv. the present or coming night. Ngayong gabi.

too, adv. also; more than enough. Man; labis; lubhâ; din; rin.

tool, n. any implement for working, cutting, shaping, etc. Kasangkapan.

tooth, n. (in most vertebrates) one of the hard bodies usually attached in a row to each jaw, serving for the mastication of food, as weapons of attack or defense. Ngipin.

toothache, n. pain in teeth. Sakit ng ngipin.

top, n. the highest point or part. Tuktok; kaitaasan.

topsy-turvy, adj. in confusion or disorder. Magulo.

torch, n. a light to be carried about or stuck in a holder. Sulo; tanglaw.

torment, n. suffering. Pahirap; parusa; pasakit.

torpedo, n. submarine projectile. Torpedo.

torrent, n. a rapid stream; an abundant and violent flow of water. Baha.

torrid, adj. very hot. Napakainit.

tortoise, n. a turtle. Pagong.

torture, n. the act of inflicting very severe pain. Labis na pagpapahirap.

toss, v. to throw; cast. Ipukol; ihagis.

tot, n. a little child. Munting bata; paslit; musmos.

touch, v. perceive by physical contact. Dampian; hipuin.

tough, adj. strong; hardy. Magayot; matigas; maganit.

tour, n. a journey to several places in succession. Biyahe; ekskursiyon; paglalakbay.

tourist, n. a traveler for pleasure. Biyahero; manlalakbay.

tournament, n. a mock fight. Torneo; paligsahan.

toward, prep. in the direction of. Patungo sa.

towel, n. a cloth or paper for wiping. Tuwalya.

tower, n. a high, slender building or structure. Moog; tore.

town, n. a community; a political division of a province. Bayan.

townsman, n. an inhabitant, or fellow inhabitant of a town. Paisano; kababayan.

toxic, adj. poisonous. Nakakalason.

toy, n. a plaything. Laruan.

trace, v. to follow the footprints or track of. Guhitan; bakasin.

track, n. a footprint or other mark left. Landas; bakas.

trade, n. commerce. Komersiyo; kalakal; gawain.

trade. v. engage in commerce. Makipagkalakalan.

trader, n. one engaged in trade or commerce. Negosyante; mangangalakal.

tradition, n. oral account transmitted from age to age. Tradisyon; kaugalian.

traduce, v. to defame; revile. Siraang-puri.

traffic, n. the coming and going of persons, vehicles; commercial dealings. **Kalakalan**; komersyo; **trapiko**; pagyayaot dito ng mga **tao,**

sasakyan o kalakal.

tragedy, n. melancholy play. Trahedya; sakuna; kasawian.

tragic, adj. sad or pathetic. Kalunus-lunos; malungkot.

trail, n. a rough path; a track. Bakas; landas; bulaos; buntot.

trail, v. draw along behind; follow the trail of. Tugaygayan; sundan; bumuntot.

train, n. a railroad locomotive and the cars connected to it. Tren; prusisyon; pila.

train, v. subject to discipline and instruction. Sanayin; turuan.

training, n. systematic exercise. Pagsasanay; pinagaralan; kinamulatan.

trait, n. a feature; quality; characteristic. Katangian; kaugalian.

traitor, n. a betrayer. Lilo; taksil; traidor.

tramp, n. a heavy tread; a vagabond who lives by begging or stealing. Bagabundo; lagalag; palaboy; mabigat na hakbang.

tramp, v. walk with a heavy step; travel about as a vagabond. Lumaboy-laboy; lumaboy; lumakad nang papadyak.

trample, v. step heavily upon. Yurakan.

trance, n. a half-conscious, dazed, or hypnotic state. Himatay; kawalang-malay.

tranquil, adj. quiet; peaceful. Tahimik; payapa.

transaction, n. performance; a deal. Transaksiyon; paguusap; pag-uunawaan.

transcend, v. to excel; surpass. Higitan; lagpasan.

transcribe, v. to copy; put into writing. Sipiin; kopyahin; isalin.

transcript, n. a written copy. Kopya; salin; sipi.

transfer, v. to convey. **Isalin**; ilipat.

translate, v. to interpret. **Isalin.**

transmit, v. to send onward or along. Ihatid; ipagbigayalam; sabihin; ipadala.

transparent, adj. permitting distinct vision through a solid substance Naaaninag; nanganganinag.

transportation, n. a means of transport. Sasakyan; transportasyon.

trap, n. a snare; stratagem. Bitag; patibong; lalang.

travel, v. make a journey. Magbiyahe; maglakbay.

traveller, n. one who travels. **Manlalakbay; biyahero.**

tray, n. a flat vessel or shallow box for holding something. Bandeha.

tread, v. to step. Hakbangan; tapakan; yurakan.

treason, n. rebellion; violation of allegiance due a state. Pagkakanulo; kataksilan.

treasure, n. hoarded wealth; anything highly valued. **Kayamanan.**

treasurer, n. one who has charge of money. Tesorero; ingat-yaman.

treaty, n. a compact. Pinagkayarian; kasunduan.

tree, n. a large perennial plant with a single permanent woody trunk. Puno; punungkahoy.

trellis, n. a lattice work. Balag.

tremble, v. to shake; shiver. Manginig.

trembling, adj. shaking; shivering. Mangaligkig; nanginginig.

tremendous, adj. marvelous; huge. Napakalaki; kasindak-sindak; kamangha-mangha.

tremulous, adj. trembling; unsteady; fearful. Nanganga-tog; nanginginig.

trend, n. tendency to go in a particular direction or course. Tendensiya; lakad; moda; hilig.

trespass, n. an offense; sin. Pagkakasala; paglaktaw; panghihimasok.

trial, n. an examination; a test. Paglilitis; pagsubok.

triangle, n. figure with three sides. Triyanggulo; tatsulok.

tribe, n. an aggregate of people united by a common ancestry; intermarriage, or allegiance. Lipi; tribu; angkan.

tribunal, n. a court of justice. Husgado; hukuman.

tribune, n. a raised platform. Tribuna; entablado.

trick, n. any method of deceiving. Enganyo; lansi; lalang.

trickle, v. to fall in drops. Pumatak; tumulo.

tricycle, n. a vehicle with three wheels. Traysikel.

trifle, n. something trivial or insignificant. Munting bagay; bagay na walang halaga.

trimming, n. ornament. Gayak; palamuti; panggilid.

trip, n. misstep; journey. Trip; talisod; maikling paglalakbay.

triple, adj. treble; threefold. Makaitlo; tatlong ulit.

triplicate, adj. threefold. Triplikado; tatlong sipi.

trite, adj. worn out; stale; hackneyed. Pangkaraniwan; palasak.

triumph, n. victory. Pagwawagi; tagumpay.

triumphant, adj. exulting. Matagumpay.

trivial, adj. worthless; light. Walang kabuluhan; di-gaanong mahalaga.

troop, n. a company; a group. Pangkat; tropa; barkada.

trophy, n. a memorial of victory. Alaala; katibayan; tropeo.

trouble, n. discomfort; inconvenience. Ligalig; trobol; gulo; kaguluhan.

troublesome, adj. vexatious. Magulo.

trough, n. long vessel for holding food or drink. Labangan.

trousers, n. pantaloons. Salawal; pantalon.

trousseau, n. bride's apparel. Mga damit na inihahanda ng babae bago ikasal.

trowel, n. a mortar tool. Panghukay; dulos.

truant, n. an idler; one who stays away from school. Pabaya; haragan; taong dipumapasok sa gawain o sa paaralan; bulakbol.

truce, n. a brief quiet; temporary peace. Pansamantalang kapayapaan.

truculent, adj. savage; cruel. Mabalasik; mabangis; malupit.

true, adj. pure; real; exact. Tunay; totoo; tapat.

truly, adv. sincerely; honestly. Matapat.

trumpet, n. a musical wind instrument. Torotot; trumpeta.

trunk, n. the main stem of a tree; the body without the head and limbs. Katawan ng punungkahoy, ng tao o ng hayop.

truss, n. a belt worn for support. Bungkos; pambenda; panali.

trust, n. confidence. Konpiyansa; pagtitiwala.

trustful, adj. confiding. Nagtitiwala.
trustworthy, adj. reliable. Mapagtitiwalaan.
trusty, adj. reliable; fit to be trusted. Tapat.
truth, n. veracity; fidelity. Katotohanan.
truthful, adj. speaking the truth, especially habitually. Tapat; mapagsabi ng katotohanan.
truthless, adj. faithless. Ditotoo; walang katotohanan.
try, v. to attempt to do or accomplish. Subukin.
trying, adj. annoying; tiring. Mahirap tiisin; mahirap; nakapapagod.
tryst, n. an appointed meeting, especially between lovers. Tipanan; pakikipagtagpo; tagpuan.
tub, n. tank-like vessel for bathing. Batya; paliguan; banyera.
tube, n. a pipe. Tubo.
tubercular, adj. of the character of a tubercle. Tuberculosa; may tisis.
tuberculosis, n. a disease affecting various tissues of the body but most often the lungs. Tisis; tibi; pagkatuyo.
tuck, n. a flat fold in cloth. Tupi; tiklop; pileges.
Tuesday, n. the third day of the week. Martes.
tuft, n. a small bunch of fibrous material, as hair, feathers or grass bound at one end. Kupete; bungkos ng balahibo na nakakabit sa puno ng sumbrero; plumahe; borlas.
tug, v. pull with force or effort. Hatakin; baltakin; batakin.
tuition, n. a fee for instruction. Bayad sa pag-aaral.
tumble, v. fall down. Mabaligtad; matumba; madapa; mabuwal.
tumid, adj. swollen; pompous. Mapintog; namamaga.
tumor, n. an abnormal swelling in the body. Tumor; bukol.
tumult, n. the commotion and uproar of a multitude. Gulo; kaguluhan; ingay.
tumultuous, adj. disorderly; noisy. Magulo; maingay.
tune, n. harmony; a melody. Tono; himig.
tune, v. adjust to a proper pitch or frequency. Iayon sa himig; gawing magkahimig; gawing magkaayon ang dalawa o higit na bagay.
tuneful, adj. melodious. Mahimig; masarap pakinggan.
tuneless, adj. unmusical; inharmonious. Walang himig; walang tono.
tunic. n. a short coat or shirt; a blouse. Damit na hanggang balakang at may paha sa baywang.
tunnel, n. an underground roadway or passage. Tanel; daan sa ilalim ng lupa.
turban, n. a headdress formed by winding a long scarf around the head. Turbante; damit na ipinupulupot sa ulo at siyang pinakasumbrero ng mga taga Silangan.
turbid, adj. clouded, opaque or muddy, as liquid. Malapot; maputik; malatak; magulo.
turbulent, adj. disturbed; riotous. Magulo; maalimpuyo; mapaghimagsik.
turf, n. sod; horse-racing. Hipodromo; lupang madamo; mumunting halamang natuyo sa putikan at ginagamit na panggatong; karerahan.

turkey, **n.** a large American fowl. Pabo.

turmoil, n. commotion; agitation. Kaguluhan; gulo.

turn, n. a movement about a center; a rotation or revolution. Liko; pagpihit; pagikot.

turn, v. move to or from a position. Ibaling; lumiko; umikot; pumihit.

turncoat, n. a person who changes his party or principles; a renegade. Taksil; lilo.

turnip, n. a plant whose roots and leaves are used as vegetables. Singkamas.

turnout, n. those who attend a meeting; output; costume; outfit. Yari; paglabas ng mga tao; aklasan; pulutong ng mga tao; mga dala-dalahan; magkaagapay na daanan sa isang makitid na lansangan.

turnover, n. rate or volume of business. Paglilipat; pagbaligtad; pagpapalit; kuweiyong magkapatong.

turpentine, n. resinous juice. Agwaras.

turpitude, n. wickedness; depravity. Kasamaan; kalaswaan.

turret, n. a small tower. Munting tore.

turtle, n. an animal having a hard shell and a soft body. Pawikan; pagong.

tusk, n. a long pointed tooth. Pangil.

tut, interj. of mild reproach. Husto na! tama na!

tutor, n. a teacher, especially one engaged in private instruction. Pansariling guro; tutor; tagapagturo; tanging guro.

tutor, v. to instruct privately. Turuan.

twaddle, v. talk in a trivial and tedious manner. Sumatsat; dumaldal.

twang, n. a sharp sound. Taginting; ingay na nakasasakit sa tainga; pagkahumal.

tweak, v. to pinch, pull or twist. Kurutin; kurutin at pilipitin.

tweed, n. a coarse woolen cloth. Magaspang na telang lanang may iba't ibang kulay at habi.

tweedle, v. to allure; to coax. Umawit o sumutsot; tumugtog ng instrumento.

tweezers, n. small pincers; a small two-pronged gripping tool. Tiyani.

twelfth, adj. 2nd after 10th. Panlabindalawa; ikalabindalawa.

twelve, adj. & n. one dozen. Dose; labindalawa.

twentieth, adj. the ordinal of the number twice ten. Pandalawampu; ikadalawampu.

twenty, adj. twice ten; a score. Beynte; dalawampu.

twice. adv. two times; doubly. Dalawang ulit; makalawa.

twig, n. shoot of a tree. Maliit na sanga.

twilight, n. the faint light before sunrise and after sunset. Takipsilim.

twin, adj. & n. one of two children brought forth at a birth. Kambal.

twine, n. a strong cord or string. Pisi; hibla; panali; tali.

twine, v. twist together; interweave. Ikirin; ibilibid; itali.

twinge, v. to torment. Kumirot; humapdi.

twinkle, v. to sparkle. Kuminang; kumislap.

twirl, v. to whirl; spin. Paikitin.

twist, n. a bend; curve or knot. Pagbaluktot; pagpilipit.

twist, v. to form by bending or curving; to pervert. Baluktutin; pilipitin.

twit, v. taunt; upbraid; reproach. Inisin; uyamin.

twitch, n. a sudden muscular contraction. Pagkibit; masakit na panginginig ng mga laman.

twitch, v. jerk suddenly, as from muscular spasm. Ikibit; manginig.

twitter, v. chirp as birds. Humuni.

two, adj. & n. one and one. Dos; dalawa.

twofold, adj. times two; double. Doble; dalawang ulit; makalawa.

two-tongued, adj. deceitful. Manlilinlang; mandaraya.

type, n. a kind or class· sort. Tipo; uri; titik ng palimbagan.

type, v. ascertain the type of; symbolize; typewrite. Magmakinilya.

typewriter, n. a machine for writing letters and characters like those produced by printing type. Makinilya.

typhoid, n. an infectious bacillic disease marked by inflammation and ulceration of the intestines. Tipus.

typhoon, n. a cyclone of the West Pacific ocean; a tornado. Unós; bagyo.

typhus, n. an acute, infectious disease caused by germs carried by fleas, lice, etc.

typical, adj. characteristic; pertaining to a type. Kumakatawan; kakanyahan ng isang uri; makauri.

typify, v. exemplify; represent by a type or symbol. Magsilbing sagisag; katawanin; maging halimbawa ng uri.

typist, n. one who operates a typewriter. Taga-makinilya.

tyrannical, adj. despotic; cruel. Malupit.

tyranny, n. despotism; unrestrained exercise of power. Paniniil; kalupitan.

tyrant, n. a despot; an absolute ruler. Manlulupig; mang-aalipin; taong malupit.

tyro, n. a beginner in learning anything. Baguhan; bagito.

tzar, n. another form for czar, former Russian emperor. Sar; emperador ng Rusya.

U

ubiquitous, adj. everywhere. Sumasalahat ng dako; nasa lahat ng dako.

udder, n. the baggy mammary gland of a cow. Suso ng baka at ng ibang mga hayop na apat ang paa.

ugliness, n. want of beauty; deformity. Kapangitan.

ugly, adj. unpleasing or repulsive in appearance. Pangit; masamang hitsura.

ulcer, n. sore discharging pus. Ulsera; sugat na nagnanaknak.

ulterior, adj. kept concealed; lying beyond. Ulteryor; lihim; di-abot.

ultimate, adj. final; highest. Ultimo; pantapos; pangwakas; panghuli.

ultimately, adv. finally, at last. Sa wakas; sa katapusan; sa huli.

ultimatum, n. a final offer; a final statement of conditions. Ultimatum; katapusang alok; huling mungkahi.

umbilical, adj. of the navel. Umbilikal; ukol sa pusod.
umbrella, n. a rainscreen; a portable screen from rain or sun. Payong.
umpire, n. a judge; a referee. Reperi; tagahatol.
unabashed, adj. not put to shame or confusion; not humbled. Di-nalulungkot; di-hamak.
unabated, adj. not diminished. Buo; ganap; di-humuhupa.
unable, adj. not able. Hindi maaari; walang kaya.
unabridged, adj. complete; not shortened. Buo; kumpleto; walang bawas.
unacceptable, adj. not acceptable or pleasing; not welcome. Di-matatanggap.
unaccompanied, adj. with no attendants. Solo; nag-iisa.
unaccountable, adj. cannot be explained. Di-mananagot; di-maisusulit; di-maipaliliwanag.
unaccustomed, adj. not habituated. Di-hirati; di-sanay; di-kinaugalian.
unadorned, adj. not decorated; not embellished. Payak; walang gayak.
unaffected, adj. with no affectation. Natural; likas.
unaided, adj. not assisted. Walang tulong; di-tinutulungan.
unalienable, adj. inalienable; not alienable. Di-maipagbibili; di-maililipat.
unalterable, adj. unchangeable; Di-mapapalitan; di-mababago.
unamiable, adj. not lovable; not adopted to gain affection. Di-kalugod-lugod; masungit.
unanimity, n. the state of being unanimous. Pagkakaisa.
unanimous, adj. of one mind. Nagkakaisa.
unanswerable, adj. not to be satisfactorily answered. Di-mapabubulaanan; di-masasagot.
unapproachable, adj. very hard to approach. Mahirap lapitan.
unarmed, adj. not having arms or armour; not equipped. Walang sandata.
unassailable, adj. not to be moved or shaken from a purpose. Di-matutulan: di-mapipintasan.
unassuming, adj. not bold or forward; modest. Di-palalo; mahinhin; mababa.
unattainable, adj. not to be obtained or gained. Di-mararating; di-makukuha; di-maaabot.
unattended, adj. not accompanied. Nag-iisa; walang kasama.
unavoidable, adj. inevitable; not to be shunned. Di-maiiwasan.
unaware, adj. not knowing; not cognizant; Di-handa; walang malay.
unbalanced, adj. not in equipoise. Di-balanse; di-timbang.
unbearable, adj. not to be born or endured. Napakabigat; di-matitiis.
unbecoming, adj. improper; indecorous. Di-angkop; di-bagay.
unbelief, n. infidelity. Kawalan ng sampalataya; di-paniniwala.
unbelievable, adj. impossible to believe. Imposible; di-mapaniwalaan.
unbiased, adj. not prejudiced; neutral. Makatarungan; walang kinikilingan.
unblushing, adj. imprudent;

destitute of shame. Di-namumula; di-nahihiya.
unbound, adj. loose; not tied. Di-natatalian; di-nakukulong.
unburden, v. to rid of a load or burden. Alisan ng daladalahan; paginhawahin.
unbutton, v. to loose the buttons of. Alisin ang pagkakabutones.
uncalled, adj. not summoned; not invited. Hindi kailangan; di-tinatawag.
uncanny, adj. eerie; weird; mysterious. Misteryoso; mahiwaga.
uncared, adj. not regarded. Walang nag-aampon; walang nag-aalaga.
unceasing, adj. continual; not intermitting. Walang patid; walang tigil.
uncertain, adj. doubtful; ambiguous. Di-maaasahan; ditiyak.
uncertainty, n. doubtfulness; dubiety. Hindi katiyakan.
unchain, v. to free from chains. Mag-alis ng tanikala.
unchangeable, adj. immutable; not subject to variation. Walang pag-iiba; walang pagbabago; di-mababago.
uncharitable, adj. harsh; censorious. Walang awa; walang habag.
uncivil, adj. not courteous; ill-mannered; rude. Bastos; walang galang.
unclad, adj. naked; without clothes. Hubô; hubad; walang damit.
uncle, n. a mother's or father's brother. Amain; tiyo.
unclean, adj. dirty. Marungis; marumi.
uncleanliness, n. the state of being unclean. Karungisan; karumihan.
uncolored, adj. not heightened in description. Walang kulay.
uncomfortable, adj. giving uneasiness; ill at ease. Di-palagay ang loob. di-maginhawa; di-komportable.
uncommon, adj. rare; infrequent. Pambihira; di-karaniwan.
uncomplaining, adj. not disposed to murmur or complain. **Kuntento;** nasisiyahan; di-dumaraing.
unconcern, n. indifference. Kawalang halaga; kawalan ng bahala.
unconnected, adj. separated. Hiwalay.
uncongenial, adj. not agreeable or pleasing. Di-kaangkop; di-makasundo.
unconquerable, adj. insuperable. Di-malulupig; walang talo; di-matatalo.
unconquered, adj. not to be subdued or brought under control. Di-matalo.
unconscious, adj. devoid of consciousness. Di-namamalayan; walang malay.
unconstitutional, adj. contrary to the constitution. Labag sa saligang batas.
uncontrollable, adj. that cannot be controlled, ruled, or restrained. Di-mapigil; dimasupil.
unconventional, adj. not according to customs. Di-naaayon sa kaugalian; walang panuntunan; impormal.
uncork, v. to draw the cork from. Alisan ng tapon.
uncouth, adj. ill-mannered; clumsy. Masagwâ; magaspang.
uncover, v. to remove a cover or covering from. Buksan; alisan ng takip.
unction, n. the act of anointing or rubbing with an un-

guent, ointment or oil. Pagpapahid ng bendita o banal na langis.

uncultivated, adj. rough or rude in manner. Di-nililinang; di-pino.

uncurl, v. to straighten out. Unatin.

undaunted, adj. fearless; intrepid. Walang gulat; malakas ang loob; di-pinanghihinaan ng loob.

undeceive, v. free from deception, misapprehension, or mistake whether caused by others or by ourselves. Dilinlangin; pagtapatan.

undeceived, adj. free from deception. Di-nilinlang.

undecided, adj. hesitating; irresolute. Salawahan; walang tiyak na pasiya.

undefiled, adj. pure; clean. Puro; dalisay; malinis.

undefined, adj. not having its limits distinctly marked or seen. Di-tiyak; walang katuturan.

undeniable, adj. indisputable; evidently true. Di-maikakaila; di-maitatatuwa; di-matututulan.

under, adv. lower. Sa ilalim.

underbred, adj. of inferior breeding or manners. Dipurong lahi; kulang sa kabutihang-asal.

underclothes, n. clothes worn under a suit or dress. Mga damit panloob.

undergo, v. to suffer; to bear. Dumanas; pagtiisan; dumaan.

underground, adj. being below the surface of the ground. Subteranyo; ilalim ng lupa.

underhanded, adj. kept secret. Sekreto; labag sa batas; lihim.

underneath, adv. in a lower place; beneath. Sa ilalim.

undernourished, adj. not sufficiently nourished. Kulang sa pagkain.

underrate, v. to rate too low; to undervalue. Hamakin; maliitin.

understand, v. to know or apprehend the meaning of. Maintindihan; unawain; mawatasan.

undertake, v. to pledge one's self to do. Ipangako; isagawa; gawin.

undertaker, n. one who directs and provides things necessary for a funeral. Tagapamahala ng mga libing; may-ari ng punerarya.

underwear, n. a wearing under the outer clothing. Mga kasuutang panloob.

underweight, adj. having too little weight. Kulang sa timbang.

underwriter, n. one who insures subscriptions to stocks or bonds. Ahente ng siguro.

undesirable, adj. not to be wished. Hindi kanais-nais; nakasusuklam.

undignified, adj. not consistent with dignity. Di-kapuripuri; di-marangal.

undress, v. take off one's dress or clothes. Maghubad; magalis ng damit.

undue, adj. improper; unworthy. Di-angkop; di-dapat; di-bagay.

unearth, v. to dig up. Hukayin.

uneasy, adj. restless; anxious. Balisa; di-mapalagay.

uneducated, adj. without formal education. Mangmang; ignorante.

unemployed, adj. having no work or occupation. Walang hanapbuhay; walang trabaho.

unemployment, n. no work or occupation. Kawalan ng

pagkakakitaan; kawalan ng hanapbuhay o gawain.

unending, **adj.** perpetual; eternal. Walang hanggan; walang katapusan.

unendurable, adj. intolerable. Di-matatagalan; di-mapagtitiisan.

unenjoyable, adj. not to be enjoying. Di-nakatutuwa; di-nakawiwili.

unenlightened, adj. not mentally or morally illuminated. Ignorante; mangmang.

unequal, adj. not equable or uniform. Hindi pareho; di-magkatulad; di-magkapantay; di-magsinlaki.

unerring, adj. committing no mistake. Di-nagkakamali.

uneven, adj. not level; not equal. Hindi patag; hindi pareho.

unexpected, adj. not expected. Hindi inaasahan.

unexperienced, adj. without experience or practice. Walang kasanayan.

unfailing, adj. not liable to fail. Di-mabibigo; tapat; walang kapintasan.

unfair, adj. not fair; not honest. Di-makatarungan.

unfaithful, adj. not observant of promises, vows, allegiance or duty. Taksil; di-tapat.

unfamiliar, adj. not well known by frequent use. Naiiba; di-kilala.

unfasten, v. to loose; to unbind; to untie. Kalagin; tastasin.

unfavorable, adj. not propitious; discouraging. Nakapipinsala; di-sang-ayon; kalaban.

unfeeling, adj. insensible. Matigas ang pusò; walang damdamin.

unfinished, adj. not complete; imperfect. Di-kompleto; di-tapos.

unfit, adj. improper; unsuitable. Di-angkop; di-bagay; walang kaya; di-kaya.

unfold, v. to lay open to view or contemplation. Ihayag; ibuka; iladlad.

unforseen, adj. not foreknown. Di-inaasahan; di-nakikita.

unforgettable, adj. incapable of being forgotten. Di-malilimot.

unforgiving, adj. implacable. Di-nagpapatawad.

unfortunate, adj. not successful; unlucky. Kapus-palad; sawing-palad.

unfounded, adj. without foundation; baseless. Walang batayan.

unfriendly, adj. not kind or benevolent. Di-malapit; di-magiliw; marahas.

unfulfilled, adj. not fulfilled; not accomplished. Di-natupad; di-tapos.

unfurnished, adj. not supplied with furniture. Walang kasangkapan.

ungainly, adj. clumsy; awkward. Walang bikas; di-maganda; kakatuwa.

ungentlemanly, adj. not becoming a gentleman. Walang galang; di-maginoo.

ungovernable, adj. incapable of being governed, ruled, or restrained. Di-masupil; di-mapamahalaan.

ungraceful, adj. wanting grace and elegance. Di-marikit; di-magandang tingnan.

ungracious, adj. unmannerly; rude. Di-kaigaigaya; walang pitagan; di-magiliw.

ungrateful, adj. not feeling thankful or showing gratitude. Ingrato; walang utang na loob.

unguarded, adj. having no guard or watch. Walang tanod; walang ingat; walang bantay.

unhappy, adj. not cheerful or gay. Di-maligaya; nalulumbay, malungkot.

unhealthy, adj. week or indisposed. Di-malusog; masasaktin.

unheard, adj. not perceived by the ear. Di-naririnig.

unhesitating, adj. not remaining in doubt; prompt. Walang atubili; tuluy-tuloy

unhitch. v. to disengage from a fastening. Kalagin; alisin sa pagkakakabit.

unhurt, adj. free from wound or injury. Walang pinsala; di-nasaktan.

unification, n. a formation into one unit. Pag-iisa.

uniform, adj. alike. Magkakaanyô; pare-pareho; magkakatulad.

unify, v. make into one. Buuin; pag-isahin; pagsamasamahin.

unimpaired, adj. not enfeebled by time or injury. Walang pinsala; walang sira.

unimportant, adj. not important; not of great significance. Di-importante; walang halaga; di mahalaga.

uninhabited, adj. not lived in; without inhabitants. Walang nakatira.

uninjured, adj. not hurt. Di-nasaktan; walang pinsala.

uninterrupted, adj. unintermitted; incessant. Tuloy-tuloy; patuloy; walang sagabal.

union, n. concord. Ang pag-iisa; kapisanan; samahan; uniyon.

unique, adj. sole; unequalled. Walang kapareho; tangi; di-karaniwan; pambihira.

unit, n. any group of things or persons considered as one. Pangkat; bahagi; yunit.

unite, v. to join; combine. Pag-isahin; magsama-sama; pagsamahin.

universe, n. all created things; the whole world. Sansinukob; sandaigdigan.

university, n. the institution of learning of the highest grade. Unibersidad; pamantasan.

unjust, adj. contrary to justice and right. Hindi-matuwid; walang katarungan; di-makatarungan.

unkind, adj. harsh; cruel. Walang awa; malupit.

unlike, adj. having no resemblance. Iba; kaiba.

unlucky, adj. not successful in one's undertakings. Kapus-palad; sawi; walang suwerte.

unmanageable, adj. beyond control. Di-makontrol; di-masupil; di-mapamahalaan.

unmarried, adj. not married; single. Soltero; binata; dalaga; walang asawa.

unmerciful, adj. inhuman; merciless. Walang awa; walang habag; malupit.

unmerited, adj. not deserved through wrong-doing. Di-nararapat; di-tapat.

unmistakable, adj. not capable of being mistaken or misunderstood. Maliwanag; di-maipagkakamali.

unmoved, adj. not changed in place; firm. Di-natitinag; di-nagagalaw; di-nahahabag.

unnatural, adj. forced; artificial. Di-natural; di-likas; artipisyal.

unnecessary, adj. needless. Di-kailangan.

unnoticed, adj. not observed, not regarded. Di-pansin.

unoccupied, adj. not possessed; not employed or taken up in business or otherwise. Bakante; walang ginagawa; walang laman; walang tao.

unpack, v. to remove a wrapper from. Alisan ng laman; alisin sa pagkakabalot.

unpaid, adj. not having received what is due. Di-pagado; di-bayad.

unpleasant, adj. not pleasant; disagreeable. Nakayayamot.

unpopular, adj. not having the public favour. Di-tanyag; di-kinagigiliwan ng marami; kinaiinisan.

unpremeditated, adj. not previously purposed or intended. Di-binalak.

unprepared, adj. not ready. Di-handa.

unprofitable, adj. useless. Walang halaga; di-pakikinabangan; walang tubo.

unpromising, adj. not affording a favorable prospect of success, of excellence, of profit. Di-maaasahan; walang pangako.

unprosperous, adj. not attended with success. Di-matagumpay; di-maunlad; di-sagana.

unprotected, adj. not protected or defended. Walang pananggalang; walang tanggulan.

unqualified, adj. incompetent. Walang kakayahan; di-angkop; di-bagay; walang karapatan.

unquestionable, adj. indubitable; certain. Tiyak; walang pasubali; di-mapag-aalinlanganan.

unreal, adj. not substantial. Di-totoo; di-tunay.

unreasonable, adj. not agreeable to reason. Walang katwiran.

unrefined, adj. not polished in manners, taste, or the like. Magaspang; magaslaw.

unreliable, adj. not to be relied or depended on. Di-mapagkakatiwalaan; di-maaasahan.

unreserved, adj frank; open. Walang inililihim.

unrest, n. restlessness; a disturbed condition. Pagkabalisa; ligalig.

unripe, adj. not mature; not ripe. Hilaw; di-hinog.

unrivalled, adj. having no rival or equal; peerless; incomparable. Walang katulad; walang kapantay.

unroll, v. to lay open or display. Alisin sa pagkakabilot; iladlad.

unruffled, adj. turbulent; ungovernable. Di-mapigil; magulo.

unruly, adj. hard to rule or control; lawless. Matigas ang ulo; magulo.

unsafe, adj. perilous; hazardous. Peligroso; di-ligtas; mapanganib.

unsalable, adj. not meeting a ready sale. Di-maipagbibili.

unsatisfactory, adj. not satisfying. Di-kasiya-siya.

unsavory, adj. tasteless; insipid. Di-masarap; walang lasa .

unscrew, v. to draw the screws from. Alisin sa pagkakaturnilyo.

unscrupulous, adj. regardless of principles. Walang ingat; di-mapagkakatiwalaan; di-maingat.

unseasonable, adj. untimely. Wala sa panahon; di-napa panahon.

unselfish, adj. not selfish or unduly attached to one's own interest. Bukas na palad· walang pag-iimbot.

unsettle, v. to make uncertain or fluctuating. Guluhin; alisin sa kinalalagyan.
unsettled, adj. unsteady or wavering; disturbed or troubled. Di-matatag; magulo; di pa ayos.
unshaken, adj. firm; steady. Di-natitinag; di-nagagalaw.
unsightly, adj. disagreeable to the eye. Masakit sa mata; pangit tingnan; di-maganda.
unskilled, adj. destitute of skill or practical knowledge. Di-bihasa; di-sanay.
unskillful, adj. having no or little skill. Walang kasanayan.
unsociable, adj. not suitable for society. Walang kapwa tao; malayo sa kapwa; di-marunong makisama.
unspeakable, adj. incapable of being spoken or uttered. Di-mabanggit; di-masabi.
unstable, adj. inconstant; irresolute. Di-matatag; mabuway.
unsuccessful, adj. having met with no success. Bigo; di-nagtagumpay.
unsuitable, adj. unfit; improper. Di-angkop; di-bagay.
unsuspected, adj. not suspected; not an object of suspicion. Pinagkakatiwalaan; di-pinaghihinalaan.
unsuspecting, adj. free from suspicion. Di-naghihinala; nagtitiwala.
untamed, adj. wild. Mailap.
unthankful, adj. ungrateful. Walang utang na loob.
untidy, adj. slovenly; disorderly. Di-malinis; magulo; walang kaayusan.
untie, v. to loosen; unfasten. Kalasin; kalagin.
until, prep. up to the time that. Hanggang.
untimely, adj. inopportune. Di-napapanahon; wala sa panahon.
untiring, adj. unwearied. Walang hinawa; walang pagod.
untold, adj. not related; not revealed. Di-masabi; di-sinasabi; di-matiyak.
untouched, adj. intangible. Di-nagagalaw; di-nahihipo.
untried, adj. not tried; not tested. Hindi pa subok.
untransferable, adj. incapable of being transferred or passed from one to another. Di-maililipat.
untrue, adj. false; not faithful to another. Mali; taksil; di-tapat; di-totoo; palso.
untrusworthy, adj. not deserving of confidence. Di-maaasahan; di-mapagtitiwalaan.
unused, adj. not accustomed. Hindi bihasa.
unusual, adj. not common; rare. Ekstraordinaryo; di-karaniwan.
unveil, v. to remove a veil from. Ihayag; alisan ng takip; alisin ang belo.
unwashed, adj. filthy. Marumi; di-nilabhan.
unwelcome, adj. not well received. Di-matatanggap; di-kanais-nais.
unwell, adj. indisposed; ailing. May sakit.
unwilling, adj. loath; reluctant. Bantulot: di-sang-ayon; di-ibig; masama ang loob.
unwise, adj. foolish; injudicious. Hangal; di-dapat.
unwrap, v. to take off a wrapper from. Alisan ng balot; alisin sa pagkakabalot.
unwritten, adj. not written. Hindi nakasulat.
up, adv. on high. Sa itaas.
upbraid, v. to charge reproachfully. Pagsabihan; sisihin; kagalitan.

uphold, v. to support. Pagtibayin; itaguyod.

upkeep, n. maintenance in a state of efficiency. Gastos; sustento; pangalaga.

uplift, v. to lift up; raise; elevate. Itaas; paunlarin.

upon, prep. up and on; on. Sa ibabaw ng; sa.

upper, adj. higher in place or position. Itaas; pang-ibabaw; higit na mabuti; kahigtan; mataas.

upright, adj. erect. Mabuti; tapat; tuwid.

uprightness, n. integrity; probity. Katuwiran; pagiging tuwid.

uprising, n. a riot; a rebellion. Paghihimagsik; himagsikan.

uproar, n. a noisy and violent disturbance. Kaguluhan.

uproot, v. to tear up by the roots; to remove completely. Bunutin, lipulin.

upstairs, adj. pertaining or relating to an upper story or flat. Sa itaas.

up-to-date, adj. modern. Moderno; makabago; husto sa oras.

upward, adj. moving or directed upward. Pataas.

urge, v. to incite; to push. Hikayatin; sulsulan; himukin.

use, n. the act of using, employing or putting to service. Kagamitan; gamit.

use, v. employ for a purpose; put to service. Gamitin.

useful, adj. valuable for use; serviceable. Makabuluhan; magagamit, kapaki-pakinabang.

usual, adj. common; ordinary. Nakagawian; karaniwan; tulad ng dati.

usurer, n. a person who lends money at an extremely high or unlawful interest. Usurero.

utility, n. usefulness. Mahalagang bagay; gamit; kapakinabangan.

utilize, v. use profitably. Gamitin; pakinabangan.

utmost, adj. extreme; furthest. Sukdulan.

utter, v. to speak. Ipahayag; sabihin.

utterance, n. issuance; manner of speaking. Pananalita; deklarasyon; sinabi.

V

vacancy, n. emptiness; unfilled position. Bakante; kawalan ng laman; gawain o tungkuling walang naghahawak.

vacant, adj. empty; void. Basyo; hindi okupado; walang laman; bakante; walang humahawak.

vacate, v. to make vacant. Iwan; alisan; gawing bakante.

vacation, n. resting time; a period of release from work. Pagliliwaliw; pagpapahinga; bakasyon.

vaccinate, v. inoculate with cowpox as protection against smallpox. Bakunahan.

vacillate, v. to waver; be irresolute. Mag-alinlangan; mag-atubili.

vacillation, n. a wavering. Pag-aalinlangan; pag-aatubili.

vacuum, n. space void of matter. Basyo; kawalan ng laman.

vagabond, n. a wanderer; a tramp. Lagalag; palaboy; hampaslupa.

vagary, n. a whim; caprice. Kapritso; sumpong.

vagrant, adj. wandering; idle. Bagamundo; palaboy; hampaslupa.

vague, **adj.** not definite, precise or clear. Hindi maliwanag; malabo.

vain, **adj.** worthless or futile; conceited. Hambog; mayabang; walang saysay.

vainglorious, **adj.** boastful. Mayabang; hambog.

vainly, **adv.** without effect; foolishly. Nang may kahambugan; nang walang saysay.

vale, **n.** low ground; a valley. Libis; lambak.

valiant, **n.** heroic; brave. Magiting; matapang.

valid, **adj.** having legal force. Maaari; tunay; totoo; may bisa; may pinagbabatayan.

valise, **n.** a bag; a small leather travelling bag. Bag; maleta.

valley, **n.** a relatively low tract of land between hills. Libis; lambak.

valor, **n.** bravery; courage. Kagitingan; lakas ng loob; tapang.

valuable, **adj.** of great value. Mahalaga.

value, **n.** price; worth; rate. Halaga.

value, **v.** regard as desireful or useful. Halagahan; pahalagahan.

valueless, **adj.** worthless. Walang halaga.

valve, **n.** any device used to control the flow of a fluid through a pipe or vent. Bálbula; manipis na takip na ginagamit na pang-impit o pampalakas ng agos o ng kuryente.

vampire, **n.** a supposed bloodsucking monster; a kind of bat. Bampira; asuwang; taong sumisipsip ng dugo ng kapwa.

van, **n.** a large covered wagon or truck. Karo; bagol; sasakyang ginagamit sa pagdadala ng mga kasangkapan.

vandal, **adj.** one nostile to art or literature. Barbaro; mapangwasak; mabangis.

vandalism, **n.** wanton destruction of things. Pananampalasan.

vanish, **v.** to disappear. Mapaparam; mawala; maglaho.

vanity, **n.** empty pride; excessive pride. Kapalaluan; labis na pagpapahalaga sa sarili; kahambugan.

vanquish, **v.** to defeat in battle or contest. Daigin; matalo; talunin.

vapor, **n.** fog; like smoke. Usok na nagmumula sa tubig na malamig o kumulo; singaw.

variable, **adj.** unsteady; tending to change; Pabago-bago; salawahan; paiba-iba.

variance, **n.** dissension; the state or fact of varying. Pagbabago; pagkakaiba; kaibhan.

variant, **adj.** diverse; different. Naiiba; iba-iba.

variety, **n.** change; diversity. Pakakaiba't iba; sarisari; pulutong na may iba't ibang bagay.

varnish, **n.** a glossy liquid. Barnis.

vary, **v.** to change; alter. Magbago; ibahin; pag-iba-ibahin.

vase, **n.** a holder or container used for ornament. Plorera.

vassal, **n.** a dependent; a feudal tenant; a subject; follower. Basalyo; alipin.

vast, **adj.** great in extent or quantity. Malaki; malawak.

vat, **n.** a large tub or vessel. Malaking batya.

Vatican, **n.** the Papal palace. Batikano; palasyo ng Papa.

vault, **n.** a chamber used

as a safe; any underground room. Bodega; malaking silid na imbakan ng alak; silid sa ilalim ng lupa; talon; lundag.

vault, v. jump or leap with the aid of the hands resting on something. Lumukso; lumundag; tumalon sa tulong ng isang tukod.

vaunt, n. boastful utterance. Kayabangan; karangyaan; kahambugan.

vaunt, v. to boast; to brag. Magyabang; magmagaling; maghambog.

veal, n. the flesh of a sheep. Ternera; karne ng tupa.

veer, v. to turn, to change. Umiwas; magbago ng tunguhin o ng kalagayan; lumihis.

vegetable, n. any herbaceous plant whose parts are used for food. Gulay.

vegetarian, n. one who eats only vegetables. Mapagkain ng gulay; taong ang tanging pagkain ay gulay.

vehicle, n. wagon; Behikulo; sasakyan.

vehement, adj. urgent; eager. Mapusok; mahigpit; matindi; malakas; maalab.

veil, n. any piece of light fabric worn over the face or head. Talukbong; lambong; belo; panakip sa ulo.

vein, n. one of the tubes that convey blood to the heart. Bena; ugat na malaki.

velocity, n. speed; swiftness. Belosidad; bilis.

velvet, n. heavy silk goods; a fabric with a thick, soft pile. Gamusa; pelus; belbet; tersiyopelo; seda o damit na may malambot at makintab na balahibo.

venal, adj. open to bribery; corrupt. Masama; madaling masuhulan; mukhang salapi.

vend, v. to sell. Magtinda; magbili.

vendetta, n. a feud. Bendikta; higanti.

vendor, n. a seller. Tagapagbili; bendor; tagapaglako; tagatinda.

veneer, n. a thin layer of fine wood or other material applied as an outer coating. Manipis na telang pampalamuti.

venerable, n. old and dignified; worthy of veneration. Benerable; kagalang-galang; kapita-pitagan.

venerate, v. to revere; regard with reverence. Sambahin; igalang.

veneration, n. reverence. Benerasyon; paggalang; pamimitagan.

vengeance, n. reverence. Bengansa; higanti.

venial, adj. that can be forgiven. Mapatatawad; hindi mabigat.

venial sin, n. an excusable or pardonable offense against God. Kasalanang benyal o magaan.

venison, n. flesh of deer. Benado; karne ng usa.

venom, n. poison; malice. Kamandag; malisya; lason.

vent, n. utterance; an outlet; an emission. Bulalás; butas; puwang.

ventilate, v. to air; let fresh air into. Ipahayag; pahanginan.

ventilator, n. an apparatus or means for changing or improving the air. Bentilador.

venture, n. a risky or daring undertaking. Pakikipagsapalaran; pagbabakasakali.

venturesome, adj. daring. Pangahas; mahilig sa pakikipagsapalaran.

veracity, n. truthfulness. Kawastuan; katotohanan.

verdict, n. judgment. Desisyon; hatol; pasiya.

verge, n. a rod; brink; edge. Tabi; gilid.

verifiable, adj. that which may be verified. Mapatotohanan; maaaring patunayan.

verify, v. to prove. Patunayan; patotohanan.

veritable, adj. true; real. Totoo; tunay.

vermilion, n. a fine red. Matingkad na pula; kulay na pulang-pula.

vernacular, adj. one's native tongue or speech. Katutubong wika; wikain.

vernal, adj. of youth or spring. Bernal; tungkol sa tagsibol; bata.

versatile, adj. many sided. Bersatil; maraming nalalaman.

verse, n. metrical composition; a poem. Berso; taludtod; tula.

version, n. a translation. Salin.

versus, prep. against. Laban.

vertebra, n. joint of spine. Bertebra; biyas ng mahabang buto sa likod.

very, adv. exceedingly; extremely. Totoong; tunay; lubha; napaka; pang-abay na nagsasaad ng pasukdol.

vespers, n. evening service. Orasyón; dasal sa dapit-hapon.

vessel, n. a dish; ship; a hollow container. Sisidlan; baso; lalagyan ng tubig o ano mang likido; bapor; sasakyang-dagat.

vest, n. a short, sleeveless garment worn by men under the coat. Tsaleko.

vestige, n. sign; trace. Bakas; palatandaan; labi.

vestry, n. church addition; a room in a church where vestments are kept. Sakristiya.

veteran, adj. experienced through long service or practice. Beterano; matanda na sa serbisyo; may kasanayan na.

veteran, n. one long experienced, as fireman, soldier, workman. Beterano; taong may matagal nang karanasan sa isang bagay o gawain lalo na sa pagsusundalo.

veto, n. the right to reject; any ban or prohibition. Beto; kapangyarihan.

vex, v. to tease; to irritate. Inisin; mayamot; mainis.

vexation, n. the act of vexing; state of being disputed. Pagpapapalit; kainisan; kayamutan.

via, prep. by way of. Sa; sa pamamagitan.

viaduct, n. elevated passage. Daang nakataas; tulay sa ibabaw ng mababang lunan.

viand, n. an article of food. Ulam; pang-ulam.

vibrate, v. quiver; resound; oscillate. Umugoy; tumaginting.

vice, prep. instead of; in place of. Sa halip ng.

vice, n. any immoral or evil practice; a bad habit. Bisyo; masamang hilig.

vice-versa, adj. the reverse; contrariwise. Gayun din naman; bais-bersa.

vicinity, n. nearness; the neighborhood. Ang karatig; ang paligid; ang dakong malapit.

vicious, adj. addicted to vice; wicked. Mapanikis; mahilig sa masama; mabisyo.

victim, n. one who suffers from a harmful agency; a dupe. Biktima; tao o hayop na sinaktan o pinatay.
victor, n. a conqueror. Ang nanalo; nagwagi; ang nagtagumpay.
victuals, n. food. Pagkain.
vie, v. to contest; to contend. Makilaban; makipagpaligsahan.
view, n. range of vision; visualization. Pagtingin; tanawin.
view, v. to look at; to consider. Tingnan; masdan.
viewpoint, n. attitude of mind. Kuro; palagay.
vigil, n. a keeping awake; watehful attention at any time. Pagtatanod; pagbabantay; paglalamay.
vigilant, adj. watchful. Maingat; laging nakabantay.
vignette, n. a small engraving; a portrait of the head and bust only. Binyeta; munting palamuting nakaguhit sa isang dahon ng aklat; maikling paglalarawan.
vigor, n. force; strength. Sigla; lakas.
vigorous, adj. full of strength. Masigla; malakas.
vile, adj. base; mean; disgusting. Mahalay; imbi; masama.
vileness, n. degradation; extreme badness. Kahalayan; kaimbihan.
vilify, v. to defame; abuse. Hamakin; siraan ng puri.
village, n. a small town; a small assemblage of houses, less than a town. Poblasyon; nayon.
villager, n. an inhabitant. Taganayon.
villain, n. the chief antagonist of the hero in a play or novel. Kontrabida; ang masamang panauhan sa isang katha; taong tampalasan.
vim, n. energy; force; vigor. Sigla; lakas.
vincible, adj. conquerable. Madadaig; maaaring matamo; magagapi.
vindictive, adj. revengeful. Bengatibo; mapaghiganti.
vine, n. climbing plant. Baging.
vinegar, n. an acid liquor; a sour liquid obtained by fermentation of fruit juices. Binagre; suka.
vineyard, n. plantation of grape vines. Ubasan; taniman ng ubas.
violable, adj. may be violated. Maaaring sirain; malalabag.
violate, v. break in upon; do violence to. Lapastanganin; sirain; labagin.
violence, n. outrage; fury. Dahas; matinding damdamin; lakas na nakawawasak.
violent, adj. forcible; vehement. Mapusok; malakas; matindi; marahas.
violet, n. any of numerous herbs bearing small short-stemmed flowers. Biyoleta.
violin, n. a fiddle; a stringed musical instrument played with a bow. Biyolin.
viper, n. venomous snake. Ulupong; bibora; isang uri ng makamandag na ahas.
virgin, n. a person, especially woman who is pure, untouched. Dalaga; birhen; babaing dalisay ang pagkababae.
virile, adj. manly. Mabulas; malusog ang pagkalalaki.
virtue, n. moral goodness. Kabaitan; kabutihan; katangian.
virus, n. contagious, poisonous matter. Birus; tagapagdala ng nakahahawang sakit.

visa, n. an official indorsement, as on a passport. Bisa.

visage, n. the countenance. Mukha; kaanyuan.

visible, adj. may be seen. Natatanaw; nakikita.

vision, n. seeing; the sense of sight. Pangmalas; paningin; pangitain.

visit, n. a friendly or official call. Bisita; pagdalaw.

visit, v. go to see (a person, place, etc.). Bumisita; dumalaw.

visitor, n. one who visits. Bisita; dalaw; panauhin.

vital, adj. essential; critically important. Lubhang kailangan; mahalaga; makabuluhan.

vitality, n. the principle of life. Lakas; lusog.

vitamin, n. special substances necessary for the proper nourishment of the body. Bitamina.

vitreous. adj. pertaining or consisting of glass. Tulad ng salamin; nag-aangkin ng katangian ng salamin.

vituperate, v. to address or find fault with abusively. Tuligsain; siraan; murahin; hamakin.

vituperation, n. censure. Pagtuligsa; pagmumura; paninira; paghamak.

vivacious, adj. gay; lively. Bibo; masigla.

vivid, adj. clearly perceptible. Buháy; nakikitang mabuti; matingkad.

vocabulary, n. words used; the words of a language collectively. Bokabularyo; talasalitaan.

vocally, adv. verbally. Bokalmente; sa pamamagitan ng tinig.

vocation, n. calling; a particular profession, business, or occupation. Bokasyon; hanapbuhay; gawain.

vociferate, v. to cry out noisily. Sabihin nang pasigaw; sumigaw; hingin nang pasigaw.

voice, n. speech-sound; expression. Pahayag; boses; tinig.

voiceless, adj. having no voice; dumb; mute. Walang tinig.

void, adj. empty; null. Walang bisa; walang laman.

void, v. nullify. Pawalan ng bisa; huwag pahalagahan.

volatile, adj. changing to vapor readily or rapidly; fickle; frivolous. Mabilis sumingaw; madaling maparam; salawahan.

volleyball, n. a game played with a large ball and a high net. Balibol.

volt, n. the unit of electromotive force. Boltahe.

voluble, adj. speaking fluently; glib. Madaldal; masatsat; masalita.

volume, n. a book, especially one of a set; a roll. Tomo; bolumen; aklat; bunton.

voluminous, adj. large in bulk; of ample size or extent. Makapal; marami; may mataas na bunton.

voluntary, adj. done on one's own accord or free choice. Boluntaryo; kusang-loob.

volunteer, n. one who enters into any service on his own free will. Boluntaryo; taong kusang-loob na naghandog ng paglilingkod.

voluptuous, adj. sensuous; seeking, affording or suggestive of pleasure. Mahilig sa kasiyahan; malibog; makalupa.

vomit, v. to eject contents of stomach through the mouth. Sumuka.

voracious, adj. ravenous; greedy. Masiba; matakaw.

vortex, n. a whirlpool. Ipu-ipo; ang pabilog na hukay na nilikha sa tubig o ano mang likido kapag pinai-ikot.

vote, n. suffrage; a ballot. Halál; boto.

vote, v. indicate a choice. Ihalal; bumoto.

voter, n. an elector; one who has a right to vote. Botante; manghahalal.

vouch, v. to attest; assert; declare. Managot; patunayan; panindigan.

voucher, n. a written evidence of payment. Botser; katibayan sa nagugol.

vouchsafe, v. bestow or grant condescendingly. Pumayag; ibigay; ipagkaloob.

vow, n. a solemn promise or pledge. Pangakong taimtim; panata; sumpa.

vow, v. promise solemnly; swear. Isumpa; gawing panata.

vowel, n. a vocal sound. Patinig.

voyage, n. a journey. Biyahe; paglalayag; paglalakbay.

vulgar, adj. common; mean; unrefined. Hindi pino; bastos; magaspang; masagwa; bulgar.

vulnerable, adj. capable of being wounded or injured. Matatablan; masusugatan.

vulture, v. a bird of prey; a large carrion-eating bird. Buwitre; isang uri ng mabangis na ibong mandaragit.

W

wad, n. a little mass of some soft material. Balumbon; tapon; munting bola ng malambot na bagay na ginagamit na pamasak; bilot ng papel.

wad, v. to form into or pack with a wad. Balumbunin; pasakan; tapalan; tapunan; sapnan.

waddle, v. walk like a duck. Lumakad ng tila pato.

wade, v. walk through water. Magtampisaw; maglunoy.

wafer, n. a thin; usually sweetened, delicate cake. Apa.

waft, v. bear or convey through a buoyant medium, as water or air. Matangay; lumutang sa hangin; lumutang sa tubig.

wag, v. move or cause to move from side to side. Pagalaw-galawin.

wage, n. rate of payment for work. Kita; suweldo; sahod.

wager, n. a bet. Pusta; taya.

wager, v. bet. Pumusta; tumaya.

wagon, n. a four-wheeled heavy vehicle. Karo; bagol; kariton.

wail, v. to grieve; lament. Humagulgól; manangis.

waist, n. the part of the human body between the ribs and the hips. Baywang.

wait, v. to stay for. Maghintay.

waiter, n. a server at table. Weyter; tagapaglingkod; tagapagsilbi sa isang karihan o kainan.

waiting-room, n. a room where you can wait. Weyting-rum; silid na hintayan.

wake, n. a vigil. Paglalamay.

wake, v. stop sleeping; become active. Gisingin.

walk, n. moderate foot pace; path; a stroll. Lakad.

walk, v. move by steps with a moderate gait. Lumakad.

wall, n. a structure of stone, brick, or other materials serving to enclose, divide, support, or defend. Tabiki; pader; dingding.

wallet, n. a bag or kit; pocketbook, especially one in which bank notes or paper lie flat. Wolet; pitaka; kartera; lalagyan ng pera.

wallflower, n. any plant of the brassicaceous genera. Isang uri ng bulaklak; babaing walang makasayaw.

wallow, v. to roll about. Maglublob.

waltz, n. a round dance in triple rhythm danced by couples. Balse.

waltz, v. to dance or move in the movement or step of a waltz. Magsayaw ng balse.

wan, adj. pale and sickly. Matamlay; maputla.

wand, n. a slender stick; a rod, especially one used by a conjurer. Tungkod; patpat; sangang payat.

wander, v. to rove; stroll; ramble. Gumala; maligaw; lumaboy.

wanderer, n. a rover. Bagamundo; palaboy; manlalakbay.

wanderlust, n. a strong desire to wander. Malaking pagkakagusto sa paglalayas.

wane, v. to grow less. Humina; magbawas; lumiit; lumipas; maparam.

want, n. poverty; lack or scarcity; is needed or desired. Nesisidad; pagnanais; pangangailangan.

want, v. feel a desire for. Magnais; mangailangan.

wanton, adj. licentious; reckless. Walang habag; mahalay; malibog; palabiro.

war, n. armed conflict among nations. Gulo; digmaan; labanan; giyera.

war, v. carry on a war. Makipagdigmaan; digmain.

warble, v. sing, as a bird. Kumanta; umawit nang nanginginig ang tinig.

warbler, n. a singer. Kantor; manganganta; mang-aawit; ibong pipit.

ward, n. the act of keeping guard; one of the sections of a hospital. Ward; alaga; tinuturuan; mga silid tulad ng sa mga pagamutan; purok.

ward, v. to guard; to defend against danger. Sanggahin; bantayan; ipagtanggol.

warden, n. a guard or guardian. Guwardiya; tagabantay; taga-alaga.

warder, n. a keeper; a guard. Tagabantay; guwardiya.

wardrobe, n. wearing apparel. Aparador ng damit.

warehouse, n. storehouse for goods. Bodega; pintungan; tinggalan ng kalakal.

warfare, n. operation against an enemy. Giyera; digmaan.

warily, adv. cautiously. Nang maingat.

warlike, adj. fit for war; fond for war. Palahamok; paladigma.

warm, adj. having a moderate degree of heat. Maalinsangan; mainit.

warning, n. cautioning. Abiso; bala; babala.

warrant, n. guaranty; sanction; justification. Patotoo; patunay; mandamyento; pagbibigay-karapatan; pananagot; pasiya.

warrant, v. to guarantee; justify. Garantiyahan; panagutan; bigyang-katwiran.

warrior, n. a soldier. Girero; mandirigma.

wart, n. an excrescence; a small hard growth on the

skin. Kulugo.

wash, n. a cleansing by water; articles to be cleansed. Labada; mga damit na labahin.

wash, v. cleanse in or with a liquid, especially water. Linisin; maghugas; maglaba.

washerwoman, n. a laundress. Labandera; manlalabang babae.

wasp, n. an insect allied to the bee. Putakti.

waste, v. devastate; ruin; squander. Sayangin; waldasin; aksayahin; sirain.

wasteful, adj. lavish; ruinous; needlessly spending or spent. Bulagsak; mangwawaldas; mapag-aksaya.

watch, n. vigil; guard; a timepiece carried in the pocket or worn on the wrist. Guwardiya; paglalamay; orasan; bantay.

watch, v. to look at attentively; keep vigil; keep guard. Tanuran; maglamay; pag-ingatan; masdan; bantayan.

water, n. a transparent, odorless, tasteless fluid, H_2O, that falls in as rain. Agwa; tubig.

waterfall, n. a cascade. Talon.

waterproof, adj. impervious or resistant to water. Di-tinatagusan ng tubig; di-nababasa.

wave, n. a ridge in the surface of a liquid. Alon.

wave, v. move to and fro; undulate; have a curved form or direction; give a signal by waving the hands. Umugoy; kulutin; paalunin; kumaway; iwagayway; magwagayway.

wax, n. a thick, sticky substance secreted by bees; any similar oily substance. Pagkit; waks; langis ng balyena o ng halaman.

way, n. method; road. Paraan; daan; pamamaraan.

wayfarer, n. a traveler on foot. Biyahero; manlalakbay; taong naglalakad sa daan.

waylay, v. to lie in wait for; attack on the way. Harangin.

wayward, adj. willful· disobedient. Suwail; matigas ang ulo.

we, pron. the first person, nominative, plural. Kami; kita; tayo.

weak, adj. feeble; lacking physical strength or endurance. Marupok; mahina.

weaken, v. make or become weaker. Manghina; pahinain.

weakly, adv. in a weak manner; sickly. Nang mahina; nang walang lakas.

weakness, n. feebleness. Karupukan; kahinaan.

wealth, n. riches. Kasaganaan; kayamanan; yaman.

wean, v. to reconcile to loss of something. Awatin; ilayo.

weapon, n. an instrument of offense or defense. Armás; sandata.

wear, v. carry or bear on the body, as clothing. Gamitin; isuot.

wearisome, adj. tedious; tiresome. Nakahahapo; nakapapagod.

weary, adj. worn out; fatigued. Hapo; pagod.

weather, n. the state of the atmosphere in regard to heat, cold, wetness, dryness, humidity, storm. Tiyempo; panahon.

weather, v. bear up against and survive. Batahin; maligtasan; pagtiisan; matalo.

weave, v. to entwine. Maglala; humabi; habihin.

weaver, n. one who weaves; one whose occupation is weaving. Manlalala; manghahabi.

web, n. a thing woven; a trap, plot, or scheme. Habi; tela; damit; bahay ng gagamba.

webbed, adj. having the digits connected by a web, as the foot of a duck or a beaver. May balat sa pagitan ng mga daliri.

wed. v. marry. Ikasal; pakasalan.

wedding-ring, n. a ring usually gold, placed by the bridegroom on the third finger of the bride's left hand at the marriage ceremony. Singsing na pangkasal.

wedlock, n. marriage; matrimony. Matrimonyo; pag-iisang-dibdib; pagkakasal; kasal.

Wednesday, n. fourth day of the week. Miyerkules.

weed, n. wild plant; a useless or characteristically unwanted plant. Sukal na damo; damo o munting halamang walang saysay.

weed, v. free from obnoxious plants. Alisan; bunutin ang sukal na damo o ang damong di kailangan.

week, n. a period of seven consecutive days. Semana; linggo.

weekday, n. any day but Sunday. Araw ng paggawa; simpleng araw.

weekly, adj. every week; occurring once each week. Lingguhan; linggu-linggo.

weep, v. to shed tears. Lumuhâ; manangis; umiyak.

weeping, adj. that weeps. Lumuluhâ; nananangis

weigh, v. determine the heaviness of; consider. Timbangin; isipin.

weight, n. degree of heaviness. Timbang; bigat.

weighty, adj. heavy; momentous. Mabigat; mahalaga.

weird, adj. supernatural; wild; uncanny. Misteryoso; kagila-gilalas; mahiwaga.

welcome, n. a kindly, warm greeting; hospitable reception. Pagbati; mabuting pagtanggap.

welcome, v. receive kindly and gladly. Batiin; tanggapin nang mahusay.

welfare, n. health, happiness and prosperity. Kagalingan; kapakanan.

well, adv. in a good, right, or worthy manner. Mabuti; magaling.

well, n. an excavation in the ground as a source of water, oil or gas. Poso; balon.

well-bred, adj. well brought up. May mabuting pinagmulan; may mabuting pinag-aralan.

well-known, adj. clearly or fully known. Laganap; bantog; tanyag.

well-to-do, adj. prosperous; wealthy. May kaya sa buhay.

welt, n. a strip of material, especially leather, standing out; a wale. Bakas ng palo o hagupit; latay.

west, n. the point where the sun sets at the equinox. Kanluran.

western, adj. pertaining to the west. Oksidental; kanluranin.

wet, adj. covered with or permeated by a moist or fluid substance. Basa.

whale, n. a fish of great size. Balyena.

wharf, n. a quay; a dock. Pantalan; daungan.

what, pron. that which. Ano.

wheat, n. any of various cereal plants whose grain is ground into flour and makes bread. Trigo.

wheel, n. circular frame or disk capable of turning on an axis. Ruweda; gulong.

when, adv. at what or which time. Kailan; nang.

when, conj. time specified as soon as. Kung.

whenever, adv. at whatever time. Sa tuwing; kailan man.

where, adv. at or in what place. Saan.

whet, v. to sharpen by rubbing. Ihasa; itagis.

which, pron. the one that. Alin.

while, conj. during or in the time that; as long as; though; whereas. Samantala; habang.

whim, n. fancy; a capricious desire. Kapritso; kahilingan.

whimsical, adj. odd. Kakatuwa; kakaiba.

whip, n. an instrument for lashing. Panghagupit; pamalo; latiko.

whirl, v. turn around rapidly rotate. Umikot; uminog.

whirlpool, n. vortex of water; a circular eddy in a body of water. Ipu-ipo; puyo ng tubig.

whirlwind, n. air whirling around and around violently. Ipu-ipo.

whiskers, n. hairs on the face. esp. that on a man's face. Balbas; bigote.

whisper, v. say under the breath; say secretly. Bumulong; ibulong.

whistle, n. a whistling sound; a device for using it. Sipol; silbato; pito.

whistle, v. make a shrill or musical sound by forcing the breath through pursed lips or air through a pipe. Sumipol; sumutsot; pumito.

white, adj. of the color of pure snow. Puti; maputi.

whiten, v. make or become whiter. Paputiin.

whither, adv. to what place; wherever. Saan.

whitish, adj. somewhat white; tending to white. Namumuti; maputi-puti.

whittle, v. cut or form with a knife; pare. Kayasin.

who, pron. what or which person; that person; those persons. Sino.

whoever, pron. no matter who. Sinuman; sino man.

whole, adj. entire; complete; all. Walang kulang; lahat; buo.

wholehearted, adj. sincere; earnest. Buong-puso; matapat.

wholesome, adj. salutary; healthy; sound-looking. Kasiya-siya; mabuti; makapagpapalusog; masarap.

whom, pron. objective case of who. Kanino.

whore, n. an unchaste woman; prostitute. Masamang babae; babaing nagbibili ng laman; patutot.

why, adv. for what reason. Bakit.

wick, n. the part of an oil lamp or candle that is lighted. Mitsa.

wicked, adj. vicious; evil; sinful. Makasalanan; masama.

wide, adj. broad; expansive. Maluwang; malapad; malawak.

widespread, adj. spread over or occupying a wide space. Laganap; kalat.

widow, n. woman whose husband has died. Biyuda; babaing namatay ang asawa; balong babae.

width, n. breadth; wideness. Luwang; lapad.

wife, n. a man's spouse. Maybahay; asawang babae.

wig, n. an artificial covering of hair for the head. Buhok na artipisyal; peluka.

wild, adj. ferocious; reckless; rash; boisterous. Mailap; marahas; magulo; mabangis.

wildness, n. savageness. Kailapan; kasalbahihan; kabangisan.

wile, n. a trick to deceive; cunning way. Pandaraya.

willful, adj. stubborn; stiff. Matigas ang ulo; sinasadya.

will, n. the faculty of conscious and deliberate action. Nasa; kagustuhan; kusang-loob; kalooban.

will, v. determine; decide. Naisin; loobin; ibigin; gustuhin; ipasiya.

willing, adj. favorably disposed; eager to serve or comply. Handa; pumayag; ibig; nais; kusa.

willingness, n. readiness. Kahandaan; kusang-loob na pagsang-ayon.

wilt, v. to wither; become limp and drooping. Malanta; maluoy.

wimple, n. hood or veil worn by nuns. Damit na linen o seda na inilalagay ng mga madre sa kanilang ulo at sa paligid ng mukha.

win, v. to gain; be victorious in. Magwagi; manalo; matamo

wind, n. a natural current of air. Hangin.

windmill, n. a mill driven by blades turned by the wind. Pahanginan; pampahangin; kasangkapan, gulong o gilingang pinaaandar ng hangin.

window, n. an opening in the wall of a building to let in light and air. Durungawan; bintana.

windpipe, n. the trachea. Lalamunan; lalaugan.

windy, adj. marked by much blowing of wind. Mahangin.

wine, n. the fermented juice of plants, specifically of the grape. Alak.

wing, n. a limb, usually occurring in pairs, by which certain animals fly. Pakpak.

winged, adj. having wings. May pakpak.

wink, n. an act of winking, Kisapmata; kindat; kurap.

wink, v. close and open the eye quickly, as a signal. Kumisap; kumurap; kumindat.

winner, n. one who wins. Ang nagwagi; ang nanalo; ang nagtagumpay.

winsome, adj. attractive; pretty. Kaakit-akit; kahali-halina.

winter, n. the cold season approximately Dec. 22 to March 21. Taglamig.

wipe, v. clean or dry by gently rubbing, as with a soft cloth. Pahirin; linisin; punasan.

wire, n. slender rod of metal. Alambre; kawad.

wiry, adj. lean but muscular; job made of wire. Parang alambre; parang kawad.

wisdom, n. sagacity. Karunungan; dunong.

wise, adj. cunning; learned; judicious. Matalino; marunong.

wish, n. eager desire or longing; the thing desired. Lunggati; hangad; nais; ibig, hiling.

wish, v. long for; desire; crave. Nasain; hangarin; naisin; ibigin; hilingin.

wit, n. cleverness; intelligence. Pang-unawa; katalasan ng isip.

witch, n. a woman with magic powers derived from evil spirits; a sorceress. Bruha; mangkukulam; manggagaway.

withdraw, v. take back; recall; retract. Retiro; umurong; iurong.

withdrawal, n. take from. Pagbawi; pag-urong.

within, adv. pertaining to the inside. Sa loob.

without, adv. on or as to the outside. Wala; sa labas.

withstand, v. to stand against; endure. Makatagal; makatiis.

witness, n. a person or thing able to give evidence, a person who saw something happen. Saksi; testigo.

witty, adj. amusingly clever in perception and expression. Matalino; matalas ang isip.

wobble, v. move from side to side. Sumuray-suray; lumakad nang patagi-tagilid.

woman, n. an adult human female. Ale; babae.

womb, n. the uterus. Uterus; palaanakan; bahay-bata.

wonder, n. a marvel; a strange thing. Admirasyon; kahanga-hangang bagay; paghanga.

wonderful, adj. marvelous. Kamangha-mangha; kahanga-hanga.

wont, adj. accustomed; in the habit. Kinagisnan; kinagawian.

woo, v. seek the favor or love of. Maniligaw; manuyo.

wood, n. the hard, fibrous substance of the body of a tree. Madera; kahoy.

woodland, n. a forest. Gubat; kakahuyan.

wooer, n. one who makes love. Manliligaw; talisuyo.

wool, n. the fleece of the sheep. Lana; balahibo ng tupa.

word, n. a sound or combination of sounds, or its graphic representation, expressing an idea. Palabra; salita.

wordy, adj. verbose; full of words. Masalita; maraming salita.

word of honor, n. a solemn promise. Tapat na pangako.

work, n. effort or exertion; job. Hanapbuhay; gawain; trabaho.

workbook, n. a book for student containing instructional materials. Workbuk.

workman, n. a man employed or skilled in some form of manual, mechanical, or industrial work. Obrero; manggagawa.

workshop, n. a shop or building in which work, especially mechanical work is carried out. Workshap, gawaan; talyer.

world, n. the earth, the universe. Mundo; daigdig.

worldly, adj. mundane; earthly. Makamundo; ukol sa daigdig; makalupa.

worm, n. any small, creeping tube-shaped animal. Bulati; uod.

worn, adj. damaged by use. Sira; gutay.

worry, n. vexation; anxiety. Alalahanin; pagkabalisa.

worry, v. cause to feel anxious; bother. Mabalisa; mag-alaala.

worse, adj. more bad. Higit na masama.

worship, n. reverence and homage to God. Adorasyon; pagsamba.

worst, adj. most bad. Ang kasama-samaan; pinakamasama.

worth, n. value of things. Presyo; halaga.

worthless, adj. useless; worth nothing. Walang silbi; walang halaga; di-pakikinabangan.

worthy, adj. deserving respect. Karapat-dapat.

wound, n. an injury to flesh or tissue. Sugat.

wrap, n. a cloak or shawl. Siyawl; balabal.

wrap, v. envelop; roll or fold around. Ibalabal; balutin.

wrapper, n. any covering; a dressing gown. Pambalot; balutan.

wrath, n. anger; fury. Galit; poot.

wreath, n. a garland; something twisted or formed into a circular band. Garlan; korona.

wreck, n. ruin or demolition of. Guho; pagkasira.

wreck, v. cause the ruin or demolition of. Lansagin; iguho; gibain; wasakin.

wreckage, n. the remains of a wreck. Labi; paglansag.

wrench, n. a violent sudden twist or jerk; a grasping tool. Liyabe; pambira; pagpilipit.

wrench, v. wrest forcibly; distort. Birahin; pilipitin; baltakin.

wrest, v. remove or seize by, or as if by violent twisting. Hatakin; agawin; baltakin.

wrestle, v. to struggle. Bunuin; makipagbuno.

wretch, n. one who is very unhappy or unfortunate. Sawimpalad; abâ; kawawa; taong di-maligaya; taong hamak.

wretched, adj. miserable. Miserable; hamak.

wriggle, v. to move the body to and fro. Mamilipit; kumislot.

wring, v. to twist; to turn. Pigain; pilipitin.

wringer, n. a device for pressing water from washed clothes. Taga-pigá; tagapilipit.

wrinkle, n. a crease; a ridge. Kunót; kulubot.

wrinkle, v. crease; pucker. Ikunot; ikulubot; gawing kulubot.

wrist, n. the joint between the hand and the forearm. Kasu-kasuan; pulso; galang-galangan.

write, v. to compose; form (letters or characters) on a surface by hand. Lumiham; sumulat.

writer, n. one who expresses ideas in writing. Awtor; manunulat.

wrong, adj. mistaken; not correct in fact. Di-tama; mali; di-tumpak.

wrongly, adv. unjustly; amiss; incorrectly. Nang mali; pamali.

wrongness, n. the state or condition of being wrong. Di-katumpakan; kamalian; kawalan ng katarungan.

wroth, adj. angry; exasperated; fretful. Ngitngit; galit; poot.

wry, adj. twisted; turned to one side. Ngiwi; tabingi.

X

xanthic, adj. yellowish. Amarilyo; kulay ginto; matingkad na dilaw.

xanthin, n. yellow coloring matter. Santina; maputing sangkap na matatagpuan sa dugo, ihi, at sa ibang katas ng tao o hayop.

xerosis, n. extraordinary dryness of the skin. Serodermya; di-pangkaraniwang pagkatuyo ng balat.

xiphoid, adj. sword-shaped Hugis-ispada.

xylograph, n. an engraving on wood. Saylograp; pag-ukit sa kahoy.

xylographer, n. one who makes an engraving on wood Saylograper; tagaukit sa kahoy.

X-ray, n. electromagnetic radiations of extremely short wave length and high penetrating power, commonly used to photograph the interior of solids and for the treatment of skin or cancerous diseases. Eks-rey; rayo-ekis; larawang kinuha sa pamamagitan ng rayo-ekis.

xylophone, n. a musical instrument having wooden bars sounded by small hammers. Saylopon; isang uri ng instrumentong pinatutunog sa pamamagitan ng dalawang martilyong kahoy; silopono.

Y

yacht, n. a pleasure ship used solely for its owner's personal purposes. Yate; sasakyang-dagat na karaniwan nang ginagamit sa pakikipagkarera sa tubig o sa pag-aaliw.

yachting, n. the practice or sport of sailing or voyaging in a yacht. Paglalayag sa pamamagitan ng yate; pagpalakad sa yate.

yank, v. to jerk. Baltakin.

yap, v. yelp; talk foolishly, or in a barking manner. Satsat; tumahol na tulad ng isang tuta.

yard, n. the ground adjoining a building: a unit of linear measure, equal to 3 feet. Patyo; yarda; bakuran; lupang sakop ng may-ari ng bahay.

yardstick, n. a calibrated stick one yard long; any standard of measurement. Medida; bara o panukat; sukatan.

yarn. n. fibers of cotton, wool, twisted together; a tale, particularly a fabricated one. Estambre; hilatsa; sinulid na estambre; kuwentong labis-labis at mahirap mangyari.

yawn, n. act of yawning; an opening, open space or chasm. Paghihikab; hikab.

yawn, v. open the mouth involuntarily in reaction from fatigue or sleepiness. Bumuka; maghikab; humikab.

year, n. the period of one revolution of the earth about the sun, about 365 days. Anyo; yir; taon.

yearly, adv. every year. Taun-taon; taunan; tuwing isang taon.

yearn, v. long for; desire strongly. Manabik; kasabikan; hangarin.

yearning, n. deep longing, especially when tinged with tenderness or sadness. Pagnanasa; pananabik.

yeast, n. a fermented substance used to leaven bread. Lebadura; pampaalsa.

yell, n. a shout or scream. Kantiyaw; sigaw.

yell, v. to cry out. Mangantiyaw; sumigaw.

yellow, adj. the color of lemons, the yolk of an egg. Amarilyo; kubarde; dilaw; duwag.

yellowish, adj. pertaining to the yellow color. Manilaw-nilaw; dilaw.

yelp, n. a sharp cry; whine. Tahol ng nasaktan.

yes, adv. a word expressing affirmation, agreement, consent. Opo; oo; oho.

yesterday, adv. the day preceding the present day. Kahapon.

yesternight, adv. last night; on the night preceding this night. Kagabi.

yet, adv. hitherto; already. Muna; pa.

yet, conj. nevertheless; notwithstanding. Gayunman; bagaman; nguni't; datapuwa't; subali't.

yield, v. produce; give up; bear (as fruit). Magdulot; sumuko; mamunga; ibigay; ipagkaloob; pumayag.

yoke, n. bond of connection. Paód; singkaw, pamatok.

yolk, n. yellow substance of an egg. Pula ng itlog; dilaw.

yokel, n. a country fellow. Probinsiyano; tagabukid.

yonder, adv. at a distance. Doon; roon; sa dako pa roon.

yore, n. long since; long ago. Noong unang panahon; noong araw; noon.

you, pron. the personal pronoun of the second person. Ka; ikaw; kayo.

young, adj. not long born. Bata.

younger, adj. a junior. Batabata; bata kaysa; higit na bata.

youngish, adj. somewhat young. Mukhang bata.

youngster, n. a youth; a young person. Bata.

your, pron. possessive form *you* used before a noun. Mo; ninyo; iyo; inyo.

yours, pron. form of *your* used predicatively or without a noun following. Ang sarili mo; iyo; inyo.

yourself, pron. you; even you. Iyong sarili; ang sarili mo.

youth, n. the period of life from puberty to maturity; adolescence. Kabataan; binata.

youthful, adj. characterized by youth. Bata; sagana sa kabataan.

yowl, n. a howl; a dismal cry. Ungal; pag-angil.

Yuletide, n. Christmas or the Christmas Season. Panahon ng pasko; Pasko.

Z

zany, n. a buffon; a clownish person; an amusing fool. Taong mapagpatawa; klaun.

zeal, n. passionate ardor; eagerness; enthusiasm. Entusiyasmo; sigasig; alab.

zealot, n. one who is fanatically earnest. Panatiko; taong lubhang masigasig; taong may maalab na paniniwala sa isang gawain o pananampalataya.

zealous, adj. diligent; full of zeal. Matiyaga; masigasig; maalab.

zenith, n. point in sky directly overhead; culmination. Taluktok; rurok; kaitaasan.

zero, n. a cipher; nothing. Sero; wala.

zest, n. keen relish; gusto; hearty enjoyment. Gana; sigla; kasiglahan; kainitan.

zigzag, n. a line or course that turns abruptly from side to side. Sigsag; guhit o daang paliku-liko.

zigzag, v. advance or form in zigzags. Sig-sagan; lumakad nang paliku-liko; magpaliku-liko; umanyong paliku-liko.

zinc, n. a bluish-white metal. Isang uri ng puting metal na may bahagyang kabughawan at madaling baluktutin o tunawin; sink.

zipper, n. sliding fastener for clothing, etc. Siper.

zodiac, n. the imaginary belt in the sky in which lie the apparent paths of the sun, moon, and principal planets. Sodiako; ang daan o landas ng araw sa langit.

zone, n. a part of the surface of a sphere lying between two parallel planes. Sakop; sona; purok.

zone, v. encircle like a belt; divide into or mark with zones. Sonahin; hatiin sa mga sona o purok.

zoo, n. an enclosure where live animals are kept for public exhibition. Su; alagaan ng iba't ibang uri ng hayop.

—

PILIPINO
INGLES

A

abá, interj. an expression of mood.
abâ, adj. reduced, miserable, wretched, mistreated, lowered,
abaka, n. a plant, the fiber from the abaca plant, hemp.
abakada, n. alphabet.
abahín, v. to remind, to inform.
abain, v. to look down upon, to scorn.
abala, n. delay, nuisance.
abalá, adj. busy, occupied.
abalahin, v. detain, keep, delay, disturb.
abaloryo, n. beadwork.
abandonada, adj. negligent.
abangán, v. wait, to time, watch for, ambush, waylay.
abaniko, n. folding fan.
abante, interj. go ahead
abasto, n. baggage.
abay, n. bridesmaid, best man, companion, attendant.
abayan, v. accompany, attend.
abdikasyon, n. abdication.
abenida, n. avenue.
abentura, n. adventure.
aberia, n. damage, mishap.
abiso, n. notice.
abla, n. surplus talk.
abó, n. ashes, remains after burning.
abóg, n. notice, noise.
aborsiyón, n. abortion.
abot, v. reached, arrived, overtaken, comprehend.
abot-isip, adv. within one's mental grasp.
abrilata, n. can opener.
absen, adj. absent.
absuwelto, adj. absolved.
abubot, n. article, thing, knick-knack.
abugado, n. lawyer, attorney.
abuhín, adj. greyish, ashen.
abuhín, v. to clean by using ashes and water.
abuloy, n. contribution, subsidy.
abuluyan, v. contribute, subsidize.
abuluyan, n. giving of contribution.
aburido, adj. worried.
abuso, n. abuse.
abutan, v. to come abreast with somebody.
abután, v. to hand, to give.
abutin, v. to be overtaken.
abut-abot, adj. continuous.
akalà, n. belief, estimate, opinion, idea.
akalain, v. believe, think,
akay-akay, v. guiding by taking one's hand.
akayin, v. direct, guide, conduct.
akbayan, v. escort, support.
akdâ, n. literary works, writings.
akin, pron. my, mine.
akitin, v. persuade, attract.
aklás, v. strike, resist.
aklasan, n. a strike of laborers, abstinence from work.
aklát, n. book.
aklatan, n. library.
akmâ, v. fit, to be applicable.
akmaán, v. to move or act in suspended motion.
akó, pron. I.

akme, n. pinnacle, height.
akuin, v. to take one's place or obligation.
akropobya, n. fear of high places.
aksayá, v. dissipate, waste, squander.
aksesorya, n. apartment house.
aksidente, n. accident.
aksyon, n. action.
akusasyon, n. blame, charge.
aktor, n. actor.
akwaryum, n. aquarium.
akyát, v. climb, ascend, go up.
ada, n. fairy.
adhikâ, n. intention, ambition, wish.
adhikaín, v. to work diligently.
adobe, n. quarrystone.
adwana, n. custom-house.
adyá, v. protect, save, liberate, defend.
adyenda, n. agenda.
adyós, n. farewell, goodbye, so long.
aga, rw. early, advance.
agád, adv. immediately, fast, right away.
agahan, n. breakfast.
agam-agam, n. doubt, suspicion, hesitancy.
agap, adj. punctual, alert, anticipating.
agas, n. miscarriage.
agaw-buhay, adj. life and death.
agawin, v. grab, take away, snatch.
aghám, n. science, study of nature.
agimat, n. belief, amulet, charm.
aginaldo, n. Christmas present.
agiw, n. spider web hanging on ceiling.
aglahî, v. despise, mock, jest.
agnás, v. melt, crumble, decay, rot.
agnos, n. locket.
agong, n. musical instrument.
agos, n. flow, gush, meandering.
agpáng, adj. applicable, fitted, suitable.
agrabyado, adj. at a disadvantage, offended, unfair.
agridulse, adj. sour-sweet.
agrimensor, n. land surveyor.
aguhilya, n. hairpin.
aguho, n. pine-like tree.
agunyás, n. dirge, lamentation, death knell.
agwantahin, v. to sustain.
agwát, n. distance, interval.
ahas, n. snake.
ahedres, n. chess.
ahente, n. agent.
ahit, n. shave.
ahitan, v. to give a shave.
ahon, v. get out (of the water)
alaala, n. remembrance, souvenir, recollection, memory.
alab, v. seethe, smolder, blaze, ardor.
alabok, n. dust.
alak ng kaligayahan, n. wine of happiness.
alak ng lakas, n. wine of strength.
alakdán, n. scorpion.
alagà, n. one taken care of, protege.
alagà, adj. well-taken care,

well-attended.
alagaan, v. to care for, protect.
alagád, n. follower, agent, disciple.
alagatain, v. to think of.
alahas, n. jewelry.
alalahanin, v. to recollect or remember.
alalayan, v. aid, lend a hand, support, sustain.
alám, v. to be aware of, understand, know.
alam, n. information.
alamáng, n. smallest of shrimps.
alamát, n. legend, folk tale, myth, belief.
alambre, n. wire.
alamid, n. mountain cat.
alampáy, n. neckerchief, shawl.
alang-alang, n. consideration, courtesy, respect.
alanganin, adj. hesitant.
alapaap, n. cloud.
alás, n. ace.
alat, **n. pulis (colloq.), policeman.**
alay, n. offering, gift, dedication, homage.
alayan, v. to offer, to give, to dedicate.
alkalde, n. mayor.
alkansiyá, n. piggy bank, money box.
alkila, v. to rent, hire.
alkitran, n. tar.
aldaba, n. door-latch.
aldabís, n. slap, strike.
aldabisín, v. to strike.
ale, n. aunt, mistress.
algodon, n. cotton.
algopobya, n. fear of pain.
alhebra, n. algebra.
alibadbád, n. dizziness, nausea, indigestion.
alibay, n. an excuse, alibi.
alibughâ, adj. unfaithful, dishonest, irresponsible.
alikabók, n. dust, sand, particles.
alige, n. fat of crabs.
aligíd, v. move around.
álilà, n. servant. maid or boy, helper.
alimango, n. crab with dark green color and sturdy shell, big crab.
alimasag, n. crab smaller than alimango.
almendras, n. almonds.
alimbukay, **n. surge of running water.**
alimpungatan, adj. restless sleep.
alimpuyó, n. tornado, whirl, whippoorwill. stormy feeling.
alimuom, n. heat, vapor.
alimura, adj. despised, hated, scorned.
alimurahin, v. to despise, to scorn.
alín, pron. which, what is.
alindóg, n. charm, beauty, loveliness.
alingasaw, n. foul odor.
alingawngáw, n. rumor, echo, news.
alinlangan, n. doubt, hesitancy, undecidedness.
alipato, n. flying ember.
alinsangan, adj. oppressive, hot, sultry.
alinsunod sa, prep. in line with, in conformity with.
alintanahin, v. to be inattentive, thoughtless.
alipin, n. slave.
alipinin, v. to make a slave of.
alipungá, n. athlete's foot, irritation between toes.

alipustâ, n. insult.
alipustaín, v. look down upon, insult, despise.
alís, rw. take away, move away, detach.
alisto, adj. alert, ready.
alitan, n. quarrel.
alitaptap, n. firefly.
alituntunin, n. rules.
aliw, n. entertainment, joy, amusement.
aliwalas, adj. neat, tidy, clean, spacious.
aliwaswás, adj. neglectful, careless.
aliwín, v. to entertain.
almasen, n. department store, bazar.
almires, n. stone mortar.
almiról, n. starch.
almusál, n. breakfast.
alók, n. offer, proposal.
alog, v. to shake.
alon, n. wave.
alpa, n. harp.
alpas, adj. loose, free.
alperes, n. chief of the civil guards of Spain.
alpombra, n. carpet.
alsahín, v. lift, remove.
altár, n. altar.
alukín, v. offer, propose.
alugbati, n. a vine, the leaves and shoots of which are used for food.
alugín, v. shake.
alulód, n. water passageway, rain gutter.
alulong, n. howling of canines.
alumnay, n. alumni.
alupihan, n. centipede.
alwan, n. relief from difficulties or hardships.
alyas, n. alias.
ama, n. father.
amag, n. mold, mildew.
amaín, n. uncle.
amasona, n. manish woman.
ambâ, n. threatening gesture.
ambág, n. contribution, offering, donation.
ambíl, rw. accustom, adapt, habituate.
ambisyon, n. ambition.
ambon, n. drizzle, light rain.
ambulansiya, n. ambulance.
ambus, n. ambush.
amihan, n. breeze.
amin, prep. our, ours.
aminin, v. to admit, to own.
amís, adj. unfortunate, offended.
amot, v. partake, share.
amo, n. head, boss.
amóy, n. scent, smell, odor.
ampalaya, n. amargoso.
ampát, n. cease, check, stop.
ampatín, v. to check, to stop.
ampáw, n. popcorn.
ampón, n. an adopted one, a protege.
ampunan, n. welfarehouse, charitable institution.
ampunín, v. adopt, take care, protect.
amukî, n. admonition.
amukiín, v. to persuade.
amuin, v. caress, domesticate, pat.
anák, n. child, son or daughter.
anakì, adj. similar, likened to.
anakín, v. to be one's godfather or godmother.
analohiya, n. analogy.
anán, n. white spots on the skin, tinea flava.

anáng, v. said, according to.
anarki, n. anarchy.
anás, v. to whisper, speak low.
anasan, n. low whispers.
anay, n. termite, white ant.
andador, n. something used to help baby to walk.
andamyo, n. gangplank, passageway.
andáp, n. flicker.
andukhâ, n. care, protection.
andukhaín, v. to care for.
ang, art. article used before a singular common noun.
angatín, v. uplift, elevate.
angkás, v. ride with another.
angkán, n. lineage, family.
angkanan, n. generation.
angkas, adj. riding together in the same vehicle.
angkat, n. consignment of merchandise.
angkinín, v. claim, usurp.
angkla, n. anchor.
angkóp, adj. becoming, adjustable, fit.
anggí, n. light shower, particles of rain.
anggulo, n. angle.
anghàng, n. state of being peppery.
anghít, n. odor.
angil, n. growl, grumble, snarl.
angilan, v. to snarl, to growl.
angís, adj. repulsive dirty.
ani, n. harvest.
anib, v. join, subscribe, unite, form.
aninag, n. shadow, form.
aninagin, v. to try to look into the darkness.
aninaw, adj. clear, transparent.
aninawin, v. look, comprehend, clarify.
anino, n. shadow.
anis, n. tiny aromatic seeds used as flavoring.
anit, n. scalp.
anito, n. soul, ghost, deity.
anluwagi, n. carpenter.
anó, prep. what.
anod, n. flow, current, drift.
antá, n. rancidity.
anták, n. bloating pain.
antas, n. degree, grade.
antala, n. delay, bother.
antalahin, v. to delay, to bother.
antíng-anting, n. amulet, charm.
antók, n. drowsiness, sleepiness.
antolohiya, n. anthology.
antukín, v. to feel sleepy, to drowse.
anunsiyo, n. advertisement.
anunas, n. sugar apple.
anyô, n. form, figure.
anyuín, v. to take the form of, to make a habit of.
apa, n. wafer.
apak, n. tread, step.
apahap, n. a variety of salt water fish with white meat.
aparador, n. clothes closet, cabinet.
apat, n. four.
apaw, adj. overflowing, full.
apawan, v. to overfill.
apdó, n. gall, bile, spleen.
apelyido, n. surname, family name.
apendisitis, n. appendicitis.

apí, adj. maltreated, harnessed, dishonored.
apid, n. adultery.
apihín, v. to maltreat, to abuse.
aplaya, n. sandy seashore.
apó, n. grandchild.
apo, n. headman, grandfather.
apog, n. lime.
apolohiya, n. apology.
apóy, n. fire, flame.
aprentis, n. a beginner.
apyan, n. opium.
aral, rw. lesson, study, teach.
aranya, n. chandelier.
araro, n. plow.
araruhin, v. to plow, to break up the soil.
aras, n. coin given by bridegroom to bride during wedding.
araw, n. day, sun.
araw-araw, adj. every day
aráy, interj. ouch.
arko, n. arc.
arkeolohiya, n. archeology.
areglado, adj. orderly, in right place.
arena, n. field of battle or conflict, a stage.
aresto, n. prosecution.
argolya, n. hoop.
arì, n. property, possession.
aringkin, n. somersault.
armas, n. weapons.
arnibal, n. thick syrup.
armi, n. army.
arsobispo, n. archbishop.
artilyeria, n. artillery.
artipisyal, adj. artificial.
aruga, n. care, attention.
arugaín, v. take care, to rear up or to work.
asada, n. hoe.
asal, n. manner, behavior, custom, habit.
asalin, v. to make a habit of, hope for.
asalto, n. surprise party.
asaról, n. hoe.
asarulín, v. to hoe.
asawa, n. wife or husband, spouse, better-half.
askád, adj. acrid, pungent.
asenso, n. promotion.
asento, n. accent.
asero, n. steel.
asikaso, adj. attentive, mindful.
asim, n. state of being sour.
asín, n. table salt.
asinán, v. to put salt.
asinan, n. place where salt is made.
asó, n. smoke.
aso, n. dog.
asoge, n. quicksilver.
aspaltado, adj. asphalted.
aspilé, n. pin.
astrolohiya, n. astrology.
astropobya, n. fear of lightning and thunder.
asuhos, n. a kind of small water fish.
asukal, n. sugar.
asunto, n. case in court.
asuwang, n. sorcerer, evil.
asotea, n. back porch.
asyenda, n. estate.
at, conj. and.
atangan, v. assist, help.
atasan, v. command, order.
ataúl, n. coffin, bier.
atáy, n. liver.
atay-atay, adv. slowly, gently.
ate, n. eldest sister.
atim, n. resignation, tolerance.
atin, pron. our, ours.
atíp, n. roof.
atis, n. sweet sop.

atras, v. to move back.
atrasado, adj. late.
atsara, n. pickles.
atsuwete, n. seeds of a plant used for coloring.
atubili, adj. hesitant, doubtful.
atupagin, v. attend, concentrate, work for.
awa, n. pity, charity, compassion, generosity.
awang, n. interval of space.
awas, n. deduction.
awatin, v. restrain, dissuade, separate.
away, n. quarrel, fight.
awdisyon, n. audition.
awit, n. song.
awitin, v. to sing.
awto, n. car.
awtobus, n. bus.
ay, v. linking verb more or less equivalent to the English to be.
aya, n. caretaker of children.
ayan, adv. there.
ayaw, v. no, not in accord.
ayon, adv. agreeable, according to, similar to.
ayos, n. a r r a n g ement, form, figure.
ayuda, n. aid.
ayungin, n. a variety of fresh water fish.
ayuno, n. fasting.
ayusin, v. to arrange.
aywan, v. no knowledge of.

B

ba, interj. an emphatic particle used in questions.
baak, n. break, split, crack.
babà, n. chin.
babâ. rw. go down, dismount.
babá, v. to rest or lean against the hands.
babád, adj. soaked.
babae, n. woman, female.
babág, n. quarrel.
babagsak, v. will fall.
babalâ, n. warning, sign, notice.
babalaan, v. to warn, to notify.
babarin, v. to soak.
babasahín, n. reading matter, readers.
babaw, n. shallowness, easiness.
babawan, v. to make shallow.
baboy, n. pig, hog.
baka, n. cow.
bakal, n. iron.
bakal-kabayo, n. horseshoe.
bakahan, n. ranch.
bakás, n. footmarks, telltale, marks, tracks.
bakasin, v. to look back and recollect.
bakasyon, n. vacation.
bakbak, adj. detached.
bakbakan, n. free-for-all fight.
bakbakín, v. remove, dislodge, take out.
bakit, adv. why.
baklá, n. dread, alarm, worry.
baklâ, adj. homosexual.
baklád, n. fishtrap.
baklî, adj. detached, broken.
bakod, n. fence, enclosure.
bakol, n. native basket, wide and big.
bakteryolohiya, n. bacteriology.
bakood, n. highland.
baks-opis, n. box-office.

bakú-bakô, adj. rough, not smooth, uneven.
bakulaw, n. man-size monkey.
bakuna, n. vaccination.
bakyâ, n. wooden shoes.
bakyaín, v. to strike with wooden shoes.
badigard, n. bodyguard.
badyet, n. budget.
badminton, n. badminton.
baga, n. live coal, embers.
bagâ, n. lungs, respiratory tract.
bagâ, n. sickness of a nursing mother (tumor on the breast)
bagá, particle used in askking questions.
bagabag, n. uneasiness.
bagal, adj. slow, sluggish, meandering.
bagamán, conj. although, however, in spite of.
bag, n. bag.
bagáng, n. molars.
bagay, adj. harmonious, suitable, fitted.
bagay-bagay, n. things, articles.
bagkús, conj. on the contrary.
baging, n. vine.
bago, adj. new, modern.
bagol, adj. unpolished, uncouth.
bagon, n. freight car.
bagoóng, n. pickled fishes.
bagót, adj. annoyed, irritated, disturbed.
bagsák, n. fall, drop.
bagsik, n. strictness.
baguhan, n. amateur, inexperienced.
baguhin, v. to remodel, to change.
baguntao, n. young man, young bachelor
baguntaón, n. New Year.
bagwís, n. wing, strength.
bagyo, n. tempest, storm.
bahâ, n. flood, overflow, inundation.
bahág, n. covering, G-string.
bahagdan, n. percentum, percentage.
bahaghari, n. rainbow.
bahagi, n. part, share, fractional part.
bahagihin, v. to divide.
bahagyâ, adv. barely, scarcely, hardly.
bahala, n. trust, care, discretion.
baháw, adj. hoarse, low, healed.
bahay, n. house, abode.
bahay-bahayan, n. toyhouse.
bahay-bata, n. uterus.
bahay-sugalan, n. gambling house.
bahid, n. taint, stain, trace, mark.
bahilya, n. set of dishes.
bahín, n. sneeze.
bahò, n. bad odor, stink.
baít, n. goodness, virtue, judgment.
baitang, n. grade, steps, degree.
bala, n. bullet.
balà, n. threat, warning.
balaan, v. threaten, warn, forewarn.
balabal, n. cloak, wrap.
balabalan, v. to cover.
balak, n. plan, scheme, project, desire.
balakang, n. hips.
balakid, n. hindrance, obstacle.
balakin, v. to plan, to

scheme.
balakubak, n. dandruff.
balag, n. arbor, trellis.
balagbag, n. cross-beam.
balagtasan, n. poetical joust in verse.
balahibo, n. feather, body hairs.
balani, n. magnetism.
balangay, n. branch, committee, party.
balangkás, n. outline, framework.
balangkasín, v. to outline.
balaraw, n. dagger.
balarilâ, n. grammar.
balasik, n. ferocity, aggressiveness, fierceness.
balasubas, adj. stingy, tightwad.
balát, n. skin, covering.
balatay, n. mark, imprint.
balatkayô, n. disguise, costume, pretention.
balatong, n. mongo bean.
balawís, n. a fierce and ferocious animal.
balay, n. house, abode.
balbás, n. beard.
balbasin, adj. with heavy beard growth.
balde, n. can, pail.
baldosa, n. tile.
balibag, n. throwing.
balík, n. return.
balì, n. break, fracture.
balikan, v. to go back.
balikan, adj. back and forth.
balikat, n. shoulder.
balikatin, v. to carry on one's shoulder.
balikukô, adj. coiled, twisted, out of shape.
balikwás, v. get up, jump up.
baligtád, adj. contrary, opposite, inside out.
báligtaran, adj. reversible.
baligtarín, v. reverse.
baliin, v. to break.
balimbing, n. star shaped fruit.
balingan, v. turn to, rely upon.
balingkinitan, adj. slender, sylph-like, trim.
balinguyngóy, n. hemorrhage of the nose.
balino, n. worry, premonition, anxiety.
balintatáw, n. pupil of the eye.
balintawak, n. Filipina dress short and informal.
balintuna, adv. unreal, contrary, unnatural.
balintuwád, v. fall upside down, false.
baling, v. to sway, to look back.
balisá, adj. agitated, worried, restless.
balisahin, v. to worry, to agitate.
balisunsóng, adj. cone-like, funnel-shaped.
balitá, n. news, information.
balitaw, n. folk dance.
balíw, adj. crazy, insane, demented.
balo, n. widow or widower.
balón, n. well, source.
balót, adj. covered, enveloped.
balota, n. ballot.
balsá, n. raft, ferry.
bálsamó, n. a healing drug, or something that soothes.
balse, n. waltz.

balták, n. pull.
baltakín, v. to pull.
balukol, adj. bent, twisted.
baluktot, adj. crooked.
balumbalunan, n. gizzard.
balut, n. fertilized egg.
balutan, n. package, bundle.
baluti, n. armor.
balutin, v. to bundle.
balyena, n. whale.
bambáng, n. ditch, canal.
bambú, n. club, piece of wood.
bambuhín, v. to club.
banaag, n. faint light, glimmer, glimpse.
banakal, n. rind of fruit.
banál, adj. pious, religious.
ban, n. ban.
banas, n. heat, sultriness.
banayad, adj. slow, moderate.
banda, n. musicians, a musical group or band.
bandana, n. a head covering similar to a scarf.
bandalismo, n. vandalism.
bandeha, n. platter, tray.
bandido, n. bandit.
bandilà, n. flag, emblem.
bangín, n. abyss, ravine.
bangís, n. ferocity.
bangó, n. fragrance, scent.
bangon, v. to wake up, rise.
bangungot, n. bad dream, nightmare.
bangungutin, v. have bad dreams.
bangús, n. milkfish.
bangán, n. granary, bodega.
bangay, n. quarrel, fight.
bangkâ, n. boat.
bangayin, v. to quarrel.
bangkáy, n. cadaver, corpse.
bangkero, n. boatman.
bangketa, n. sidewalk.
bangkò, n. bench.
bangkuwáng, n. coarse mat.
banggain, v. collide, clash.
banggerahán, n. dish stand.
banggít, n. mention, citation.
banggitín, v. to mention.
bangháy, n. outline, sketch, plot, plan.
baníg, n. mat, floor covering.
banigín, v. to use as a mat.
banlág, adj. with defective eyesight, squinting.
banlî, n. scalding.
banlián, v. to clean with boiling water.
banság, adj. well-known.
bansot, adj. stunted.
bantá, n. threat, design.
bantás, n. punctuation.
bantasán, v. to punctuate.
bantáy, n. watch, guard.
bantayán, v. to guard.
bantayog, n. monument.
bati, n. congratulation.
bantô, v. mix with water.
bantóg, adj. well-known, famous, popular.
bantot, n. stink.
banyaga, n. foreigner.
banyo, n. bathroom.
banyós, v. bathe.
bao, n. empty coconut shell.
baon, n. provision.
bapor, n. ship.
bará, n. obstruction, hindrance.
bara, n. measurement (80 cm. long).
baraka, n. market place.
baraha, n. playing card.
baraso, n. arm.
barbero, n. barber, hair-

cutter.
barbekyu, n. meat roasted by pieces.
baríl, n. gun.
bariles, n. barrel.
barilya, n. barrel.
barnís, n. varnish.
barò, n. dress, clothes.
barong tagalog, n. men's shirt with stiff collar and cuffs. (Filipino costume)
baruan, v. to put on a dress.
barung-barong, n. hut, shanty.
baryá, n. loose change.
basâ, adj. wet, moist.
basa, rw. read.
baság, adj. broken, cracked.
basag-ulo, n. trouble, altercation.
basahan, n. rag.
basahin, v. to read.
basaín, v. to wet.
basal, adj. brand-new, virgin, young.
basalyo, n. vassal.
basbasán, v. bless.
basi, n. wine from sugarcane.
basket, n. basket, container
basketbol, n. basketball, game of ball.
baso, n. drinking glass.
bastidor, n. embroidery hoop.
batà, n. child, young.
batá, v. bear, suffer.
bata, n. gown.
bataán, n. house helper, servant.
batak, n. pull.
batakin, v. to pull.
batalán, n. kitchen and washing place.
batás, n. law, constitution.
batasan, n. law-making body.
batasang-bayan, n. national legislature.
batayan, n. basis, foundation.
batbát, adj. replete, full of, covered.
baterya, n. battery.
Bathalà, n. God.
batí, n. beating of eggs
batì, n. salutation or greeting.
batibot, adj. sturdy, robust, small.
batik, n. taint, spot.
batikan, v. to besmirch.
batikos, n. hitting with a cudgel.
batíd, v. know, to learn.
batiin, v. greet.
batingaw, n. bell.
batis, n. brook, spring.
bató, n. small flat stone or brick used in playing kasoy seeds, stone.
batok, n. nape.
batukan, v. to strike on the nape.
batugan, adj. lazy, good-for-nothing, shameless.
batuhan, adj. rocky.
batuhín, v. to stone.
batyâ, n. shallow wide washing tub.
baul, n. a chest.
bawal, rw. prohibited, forbidden.
bawang, n. garlic.
bawas, n. reduction, decrease.
bawasan, v. to lessen, reduce, diminish.
bawi, rw. regain, retract.
bayabas, n. guava.
bayad, n. pay.
bayâd, adj. already paid.
bayan, n. country.
bayani, n. hero.
bayaran, v. to pay.

bayáw, n. brother-in-law.
bayawak, n. field lizard.
bayawín, v. to make one his brother-in-law.
baybáy, n. spelling, seashore.
baybayín, v. to spell.
bayolens, n. violence.
bayóng, n. native basket made of palm strips.
baywáng, n. waist.
bekon, n. bacon, salted and smoked meat.
benda, n. bandage.
bendita, n. holy water.
benditahan, v. to bless.
benggador, n. avenger.
benggansa, n. vengeance.
berso, n. verse.
besbol, n. baseball.
beses, n. times.
beterano, n. veteran.
bías, n. internode of bamboo or cane, space between joints.
bibi, n. duck.
bibig, n. mouth.
bibingka, n. native cake.
bibitayán, n. place of execution.
bibiyenanín, n. in-laws-to-be.
bibliograpo, n. bibliography.
bibliya, n. bible, sacred writings of Christianity.
bikas, n. looks, appearance.
bikíg, n. clog in the throat.
bigkís, n. bundle.
biko. n. glutinous rice cooked with coconut milk.
bidiyelantes. n. vigilantes.
bigas, n. rice.
bigát, n. weight.
bigáy, rw. give, endorse.
bigay-alám, v. to inform, advise
bigáy-kaya, n. full range, unstinted support, dowry.
bigkasin, v. to recite, pronounce.
bigkisín, v. to bundle.
bighanì, n. attraction, charm.
biglâ, adj. sudden, abrupt, immediate.
biglaín, v. to shock.
biguín, v. to dissappoint.
bigô, n. failure, disappointment.
bigote, n. mustache.
bigti, adj. strangled, hanged.
bihag, n. captive, prisoner.
bihasa, adj. accustomed, civilized, experienced.
bihasahin, v. to accustom.
bihirà, adj. unusual, few, not common.
bihís, adj. dressed up.
bihis, n. dress, wearing apparel.
bihisan. v. to dress up.
bihon, n. white rice noodles.
biík, n. small pig, suckling.
biIád, v. to bleach, dry, expose.
bilanggo, n. prisoner.
bilangguan, n. prison.
bilangin, v. to count.
bilao, n. winnowing basket.
bilang, n. number.
bilás, n. relation of brothers' wives or sisters' husbands.
bilasâ, adj. stale, spoiled.
bilhin, v. to purchase.
bilí, rw. buy, purchase.
bilib, v. believed.
bilin, n. a request, instruction.
bilis, n. alertness, swiftness.
bilisán, v. to move fast.
bilóg, adj. round, circular.
bilot, n. package.
biloy, n. dimple.

bilugan, adj. plump.
bilugin, v. to make round.
bimbín, rw. detain, retain.
binabaé, n. sissy, hermaphrodite, homosexual.
binalatkayuan, v. disguised.
binanggit, v. mentioned.
binaril, v. shot.
binasbasan, v. blessed.
binat, rw. strain, weaken, relapse.
binatà, n. bachelor, single, young man
binati, v. greeted.
binatóg, n. boiled corn.
bindisyón, n. blessing, benediction.
bindisyunán, v. to bless.
binhî, n. seedling.
binhián, v. to breed, to sprout.
binibilang, v. counting.
binibini, n. young maiden, Miss.
bininyagán, v. was baptized.
binlid, n. small grain of rice.
binlirán, v. to remove small grains of rice.
binta, n. Moro boat.
bintana, n. window.
bintáng, n. suspicion.
binitay, v. executed.
binti, n. leg.
binyág, n. baptism.
binyagan, n. Christian.
bingí, adj. deaf.
bingit, n. edge, rim.
bingót, adj. with broken edge.
bingwít, rw. tackle.
binudburan, v. sprinkled.
birá, n. violent stroke.
birang, n. head kerchief.
birò, n. joke, jest.
birtud, n. virtue.
biruán, n. joking mood.
bisà, n. effect.
bisaklát, adj. opened wide.
bisagra, n. hinge.
bisalà, n. mistake.
biskotso, n. toasted bread.
bisikleta, n. bicycle.
bisig, n. arm.
bisiro, n. colt.
bisita, n. guest.
bisperas, n. eve.
bista, n. hearing in court.
bistay, n. shallow round basket with large mesh.
bisugo, n. fish with pinkish scales.
bisyo, n. vice, habit.
biták, n. crack on the ground.
bitag, n. trap.
bitáw, n. cockfighting.
bitawan, v. to let loose, free.
bitay, n. hanging or electrocution.
bitbít, n. baggage.
bitbitín, v. to carry, hold.
bitin, rw. suspend.
bitiwan, v. to release.
bitones, n. button.
bitsin, n. flavoring powder.
bituka, n. intestines.
bituin, n. star.
biya, n. goby.
biyák, adj. broken, opened, cracked.
biyakín, v. to break, to crack.
biyakin, adj. easily broken.
Biya-krusis, n. Way of the Cross.
biyahe, n. trip, journey.
biyayà, n. mercy, grace.
biyayaan, v. to grace.
biyenán, n. mother-in-law, father-in-law.
biyolohiya, n. biology.
biyuda, n. widow.

biyulin, n. violin.
bloke, n. block.
bobo, adj. fool, dumbhead.
bokasyon, n. vocation.
boksing, n. boxing.
bola, n. ball.
bolahin, v. to fool, roll.
bolpen, n. ballpen.
bomba, n. bomb.
bómbahín, v. to bomb.
bombero, n. fireman.
boo, v. to boo.
borador, n. rough draft.
borlas, n. tassel.
boses, n. voice.
bote, n. bottle.
boto, n. vote.
botohin, v. to vote for.
boykot, n. boycott.
brandi, n. brandy.
bruha, n. witch.
bubog, n. broken glass.
bubót, n. unripe fruit.
bugbugin, v. to beat.
bubuli, n. field lizard.
bubungán, n. roof.
bubuwít, n. rat.
bubuyog, n. bumblebee.
buká, adj. open.
bukakà, adj. with open legs.
bukadkád, adj. unfolded, opened.
bukal, n. fountain, spring.
bukana, n. front.
bukáng-liwaywáy, n. dawn, sunrise.
bukas, n. tomorrow.
bukás, adj. open.
búkasan, n. opening.
bukayò, n. sweetened coconut gratings.
bukbók, n. weevil.
bukid, n. field, farm.
buklatin, v. to open.
buklaw, n. goiter.
buklód, n. binding tie.
buklurín, n. to unite.
buko, n. bud node.
bukó, n. young coconut.
bukód, v. separate.
bukol, n. swelling, boil.
bukulan, v. to sock, to swell.
budbód, n. sprinklings, give-away.
budburán, v. to sprinkle, to scatter.
budhî, n. conscience, disposition.
bugá, v. to spill out.
bugahán, v. to blow out of the mouth.
bugaw, n. go-between.
bugawin, v. to shoo away.
bugbugan, n. riot, free-for-all.
bugbugín, v. beat, to mangle, to bruise.
bugháw, adj. blue.
bugók, adj. spoiled, rotten.
bugnót, adj. irritated, restless.
bugnutin, n. a person who is easily piqued.
bugtóng, n. riddle, puzzle.
bugsô, n. passionate outburst.
buhaghag, adj. porous, expanded, careless.
buhangin, n. sand.
buhat, prep. from, since.
buhawì, n. whirlwind, tornado.
buhay, n. life, living, story, plot.
buhayín, v. to bring to life, to grow.
buhò, n. a species of bamboo.
buhók, n. hair.
buhól, n. knot, tie.
buhóng, n. coward, knave, villain.
buhos, n. pouring.
buhukán, v. to hold, pull or

cut the har.
bulâ, n. bubble, foam.
bulaán, adj. & n. liar.
bulak, n. cotton, sterilized cotton.
bulakbol, adj. truant.
bulaklák, n. flower.
bulador, n. kite.
bulág, n. blind person.
bulagâ, n. surprise, unawareness.
bulagaín, v. to take by surprise, catch unaware.
bulagin, v. to make blind, take away the sight.
bulagsák, adj. careless, wasteful, disorderly.
bulagtâ, adj. down and out, unconscious.
bulahaw, n. noise, tumult.
bulahawin, v. to disturb, to awaken.
búlalakaw, n. shooting star or planet.
bulalás, n. uncontrollable expression of feeling.
bulanláng, n. native dish of different vegetables, seasoned with bagoóng.
bulaos, n. pathway through the hills.
bulastóg, adj. vulgar, mean.
bulati, n. earthworm.
bulatlatín, v. to rend open, to examine in detail.
buláy-bulayin, v. to think or reflect over.
bulkan, n. volcano.
buldoser, n. bulldozer.
buli, v. to smooth out.
bulik, n. black-and-white colored rooster.
bulíd, v. to bring about a fall.
bulig, n. medium-sized mud fish.
bulilit, n. a small, dwarf-like person.
bulislís, adj. partly opened or showing.
bulô, n. a young calf or carabao.
bulo, n. floss covering of stems, leaves and fruits.
bulók, n. graft, rottenness.
bulól, adj. stammering.
bulòng, n. whisper.
bulós, n. a bundle or a bolt.
bulsá, n. pocket.
bulto, n. unit of packaging.
bulubod, n. rice in the stalk.
bulubundukin, adj. mountainous, hilly.
bulukín, v. to keep spoiled.
bulugan, n. male of the species.
bulung-bulungan, n. whispers, rumors.
bulusok, n. sudden sinking.
bulutong, n. smallpox.
bulutungin, v. to contract smallpox.
bulwagan, n. hall, sala, meeting place.
bulyawán, v. to shout or rebuke.
bumabâ, v. descended.
bumagsak, v. fell.
bumabati, v. greets, greeting.
bumbóng, n. hollow or elongated bamboo container.
bumbunan, n. the soft part of a baby's head.
bumibili, v. buying.
bumúbulós, v. falling out of a hole.
bumukod, v. separate.
bundát, adj. over-satisfied.
bundok, n. mountain.
bundulín, v. to bump, to collide.
buni, n. eczema, herpes.
bunö, n. wrestling.
bunót, n. coconut husk used for polishing floors.
bunsô, n. youngest among

the children.
bunsod, n. launching.
buntál, v. strike (with fist), to box.
buntis, n. pregnant.
buntón, n. heap.
buntong-hiningá, n. sigh.
buntót, n. tail, the end part.
buntután, v. to follow thru, to stalk, to put a tail on.
bunutin, v. to pull out, pull at roots.
bunyî, rw. acclaim, celebrate.
bunga, n. result, fruit, bettle nut.
bungangkahoy, n. fruit.
bungad, n. opening, commencement.
bungal, adj. toothless.
bungalngalán, v. to talk loudly or vociferously.
bunganga̖, n. big mouth.
bungangaán, v. to lecture.
bungang-araw, n. skin eruption caused by prickly heat.
bungang-isip, n. figment of the mind.
bungang-tulog, n. hazy sleep or dream.
bungkál, n. diggings, a mound.
bungkalín, v. to examine, dig, open.
bungkos, n. bundle, package.
bunggô, v. to jolt, bump.
bungî, adj. toothless.
bungisngís, adj. easy to laugh or giggle at anything.
bungô, n. skull.
bungulan, n. the biggest species of banana.
bunton, n. pile.
buntung-hininga, n. sigh.
buô, n. whole, complete.
buod, n. gist.
bupeté, n. lawyer's office.
burá, n. erasure.
burak, n. mire.
burahin, v. to erase, to take away marks.
burda, n. embroidery.
burok, n. yolk.
buról, n. hill.
bus, n. bus, autobus.
busá, v. to roast.
busabos, n. slave, servant, serf.
busál, n. muzzle.
busalsál, adj. slovenly, without order.
busil, n. core of wood.
busilak, adj. immaculate.
businа, n. sounding horn.
busisì, adj. particular, fastidious.
buslô, n. basket.
busóg, adj. satisfied, full.
buson, n. mailbox.
butás, adj. pierced, perforated, bored.
butas, n. hole, leak.
butasin, v. to bore, pierce.
butáw, n. fee, contribution.
butete, n. a species of fish with expanded body.
buti, n. goodness, well-being.
butikî, n. house lizard.
butihin, v. to make good, to take seriously.
butihín, adj. good, gentle.
butil, n. grain.
butingtingín, v. to examine in detail, to work on a thing minutely.
butlig, n. wen.
butó, n. bone, seed.
butuan, n. a variety of seeded banana.
buuín, v. to complete, to put together.

butones, n. button.
buwagín, v. to tear down, demolish, destroy.
buwál, n. fall.
buwán, n. moon, month.
buwán-buwán, adj. monthly, regularly each month.
buwáy, n. unsteadiness.
buwaya, n. crocodile.
buwenas, adj. good.
buwíg, n. bunch of bananas, cluster.
buwís, n. tax, contribution or tribute.
buwisán, v. to rent or lease.
buwisit, adj. unlucky, annoying, bad luck.
buwisitin, v. to annoy, disturb, irritate.
buwitre, n. vulture.

K

ka, pron. personal pronoun, second person, singular, nominative and objective.
kaabalahán, n. trouble, disturbance, annoyance.
kaabug-abog, n. suddenness.
kaanak, n. relative, kin.
kaakibat, n. opponent.
kaalamán, n. knowledge, information.
kaangkan, n. person of the same clan or ancestry.
kaapihán, n. oppression, unfairness.
kaarawan, n. birthday.
kaasiman, n. sourness.
kabá, n. fear, worry, premonition.
kababalaghán, n. miracle, something unbelievable.
kababata, n. fellow young people, childhood friend.
kababayan, n. townmate, from the same country.
kabaka, n. opponent.
kabag, n. gas pain in the stomach.
kabaitan, n. goodness.
kabalalay, adj. parallel, in line with.
kabalat, n. person of the same color of skin.
kabalyero, adj. chivalrous.
kaban, n. clothes closet.
kabanata, n. chapter.
kabaong, n. coffin.
kabaret, n. dance hall.
kabatas, n. policeman.
kabasi, n. a variety of fish with many bones.
kabantugan, n. fame.
kabataan, n. youth.
kabalintunaan, n. paradox.
kabayanan, n. town proper, municipality.
kabayanihan, n. heroism.
kabayo, n. horse.
kabayuhán, n. cavalry.
kabayuhin, v. to sit or ride over.
kabesa, n. headman or tax collector for a group of families, chief.
kabibi, n. clam, shell.
kabig, n. follower, soldier.
kabigin, v. to pull toward self.
kabiguan, n. disappointment.
kabihasnan, n. civilization.
kabilâ, adj. the other side.
kabilán, adj. not in symmetry, unequal.
kabilanin, adj. partial, changeable.
kabisa, n. head or chief.
kabisera, n. capital.
kabisote, adj. dull-headed.
kabit, n. part of, connection.
kabo, n. corporal.
kabóg, n. hollow sound.

kabuté, n. mushroom.
kabuluhán, n. worthiness.
kabutihan, n. goodness.
kabuyaw, n. orange, fruit with bumps.
kabulaanan, n. lie, falsehood.
kabuwisitan, n. irritation, annoyance.
kabyawan, n. sugarcane mill.

kaka, n. older relative.
kakahuyan, n. woods, trees.
kakaibá, adj. strange, different, out of place.
kakanán, n. eating place of a house.
kakanggatâ, n. pure substance from liquids, coconut.
kakanin, n. tidbits.
kakayurin, v. will scrape.
kakila-kilabot, adj. terrible, horrible, spine-tingling.
kakilala, n. acquaintance.
kakinisan, n. smoothness.
kadkarín, v. to unfold, spread.

kadahupan, n. scarcity.
kadang-kadang, n. disease of coconut trees.
kadena, n. chain.
kadete, n. cadet.
kadugo, n. fellow of the same bloodline.
kadyos, n. pigeon peas.
kadigma, n. enemies to fight against.
kadluan, n. source.
kadyutín, v. to pull jerkily.
kagabí, adv. last night.
kagalang-galang, adj. respectable, honorable.
kagalit, n. enemy.
kagampán, adj. in the maturity of pregnancy.
kagálingan, n. welfare.
kagandahan, n. beauty.
kagát, n. bite.
kagawad, n. member.
kágawarán, n. department or bureau.
kaginhawahan, n. comfort.
kaginsa-ginsá, adv. all of a sudden, suddenly.
kagípitan, n. difficulty.
kagitingan, n. heroism.
kagitnâ, n. equivalent of 1 liter and a half.
kagubatan, n. wilderness, forest.
kagyat, adv. immediately, at once.
kaháhantungan, n. destiny, end.
kahalagahan, n. importance, value.
kahapisan, n. sadness, melancholia.
kahanga-hanga, adj. wonderful.
kaharian, n. kingdom.
kahera, n. lady cashier.
kahig, n. scratch, mark.
kahigin; v. to scratch, to mark.
kahiniyan, n. shame.
kahilingan, n. request.
kahimanawarì, n. God grants, goodluck.
kahinahunan, n. calmness.
kahinatnan, n. eventuality.
kahindik-hindik, adj. fierce.
kahirapan, n. difficulty, poverty.
kahit, conj. although, even if, no matter what.
kahol, v. bark.
kahón, n. box.
kahoy, n. wood, fuel.
kahulugán, n. meaning of, result of.
kahusayan, n. efficiency,

kabuhayan, n. state or manner of life.

dexterity.
kahuyin, v. to pick up for fuel.
kaibahán, n. difference, strangeness.
kaibig-ibig, adj. lovely.
kaibigan, n. a friend.
kaibiganin, v. to befriend.
kaibuturan, n. innermost, deepest part.
kaiga-igaya, adj. pleasing, attractive.
kaigsian, n. shortness, dullness.
kailaliman, n. underneath.
kailán, adv. when, how soon.
kailangan, adj. needed, necessary.
kailanganin, v. to need.
kailanmán, adv. whenever.
kailanmán, adv. evermore.
kain, rw. eat.
kainán, n. feast, banquet, dining room.
kainaman, n. average, sufficiency, neatness.
kaing, n. bushel basket of woven bamboo.
kaingin, n. soil cultivation on hillsides, forests.
kainggitan, n. envy.
kainin, v. to eat.
kainisán, n. irritation.
kaintindihan, n. one of the same opinion and plans.
kait, v. to take away, to refuse, to withdraw.
kaituktukan, n. the summit, the top.
kalaanan, n. region that is not inhabited.
kalabasa, n. squash, failure.
kalabasan, n. result, effect.
kalabáw, n. water-buffalo, carabao.
kalabít, n. sudden or jerky touch of the fingers.
kalabitín, v. to touch jerkily.
kalabóg, n. the thud of a fall.
kalaboso, n. prison.
kalakal, n. merchandise, business, commerce.
kalakalan, n. trade.
kalakalin, v. to commercialize.
kalakarán, n. fad, fashion, practice.
kalakián, n. full-grown.
kaladkád, n. a pick-up, an easy-to-get person.
kaladkád, v. to haul along, to pull.
kalágitnaan, n. middle, halfway.
kalaguyo, n. intimate friend, partner.
kalahati, n. one-half.
kalahi, n. fellow of the same race.
kalalakihan, n. a group of men, male.
kalaliman, n. depth.
kalamnan, n. joul.
kalamansi, n. citrus fruit.
kalambre, n. cramp.
kalampag, n. noise produced.
kalamay, n. sweetened rice.
kalamayin, v. to be brave, to take hardship for granted, to sweeten.
kalan, n. cooking stove.
kalang, n. wedge.
kalangan, v. to put a wedge.
kalangitan, n. heaven, ecstacy.
kalansay, n. skeleton.
kalansing, n. tinkling sound of falling coins.
kalantariin, v. to talk scandalously of another.
kalantóg, n. jerking noise.
kalantugín, v. to jerk.

kalapati, n. a dove.
kalarô, n. playmate.
kalás, adj. loose, not tied up.
kalasag, n. shield, armor.
kalasín, v. to untie, to unbind.
kálasin, adj. easily untied.
kalasingán, n. drunkenness.
kalat, n. scatterings, disorderliness.
kalát, adj. widespread, rumored.
kalatan, v. scatter, to throw.
kalatas, n. letter, missive.
kalatis, n. extremely soft noise.
kalatog-pinggan, n. gatecrasher.
kalawang, n. rust.
kalawit, n. scythe.
kalayaan, n. liberty, freedom.
kalaykáy, n. rake.
kalaykayín, v. to rake, to scatter.
kalbaryo, n. calvary.
kalbó, adj. bald-headed.
kaldera, n. kettle.
kaldo, n. broth.
kalesa, n. rig.
kalibkíb, n. copra.
kalikasán, n. nature.
kalikawin, n. to stir.
kalikot, n. an instrument used for poking or pulverizing.
kalidad, n. quality, character.
kaligkig, n. shivering due to extreme cold.
kalihim, n. secretary.
kálihimán, n. secretarial office.
kaliluhan, n. treachery.
kalimutan, v. forget.
kalindaryo, n. calendar.
kalingà, n. act of looking after someone.
kalingain, v. to care for, to help.
kalingkingan, n. the smallest among the four fingers, fore-finger.
kalipi, n. fellow of the same lineage or bloodline.
kalipunán, n. association, society, club, federation.
kalis, n. sword.
kaliskís, n. scales of fishes or animals.
kaliskisán, v. to take away the scales. to look over for an impression.
kaliwa, n. left.
kaliwete, adj. left-handed.
kalmante, adj. sedative, soothing.
kalmót, n. scratch.
kalmutan, n. fight wherein body scratching or hair pulling is in order, as women's fight.
kalmutín, v. to scratch fiercely.
kalò, n. pulley.
kalong, rw. to carry on one's lap.
kaloob, n. gift, blessing.
kalungkong, v. carried in a protective embrace.
kalsada, n. street.
kalsador, n. shoehorn.
kalsunsilyo, n. shorts, inner pants.
kaltas, adj. removed, deducted, taken advantage.
kaluban, n. sheath.
kalugud-lugud, adj. agreeable, pleasant.
kalupi, n. pocketbook.
kalupitan, n. cruelty.

kaluskós, n. rustling noise.
kalusugan, n. health.
kalye, n. street.
kalyo, n. corn on toes.
kaluto, n. recipe.
kamaksi, n. cricket.
kama, n. bed.
kamag-anak, n. relative.
kamalig, n. granary, small hut.
kamamamamayan, n. fellow citizen.
kamandág, n. poison.
kamangmangán, n. ignorance, illiteracy.
kamanyáng, n. incense.
kamao, n. the back of the hand.
kamaron, n. shrimps.
kamarote, n. berth.
kamátayan, n. death.
kamatis, n. tomato.
kamaw, n. native clay, bowl, handscape.
kamáy, n. hands.
kamayán, v. to shake hands at work.
kamayín, v. to use the hands.
kamí, pron. we.
kamiseta, n. undershirt.
kamison, n. chemise.
kamot, n. scratch.
kamote, n. sweet potato.
kamoteng-kahoy, n. cassava.
kampanà, n. bell.
kampanaryo, n. belfry.
kampanya, n. campaign.
kampeonato, n. championship.
kampilan, n. cutlass, long bolo of the Moros.
kampít, n. a big kitchen knife.
kampihán, v. to take side with another.
kampo, n. camp.
kampón, n. follower, tribe.
kamposanto, n. holy place, cemetery.
kampupot, n. a shrub with sweet-smelling white flowers.
kamtán, v. to possess, to acquire.
kamunduhán, n. worldliness, passion, sex.
kamusmusán, n. innocence, childhood.
kamuwangan, n. ignorance.
kamutin, v. to scratch.
kamya, n. a species of flowers with long white petals exuding a fragrant scent.
kamyas, n. small, sour, green fruit.
kanaín, v. to fight, to grapple with.
kanál, n. ditch, canal.
kanan, n. right.
kanawín, n. to dilute, to dissolve.
kandado, n. lock.
kandangaok, n. heron.
kandidato, n. candidate.
kandilà, n. candle.
kandili, n. protection, care.
kandilihin, v. to care for, to bring up.
kandirít, n. hop.
kandong, rw. held on one's lap.
kandungan, n. lap.
kandungin, v. place upon one's lap or care.
kandurô, n. snipe.
kanela, n. cinnamon.
kaní-kanilá, v. to divide,

to have one's own.
kanilá, pron. their, theirs.
kanin, n. rice.
kanina, adv. a little while ago.
kanino, pron. to whom, for whom, whose.
kanyá, pron. his, her, him.
kanlóng, adj. out of the way, protected.
kanluran, n. west.
kanser, n. cancer.
kantá, n. song.
kantahín, v. to sing.
kantero, n. bricklayer, mason.
kantiyáw, n. rooting, vexation.
kantiyawán, v. to root, to annoy or vex.
kanugnog, adj. adjacent.
kanyón, n. cannon.
kanyunín, n. to bomb.
kangkóng, n. a vegetative leafy plant thriving on water.
kangrena, n. gangrene.
kangina, adv. a short time ago.
kanino, prep. to whom, whose.
kapa, n. cloak.
kapabayaán, n. neglect, inattention.
kapág, adv. if when.
kapagdaka, adv. immediately, right away.
kapahamakan, n. sudden mishap, misfortune.
kapahintulután, n. permission.
kapaín, v. to grope, to feel.
kapal, n. thickness.
kapalaran, n. fortune, faith, life.
kapanatagan, n. repose.
kapansanan, n. accident, obstruction, sickness.
kapanganiban, n. danger.
kapangyarihan, n. power, authority.
kaparangan, n. prairie, meadow, woods.
kapararakan, n. advantage, benefit.
kapasiyahan, n. decision, resolution.
kapatas, n. overseer.
kapatíd, n. brother or sister.
kapátiran, n. association, fraternity.
kapayakán, n. simplicity.
kapayapáan, n. peace, rest.
kapkap, adj. feeling out or frisking.
kapé, n. coffee.
kapighatián, n. sorrow, misfortune.
kapilas, adj. like, similar.
kapintasan, n. defect.
kapís, n. window panes made from shells.
kapisanan, n. society, party, federation.
kapisanin, v. to live together with.
kapit, n. hold, grasp.
kapitan, n. captain, a title used in addressing a governadorcillo.
kapitá-pitagan, adj. deserving respect, respectful.
kapitbahay, n. neighbor.
kapón, adj. castrated.
kapós, adj. poor, insufficient, not enough
kapote, n. raincoat.
kapritso, n. whim, fancy.

kapunín, v. to castrate.
kapulungin, v. to meet, to talk with.
kapuná-puná, adj. noticeable, conspicuous.
kapupunán, n. addition, filler.
kapurihan, n. glory.
kapuri-puri, adj. praiseworthy, noteworthy.
kapusín, v. to be short of.
kapusukán, n. aggressiveness, heat, state of emotional upheaval.
kapuwá, n. both, the two.
kapuwá-batá, n. childhood friend.
kapuwa-tao, n. acquaintance, fellow human being.
kara, n. face or head side of a coin.
karakara, n. game of tossing coins.
karagdagan, n. additional.
karaingan, n. supplication, complaints.
karálitaán, n. poverty, wretchedness.
karamelo, n. caramel.
karate, n. karaté.
karapatdapat, adj. worthy, proper.
karagatan, n. the whole ocean, the seas.
karampot, adj. of small quantity.
karatula, n. signboard.
karapatán, n. right of, privilege.
karangalan, n. honor.
karaniwan, adj. ordinary, everyday happening.
karapat-dapat, adj. suited to, deserving of.
karat, n. carat, unit of gems weight.
karayom, n. needle.
karbon, n. coal.
karburo, n. carbide.
kardenal, n. Cardinal, a prince of the Church.
karetilya, n. wheelbarrow.
karga, rw. carried as a load, load.
karera, n. race.
karí-karí, n. native stew of cow's entrails.
karikatura, n. cartoon.
kariktan, n. beauty.
karidad, n. charity.
kárihan, n. eating place, restaurant.
karilagan, n. gorgeousness.
karilyo, n. shadow play.
karima-rimarim, adj. abhorrent.
karimlán, n. darkness.
karinyo, n. fondness.
karit, n. sickle.
karitela, n. native buggy.
karitón, n. a two-wheeled cart pulled by animals or men.
karnabal, n. carnival.
karne, n. meat.
karo, n. car.
karós, adj. restless, hasty, unrefined.
karosa, n. chariot.
karpeta, n. carpet.
karpintero, n. carpenter.
kartelon, n. poster, placard.
kartilya, n. a kindergarten primer book.
karton, n. pasteboard.
kartulina, n. bristol board.
kartutso, n. cartridge.
karsel, n. jail, cell, prison.
karugtóng, n. continuation, addition.
karunungan, n. knowledge.
karuwahe, n. carriage.

kasabihán, n. saying, proverb.
kas, n. cash.
kasa, n. firm, commercial house.
kasál, n. wedding.
kasalanan, n. fault, sin.
kasalukuyan, n. now, currently.
kasalungát, n. adversary, opponent.
kasama, n. companion.
kasamá, n. tenant.
kasamahìn, v. to go with, to live with.
kasangkapan, n. tool, furniture, furnishings.
kasangkapanin, v. to use as tool of.
kasangkót, n. accomplice.
kasanggunì, n. member, adviser.
kasanggunián, n. advisory board.
kasanlingán, n. morality.
kasarinlán, n. independence.
kasapì, n. member.
kásasapitan, n. end, result.
kasawian, n. misfortune.
kasayahan, n. joy, festivity, celebration.
kasaysayan, n. history.
kaskó, n. barge.
kaskas, adj. scraped off.
kaskasero, n. speed maniac.
kaskasín, v. wipe out.
kasera, n. landlady.
kasi, n. dear person.
kasibulán, n. prime of life, youthfulness.
kasikatan, n. height of success, popularity.
kasilyas, n. latrine house.
kasilyo, n. cottage cheese.
kasimbigát, adj. of the same weight as.
kasinghirap, adj. as difficult as.
kasinlakí, adj. as big as.
kasingsaráp, adj. as delicious as.
kasino, n. gambling house.
kasintaas, adj. as tall as.
kaso, n. case in court.
kasóy, n. cashew.
kastanyás, n. chestnut.
kastilà, n. Spaniard, Spanish.
kastilalóy, adj. like a Spaniard.
kasú-kasuán, n. bone joints.
kasuklam-suklam, adj. repulsive.
kasulatan, n. writings, document.
kasulatán, n. correspondent.
kásunduan, n. contract.
kasunduín, v. to contract with.
kasundô, adj. cooperative, harmonious.
kasya, adj. enough.
katabí, prep. beside.
katabilán, n. talkativeness.
katakana, n. Japanese alphabet.
kataka-taka, adj. strange.
katád, n. leather.
katagâ, n. particle.
katahimikan, n. silence, rest.
katál, n. trembling.
katala, n. a species of white parrot.
katalagahan, n. natural law, nature.
katalogo, n. catalogue.
katalunán, n. loss.
katám, n. carpenter's plane.
katamtaman, adj. just suf-

ficient, enough

katamaran, n. indolence, laziness.

katampatan, n. quality, characteristics.

katandaan, n. old age.

katapatan, n. sincerity.

katapangan, n. bravery.

katapusán, n. the end.

katarungan, n. justice

katas, n. juice.

katatagan, n. steadiness.

katatawanan, n. humor, joke.

katawan, n. body.

katawanin, v. to represent somebody, to work for somebody.

katawá-tawá, adj. funny.

katay, n. slice of meat.

katayin, v. slaughter for food.

katedral, n. cathedral.

katerba, n. multitude.

katesismo, n. catechism.

kathâ, n. works, fiction writings.

kathaín, v. to write about.

kathambuhay, n. biography.

katí, n. low tide.

katí, n. itch.

katibayan, n. strength of, proof, evidence.

katimbang, n. equivalent, of the same weight or value.

katig, n. outriggers.

katihan, n. dry land.

katiín, v. to test the durability of the eggshell by striking gently against the teeth, to entice, to allure.

katimpián, n. restraint, control.

katingán, n. cooking pot.

katiningan, n. sobriety, serenity.

katipunan, n. collection, federation.

katipan, n. fiance or fiancee.

katitikan, n. minutes of a meeting.

katiting, adj. very tiny or minute.

katiyakán, n. definiteness,

katiyaw, n. young rooster.

katiwalà, n. overseer, manager.

katiwalian, n. graft, corruption.

katiwasayan, n. security.

katók, n. knock.

katoto, n. friend.

katotohanan, n. truth, veracity.

katumbas, adj. equivalent to.

katukayo, n. one possessing the same name or nickname.

katulad, adj. having the same features.

katungkulan, n. duty, obligation.

katunggali, n. opponent.

katuparan, n. fulfillment.

katusuhan, n. trait of being wise.

katuusan, n. computation, total.

katuwaan, n. merriment, enjoyment.

katre, n. bed.

katsá, n. unbleached muslin.

katukín, v. to knock.

katulong, n. attendant, helper.

katutubò, adj. natural, in-

born characteristic.
katuturán, n. answer, value, import.
katuwâ, adj. queer, out of the ordinary.
katuwaan, n. merriment.
katuwiran, n. reason, right.
katuwirán, adj. straightness.
kaugali, adv. having the same characteristics.
kaugalián, n. custom, tradition.
kaugnáy, n. continuation, related to.
kaululan, n. folly.
kaunín, v. to fetch.
kaunlaran, n. progressiveness.
kauntián, v. to decrease, to diminish.
kausáp, n. one who is responsible in answering for a contract, the other fellow in a conversation.
kausapin, v. to talk to.
kawa, n. large caldron.
kawad, n. wire.
kawág, n. hand or leg movements.
kawal, n. soldier.
kawalán, n. poverty, wretchedness.
kawaláng-awa, n. heartlessness.
kawalì, n. frying pan.
kawan, n. group, multitude.
kawangki, adj. similar to something.
káwanggawá, n. charity.
kawaní, n. clerk, employee.
káwanihan, n. bureau.
kawatan, n. robber.
kawawà, adj. pitiful.
kawawaan, n. no meaning.
result or conclusion.
kawayan, n. bamboo.
kawayanán, n. cluster of bamboo trees.
kawikaan, n. adage.
kawil, n. hook for fishing.
kawing, n. link of a chain.
kawit, n. hook, grapnel.
kaya, n. ability.
kayâ, conj. for this or that reason.
kayag, n. invitation.
kayamanan, n. riches, affluence.
kayamuan, n. ostentation, luxury.
kayamután, n. annoyance.
kayanin, v. to assume, to do all work.
kayas, n. act of shaving off.
kayasin, v. to scrape, to smooth.
kayapalà, adv. maybe, perhaps, so it is.
kayó, pron. you (pl.).
kayo, n. fabric, textile.
kayod, n. scraping.
kaysá, adv. than.
kayumanggí, n. brown.
kayungkóng, v. to cuddle up.
kayurin, v. to grate.
keso, n. cheese.
kendi, n. candy.
kerida, n. paramour, mistress.
ketongin, n. leper.
ketsup, n. catsup.
kibít, n. slight but sudden jerky motion.
kibô, n. movement, action.
kibot, n. throb.
kikil, n. file.
kikilan, v. to bleed, to take advantage.

kikiling, v. will side with.
kíkisáp-kisáp, adj. flickering, to close and open.
kidlát, n. lightning.
kilabot, n. terror.
kilabutan, v. tremble.
kilala, adj. well known, popular.
kilalanin, v. to find out, to identify.
kilatis, n. sound of ticking.
kilay, n. eyebrows.
kilik, rw. carried against the hipside.
kilikili, n. armpit.
kilikin, v. to carry on one side, as a baby.
kilig, n. shiver, shudder.
kilíng, adj. tilted, not in line.
kilitî, n. ticklishness.
kilos, n. action, movement.
kilusan, n. activity.
kilusin, v. to move, to take action.
kimáy, adj. twisted (arm).
kimkím, adj. possessing of.
kimika, n. chemistry.
kimî, adj. shy, timid.
kimono, n. lounging robe.
kimpál, n. concentrated group, lump.
kiná, art. to, to one's place.
kinákapatíd, n. godbrother or godsister.
kinagawian, n. what one has been accustomed to do.
kinagigiliwan, v. is pleased with.
kinaiinggitan, v. is envious of.
kinamumuhian, v. being hated by.
kinähanggahán, n. end, result, terminal.
kináhinatnán, n. end, result.
kinálalagyán, n. hiding place.
kinalkál, v. have worked out, have strewn about.
kinamulatan, n. birthplace, environment.
kináng, n. brightness, brilliance.
kinapal, n. creation.
kinatha, v. wrote, published.
kináumagahan, adv. next morning.
kinikilingan, adj. favored.
kinina, n. quinine.
kinis, n. smoothness, refinement.
kiniskis, v. rubbed in order to polish.
kinsena, adj. every fifteen days.
kintáb, n. brilliance.
kintal, n. impression, mark.
kintsay, n. Chinese celery.
kingke, n. petroleum wick lamp.
kipkip, rw. carried under the armpit.
kipil, adj. pressed down tightly.
kirat, adj. with palsied eyelids.
kiri, adj. flirtatious.
kirot, n. stinging pain.
kisap-matá, n. instant, in the wink of an eye.
kisáy, n. convulsion.
kiskís, v. to rub against another.
kisig, n. elegance.
kislap, n. sparkle.
kita, pron. you and I.
kita, n. earnings.

kitang-kita, adj. visible, in full view.
kiti, n. chicks.
kitikití, n. pupa of a mosquito.
kitid, n. breadth, narrowness.
kitiran, v. to make narrow.
kitlán, v. to kill, to snuff out.
kolorum, adj. colorum, unlicensed.
klaustro, n. cloister.
klaustropobya, n. claustrophobia.
kleptomania, n. kleptomania.
klerigo, n. clergyman.
klero, n. clergy.
kliente, n. client.
koboy, n. cowboy.
klima, n. climate, weather.
klinika, n. clinic.
klip, n. clip.
kobre-kama, n. bedspread.
kodak, n. small camera.
kola, n. glue.
kolehiyo, n. college, school.
kolorete, n. rouge.
komadrona, n. midwife.
konsulado, n. consulate.
kongreso, n. congress, public meeting of the masses.
kontrata, n. contract, arrangement.
korporasyon, n. corporation, religious sect.
kubyerta, n. deck.
korona, n. crown.
kolektor, n. collector.
kolyar, n. collar.
komedya, n. a comical skit.
komite, n. committee.
komposisyon, n. composition.
kontrol, n. control.
kras, n. crash.
kriminal, n. criminal.
kronolohiya, n. cronology.
kubkób, v. to beleaguer, to encircle, to surround.
krisis, n. crisis.
kubyertos, n. table-silver.
kuko, n. fingernail.
kúkuti-kutitap, adj. flickering, dying out (as in lights).
kudkuran, n. scraper or grinder.
kudlít, n. apostrophe.
kudyapî, n. harp, lyre.
kuhilà, n. traitor.
kuhól, n. snail.
kulabà, n. filmy mist that settles on eyes of persons about to die.
kúlahan, n. bleaching place.
kulahín, v. to bleach.
kulalat, adj. the last in a group, the hindmost.
kulam, n. witchery.
kulambô, n. mosquito net.
kulambuán, v. to cover with a mosquito net.
kulamin, v. to bewitch.
kulang, adj. short, not complete.
kuláng-kuláng, adj. narrow-minded, with shortages.
kulangot, n. dried mucus.
kulanì, n. swelling in the groins.
kulantró, n. native medicinal seeds used against chicken pox.
kulapulan, v. to besmear.
kulasisi, n. small parrot.
kulasyon, n. abstinence.
kulata, n. butt of rifle.
kulay, n. color.
kulay-ginto, adj. golden.
kulayan, v. to color or render with colors.

kulig, n. suckling pig.
kuliglíg, n. cicada.
kuliling, n. bell, chime.
kulimlím, adj. downcast melancholy, cloudy, dim, hazy.
kulisap, n. bug, insect.
kuliti, n. stye (in the eye).
kulô, n. boiling point.
kulob, n. wrappings, cover.
kulóg, n. thunder.
kulót, n. curl, wave.
kulubóng, n. covering, shelter.
kulubót, n. wrinkle.
kulubutín, v. to wrinkle.
kulugó, n. wart.
kúluguhin, adj. having plenty of warts.
kulungan, v. to cover up.
kulungán, n. cell.
kulungín, v. to imprison, to surround.
kuluntóy, adj. faded, folded.
kúlutan, n. beauty shop.
kulutín, v. to curl, to wave.
kulyahín, v. to bump.
kumákahól, v. barking.
kumare, n. term used between a child's godmother and his parents.
kumbabà, n. humiliation, submission.
kumbento, n. convent.
kumatok, v. to knock.
kumbidado, n. one who is invited.
kumbidahín, v. to invite.
kumindat, v. to wink one eye.
kumintang, n. pre-Spanish Tagalog epic.
kumón, n. latrine.
kumot, n. blanket.
kumpare, n. term used between a child's godfather and his parents.
kumparsa, n. a string band.
kumpás, n. action, movement, musical gesture.
kumpasín, v. to gesture.
kumpay, n. beat, rhythm.
kumpíl, n. confirmation.
kumpisál, n. confession.
kumpisalan, n. the confessional.
kumpisalín, v. to make one confess.
kumpit, n. a type of swift Moro vinta.
kumpleanyo, n. birthday.
kumpól, n. a bunch, a gathering.
kumpulín, v. to gather, to make a cluster.
kumpunihín, v. to repair.
kumustá, n. hello, how are you.
kumustahan, n. greetings, welcome.
kumustahín, v. to greet one, to courteously inquire of one's health.
kumutan, v. to cover with a blanket.
kunat, adj. tough.
kundangan, adv. due to, because of.
kundangan, n. respect, consideration.
kundî, prep, because of, but.
kundiman, n. a love ditty, a red clothing.
kundól, n. a species of fruit, usually used for making sweets, caramel, etc.
kuneho, n. rabbit.
kunin, v. fetch, procure.
kunót, n. wrinkle, fold.

kunsumisyon, n. vexation, exasperation.
kunsumo, n. consumption.
kuntil-butil, n. too many unnecessary details or delays.
kunwarì, n. pretension.
kunwarì, adv. as if.
kung, prep. when, if.
kung hindî, adv. if not.
kupad, n. sluggishness.
kupás, adj. fading, disappearing.
kupasín, adj. easily fading.
kupkóp, n. protection, shelter, help.
kupkupín, v. to protect.
kupi, adj. folded, doubled.
kuping, adj. dented.
kupido, n. god of love, cupid.
kupit, n. filching, pilfering.
kupitan, v. to filch.
kupón, n. coupon, an ally.
kuponan, n. team, group.
kura, n. parish priest.
kurál, n. corral.
kuráp, n. blink.
kurbata, n. necktie.
kurkubado, adj. humpbacked.
kurdon, n. round cord.
kuripot, adj. stingy.
kurót, n. pinch.
kursó, n. diarrhea, stomach trouble.
kurso, n. course, career.
kursunada, n. impulse in the heart, a liking.
kurta, adj. curdled.
kurtina, n. curtain.
kuru-kurò, n. opinion.
kuru-kuruín, v. to think over.
kurús, n. cross.
kúrutan, n. pinching one another.
kurutín, v. to pinch.
kuryente, n. current.
kusa, n. initiative.
kusain, v. to take the initiative.
kuskós, n. rub, silly pretensions.
kuskusan, n. doormat, wiper.
kuskús-balungos, n. uselessness, superfluity.
kuskusín, v. to rub, to scrub.
kusina, n. kitchen.
kusinero, n. cook.
kusinilya, n. gas stove.
kusíng, n. half-centavo in coin.
kusot, n. shavings from woodwork.
kustilyas, n. pork chops.
kusutin, v. to crumple, to clean, to rub.
kutá, n. fort.
kutád, adj. immature, inexperienced.
kuteho, n. listings, bulletin.
kuting, n. kitten.
kutis, n. skin, complexion.
kutitap, n. blinking of numerous tiny lights.
kutsi-kutsi, n silly excuses.
kutkutin, n. diggings, scrapings.
kutkutín, v. to dig, to scrape.
kuto, n. hair bug, louse.
kutób, n. hunch, feeling, premonition.
kutós, n. a rap or light

knock on the head.
kutubán, v. to have a hunch, to suspect.
kutuhin, adj. having plenty of lice.
kutusán, v. to rap, to give a light knock (on the head).
kutsara, n. spoon.
kutsarahin, v. to use a spoon.
kutsaron, n. soup ladle.
kutsero, n. driver of a rig.
kutson, n. cushion.
kutsilyo, n. table knife
kutsilyuhin, v. to knife.
kutsinta, n. steamed rice batter.
kutyâ, n. ridicule.
kutyaín, v. to mock, to despise.
kuwako, n. smoking pipe.
kuwaderno, n. notebook.
kuwadra, n. stable for horses, a barn.
kuwadrado, n. square.
kuwadro, n. frame.
kuwago, n. owl.
kuwán, n. indefinite expression commonly used in lieu of names.
kuwarta, n. money.
kuwártahín, v. to turn into money, to commercialize.
kuwartel, n. quarter, cell.
kuwarto, n. room, partition.
kuwarto, adj. the fourth.
kuweba, n. cave.
kuwelyo, n. collar.
kuwelyuhín, v. to make into a collar of.
kuwenta, n. importance, value, account.
kuwentista, n. story teller.
kuwento, n. a story, a narration.
kuwentuhan, n. story telling among a group.
kuwerdas, n. strings, cords.
kuwérdasán, v. to string, to place cords.
kuwero, n. leather.
kuwestiyon, n. question, problem.
kuwintás, n. necklace, a string of.
kuwintasán, v. to put a necklace, to string around.
kuwitib, n. small, red ants.
kuwitis, n. fireworks.
kuworum, n. quorum.
kuwota, n. quota.
kuya, n. term used in calling the eldest brother.
kuyakoy, n. the swinging movement of the legs when seated, or drumming.
kuyad, n. slowness.
kuyad-kuyad, adj. very, very slow.
kuyapit, v. to hold on tightly.
kuyapò, n. a species of water plants that thrive on river waters.
kuyog, n. a swarm of, throng.
kuyóm, adj. clenched, held tightly together, compressed.
kuyukot, n. coccyx, back.
kuyumad, n. tiny young lice.
kuyumín, v. to clench, to keep to oneself.

D

daanbakal, n. railroad track.
daán, n. road, street.
daanán, v. to pass by.
dabog, n. movement showing displeasure or anger.

dabugan, v. to walk heavily in a stamping manner.
dakilà, adj. great, majestic, sublime.
dakilain, v. to honor, to pay homage.
dakipan, n. arrest, apprehension.
dakipín, v. to arrest, to apprehend.
dako, n. part of.
dakót, n. grasp, handful.
daklutín, n. to grasp.
daklutan, n. kidnapping.
dakutin, v. to pick up.
dagâ, n. mouse.
daganán, v. to put over one's weight, to pile over.
dagat, n. sea.
dagat-dagatan, n. a small lake.
dagdág, n. increase, addition.
dagdagán, v. to increase, to add some more.
dagison, n. act of moving closer together.
dagit, n. something snatched or caught.
dagitab, n. sparkle of flame.
dagitin, v. to snatch, to prey upon.
daglat, n. abbreviation.
daglî, adv. immediately, at once.
dagok, n. a pounding, a strike, misfortune.
dagok ng kapalaran, n. misfortune, bad luck.
dagsâ, n. heavy output, abundance.
dagsaán, v. to come in a throng.
dagukan, v. to pound or strike with closed fist.
dagtâ, n. sap.
dagundóng, n. thunderlike vibration.
dahan-dahan, adv. slowly, softly.
dahan-dahan, v. to do something softly, slowly.
dahás, n. force, violence.
dahil, conj. because.
dahilig, n. large slope.
dahon, n. leaf.
dahop, adj. in want, poor, needy.
dahumpalay, n. green whip snake colored like the leaves of rice plant.
daigdíg, n. world, universe.
daigín, v. to surpass, beat.
daing, n. fish sliced open and dried up.
daíng, n. lamentation, supplication.
dáingan, n. one who usually soothes the afflicted.
daingán, v. to plaint, to give one's complaint or supplications to another.
daít, n. contact.
dala, n. fishing net.
dalâ, adj. experienced, have received a lesson.
dalá-dalá, v. being taken, carried.
dalá-dalahan, n. baggage, gifts, give-aways.
dalag, n. mudfish.
dalaga, n. a matured girl at marriageable age.
dalagang-bukid, n. girl of the field, a species of edible fish.
dalagang-bahay, n. a maid who loves to stay at home most of the time.
dalagang-bayan, n. maid of the city.
dalahikan, n. isthmus.
daláhirà, n. gossiper, rumor-monger.
dalahirain, v. to gossip or relate all over.

dalahit, n. an attack of intense coughing.
dalaín, v. to render impotent due to fear or punishment.
dalamhatì, n. sorrow, affliction.
dalámpasigan, n. shore, bank.
dalang, n. sparseness, infrequency.
dalangin, n. prayer.
dalanginan, v. to pray, to supplicate.
dalás, n. frequency.
dalasín, v. to speed u, to make haste.
dalatan, n. dry land.
dalaw, n. visitor, guest.
dalawá, adj. two.
dalawahín, v. to make two, to pair.
dalawampú, n. & adj. twenty.
dalawin, v. to visit.
daldál, n. glibness, talk.
daldalero, adj. talkative, glib talker.
dali, n. inch.
dali, n. quickness, promptness.
dali-dalí, adj. hurriedly, hastily.
dalí-daliín, v. to hurry, to make haste.
daliri, n. finger.
daliriin, v. recount, to relate in anger.
dalirutin, v. to stir up.
dalisay, adj. pure, clean.
dalisayin, v. to make pure, to render clean.
dalít, n. narration, psalm.
dálitâ, adj. poverty, suffering.
daló, n. attendance.
dalos, n. rashness, haste.
daloy, n. flow, ooze.
dalubhasà, adj. expert, wise.
dalubwika, n. linguist.
daluhán, v. to succor, to help.
daluhong, n. attack.
daluhungin, v. to attack.
daluyan, v. to flow.
dáluyan, n. canal, pipe.
daluyong, n. surge or swell of the sea.
damahán, n. checkerboard.
damahín, v. to feel, to realize.
damahuana, n. gallon.
damayan, v. to help one another, sympathize.
damba, n. rising on hind legs.
dambanà, n. altar.
dambóng, n. plunder.
dambuhalà, n. monster.
dambungán, v. to pillage or rob.
damhín, v. to feel.
dami, n. great number.
damihan, v. to render more, to increase.
damít, n. cloth, clothing.
damitán, v. to dress up.
damó, n. grass.
dampa. n. hut, hovel.
damot, n. stinginess.
dampi, n. light and gentle touch.
damputín, v. to pick up.
damuhán, n. grassy meadow.
damulag, n. a carabao.
danak, n. copious shedding.
danasin, v. to experience.
dantaón, n. century.
dantayán, v. to rest one's body against another.
danyos, n. damage.
dangál, n. honor.
dangkalín, v. to measure with the length of the outspread fingers.
daóng, rw. to anchor, to

go ashore.
daop, adj. joined or closely touching together.
dapa, n. flounder, flat.
dapat, v. must, proper.
dapdap, n. Indian coral tree.
daplís, n. a miss, out of target.
daplisán, v. to strike or rub slightly.
dapò, n. orchid.
dapóg, n. cooking stove.
dáraán, v. will pass.
dapyó, n. blow, pat, dab.
darák, n. rice bran.
darag, n. rude manner or action.
darang, n. exposition to heat of flames.
daratal, v. will arrive.
dasál, n. prayer.
dátapwâ, adv. but, however.
datu, n. chief of a muslim village.
dasalín, v. to pray.
datig, n. lining.
datíng, n. arrival.
datnín, v. to reach.
datos, n. data.
dawag, n. thorny path.
dawdawín, v. to dip into a liquid with the finger.
daya, n. deceit, fraud.
dayang, n. term for princess.
dayami, n. straw, dried rice stalks.
dayap, n. lime.
dayber, n. diver.
dayo, n. foreigner.
dayukdók, n. a hungry person.
dayuhan, n. a stranger.
dayuhin, v. to immigrate.
debate, n. debate, dispute.
dekano, n. dean.
dekalogo, n. decalogue.
delantera, n. front, facade.
delikado, adj. fastidious.
demanda, n. accusation, claim, a suit.
demo, n. demonstration, protest march.
deposito, n. deposit.
deyt, n. date.
dî, adv. not (aphaeresis of **hindî**).
dibdíb, n. breast.
diborsiyo, n. divorce, legal dissolution of the marriage bond.
dibisyon, n. division.
dibuho, n. sketch, drawing.
dikdik, adj. pulverized.
dike, n. dam, dike.
dikín, n. round wedge for bases of cooking pots.
dikít, n. beauty, attachment.
diko, n. the term used in calling an elder brother.
dikya, n. jellyfish.
didál, n. thimble.
diga, n. idle talk.
digmâ, n. war.
digmaín, v. to wage a war.
diín, rw. press heavily, emphasis.
diinán, v. to press, to emphasize.
diit, n. slight pressure on something.
dilà, n. tongue.
dilag, n. beauty, splendor.
dilaw, n. yellow ginger. tumeric, yellow color.
dilidili, n. sense, feeling, understanding.
dilídilihin, v. to think, to meditate.
diligin, v. to water.
dilihensiya, n. ability to find ways and means.
dilím, n. darkness.
dilimín, v. to be caught by night time.

dilis, n. anchovy.
dilubyo, n. deluge.
di-mabilang, adj. innumerable, numerous.
di-mabuti, adj. bad, false.
di-mainam, adj. not good, not suitable.
di-malasa, adj. with a flat taste.
di-malirip, adj. inconceivable, hazy.
di-maliksí, adj. not fast, not active.
di-malimot, adj. unforgettable.
di-mapusyáw, adj. bright-colored.
di-masayod, adj. immeasurable.
dimiti, n. resignation.
di-tuwiran, adj. indirect.
dimonyo, n. devil.
dimon, n. after-delivery period.
din, (rin), adv. also.
dinamitan, v. put on clothes.
díngding, n. partition, sides.
dindingán, n. wall sides.
dini, adv. here.
dinilaan, v. licked.
dinigma, v. besieged.
dingal, n. dazzle, brilliance, pageantry.
dipa, n. the stretch of both arms.
diputado, n. representative.
direktor, n. director.
diskurso, n. speech.
disenyo, n. design.
disimulado, adj. unnoticeable.
distrito, n. district.
dito, adv. here (near the speaker, farther than in "dini").
ditsé, n. term used in addressing elder sister.
ditso, dyudo. n. ju-jitsu.
diwà, n. spirit, soul, thought.
diwatâ, n. fairy, goddess.
diyán, adv. there (far from the speaker and near the person addressed).
diyamante, n. diamond.
Diyana, n. goddess of the moon, Diana.
diyalogo, n. dialogue.
diyanitor, n. janitor.
diyarea, n. diarrhea.
diyaryo, n. newspaper.
diyatà, adv. really, truly.
diyeta, n. prescribed or regulated meal, diet.
Diyos, n. God, Deity.
diyunyor, adj. junior. Jr.
diyusín, v. to pay homage.
doble, adj. double.
dolyar, n. dollar.
Dominiko, n. & adj. Dominican, religious group.
domino, n. game of dominoes.
donselya, n. damsel, chaste woman, virgin.
donya, n. madam.
doón, adv. there (far from both the speaker and the person addressed).
dormitoryo, n. dormitory.
dote, n. dowry.
duke, n. duke.
drayber, n. driver.
dukhâ, n. poor, lowly person.
dukláy, n. branch.
duklayín, v. to reach thru the branches.
duktor, n. doctor.
dukutin, v. to pull out.
dukwang, n. act of reaching for something.
duda, n. doubt.
dugô, n. blood.
dugtong, n. joint, connection.

duguán, adj. bloody, smeared with blood.
duhapang, adj. eager and uncontrollable due to desire, greedily.
duhat, n. blackberry.
dulà, n. drama.
dúlaan, n. theater.
dulang, n. low table for squatting positions.
dulás, n. slip, slipperiness.
duling, adj. cross-eyed.
dulingás, adj. mischievous, bewildered.
dulo, n. end.
Dulong-Silangan, n. Far East.
dulot, n. offer, bring.
dulutan, v. to offer.
dumaán, v. passed.
dumagsâ, v. become abundant, come in numbers.
dumalaga, n. at puberty age, teenage.
dumaloy, v. to flow.
dumanas, v. to experience.
dumapò, v. alighted.
dumaraing, v. complaining.
dumí, n. dirt.
dumihán, v. to render dirty.
dumihan, n. garbage pile, waste basket, latrine.
dumilat, v. to open the eyes.
dumog, adj. absorbed in the fulfillment of one's task.
dumukot, v. to dig into the pocket.
dumuduwál, v. vomiting.
dumugin, v. to rush at.
dumulóg, v. to come to the table (to eat).
dunong, n. knowledge.
dungaw, rw. look out of the window.
dunggól, n. jab.
dunggulín, v. to jab.
dunghalín, v. to look out.
dungis, n. dirt.
dungô, adj. timid, shy.
duplikado, n. & adj. duplicate.
duplo, n. poetical game or contest.
dupok, n. fragility.
dupong, n. firebrand.
dura, n. saliva.
durò, n. prick.
duróg-duróg, adj. pulverized.
durugin, v. to pulverize.
dúrungawan, n. window, lookout.
dusa, n. suffering, affliction.
dustâ, n. abuse, insult.
dustain, v. to abuse, to insult, to look upon.
dutsa, n. the sprinkler in a shower bath.
duwág, adj. coward.
duwal, n. gas expulsion from stomach.
duwelo, n. duel.
duwende, n. elf.
duyan, n. cradle.
dyanket, n. junket.
dyip, n. jeep.
dyipni, n. jeepney.

E

ebanghelyo, n. gospel.
ebidensiya, n. evidence.
eklipse, n. eclipse.
eksakto, adj. exact.
ekstra, n. extra.
eksployt, v. exploit.
eksray, n. X-ray.
ekwetor, n. equator.
eksamen, n. examination.
edád, n. age, era.
edipisyo, n. edifice.
edisyon, n. edition.
ehe, n. axle.
ehemplo, n. example.

eleksiyon, n. election.
embahada, n. embassy.
embahadór, n. ambassador, sp., representative of a nation in other countries.
embargo, n. seizure.
embudo, n. funnel.
empanada, n. fried turnover with flaky crust and a variety of meat fillings.
emigrasyon, n. emigration.
empatso, n. indigestion.
emperdible, n. safety pin.
emplasto, n. poultice, plaster.
emir, n. ruler, governor.
engkantada, n. enchantress.
ensalada, n. salad.
ensayo, n. rehearsal.
entablado, n. stage.
entrada, n. entrance.
entrega, n. delivery, surrender.
entresuwelo, n. room in the first floor of the house.
entomolohiya, n. entomology.
epekto, n. effect.
epidemya, n. epidemic.
episyensiya, n. efficiency.
episyente, adj. efficient.
eredero, n. heir, heiress.
erehe, n. heretic.
ermita, n. hermitage.
eskala, n. scale.
eskaparate, n. show window of a store.
eskinita, n. an alley.
eskirol, n. scab.
eskopeta, n. shotgun.
eskuwala, n. carpenter's square.
eskuwelahán, n. school house, institution.
esmeralda, n. emerald.
esperma, n. white candle.
espinghe, n. sphinx.
espiritu, n. spirit.
espiya, n. spy.
espongha, n. powder puff.
esposo, n. husband, spouse.
espuma, n. froth, foam.
estante, n. shelf.
estapa, n. swindle.
estremadura, n. a region in south western Spain.
espada, n. sword, sp.
estátuwá, n. statue, sp.
estandard, n. standard.
estopado, n. fried pieces of meat cooked in spices.
estrelya, n. star.
estrayk, n. strike.
estudyante, n. student, sp.
eter, n. ether.
eto, (heto) adv. here.

G

gaán, n. easiness, lightness.
gaanán, v. to ease, to lighten.
gaano, adv. how much.
gabáy, n. guide, support.
gabayán, v. to support.
gabí, n. night, evening.
gabi, n. yam.
gabihín, v. to be caught by night time.
gabinete, n. cabinet.
gabok, n. dust or ash particle.
gadgad, adj. shelled out.
gaga, n. fool, girl simpleton.
gagá, v. to appropriate, to usurp.
gagád, n. imitation.
gagambá, n. spider.
gagarín, v. to imitate.
gahasà, n. recklessness, force, rape.
gahasain, v. to force, to violate.
gahì, n. rupture, rip.

gahiin, v. to rip, to rupture.
gahisin, v. to subdue.
gahól, adj. short of time.
gahulín, v. to be short of time.
galâ, n. traveler, widely-travelled, out in street.
galák, n. joy.
galamáy, n. helper, appendage.
galante, adj. gallant, chivalrous.
galang, n. respect.
galáng, n. bracelet.
galangin, v. to respect.
galapong, n. rice flour batter.
galás, n. roughness.
galáw, n. movement.
galawín, v. to move.
galî, n. exhilaration.
galíng, n. amulet, charm, excellence.
galís, n. dobie itch.
gálisin, adj. full of itches.
galit, n. anger.
galitin, v. to make angry.
galos, n. scratch, mark.
galunggong, n. big bodied round scad.
galusan, v. to scratch.
galyetas, n. a kind of biscuit.
gamay. n. habituated.
gambalá, n. disturbance.
gambalain, v. to disturb.
gamit, n. use, utility.
gamitin, v. to use, to utilize.
gamót, n. medicine.
gampanán, v. to fulfill one's duty, to act.
gamutan, n. treatment.
gamutín, v. to treat.
gana, n. profit, appetite.
ganahan, v. to whet one's appetite, to be interested.
ganansiya, n. profit.
ganap, n. complete.
gandá, n. beauty.
gandahán, v. to make beautiful, to beautify.
ganid, adj. stingy, beastly.
ganít, adj. tough.
ganitó, adv. like this.
ganoón, adv. like that.
gansâ, n. goose.
gansál, n. odd number.
gantí, n. retaliation, reply.
gantihín, v. to reciprocate.
gantimpalá, n. prize, reward.
gantimpalaan, v. reward.
gantsilyo, n. crochet.
ganyak, v. to induce.
ganyán, adv. like that.
gaod, n. row.
gapangin, v. to crawl, creep, climb.
gapák, adj. ripped.
gapasán, n. harvest time.
gapasin, v. to harvest.
gapî, adj. subdued, overpowered.
gapiin, v. to overpower.
gapok, adj. rotten inside.
gapos, n. tie, binding.
gapusin, v. to bind, to tie up.
garà, n. pomposity, style, brilliancy.
garaan, v. to make stylish or pompous.
garahe, n. garage.
garalgal. n. gargling sound.
garantiyá, n. guaranty, pledge.
garapa, n. wide-mouthed bottle, dobie itch.
garapinyera, n. ice-cream freezer.
garbansos, n. chick pea.
gargantilya, n. necklace.
garíl, adj. stuttering.
garing, n. ivory.
garote, n. cudgel, bludgeon.

gas, n. gas.
gasláw, n. vulgarity, inhibition.
gasgás, n. scratches.
gasó, n. recklessness, prankishness.
gaspang, n. coarseness.
gastado, adj. worn-out by much use.
gastador, n. spendthrift.
gastos, n. expense.
gatâ, n. pure juice.
gatangan, v. to measure with chupa.
gatas, n. milk.
gatpuno, n. chief, mayor.
gatlâ, n. mark, pointer.
gatungan, v. to increase the fire.
gatong, n. fuel.
gatol, n. intermittent stops.
gawâ, n. occupation, work.
gawaan, n. place of work, factory.
gaway, n. witchcraft.
gawayin, v. to practice sorcery on.
gawgáw, n. starch.
gawi, n. habit, custom.
gawî, n. direction.
gaya, n. imitation.
gayák, n. decoration.
gayahin, v. to imitate.
gayatín, v. to slice into very thin pieces.
gayuma, n. allure, charm.
gerero, n. warrior.
giyera, n. war.
gibâ, adj. demolished, ruined.
gibaín, v. to demolish.
gibík, n. shout for help.
gigil, n. act of gritting the teeth when controlling emotion.
giikan, n. threshing machine.
giit, v. to insist.
gilalás, n. wonder, surprise.
gilas, n. gallant action.
gilik, n. rice straws.
gilid, n. rim, edge.
gilingán, n. grinder.
gilingin, v. to grind.
gilit, n. incision, cut.
giliw, n. term of affection.
gimbalín, v. to surprise, to disturb the peace.
ginágagád, v. being imitated.
ginang, n. matron, married woman (Mrs.).
ginatan, n. a dish cooked with coconut milk.
gináw, n. coldness.
ginhawa, n. physical comfort.
ginimbal, v. shocked.
ginintuán, adj. golden.
ginisa, adj. sauteed.
ginoó, (g.) mister, sir (Mr.)
gintô, n. gold.
ginúgunamgunam, v. recalling.
gipit, adj. wanting or lacking in space.
giray, n. staggering.
giri, n. affected strutting around.
gisá, v. to stew.
gisado, adj. having been stewed.
gisíng, adj. wide awake.
gisingin, v. to awaken.
gitara, n. guitar.
gitarahan, v. to serenade with a guitar.
gitlá, n. shock, fright.
gitling, n. hyphen.
gitgit, v. to crowd, shove.
gitlahín, v. to shock, to frighten.
giting, n. heroism, excellence.
gitnâ, n. middle, midst.

Gitnang-Silangan, n. Middle East.
giwang, n. rocking.
giya, n. guide.
giyagis, adj. afflicted (by).
gobernadorsilyo, n. petty officer.
gobyerno, n. government.
golp, n. golf.
gora, n. cap.
goto, n. ox or cow tripe.
grapt, n. graft.
graba, n. gravel.
grasya, n. grace.
grasyosa, adj. graceful.
gripo, n. faucet.
grogi, adj. groggy.
gubat, n. forest, woods.
gudtaim, n. goodtime.
gugò, n. gogo bark used for cleaning the hair.
gugol, n. expenses.
guguan, v. to cleanse the hair with gogo bark or with bath soap.
gugulan, v. to finance or to invest money.
guhit, n. line, sketch.
guhitan, v. to make a line, to make a sketch.
guhò, n. crumbling, collapse, demolition.
guhuin, v. to demolish.
gulaman, n. agar-agar, seaweed.
gugulatin, v. will surprise.
gulang, n. maturity, age.
gulanít, adj. tattered, worn out.
gulapay, adj. overworked, weak.
gulat, n. fright, shock.
gulatin, v. to surprise, to frighten.
gulay, n. vegetable.
gulilát, adj. panicky.
gulo, n. riot, disorderliness.
gulok, n. a bolo used for heavy cuttings.
gulod, n. slope of the hill.
gulóng, n. wheel turn.
gulugód, n. backbone.
guluhín, v. to confuse, to bring to disorder.
gulungan, v. to run over.
gulunggulungan, n. windpipe, throat.
gumaán, v. to become light.
gumagapang, v. creeps, creeping.
gumimbál, v. to shock, to frighten.
gumon, n. addiction.
gunggong, adj. stupid.
guryon, n. small kite.
guwapo, adj. handsome.
guya, n. young of carabao.
guyam, n. ant.
gumuho, v. to crumble, destroyed.
gunamgunam, n. meditation, recollection.
gunawin, v. to devastate, to dissolve.
guniguní, n. imagination, presentiment.
gunitâ, n. reminiscence, memory.
gunitaín, v. to remember, to recall.
guntíng, n. scissors.
guntingín, v. to cut or stab with scissors.
gunggóng, adj. foolish, stupid, feeble.
gupit, n. haircut.
gupitán, v. to cut the hair, to trim.
gupô, adj. weak, shattered, demolished.
gurò, n. teacher.
gusalì, n. building.
gusgusin, adj. dirty and in rags.
gusót, adj. crumpled, confused.

gusutín, v. to crumple, to confuse.
gutáy, adj. torn, shattered.
gutáy-gutáy, adj. torn, shredded.
gutayín, v. to tear, to shred.
gutom, n. hunger.
gutumin, v. to render hungry.
guwáng, n. crevice, hollow.
guwantes, n. glove.
guyabano, n. sour sop.
guwardiya sibil, n. civilguard.

H

habà, n. length.
habâ, adj. elongated.
habaan, v. to lenghten.
habag, n. compassion.
habagat, n. wind from the west.
habang, adv. while.
habi, n. weave.
habi, adj. woven.
habihán, n. loom, weaving instrument.
habiin, v. to weave.
habilin, n. will, instructions.
habla, n. a court suit.
habol, n. hurry in overtaking somebody, postscript.
habong, n. lean-to shelter, temporary roofing.
hakà, n. idea, suspicion.
haka-hakà, n. supposition.
hakbáng, n. step, measure.
hakot, n. load, baggage.
hakutin, v. to gather, tc take delivery for transfer.
hadláng, n. barrier, obstacle.
hadlangán, v. to stop, to cause an obstacle.
hagad, n. motorcycle, cop.
hagarin, v. to overtake, to follow thru.
hagkan, v. to kiss.
hagkis, n. stroke of whip or lash.
hagdán, n. ladder, staircase.
hagdanán, v. to build a ladder.
hagibís, n. fast runner.
hagilapin, v. to look for, to search for.
haging, n. buzz, hiss.
hagip, adj. hit or caught by a moving body.
hagis, n. throw.
hagisan, v. to throw.
hagok, n. gasp.
hagod, n. rub, caress.
hagpós, adj. loose.
hagulgól, n. weeping, loud cry.
hagunót, n. turbulency, fierceness.
hagurin, v. to rub, to caress.
halaán, n. edible clam.
halabós, adj. boiled and dried.
halakhák, n. laughter.
halakhakán, v. to laugh at.
halagá, n. price, importance, value.
halagahán, v. to price, to praise.
halaghag, adj. neglectful without care.
halál, n. vote.
halál, adj. elected.
hálalan, n. election.
halaman, n. plant.
hálamanán, n. garden.
halang, n. obstruction, fence.
haláng, n. one who does not value life or convention.
halangan, v. to place an

obstacle, to fence.
halas, n. scratch on skin caused by sharp blades of grass.
halatâ, n. perception, inkling.
hálatain, adj. easy to perceive.
halataín, v. to find out, to sound out.
halatáng-halatâ, adj. too open, not cautious, very noticeable.
haláw, n. translation from an original.
halawín, n. to condense or translate.
halay, n. indecency.
halayhay, n. file, row.
halayin, v. to shame, to place one in an indecent position.
haleya, n. jam.
halibas, n. throw, hurl.
halík, n. kiss.
halika, v. come over.
halikán, v. to kiss.
haligi, n. post, pillar.
haligihan, v. to place a support, or piece of wood.
halili, n. replacement.
halimaw, n. beast.
halimbawà, n. example.
halimhimán, v. to hatch.
halimuyak, n. fragrance.
halina, adv. all right, go on.
haling.adj. foolish, mad.
halinghíng, n. moan.
haliparót, adj. uninhibited, vulgar.
haló, n. hello.
halo, n. pestle.
halò, n. mixture.
halos, adv. almost.
halubilo, n. noisy crowd or multitude.
halukay, n. disorderly bundle.
halukayin, v. to ransack.
halu-halò, n. a refreshment of a mixture of sweets, ice and milk.
halukipkíp, n. indifference shown by folding the arms.
haluin, v. to mix, to stir.
halumigmíg, adj. moist.
halungkatín, v. search.
hamak, adj. lowly.
hamakin, v. to belittle.
hambalos, n. blow, beating.
hambalusin, v. to beat with a cane or piece of wood.
hambog, adj. boastful.
hamóg, n. dew.
hamon, n. challenge.
hamón, n. ham, smoked pork.
hampasín, v. to strike.
hampáslupà, n. vagabond, hobo.
hamunin, v. to challenge.
hanap, n. object of search.
hanapbuhay, n. work, occupation.
hanapin, v. to look for, to search.
hanay, n. row, line.
handâ, adj. prepared, ready.
handaan, n. feast, gathering.
handóg, n. gift.
handugán, v. to render a gift or to celebrate.
handusáy, adj. shocked, weary, tired.
hanip. n. flea.
hangál, adj. stupid.
hanggang, prep. until.
hangganan, n. border, end of the trail.
hangarin, n. desire, wish.
hangin, n. wind.
hanging palay-palay, n. gentle breeze.

hanging payagpag, n. severe wind.
hanglay, n. taste of uncooked vegetables.
hangò, adj. adapted.
hangós, adj. out of breath.
hantungan, n. destination.
hapag, n. table, floor.
hapáy, adj. bankrupt, defeated.
hapdî, n. smarting pain.
hapis, n. sorrow, anguish.
hapís, adj. afflicted, sorrowful.
hapít, adj. fittingly close.
haplít, rw. quicken.
haplitín, v. to lash, to eat voraciously.
haplós, n. caress.
haplusín, v. to caress, to massage.
hapò, n. weariness, tiredness.
hapò, adj. tired, weary.
hapon, n. afternoon.
Hapón, n. Japanese, Japan.
hapunan,n. dinner.
hapunán, n. roosting place of chickens.
haragan, n. loiterer.
harana, n. serenade.
harang, n. obstruction.
harangin, n. holdup.
harangan, v. to stop, to waylay.
hárapan, n. front, face to face.
harapín, v. to devote, to confront.
hardin, n. garden.
harì, n. king.
harí-harian, adj. acting like a king.
harina, n. flour.
harót, adj. prankish.
hárutan, n. merry disturbance.
harutín, v. to play pranks on one.
hasâ, adj. sharpened.
hasâ, adj. sharpened, experienced.
hasa-hasâ, n. mackerel.
hasain, v. to sharpen, to secure experience.
hasang, n. gills of fishes.
hasík, n. seedling, sowing.
hatak, n. towing.
hataw, n. thrashing.
hatid, n. conduction.
hatiin, v. to divide.
hatinggabí, n. midnight.
hatinggabihín, v. to be overtaken by midnight.
hatol, n. decision.
hatulan, v. to render a decision.
hawa, n. contagion, infection.
hawak, n. hold, grasp.
hawak, adj. under someone's possession.
hawakan, v. to take hold.
hawás, adj. thin and longish.
hawig, adj. similar to.
hawla, n. cage.
hayaan, v. to allow or let.
hayág, rw. to make known.
háyagan, adj. openly.
hayán, adv. there it is.
hayap, adj. keenness.
hayók, adj. greedy, hungry.
hayop, n. animal.
hayway, n. highway.
hayupan, n. animal-raising.
hibáng, adj. delirious.
heko, n. dark sauce from salted shrimps.
hele, n. lullaby.
henyo, n. genius.
Hermana Mayor, n. one who takes care of a fiesta or a procession and reimburses all expenses.
hibik, n. lamentation, love

proposals.
hiblá, n. thread, fiber.
hibò, n. seduction.
hikà, n. asthma.
hikab, n. yawn, sleepy movement.
hikahós, adj. short, poor.
hikain, adj. asthmatic.
hikaw, n. earrings.
hikawan, v. to put earrings.
hikayat, n. persuasion.
hikayatin, v. to persuade, to attract with arguments.
hikbî, n. sobbing.
hidhíd, adj. stingy.
hidwâ, adj. wrong, astray.
higâ, v. to lie down.
higad, n. caterpillar.
higante, n. giant.
higantí, n. revenge.
higera, n. fig tree.
higing, n. cue, rumor.
higít, v. to have more, surpass.
higop, n. sip.
higpít, adj. strictness, tightness, tighten.
higupin, v. to sip.
hihigan, n. bed.
hihip, n. blower.
hila, n. pull, cargo.
hilab, n. swell, bulge.
hilakbót, n. terror, fear.
hilagà, n. north.
hilagang-silangan, n. northeast.
hilagang-kanluran, n. northwest.
hilahil, n. hardships.
hilahin, v. to pull, to tow.
hilahód, adj. dragging, crawling.
hilam, n. eye pain due to acid from soap or lye.
himala, n. miracle, wonder.
hilamusan, v. to wash the face.
hilát, adj. stretched out.
hilatà, adj. lying down carelessly.
hilatsa, n. thread unravelled from cloth.
hiláw, adj. uncooked, not ripe.
hilawín, v. to render uncooked.
hilbana, n. baste stitch.
hilera, v. to place in a row.
hilera, n. file, row.
hilì, n. envy.
hilík, n. snore.
hilig, n. tendency, liking, inclination.
hiliin, v. to ask another to do one's work.
hilingín, v. to request, to petition.
hilís, n. cut, movement when playing the violin.
hilisin, v. to cut in slanting or oblique direction.
hilo, n. dizziness, nausea.
hilod, n. scrubbing.
hilom, n. closing or healing of a wound.
hilot, n. midwife.
hiluhin, v. to make one dizzy.
hilurin, v. to scrub.
hilutin, v. to massage.
himakás, n. parting.
himagas, n. dessert.
hímagsikan, n. revolution.
himalâ, n. miracle.
himas, n. caress.
himasin, v. to caress.
himasmasán, v. to bring into conscious state.
himasok, n. meddling.
himatáy, n. fainting.
himatayín, v. to faint or swoon.
himaymay, n. fiber.
himbíng, n. deep slumber.
himig, n. melody.

himigan, v. to compose.
himok, n. persuasion.
himod, n. lapping or licking.
himpapawíd, n. sky or air spaces.
himukin, v. to persuade.
himpíl, n. stop.
himulmól, n. thread or feathers when plucked out.
himurin, v. to lick.
himutók, n. resentment.
hinà, n. weakness.
hinakdal, n. request for aid, protection or patronage.
hinagap, n. idea, expectation.
hinagapin, v. to expect, to think.
hinagpís, n. sorrow.
hinagupit, v. struck continuously.
hinahadlangan, v. obstracting.
hinahon, n. calmness.
hinahunin, v. to calm down.
hinaíng, n. supplications.
hinalà, n. suspicion.
hinalain, v. to suspect.
hinalikán, v. kissed.
hinalughog, v. ransacked.
hinampó, n. resentment.
hinanakít, n. grudge.
hinangin, v. to weld.
hinay-hinay, adj. very slowly.
hinatulan, v. condemned.
hináw, v. to dip or wash hands.
hinawa, n. surfeit, boredom.
hinawan, v. cleared.
hinayang, n. regrettable loss.
hindî, adv. no, not.
hindik, n. continuous and agonizing hard breathing.
hinete, n. jockey, horseman.
hinhin, n. refinement, modesty.
hinimok, v. persuaded.
hiningá, n. breath.
hinlalakí, n. thumb.
hinlóg, n. relative.
hinlalatò, n. middle finger.
hinóg, adj. ripe.
hintáy, rw. wait for.
hintayan, n. station.
hintô, n. stop.
hintuturò, n. index finger.
hinuko, n. cutting of finger or toe nails.
hinudyatán, v. signalled.
hinugín, v. ripen.
hínugan, n. place where fruits are ripened.
hinugot, v. pulled out, withdrawn.
hinuhà, n. conclusion.
hinuhain, v. to conclude.
hinuhod, n. agreeableness.
hingà, n. breath.
híngahan, n. confidant.
hingal, adj. gasping, panting.
hingalo, n. death agony.
hingalay, rw. rest.
hinggil, prep. regarding something.
hingín, v. to ask for or request.
hipag, n. sister-in-law.
hipan, v. to blow.
hipò, n. touch.
hipon, n. shrimps.
hipuin, v. to touch.
hirám, rw. borrow, lend.
híraman, n. act of borrowing, favors.
hiramin, v. to borrow.
hirang, rw. select.
hirangin, v. to choose, to appoint.
hirap, adj. difficult, hard, poor.

hirati, adj. accustomed.
hirinan, v. to be choked
hitik, adj. bent due to weight, full, heavy.
hitâ, n. gain.
hitâ, n. thigh.
hitana, n. female gypsy.
hititín, v. to suck, to smoke.
hito, n. a variety of fresh water catfish.
hitsura, n. figure, form. looks.
hiwà, n. cut.
hiwagà, n. mystery.
hiwain, v. to cut.
hiwalayán, v. to separate, to part from.
hiwaláy, adj. separated, apart.
hiwatig, n. knowledge, perception.
hiwatigan, v. to found out, to perceive.
hiyâ, n. shame.
hiyáng, adj. good, agreeable.
hiyaín, v. to put to shame.
hiyás, n. jewelry.
hiyasan, v. to adorn.
hiyáw, n. shout.
hiyawán, v. to shout.
hô, a variant of pô.
holdap, n. holdup.
holdapin, v. to waylay and rob.
homisted, n. homestead.
hording, n. hoarding.
hubád, adj. naked.
hubarán, v. to undress.
hubô at hubád, adj. naked totally.
hubog, n. shape, form.
hubugin, v. to form, to shape.
hukay, n. grave, digging.
hukáy, adj. dug, excavated.
hukayín, v. to dig.
hukbó, n. army.
hukóm, n. judge.
hukót, adj. bent, hunched.
húkuman, n. court of justice.
húkumán, v. to render justice.
hudas, n. traitor.
hudyát, n. sign.
hudyatán, v. to signal.
hudyatan, n. password.
Hudyo, n. Jew
hugas, n. wash water.
hugasan, v. to wash.
hugasán, n. washtub.
hugis, n. shape, outline, form.
hugisan, v. to outline, to form.
hugong, n. humming in the ear.
hugos, n. rush, stampede
hugot, n. draw.
hugutin, v. to draw out, to pull out.
hulà, n. guess, prediction.
hulaan, v. to predict.
hulas, n. melting.
huli, n. catch.
hulí, adj. late.
hulihán, n. raid, arrest, back.
hulihin, v. to catch.
hulog, n. installment, fall.
hulmahan, n. molding, casting.
hulmahín, v. to mold.
hulugán, n. selling on installment plan.
huluin, v. to discern.
humahampas, v. dashing against.
humáhangós, v. panting.
humál, adj. speaking through the nose.
humangga, v. to end.
humayo, v. to go away, depart.
humanay, v. to form a

line.
humapon, v. to roost.
humihina, v. getting weak.
humila, v. to pull.
humilig, v. to incline.
humpák, adj. hollow.
humpáy, n. rest, cessation.
humpayán, v. to cease, to rest.
humugong, v. whizzed.
humupâ, v. to subside.
huni, n. chirping.
hunâ, adj. frailty or structure.
hunos, n. skin peelings, molt. as of reptiles.
hunusdilì, n. control, prudence.
hunyangò, n. chameleon.
hunkág, adj. without contents.
hungháng, adj. stupid, feeble-minded.
huntahan, n. conversation.
hupâ, n. decrease.
hurado, n. jury.
huramentado, n. person who runs amuck.
hurnal, n. installment.
hurnó, n. oven.
husgado. n. court.
hustó, adj. sufficient, right, fitted.
hustuhán, v. to complete.
hutnutin, v. to suck, to take advantage of.
hutukin, v. to discipline, to mold.
huwád, adj. counterfeit, fake.
huwág, v. prohibitive particle, do not.
húwaran, adj. a model.
huwarín, v. to counterfeit.
huwego, n. set of furniture.
huweteng, n. a number pairing game.
huwes, n. judge, magistrate.
Huwebes, n. Thursday.

I

ibá, pron. other, another.
ibabâ, v. to lower, to put down.
ibabad, v. to soak.
ibabaon, v. will bury.
ibabaw, n. top, on top of.
ibabawan, v. to top over.
ibatay, v. to base on.
ibayo, n. other side, opposite side.
ibayó, v. to double, to pound.
ibig, n. like, desire, wish.
ibigin, rw. to like, want, love.
ibilad, v. to spread to dry.
ibinit, v. to make taut (as an arrow).
ibis, n. unloading.
ibitin, v. to hang up.
ibon, n. bird.
ibubô v. to spill, to shed.
ibunsód, v. to launch.
ibunyag, v. to reveal.
iká, adj. a prefix.
iika-ika, adj. limping.
ikabúbuti, n. goodness, welfare.
ikaila, v. to deny.
ikaliligtás, n. safety.
ikasampu, adj. tenth.
ikasásamâ, n. destruction.
ikáw, pron. you (singular).
ikid, n. coil, roll.
ikinamuhi, n. was the cause of one's displeasure.
ikinararangal ko, adj. I have the honor to.
ikinindat, v. winked.
ikirin, v. to coil, to roll.

ikit, n. inward turn, roll.
ikli, rw. shortness.
ikom, adj. closed.
ikot, n. centrifugal or outside rotation.
ididilig, v. to be watered.
idlip, n. short sleep, nap.
idinaos, v. held.
igawad, v. to offer, to give.
igkás, adj. recoiling, springy.
igíb, v. to fetch water.
igláp, n. instant jump.
iglesya, n. church.
ignoransiya, n. ignorance.
ignorante, adj. ignorant.
igsi, n. shortness.
igtád, n. sudden jump or move.
ihagis, v. to throw.
ihanay, v. to relate, to place in a row.
iharáp, v. to bring forward.
ihawín, v. to roast.
ihayag, v. to be made public, to relate.
ihi, n. urine.
ihit, n. fit, convulsion.
ihiyene, n. hygiene.
iisá, adj. only one.
iladlád, v. unfurl.
ilag, n. side movement to parry on object.
ilagan, v. to avoid.
ilagáy, v. to put, to place.
ilalim, prep. beneath.
ilang, n. open, uninhabited space, wilderness.
ilán, adv. how many.
ilán-ilán, adj. very few.
iláng-iláng, n. fragrant flower with long, yellow petals.
iláp, n. act of being untamed.
ilat, n. a brook.
ilathalà, v. to publish, to make public.
ilaw, n. light.
ilawán, n. lamp.
ilawan, v. to light.
iling, n. shaking of the head in denial or disapproval.
ilit, n. confiscation of property.
ilog, n. river.
ilóng, n. nose.
imbabáw, n. pretense, superficiality.
imahen, n. image, statue.
imbák, n. stocks, preserves.
imbakín, v. to stock up, to preserve.
imbáy, n. swing of the arms, the arms in motion.
imbí, adj. miserable, mean.
imbót, n. greed.
imík, n. talk.
imikán, v. to talk with.
impeksiyon, n. infection.
impertinente, adj. impertinent.
impiltraytor, n. infiltrator.
impromto, adj. impromtu, not prepared.
imperyo, n. empire.
impis, adj. shrunken, deflated.
impít, n. pressure, tightness.
impitín, v. to tighten.
impiyerno, n. hell.
impó, n. grandmother.
impók, n. savings.
impormál, adj. informal.
impormasyón, n. information.
imperyalismo, n. imperialism.
impukín, v. to save.
imulat, v. to open one's eyes to teach.
inâ, n. mother.

inaalagaan, v being taken care of.
inakáy, n. brood.
inaglahi v. ridiculed.
inahin, n. hen.
inam, n. neatness, harmony.
inamín, v. admitted.
inampalan, n. júdge in a contest.
inangkin, v. claimed.
inát, n. stretchings.
imbestmen, n. investment.
inbestigasyon, n. investigation.
indák, n. movement in rhythm.
indayog, n. rhythm.
inersiya, n. inertia.
inday, n. young girl.
inhenyero, n. engineer.
iniatas, v. ordered.
inidoro, n. water-closet.
inihaw, n. broiled.
ininín, v. to put into right degree of heat.
iníp, adj. impatient.
inís, adj. irritated, suffocated.
inisín, v. to irritate, to suffocate.
init, n. heat.
iniwagwag, v. to take off by shaking.
inog, n. revolution.
inom, v. to drink.
insó, n. term used in calling the wife of an elder brother.
inspirado, adj. inspired.
insulto, n. insult.
interes, n. interest.
interbyu, n. interview.
intindí, n. understanding.
intindihín, v. to understand, to listen.
itaboy, v. to drive.
itinalaga, adj. destined.
introduksiyon, n. introduction.
inuhín, v. to take notice of.
inulit, v. repeated.
inumin, n. something to drink.
inumín, v. to drink.
inunan, n. placenta.
inusig, v. investigated.
inutil. adj. disabled. useless.
inút-inutín, v. to go slowly by degrees.
inutusan, v. was sent on an errand.
inúusig, n. being prosecuted.
inuyat, n. thickened extracted juice of sugar cane.
inyó, pron. your, yours (both plural and second persons, singular, respectful).
inyuhín, v. to own.
ingat, n. care, protection.
ingatan, v. to take care.
ingat-yaman, n. treasurer.
ingay, n. noise.
ingayan, v. to make noise.
inggit, n. envy.
ipa, n. chaff of rice grains.
ipaseguro. v. to have someone be insured.
ipatungkol, v. to cause to be attended to.
ipaubayà, v. to entrust.
ipapuputol, v. will order to cut.
ipikít, v. to close (as the eyes).
ipil, n. hardwood tree used in house construction.
ipinag-utos, v. ordered.
ipinagbabawal, v. prohibited.
ipinugal, v. tied.
ipis, n. cockroach.

ipit, n. pinch, pressure.
ipitin, v. to pinch, pressure.
ipod, v. to move over while sitting.
ípon, n. heap, pile.
ipot, n. dropping of fowls and animals.
ipu-ipo, n. cyclone, whirlwind.
iral, n. actuality.
irap, n. sullen look.
iri, n. muscular forcing in moving the bowels.
isá, n. & adj. one.
isáng-katló, n. one-third.
isangguni, v. to consult.
isanla, v. to pawn.
isaulî, v. to return.
iskrip, n. script.
iskursiyon, n. excursion, picnic.
iskuwad, n. squad, small number of soldiers.
isdá, n. fish.
isi, adj. easy.
isinakdal, n. filed a case in court against.
isinalpók, v. dipped.
isinama, v. took along.
isinamâ, n. something that made one wrong or bad.
isinaulî, v. returned.
isiningkaw, v. yoked.
isinumpâ, v. cursed.
isinuót, v. put on.
isip, n. thought, mind.
isipan, n. sense.
isipin, v. to think, to reflect.
isíp-isipin, v. to just think about.
is-is, n. sandpaper-like leaves.
isiwalat, v. to reveal.
ismíd, n. sneer.
isod, n. act of moving up or away in position.
ismirán, v. to sneer.

istaka, n. stake, picket.
istasyon, n. station.
istatwa, n. statue.
isyu, n. issue.
estapa, n. estafa.
isuplong, n. to report.
ita, n. negrito.
itaás, n. upstairs.
itaás, v. to hold high.
iták, n. bolo.
itapon, v. to throw away.
itatag, v. to found or organize.
itatuwâ, v. to deny.
iti, n. dysentery.
itik, n. duck.
itihin, v. to snatch, to pilfer, to become sick of dysentery.
itím, adj. black.
itimán, adj. with predominant black color.
itimín, v. to blacken.
itinátalagá, v. placing oneself at the mercy of faith.
itindig, v. to adjourn.
itinudla, v. shot.
itlóg, n. egg.
itó, pron. this.
itudlà, v. to aim at.
itumbás, v. to substitute for something, to compare.
iwa, n. stab, slash.
iwanan, v. to entrust to somebody.
iwas, n. evasion, parry.
iwasák, v. to destroy.
iwasan, v. to parry, to evade.
iwi, n. taking care of an animal for someone else.
iyák, n. cry, sob.
iyakan, v. to cry over.
iyakin, adj. cry-baby, often crying.
iyán, pron. that (near the

iyó, pron. yours.
iyón, pron. that, over there.

L

laan, adj. reserved for.
laáng-gugulín, n. money set apart for expenses, budget.
laba, n. washing of clothes.
labada, n. clothes given or taken for washing.
lababo, n. sink.
labak, n. low region.
laban, n. game, fight.
labaha, n. razor.
lábahan, n. washing place, washing tub.
labahita, n. sturgeon.
labág, adj. against, in violation of.
labanan, v. to fight, to oppose.
labanós, n. radish.
labangán, n. feeding. trough for pigs or horses.
labás, adv. out, outside.
labasán, v. to issue forth, to come out.
labatiba, n. enema.
labatibahin, v. to give an enema.
labhán, v. to wash.
labì, n. lips.
labî, n. remains, left-over.
labian, v. to scorn.
labingsiyám, n. & adj. nineteen.
labintadór, n. firecrackers.
labing-isá, n. & adj. eleven.
labis, n. surplus, overage.
labisan, v. to make more than sufficient.
labis-labis, adj. more than sufficient, excessive.
labnot, adj. plucked out.
labò, n. dimness, turbidity.
labog, n. oversoftness of consistency due to overcooking.
labong, n. bamboo shoot.
labsak, n. softness and stickness of consistency.
labuín, v. to dim, to make turbid.
labusaw, n. turbid, muddy.
labuyò, n. wild fowl.
lakad, n. walk, stride, engagement.
lakambini, n. muse.
lakán, n. lord, chieftain.
lakandiwà, n. judge in a poetic joust.
lakarin, v. to work for, to negotiate.
lakas, n. strength.
lakdawan, v. to omit, to leave out.
lakip, n. enclosure, as in a letter.
lakò, n. things to sell.
laksâ, n. ten thousand.
laksante, adj. laxative.
lagabláb, n. blaze.
lagak, n. deposit, bail.
lagalág, adj. wandering, roving.
laganap, adj. widespread.
lagapak, n. resounding noise of something falling.
lagarì, n. saw.
lagás, adj. fallen (as leaves).
lagaslasan, n. rapids.
lagariin, v. to saw.
lagasin, v. to pick out, to destroy.

lagaslás, n. swift flowing of a brook.
lagáy, rw. put, place.
lagkít, adj. starchy, sticky.
lakatan, n. a variety of banana.
lagkitan, n. glutinous corn.
lagdâ, n. signature.
lagì, adv. often, oftentimes.
lagím, n. extreme sorrow, terror.
lagitík, n. lash or creak of a whip.
lagläg, n. drop, failure.
lagnát, n. fever.
lagnatín, v. to have fever.
lago, n. luxuriant growth.
lagok, n. gulp.
lagom, n. all-inclusive comprehension.
lagós, adj. penetrating.
lagot, adj. snapped off, cut off.
lagpák, n. fall.
lagpakán, v. to cause to fall.
lagunlóng, n. sound of falling water.
lagusin, v. to cover all.
lagús-lagusan, adj. easily penetrable.
lahad, n. narration, statement.
lahát, n. all, everybody.
lahì, n. race.
lahiin, v. to find out the parentage.
lahò, n. oblivion.
lalâ, adj. serious.
lalaki, n. male, man.
lalagukan, n. trachea.
lalamunan, n. throat.
laláng, n. artifice, creation.
lalangín, v. to create.
lalaugan, n. esophagus.
lalawig, v. to be continuous.
lalawigan, n. province.
lalim, n. depth, seriousness.
laliman, v. to deepen.
lalos, adv. all together.
lamad, n. membrane.
laman, n. meat.
lamáng, adj. have an advantage over. adv. only.
lamangán, v. to fool, to take advantage of.
lamás, adj. mussed.
lamasin, v. to muss or crumple, breakage.
lamat, n. crack in glassware as the beginning of a break.
lamay, n. vigil, night work.
lamayan, n. night vigil over a departed.
lamayin, v. to work throughout the night.
lambak, n. valley.
lambanog, n. wine from coconut water.
lambát, n. net.
lambayog, n. hanging cluster of fruit.
lambingan, n. affectionate; tete-a-tete.
lambingán, v. to caress, to render affectionate.
lambitinan, v. to hang on.
lambóng, n. mouring mantle.
lambót, n. tenderness.
lamig, n. coldness.
lamigán, v. to soften, to control oneself.
lamlám, adj. flickering.
lamóg, adj. overhandled.
lamon, n. voracious eating.
lampá, adj. feeble, weak.
lampahín, v. to weaken.
lámpará, n. light, lamp.
lampás, adv. beyond. adj. penetrating.
lampasán, v. to go over or beyond.

lampong, n. jealous howling of cats.
lamukos, v. to crush or crumple.
lamukot, n. edible part of nangka fruit.
lamugín, v. to manhandle till soft or battered.
lamunin, v. to eat greedily.
lamuyutin, v. to convince, to render easy.
lamya, n. oozy or caressive manner of talking.
lamyós, n. caress.
lana, n. wool.
landás, n. path.
landasín, v. to make a pathway.
landáy, n. shallowness.
langgam, n. ant.
langgamín, v. to render accessible to ants.
langgonisa, n. native sausage.
langís, n. oil.
langisán, v. to oil, to smoothen.
lángisan, n. oil factory.
langitngit, n. creak.
langóy, rw. swim.
lánguyan, n. swimming contest.
lansá, adj. fishy taste.
lansangan, n. street.
lanság, adj. dissolved, destroyed.
lansagín, v. to destroy, to dissolve.
lansihan, n. a game of tricks.
lansungan, n. native steamer.
lantá, adj. withered.
lantak, n. violent attack or onset.
lantahín, v. to wither.
lantád, adj. wide open, exposed.
lantay, adj. pure, unalloyed.
lantik, n. graceful bend or curve.
langkay, n. small flock or group.
langgas, n. dressing or washing of wound.
langib, n. scab of wounds.
laon, n. delay.
laón, adj. old, of a long time.
laós, adj. useless, obsolete.
lapad, n. width.
lapág, n. floor.
lapang, n. big piece of meat.
lapastangan, adj. blasphemous, disrespectful.
lapastanganin, v. to act without due-respect.
lapát, n. fine strips of bamboo.
lapat, adj. well adjusted.
lapatan, v. to render treatment or punishment.
lapay, n. spleen.
lapian, n. party (politics).
lapida, n. gravestone.
lapit, n. nearness.
lapitan, v. to come near, to offer.
lapnos, adj. flayed, excoriated.
lapot, n. thickness.
lapis, n. pencil.
lapu-lapu, n. sea bass or grouper.
larangan, n. the field of.
larawan, n. image, picture.
larawang-diwà, n. imaginary picture.
laruán, n. toy, a game.
láruan, n. playground, gaming place.
laruín, v. to play with.
lasapín, n. to taste, to experience.

lasáp, n. taste.
lásingan, n. bar, drinking place.
lasingín, v. to make one drunk.
laslás, n. rip.
lason, n. poison.
lasunin, v. to poison.
laswâ, n. indecency.
latâ, n. weariness.
lata, n. can.
latak, n. residue.
latag, n. spread.
latay, n. welt, mark.
latayan, v. to mark, to produce welt.
lathalà, n. publication.
latian, n. swamp.
latik, n. residue of coconut milk.
látiko, n. a whip.
laurel, n. olive.
lawà, n. lake.
lawâ, adj. wet, full of water.
lawaan, n. lagoon.
lawain, v. to wet, to render wet.
lawak, n. area, extent.
lawakan, v. to spread out, to think farther.
laway, n. saliva.
lawig, n. duration.
lawin, n. hawk.
lawít, n. something suspended or hanging.
lawitán, v. to give a favor or attention.
layà, n. freedom, liberty.
layák, n. rubbish.
layag, n. sail.
layás, adj. vagabond.
layaw, n. ostentation, too much favors.
laylay, adj. hanging weakly.
layò, n. distance.
layon, n. aim.
layuán, v. to move away from.
layunin, n. aim.
leeg, n. neck.
legwas. n. league.
lei, n. law, commandment.
lehiyon, n. legion.
lente, n. flashlight.
letra, n. letter.
letrahán, v. to letter.
leyenda, n. legend.
libák, n. humiliation, mockery.
libág, n. body dirt.
liban, v. to postpone.
libangan, n. recreation, amusement.
libangín, v. to amuse.
libid, n. coiling.
libíng, n. burial.
libingan, n. cemetery.
libís, n. slope.
liblíb, n. hidden spot.
libo, n. thousand.
libog, n. sex, passion, aroused desire.
libró, n. book.
likas, n. exodus, evacuation.
likas, adj. natural, inborn.
likha, adj. created.
liksi, n. quickness.
liksiyón, n. lesson.
liempo, n. side bacon belly.
lider, n. leader.
ligalíg, adj. troubled, uneasy.
ligalig, n. trouble, molestation.
ligaligin, v. to make trouble.
ligamgám, n. worry, perturbation, state of being tepid, as in water.
ligas, n. garter.
ligat, n. glutinousness.
ligaw, n. suitor.
ligáw, adj. astray.
ligawan, v. to court.
ligaya, n. happines.

ligiran, v. to surround.
ligò, rw. bath.
ligoy, n. wordiness, verbosity.
ligpitín, v. to keep away.
ligtás, rw. free, safe.
ligwak, n. spill.
liha, n. sandpaper.
lihâ, n. segment of a fruit.
liham, n. letter.
lihaman, v. to write a letter to.
lihí, n. conception.
lihim, n. secret.
lihimin, v. to talk secretly.
lihiyá, n. lye.
liit, adj. small, tiny.
liitan, v. to make smaller, decrease.
likás, adj. natural.
likhâ, n. something created.
likhaín, v. to create.
likô, adj. wrong. n. turn.
likód, n. back.
liksí, n. fastness, agility.
liksihán, v. to go fast.
likù-likô, adj. winding, mazy.
likutín, v. to tamper.
lilim, n. shade.
liliman, v. to put a shade.
lilip, n. hemstitch.
lilís, v. to roll up sleeves or trousers.
lilisán, v. to lift up.
lilo, adj. unfaithful.
lilukin, v. to carve.
limahid, adj. untidily dressed.
limampû, n. & adj. fifty.
limasín, v. to ladle out.
limatik, n. leech, sucker
limbág, n. publication.
limbás, n. bird of prey.
limit, n. frequency.
limlim, n. brooder heat or temperature.
limlimán, v. to hatch.
limós, n. alms.
limot, n. forgetfulness.
limpák, n. lump.
limpi, adj. gathered together.
limunada, n. lemonade.
limusán, v. to give a contribution.
limutin, v. to forget.
linamnám, n. savor, taste.
linangín, v. to cultivate.
linaw, n. clearness.
linawin, v. to make clear.
lináp, n. fatty scum.
linaw, n. clearness.
lindól, n. earthquake.
linggatong, n. perturbation.
lingkisin, v. enfolded.
linggó, n. week, Sunday.
lingguhan, adj. every week.
linggû-linggó, adj. every week.
lingunin, v. to turn one's head around.
lingíd, adj. unknown.
lingkód, n. service, one ready to serve.
linilok, v. sculptured.
liningin, v. to think over, meditate.
linis, n. cleanliness.
linisin, v. to clean.
linlang, n. deceit, fraud.
linlangín, v. to mislead.
linsád, n. dislocation.
linso, n. linen cloth.
linsól, adj. unfortunate.
lintâ, n. leech.
lintík, n. lightning.
lintikán, v. to be under troubles.
lintos, n. blister from friction.

lingunín, v. to look back.
lipád, n. flight.
lipanà, adj. all around, in plenty.
liparín, v. to fly.
lipás, adj. out of season.
lipì, n. lineage.
lipì, n. ancestry.
lipstik, n. lipstick.
lipol, n. extinction.
lipon, n. crowd, gathering.
lipos, adj. full.
lipunan, n. society.
lira, n. lyre.
lisa, n. eggs of lice, nits.
liston, n. band, ribbon, tape.
lisyâ, adj. erroneous.
lisyain, v. to commit error or mistake.
litaw, adj. visible, obvious.
litid, n. ligament.
litis, n. trial in court.
lito, adj. confused.
liwaliw, n. taking a pleasure trip.
liwasan, n. plaza.
liyab, n. blaze, flame.
liyag. n. beloved.
liyo, n. dizziness.
lohika, n. logic.
lomo, n. loin.
lobo, n. wolf.
longganisa, n. pork sausage.
loob, n. inside.
looban, n. yard
loobín, v. to make one feel.
loobin, n. feeling.
loók, n. bay.
loro, n. parrot.
losa, n. porcelain.
luad, n. clay.
lubák, n. rut.
lubag. n. pacification, lull.
lubagin, v. to calm oneself.
lubalób, n. an addict of vice, standby.
lubáy, n. stop, cessation.
lubayan, v. to stop, to cease.
lubayán, adj. serious, grave.
lubha, adv. excessively, very much.
lubid, n. rope.
lubirin, v. to rope.
lublób, v. to wallow.
lubóg, adv. submerged.
lubós, adv. completely.
lubusan, adv. completely, absolutely.
lukbutan, n. pocket.
luklók, v. to be seated.
luklukan, n. seat.
luko, n. insane.
lukob, n. act of sheltering or giving shelter.
lukót, adj. crumpled.
luksâ, adj. black, in mourning.
luksó, n. jump.
luksuhín, v. to hurdle.
luktón, n. young locust.
lukuban, v. to protect, to bring under one's discipline.
ludlód, n. dale, green spot.
lugà, n. pus in the ear.
lugál, n. plaee.
lugamî, adj. prostrate with grief.
lugás, adj. fallen off.
lugaw, n. rice gruel.
lugawin, v. to make rice gruel.
lugay, adj. hanging loose.
lugi, n. loss.
luglugín, v. to shake.
lugó, adj. weak.
lugód, n. delight, pleasure.
lugsô, v. to destroy.
luhà, n. tears.
luho, n. luxury.

lumagô, v. to become luxuriant in growth.
lumahok, v. join.
lumalalo, v. increasing.
lumalabag, v. going against, violating.
lumayo, v. go away.
lumusong, v. to go to a lower place as in water.
luhód, v. to kneel.
luhog, n. request, imploration.
lula, n. vertigo, seasickness.
lulan, n. capacity.
lulanan, v. to fill with cargo.
lulod, n. shin.
lulunín, v. to swallow, to roll.
lumà, adj. old, stale.
lumalâ, v. to become worse.
lumabág, v. to violate.
lumabas, v. to go out.
lumálalâ, v. aggravating.
lumalamon, v. devouring.
lumanay, n. mildness, gentleness.
lumapit, v. to get near.
lumbáy, n. sorrow.
lumbó, n. round drinking cup, usually a coconut shell.
lumawig, v. to prolong.
lumot, n. moss.
lumayas, v. to go away.
lumayô, v. to go farther away.
lumikas, v. to evacuate.
lumikha, adj. created.
lumingon, v. to turn one's head.
lumipas, n. the past.
lumipas, v. passed by.
lumitáw, v. to appear.
lumpó, adj. totally or partially paralyzed.
lumulan, v. to ride in.
lumundag, v. to jump.
lunas, n. remedy.
lundáy, n. boat.
Lunes, n. Monday.
lúneta, n. moonlight park.
lungad, n. spewings of milk or food.
lungkot, n. sadness.
luningning, n. glitter, brilliance.
lunggâ, n. hole, burrow.
lunggatî, n. desire, wish.
lunó, adj. boneless, soft.
lunos, n. compassion.
lunsód, n. city.
luntian, adj. green.
lunurin, v. to drown.
luom, adj. covered airtight.
luóy, adj. faded, wilted.
lupà, n. earth, ground.
lupak, adj. crushed by pounding.
lupagi, adj. in a squatting position.
lupain, n. land of, kingdom.
lupalop, n. sphere.
lupaypáy, adj. weakened.
lupî, n. fold.
lupig, rw. vanquished.
lupít, n. cruelty.
lupon, n. a group, a committee.
lurâ, n. saliva.
luraán, v. to spit on.
luráy, adj. destroyed.
lurayín, v. to destroy, to render into smithereens.
lurok, v. to understand one's idea or opinion.
lusak, n. muddy place, mire, immorality.
lusakin, v. to render muddy.
lusáw, v. to melt, to dissolve.
luslos, n. hernia, rupture.
lusob, n. attack.

lusót, adj. having holes.
lusót, v. to pass through.
lusong, n. wooden mortar.
lusubin, v. to attack.
lúsutan, n. opening, a slip thru.
lusután, v. to slip. pacify.
lúsutan, n. passage.
lutang, rw. to drift, to float.
lutás, adj. concluded, finished.
lutasín, v. to terminate, to solve.
luting, n. looting.
lutóng, adj. brittle.
lutungán, v. to make crisp.
lutò, n. menu, recipe.
lutuán, n. kitchen, stove.
lutuin, v. to cook.
luwà, v. to emit, to eject.
luwâ, adj. protruding.
luwagán, v. to loosen, to make room.
luwál, n. something born or produced.
luwalhatì, n. happiness, ecstasy, glory.
luwalhatiin, v. to celebrate, to glorify.
luwás, v. to go to the city or the town.
luwasan, n. center of the town, downstream.
luwát, n. tardiness.
luya, n. ginger.
luylóy, adj. *loosely hanging.

M

maáarì, v. possible, will do.
maabutan, v. to be overtaken.
maabután, v. to be able to hand over.
maaga, adj. early.
maagap, adj. punctual, everready.
maagos, adj. swift, running, as water.
maalab, adj. heated, warmed.
maalalahanin, adj. thoughtful.
maalam, adj. wise.
maalat, adj. salty.
maalamát, adj. rich in legends.
maalindog, adj. extremely beautiful.
maalinsangan, adj. hot, sultry.
maalwán, adj. easy.
maamò, adj. domesticated, tame.
maantá, adj. rancid.
maantak, adj. continually very painful.
maáng-maangan, adj. ignorance.
maanggó, adj. sour (as of milk).
maapóy, adj. fiery.
maapulà, v. to stop, check.
maasim, adj. sour.
maawaín, adj. merciful.
maaya, adj. pleasant.
mabalasik, adj. wicked, evil, mean-eyed.
mababá, adj. humble.
mababaw, adj. shallow.
mabagal, adj. slow.
mabagót, v. to be bored.
mabagsík, adj. fierce.
mabaít, adj. virtuous.
mabalasik, adj. ferocious.
mabanás, adj. sultry.
mabangis, adj. fierce, wild.
mabahò, adj. with a bad smell.
mabangó, adj. fragrant.
mabibíg, adj. talkative,

big-mouthed.
mabibigat na gawain, n. hard work, difficult.
mabigát, adj. heavy.
mabiglâ, v. to be taken by surprise.
mabigô, v. to be disappointed.
mabilí, adj. saleable.
mabilís, adj. swift, cunning.
mabilog, adj. spherical, rounded.
mabinì, adj. full of modesty, gentle.
mabisà, adj. effective.
mábubô, v. to spill.
mabuhay, n. long live.
mabulaklák, adj. flowery.
mabulo, adj. full of pricky hair, (in plants)
mabuti, adj. good.
mabuwáy, adj. unbalanced.
makabago, adj. modern.
makabayan, adj. patriotic, civic-minded.
makagitaw, v. to excel, to be able to stand out.
makálawá, adv. twice.
makalawá, n. day after tomorrow.
makalag, v. to be untied.
mákaligtaán, v. to omit, to not include
makalimot, v. to forget.
makálulón, v. to swallow accidentally.
makalumà, adj. old-fashioned, prudish.
makalupà, adj. earthly, materialistic, sexy.
mákaniíg, v. to have a tete-a-tete, to converse intimately with.
makapaghiganti, v. to avenge.
makapaglálatang, v. to be the cause of kindling.
makapál, adj. thick, heavy.
makapamoók, v. to be able to fight against.
makapangahas, v. to be bold, to be daring.
makasalanan, adj. full of sins.
makasimsim, v. to taste, to sip.
makatkát, v. to remove, to efface.
makátipák, v. to make a big gain.
makatuwiran, adj. reasonable.
makilbaka, v. to fight with.
makihati, v. to share with.
mákiná, n. machine, Sp.
makináng, adj. brilliant, glittering.
makinilya, n. typewriting machine.
makinis, adj. smooth.
makinista, n. machinist.
makipag-alít, v. to quarrel with.
makipagkasundo. v. to agree, to patch up.
makipisan, v. to live with.
makipot, adj. narrow, tight.
makirot, adj. extremely painful.
makisanib, v. to join, to be a member.
makisig, adj. dressy, elegant.
makislap, adj. sparkling.
mákita, v. to see by chance.
makitid, adj. narrow.
makitil, v. to cut, to kill.
makiusap, v. to plead, to make a request.
makopa, n. a bell shaped fruit.
maktulin, adj. peevish.

madagsâ, adj. hurried, bustling.
madagtâ, adj. full of resin.
madalang, adj. less frequent, thin.
madalás, adv. often, frequently.
madaldál, adj. talkative.
madalî, adj. easy, prompt.
mádalian, adj. hurrying up, in short notice.
madalita, adj. full of suffering.
madaluhong, adj. easy to attack, ready to help.
madamdamin, adj. full of emotion.
madapâ, v. to stumble.
madasalin, adj. prone to praying, religious.
madayà, adj. full of deceit.
madiláw, adj. yellowish.
madilím, adj. dark, obscure.
madlâ, n. public.
madrasta, n. stepmother.
madulás, adj. slippery, elusive.
madyong, n. mahjong.
maestra, n. teacher (female).
maestro, n. teacher (male), instructor.
maestruhán, v. to teach.
magâ, adj. swollen.
mag-aalahas, n. jeweler.
mag-aamá, n. father and children.
magaán, adj. easy, light.
mag-alaala, v. to be anxious.
magalang, adj. courteous, respectful.
magalíng, adj. excellent, good.
mag-anak, n. family.
magandá, adj. beautiful.
mag-apuháp, v. to grope for.
magarà, adj. pompous, dressy.
mag-aral, v. to study, to learn.
mag-asawa, n. husband and wife.
mágasín, n. magazine.
magasó, adj. mischievous.
magatô, v. to be worn out.
mag-atubili, v. to hesitate.
magayót, adj. tough.
magayuma, v. to be charmed.
magbalik, v. to come again.
magbungkal, v. to dig.
magbatá, v. to bear, to carry thru.
magbayad, v. to pay.
magbigáy, v. to give, to extend.
magbigtí, v. to hang oneself.
magbihis, v. to change one's clothes, to dress up.
magkábilâ, n. both sides.
magkabilán, adj. not in alignment, dissimilar.
magkabisa, v. to take effect.
magkagalít, n. enemies.
magkurlís, v. to be scratched.
magkakilala, n. acquaintances.
magkalaguyò, n. friends, lovers.
magkamukhâ, adj. resembling each other.
magkanlóng, v. to hide.
magkano, pron. how much.
magkapatíd, n. brothers, members of a brotherhood.
magkápatiran, n. brotherhood.
magkasama, n. companions.

magkásamaan, v. to be in bad terms
magkasi, n. sweethearts.
magkátotoó, v. to come true.
magkikita, v. will see each other.
magkikiyâ, v. to gesticulate.
magkulang, v. to be lacking, to forget.
magkuwento, v. to relate a story.
magdahilan, v. to give some excuse.
magdalá, v. to carry, to possess.
magdaláng-awà, v. to be compassionate.
magdaláng-hiyâ, v. to be ashamed.
magdaláng-tao, v. to be pregnant.
magdamág, adv. all night long, throughout the night.
magdarayà, adj. dishonest.
magdaragat, n. seaman, mariner.
maghampaslupà, v. to be a hobo, to become a vagabond, to idle.
maghapon, adv. all day long.
maghiganti, v. to revenge.
maghilom, v. to heal (as a wound).
mag-inà, n. mother and child.
magiging, v. will become.
magiliw, adj. affectionate.
maginâw, adj. chilly, cold.
maging, v. to be.
magíng, prep. even, whether.
máginoó, n. gentleman.
mágising. v. to be awakened.
magiting, adj. heroic.
maglakô, v. to sell by carrying goods around.
maglalagos, v. will pierce.
maglagalág, v. to travel endlessly.
maglarô, v. to play.
maglimos, v. to give alms.
maglinis, v. to clean up.
magmaliw, v. to be lost, to pass by.
magmaáng-maangan, v. to pretend not to know.
magmalasakit, v. to put interest in, to care for.
magmanmán, v. to watch out, to detect.
magmatúwid, v. to justify one's own fault.
magnanakaw, n. robber, thief, holdupper
magnilay, v. to reflect, to meditate.
magpaalam, v. to bid goodbye.
magpahuli, v. to go behind.
magpailanláng, v. to go up in the air, to imagine.
magpalibut-libot, v. go about.
magpalimos, v. to beg.
magpalusog, v. to be healthy.
magparangál, v. to honor oneself, to fete another.
magparangalan, v. to show off.
magpasyál, v. to promenade, to take a walk.
magpatiwakál, v. to commit suicide, to kill oneself.
magpatuloy, v. to continue.
magpaumat-umat, v. to procrastinate.

magpaunlák, v. to accede, to give in, to give favor.
magsaka, v. to cultivate the soil, to farm.
magsasaka, n. farmer.
magsikap, v. to work diligently.
magsimba, v. to go to church.
magsipag, v. to be busy, to be industrious.
magsisi, v. to repent.
magsiwalat, v. to expose, to explain.
magsiyasat, v. to investigate.
magsugal, v. to gamble.
magsulsí, v. to mend torn garments.
magtaksil, v. to turn traitor.
magtagál, v. to last long.
magtahán, v. to stop crying, to stay at home.
magtahí-tahî, v. to fabricate.
magtampisáw, v. to walk barefooted in a muddy place.
magtanan, v. to run away, to elope.
magtanghál, v. to stage, to present.
magtanggál, v. to cut off, to disconnect, to lay off.
magtanggól, v. to defend.
magtaním, v. to plant.
magtapon, v. to throw away.
magtiis, v. to suffer, to endure.
magtimpi, v. to endure.
magtindig, v. to erect.
magtitingì, n. retail seller.
magtugot, v. to yield, to stop.
magtulóg, v. to sleep the whole time.
magtulot, v. to let by.
magulangan, v. to be taken advantage of.
mágulantang, v. to be awakened suddenly.
magulat, v. to be surprised.
mag-ulat, v. to account, to relate.
mag-ulayaw, v. to converse intimately.
maguluhan, v. to be in trouble.
magulumihanan, v. to be upset, to be surprised.
magunita, v. to come to mind, to recollect.
mag-usap, v. to converse, to talk.
magwagi, v. to win.
mahagway, adj. tall and well-proportioned.
mahal, adj. dear, expensive.
mahalaga, adj. important, valuable.
mahalay, adj. vulgar, obscene.
mahalayan, v. to feel depraved.
mahalín, v. to be infatuated, to love.
mahalin, v. to love, to lavish affection.
mahapdî, adj. painful.
maharlika, adj. noble, aristocratic.
mahayap, adj. piercing.
mahibáng, v. to go mad.
mahigpít, adj. strict, tight.
mahilig, adj. inclined to.
mahimláy, v. to fall asleep.
mahinà, adj. weak.
mahinahon, adj. prudent.
mahinusay, adj. orderly, properly.
mahirap, n. a poor one, a lowly one.
mahirap, adj. hard, diffi-

cult.
mahirapan, v. to be subjected to hardships.
máhistrado, adj. judge magistrate.
mahitík, v. to be laden with fruits.
mahitít, v. to suck.
mahiwagà, adj. mysterious.
mahiya, n. magic.
mahusay, adj. good, well-placed.
maiklî, adj. short.
máidlíp, v. take a nap accidentally.
maigaya, adj. delightful, happy.
maigi, adj. all right, enough.
maigting, adj. taut, full of.
mailáp, adj. elusive, untamed.
maimbót, adj. stingy, full of greed.
maimpók, adj. thrifty, economical.
mainam, adj. nice.
mainíp, v. to feel impatient.
mainit, adj. hot, fiery.
maingat, adj. careful.
maingay, adj. noisy.
mainggitin, adj. envious, full of envy.
maipagsanggaláng, v. to protect.
maipagtírik, v. to light candle as offering.
mairog, adj. loving, sweet full of love.
mais, n. corn.
malabay, adj. spreading, luxuriant.
malabigà, adj. full of gossips.
malabis, adj. exaggerated deeply felt.
malabò, adj. not clear.
malakás, adj. strong.
malakí, adj. big, enormous.
malagkít, adj. sticky.
malagihay, adj. half-dry.
malahiningá, adj. tepid.
malaibay, adj. tipsy.
malalâ, adj. grave.
malalim, adj. deep.
malamán, adj. fleshy.
malambíng, adj. caressing, affectionate.
malambót, adj. soft.
malamíg, adj. cold.
malamlám, adj. dim.
malanság, v. to be dissolved.
malantá, v. to be wilted.
malaon, adj. after a time.
malapad, adj. broad.
malapit, adv. near.
malapot, adj. thick.
malas, n. bad luck.
malasa, adj. tasty, delicious.
malasakit, n. protective concern.
malasado, adj. half-cooked.
mala-sebo, adj. sour-sweet.
malat, n. hoarseness.
malawak, adj. wide.
malawig, adj. prolonged.
malay, n. knowledge, information.
malayò, adj. far.
malay-tao, n. consciousness.
maleta, n. valise.
mali, n. error, oversight.
malî, adj. wrong.
malibag, adj. dirty.
malikmatà, n. vision, apparition.
malikót, adj. mischievous.
maliksí, adj. quick, agile.
máligáw, v. to go astray.
maligaya, adj. full of happiness.
maligoy, adj. long round-

about.
maliít, adj. small.
malilim, adj. shady.
malinis, adj. clean, pure.
malinamnam, adj. tastes good.
malipol, v. to be annihilated.
malirip, v. to understand.
malitó, v. to be confused.
malituhín, adj. easily confused.
maliwanag, adj. brilliant, lighted.
maliwanagan, v. to understand, to be cleared of.
maliyáb, adj. full of blaze.
malubhâ, adj. serious.
malukóng, adj. concave.
malugod, adj. cordial.
maluningning, adj. scintillating.
malumanay, adj. slow, soft.
malungkot, adj. sad, sorrowful.
malungkutín, adj. always sad.
malupít, adj. cruel, stern.
maluráy, v. to be destroyed into pieces.
malusóg, adj. strong, healthy.
malutóng, adj. brittle.
maluwalhati, adj. glorious.
maluwag, adj. loose.
maluwáng, adj. wide, roomy.
maluwát, adj. too long, long delayed.
mamà, n. address used for elderly men with whom the speaker is not familiar.
mamád, adj. without feeling.
mamamayan, n. citizen.
mambubuwis, n. taxpayer.
mamangka, v. to go riding in a boat.
mamarang, n. a variety of edible mushroom.
mamay, n. a nurse.
mámayâ, adv. by and by.
mamimili, n. buyer.
mamintás, v. to find fault with.
mamirinsá, v. to iron clothes.
mamiyapis, v. to cringe.
mamon, n. sponge cake.
mamuhay, v. to live.
mamumuksa, n. plunderer
mamutawì, v. to speak out.
manakop, v. to conquer.
manalig, v. to believe in.
manaluntón, v. to follow.
mánanakop, n. conqueror.
manánagano, v. will predominate.
mánanaliksik, n. researcher.
manas, n. beri-beri.
manatili, v. to remain.
mandala, n. conical heap of palay in the stalk.
mandirigmâ, n. warrior.
mang-aawit, n. singer, minstrel.
manedyér, n. manager.
maneho, v. manage, to run.
mangabayo, v. to go riding on horseback.
manggá, n. mango.
manggagamot, n. doctor, physician.
manggagawà, n. laborer, worker.
mangkok, n. bowl.
mangkukulam, n. sorcerer, witch.
mangangalakal, n. merchant.
manggàs, n. sleeve.
manghâ, n. surprise.
mangingibig, n. suitor.
manghuhula, n. fortune teller.
manghuhuthót, n. profit-

eer.
mangmáng, n. ignorant.
mangulila, v. to be lonely.
mangulubót, v. to shrivel.
mangumpisál, v. to confess.
mangyari, v. to occur, to take place.
mamumuhunan, n. capitalist, investor.
mamuno, v. to lead.
manaka-naka, adv. once in a while.
manî, n. peanut.
manhíd, n. numbness.
manibálang, adj. mature.
manikà, n. doll.
manipesto, n. manifesto.
maningníng, adj. brilliant.
manipis, adj. thin.
maniwalà, v. to believe.
manlalakbay, n. traveler.
mangangalakal, n. businessman.
manghimagsik, v. rebel.
manligaw, v. to pay court.
manlupaypáy, v. to droop, to feel weary.
mano, n. right.
manók, n. chicken.
mantekilya, n. butter.
mantél, n. tablecloth.
mantsá, n. stain, dirt.
mánukan, n. poultry.
mánunubos, n. redeemer.
manugang, n. son or daugther-in-law.
manugangin, v. to make one's son or daughter-in-law.
manunungkulan, n. official.
manunudla, n. archer
mapagkamkám, adj. greedy, grabbing.
mapagkandili, adj. solicitous, protective.
mapagmataás, adj. proud.
mapagpaimbabaw, adj. hypocritical, deceitful.
mapagsamantalá, adj. opportunistic, grabbing.
mapagtitiwalaan, adj. can be trusted.
mapag-unawà, adj. understanding.
mapamighani, adj. alluring, entrancing.
mapamihag, adj. captivating.
mapanaghiliín, adj. envious.
mapanatili, v. maintain.
mapangamkám, adj. avaricious, greedy.
mapanghalina, adj. fascinating.
mapanggayuma, adj. bewitching.
mapangilagan, v. to get rid of, to beware of.
mapangláw, adj. sad, gloomy.
mapang-uyám, adj. sarcastic.
mapanudyó, adj. inclined to teasing.
mapanuri, adj. wary.
mapápaknít, v. will be detached, to be disconnected.
maparam, v. to cause to disappear.
mápariwarà, v. to be misled.
mápatanyág, v. to be made famous.
mapawì, v. to vanish.
mapayapà, adj. peaceful.
mapilit, adj. insistent.
mapilitan, v. to be forced to.
mapitagan, adj. respectful.
mapunahin, adj. critical, observant.
mapungay, adj. lambent.
mapuról, adj. dull.

maputî, adj. white.
maputlâ, adj. pale.
marahan, adv. softly.
marahás, adj. aggressive.
marahil, adv. maybe.
maralitâ, adj. poor.
maramay, v. & adj. to be involved, helpful.
maramdamin, adj. sensitive.
marami, adj. much, many, plenty.
máramihan, adj. in large quantities, wholesale.
maramot, adj. selfish, stingy.
marangál, adj. honorable.
maranasan, v. to experience.
marangál, adj. worthy of respect.
marangya, adj. magnificent, showy.
marapat, adj. worthy.
marawal, adj. dirty, gloomy, disgusting.
marká, n. mark, trade mark.
markahán, v. to mark.
marikít, adj. pretty.
marilág, adj. bright hand some, elegant.
marinero, n. sailor.
maringal, adj. elegant, solemn.
marinig, v. to hear.
mariposa, n. butterfly.
marmol, n. marble.
Marte, n. god of war, Mars.
Martes, n. Tuesday.
martilyo, n. hammer.
martilyuhín, v. to hammer.
marubdób, adj. ardent, passionate.
marumì, adj. dirty, impure.
marungis, adj. bad, mean, dirty.
marunong, adj. wise, intelligent.
marupók, adj. fragile, weak.
masa, n. dough, mass, common people.
masakím, adj. grabbing, greedy.
masakít, adj. painful.
masakláp, adj. bitter, unpleasant.
masaksihán, v. to witness.
masagabal, adj. full of obstructions.
masaganà, adj. prosperous, bountiful.
masahin, v. to make a dough.
masahe, n. massage.
masahol, adj. worse than.
masairán, v. to go broke.
masalitâ, adj. talkative.
masamâ, adj. bad, evil.
masamaín, v. to feel bad.
masamyó, adj. fragrant.
másangkót, v. to be involved.
masansalà, v. to be stopped from doing something.
masaráp, adj. tasty, delicious.
masamang-loob, n, bandits, robbers.
masasanglâ, v. to be pawned.
masawî, v. to meet misfortune.
masayá, adj. cheerful.
maskada, n. chewing tobacco.
masdan, v. to look very carefully.
maselang, adj. very particular, fastidious.
masetas, n. potted plants.

masid, v. to observe closely.
masidhî, adj. intense, vehement.
masigasig, adj. industrious, diligent.
masigid, adj. intense.
masiglá, adj. gay, lively.
masilaw, v. to be dazzled.
masilungan, v. to serve as shady shelter.
masíndakin, adj. easily frightened.
masinop, adj. industrious, practical, economical.
masinsín, adj. compact, very close.
masinsinan, adj. serious, hearty.
masipag, adj. diligent, hardworking.
masisilawin, adj. easily dazzled by outward appearance.
masiyasatín, adj. inquisitive, full of curiosity.
masunurin, adj. obedient.
masunggáb, adj. always ready to grab, greedy.
masungit, adj. ill-tempered.
masunurin, adj. obedient.
masurì, adj. critical, analytic.
masuyò, adj. full of affection, obliging.
masyado, adj. extreme, excessive.
matá, n. eyes.
mataás, adj. high, tall, well-known.
matabâ, adj. fatty, stout.
matabáng, adj. without salt, tasteless.
matabíl, adj. talkative.
matakaw, adj. greedy, voracious.
matadero, n. slaughterhouse
matagál, adj. taking a long time, for quite a time.
mátagalan, adj. durable, for a period of time.
matagintíng, adj. resounding, full pitch.
matahan, adj. big-eyed.
mataimtim, adj. full of faith, fervent.
matalas, adj. sharp, aggressive, keen.
matalik, adj. intimate, close.
matalino, adj. talented, clever, wise.
matambók, adj. protruding, bulky.
matamis, adj. sweet, full of melody.
matamláy, adj. spiritless, indisposed.
matampuhin, adj. sensitive.
matamo, v. to obtain.
matandâ, adj. old, matured.
matandain, adj. keen memories, easy to remember.
matangkad, adj. lanky.
matangos, adj. long and pointed.
mataós, adj. sincere.
matapang, adj. brave, courageous.
matapát, adj. honest, loyal.
matapatin, adj. honest, trustworthy.
matatág, adj. steady, stable, strong.
matátagalán, v. endure.
matatap, v. to realize, to learn.
matatás, adj. fluent, talkative.
matauhan, v. to recover sense.
matayog, adj. high, high-toned.
matematìka, n. mathema-

tics.
matigas, adj. hard, fighting, unmovable.
matimtiman, adj. constant, devoted.
matimyás, adj. full of devotion.
matindí, adj. serious, strong.
matingkád, adj. strong colored, bright, brilliant.
matiník, adj. full of thorns, rough.
matining, adj. high and full voice.
matinis, adj. shrill, high-pitched.
matino, adj. full of common sense, normal.
matipunò, adj. healthy and strongly built.
matiyagâ, adj. patient, persevering.
maton, n. bully, browbeater.
matrikula, n. tuition fee.
matris, n. uterus.
matyagán, v. to follow up.
matubig, adj. wet, full of water.
matubò, adj. profitable, productive.
maukol, v. to belong.
matumal, adj. stale, slow, not saleable.
mátuntón, v. to trace to one's hiding place.
matunóg, adj. resounding, clever.
matupad, v. to go through.
matupok, v. to be burned.
matuwâ, v. to be glad.
matuwain, adj. affectionate.
matwid. n. reason, argument.
matwíd, adj. straight, right.
mauhaw. v. be thirsty.
mauhawín, adj. getting thirsty easily.
maulán, adj. rainy.
maulinigan, v. to hear.
maulit, adj. repetitious.
maunlád, adj. progressive, productive.
mausisà, adj. curious, inquisitive.
mawalâ, v. to be lost.
may, v. having, possessing.
maya, n. sparrow.
mayabong, adj. luxuriant, thriving.
may-akdâ, n. author.
mayaman, adj. rich, opulent.
mayá-mayâ, adv. later.
mayapá, adj. insipid.
may-arì, n. owner.
may-kabuluhán, adj. of significance, important.
may-kalintikán, adj. full of mischief, wily.
may-kalokohan, adj. humorous, playful, jesting.
maykapangyarihan, n. authorities.
maygawâ, n. author, constructor.
maypakanâ, n. one who instigates.
may-pasak, adj. clogged.
mayroon, v. having, possessing, there is, there are.
maysakít, n. patient, one who is sick.
mayumi, adj. modest, demure.
mekaniko, n. mechanic.
medalya, n. medal.
medisina, n. medicine.
medikó, n. doctor.
medida, n. tape.
medyas, n. socks, stocking.
medyo, adj. half, **semi.**
meteorolohiya, n. meteorology.

mga, (manga) art. article placed before a noun, to denote plurality.
milyon, n. million.
mina, n. mine, riches.
minámahál, n. beloved.
minindál, n. afternoon snack.
minsan, adv. once.
minsanan, adj. just one time, once.
mintis, adj. failed.
minulán, v. began.
minura, v. scolded with abusive language.
minuto, n. minute.
mírindal, n. light repast between lunch and supper.
miron, n. spectator.
misa, n. mass.
misay, n. beard.
mistulà, adj. similar to, like.
mithì, adj. objective, wish.
mithiin, n. aspiration.
miting, n. meeting, gathering.
mitra, n. mitre.
mitsa, n. wick.
mitolohiya, n. mythology.
Miyérkulés, n. Wednesday.
mo, pron. by you.
moda, n. fashion, style.
modelo, n. model.
modo, n. manner.
molestiya, n. bother.
molotobam, n. molotov-bomb.
momo, n. bogeyman.
moog, n. fort, defense, tower.
morpolohiya, n. morphology.
Moro, n. Moro.
mukhâ, n. face.
mukhang-bangkay, adj. cadaverous.
mukhang patay, adj. deathlike.
muhî, n. irritation, repugnance.
muhon, n. boundary marker.
mulâ, adv. since then, since that time.
mulawin, n. molave tree.
muleta, n. crutch.
muli, adv. once more, again.
multa, n. fine.
multó, n. ghost.
mumo, n. left-over during eating, particle.
mumog, n. gargle.
muna, adv. first move.
mundó, n. world, Sp.
mungkahì, n. suggestion, motion.
munì, n. sensible thought.
muntî, adj. small.
muntík, adv. almost, nearly.
munukala, n. idea, plan.
mura, adj. cheap, not costly.
murahin, v. condemn, to scold.
muralya, n. rampart, wall.
musa, n. muse.
musang, n. civet cat.
músikó, n. musician.
musmós, adj. innocent, young.
mustasa, n. mustard.
mutà, n. secretion of the eyes, knowledge.
mútain, adj. having or full of eye secretion.
mutyâ, n. pearl, loved one.
musika, n. music.
museo, n. museum.
muwang, n. sense, grasp, understanding.

N

na, n. an article used to connect the modifier

with the modified, an adverb of time equivalent to ready, now.
naaakit, v. being attracted.
naaangkop, adj. fit.
naaalang-alang, v. to be taken into consideration.
naaamís, v. being disappointed.
naaalaala, v. to be remembered, to be recollected.
naáanod, v. to be carried away by the current.
naawà, v. took pity on.
nabagabag, adj. to be filled with compassion.
nabagbág, adj. demolished, broken up.
nabalam, v. delayed.
nabalták, v. to be pulled.
nabigo, v. failed, did not succeed.
nabigla, v. taken by surprise.
nabunyag, v. revealed.
nábihag, v. to be taken as captive, to be charmed.
nakaalís, v. to be able to get away, had gone.
nakaambâ, adj. threatening in suspended motion.
nakakíkilitî, v. to be feeling ticklish.
nakalimot, v. forgot.
nakaut, n. knockout.
nakalúlumbáy, adj. sorrowful.
nakamúmuhì, adj. disgusting, irritating.
nakamúmulás, adj. escaping out of.
nakapandidiri, adj. loathsome.
nakapanghíhila, adj. attracting, persuading.
nakapanghíhilakbót, adj. horrible, frightening.
nakararami, n. majority.
nakapanghíhinayang, adj. regrettable.
nakararahuyo, adj. enticing.
nakapinid, adj. closed, locked.
nakasakáy, v. riding.
nakasalalay, adj. placed on a shelf or any protruding base.
nakasalamín, adj. with glasses placed on or hanging on a base.
nakasalampáy, adj. carelessly hanged on.
nakasalampák, adj. sitting down carelessly on the floor.
nakasalig, v. based on, patterned after.
nakasampáy, adj. draped, hanging on the line.
nakasangkót, v. involved in.
nakasísiguro, adj. sure of.
nakasísindák, adj. frightful.
nakasísinók, adj. to be fed up.
nakatanghód, adj. looking or witnessing something in anticipation.
nakatatakot, adj. fearful.
nakatátandâ, adj. older than the rest.
nakatátantiya, adj. full of estimate.
nakatátarók, adj. with full knowledge of.
nakatigháw, v. was able to quench, recover.
nakatirá, v. living, residing.
nakatítiyák, adj. to be sure of.
nákatulog, v. fell asleep.
nakatulóy, v. was able to enter.
nakatutulig, adj. stunning, stupefying, deafening.

nakaw, adj. stolen, pilfered.
nakawalâ, v. was able to get away.
nakidigma, v. fought.
nakíkimatyág, v. to observe with.
nakíkisalamuhà, v. mixing with others.
nakíkisama, v. to be in company with others.
nakíkiugalì, v. adopt the custom of the locality.
nakipagitan, v. acted as intermediary.
naknak, adj. abscessed.
nádaganán, v. buried, placed under.
nádampî, v. was touched lightly.
nadirimlán, v. in darkness, in confusion.
nag-aalinlangan, v. doubting.
nag-áalsá, v. to strike, to talk loudly.
nag-áaral, v. studying, learning.
nag-áatubilí, v. hesitate.
nagahís, v. to be defeated.
nagalaw, v. moved.
nagalit, v. to get angry.
nagalusan, v. to be bruised.
nagansál, adj. to be uneven.
nagantihán, v. to be able to reciprocate or to revenge.
naganyák, v. to be induced.
nagbábadhâ, v. indicating, foretelling.
nagbábadyá, v. relating or speaking of.
nagbábagwís, v. developing wings.
nagbábalak, v. planning, thinking.
nagbábalík, v. returning.
nagbalatkayo, v. disguised.
nagbantáy, v. guarded.
nagbíbirô, v. to be in a joking mood.
nagbihis, v. dressed.
nagbíbiruán, v. joking with each other.
nagbúbuhat, adv. issuing from, coming from.
nagbúbuhát, v. using force, lifting.
nagbúbunót, v. husking (as in cleaning the floor), pulling out plants.
nagbunsód, v. started, made to do.
nagbuntúng-hiningá, v. sighed.
nagkaguló, v. to become disorderly.
nagkasira, v. quarreled.
nagkátinginan, v. looked at each other.
nagkautang, v. was in debt.
nagkiskís, v. struck as a match rubbed together.
nagdaóp, v. clasped both hands together.
nagdasal, v. prayed.
naggágapang, v. crawling around.
nagising, v. woke up.
nagustuhan, v. liked, enjoyed.
nagugutom, adj. hungry.
naghágikgikan, v. giggled.
naghálikan, v. kissed each other.
naghamók, v. locked in combat.
naghampasan, v. beat or struck each other.
naghanáp, v. searched, looked for.
naghanay, v. lined up or placed in a row.
naghikab, v. yawned.
naghíhilamos, v. washing the face.
naghimala, v. showed a miracle.

naghíhintayan, v. waiting for each other.
nahihimbing, v. sleeping soundly.
naghilatà, v. sitting or lying idly around.
naghimatay, v. fainted.
naghingalô, v. to breathe out one's last.
naghintô, v. stopped.
nagibâ, v. destroyed.
nag-ibá, v. to change, to be different.
nag-indá-indayog, v. is or are swaying.
nágisíng, v. awakened.
naglagos, v. pierced.
naglíliparan, v. flying about.
naglilipatan, v. moving out.
naglipanà, v. scattered all around.
nagluksa, v. mourned.
nagpagibík, v. called for help.
nagpuyos, v. raged.
nagsásabóg, v. spreading.
nagsásabong, v. fighting in the way of roosters.
nagsásaing, v. cooking rice.
nagsísibák, v. splitting wood.
nagsísiilag, v. dodging, evading.
nagsísiláb, v. blazing.
nagsisipanginig, adj. trembling.
nagtagál, v. lasted a long time.
nagtagò, v. hid oneself.
nagtalik, v. were intimate.
nagtátamasa, v. enjoying.
nagtapat, v. told frankly.
nagtawanan, v. laughed together.
nagtilád, v. break up into small pieces.
nagtilaukan, v. crowed.
nagtipanan, v. made a date.
nágulantáng, v. awakened abruptly.
nágulat, v. taken by surprise.
nag-ulat, v. accounted for.
nagulumihanan, v. to be taken by surprise or wonder.
nag-unat, v. straightened.
nag-usap, v. conversed.
nagwalang-bahala, v. feigned indifference.
nagyakág, v. to persuade, to have invited.
nagyakap, v. embraced each other.
nahapis, v. saddened.
nahatì, v. divided.
nahíhibang, adj. delirious.
nahihilo, v. feeling dizzy.
náhíhimláy, adj. sleeping, resting.
nahihiya, adj. feeling embarassed.
nahintakutan, adj. become afraid.
nahulaan, v. guessed.
nahuli, v. caught.
náhulí, adj. to have arrived late.
naíkulá, v. was bleached.
náikulóng, v. was imprisoned, crowded in.
naíinggít, v. envying.
naìlapat, v. was closed tightly.
náiligtás, v. was saved.
náintindihán, v. understood.
naipadpád, v. floated by the sea, carried by.
náipit, v. caught between two bodies.
nais, n. desire.
naisin, v. to thought of.
naitalâ, v. was recorded.

náitakwíl, v. place aside, discarded.
naitanan, v. was able to elope, escape.
nálabasán, v. have come across something.
nálalabî, n. remainder, left-over, remains.
nálalaman, v. know, learn.
nalálamangán, v. be at a disadvantage, have advantage over another.
nalálarawan, v. illustrated.
naliligalig, v. being perturbed.
naliligid, v. surrounded. encircled.
nalúlugás, v. in state of falling o withering.
nalúlumà, v. state of being out of date, getting spoiled.
nalúlungkót, v. in state of sadness.
naluóy, v. withered.
namamaga, adj. swollen.
namámalakaya, v. fishing with boats.
namámalantsa, v. ironing clothes.
namán, adv. in like manner again.
namanghâ, v. surprised.
namatáy, v. died.
namatayán, v. bereaved.
namayani, v. to reign, to be dominant.
namimilí, v. buying or purchasing.
namimilipit, v. recoiling.
namin, prep. our, by us.
namintanà, v. stayed thru the window.
namnám, n. flavor, taste.
namnamín, v. to enjoy pleasant taste.
nanà, n. pus.
nananahimik, adj. dead.
nanain, v. to contain pus.
nanandata, adj. armed.
nanaog, v. went down, came down.
nanay, n. mother.
nanay-nanayan, n. like a mother or acting like a mother.
nang, adv. when, by.
nangahimbing, adv. asleep.
naníningaláng-pugad, v. going on adolescent manhood.
nangalay, v. to be fatigued, to feel tired.
nangamitas, v. pick, picking.
nangangatal, adj. shivering.
nangángalmót, v. scratching, clawing.
nangángasera, v. boarding, lodging.
nangkâ, n. jackfruit.
nanghihilakbot, v. terrified.
naniwalà, v. believed.
nanlisik, v. looked sharply and angrily.
nanlupaypay, adj. become weak.
nangangaligkig, v. trembling with cold.
nanggigigil, adj. in state of trying to control anger or hate.
nangíngilag, v. avoiding, fearing.
nanggilalás, v. was stupefied.
nanguha, v. picked, collected.
nangunyapit, v. clung to.
nangyari, v. happened.
nápakabangís, adj. ferocious, wild.
nápakabantóg, adj. terribly popular, very famous.
napakasál, v. got married.

napagbintangan, v. suspected.
napahinuhod, v. allowed oneself to agree or be induced.
nápalibíng, v. was buried.
napalinggít, v. was able to decrease, to make diminutive.
nápansín, v. notice, took cognizance of.
náparamay, v. to get involved.
naparito, v. sent here, came here.
nápariyán, v. came over here (near).
naparoól, v. to have met misfortune, to be in bad luck.
nápasuntók, v. to strike with clenched fist.
napaigtad, v. to move suddenly.
nápayukayok, v. bowed in discouragement, lowered one's head in drowsiness.
napulpol, v. was dulled.
napulupot, v. to get tied around.
naputol, v. cut off.
nararapat, adj. proper, appropriate.
naríirimarim, v. affected with loathing, feeling disgusted with nausea.
nárító, adv. is here.
naroón, adv. is there (far from speaker and person spoken to).
narses, n. nurse.
nasa, v. is there.
nasà, n. desire, wish.
násaán, v. where.
nasain, v. to desire.
nasalantâ, v. damaged, destroyed.
nasalubong, v. met on the way.
nasasabík, adj. anxious, eager.
násipà, v. was kicked.
nasisiyahan, adj. contented, satisfied.
nasok, v. to have entered.
násulyapán, v. seen accidentally.
natambad, v. exposed.
natarók, v. comprehend, understood.
natatakot, adj. afraid of frightened.
natatagò, v. hidden.
natibág, v. crumbled, demolished.
natin, pron. ours.
natinag, v. have been moved or shaken.
nátirá, v. left, have been left.
natitirá, v. living or residing.
nátiwalág, v. fired, dismissed.
natuklasan, v. discovered.
natuksó, v. tempted, attracted.
nasyonal, n. national.
natunaw, v. melted, dissolved.
naunsiyamì, v. stopped in growth, stunted.
nawalan ng tiwala, adj. lost confidence.
nayon, n. town, municipality, barrio.
nebi, n. navy.
nené, n. common term for a female baby or girl.
negosyo, n. business venture.
nerbiyos, n. feeling of nervousness.
ni, a particle placed before personal proper nouns in genitive (singular).

niknik, n. a species of tiny blood-sucking insect.
niíg, n. friendly or affectionate chat.
nilá, pron. of them, by them.
nilaga, n. boiled.
nilaláng, n. creation (as human being).
nilalik, v. fashioned, carved.
nilikhâ, v. created.
nilílimot, v. trying to forget.
nilílitsón, v. being roasted, as a pig.
nilugawan, adj. cooked with boiled rice.
nilúlunggatî, v. wishing for fervently.
ninang, n. godmother.
nino, pron. whose.
ninong, n. godfather.
ninuno, n. grand parents, ancestors.
ninyó, pron. for your, by you (plural or respectful singular).
ningas, n. flame, blaze, ignition.
ningas-kugon, adj. symbolically, short-lived, as burning cogon grass.
ningning, n. brilliance.
nipís, n. thinness.
nisnís, adj. frayed, bruised.
nitso, n. niche.
niyakap, v. embraced, hugged.
niyóg, n. coconut.
niyugan n. coconut plantation.
niyurakan, v. went boldly over one's dignity.
niyúyungyungán, v. coming over or above any object.
nobatos, adj. & n. novice, greenhorn.
nobela, n. novel, story.
nobena, n. devotion consisting of nine days prayer.
noó, n. forehead.
noón, adv. at that time.
nota, n. note on a musical score.
nunal, n. mole.
nuno, n. grandparents.
nunong babae, n. grandmother.
nunong lalaki, n. grandfather.
núnukál, v. will spring forth.
nupô, v. sat down.
nuynuyín, v. to reflect, to think over.
ng, pron. twelfth letter of the Tagalog alphabet, a consonant pronounced **ngâ**.
ngakngak, n. cry of child during sulkiness.
ngâ, emphatic particle meaning please, so really, truly, in fact, etc.
ngabngabin, v. to devour in eating, to gormandize noisily.
ngalan, n. name.
ngalandakan, v. to talk or shout scandalously.
ngalangalá, n. palate.
ngalay, n. numbness.
ngaligkíg, n. shiver, tremble.
ngalingali, adv. almost, on the verge of.
ngalit, n. fury.
ngalót, n. mastication.
ngalumatá, n. deepened eyes with marks around due to illness or lack of sleep.

ngani-ngani, n. swerving, faltering.
ngangá, n. opening of mouth or wound.
ngangà, n. the chewing of buyo.
ngapa, v. to grope in the dark.
ngasáb, n. movement of mouth and making noise while eating.
ngasngás, n. noise, superfluous talk.
ngatâ, v. to chew very finely.
ngatál, n. trembling.
ngawâ, n. loud but empty talk, howl of crying children.
ngawngaw, n. superfluous or unnecessary talk.
ngawit, n. numbness from tension or exhaustion.
ngayón, adv. now, at present.
ngibit, n. chill, grimace due to coldness.
ngiki, n. chill, coldness due to fever.
ngiló, n. painful feeling due to the setting of the teeth on edges.
ngimi, n. bashfulness.
nginig, n. trembling.
ngipin, n. teeth.
ngisi, n. giggling.
ngisngis, n. giggle.
ngitî, n. smile.
ngitian, v. to smile.
ngitngít, n. irritation, suppressed or controlled rage.
ngitngitán, v. to vent suppressed fury on something.
ngiwî, adj. twisted, out-of-place mouth.
ngiwián, v. to move the mouth out of place.
ngiyáw, n. noise or mewing of cats.
ngiyawan, v. to produce irritating noise as that of cats.
ngiyawan, n. mewing of two or more cats.
ngongò, n. one who speaks with a twang due to nasal disorder.
ngudngod, n. to injure one's snout or nose.
nguni't, prep. but.
ngusò, n. upper lip.
ngusuan, v. to move the upper lip, higher or pointedly.
nguyâ, n. chewing.
nguyaín, v. to masticate.

O

o, oh, interj. o, oh.
obispo, n. bishop.
obrero, n. laborer.
okoy, n. native delicacy with such ingredients as mongo sprouts, shrimps and spiced with vinegar and garlic.
ohò, adv. variation ot opò.
oo, adv. yes.
opereytor, n. operator.
orasán, n. watch.
oras, n. hour, Sp.
orasan, v. to time.
order, n. order.
oregano, n. Mexican sage.
orihinál, n. original, Sp.
ortograpiya, n. ortography.
oy, interj. Hello there, Hey you.
oyayi, n. lullaby.

P

pa, a prefix to express manner.
paá, n. foot.
paabot, v. to allow oneself to be overtaken.
paahín, v. kick, to use the feet.
paalam, n. good-bye, farewell.
páalaman, n. act of bidding good-bye.
paalám, v. to inform, to advise.
paanán, n. at the foot.
paano, pron. how.
páaralan, n. school, schoolhouse.
páaraláng-bayan, n. public school.
paayap, n. cowpea.
paayon, adv. in the same direction.
pabagsak, n. tip, bribery.
pabalat, n. covering.
pabango, n. perfume, scent.
pabanguhán, v. to put perfume, to sprinkle with perfume.
pábanguhan, n. perfume factory.
pabanguhín, v. to give a scented or delicious odor.
pabaon, n. send-off gift.
pabahay, n. house allowance.
pabayaan, v. to neglect, to let alone.
pabayâ, adj. careless, neglectful.
pabrika, n. factory.
pabula, n. fable.
pabuyà, n. payment, tip.
pakakak, n. trumphet.
pakámahalín, v. love dearly.
pakamáy, adv. with the use of the hands.
pakana, n. plan, scheme.
pakanin, v. feed.
pakawalan, adj. let free.
pakay, n. objective, aim.
pakikibaka, n. struggle, fight.
pakikihamok, n. battle, strife.
pakikipagkapwà, n. social intercourse.
pakimkím, n. gift or money given during a baptism.
pakimkimán, v. to give a gift or sum of money.
pakinabang, n. profit, benefit.
pakinabangan, v. to make profitable.
pakitang-gilas, n. showing off.
pakitang-tao, n. appearance, hypocrisy, pretense.
pakiusap, n. entreaty.
pakiusapan, v. entreat, to ask for favor.
pakla, n. acerbity, tartness.
pakli, v. to reply, to answer.
pakò, n. nail.
pakpák, n. wing.
paksâ, n. subject matter, topic.
paksáng-aralín, n. subject.
paksíw, n. a native dish with vinegar.
pakumbabâ, n. humility, submission.
pakundangan, n. respect.
pakundanganan, v. to respect, to be considerate.
pakutya, adv. with sarcasm.
pakwán, n. watermelon.
pakyáw, n. wholesale.
pakyawín, v. to purchase wholesale.
padaán, v. to have one's way.

padaplís, adv. indirectly, sideways.
padaplisán, v. to box sideways or indirectly.
padér, n. wall.
padparín, v. to be carried away by wind or water.
padrasto, n. step-father.
padyak, n. act of stamping.
pag-aani, n. harvest time.
pag-aarì, n. property.
pag-aaruga, n. taking care of.
pagado, adj. paid, settled.
pagador, n. paymaster.
pagál, adj. tired, fatigued.
pagalín, v. to tire.
pagamutan, n. clinic, dispensary.
pag-angkat, n. importing of goods.
pag-asa, n. hope.
pag-asam, n. anticipation.
pagaw, n. hoarseness.
pagbaka, n. act of fighting.
pagbubulay-bulay, n. reflection.
pagbubunyî, n. celebration, exaltation.
pagbulay-bulayin, v. to reflect on, to think over.
pagkabinat, n. state of having a relapse.
pagkabigo, n. disappointment.
pagkabuhay, n. livelihood, food.
pagkakákilanlán, n. means of identification, identity.
pagkakánulô, n. act of being a traitor, treason.
pagkakapantay-pantay, n. equality.
pagkakapatiran, n. brotherhood.
pagkakátaón, n. chance, opportunity.
pagkakátiklóp, n. state of being folded, fold.
pagkakawangis, n. similarity, likeness.
pagkadayukdók, n. hunger.
pagkaibay, n. nausea.
pagkain, n. manner of eating, food.
pagkainis, n. exasperation.
pagkalingà, n. care, protection, adoption.
pagkamámamayán, n. citizenship.
pagkampáy, n. act of flying (with wings).
pagkamuhì, n. state of being disgusted, disgust.
pagkasi, n. act of loving, affection.
pagkasuya, n. surfeit due to tastiness.
pagkatao, n. being, human nature.
pagkatapos, adv. afterwards, then.
pagkayamot, n. vexation, annoyance.
pagkasalanta, n. being damaged.
pagkít, n. wax.
pagkurú-kuruin, v. to think over and over.
pagdaka, adv. immediately, at once.
pagdadahóp, n. poverty.
pagdaraya, n. tricks.
pagdiriwang, n. celebration.
paghangà, n. admiration.
pagi, n. ray-fish.
pag-ibig, n. love.
pagitan, n. interval.
pagitawin, v. to allow to stand out.
paglalakbáy, n. journey, voyage.
paglalahad, n. presentation.
paglalambitin, n. hanging.

paglambitinan, v. to hang on to.
paglalarawang-tauhan, n. characterization.
paglalaway, n. salivation.
paglalayag, n. voyage.
paligsahan, n. contest.
paglilibáng, n. recreation, spare time.
paglilibíng, n. interment, burial.
paglilimahid, n. dirtiness, slovenliness.
paglilimás, n. drying, act of letting the water flow out of a ditch or a small stream.
paglilitis, n. trial, hearing.
pagluhà, n. tears, teary supplication.
pagluhog, n. entreaty.
paglunók, n. act of swallowing.
paglusob, n. aggression.
pagmamahal, n. love, affection.
pagmamatigas, n. persistence.
pagngingitngit, n. deep resentment.
pagngangalit, n. rage, fury.
pagod, n. tiredness.
pagpagín, v. to shake off.
pagpapahirap, n. torture.
pagpapakasakit, n. sacrifice.
pagpapadala, v. sending.
pagpapalakí, n. bringing up.
pagpapalayaw, n. indulgence.
pagpapalistá, n. registration.
pagpapálitang-kurò, n. discussion, open forum, exchange of opinion.
pagpaparayâ, n. act of tolerance.
pagpapatiwakal, n. suicide.
pagpapatubo, n. act of causing to grow.
pagparito, n. act of coming here.
pagsasakit, n. exertion of effort.
pagsasagupà, n. encounter, meeting.
pagsasanay, n. exercise.
pagsasaulî, n. return.
pagsasawa, n. surfeit due to abundance.
pagsauláng-loób, v. to regain consciousness or courage.
pagsilang, n. birth.
pagsisiyasat, n. investigation.
pagtapak, n. way of stepping.
pagtalikód, n. turn-about, refusal.
pagtaliwakás, n. retraction, evasion.
pagtalimuáng, n. about-face, denial.
pagtalunan, v. to argue about, to discuss.
pagtangkilik, n. act of supporting, patronage.
pagtataká, n. wonder, surprise.
pagtataksil, n. deceit, treachery.
pagtatalo, n. discussion, argument.
pagtatama, n. coordination.
pagtatamasa, n. bounty, productivity, enjoyment.
pagtatampók, n. act of emphasizing, act of popularizing.
pagtatangkilikán, n. cooperation, mutual aid.
pagtuligsâ, n. act of criticizing, criticism.
pagtunggâ, n. act of drinking.

pagtutungayaw, n. act of anger, beration.
pagtutulin, n. haste, speed.
pagurin, n. to tire.
pag-uugalì, n. habit, custom.
paha, n. girdle, band.
pahám, n. wise man, sage.
pahamak, n. saboteur.
pahát, adj. thin, meager.
pahayag, n. article, order.
páhayagán, n. newspaper, daily.
pahiga, adj. horizontal.
pahimakás, n. farewell.
pahimakasán, v. to terminate, to end.
pahina, n. page.
pahingá, n. rest.
pahingahín, v. to rest.
pahingalay, n. relaxation.
pahintulot, n. permission.
pahintulutan, v. to allow, to permit.
pahinuhod, n. acquiescence.
pahirin, v. to wipe off.
paimbabaw, adj. superficial, simulated.
paít, n. bitterness.
pain, n. bait.
paineta, n. decorative comb.
palà, n. shovel, spade.
palá, interj. an interjectional particle used to express surprise.
palababahán, n. window sill.
palabok, n. spice, flattery.
palabukan, v. to spice thickly, to flatter.
pairugan, v. to accede.
palakâ, n. frog.
palakad, n. policy, current practice.
palakhín, v. to let grow, to increase.
palad, n. palm, faith, luck.
palág, n. spasm, intermittent or sudden movements.
palágarián, n. sawmill.
palagáy, n. idea, opinion.
pálagayan, n. comradeship, friendship.
palág-palág, adj. moving, shaky, restless.
palahaw, n. scream, shout.
paláhudyatan, n. system of signals, sign.
paláisdaan, n. fishery, fishpond.
palalò, adj. boastful. proud.
palamán, adj. insinuation, stuffing, contents.
palamara, adj. ungrateful, unfaithful.
palamuti, n. decoration.
palanas, n. rocky or stony shore.
palanggana, n. wash basin.
palapa, n. pulpy leaf of plants like the banana.
palapag, n. floor, story of a building.
palápintasin, adj. critical.
palarâ, n. tinsel, tinfoil.
palarin, v. to be in good luck.
palaruan, n. playground.
palarindingan, n. wall.
palás, adj. clipped.
palasak, adj. common.
palasô, n. arrow.
palaspas, n. fancily woven palm leaves blessed on Palm Sunday.
palasyo, n. palace, Sp.
palaták, n. clacking noise from the tongue to express admiration or regret.
palátuntunan, n. program.
palay, n. rice plant.

palayain, v. to set free.
palayaw, n. nickname.
palayawin, v. to pamper, to rear in indulgence.
palayók, n. earthen pot for cooking.
palengké, n. public market.
palibís, adj. going downward.
palikpík, n. fin.
palikuran, n. toilet.
paliguán, n. bathroom.
paligid, n. surrounding, circle.
paligò, n. bath.
paligsahan, n. contest.
paliguan, v. to bathe.
palihan, n. anvil.
palihís, adj. deviating from the correct path.
palíng, adj. tilted.
palitada, n. cement mortar.
palito, n. toothpick.
palma, n. palm.
palò, n. stroke, beat.
palong, n. cock's comb.
paltík, n. a home made gun.
paluin, v. to strike, to beat.
palu-palo, n. paddle for cleaning clothes.
palupo, n. ridge of roof.
palupuhan, v. to construct a ridge for the roof.
palusong, n. planting time.
palya, n. absence, omission.
pama, n. fame, renown.
pamagát, n. title, caption.
pamahalaan, n. government.
pamahayan, v. to turn into a dwelling.
pamahiin, n. superstition.
pamahiran, n. hand towel.
pamalo, n. stick used for whipping.
pamamahay, n. home.
pamamanas, n. swelling of the body due to beriberi.
pamangkin, n. nephew, niece.
pamanhík, n. entreaty.
pamanhikán, v. to entreat.
pámantasan, n. university.
pamilihan, n. market.
paminggalan, n. cupboard.
pamintá, n. pepper.
pampáng, n. shore.
pampánitikán, adj. literary.
pambihira, adj. rare, seldom.
pamuhatan, n. heading of a letter.
pamutat, n. side dish for the regular menu.
panà, n. bow and arrow.
panaderyá, n. bakery, a house for baking.
panaghilì, n. envy.
panaghilian, v. to envy.
panaghóy, n. weeping.
panaginip, n. dream.
panahian, n. sewing box.
panahón, n. time.
panain, v. to shoot with bow and arrow.
panalangin, n. prayer.
panambitan, n. wailing lament.
pananamít, n. dress.
panarili, adj. private.
panata, n. vow.
panatilihin, v. to make permanent.
panauhin, n. visitor.
panawan, v. to leave.
panáy, adj. continuous.
panayám, n. conference.
pandák, n. a midget.
pandakót, n. dustpan.
pandáy, n. blacksmith.
pandesal, n. bread rolls slightly salted.
pandilatan, v. to glance at with widely open eyes.
panibughò, n. jealousy.

panig, n. side.
panigan, v. to side with.
panik, n. panic.
pâniki, n. a bat.
panimulà, adj. beginning.
paninigas, n. hardening, solidification.
panís, adj. spoiled.
panisin, v. to render spoiled.
panistís, n. instrument used for operation, scalpel.
paniwalà, n. belief.
paniwalaan, v. to believe.
panlahat, adj. general.
panlisikan, v. to look at with bulging eyes.
panlukbutan, adj. purposely for pocket keeping.
panót, adj. bald.
pansimbá, adj. for church wear.
pansín, n. attention, notice.
pansít, n. noodles.
pansol, n. spring of water that gushes out from a high source.
pantal, n. wheal, welt, wale.
pantas, n. genius.
pantig, n. syllable.
pantiyón, n. cemetery.
pantóg, n. bladder.
pantalan, n. harbor.
pantulog, n. night gown.
panukalà, n. proposition.
panukat, n. gauge.
panunudyo, n. mockery, jest.
panunumbalik, n. return, coming back.
panunurì, n. criticism, inspection.
panunuyò, n. act of ingratiating oneself, wooing.
panutsa, n. caked peanut and molasses.
panyô, n. handkerchief.
panga, n. jaw.
pangakò, n. promise.
pangakuan, v. to promise.
pangahán, adj. with prominent jaws.
pangahás, adj. to be aggressive, to take the risk.
pangalan, n. name.
pangalanan, v. to christen, to name.
pangambá, n. fear, worry.
pangambahan, v. to fear.
panganay, n. the eldest.
panganib, n. danger.
panganganak, n. giving birth to.
panganiban, v. to be afraid of.
panganorin, n. atmosphere.
panganyayà, n. ruin, misfortune.
pangangalakal, n. business.
pangarap, n. dream.
pangat, n. fish cooked in little water and salt.
pangáw, n. handcuffs.
pangkát, n. party, group.
pangkó, n. anything carried in the arms.
pangkuhin, v. to carry a person in one's arms.
panggagagá, n. usurpation.
panggantsilyo, n. crochet hook.
panggatong, n. firewood.
panghí, n. offensive odor of urine.
pangil, n. tusk.
pangimbulo, n. jealousy, spite, grudge.
panginoón, n. master.
pangingilin, n. abstinence.
pangit, adj. ugly.
pangitain, n. omen.
pangláw, n. solitude, solitariness.
pangmámamamayán, adj. civic, for the community.
pangnán, n. basket.

pangos, v. to chew (fibrous matters).
pang-ukol, n. preposition.
pang-ulo, n. heading.
pangulo, n. president.
pangulong-bayan, n. capital city.
pangungulila, n. loneliness, state of being orphaned.
pangyayari, n. happenings, event.
panimdim, n. profound sorrow, misgiving.
pantas, n. genius, wise man.
paos, n. raucousness (of voice).
papak, adj. eaten unaccompanied by rice.
papag, n. bamboo bed.
papawirin, n. firmament.
papél, n. paper.
papet, n. puppet.
papintasán, v. to have criticized, smeared.
papiro, n. papyrus.
para, prep. for, reserved for.
pantubos, n. ransom.
paraan, n. way, method.
parada, n. parade.
paraiso, n. paradise.
parali, n. defamation, hurtful rumors.
paraluman, n. muse.
parang, n. forest, mountainous regions.
parangal, n. an act of honoring.
parangalán, v. to fete, to honor.
paratang, n. false incrimination, accusation.
paratangan, v. to accuse.
parati, adj. from time to time, continuous.
paratingín, v. to extend.
paraw, n. sail boat.
pareha, n. pair.
pareho, n. equivalent, similar, equal.
pari, n. priest.
parikít, n. firewood.
parilya, n. broiler.
pariníg, n. insinuation.
parirala, n. phrase.
parisukat, n. square.
paról, n. lantern, lamp.
parola, n. lighthouse.
parunggít, n. derogatory remarks.
parunggitán, v. to remark hurtingly.
paruparó, n. butterfly.
parusa, n. punishment.
parusahan, v. to punish.
pasa, n. bruise, black and blue marks.
pasak, n. stopper, plug.
pasahe, n. fare.
pasahero, n. passenger.
pasamano, n. window sill.
pasan, adj. carried on the shoulders.
pasaring, n. insinuation.
pasasa, adj. enjoying the abundance of.
pasanin, n. load.
paseguro, v. to have oneself insured.
pasigan, n. coast, shore.
pasimulâ, n. beginning.
pasimulâ, n. head, one who leads.
pasimuno, n. leader in an undesirable affair.
pasinayà, n. inauguration.
pasintabi, n. apology.
pasismo, n. fascism.
pasiyá, n. decision.
pasiyók, n. whistle.
paslít, n. young innocent, boy or girl.
pasò, n. burn, scald.
pasô, n. plant or flower pot.

pasok, rw. enter, go in.
pasok, n. entrance, time of being in.
pasók, adj. entered in, already in.
paspasán, v. to dust.
paspasan, n. fight, free-for-all.
pasta, n. filling (of teeth).
pastilyas; n. rolled sweet paste used as dessert.
pastol, n. shepherd.
pasubalì, n. dissenting action.
pasukán, n. school days, doorway.
pasuin, v. to burn.
pasumalá, adv. at random.
pasumalâ, n. chance.
pasunod, n. discipline.
pasuwit, n. whistle, signal.
pasyalan, n. promenade, park.
pasyon, n. the life of Christ in vernacular verse.
pata, n. foot, hocks.
pataán, n. reserve, allowance.
paták, n. drop.
pátakarán, n. by laws, regulations.
paták-paták, adj. by drops.
patalastas, n. notice.
patag, adj. level, smooth.
patalím, n. pointed weapon.
patáng-patá, adj. terribly exhausted.
patani, n. lima bean.
patas, adj. draw.
patatas, n. potato.
patawan, v. to put a weight.
patawa, n. parody.
patáy, n. dead.
patáy-gutom, adj. ravenous.
patí, adv. even, also.
patibóng, n. trap, decoy.
patihayâ, adj. lying on one's back.
patilya, n. side-whiskers, sideburns.
patíng, n. shark.
patinga, n. collateral.
patirín, v. to trip, cut.
patis, n. brine.
patiwarík, adj. head down and feet up.
patiyad, adj. standing on toes.
patláng, n. intermission, blank.
patnubay, n. guide.
patnugot, n. director.
pato, n. duck.
patola, n. sponge gourd.
patolohiya, n. pathology.
patong, n. interest.
patpát, n. split of bamboo.
patpatin, adj. thin, weak.
patubig, n. irrigation.
patuloy, adj. continuous.
patulugin, v. cause to sleep.
patumanggâ, n. respite.
patusin, v. to throw.
patuyuan, n. drying place.
patyo, n. inner yard.
paumanhin, n. toleration, allowance.
páuná, n. advance, warning.
paunawa, n. notice.
pausisà, adv. inquiringly.
pawid, n. nipa palm, the leaves of which are used for thatching roof.
pawis, n. sweat.
pawisán, adj. full of sweat.
pawisan, v. to induce sweat to come out.
payák, adj. simple, pure.
payagan, v. to allow, to permit.
payagpag, n. flapping of wings.
payapà, adj. peaceful.

payapain, v. to calm down.
payapang bayan, n. heaven.
payaso, n. clown.
payát, adj. thin.
payo, n. counsel, advice.
payong, n. umbrella.
paypáy, n. abaniko.
paypayán, v. to fan.
payrol, n. payroll.
payuhan, v. to give counsel.
payungan, v. to put an umbrella.
pekas, n. freckles, spots.
pekasin, adj. full of freckles.
pedestriyan, n. pedestrian.
pedido, n. order for goods.
pelikula, n. movie-film.
peligroso, adj. dangerous, risky.
peluka, n. wig.
penoy, n. unfertilized hard-cooked egg.
pensiyon, n. pension.
perdigones, n. pellets for rifles.
pertil, n. fertile.
pesa, n. a native dish.
peste, n. epidemic.
pestihín, v. to pester, to disturb.
petsay, n. chinese leafy vegetable.
pika, n. pike.
piket, n. picket.
pikî, adj. knock-kneed.
pikô, n. a game played by children.
pikot, adj. cornered.
pigaín, v. to press.
pighatî, n. profound sorrow.
pigî, n. buttock.
pigil, adj. controlled.
pigilin, v. to detain, to stop.
pigíng, n. banquet.
pigipitin, v. to put pressure.
piglás, n. struggle.
pigsá, n. boil.
pigsahin, adj. full of boils.
pigtás, adj. ripped.
pihado, adv. surely, certainly.
pihikan, adj. fastidious, exacting.
pihit, n. turn.
pihitin, v. to turn.
piitan, n. cell.
piitin, v. imprison.
pila, n. file.
pilak, n. silver.
pilansík, n. splashes.
pilantík, n. jerky whip, innuendo.
pilas, n. rip, tear.
pilasin, v. rip.
pilay, n. lameness, broken bones.
pilì, adj. choiced, selected.
pilibustero, n. filibuster.
pilik-matá, n. eyelash.
piliin, n. to select.
piling, n. the side.
pilíng, n. bunch or cluster.
pilipit, adj. twisted.
pilit, adj. forced.
pilitin, v. to force, to insist.
pilolohiya, n. philology.
pilosopiya, n. philosophy.
pimiento, n. sweet pepper.
pinakamatalik, adj. most intimate.
pinakamatapang, adj. bravest.
pinahihintulutan, v. permitting, allowing.
pinagmulan, n. origin, source.
pinagmulan, n. source.
pinagsanib, n. joined, united.
pinagsikapan, v. tried diligently.
pinag-usig, v. prosecuted.
pinahuli, v. was ordered to

be caught.
pinahulmá, v. molded.
pinainam, v. to make much nicer or better.
pinainóm, v. given a drink.
pinalabò, v. caused to become dim.
pinalalagi, v. caused to remain.
pinalaló, v. make worse, to increase.
pinalayà, v. was given freedom.
pinalayas, v. ordered to leave.
pinalò, v. was beaten.
pinandidirihan, v. shunned.
pinanggagalingan, n. source.
pinangát, n. a native menu consisting of boiled fish with tomatoes, kalamansi and lard.
pinangkó, v. carried (in the arms).
pinápalad, adj. lucky, being fortunate.
pinapangalisag, v. to have cause one's hair to stand on ends.
pinarusahan, v. punished.
pinasaringan, v. insinuated, insulted.
pinasláng, v. abused, beaten.
pinatuyô, v. was dried.
pinawà, n. colored, husked rice, unpolished.
pinawalán, v. was allowed to get away.
pinawaláng-sala, v. acquitted.
pinakbet, n. an Ilocano dish.
pindang, n. jerked beef.
pindót, n. tight hold, squeeze.
pindutin, v. to hold tight, to squeeze.
pinid, adj. closed.
pinipig, n. pounded highland rice deliciously scented.
pino, adj. finely powdered.
pinsan, n. cousin.
pinsalà, n. damage.
pinsíl, n. painter's brush.
pinsalain, v. to damage.
pintá, n. paint.
pintakasi, n. patron saint.
pintahán, v. to paint.
pintas, n. fault, flaw.
pintasán, v. to criticize adversely.
pintíg, n. throb, beat.
pintigin, v. cause to beat.
pintog, n. swelling.
pintuan, n. doorway.
pintuhuin, v. to woo, to adore.
pintungan, n. warehouse.
pinulot, v. picked up.
pinunò, n. officer, head.
pinunô, v. filled.
pinupupol, v. gathering.
pinyá, n. pineapple.
pinyahan, n. pineapple plantation.
pingas, n. a small break at the edge.
pingás, adj. broken, dented.
pingasin, adj. to cause to indent.
pinggá, n. a pole used to balance two weights.
pinggán, n. plate.
pingkáw, adj. with crooked arms.
pimpong, n. ping-pong game.
pingkian, n. friction.
pingkít, adj. half-closed eyes.

pinupuri, v. flattering, praising, honoring.
pipi, adj. dumb.
pipino, n. cucumber.
pipís, adj. compressed, flat.
piramid, n. pyramid.
piraso, n. a piece.
pirasuhin, v. to cut a piece of.
pirinsahín, v. to press or iron.
piring, n. blindfold.
piringán, v. to cover the eyes.
pirmá, n. signature.
pirmahán, v. to sign.
pirot, n. act of pinching with the fingers and twisting.
pirurutong, n. a species of dark-colored rice.
pisak, adj. one-eyed.
pisaín, v. to hatch.
pisanin, v. to put together.
pisara, n. blackboard.
piskál, n. fiscal, judge.
pisi, n. string.
pisil, n. hold, press.
pisngí, n. cheek.
piso, n. one peso.
pisón, n. steam roller.
pispis, n. remnants of what is eaten.
pistá, n. fiesta, celebration.
pitak, n. column.
pitada, n. blast of a siren.
pitagan, n. respect, courtesy.
pitahin, v. to desire, to wish for.
pithayà, n. ambition, desire.
pitís, adj. tight.
pito, n. whistle.
pitó, n. seven.
piton, n. python, a serpent.
pitpitín, v. to flatten, to pound.
pitsa, n. chips.
pitsel, n. pitcher (for water).
pitser, n. pitcher for a game of baseball.
pitso, n. breast of fowl or animal.
pituhan, v. to whistle at.
pitumpû, n. & adj. seventy.
plasma, n. plasma, blood.
plorera, n. flower vase.
piyansa, n. surety, bail, bond.
piyansahan, v. to bail for.
piyapis, adj. cornered by sudden attack of the enemy.
piye, n. foot measure.
piyon, n. unskilled or semi-skilled worker.
piyudalismo, n. feudalism.
plaka, n. disc (phonograph record).
plansa, n. laundry iron.
plataporma, n. basic platform.
platero, n. silversmith.
plegarya, n. prayer, supplication.
plema, n. phlegm.
pluma, n. pen. Sp.
plumahe, n. plume, plumage.
plumero, n. feather duster.
po, a particle used in respectful address, Sir or Madam.
pobya, n. phobia, morbid fear or dread.
poder, n. power, authority.
pogí, n. handsome.
pohas. n. sheet (of paper).
ponda, n. eating house.

poók, n. district, place.
poón, n. Lord.
poonin, v. to worship.
poót, n. hate, fury.
pormal, adj. formal, severe.
poso-artesyano, n. artesian well.
poso-negro, n. septic tank.
pospas, n. rice gruel with chicken.
posporo, n. match stick.
prasko, n. flask.
prenda, n. pledge.
prito, adj. fried.
prinsa, n. charcoal heated flat-iron.
propitiring, n. profiteering.
proteksyon, n. protection.
prusisyon, n. procession.
primyer, n. premier.
psikolohiya, n. psychology.
pukawin, v. to waken.
puknatán, v. to cease, to rest.
pukpukan, n. free-for-all combat.
pukpukín, v. to hit, to hammer.
puksain, v. to destroy, to liquidate.
pukyutan, n. honeybee.
pudpód, adj. worn out.
puga, n. flight, escape.
pugad, n. nest.
pugayan, v. to salute, to abuse.
pugo, n. quail.
pugong, n. piece of cloth used as head covering.
pugót, adj. without head.
pugtô, v. to cut off.
pugutin, v. to behead.
puhunan, n. capital, investment.
puhunanin, v. to invest.
pulá, adj. red.
pulà, n. hurtful criticism.
pulaan, v. to besmirch, to stain.
pulbós, n. powder.
pulgada, n. inch.
pulikat, n. cramps.
pulido, adj. polished, neat.
pulís, n. policeman.
pulô, n. small island.
pulok, n. the bristling feathers on the neck of a rooster.
pulong, n. meeting.
pulot, n. molasses.
pulpitó, n. church pulpit.
pulso, n. pulse.
pulubi, n. beggar.
puluhán, n. hilt.
pulungin, v. to call a meeting.
pulupot, adj. winding.
pulutan, n. appetizer taken with wine.
pulút-gatâ, n. honeymoon.
pulutong, n. group.
pumakyaw, v. to buy by wholesale.
pumailangláng, v. to go up in the air, to spread out.
pumalit, v. changed, changed places.
pumanaw, v. died, lost.
pumanhík, v. to go up (a house), to ascend.
pumápaling, v. is inclined, siding with.
pumarito, v. came here (near).
pumaroón, v. went there (far).
pumikit, v. to close the eyes.
pumpon, n. bouquet.
pumúpusyáw, v. becoming pale, fading.
pumustá, v. bet on.
pumuták, v. to make irritating noise like the chickens.
pumutók, v. burst

puna, n. notice, observation.
púnahin, adj. easily noticeable.
punasan, v. wipe.
punda, n. pillow slip.
punebre, n. funeral march.
punerarya, n. funeral parlor.
punit, adj. tear, torn.
punitin, v. to tear.
punít-punít, adj. torn.
punlâ, n. seedling.
punlô, n. bullet.
punó, n. tree, leader.
punong-salitâ, n. preface.
punso, n. ant hill.
punta, n. direction.
puntahán, v. to go over there.
puntirya, n. aim.
punto, n. period, point.
punung-gurò, n. head teacher, principal.
punúng-punô, adj. totally filled.
pungas, adj. reeling confusedly while half-asleep.
pungos, n. cut.
punyós, n. cuffs.
pungayan, v. to look languidly.
punung-bayan, n. town head.
puntód, n. grave, mound.
pupog, n. assault.
purihin, v. to appreciate, to praise, to flatter.
purók, n. district.
puról, adj. blunt.
pusà, n. cat.
pusa-pusà, n. one who serves wily to attain his selfish ends.
pusalì, n. mire.
pusikít, adj. very dark.
puslit, n. squirt, gate-crasher.
pusò, n. heart.
puso ng saging, n. banana inflorescence.
pusok, n. aggressiveness, impetuosity.
pusod, n. navel.
pusta, n. bet, stake.
pusunin, adj. big-bellied.
puspós, adj. full of, complete.
puta, n. whore, prostitute.
puták, n. cackle.
putahe, n. servings, menu.
putá-putakî, adj. sporadic.
putî, adj. white.
putik, n. mud.
putikán, adj. muddy.
putihin, v. to kill, to cut.
putlain, adj. pale.
puto, n. steamed rice cake.
putók, n. explosion.
putól, adj. cut off.
putong, n. head gear.
putót, n. short pants.
putót, adj. bent, full of weight.
putsero, n. dish of boiled meat and vegetables.
putulin, v. to cut, to discontinue.
puwáng, n. crack, space.
puwersa, n. force, strength.
puwes, conj. therefore, then.
puwíng, n. foreign matter in the eyes.
puwít, n. anus.
puyát, adj. sleepless.
puyó, n. cowlick on the head.

R

raketa, n. racket.

raket, n. racket, extortion.
radyo, n. radio.
raha, n. rajah.
rahuyò, n. attraction, charm.
rahuyuin, v. to entice.
rali, n. rally.
rambutan, n. native liches.
ramdám, (damdam), n. feeling.
rantso, n. ranch.
rangyâ, n. splendor.
raso, n. silky fabric or clothing material.
raspa, v. to scrape, rasp.
rasyón, n. ration.
raw (daw), adv. it is said.
rayos, n. wheel spokes.
rayot, n. riot, violent public disturbance.
rayuma, n. rheumatism.
rebentadór, n. firecracker.
rebosado, n. & adj. dipped in or covered with batter.
rebisino, n. a kind of game of cards usually indulged in during vigils.
rekado, n. subordinate ingredients added to the principal.
rekisa, n. inspection by looking into containers.
reklamo, n. claim, complaint.
rekurida, n. rounds.
rekwa, n. multitude, pack of things.
rekwerdo, n. remembrance.
reduksiyon, n. reduction
regla, n. menstruation, rule.
reglahan, v. to rule, to regulate.
relyeno, adj. stuffed.
relihiyon, n. religion.
renda, n. rein.
rendahan, v. to rein, to let loose.
repinado, adj. ground fine.
reporma, n. reform.
report, n. report.
resulta, n. result.
reseta, n. medical prescription.
restawran, n. an eating place, restaurant.
reto, n. a challenge, a bet.
retuhin, v. to bet, to challenge.
reyna, n. queen.
riboiber, n. revolver.
ribon, n. ribbon.
ribulusyón, n. revolution.
rikargo, n. penalty.
rikarguhán, v. to penalize.
rikisa, n. a search.
rikisahin, v. to search.
rigalo, n. gift, offering.
riles, n. rail, railway.
rilós, n. watch.
rimarim, n. disgust, nausea.
rimas, n. native breadfruit.
rimatse, n. rivetting.
rin, (din), adv. also.
ripa, n. lottery.
ripaso, n. review.
ripeke, n. peal of bells.
ripinado, n. refined sugar.
ripolyo, n. cabbage.
riserbasiyón, n. reservation.
risés, n. recess.
riseta, n. prescription.
risibo, n. receipt, acknowledgment.
ritaso, n. remnants.
ritirado, n. retired.
ritoke, n. retouch.
riwasâ, n. riches.
ronda, n. night patrol.
rondalya, n. string orchestra.
ropero, n. dirty linen basket.
rosaryo, n. rosary, Sp.
roskas, n. screw.
rubi, n. precious stone,

brilliant red.
rumáragasâ, v. in a hurry.
rurók, n. rw. summit, highest point.
ruta, n. route, itinerary.
ruweda, n. wheel.

S

sa, prep. a preposition used to form adverbial phrases of place.
sa kanan, adv. on the right.
sa kaliwa, adv. on the left.
sa pagitan, adv. between.
sa gitna, adv. in the middle.
sa kalagitnaan, adv. in the very center.
sa tabi, adv. on the side.
sa ibabaw, adv. on top.
sa itaas, adv. above.
sa kaitaasan, adv. on the very top.
sa taluktok, adv. on the summit.
sa ibaba, adv. below.
sa ilalim, adv. under.
sa ilaya, adv. uptown.
sa libis, adv. lower part.
saád, n. answer, reply.
saán, adv. where.
saanmán, adv. whenever.
saba, n. a species of banana plant.
sabakan, v. to attack.
sabád, n. interruption.
Sábado, n. Saturday.
sabana, n. grassy plain.
sabáy, adj. at the same time.
sabayan, v. to accompany.
sabáw, n. broth.
sabik, adj. eager.
sabihin, v. to say.
sabi-sabi, n. rumors.
sabitan, v. to hang.
sabitán, n. hanger.
sabog, n. scattering, sowing.
sabón, n. soap.
sabong, n. cockfight.
sabungan, n. cockpit.
saboy, n. splattering, splashing.
sabsab, n. manner of eating peculiar to hogs and dogs.
sábukót, adj. with disheveled hair.
sabunutan, v. to pull by the hair.
sabwatan, n. secret agreement, connivance.
sakali, adv. in case of.
sakalín, v. to choke.
sakáng, adj. bow-legged.
sakate, n. fodder, grass.
sakáy, rw. to ride in or on.
sakbat, n. band from the shoulder across the chest.
sakdál, adj. extremely.
sakdál, n. lawsuit.
sakím, adj. greedy.
sakitin, v. endeavor.
sakit ng loob, n. rancor.
sakláp, n. bitterness.
sakláw, n. under the authority of.
saklolo, n. aid, help.
saklolohan, v. to help, give aid.
sakmalan, n. grabbing or snatching among a group.
saknóng, n. stanza.
sako, n. bag.
sakong, n. heel bone.
sakóp, n. subject.
sakripisyo, n. sacrifice.
saksí, n. witness.
saksihán, v. to witness.
saksakín, v. to stab.
saksakan, n. stabbing affray.
sakunâ, n. calamity, misfortune, accident.
sadyaín, v. to do purposely.

sagad, adj. at the height of impressive activity.
sagabal, n. impediment, hindrance, obstacle.
sagadsád, adj. skidding.
sagala, n. maiden in costume joining the Lenten procession.
sagap, n. something scooped from just below the surface of water.
saganà, adj. plenty.
sagasaán, v. to overrun.
sagi, n. light touch while in motion or while passing by.
sagisag, n. emblem.
sagitsit, n. hissing or whizzing sound.
sagiin, v. to collide, to pass by.
sagó, n. tapioca.
sagót, n. answer, reply.
sagpang, n. act of snatching with the mouth.
sagutin, v. to answer.
ságutan, n. argument, discussion.
sagupain, v. to face, to encounter.
ságupaán, n. encounter, battle.
saglít-saglít, adv. in snatches.
saglitín, v. to get in touch immediately.
sagwán, n. paddle.
sagwíl, n. obstacle.
saha, n. strips of abaca or banana plant.
sahíg, n. floor.
sahing, n. white sticky resin.
sahóg, n. fish or pork cooked with vegetables.
sahól, adj. wanting, lacking.
sala, n. sin, living room.
sala, adj. wrong, mistaken.
salâ, adj. sieved, filtered.
salabat, n. ginger tea.
salabid, n. obstruction.
salain, v. to screen, to eliminate, to filter.
salaán, n. sieve.
salakay, n. assault, attack.
salakayín, v. to attack.
salakot, n. a head wear.
salaksak, n. probing or puncturing with a long and slender instrument.
salaghati, n. resentment, indignation.
salagimsim, n. premonition, fearful foreboding.
salagín, v. to parry a blow or a strike.
salalay, n. prop, under layer.
salamangká, n. trick or swiftness of hands, dexterity.
salamat, n. thanks.
salamín, n. mirror.
salaminín, v. to look into a mirror of oneself.
salamisim, n. bitter-sweet memories.
salansán, n. pile.
salansangín, v. to contradict, to argue.
salanggapang, n. rogue.
salantâ, adj. damaged, weakened.
salantaín, v. to break down, to go to wreck and ruin.
salang, adj. placed over stove or fire in process of cooking.
salapáng, n. harpoon.
salapiín, v. to make or turn into money.
salapî, n. money.
salapian, n. monetary exchange.
salarin, n. criminal, culprit.
salas, n. living room.

salát, adj. lacking, short of.
salatín. v. to feel, to touch.
salaula, adj. filthy, unclean.
salawál, n. short underwear.
salawalán, v. to put on pants.
saláwikaín, n. a proverb.
salaysáy, n. narration, exposition.
salaysayin, n. short story.
salbabida, n. life-preserver.
salero, n. salt-shaker.
saligán, n. basis, foundation.
saligángbatás, n. constitution.
salimuot, adj. messy, confusing.
salin, n. translation, generation.
salinan, v. to transfer, to pour into.
salisí, adj. alternate, not in line.
salisód, adj. dragging (of feet).
salitâ, n. word.
salitaín, v. speak, to express.
salitaan, n. discussion, talk.
salitre, n. saltpetre.
saliw, n. accompaniment.
saliwâ, adj. mistaken, misdirected, inverted.
saliwan, v. to accompany.
salo, v. to partake or eat together.
salok, n. fetching of water.
salop, n. ganta.
salot, n. pestilence.
salpok, n. collision, impact, bump.
salsa, n. sauce.
salubsob, n. splinter embedded in the skin.
salukin, v. to scoop, to fetch.
saluno, n. person sent to meet midway someone coming.
salungát, adj. contradictory, opposed.
salungatín, v. to oppose, to contradict.
salungatan, n. opposition.
salu-salo, n. banquet, dinner.
salungahin, v. to go uphill or upriver.
samâ, adj. bad.
samakalawa, adv. day after tomorrow.
samaín, v. to meet bad luck.
samá, n. party to an understanding.
samahan, v. to go with, to accompany.
samahán, n. society, organization, party, union.
sámahan ng seguro, n. insurance firm.
sama-sama, adv. altogether.
samantala, adv. meanwhile, in the meantime.
samantalahín, v. to be opportunistic, to take advantage of.
sambahín, v. to worship, to venerate.
sambahan, n. place of worship.
sambahayán, n. household.
sambalilo, n. hat.
sambalilong bakal, n. helmet.
sambilatin, n. to grab, to snatch.
sambít, n. emotional utterance.
sambitlaín, v. invoke.
sambulat, adj. scattered, in confusion.
sambutin, v. to catch.

samíd, n. choking.
samo, n. supplication, entreaty.
sampû, n. & adj. ten.
samsamín, v. to confiscate, to gather.
sampal, n. slap on the face.
sampalín, v. to spank.
sampalok, n. tamarind.
sampáy, n. hanging.
sampayan, n. clothes-line.
sampan, n. champagne.
samsamin, v. confiscate.
samyô, n. fragrance, scent.
sanaysáy, n. essay.
sanáy, adj. experienced, well-practiced.
sanayin, v. to practise, to train.
sandaan, n. & adj. a hundred.
sandaigdigan, n. the whole world.
sandalan, n. a place where one leans or reclines.
sandalán, v. to recline.
sandali, n. moment, minute.
sandalian, adj. for a short time limit.
sandaliin, v. to borrow for a moment.
sandat, adj. full, replete, satiated.
sandata, n. arms.
sandatahán, adj. armed, fully equipped.
sandig, v. to recline.
sandók, n. ladle.
sandukín, v. to dip out as of a ladle.
sanhî, n. cause.
sanidad, n. person employed to maintain sanitation.
sanlâ, n. pledge, collateral.
sanduguan, n. blood compact.
sanlaan, n. pawnshop.
sanlibo. n. one thousand.
sansalain, v. to stop, to obstruct.
sansé, n. term used in calling an older relative (3rd girl in family).
sansinukob, n. universe, earth.
santo, n. saint, holy person, Sp.
santuhín, v. to venerate, to worship.
sangá, n. branch, twig.
sangkatauhan, n. humanity.
sangko, n. term used in calling an elder brother.
sanwits. n. sandwich.
sanggunián, n. advisory body, oracle.
sanggunîin, v. to secure advice.
sanghaya, n. honor, dignity.
sangmaliwanag, n. the world.
sangsang, n. strong agreeable odor.
sapà, n. brooklet, shallow river.
sapal, n. residue (after extracting the juice).
sapakatin, v. to have an understanding, to plan together.
sapalaran, n. taking of chances or risks.
sapantahà, n. presumption.
sapát, adj. enough, sufficient, fitting, just right.
sapian, v. to strengthen.
sapí-sapí, adj. one layer after another.
saplot, n. a covering for

the body.
sapó, adj. carried by propping up from below.
saplután, v. to clothe.
sap-sap, n. slipmouth.
saragate, n. rascal, rogue.
saráp, n. savor.
sarapán, v. to render nicely, to make delicious.
sarhán, v. to close.
sarili, n. one's own self.
sarilinin, v. to keep to oneself.
sarilinan, adv. in private.
sari-sarì, adj. various, miscellaneous.
sariwà, adj. fresh.
sariwain, v. to recollect, to reminisce.
saro, n. cup.
sasá, n. a native palm found in swamps.
sasakyan, n. vehicle.
sasal, n. intensity of aggravation.
sastre, n. tailor.
sawá, n. boa constrictor.
sawâ, n. surfeit, having more than enough.
sawali, n. woven split bamboo strips, used for walling.
sawatain, v. to check, to stop.
sawayín, v. to prohibit.
sawi, adj. unfortunate, unlucky.
sawsaw, v. to dip into liquid just wetting it.
saya, n. Filipino loose skirt.
seks, n. sex.
seksi, adj. sexy.
sayad, adj. aground, close to the ground.
sayang, interj. expression of regret.
sayangin, v. to spoil, to misuse.
sayáw, n. dance.
sayáw, v. to dance, to accompany with rhythm.
sáyawan, n. dance party, dance orgy.
saysáy, n. worth, value.
sebo, n. tallow, fat.
sekreta, n. detective.
senado, n. senate.
sensilyo, n. loose change.
senyor, n. señor, a gentleman.
segurado, adj. insured.
seguridad, n. security, assuredness.
sekta, n. sect.
senopobya, n. xenophobia.
sereno, n. night watchman.
sermon, n. sermon, counsel.
sertipiko, n. certificate.
setro, n. scepter.
serye, n. series, episode.
sesyon, n. session.
si, art. article placed before personal pronouns in the nominative singular.
sibà, n. greed.
sibak, n. act of splitting.
sibakín, v. to cut, to split with a big ax.
sibasibin, v. to attack as of a pig.
sibát, n. spear.
sibatín, v. to spear, to throw as a spear.
sibihan, v. to build a lean-to.
sibilyan, n. civilian.
siból, n. bud, spring.
sibsib, n. late sunset.
sibuyas, n. onion.
sikad, n. backward kick.
sikap, n. industry, sipag.
sikapin, v. to work diligently.
sikat, n. rays.
sikdó, n. a violent palpita-

tion of the heart.
sikhay, n. assiduity.
sikíp, adj. crowded, tight.
siklot, n. a game using pebbles — similar to jackstone.
siklutín, v. to toss up and down.
siko, n. elbow.
siksík, adj. stuffed, packed tight.
siksikín, v. to pack full.
sikuhín, v. to elbow strongly.
sidhâ, n. constancy of diligence.
sidhi, n. intensity.
sigâ, n. bonfire, goon.
sigaán, v. to smoke, to burn.
sigabo, n. sudden onslaught.
sigalót, n. complication, quarrel.
sigasig, n. conscientiousness,
sigáw, n. shout, cry.
sigawán, n. a din, clamoring noise.
siglá, n. enthusiasm, an act of being active.
siglahán, v. to fill with enthusiasm.
siglo, n. century.
signos, n. fatal sign.
sigurado, adj. assured.
siguro, adv. perhaps, maybe, Sp.
sigwa, n. storm at sea.
sihang, n. jaw.
sihangan, v. to open by force with an instrument.
siilín, v. to oppress.
siít, n. small thorny branches of bamboo.
silá, pron. they.
silain, v. to prey upon.
silabán, v. to build a blaze.
silakbó, n. outburst of emotion.
silahis, n. ray.
silam, n. eye irritation (by soap or the like).
silangan, n. east.
silanganin, adj. oriental.
silát, n. slits on floorings.
siláw, n. & adj. dazzled.
silayan, v. to visit, to look over.
silbato, n. whistle.
silbi, n. use, utility.
sili, n. pepper.
silíd, n. room, compartment.
silid-tulugan, n. bedroom.
silipin, v. to peep, to look through a crevice.
silíd-aralán, n. classroom.
silò, n. noose.
silong, n. lower part of a building.
silungán, n. rain or sun shed.
silya, n. chair.
sima, n. quill or feather at end of arrow.
simbahan, n. church.
simboryo, n. tower.
simangót, adj. sour or distorted.
simi, n. refuse or remnants of fish fallen on the table.
simoy, n. breeze,
simsimín, v. to suck, to pluck.
simulâ, n. beginning.
simutín, v. to pick out everything.
simyento, n. cement.
sinalakay, v. attack.
sinaluhan, v. partook.
sinandatahan, v. armed.
sinangag, n. toasted cooked rice.
sinamay, n. fabric made of abaca fiber.
sinamsám, v. confiscated.

gathered.
sindak, n. fright, terror.
sinindak, v. frightened.
sinelas, n. slippers.
sinapupunan, n. within one's care.
sining, n. art.
sindák, n. fright.
singaw, n. vapor.
siniguelas, n. spanish plum.
sinilabán, v. scorched.
siniyasat, v. examined closely.
sino, pron. who.
sinok, n. hiccough.
sinsin, n. density of growth.
sinuhin, v. to ask for identity.
sintá, n. loved one.
sintahín, v. to make love to.
sintahan, n. love affair.
sintido, n. sense, feeling.
sinturon, n. belt.
sinulid, n. thread.
sinulsulan, v. induced.
sinungaling, n. liar.
sinuway, v. disobeyed.
singa, n. mucus expelled from the nose.
singasing, n. hiss.
singáw, n. vapor, exhuded scent.
sing-ibig, n. sweetheart, lovers.
singkad, adv. exactly, fully, completely.
singkamás, n. turnip.
singkawán, v. to put harness on.
singkil, n. jostling with the elbow.
singkit, adj. slit-eyed.
singko, n. five centavos.
singhal, n. loud vocal outburst of anger.
sipa, n. kick.
sipag, n. industry.
sipatin, v. to look carefully.
siper, n. zipper.
sipì, n. copy.
siphayò, n. disappointment.
sipilyo, n. brush.
sipilyuhín, v. to brush.
sipit, n. tongs.
sipsipín, v. to suck.
sipón, n. cold.
sipunin, adj. afflicted with cold easily.
sipunín, v. to catch cold.
sirâ, adj. torn, shredded.
sirain, v. to break, to destroy.
sirko, n. circus, acrobatics.
sirena, n. mermaid.
siruhano, n. surgeon.
sisante, adj. dismissed from office.
sisi, n. reproach, regret.
sisidlan, n. container.
sisihin, v. to reproach.
sisirin, v. to dive.
sisiw, n. small chicken.
siste, n. jest, joke.
sistema, n. system.
sitaw, n. pod-bearing vegetable.
sitsít, n. gossip.
siwang, n. small opening.
siya, n. saddle.
siyá, pron. personal pronoun, third person, singular nominative.
siyaho, n. elder sister's husband.
siyám, n. nine.
siyáp, n. chirp of the chickens.
siyaping, n. shopping.
siyamnapû, n. ninety.
siyudad, n. city. Sp.
sisiyáp-siyáp, adj. chirping intermittently.
sobra, adj. excess
soo, n. zoo.

soopobya, n. zoophobia.
subain, v. not to pay intentionally.
subalì, prep. but.
subasob, adj. facing downward.
subasta, n. public auction.
subaybayán, v. to follow secretly.
subuan, v. to place into one's mouth, to place materials into a machine.
subo, n. a portion of food enough for a mouth.
subok, n. test
subukan, v. to test.
subukin, v. to try.
subyang, n. obstruction, a thorn.
suka, n. vomiting.
suká, n. vinegar.
sukal, n. heap of dirt.
sukáb, adj. dishonest, treacherous.
sukatán, n. measurer, tape measure.
sukatan, n. measurement.
sukbit, adj. carried inserted under top edge of skirt or trousers.
sukì, n. client, patron.
suklám, n. loathing.
sukláy, n. comb.
sukuban, v. spread over.
suklî, n. change.
suklián, v. to give the change.
suklian, n. reciprocal arrangements.
suklob, n. cover with encasing around sides.
sukol, adj. cornered, driven to a corner or a wall.
sukursál, n. distributing office.
sugál, n. game of chance.
sula, n. a precious stone.
sugalan, n. gambling house, casino.
sugalán, v. to gamble with.
sumalok, v. fetch water in a pail.
sugapa, adj. inveterate drunkard who yells around habitually when drunk.
sugarol, n. gambler.
sugat, n. wound.
sugatán, adj. wounded.
sugatan, v. to wound.
sugid, n. diligence, persistence.
sugo, n. delegate, ambassador.
sugpuin, v. to nip at the bud.
suhà, n. pomelo.
suhay, n. prop, support.
suhayan, v. to support.
suhol, n. bribe, enticement.
suhulan, v. to bribe.
sulat, n. letter.
sulatin, v. to write.
sulimpat, adj. squint-eyed.
sulitin, v. to account for, to examine.
sulô, n. torch.
sulok, n. corner.
sumama, v. to go with.
sumamò, v. to appeal.
sumapayapà, v. rest in peace.
sumásampalataya, n. one who keeps faith.
sumbóng, n. report, complaint.
sumimangot, v. to scowl.
sumingáw, v. evaporate.
sumuskribi, v. to subscribe.
sulong, v. to advance.
sulsí, n. mend.
sulyap, n. glance.
sumúsulák, adj. shimmer-

ing, blood seemingly rising up to the head.
sumibol, v. to grow.
sumpóng, n. periodic manifestation, tantrum.
sumpungin, adj. changeable, fickle.
sumusumpa, v. swearing.
sumpâ, n. pledge, vow.
sumpaín, v. to condemn.
sumpit, n. blowgun.
sundalo, n. soldier.
sundáng, n. long dagger.
sunduin, v. to fetch, to go after.
sundót, n. puncture.
sundutín, v. to puncture.
supilin, v. to subdue.
sunok, n. surfeit.
sunód, adj. in accordance with.
sunurín, adj. obedient, following orders.
sunog, n. fire, conflagration.
sunóg, adj. burnt.
sunugin, v. to burn.
sunong, n. something carried on the head.
sunungin, v. to carry on one's head.
suntók, n. fistic blow.
suntukín, v. to box.
suntukan, n. fistic fight.
sunggáb, n. grab.
sunggabán, v. to grab.
sungay, n. horn.
sungayán, adj. discourteous, insolent.
sungkî, adj. irregular growth of teeth.
sungkít, n. pole and hook for picking fruits.
sungkitín, v. to gather fruits with a hook.
sungít, adj. irritable.
sungót, n. feelers or antennae.
sunud-sunod, adj. successive.
suubin, v. to fumigate.
suob, n. fumigation.
suong, v. to place one towards danger.
suót, n. habiliments, dress.
suutan, v. to wear, to put on.
supá, n. sofa.
supalpal, n. something covering the mouth.
supíl, adj. controlled, disciplined.
supil, n. something that controls the hair.
supilin, v. to discipline.
supisyente, adj. sufficient.
suplado, adj. swelled-up, conceited.
suplíngán, v. to have sprouts.
supot, n. bag, sack.
suputin, v. to make into a sack.
suray, n. staggering, tottering.
surì, n. test, examination.
suriin, v. to look into, examine.
surián, n. an institute for the study of arts and sciences.
surot, n. bedbug.
surutin, n. to be filled with bedbugs, to point with the fingers while reprimanding.
suskrisyon, n. subscription.
susì, n. key.
suso, n. breast, nipple.
susô, n. snail.
susuhan, v. to set to fire.
susog, n. amendment.
suson, n. second layer.
susugan, v. to amend.
susun-susón, adj. double, laying one upon another.
sustansiyá, n. substance.

sutlâ, n. silk.
sutlain, adj. silky.
sutsót, n. irritated whistle.
sutsután, v. to whistle at.
suwagín, v. to thrust with the horn.
suwaíl, adj. insolent.
suwayin, v. to disobey.
suwelas, n. soles.
suweldo, n. salary, compensation.
suwelduhán, v. to give salary.
suwitik, adj. sly, artful.
suyà, n. disgust.
suyáng-suyâ, adj. disgusted.
suyuin, v. to make or render oneself into the favor of another.
suyod, n. fine-toothed comb, weaver's comb, harrow.
suyurin, v. to comb.

T

taas, n. height.
taasan, v. to elevate, to make high.
taal, n. native of.
tabâ, n. fat, obesity.
tabák, n. bolo.
tabako, n. cigar, tobacco.
taban, n. hold.
tabanan, v. to hold.
tabáng, n. tastelessness.
tabangán, v. to make tasteless.
tabas, n. cut, style.
tabí, n. side.
tabike, n. partition, wall.
tabihán, v. to sit beside.
tabing-dagat o tabindagat, n. seashore.
tabigin, v. to push aside.
tabi-tabingî, adj. disproportioned.
tabíl, adj. talkative.
tabing, n. screen.
tabingan, v. to put a screen.
tabingî, adj. without symmetry.
tabó, n. a small water container.
tablá, n. woodboard, draw.
tabsíng, n. tide.
taka, n. amazement, astonishment.
takal, n. measure.
takalan, v. to measure.
takám, n. longing, desire.
takapán, v. to bawl out.
takas, n. escape.
takasan, n. to leave behind.
takaw, n. greediness.
takaw-alat, adj. preference for salty foods.
takaw-tamis, adj. sweet-tooth.
takbá, n. clothes chest.
takbó, n. run, driving.
takdâ, n. limit.
takdáng-aralín, n. assignment.
takigrapiya, n. stenography.
takigrapo, n. stenographer.
takilya, n. ticketbooth.
takíp, n. cover.
takipsilim, n. twilight.
taklób, n. covering.
taklubán, v. to cover the top.
taksil, n. traitor.
takot, n. fear.
takutin, v. to frighten.
tadhaná, n. fate, provision.
tadtád, adj. chopped.
tadtarín, v. to chop.
tadyakán, v. to kick forcefully.
tadyáng, n. rib.
tagá, rw. from, originated from.
taga-ayos, n. arranger, pacifier, manager.

tagaingat-yaman, n. treasurer.
tagák, n. heron.
tagál, n. duration.
tagalán, v. to cause to be long.
taganás, adj. all of everything.
tagapag-alagà, n. caretaker.
tagapagkalinga, n. guardian.
tagapaglingkod, n. one who renders service.
tagapag-tatag, n. one whose duty is to found or organize.
taghóy, n. lament.
tagapamayapà, n. sergeant-at-arms.
tagasulit, n. examiner.
tagarito, n. a native of a place.
tagasurì, n. auditor.
tagausig, n. prosecutor.
tagdán, n. a flagpole.
taghóy, n. lamentation.
tag-init, n. summer.
tagintíng, n. noise created by two metallic objects.
tagubilin, n. recommendation, instruction.
taglamíg, n. cold season, winter.
tagistís, n. drip.
tagláy, v. to carry along.
tagô, adj. hidden.
taguán, n. hide and seek.
tagubilin, n. charge, order, instruction.
tagpasín, v. to cut down.
tagpî, n. patch.
tagpô, n. scene.
tagpuan, n. rendezvous.
tagsiból, n. spring time.
tagubilin, n. order, instruction.
tagubilinan, v. to order, to instruct.
tagulabáy, n. blotches on the skin.
tagulamín, n. mildew.
tagumpáy, n. victory.
taguri, n. appellation, title, name.
taggutom, n. famine.
tahakin, v. to follow up, to explore.
táhanan, n. residence, home.
tahán, v. to stop
tahî, n. sewing.
tahiín, v. to sew.
tahilan, n. beam of a house.
tahimik, adj. peaceful.
tahipín, v. to winnow.
tahíp, n. palpitation.
tahól, n. bark.
tahulán, v. to bark at.
tahure, n. soybean curd.
taimtím, adj. devoted, hearty.
talà, n. big star.
talâ, n. notation.
tálaan, n. list, writing book.
talà, v. note down, record.
taláarawán, n. diary.
talabá, n. oysters.
talakay, v. to expound.
talaksán, n. a big pile.
talagá, adv. naturally.
talámbuhay, n. biography.
talámpakan, n. sole.
talampás, n. plateau.
talangka, n. tiny fresh water crabs.
talas, n. keenness.
talastás, v. to understand.
tálataán, n. stanza, paragraph.
talátinigan, n. dictionary.
tali, n. knot, tie.
talian, v. to tie.
talikdán, v. to turn one's back to.
taliba, n. guard, herald.

talibaan, v. to guard.
talinghagà, n. allegory, figure of speech.
talím, n. sharpness.
talimán, v. to sharpen.
talimusak, n. small fish of the goby family.
talino, n. talent.
taling, n. mole, mark.
talipandás, adj. fickle.
taliwas, adj. opposite.
talón, n. falls, waterfall.
talón, v. to jump.
talóng, n. eggplant.
talop, n. skin, peelings.
talóp, adj. skin peeled.
talupan, v. to peel.
talós, n. comprehended.
talusín, v. to understand.
talusaling, adj. hard to please, sensitive.
talsík, n. splash.
talsikán, v. to be splashed, to be weeded out, to scamper away.
taludtód, n. line (as in verse).
talukbóng, n. headgear, veil.
talulot, n. petals.
talukbungán, v. to cover the head.
talukab, n. crabshell carapace.
talukap, n. eyelid.
taluktók, n. top, summit.
talumpatì, n. speech.
talúmpatián, v. to deliver a speech.
talumpatian, n. speech making.
taluntunín, v. to follow.
taluntunan, n. rules, regulation.
talyasì, n. vat.
tamà, adj. right, correct.
tamaan, v. to hit squarely.
tamád, adj. lazy, indolent.
tamád-tamaran, v. to pretend to be lazy.
tamarín, v. to feel lazy.
tampipe, n. chest for clothes.
tampulan, n. target.
tambak, n. heaping up.
tambô, n. a broom.
tamburín, n. gold necklace.
tanán, adj. all, everyone.
tanáw, n. sight, outlook.
tanawín, v. to look, to sight.
tánawin, n. scenery.
tanawan, adj., visible from one point to another.
tandâ, n. mark, sign, age.
tandâ, n. old people.
tandaán, v. to remember.
tandáng, n. rooster.
tanikalà, n. chain.
tanikalaán, v. to bind with chains.
taním, n. plant.
taning, n. limitation in time.
taningan, v. to fix a day, to limit.
tanóng, n. question, inquiry.
tanungan, n. questioning, questionnaire, counselor.
tanungín, v. to question, to inquire.
tanso, n. copper.
tantiyá, n. estimate, calculation.
tantiyahín, v. to estimate, to feel out.
tangá, adj. stupid.
tangà, n. clothes moth.
tangan, n. something held.
tanganan, v. to hold.
tanyág, adj. famous, well known.
tangáy, n. object that is carried along.
tangayín, v. to carry an

object on leaving.
tangkád, adj. tall.
tangkaín, v. to intend, to plan out.
tangkáy, n. stem.
tangkás, n. bundle.
tangkilik, n. support.
tangkilikin, v. to support.
tangkilikán, n. mutual aid, society.
tanggáp, rw. accept, receive.
tanggapan, n. office.
tanggapín, v. to accept.
tanggál, adj. loose, disconnected.
tanggalín, v. to strike out, to disconnect.
tanggalin, adj. easily disconnected.
tanggihán, v. refuse.
tanggulan, n. defense, device.
tanghál, n. show, display.
tanghalì, n. noon.
tanghaling-tapát, n. midday.
tanghalian, n. lunch.
tangì, adj. special.
tangláw, n. light, lamp.
tanglawán, v. to light, to bring out a lamp.
tangô, n. confirmation by nodding.
tanguán, v. to say yes by a nod, to confirm.
tanod-pinto, n. porter.
tao, n. human being.
taong-bayan, n. citizen.
taong-bansa, n. nationals of a country.
taong-sakop, n. subject.
taong-lambak, n. people of the valley.
taong-dayami, n. scarecrow.
taong-dambuhala, n. human monster.
taong-pulà, n. person of the red race.
taong-abók, n. human fossil.
taong-ilaya, n. people of the hinterlands.
taong-lakád, n. pedestrian.
taong-lalawigan, n. provincial people.
taong-labás, n. outsider.
taong-lupa, n. earthman.
tapa, n. meat that is dried or smoked.
tapahin, v. to smoke out.
tapak, n. footsteps.
tapák, adj. barefooted.
tapang, n. bravery.
tapangan, v. to feel brave.
tapát, adj. faithful, frank.
tapatan, adj. opposite.
tapatin, v. to confess, to talk frankly.
tapayan, n. large water container.
tapón, n. cork.
tapon, n. a stranger, an orphan, an outcast.
tapós, n. finish, end.
tapós, n. end of the nine-day prayers for a departed.
tapusin, v. to finish, to end.
trabaho, n. occupation.
tarantado, adj. confused, out of the senses.
tarás, n. sharpness, effrontery.
tarì, n. pointed spur used in cockpits.
tarík, adj. steep.
tarós, n. care, consideration.
tasa, n. estimate, a cup.
tasahan, v. to appraise.
tastás, adj. unstitched.
tastás, n. loose stitches.
tastasín, v. to loosen the sewing.

taták, n. stamp, brand.
tatakán, v. to mark, to put a label.
tatay, n. affiliation for father.
tatág, n. stability.
tatáy-tatayan, n. pretending to be the father.
tatló, adj. & n. three.
tatluhan, adj. capacity for three.
tatluhin, v. to make or increase to three.
tatlumpû, adj. & n. thirty.
tatsulok, n. triangle.
tau-tauhan, n. puppet.
tauhan, n. followers.
tausi, n. salted soybeans.
tawa, n. laughter.
tawag, n. call.
tawagin, v. to call.
táwanan, n. laughter in a group.
tawanan, v. to laugh at.
tawas, n. alum.
taynga, n. ear.
tayo, pron. we.
tayô, n. stand.
tayp, n. type.
tayuán, v. to stand for, to guarantee.
teknolohiya, n. technology.
tibág, n. demolition.
tibay, n. strength, durability.
tibayan, v. to strengthen, to be courageous.
tibò, n. broken glass.
tibók, n. beat, palpitation.
tibukán, v. to feel, to palpitate.
tikas, n. bearing, form, figure.
tikasan, v. to make one's bearing attractive.
tikatík, adj. continuous but slow patter of raindrops.
tikbalang, n. phantom, a hairy monster.
tiket, n. ticket.
tikim, n. taste.
tikis, adj. intentional, purposely.
tikisan, n. something done purposely.
tikisín, v. not to care purposely.
tiklóp, n. fold.
tiklupín, v. to fold.
tiklupin, adj. easily folded, made to be folded.
tiklúp-tuhod, adj. sincere, soulful, submissive.
tikóm, v. to close, to gather closely.
tikoy, n. a chinese cake.
tigáng, adj. dry, arid.
tigás, n. hardness, strength.
tigasán, v. to harden.
tigíb, adj. full, loaded.
tigil, n. stop-over.
tigisin, v. to squeeze, to let flow.
tigmák, adj. soaked or wet.
tigpasín, v. to cut.
tigre, n. tiger.
tiisin, v. to bear, to tolerate.
tila, adv. maybe, perhaps.
tilà, n. ceased.
tilamsík, n. splatter.
tilamsikán, v. to splatter.
tilaok, n. crowing.
tilarín, v. to chop into pieces.
tilaukan, v. to crow.
tílaukan, n. crowing of cocks in the morning.
tilî, n. a shrill shout caused by fright, pain or shock.
tílian, n. a medly of frightened shouts or angry innuendoes.

tilián, v. to shout at somebody in anger or fury.
tim, n. team.
timbáng, n. weight, equal.
timbangan, n. balance.
timbangín, v. to weigh, to balance.
timog, n. south.
timog-silangan, n. southeast.
timog-kanluran, n. southwest.
timpalák, n. contest.
timpiín, v. to hold under control.
timyás, adj. purity.
tinà, n. blue dye.
tinagin, v. to move, to transfer.
tinalì, n. fighting cock.
tinamisán, v. sweetened.
tinapá, n. smoked fish.
tinapay, n. bread.
tinátamasa, v. is enjoying.
tinawag, v. called.
tindá, n. merchandise.
tindahan, n. store.
tindíg, n. stand, posture.
tiník, n. thorn.
tinidór, n. fork.
tinig, n. voice.
tining, n. residue, sediment.
tinítirhán, n. address, residence.
tiniyák, v. to make sure.
tingkád, n. brightness of color.
tingkarán, v. to brighten the color.
tingkayád, v. to sit on one's heels.
tingalaín, v. to look up.
tinggalín, v. to preserve.
tinghóy, n. oil lamp with wick.
tingian, n. retail.
tingî, v. to sell at retail.
tingín, rw. see, look.
tingnan, v. to look at.
tingtíng, n. stick from native brooms.
tinubuan, n. native place of birth.
tinubuan, v. to have or to contact a disease.
tinuhog, v. strung together.
tinupi, v. folded.
tinupok, v. burned.
tinuran, v. mentioned.
tinyente, n. lieutenant.
tipaklóng, n. grasshopper.
tipanan, n. meeting place of a group.
tipunin, v. to collect, to gather.
tira, n. left over.
tirá-tirahan, n. left-overs.
tirhán, v. to leave something.
titikhím, v. will cough (artificially).
titik, n. letter of the alphabet.
titser, n. teacher.
titig, n. stare, look, without winking.
titis, n. live sparks from a burning cigarette or lighted match sticks.
tiwa, n. worms of the intestine.
tiwalà, n. trust.
tiwalî, adj. wrong, incorrect.
tiwarík, adj. upside down.
tiwasáy, adj. peaceful, composed.
tiyá, n. aunt.
tiwasayín, v. to compose.
tiyák, adj. certain, sure.
tiyakin, v. to ascertain, to be sure of.
tiyagâ, n. perseverance.
tiyán, n. stomach.
tiyanì, n. tweezers.
tíyapan, n. appointment, date.

tiyapín, v. to date, to engage.
tiyó, n. uncle.
tiyuhin, n. many uncles.
toge, n. sprouted mongo.
tokwa, n. soybean cake.
tong, n. a bribe.
tosino, n. bacon.
toyo, n. soy sauce.
totoo, adj. true.
totohanin, v. to make true.
trahedya, n. tragedy, Sp.
traysikel, n. tricycle.
tren, n. train.
trensera, n. trench.
tribunal, n. municipal building.
trono, n. throne.
troso, n. timber.
tubig, n. water.
tubigan, v. to water, to add water.
tubó, n. sugar cane.
tubò, n. profit, gain.
tubò, adj. growth, sprout.
tubuan, v. to have sprout.
tubugán, n. place or object where needles and pins are stuck to.
tubusín, v. to redeem.
túbusan, n. privilege of redemption.
tukâ, n. bill, peck.
tuklás, n. discovery.
tuklasín, v. to discover.
tukláw, n. bite of (a snake).
tuklóng, n. provisional chapel.
tukod, n. support, prop.
tukuran, v. to prop.
tukoy, n. object, aim.
tukuyin, v. to point out, to specify.
tuksó, n. temptation.
tuksuhín, v. to tempt.
tudlâ, n. aim.
tudlíng, n. furrow, column.
tugapay, v. pursue.
tugatog, n. height, highest point.
tugma, n. rhyme.
tugî, n. tubers.
tugón, n. reply.
tugunín, v. to make a reply.
tugunan, n. exchange of responses.
tugtugin, n. music.
tugtugin, v. to play on.
tugtugan, n. concert, a band playing.
tuhod, n. knee.
tuhugin, v. to pierce thru, to string.
tuhurín, v. to kick with the knee.
tulalà, adj. ignorant, simple.
tulâ, n. poem.
tulaín, v. to recite as a poem.
tulaan, n. recitation of poetry.
tuláy, n. bridge.
tulayán, v. to cross the bridge.
tuldik, n. accent.
tuldikán, v. to accentuate.
tuldók, n. period.
tuldukán, v. to place a period.
tulíg, adj. deafened by shock.
tuligín, v. to shock, to render deaf.
tuligsaín, v. to criticize.
tuligsaan, n. an exchange of destructive criticism.
tulin, n. speed.
tulingag, adj. stupefied.
tulís, adj. pointed.
tulisan, v. to make pointed, to sharpen.
tulisán, n. bandit, robber.
tulò, n. leak, drip.

tulóg, adj. asleep.
tuluan, v. to be wet due to drips.
tulog, v. to sleep.
tulugán, n. bedroom.
tulong, n. aid.
tulóy, v. to go thru.
tuluyán, v. to continue, to lodge with.
túluyan, n. prose.
tulyá, n. smallest clam.
tulyapis, n. unsubstantial grain.
tumabí, v. to get out of the way, sit beside someone.
tumakas, v. to escape.
tumagistís, v. fall freely (as tears).
tumaláb, v. to take effect.
tumalikod, v. to turn one's back.
tumalima, v. to obey.
tumalón, v. to jump.
tumalungkô, v. squat.
tumanà, n. vegetable patch.
tumanod, v. to keep guard.
tumumbá, v. to tumble.
tumbalik, adj. inverted.
tumbalikín, v. to reverse.
tumbás, n. equivalent.
tumbasín, v. to equalize, to give an equivalent.
tumila, v. to cease, as rain.
tumindig, v. stood up.
tumbukan, n. collision.
tumbukín, v. to strike against an object.
tumarók, v. fathom.
tumbóng, n. anus.
tumimò, v. lodge.
tumpák, adj. correct.
tumpakín, v. to correct.
tumugot, v. to yield.
tumulalà, v. to stand by stupidly.
tumulóy, v. to go on, drop in.
tumalilis, v. to leave sideways.
tumantiyá, v. to estimate, to ascertain.
tumok, n. thickness of grass.
tumuntóng, v. to stand on, to step on.
tumungó, v. to look downwards.
tumunggâ, v. to drink.
tumutol, n. object, objection.
tunáw, adj. melted, dissolved.
tunawin, v. to dissolve.
túnawan, n. a basin or pot for melting purposes.
tunay, adj. true, genuine.
tunton, rw. trail, trace.
tuntungan, n. a raised platform on which one stands.
tuntungán, v. to step on, to cover (as a pot).
tuntunin, n. rule.
tunggain, v. to drink to the last drop.
tunganga, adj. indifferent, curious.
tungayaw, n. insulting and dirty language.
tungayawin, v. to insult with dirty language.
tungkabín, v. to force open with a device.
tungkód, n. stick, cane.
tungkól, adv. in reference to.
tungkulin, n. obligation, duty.
tungkulin, v. to assume.
tunggák, adj. unfit.
tunggali, n. dispute.
tunghan, v. to look down-

wards.
tunghayán, v. to scan or look carefully.
tungó, adj. stooped, bowed.
tunguhin, v. to go in the direction of.
tunóg, n. sound.
tuód, n. stump.
tuon, n. pressure steadied by force at hand or foot.
tuós, n. settlement.
tupa, n. sheep.
tuparín, v. to fulfill.
tupók, adj. burned.
turbante, n. turban.
turista, n. tourist.
turít, n. young cow.
turít, adj. confused, dazed.
turnilyo, n. screw.
turò, n. teachings, instruction, point.
turumpó, n. top.
tusino, n. bacon.
túso, n. astute, wily.
tusok, n. prick.
tustós, n. allowance.
tustusán, v. to support.
tusukan, n. object of.
tusukin, v. to prick.
tuta, n. puppy.
tutukan, v. to point a gun on somebody.
tutol, n. opposition, objection.
tutulan, v. to oppose, to object.
tutóng, n. burnt part of boiled rice.
tutungán, adj. full of burnt rice.
tutóp, n. trimming.
tutupán, v. to put on trimming.
tutubí, n. dragonfly.
tutulí, n. earwax.
tuusín, v. to liquidate, to settle.
tuwâ, n. gladness.
tuwakang, n. large anchovies.
tuwalya, n. towel.
tuwád, adj. upside-down.
túwangan, n. coordination.
tuwangán, v. to help.
tuwang-tuwa, adj. very happy.
tuwáng-tuwáng, adj. helping each other.
tuwì, adv. often.
tuwíd, adj. straight.
tuwirin, v. to follow, straighten.
túwiran, n. a straight path.
tuya, n. sarcasm.
tuyaín, v. to mock.
tuyô, adj. dried.
tuyuín, v. to dry.
tuyót, adj. totally dried.

U

ubanin, adj. full of grey hairs.
ubas, n. grapes.
ubó, n. cough.
ubok, n. white clay used for painting.
ubod, n. core, pith.
ubod, adj. completely, full of.
ubós, adj. exhausted, consumed.
ubusin, v. to consume.
uká-ukâ, adj. full of ruts.
ukâ, adj. worn out, dug up, rotten.
uká-ukà, adj. full of ruts
ukain, v. to dig out.
ukilkíl, v. to ask persistently.
ukol, prep. in connection with.
uban, n. greyish hair.
udyók, n. inducement.
udyukán, v. to urge, to

induce.
ugà, n. rw. shake.
ugain, v. to shake.
ugalì, n. habit, custom.
ugaliin, v. to adopt as a habit.
ugát, n. root.
ugit, n. rudder, helm.
ugmâ, adj. fitting.
uhaw, n. thirst.
uhawin, v. to become thirsty.
uhâ, n. cry of a new baby.
uhales, n. buttonhole.
ugnáy, n. joint, connection.
ugnayín, v. to join, to connect.
ulam, n. viand.
ulamin, v. to use as a viand.
ulap, n. clouds.
ulat, n. report.
ulbo, n. pig pen.
ulì, adv. once more.
ulián, adj. forgetful due to age.
ulikbâ, adj. black.
ulinig, v. to listen, to hear.
ulila, n. orphan.
ulirán, adj. ideal.
ulit, n. repetition.
ulí-ulì, adv. next time.
uliuli, n. eddying water.
ulyanin, adj. forgetful.
ulo, n. head.
uluhán, n. head, part, with a big head.
ulunán, adv. at the head, in the direction of the head.
ulók, n. incitement.
ulukán, v. to incite.
ulóg, n. shake.
ulugín, v. to shake.
ulól, n. insane, fool.
ulupóng, n. poisonous snake.
ulusín, v. to pierce.
ulutan, n. a place in the cockpit where the match is made.
umaasa, v. hopes, hoping.
umakyat, v. to go up.
umaga, n. morning.
umagahin, v. to be caught by dawn.
umagtíng, v. to vibrate.
umahon, v. to go to a higher place.
umalalay, v. to support, to prop.
umalimbukáy, v. to surge, as water.
umalingasaw, v. to spread out, to give strong odor.
umalingawngáw, v. to be repeated in whispers.
umalís, v. went away, departed.
umalíw, v. console.
umaliw-iw, v. to bubble like a brook.
umangkat, v. to buy by importing.
umayon, v. to agree.
umibís, v. alighted.
umíd, adj. tongue-tied.
umidlíp, v. to take a nap.
umigíb, v. to fetch water.
umilag, v. to avoid, to parry.
umiikot, v. turning around.
umiiyak, v. crying.
umilandáng, v. to be thrown far.
umiláp, v. to become elusive, to become wild.
umilíng, v. shooks one's head.
umirap, v. to look at angrily.
umisip, v. to think.
umít, n. pilfered goods.
umitán, v. to steal something from another.

umitín, v. steal, to pilfer.
umpok, n. group.
umudlót, v. to stop on one's tracks.
umugin, v. to beat together.
umugong, v. to resound, to thunder.
umulán, v. to rain.
umumaga, v. to become morning.
umumbók, v. to swell.
umumít, v. to steal, to pilfer.
umungol, v. to grunt.
umungós, v. sprouted.
umuntág, v. to remind.
umurong, v. to go back, to shrink, to retreat.
umusig, v. to go after one.
umuslî, v. to stick out.
umuwî, v. to go home.
una, adj. first.
unahan, v. to go first.
unahán, n. front.
unan, n. pillow.
unano, adj. dwarf.
unat, n. straightness.
unawà, n. comprehension, notice.
unawain, v. to comprehend, to understand.
unós, n. strong breeze.
union, n. union.
unsiyamì, adj. stunted in growth.
unsiyamiin, v. to cause one's growth or enthusiasm, to cease.
untagin, v. to repeatedly ask.
unti-unti, adj. little by little.
untóg, n. bump.
untugin, v. to bump.
ungal, n. howl.
ungalan, v. to howl at.
ungás, n. simpleton, stupid person.
unggóy, n. monkey.
uod, n. worm.
upa, n. payment, fee.
upasalà, n. vituperation, accusation.
upasalain, v. to accuse, to suspect.
upo, n. gourd.
upô, n. sitting position.
upuán, v. to sit on.
úpuan, n. seat.
urì, n. kind, quality.
uriin, v. to classify.
urirà, adj. inquisitive.
urungan, v. to back out.
usá, n. deer.
usad, n. crawl
usapan, n. conversation, chat.
usapín, n. case in court.
usbóng, n. young shoot.
usbungán, v. to produce young shoots, to cut young shoots.
uso, n. mode, style.
usok, n. smoke.
usukan, v. to smoke.
usuhin, v. to put on a new style.
utak, n. brains.
utál-utál, adj. stammering.
utang, n. indebtedness.
utangin, v. to be in debt.
utasín, v. to finish.
utáy-utayín, v. to finish little by little.
utos, n. order, command.
utusán, n. maid, servant.
utusan, v. to order, to send on an errand.
utu-utu, n. imbecile.
uugúd-ugód, adj. weak, trembling.
uurin, v. to be filled with worms.
uwî, n. something brought

home.
uwián, v. to bring home something.
uyám, n. mockery, sarcasm.
uyamín, v. to mock, be sarcastic.
uyayi, n. lullaby.

W

wakás, n. end, finish.
wakasán, v. to end.
wakwák, adj. exposed, opened.
wagás, adj. faithful, sincere.
wagaywáy, v. to flutter.
waglít, v. to mislay.
wagwagan, n. splashing of water in pool, river or sea.
wagwagín, v. to shake in the wind or in water.
walâ, adj. absent.
walaín, v. to lose.
waláng-anumán, an expression used when being thanked.
walang kamatayan, adj. immortal.
waláng-habas, adj. unrestrained.
waláng-hanggán, adj. eternal.
waláng-hiyâ, adj. shameless.
walang-hugis, adj. shapeless.
waláng-humpáy, adj. without ceasing.
walang-lasa, adj. tasteless.
waláng-walâ, adj. bereft, poor.
walát, adj. destroyed.
walís, n. broom.
walisán, v. to clean with a broom
waló, n. eight.
wáluhan, adj. with a capacity for eight.
wastô, adj. correct, right.
wastuín, v. to correct, to put in order.
waták-waták, adj. scattered.
watasin, v. to understand.
watawat, n. flag, emblem.
wawá, n. small river, confusion, nonsense.
wáwalaing-bahalà, v. will not value.
welga, n. strike, a refuse by the employees to work.
wikà, v. & n. said, language.
wikain, v. to say.
wilíg, n. sprinkling.
wiligán, v. to sprinkle water on.
wilíng-wilí, adj. feeling at home.
windáng-windáng, adj. tattered, torn.
wisík, n. spray.

Y

yabág, n. footstep.
yabang, n. boastfulness.
yabong, n. growth.
yakag, n. inducement.
yakagin, v. to induce, to ask.
yagít, n. rubbish.
yaman, n. riches, wealth.
yamang, adv. inasmuch as.
yamót, n. & adj. annoyance, irritation, piqued.
yamungmóng, n. expansion, enlargement.
yamutín, v. to annoy, to pique.
yamutmót, n. trash.
yanki, n. yankee.

yanigín, v. to shake, to vibrate.
yaón, pron. that.
yapák, n. footsteps, foot prints.
yapák, adj. barefooted.
yapakan, v. to step on.
yapós, n. embrace.
yapusín, v. to embrace.
yápusan, n. necking.
yarì, n. product, produce.
yarì, n. & adj. manufactured, made, finished.
yariin, v. to make.
yatà, adv. maybe, perhaps.
yayà, n. invitation.
yayain, v. to invite, to persuade.
yayamang, adv. since.
yayat, adv. emaciated.
yero, n. galvanized iron.
yelo, n. snow, ice.
yeso, n. chalk.
yoyò, n. yoyo (toy).
yukayok, adj. crestfallen.
yukô, n. stoop.
yukod. adj. stooped.
yukuán, v. to stoop.
yugyóg, n. shaking.
yugyugin, v. to shake.
yumakag, v. to call, to invite.
yumao, v. died, went away.
yumì, n. modesty, meekness.
yungíb, n. cave.
yungyungán, v. to shelter, to protect.
yupapà, n. submission.
yupî, n. distortion.
yupî-yupî, adj. distorted. flattened.
yupiín, v. to distort.
yurak, n. motion of trampling.
yurakan, v. to trample.
yutà, n. a hundred thousand.
yutyutín, v. to shake continuously.

MGA TAMBALANG SALITA

COMMON DOUBLE EXPRESSIONS

abut-dili, adj. very serious that remedy may come on time.
agaw-buhay, adj. about to expire, breathing one's last.
agaw-tulog, adj. beginning to drowse.
ahas-tulóg, n. a species of a non-poisonous snake.
anák-araw, n. a very exceptionally white being who cannot look at the sun.
anák-pawis, n. one who is born of poverty, poor one.
aklatang-bayan, n. a public library.
asal-hayop, adj. ferocious, like an animal.
asal-alipin, adj. having the characteristics of a slave, ignorant, stupid, submissive.
bantáy-salakay, n. one who does the robbing or pilfering of what he is guarding.
bagong-bayan, n. a newly created city or town.
bahay-sanlaan, n. a pawnshop.
bahay-kubo, n. a native hut, especially in the field
balátkayô, n. pretense, costume, a mask.
balát-sibuyas, adj. sensitive like the onion skin, very transparent.
balik-aral, n. a review.
batong-buhay, n. a kind of stone that is unbreakable.
bigláng-yaman, n. one who becomes rich accidentally.
bagong-tao, n. a young man.
binatang-taring, n. a brave boy, a stylish young man.
bungang-araw, n. skin rash that gives painful itches.
buóng-pusò, adj. heartfelt, heartily.
bungangkahoy, n. fruits.
bukáng-bibíg, n. subject or topic of rumors.
buntóng-hiningá, n. deep and soulful breathing.
bukáng-liwaywáy, n. dawn.
buhay-alamáng, adj. a poor life full of daily struggles.
kabatakáng-kumot, n. a very close friend.
kabígayang-loób, n. reciprocity, reciprocal neighbors.
kabunggóng-balikat, n. friends who go out together and at all occasions.
kadáupang-palad, n. a close acquaintance.
kapit-tukô, n. close hold or embrace, very tight.
katápatang-lihim, n. a confidant, a secret acquaintance.
kaútutang-dilà, n. a secret intimate, a confidant,
kisáp-matá, n. an instant, the blink of an eye.
kumain-dili, adj. without appetite due to illness, without things to eat.
dahong-palay, n. a poisonous snake that assumes the likeness of the palay

dalagang-bukid, n. a girl of the field or the province, a species of an edible fish.

dálang-tao, adj. on the family way.

daláng-hiyâ, adj. feeling awkward or ashamed.

dapit-hapon, n. sunset, sundown.

hampás-lupa, n. a vaga bond, a hobo.

hatinggabí, n. midnight.

hubog-kandilà, adj. long and tapering (fingers) like a candle.

lagpás-tuhod, adj. above the knees.

ligong-pato, n. bathing without wetting the head.

makadurog-pusò, adj. sorrowful, heart-touching.

makalagiág-matsíng, adj. looking at somebody long and soulfully; looking with unexpressed feeling.

mayroóng-walá, n. a rich man who live like a poor man.

nagmúmurang-ka m a t i s, adj. (a girl) during the conceiving period.

naníningaláng-pugad, adj. a boy out to woo or make love.

ningas-kugon, adj. enthusiastic at the beginning but with short-lived enthusiasm.

pakiharapan-dili, adj. unwilling to entertain.

pakitang-tao, adj. showy, full of pretense.

palipád-hangin, n. boastings, flattery.

pangulong-lunsód, n. the capital city.

patáy-gutom, adj. wretched and poor, hungry.

pipit-pusó, n. a species of bird.

pulut-gatá, n. honeymoon.

sampáy-bakod, adj. amateurish, inexperienced.

sawing-palad, adj. without luck, unfortunate.

sinag-talá, n. rays of the star.

sising-alipin, adj. remorseful, full of remorse as in the manner of slaves.

talisuyó, n. one who does the wooing or impression of another on the object of affection.

tiklóp-tuhod, adj. submissive, full of entreaties, humble.

tawang-aso, adj. a mocking or jesting smile.

tigib-dusa, adj. mournful.

ubos-kaya, adj. expensive and luxurious undertakings without sparing the costs.

urong-sulong, adj. hesitating, unsure.

waláng-mayroón, n. a poor man who lives like a rich man.

APPENDIX

Words Written Alike But With Different Meanings
Everyday Common Words For Home School and Office
Astronomical Terms
Geological Terms
Common Terms In the Household
Fishery Terms
Names of Government Offices
Diploma Terms
Physics, Chemistry, Biology And Social Sciences Terms
Terms For Frequency, Distance and Monetary Units
Mathematical Terms

MGA SALITANG MAGKAKATULAD NG BAYBAY NGUNI'T MAGKAKAIBA NG TULDIK, KAHULUGAN, AT BIGKAS:

Words written alike but with different meanings.

aba — pandamdam — Interjection.
aba — poor

ako — I
akò — guarantee

araw — sun
araw — day

baba — chin
baba — go down

bakal — iron
bakal — to plant ice

bakas — financial partnership
bakas — financial prints

baga — lungs
baga — ember

bala — ammunition
bala — threat

balita — news
balita — known (magkaisa ng bigkas)

balot — wrapping
balot — preserved egg.

bao — coconut shell
bao — widow (magkaisa ng bigkas)

bara — measure
bara — obstruction

basa — wet
basa — read

bata — gown
bata — child

bataw — kind of bean
bataw — partial

bilog — circle
bilog — round

bukas — open
bukas — tomorrow

buko — bud
buko — joints

buhay — life
buhay — alive, living

buli — polish
buli — puri

bulo — hairs
bulo — a young carabao

busog — arrow
busog — satisfied

butas — hole
butas — perforated

buto — bone
buto — seed

kasama — companion
kasama — tenant

kati — low tide
kati — itchiness
kati — test of durability of the egg shell

kaya — ability, weal
kaya — for this reason; that is why

kayo — fabric
kayo — you

kiling — inclination
kiling — inclined, tilted

kita — seen, visible
kita — salary, wages (magkaisa ng bigkas)
kita — you and I

kusot — shavings
kusot — crumpled

daing — fish sliced open, salted & dried
daing — supplication

gabi — edible tuber
gabi — night, evening

gala — stroll
gala — wanderer, rover

galang — respect
galang — bracelet

galing — came from
galing — excellence

galit — anger
galit — angry

gamit — use, utility
gamit — used, second hand

gulat — fright, shock
gulat — frightened

gulong — roll about
gulong — wheel

gutom — hunger
gutom — hungry

haba — length
haba — lengthened

hamon — challenge
hamon — hamon

hapon — afternoon
Hapon — Japan

huli — captive
huli — late

labi — remnant
labi — lips

ligaw — suitor
ligaw — stray

pasa — go
pasa — bruises

pato — goose
pato — a kind of game

pito — whistle
pito — seven

pula — red
pula — bad reputation

puno — trunk
puno — full

puti — white
puti — cut off

putol — a piece
putol — cut off

sakit — pain
sakit — suffering

saya — skirt
saya — happiness

subo — mouthful
subo — boiling (as of rice)

suso — breast
suso — snail

tayo — we
tayo — stand

tubo — chimney
tubo — gain

tuloy — transient
tuloy — will be held

uhaw — thirst
uhaw — thirsty

upo — white squash
upo — sit down

KARANIWANG MGA PANGALANG PANG-ARAW-ARAW

Everyday Common Terms

MGA BAHAGI NG KATAWÁN NG TAO	PARTS OF THE HUMAN BODY
Alak-Alakan	Hock
Apdó	Gall
Atáy	Liver
Babá	Chin
Bagá	Lungs
Balát	Skin
Balintatáw	Eyeball
Batok	Nape
Balikat	Shoulder
Balakáng	Hip
Balagat	Clavicle
Baywáng	Waist
Bagáng	Molar
Bibíg	Mouth
Bisig	Arm
Bituka	Intestine
Bintí	Leg
Bukung-bukong	Ankle
Kalamnán ng binti	Calf of the leg
Bukó ng daliri	Joint or knuckle of the fingers
Bungó	Skull, cranium
Bumbunan	Top of the head
Buhók, balahibo	Hair
Butó	Bone
Kanang bisig	Right arm
Kaliwáng bisig	Left arm
Katawán	Body
Kalingkingan	Little finger
Kamáy galang-galangán	Wrist
Kamáy	Hand
Kilay	Eyebrow
Kilikili	Armpit
Kukó	Nail
Daliri	Finger
Daliring panggitnâ	Middle finger

Daliring-sinsingan	Ring finger
Daliri ng paá	Toe
Dilà	Tongue
Dibdíb	Breast, chest
Dugô	Blood
Gilagid	Gum
Gulugód	Spinc, backbone
Gulung-gulungan	Esophagus
Hinlalakí	Thumb
Hintuturò	Forefinger, index finger
Hità	Thigh
Ilóng	Nose
Labi	Lip
Lalamunan	Throat
Lamán	Flesh
Lamad	Membrane
Liíg, Leég	Neck
Likód	Back
Litid	Tendon
Matá	Eye
Mukhâ	Face
Noó	Forehead
Ngalangalá	Palate
Ngipin	Tooth
Ngusò	Upper lip
Paá	Foot
Palad ng kamáy	Palm of the hand
Pantóg	Bladder
Pilikmatá	Eyelash
Pilipisan	Temple
Pisngi	Cheek
Pigi	Buttock; hip
Pulsó	Wrist
Pusón	Abdomen
Puso	Heart
Puwít	Anus
Pusod	Navel
Sakong	Heel
Sikmurà	Stomach
Singit	Groin
Sihang, pangá	Jawbone
Siko	Elbow
Suso	Breast
Talampakan	Sole of the foot
Tadyáng	Rib
Tagiliran	Side
Tainga	Ear
Tiyán	Belly, abdomen

Tuhod	Knee
Ulo	Head
Ugát	Vein
Utak (sa butó)	Marrow
Utak (sa ulo)	Brain

SALITA AT MGA BAGAY-BAGAY NA PANG-ESKUWELA	**SCHOOL TERMS AND ARTICLES**
Akdà, gawâ	Work, literary work
Aklàt	Book
Alagád, ináaralan, tinúturuan	Pupil, disciple
Antás	Grade, degree
Bandilà, watawat	Flag
Bangkô	Bench
Bangháy	Rough drawing
Basket	Basket
Kahón	Box, chest
Karunungan	Science
Kasiningan	Arts
Katinig	Consonant
Klase	Class
Klaseng mababà	Junior class
Klaseng mataás	Senior class
Koléhiyó	College
Kuwadro	Picture-frame
Kuwarto, silíd	Room
Kuwít	Apostrophe, comma
Dibuho	Drawing
Guhit	Stroke, dash, line
Gurò, tagapagturo	Teacher
Historya	History
Labanán, páligsahan	Contest
Lamesa, mesa	Table
Lapis, panulat	Pencil
Larawan, kuwadro	Picture
Liksyón	Lesson
Liham	Letter
Listá, listahán	List
Orasán, relós	Clock, watch
Páaralán, iskuwelahán ...	School
Páaraláng bayan	Public school

Páaraláng mataas	High School
Paaralang-panggitna ...	Intermediate School
Paaraláng pribado	Private school
Palátuntunan	Program
Tinta	Ink
Tintahan	Inkstand
Tisà, yeso	Chalk
Tálaan	Register
Titik	Letter
Upán, uupán	Seat

KALIKASAN AT HEOGRAPYA	**NATURE & GEOGRAPHICAL TERMS**
Alon, daluyong	Wave
Alapaap	Cloud
Ambón	Drizzle
Bahaghari	Rainbow
Buhawì	Hurricane
Bagyó	Typhoon
Busilak o yelo	Snow
Barometro	Barometer
Batis	Fountain
Bukál, labón	Spring
Bató	Stone, rock
Bangkutà	Reef
Bundók	Mountain
Buról, tugatog	Hill
Bulkán	Volcano
Baybáy, dalampasigan ...	Coast, shore
Kalawakan	Continent
Kapuluán	Islands, archipelago
Kaparangan	Woods, forest
Kanál	Canal
Kati ng tubig	Low-water
Klima	Climate
Kidlát	Lightning
Kulóg	Thunder
Karagatan	Ocean
Kapatagan	Plain
Kahuyán	Grove
Dagat	Sea
Dalampasigan	Beach, strand
Dalat, dalatan, lupaín	Land
Dagatan	Gulf
Delta	Delta

Dagitab .... Electricity
Dagundóng ng kulóg .... Thunderclap
Globo .... Globe
Gulod .... Mountain chain
Gubat .... Jungle
Hamóg .... Dew
Hangin .... Air, wind
Hidrogeno .... Hydrogen
Himpapawíd .... Air, clouds
Hulò .... Source
Ilog na pasukán .... Inlet
Ilog na lábasan .... Outlet
Iláng .... Desert, wilderness
Ipu-ipo .... Whirl, whirlwind
Ilat .... Rill
Ilog .... River, stream
Lakí ng tubig .... High-water
Latì .... Swamp
Lawà .... Lake
Lupà .... Ground
Lupà, sanlibután .... Earth
Libís .... Valley
Look .... Bay
Lungos .... Creek
Lindol .... Earthquake
Lintík .... Thunderbolt
Lusong .... Downhill
Mina .... Mine
Minahán .... Mineral deposit
Matabáng lupà .... Fertile soil
Minerál .... Mineral
Mityoro .... Meteor
Mainit .... Hot, warm
Munson .... Monsoons
Malamig .... Cool
Mayuming hangin .... Soft wind
Malakas na hangin ..... Strong wind
Maragsang hangin ...... Impetuous wind
Nitrogeno .... Nitrogen
Oasis .... Oasis
Oksigeno .... Oxygen
Patag .... Level
Pulô .... Island
Puntód .... Sandbank
Páagusan, páanuran .... Channel, drain
Salungâ .... Uphill
Sapà .... Marsh

APOLLO-11 LAUNCH -- The giant Saturn V rocket blasts off the launch pad at Cape Kennedy in Florida July 16 starting Apollo-11 astronauts Neil Armstrong, Michael Collins and Edwin Aldrin on their way to the Moon. PHOTO FROM IPS (69-2751)

Saluysoy	Brook
Simoy	Breeze
Sigwâ	Storm
Tubig	Water
Talón ng tubig	Cascade, waterfall
Taluktók, tagaytáy	Summit, peak, top
Tangwáy, tangos	Point
Tagudtód ng mga bundók .	Ridge of mountains
Temperatura	Temperature
Termometro	Thermometer
Tubig na tabáng	Fresh water
Tubig na alat	Salt water
Tubig na palaki	Floodtide
Tubig na pakati	Ebbtide
Usok	Smoke, steam, vapor
Ulap	Fog, clouds
Ulán	Rain
Wawà	Mouth of the river

MGA SALITA SA ASTRONOMIYA	**ASTRONOMICAL TERMS**
Agwat	Distance
Araw	Sun
Amihan	East wind
Araw at gabi	Day and night
Balabalaing anyô ng buwán	Different phases of the moon
Bagong buwán	New moon
Benus	Venus
Buntala	Planet
Kanluran	Occident, west
Kalendaryo	Calendar
Kabilugan ng buwán	Full moon
Diyametro	Diameter
Disko	Disc
Ekinoksiyo	Equinox
Ekwadór	Equator
Habagat	West wind
Hapon	Afternoon, evening
Hatinggabi	Midnight
Hilagà	North
Hilagang-silangan	Northeast
Hupitér	Jupiter
Langit	Sky, heaven
Lahò, paglalahò	Eclipse
Lahong pangkát	Partial eclipse
Lupà	Earth

Linggo	Sunday
Liwanag	Light, clearness
Madalíng-araw	Dawn
Maghapon	All day
Magdamág	All night
Marte	Mars
Merkuryo	Mercury
Miridyano	Meridian
Minuto	Minute
Orbitá, ang daán ng isang buntalà	Orbit
Oras	Hour
Palaking buwán	Crescent moon
Pagpihit ng lupà	Turning of the earth
Pagkilos sa pagpihit	Movement of rotation
Pagsikat ng araw	Sunrise
Paglubóg ng araw	Sunset
Panahón	Time, weather
Petsa	Date
Sandaigdig	Earth
Sanglinggó, semana (7 araw)	Week
Sanlibután	Universe
Saturno	Saturn
Segundo	Second
Siklo	Cycle
Signo ng sodyako	Sign of the zodiac
Silangan, silanganan	Orient, east
Sinag ng araw	Sun's rays; sunbeam
Soltisyo	Solstice
Sona, mga sona	Zone, zones
Sonang mainit	Torrid zone, hot zone
Sonang malamig	Frigid zone, cold zone
Takipsilim	Dusk
Tag-aráw	Dry season
Tagginàw	Winter
Tag-ulán	Wet season
Talà	Heavenly body
Taludtód	Line
Tanghalì	Noon
Taón	Year
Taóng bisyesto	Leap year
Timog	South
Timog-kanluran	Southwest
Timog-silangan	Southeast
Trópikó	Tropic
Umaga	Morning

Lunes	Monday
Martés	Tuesday
Miyérkolés	Wednesday
Huwebes	Thursday
Biyernes	Friday
Sábado	Saturday
Enero	January
Pebrero	February
Marso	March
Abríl	April
Mayo	May
Hunyo	June
Hulyo	July
Agosto	August
Setyembre	September
Oktubre	October
Nobyembre	November
Disyembre	December

MGA KATAWAGANG PANGHEOLOHIYA
Geological Terms

ENGLISH	PILIPINO
abrade	maagnas; magasgas
abrasive	abrasibo; nakaaagnas; na kagagasgas
accessory mineral	gamit na mineral
acicular	hugis karayom; matulis
acid	ásido; áksido
acidic	mapait
adamantine	diamantino
agate	agata
agglomerate	mamuo
alabaster	alabastro
albite	albatita
albitization	albititasyón
alkali	álkali
alluvial plain	kapatagang banlik
altitude	taas
alumina	alúmina
amorphous	walang hugis
angular unconformity	di-kaayusan sa panulukan
anhydrite	anidrita
anthracite	antrasita
anticline	antiklina

apatite	apatita
arkose	arkos
asbestos	asbestos
asphalt	aspalto
atoll	atalón
augite	augita
aureole	aureola, balantok
barrier reef	sanggang kabatuhang naka-paligid
basalt	basalto
base metals	mga saligáng metál
batholith	batolito
bauxite	bauhita
bedded deposit	susun-susong deposito
bedding	suson o patong
bedrock	palanas
bitumen	betún, bitumen
bitumenous coal	karbon bituminoso
black sand	itim na buhangin
black lava	itim na laba
briccia	briksiya, *briccia*
b.t.u.	b.t.u.
building stone	batóng panggusali
calcite	kalsita
calvarious deposits	mga depositong bunguan
cambrian period	panahong kambriyano
canyon	sabak
carbonation	karbonasiyon
carbonaceous rocks	mga batong karbonoso
carbonization	karbonisasiyon
cenozoic era	panahong senesoiko

PILING MGA TALASALITAAN

SELECTED WORDS

chalk	kreta; tisa
chert	tsert; *chert*
chlorite schist	eskuistong may klorita
cinder	bagay na di nag-aabo; kar-bon; eskoriya
cinder cone	talulo (ng bulkan) na may eskoriya
clastic rocks	mga batong klastiko
clay	luwád, luád
clay minerals	mga mineral na luwad
cleavage	pagkakahati
coal measures	mga sukat sa karbón
corase gained	
cobble	batong bilog; giharo
cohesion	paninikit
columnar basalt	basaltong kama-kama

MOON FLAG -- One of the first assignments of Apollo-11 commander Neil Armstrong on the surface of the Moon will be to plant the United States Flag. The nylon emblem, size .9 by 1.5 meters on a 2.4-meter staff, is strapped to the ladder on the lunar landing vehicle during the flight-out. A spring-loaded wire holds it open.

Photo from IPS (69-2737)

compaction	kasigsigan
competent	matauli; mapagtauli
complex	langkapan; masalimuót
composite vein	busigsig na ugat
conchoidal	kondoideo
concretion	pamumuo; pagkabuo
conformity	kaangkupan; pagkakaangkop
conglomerate	mabuo; mamuo
consequent stream	kasunod na daloy (batis)
contact	
contact metamorphic deposits	
continental shelf	kalunasan ng sanlupalop
contour interval	agwat ng liko
contour line	likong guhit
contour map	mapa ng liko
coquina	kokina; *coquina*
coral limestone	apog na galing sa bulaklak ng bato
coral reef	mga bato't bulaklak ng batong nakapaligid
coral sand	buhanging mabulaklak-bato
coralline	koralina
cordillera	tagaytay
core drilling	ugnay
correlate	umugnay; tumugma; umagpang
correlation	pagkakaugnay; pagkakatugma; pagkakaagpang
corrosion	pagkaagnas
corundum	korindon
country rock	batumbukid
creek	sapa; batis
crest line	guhit sa tuktok
cretaceous period	panahong kretasyo (Kast.)
cross bedding	pakurus na pagkakasapin-sapin
cross section	bahaging hating-krus
crust	(ibabaw-ng-lupa) krast; *crust;*
cryptocrystalline	kortera
crystal	kriptokristalino
crystalline rock	kristal
crystalization	batong kristal
cycle of erosion	pagkikristal
cyclothem	panahunan ng pagkaagnas
dacite	desayt; *dacite*
decay	mabulok; pagkabulok
deformation	pagkasira ng hugis
degradation	pagbaba ng uri o antas

MGA KATAWAGANG PANGHEOLOHIYA

GEOLOGICAL TERMS

delta	delta
dendrite	dendrita
deposition	pagdedeposito; nadedeposito
depression	labák; lubák
desert	disyerto; iláng
devitrification	debitripikasiyon
devonian	deboniyano
diabase	diyabasa
diastem	diyastem; dayastem
diastrophism	diyastropism; *diastrophism*
diatom	diyatomea; liya
diatomaceous earth	lupang madiyatomea
differentiation	pagkakaiba-iba; pag-iba-iba
dike	pilapil; saplad; dike; rampa
dimension stone	batong panukat
diorite	diyorita
dip	dip
dip fault	dip polt; *dip fault*
dip slip	dip islip; *dip slip*
disconformity	di-pagkaangkop; di-pagkaayos; dipagkatugma
disintegrate	pagkakahiwahiwalay; pagkaagnas
dislocation	pagkaligaw ng makapal na kabatuhan
dissected	hatiin; pag-ataro; suriin
disseminated ore deposits	kalat na mga deposito ng inang bato
disturbance	kaguluhan
dolerite	dolerita
dolomite	dolomíta
dome	yungib; kuweba
drag	drag
drainage	desagwe; pagpapatubig
dune	duna
dunnite	dunita
earth movement	galaw ng daigdig
ecolean deposits	mga depositong ecoliko
eclogite	eklodyayt; *eclogita*
ecology	ekolohiya
economic geology	heolohiyang pangkabuhayan
elevation	taas; kataasan; ayos; itsura
embayed coasts	mga baybay—dagat na lunaw
enrichment	pagpapayaman
eocene	eoseno
eolian deposits	mga depositong eoliko
epeírogenetic	

epicenter	gitnang-gitna; episentro
epidote	epidota
epithermal deposits	depositong epitermal
epoch	panahon; époka
epeirogenetic	epeirohenetiko
equiangular	parisulok
era	panahon
erode	maagnas
erosion cycle	panahunan ng pagkaagnas
erosion surface	ibabaw (ng bagay) na naaagnas
eruption	pagsabog; pagputok
evaporites	tarik ng burol
exfoliate	lagasin

PILING MGA TALASALITAAN

SELECTED WORDS

exfoliation	pagkalagas
exposure	pagkahantad; pagkatiwangwang
extrusion	pag-usli
fault	palya (kast. *falla*)
fault-line	palyadong linya
fauna	hayop
feldspar	peldespato
field map	mapang panlarangan
fine-grained	binuti-na-pino
fissure	makipot na butas
fixed carbon	karbonong hindi sumisingaw
flagstone	laha; lantsa
flint	pingkian
floodplain	kapatagang-bahaan
flow banding	
flow structure	
fold	tupi; tiklop
foliation	batimiyento
foraminefera	poramenapera; *foramenafera*
formation	pagbubuo; pagkabuo
fracture	nahihiwalay
fracture zone	hiwalay (bahagi, pook)
fuller's earth	galaktita
gabbro	gabro
garnet	granate
geanticline	heantiklinikal
gem	hiyas
gem stone	batong hiyas
geochemistry	heokimika
geode	heoda
geography	heograpiya

geologic age	panahong heolohiko
geologic column	kolumna heolohiko
geologic formation	pagbubuo (o pagkabuong) heolohiko
geologic horizon	heolohikong guhit-tagpuan
geologic map	mapa ng panheolohiya
geologic section	bahaging heolohiko o pangkat sa heolohiya
geologic thermometer	termometrong heolohiko
geologist	heólogo
geology	heolohiyo
geomorphic cycle	panahunang heomorpiko
geomorphology	heomorpolohiya
geophysical prospecting	paghahanap na heopisiko
geophysics	heopisika
geosyncline	heosinklinal
geothermal	heotermal
geyser	geyser
glass	bubog; salamin
glassy texture	salat-bubog
glauconite	glawkonayt, *glauconite*
gneis	*gneis*
gneissic	*gneisiko*
gossan	gosan, *gossan*
gouge	pait
graben	graben
gradation	bai-baitang
grade	uri; baitang
graded	nauuri; bai-baitang
grain	butil; grano

MGA KATAWAGANG PANGHEOLOHIYA

granite	granito
granite porphyry	porpidong granito
granitic rocks	mga batong granito
granitization	
graphic texture	buhay na buhay na salat
graywacke	grewak, *graywacke*
greenstone	hade
groundmass	kapal-lupa
ground water	tubig-lupa
gypsum	yeso
hanging wall	bubong ng yungib o kuweba
hardness	katigasan; tigas
headward erosion	
heavy minerals	mabibigat na mineral
hematite	hematites
hiatus	maluwang na butas; hayatus *hiatus*

historical geology	heolohiyang pangkasaysayan
hogback	taluktok; batuk-baka
homocline	omoklinal; *homocline*
hornblende	ornablenda
hornfels	hornpels, *hornfels*
hoist	itaas; makinang pantaas
hydration	idrasiyon
hydrolic cycle	panahunang idroliko
hydrology	idrolohiya
hydrosphere	idrospera
hydrothermal alteration	pagbabagong idrotermal
hypersthene	haypersten, *hypersthene*
hypogene	ipohéniko
hypothermal deposits	mga depositong ipotermal
igneous	nagniningas; nagliliyab
ilmenite	ilmenayt; *ilmenite*
inclusion	pag-uuri-uri; pagpapangkat-pangkat; pagsasama-sama
incompetent fold	
index fossil	patnubayan kalansay
intrusive rock	mga kabatuhang ligaw
isostasy	isostasiya, *isostasy*
jasper	haspe
joint	sugpong
joint system	pamaraang sugpungan
jarassic period	panahong hurásiko
kaolin	kaolín
kaolin minerals	mga mineral na kaolín
kaolinization	kaolinisasiyon
key bed	unang sapin
labradorite	labradorita
lampophyre	batong-sala; batunsala
lapille	
laterite	laterita
lava	laba
law of superposition	batas ng pagkakapatung-patong o pagkakasuson-suson
layer	suson; patong
lignite	lignito
limestone	batong-apog
lineation	lineasiyon
litteral	kalát o tibág
lode	(minahang) dulangan
mafic	mapik, *mafic*

GEOLOGICAL TERMS

magnetite	magentita

mantle rock	
marble	marmol
massive	mabigat
medium-grained	mala-binutil
mesothermal	katamtamang init
mesozoic era	panahong mesosoiko
metallic metal	metalikong metál
metallic lustre	kaningningingang metalikò
metamorphic rock	batong metamórpiko
metamorphism	metamorpismo
metasediments	mga tila latak
metavolcanics	metabulkan; *metavolcanics*
meteorites	meteoritó
mica	mika
mica schists	mikasita
microlite	mikrolito
mineral deposit	mga depositong mineral
mineral water	tubig na mineral
mineralization	mineralisasiyon
mineralogy	mineralohiya
miocene epoch	panahong miyoseno
mississipian period	panahong *Mississipian*
montmorillonite	
monzonite	monsonayt, *monzonite*
mother lode	inang (minahang) dulangan
mountain range	tagaytay
muck	taong-hayop
mud cracks	mga maliliit na butas sa putik
muscovite	muskobita
norite	norayt, *norite*
obsidian	obsidiyana
oilfield	langisan
oil shale	batong-langis
olivine	olibino
olitic	olitiko
order of crystallization	ayos ng kristalisasiyon
ordovician period	panahong ordobisiyan o *ordovician*
ore	inang-bato
ore body	katawan ng inang-bato
ore deposits	mga depositong inang-bato
ore minerals	mga inang-batong minerál
ore shoots	mga sanga ng inang-bato
orthoclase	ortoklasa
outcrop	aploramiyento
oxbow lake	lawang hugis-U
oxidation	oksidasiyon
paleontology	paleontolohiya
paleozoic	paleoscko
parting	hati ng suson o patong
peat	turba

pegmatite	pegmatita
peneplain	kalunasang lupa
pennsylvanian	pensilbano
peridotite	peridotita
perlite	perlita
permeability	pagkamalusutin
pernian period	panahong perniyan o *pern ian*
petrifaction	petripaksiyon; pagsasakalan say
petrify	magsakalansay; magıng ka lansay

MGA KATAWAGANG PANGHEOLOHIYA

petrofabric analysis	pagsusuri sa himaymay-bato
petrography	petrograpiya
petroleum	petroleo
petroleum geology	heolohiyang pampetroleo
petrology	petrolohiya
phanerites	mga minang nasa ibabaw ng lupa
phosphate rock	batong pospato
photogrammetry	potogrametriya; *photogrum metry*
phyllite	pilayt, *phyllite*
physical geology	heolohiyang pisiko
pillow lava	
pitchstone	bubog-bulkan
placer	(minahang) tibág
plagioclase	plahiyoklasa
plasticity	kalabuhán
plateau	talampas
platy structure	kayariang lapád
playa	playa
pleistocene	pleistoseno
pliocene	pliyoseno
porosity	pagkamabutas; porosidad
porphery	porpido
prospecting	paghahanap, panunuklas
pumice	pumita
pyrite	pirita
pyritization	piritisasiyon
pyroxine	piroksen
quarry	tibagan
quarrying	pagtitibag
quartz	kuarso
quartz monzonite	kuarsong monsonayt
quartzite	kuarsita
quicksand	kuminoy

reconnaisance phism	paggalugad
recrystallization	rekristalisasiyon
reef	tagaytay-bato sa tubig
regional metamorphism	metamorpismong pampurok
relief	kalatagan
repetition of beds	pagkakasulit ng mga suson
replacement deposits	mga kahaliling deposito
residual	tirá
rhyolite	royolayt, *rhyolite*
river piracy	
rock salt	asing-bato, asinbato
rock forming mineral	mineral na nagiging sanhi ng pagiging bato
regional metamorphism	
saddle	aluyan o duyan
saline deposits	mga depositong maasin
salt dome	yungib ng asin
saltation	pag-aasin
sand dune	dunang buhangin
sand stone	buhanginbato
schist	eskuisto
schistesity	
schistose	eskuistoso
scoria	escoriya
sedimentation	paglalatak
seismic	sanhing - lindol
serpentine	serpentina
serpentinization	serpentinasasiyon
shale	eskuisto

PILING MGA TALASALITAAN

SELECTED WORDS

shiled volcano	
silica	silise, silika, *silica*
silicates	silikato
silification	
sill	
silurian period	panahong siluriyano
skarh	
slaking	pagkahalo sa tubig
slate	munting pisara
slaty	pisarenyo
slickenside	
slump	maruming pook
soda	soda
sorting	pag-uuri-uri; pagpapang kat-pangkat
spheroidal	mabilog
spherulite	munting bilog
stockwork	
stalactite	estalaktita

stalagmite	estalagmita
stratification	estratipikasiyon
stratigraphy	estratigrapiya
stress minerals	
strike	tunguhin ng suson (o patong)
structural geology	heolohiyang pangkayarian
structural relief	kalatagang pangkayarian
structure contour	hugis ng kayarian
subsurface map	mapa ng ilalim ng kalatapan
supergene	
survey	paggalugad.
swamp	latian
syncline	sinklinal
syngentic	
tabular ore body	katawang lapad ng inang-bato
talus	guho
tektite	
tenor	
terrace	
terrain	malawak na lupain
tertiary period	panahong tersiyoriyo
texture	salát
tin section	pangkat ng lata
time scale	panukatan ng panahon
time strategraphic unit	
topaz	topasiyo
topographic map	mapang topograpika
topography	topograpiya
sopsoil	lupang pang-ibabaw
tourmaline	turmalina
trap	basalto
travertine	trabertino
tremolite	puting ornablenda
triassic period	panahong triyasikon
trilobite	trilobites
tripoli	tripol
tuff	
ultrabasic	
unconformity	di-kaangkupan; di-kaayusan
vadose	

MGA KATAWAGANG PANGHEOLOHIYA

varves	
vein	ugat; sanga
vein deposits	mga sangang deposito
vein quartz	sangang kuarso
vein system	sanga-sanga
vesicular	besikular
vitreous	(sa o ng) bubog
vitrification	pagbububog

volcanic	(sa o ng) bulkán
volcanic ash	abo ng bulkan
volcanism	bulkanismo
volcanology	bulkanolohiya
vuggy	
water-bearing formation	pagkábuong nagtataglay ng tubig
water course	agos ng tubig
water table	balong
wall log	
wind abrasion	pagkaagnas sa hangin
wollastonite rock	batóng *wollastonite*
zeolite	
zeolitization	
zircon	sirkón
zone of deposition	pook ng mga deposito
zone of erosion	pook ng pagkaagnas
zone of fracture	pook ng nahihiwalay (na mina)
zone weathering	pook ng pagkabasa, pagka tuyo, atb.
zone of saturation	pook ng pagkababad
quartz	kuarso
siliceous clay	silisiyong luad
volcanic dust	alikabok ng bulkán
millstones	gilingan
grindstones	hasaan
asbestos	asbestos
barites	baritina
cement materials	mga kagamitan sa semento
clay luod	luad
foundry clay	luad sa pagmomolde (ng bakal)
bleaching clay	luad sa pagkukula
glass sands	buhanging bubog
gypsum	yeso
lime	apog
magnesite	magnesita
mineral pigment	kulay ng mineral
nature bitumens	mga katutubong bitún
potash	potasa
salt	asin
sulphur	asupre
calcined shells	
trondojomite	
greenstone	hade
dacite	daysayt, *dacite*
dunnite	dunita
gold	ginto
silver	pilak
platinum	platino
copper	tanso
lead	tingga

zinc	sink
iron	yero
magnetite	magnetita

MGA KATAGANG PAMAHAYAN

MGA SALITA SA PANANAMIT AT MGA HIYAS	TERMS FOR CLOTHING & JEWELRY
Alampáy	Shoulder kerchief
Aspilé	Pin
Barò	Shirt, camisa (Sp.) clothes
Barong tagalog	Filipino national costume
Birang, panyô	Kerchief
Balabal	Cloak, mantle, cover
Bakyâ	Wooden shoes
Bitones	Button
Bahág	G-string
Kamiseta	Undershirt
Kayo, damít	Fabric
Kamisola	Dress
Kamisón	Chemise
Kurbata	Necktie, cravat
Kuwintas	Beads, necklace
Kalsitín	Small stocking
Damit, pananamít, kasuután	Dress, clothes, garment
Galáng	Bracelet
Guwantes	Glove
Hikaw	Earring
Laso, talì	Knot, ribbon
Lambóng	Veil, mantle
Medyas	Stockings
Panyô, panyulito	Handkerchief
Panyulón	A long square shawl
Pamaypáy	Fan
Payong	Umbrella
Pamigkís	Girdle
Relós	Watch
Salawál	Inside pants
Saya; patadyóng	Skirt
Sintás	Ribbon
Sinturón	Belt
Sapatos	Shoes
Sinelas, tsinelas	Slippers
Sukláy	Comb

Suyod	A close comb for taking out lice
Singsíng	ring, finger-ring
Tungkód, bastón	Walking stick, cane
Tapis	Outside cover or apron

MGA SALITÁ UKOL SA PAGKAIN	**FOOD TERMS**
Adobo	Fried meat or pork seasoned with vinegar and garlic
Agahan, almusál	Breakfast
Asukal, asukar	Sugar
Alak	Wine
Asado	Roast meat
Asin	Salt
Bigás	Rice
Biskotso, biskuwit	Biscuit
Baboy (karné ng baboy) .	Pork
Bungangkahoy	Fruit
Balunbalunan	Gizzard
Bagoóng	Fish or small shrimps in brine
Bistéк	Beefsteak
Kanin	Cooked rice
Karné	Meat
Karnéng inihaw	Roast meat
Karneng pinirito	Fried meat
Karnéng inihaw sa parilya	Broiled meat
Karnéng ginisá	Hashed meat
Karné ng baka	Beef
Karné ng tupa	Mutton
Karné ng bulô	Veal
Karné ng usá	Venison
Keso	Cheese
Karamelo	sugar-candy, caramel
Kustilyas, tadyáng ng baboy	Pork-chop
Dumalaga (Manok)	Pullet, chicken
Gatas	Milk
Gulay	Vegetable
Ginatán	A kind of liquid food with coconut milk and sugar
Galapóng	Rice flour
Harina	Flour
Hamón	Ham
Himagas	Dessert

Hapunan	Supper
Iskabetse	Pickled fish
Itlóg, mga itlóg	Egg, eggs
Isdâ	Fish
Istupadong karné	Stewed meat
Linagang manók	Boiled chicken with vegetables
Linugaw	Gruel, or the liquid cooked rice
Litsón	Roasted pig
Linagang karné	Boiled meat with vegetables
Manók (inahín)	Hen
Matamís	Sweets
Mirindál	Merienda
Mantiká	Lard; butter
Mantikilya	Butter, margarine
Mumo	Scrap morsel
Pagkain	Food, meal
Pag-inóm	Drinking
Pamutat	Vegetables, leaves or fruits that are eaten with viands
Pata	Hock, foot
Patís	A kind of brine
Pispis	Scrap;
Pulót	Honey
Prito	Fried meat or fish
Pritada	Fried pork, meat or fish seasoned with garlic, tomatoes and onions.
Pesà, pinesà	Boiled fish, chicken or hen, the broth of which is seasoned with a bit of ginger and some spices.
Pinangát	Boiled fish with a little salt and tomatoes.
Pospas	A kind of gruel with hen or chicken.
Paksíw, pinaksíw	A kind of boiled fish or pork, the broth of which is seasoned with vinegar and other spices.
Sabáw	Broth
Sukà	Vinegar
Sinigáng	Boiled fish or meat, the

broth of which is seasoned with the juice of tamarind fruit or some other sour fruit, onions, tomatoes, and a little salt.

Saging .... Banana

Surbetes .... Ice Cream

Suwám .... Pesà seasoned with lard

Sinaing .... Cooked rice

Sopas .... Soup

Tsokulate .... Chocolate

Tinapay .... Bread

Tubig .... Water

Tusino, inasnáng baboy Salted pork, bacon

Tadtarín .... Minced meat

Tinola .... Boiled hen or chicken with upo, dressed with lard, garlic, ginger and some other spices.

Torta .... A round cake made of various ingredients.

Tortilya .... Fried potatoes and scrambled eggs.

Tortilyang itlóg ...... Omelet

Tanghalian .... Lunch

Ulam .... Viand

MGA BAGAY-BAGAY NA PAMBAHAY AT PANGKUSINA — HOUSE & KITCHEN THINGS

Almirés .... Mortar

Alulód .... Spout

Aklatan .... Library

Aranya .... Chandelier

Apuyan .... Lime-kiln

Araro .... Plow

Asaról, asada .... Hoe, mattock, spade

Bahay .... House

Batalán .... Washing place of a home

Baytáng .... Step (of a staircase).
Bubungán .... Roof
Balisbisan .... Eaves
Baníg .... Mat
Bangâ .... Jar
Batyâ .... Wash basin
Bayóng .... Sack, bag
Basket .... Basket
Bakol .... Square basket
Bílao .... Round basket
Buslô .... Egg-basket
Bareta, lingkáw .... Small bar
Bistáy .... Sieve, cribble
Kusinà .... Kitchen
Kasangkapan .... Furniture
Komodá .... A clothes-press; bureau
Katre .... Bedstead
Kulambô .... Mosquito net
Kumot .... Blanket
Kubóng, kulubóng ...... Veil, mantle
Kalán .... Stove
Kasangkapan .... Tool
Kabán, baúl .... Trunk
Kopa .... Cup
Kubyertos .... Table-service
Kutsara .... Spoon
Kutsilyo .... Knife
Kahoy .... Wood
Karo .... Car
Karosa, karwahe, kotse .. Carriage
Karumata .... Carromata (Sp.)
Karitón, karitela .... Cart
Kawalì .... Frying-pan
Kainán .... Dining-room
Kandilà .... Candle
Karayom .... Needle
Katám .... Plane
Kikil .... File (a kind of tool)
Dùrungawán .... Window
Dingding .... Wall
Duyan .... Hammock
Dapóg .... Hearth
Dulang .... Table
Dinulang .... Dish

Dambana, altàr	Altar
Didál	Thimble
Gunting	Scissors
Gusalì	Building
Gusì	A china jar, a chamber-pot
Gatang	Chupa
Gilingán	Grinder
Grado ng bahay	Story
Gulóng	Wheel
Haligi	Post; pillar; column
Hagdanan	Staircase, stairs
Hihigán	Bed
Hurnó	Oven
Hilamusán	Basin
Hawlá	Cage
Ilaw	Light
Istante	Shelf, bookshelf
Ibabâ ng bahay	Downstairs
Itaás ng bahay	Upstairs
Ihawán	Gridiron, broiler
Larawan	Picture, image, effigy
Lámpará	Lamp
Langís	Oil
Lubid	Rope
Lagarì	Saw
Lumbó	A kind of dipper
Mantél	Tablecloth
Mangkók	Bowl
Pinggán	Plate
Pintô	Door, gate
Padér	Wall
Palasyo	Palace
Palababahan	Ballustrade
Palayók	Pot
Plato	Plate
Palakól	Axe, hatchet
Palihán	Anvil
Panghikwát	Lever
Pangalawit	Hook
Pambutas	Borer
Plantsa, pirinsá	Iron
Pundá ng unan	Pillowcase
Pisi, leteng	Small rope, string
Panambil, tambíl	Awning
Pangnán	A small fish-basket
Pang-ahit	Razor, clasp-knife
Pánabihán, pálikuran	Water-closet, privy-house
Sasakyáng may gulóng ..	Vehicle

Sahig, lapagan	Floor
Sampayan	Perch, hanger
Suhay, tukod	Prop
Saro	A small jar
Sandók	Ladle
Sipit	Tongs; pincers
Suklób	Pot lid
Salóp	Ganta
Salas	Hall, parlor
Salang marmól	Marble hall
Salamín	Looking-glass
Salamín sa matá	Spectacles, eye glasses
Sepilyo sa ngipin	Toothbrush
Sinulid	Thread
Sutlâ	Silk
Sabón	Soap
Susì	Key
Silong	Ground-floor; downstairs
Talaró, timbangan	Balance, a pair of scales, scale
Tabò	A kind of tumbler made of coco-shell
Tubo	Tube
Tabing	Curtain; veil
Tanikalâ	Chain; fetters
Timbâ	Pail
Tapayan	A large jar
Tinidór	Fork
Tarì	Cock-knife
Unan	Pillow

MGA KATAWAGAN SA PANGINGISDA

(Fishery Terms

ENGLISH	PILIPINO
agar-agar	**gulaman**
algae	**lumot**
bag net	**basnig**
barricade	**pangharang, habing, bating hibasan**
brackish water	**tubig-alat, magkahalong tubig-alat at tubig-tabang**
brook	**sapa; batis**
blanket net	**paduyan**
cast net	**dala**

coastal — baybayin
cover net — panaklob, sukob
cover pot — salakáb, sima
crab lift net — bintól
creek — munting ilog, sapa, batis
Danish trawl — taksáy-Dinamarka
deep sea — dagat, karagatan
dip net — panadiyók
drag seine or long haul — salap o sinsoro
drift net — pantí, paanod
drive-in-net — kulokutok
filter net — dayakus, rayukus, diyakos
fingerling — hátiran
fish corral — baklád
fish fry — kawág-kawág, anák isdâ
fish planting — pagpapabinhî (ng isdâ)
fish pond — palaisdaan
fish pot — bubo (ng isdâ)
fish preservation — pangangalagà ng isdâ, pagiimbák ng isdâ
fish shelter — bumbón, talaksán (ng isdâ
fish stocking — pag-aalagà (ng isdâ)
fish transplanting — paglilipat ng isdâ
fish trap — paluob, panloób
floating fish shelter — pugad-pugad
fresh water — tubig-tabáng, dagat tabáng
fry ground — pabinhian
fyke net — panalang-dagat, alawâ
gill net — paningahan
goby pot — bubo (ng biyâ)
handlines — kawil, paluway (isahang tagâ)
harpoon — panibát, salapáng
hook — panikwát, suligì; tagâ
inshore — tabing dagát
hoop net — bukatót, bikatót
jigger — galay
lake — lawà
lever net — salambáw
long line — kitáng
marshes — latian
multiple handline — kawil (maramihang tagâ)
net — lambát
nursery pond — álagaán o palakihang lawà

PILING MGA TALASALITAAN

SELECTED WORDS

offshore	laót
pole and line	bingwit o biwas
pond	lawà
pool	sapà
purse seine	kubkob
push net	sakág (maging sa hipon o isdâ)
rake and dredges	pangahig, kalaykáy, kaladkád
reef seine	ligkáp
rice paddies	pitak ng palay, pinitak
ring net	talakop
river	ilog
river fish corral	paluksó
round haul seine	sapyáw
scoop	panalok, salap, salok
scoop seine	gayad
sea water	tubig alat, dagat alat
seeding	pagpapabinhi (ng isdâ)
seine	pukot (maliit)
shallow water corral	siid
shrimp lift basket	talabóg
shrimp pot	bubo (ng hipon)
shrimp shelter	bumbón (ng hipon)
skimming net	anud-sulóng
snare	panilo, bitag, patibóng
spawn	salapáng, sibát
spear	pangingitlóg ng isdâ
stop seine	salapáng, sibát
stream	pangulóng
trammel net	batis, ilog
trap net	trasmalyo
trawl	bakládna lambát
troll line	taksáy
tuck seine	sibid-sibid o pahila
	pukot laot, pukot na malaki

MGA KATAGANG GAMIT SA PAMAMAHAYAN

Local Terms Used in Home

—A—

agahan — breakfast
alampay — shawl
almires — mortar
aliwin — comfort
alugin — shake
anit — scalp
aranya — chandeñer
asin — salt
asukal — sugar

—B—

balabal — shawl
balak — plan, project

balakubak — dandruff
balangkas — structure
balumbalunan — gizzard
bandeha, bandehado—tray
bañgan — jar
baro — garment
basura — garbage, trash
batalan —a place for washing in the home
batihin — beat
bayo — pound
blusa — blouse
burara — sloppy, untidy
buwig — bunch

—K—

kaakit-akit — attractive
kaban, baul — chest
kabuyaw — wild orange
kakaiba — unique
kagamitan — equipment
kalan — stove
kamiseta — undershirt
kamison — slip, chemise
karamelo — caramel, hardened sugar
karayom — needle
kawali — frying pan
kinchay — celery
kisame — ceiling
kubyertos — silverware
kulay — color
kuskusin — scrub
kustilyas — pork chop
kutis — complexion
kuwelyo — collar
kuwintas — necklace

—D—

dambana — altar
damit — garment, clothes
dibuho — design
di-karaniwan — unique
didal — thimble
dikdikin — mince, pound
dinding — wall
dumalaga — pullet
durungawan, bintana window
duyan — hammock, cradle

—G—

galapong — rice flour, ground rice
gampanan — perform
gana — appetite
gantsilyo — crochet
gatang — chupa
gilingin — grind
gripo — faucet

—H—

hasang — gills
hilaw — raw
hilbana — basting
himagas — dessert
hugasan — lavatory
huwaran — pattern

—I—

ilaw — light
istante — shelf

—L—

lakas — energy
laksante, purga — **laxative**
laso — ribbon
laylayan — hem
linugaw — rice gruel
lintos — blister
lipak — corn

—M—

makina — machine
magkula — bleach
malansa — fishy
masustansiya — nutritious
matibay — durable
maysakit — patient
miki — noodles
miso — paste made of fermented soy beans
miswa — fine noodles
mumo — crumbs, food

especially rice, dropped on the table
mura — inexpensive
mustasa — mustard

—N—

nakahahawa — communicable
nalalabhan — washable
narumhan — soiled

—P—

pakikipagtulungan, pakikisama — cooperation
pagbababad — soaking
pagbabanli — scalding
pagbabayo — pounding
pagkakabagay-bagay — harmony
pagkayod, pagkaskas — scrape
paggigisa — sauteing
paghihimay — stringing, shelling
paghiwa — to slice
pagpiga — to squeeze
pagpipilas-pilas — shredding
pagsala — strain
pagtitipid — economy
palda — skirt
paltos — blister
pamimili — shopping
pampagana — appetizer
pantulog — nightgown, sleepwear
parusa — punishment
pawis — perspiration
pinakuluan — sterilized
pispis — crumbs
pospas — rice gruel with chicken
pulot — honey

—S—

saya — skirt
singkamas — turnips
sulsi — darn
sukatan, panukat — gauge

—T—

talatakdaan — schedule
tagpi — patch
tela — cloth
timpla — flavor
tortilya — omelet
tosino — bacon
tustahin — toast

—U—

umikli, umurong — shrink
ulang — lobster

—Y—

yantok, uway — rattan

MGA NGALAN NG TANGGAPAN NG GOBYERNO

SOLAR WIND EXPERIMENT -- Apollo-11 astronaut Edwin Aldrin deploys the Solar Wind Composition Experiment on the surface of the Moon. The experiment was folded up at the end of the visit and returned to Earth. At right is the lunar landing vehicle. Neil Armstrong took this photograph. The two spacemen made their historic visit on July 20-21. Photo from IPS (69-3089)

ENGLISH	PILIPINO
Agricultural Credit Administration	Pangasiwaan ng Pagpapautang sa Pagsasaka
Civil Aeronautics Administration	Pangasiwaan ng Aeronautika Sibil
Claims, Adjudication and Disposal Administration	Pangasiwaan ng Paghahabol, Paglilitis at Pagpapasiya
Electrification Administration	Pangasiwaan ng Elektripikasyon
Land Reform Project Administration	Pangasiwaan ng Proyektong Reporma sa Lupa
National Irrigation Administration	Pambansang Pangasiwaan ng Patubig
National Land Reform Administration	Pambansang Pangasiwaan ng Reporma sa Lupa
Land Tenure Administration	Pangasiwaan ng Panghahawakang Lupa
National Civil Defense Administration	Pangasiwaan ng Pambansang Tanggulang Sibil
National Resettlement & Rehabilitation Administration	Pambansang Pangasiwaan ng Paglilipat-Tahanan at Rehabilitasyon
Philippine Coconut Administration	Pangasiwaan ng Niyog ng Pilipinas
Philippine Tobacco Administration	Pangasiwaan ng Tabako ng Pilipinas
Philippine Virginia Tobacco Administration	Pangasiwaan ng Tabakong Virginia ng Pilipinas
Reforestation Administration	Pangasiwaan ng Muling Pagpapagubat
Rice and Corn Administration	Pangasiwaan sa Bigas at Mais
Social Welfare Administration	Pangasiwaan ng Kagalingang Panlipunan
Sugar Quota Administration	Pangasiwaan ng Kota sa Asukal
Food and Drug Administration	Pangasiwaan ng Pagkain at Gamot
Custody and Disposal Administration	Pangasiwaan sa Pag-iingat at Pagpapasiya
Land Authority	Pangasiwaan sa Lupa

Mindanao Development Authority	**Pangasiwaan ng Pagpapaunlad ng Mindánao**
National Cottage Industries Development Authority	**Pambansang Pangasiwaan ng Pagpapaunlad ng mga Industriyang Pantahanan**
National Waterworks and Sewerage Authority	**Pambansang Pangasiwaan ng Tubig at Alkantarilya**
Abaca Development Board	**Lupon ng Pagpapaunlad ng Abaka**
Anti-Dummy Board	**Lupon Laban sa Pantalya**
Board of Censors for Motion Pictures	**Lupon ng mga Sensor sa Pelikula**
Civil Aeronautics Board	**Lupon ng Aeronautika Sibil**
Civil Service Board of Appeals	**Lupon ng Paghahabol sa Serbisyo Sibil**
Deportation Board	**Lupon sa Deportasyon**
Embroidery and Apparel Control and Inspection Board	**Lupon ng Pangangasiwa at Pagsusuri ng Burda at Damit**
Fair Trade Board	**Lupon ng Maayos na Komersiyo**
Games and Amusement Board	**Lupon ng mga Laro at Libangan**
Gold Mining Industry Assistance Board	**Lupon ng Tulong sa Industriya ng Mina ng Ginto**
National Advisory Board on Health	**Pambansang Lupong Tagapayo sa Kalusugan**
Board of Industries	**Lupon ng mga Industriya**
Board of Liquidators	**Lupon ng mga Likidador**
Board of National Education	**Lupon ng Pambansang Edukasyon**
Board of National Pantheon	**Lupon ng Pambansang Libingan**
National Science Development Board	**Pambansang Lupon sa Pagpapaunlad ng Agham**
Board of Pardons and Parole	**Lupon ng Patawad at Parol**
Board on Pensions for Veterans	**Lupon sa Pensiyon ng mga Beterano**
Producers Incentives Board	**Lupon ng Pagganyak sa mga Produktor**
Rice and Corn Board	**Lupon sa Bigas at Mais**
Board of Technical Surveys and Maps	**Lupon ng mga Teknikong Pagsukat at Mapa**

Board of Travel and Tourist Industry	**Lupon ng Industriya sa Paglalakbay at Turista**
Philippine Veterans Board	**Lugon ng mga Beterano ng Pilipinas**
Bureau of Agricultural Economics	**Kawanihan ng Ekonomiya sa Pagsasaka**
Bureau of Animal Industry	**Kawanihan ng Paghahayupan**
Bureau of Buildings and Real Property Management	**Kawanihan ng Pamamahala ng mga Gusali at Ari-ariang Real**
Bureau of Census and Statistics	**Kawanihan ng Senso at Estadistika**
Bureau of Coast and Geodetic Survey	**Kawanihan ng Pagsukat Baybayin at Heodesiko**
Bureau of Commerce	**Kawanihan ng Komersiyo**
Bureau of Customs	**Kawanihan ng Aduwana**
Bureau of Dental Health Services	**Kawanihan ng Lingkuran sa Kalusugan ng Ngipin**
Bureau of Disease Control	**Kawanihan ng Pagsugpo sa Sakit**
Bureau of Fiber Inspection Service	**Kawanihan ng Lingkuran sa Pagsusuri ng Himay-may**
Bureau of Forestry	**Kawanihan ng Paggugubat**
Bureau of Health Services	**Kawanihan ng Lingkurang Pangkalusugan**
Bureau of Immigration	**Kawanihan ng Pandarayuhan**
Bureau of Internal Revenue	**Kawanihan ng Rentas Internas**
National Bureau of Investigation	**Pambansang Kawanihan sa Pagsisiyasat**
Bureau of Labor Relations	**Kawanihan ng Pagsasamahan sa Paggawa**
Bureau of Labor Standards	**Kawanihan ng Pamantayan sa Paggawa**
Bureau of Lands	**Kawanihan ng mga Lupain**
Bureau of Medical Services	**Kawanihan ng Lingkuran sa Panggagamot**
Bureau of Mines	**Kawanihan ng mga Minahan**
Bureau of Plant Industry	**Kawanihan ng Paghahalaman**
Bureau of Posts	**Kawanihan ng Koreo**

Bureau of Prisons	**Kawanihan ng mga Bilangguan**
Bureau of Private Schools	**Kawanihan ng mga Paaralang Pribado**
Bureau of Public Highways	**Kawanihan ng Lansangang Bayan**
Bureau of Public Schools	**Kawanihan ng mga Paaralang Bayan**
Bureau of Public Works	**Kawanihan ng mga Pagawaing Bayan**
Bureau of Quarantine	**Kawanihan ng Kuwarentenas**
Bureau of Records Management	**Kawanihan ng Pamamahala ng mga Kasulatan**
Bureau of Research and Laboratories	**Kawanihan ng Pananaliksik at mga Laboratoryo**
Bureau of Standards	**Kawanihan ng mga Pamantayan**
Bureau of Soils	**Kawanihan ng Lupa**
Bureau of Supply Coordination	**Kawanihan ng Ugnayan sa Panustos**
Bureau of Telecommunications	**Kawanihan ng Telekomunikasyon**
Bureau of Treasury	**Kawanihan ng Ingatangyaman**
Bureau of Vocational Education	**Kawanihan ng Edukasyong Bokasyonal**
Weather Bureau	**Kawanihan ng Panahon**
Bureau of Women and Minors	**Kawanihan ng mga Babae at Menor**
Bureau of Workmen's Compensation	**Kawanihan ng Bigaypala sa mga Manggagawa**
Anti-Smuggling Action Center	**Sentro ng Kilusan Laban sa Kontrabando**
Disease Intelligence Center	**Sentro ng Kabatiran sa Sakit**
Food and Nutrition Research Center	**Panaliksikan ng Pagkain at Nutrisyon**
National Coordinating Center for the Study & Development of Filipino Children and Youth	**Pambansang Sentrong Ugnayan sa Pag-aaral at Pagpapaunlad ng mga Bata't Kabataang Pilipino**

MGA TANGGAPAN NG GOBYERNO

National Media Production Center	**Pambansang Sentro sa Kabatirang Madla at Paglalathala**
Philippine Atomic Research Center	**Sentro ng Pananaliksik Atomika ng Pilipinas**
Agricultural Productivity Commission	**Komisyon ng Pagpapasagana ng Ani sa Pagsasaka**
Agricultural Tenancy Commission	**Komisyon ng Pagsasamahang Pansakahan**
Commission on Appointments	**Komisyon sa mga Paghirang**
Asian Good Neighbor Relations Commission	**Komisyon ng Mabuting Pagsasamahan ng mga Bansang Asyano**

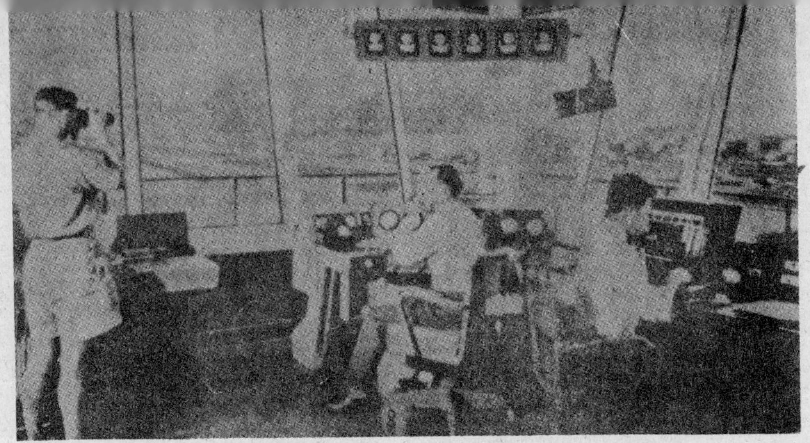

Philippine Atomic Energy Commission	**Komisyon ng Lakas Atomika ng Pilipinas**
Budget Commission	**Komisyon ng Badyet**
Civil Service Commission	**Komisyon ng Serbisyo Sibil**
Code Commission	**Komisyon sa Kodigo**
Commission on Elections	**Komisyon sa Halalan**
Home Financing Commission	**Komisyon ng Pamumuhunang Pantahanan**
Joint Legislative-Executive Tax Commission	**Magkasanib na Komisyong Tagapagbatas-Tagapagpaganap sa Buwis**
Land Registration Commission	**Komisyon ng Patalaan ng Lupain**
Land Transportation Commission	**Komisyon ng Transportasyong-Lupa (Komisyon ng Sasakyang-dalatan)**
National Heroes Commission	**Komisyon ng mga Pambansang Bayani**
National Historical Commission	**Pambansang Komisyong Pangkasaysayan**
Commission on National Integration	**Komisyon sa Pambansang Integrasyon**
National Planning Commission	**Komisyon ng Pambansang Pagpaplano**
Police Commission	**Komisyon ng Pulisya**
National Shrines Commission	**Komisyon ng mga Pambansang Dambana**
Philippine Fisheries Commission	**Komisyon ng Pangingisda ng Pilipinas**

National Water and Air Pollution Commission	**Pambansang Komisyon ng Pagsugpo sa Pagkalalin ng Tubig at Hangin**
Peace and Amelioration Fund Commission	**Komisyon ng Pondong Pangkapayapaan at Pagpapabuting-kalagayan**
Public Service Commission	**Komisyon ng Lingkurang Bayan**
Reparations Commission	**Komisyon ng Reparasyon**
Securities and Exchange Commission	**Komisyon ng mga Panagot at Palitan**
Tariff Commission	**Komisyon ng Taripa**
Tenancy Mediation Commission	**Komisyong Tagapamagitan sa Panakahan**
UNESCO National Commission of the Philippines	**Pambansang Komisyon ng UNESCO sa Pilipinas**
Veterans Claims Commission	**Komisyon ng Paghahabol ng mga Beterano**
Commission on Volcanology	**Komisyon sa Bulkanolohiya**
Workmen's Compensation Commission	**Komisyon ng Bigaypala sa mga Manggagawa**
Committee on Anti-Filipino Activities	**Komite sa mga Gawaing Laban sa Pilipino**
Export Control Committee	**Komite ng Kontrol sa Pagluluwas**
Philippine Heraldry Committee	**Komite sa mga Panandang Sagisag ng Pilipinas**
Philippine Historical Committee	**Komiteng Pangkasaysayan ng Pilipinas**
Presidential Committee on Executive Performance	**Komite ng Pangulo sa Panuparang Tagapagpaganap**
Presidential Committee on Relief and Rehabilitation	**Komite ng Pangulo sa Tulong at Panauli sa Mabuting Katayuan**
Regional Land Reform Committee	**Komiteng Pampurok sa Reporma sa Lupa**
Committee on Schoolhouse Program	**Komite sa Palatuntunan sa Gusaling-Paaralan**
National Parks Development Committee	**Komite sa Pagpapaunlad ng mga Pambansang Parke**
National Development Company	**Kompanya ng Pambansang Pagpapaunlad**

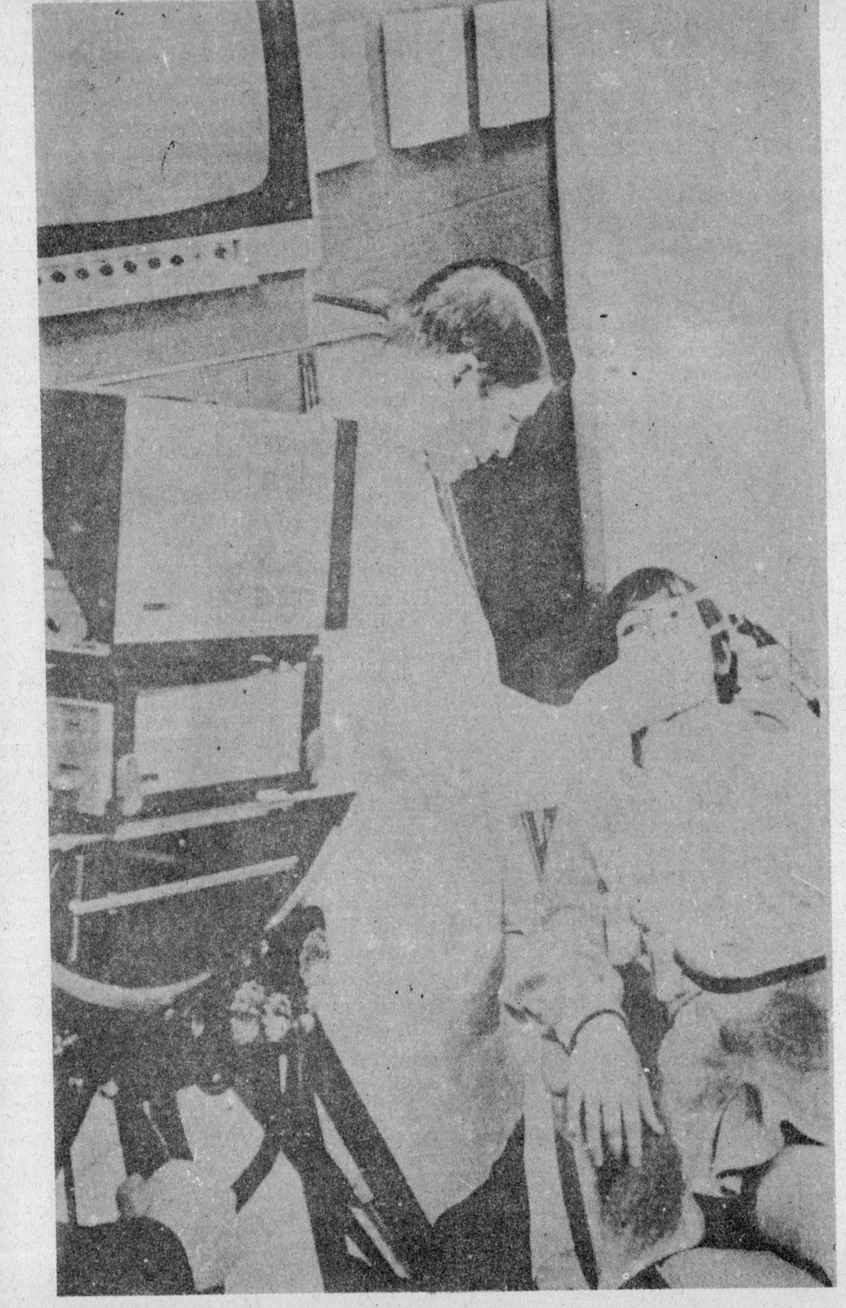

Special National Committee on Statistics on Filipino Child-Youth Development and Welfare	**Tanging Pambansang Komite sa Estadistika sa Pagpapaunlad at Kagalingan ng Bata-Kabataang Pilipino**
Abaca Corporation of the Philippines	**Korporasyon sa Abaka ng Pilipinas**
Manila Gas Corporation	**Korporasyon sa Gas ng Maynila**
National Marketing Corporation	**Pambansang Korporasyon ng Pagsasapamilihan**
National Power Corporation	**Pambansang Kompanya ng Elektrisidad**
National Shipyard and Steel Corporation	**Pambansang Korporasyon sa Basadero at Asero**
People's Homesite and Housing Corporation	**Korporasyong Bayan sa Panahanan at Pagpapabahay**
Council of Administrative Management	**Sanggunian ng Pamamahalang Pampangasiwaan**
Development Council	**Sanggunian ng Pagpapaunlad**
Irrigation Council	**Sanggunian ng Patubig**
Labor Management Advisory Council	**Sangguniang Tagapayo sa Pamamahala sa Paggawa**
National Agricultural Council	**Pambansang Sanggunian sa Pagsasaka**
National Economic Council	**Sangguniang Pambansa sa Kabuhayan**
National Land Reform Council	**Pambansang Sanggunian ng Reporma sa Lupa**
National Security Council	**Sangguniang Pambansa sa Kapanatagan**
Peace and Order Council	**Sanggunian sa Kapayapaan at Kaayusan**
Council of State	**Sanggunian ng Estado**
Rice and Corn Production Coordinating Council	**Sangguniang Tagapag-ugnay sa Produksiyon ng Bigas at Mais**
Rural Broadcasting Council	**Sanggunian sa Pagbabalitang Pangkabukiran**
Court of Agrarian Relations	**Hukuman ng Pagsasamahang Pansakahan**
Court of Appeals	**Hukuman ng Paghahabol**

Court of First Instance	**Hukumang Unang Dulugan**
Court of Industrial Relations	**Hukuman ng Pagsasamahang Industriyal**
Juvenile and Domestic Relations Court	**Hukuman sa Kabataan at Pagsasamahang Pantahanan**
Supreme Court of the Philippines	**Kataas-taasang Hukuman ng Pilipinas**
Court of Tax Appeals	**Hukuman ng Paghahabol sa Buwis**
Department of Agriculture and Natural Resources	**Kagawaran ng Pagsasaka at Likas na Kayamanan**
Department of Commerce and Industry	**Kagawaran ng Komersiyo at Industriya**
Department of Education	**Kagawaran ng Edukasyon**
Department of Finance	**Kagawaran ng Pananalapi**
Department of Foreign Affairs	**Kagawaran ng Suliraning Panlabas**
Department of General Services	**Kagawaran ng Lingkurang Panlahat**
Department of Health	**Kagawaran ng Kalusugan**
Department of Justice	**Kagawaran ng Katarungan**
Department of Labor	**Kagawaran ng Paggawa**
Department of National Defense	**Kagawaran ng Tanggulang Bansa**
Department of Public Works and Communications	**Kagawaran ng Pagawaing Bayan at Komunikasyon**
Office of Apprenticeship	**Tanggapan ng Pagsasanay sa Gawain**
Cooperative Administration Office	**Tanggapan ng Pangangasiwa ng Kooperatiba**
Office of Economic Coordination	**Tanggapan ng Ugnayang Pangkabuhayan**
Office of Agrarian Counsel	**Tanggapan ng Abogado ng Pagsasamahan sa Lupa**
Executive Office of the President	**Tanggapang Tagapagpaganap ng Pangulo**
General Auditing Office	**Tanggapan ng Pangkalahatang Pag-aaudit**
Office of the Government Corporate Counsel	**Tanggapan ng Abogado ng mga Korporasyong Pampamahalaan**

Office of the Insurance Commissioner	**Tanggapan ng Komisyonado ng Seguro**
Office of Manpower Services	**Tanggapan ng Lingkurang Lakas-tao**
Office of National Planning	**Tanggapan ng Pambansang Pagpaplano**
Philippine Charity Sweepstakes Office	**Tanggapan ng Swipstik ng Kawanggawa sa Pilipinas**
Philippines Patent Office	**Tanggapan ng Patente sa Pilipinas**
Office of Political and Cultural Affairs	**Tanggapan ng mga Suliraning Pampulitika at Pangkultura**
Radio Control Office	**Tanggapan ng Pamamahala ng Radyo**
Office of the Solicitor General	**Tanggapan ng Prokurador Heneral**
Office of Statistical Coordination and Standards	**Tanggapan ng Ugnayan at Pamantayang Estadistiko**
Office of the Undersecretary for Health and Medical Services	**Tanggapan ng Pangalawang Kalihim sa Lingkurang Pangkalusugan at Panggagamot**
Office of the Undersecretary for Special Health Services	**Tanggapan ng Pangalawang Kalihim sa Tanging Lingkurang Pangkalusugan**
Office of the Vice President	**Tanggapan ng Pangalawang Pangulo**
Office of Vocational Rehabilitation	**Tangapan ng Rehabilitasyong Bokasyonal**
Parks and Wildlife Office	**Tanggapan ng mga Parke at Buhay-Iláng**
Wage and Position Classification Office	**Tanggapan ng Pag-uri ng Sahod at Tungkulin**
Armed Forces of the Philippines	**Sandatahang Lakas ng Pilipinas**
Bataan National Shipyard	**Pambansang Baradero sa Bataan**
Civic Action in the Philippines Against Smuggling	**Kilusang Sibiko sa Pilipinas laban sa Kontrabando**
Central Bank of the Philippines	**Bangko Sentral ng Pilipinas**

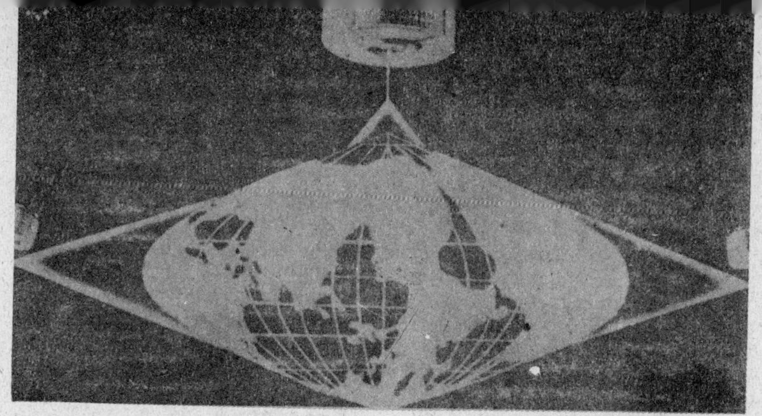

Presidential Electoral Tribunal	**Pampangulong Hukumang Elektoral**
Quirino Memorial Hospital	**Pang-alaalang Pagamutang Quirino**
Senate Electoral Tribunal	**Hukumang Elektoral ng Senado**
Social Security System	**Paseguruhan ng Kapanatagang Panlipunan**
University of the Philippines	**Pamantasan ng Pilipinas**
Veterans Memorial Hospital	**Pang-alaalang Pagamutan ng mga Beterano**
Regional Health Office No.—	**Pampurok na Tanggapang Pangkalusugan Blg.—**
Dr. J. R. Reyes Memorial Hospital	**Pang-alaalang Pagamutang Dr. J. R. Reyes**
Philippine Army	**Hukbong Sandatahan ng Pilipinas**
Philippine Navy	**Hukbong Dagat ng Pilipinas**
Philippine Air Force	**Lakas Himpapawid ng Pilipinas**
Philippine Constabulary	**Konstabularya ng Pilipinas**
Philippine Military Academy	**Akademya Militar ng Pilipinas**
First Judicial District	**Unang Distritong Panghukuman**
Second Judicial District	**Ikalawang Distritong Panghukuman**
Third Judicial District	**Ikatlong Distritong Panghukuman**

Accountant	**Tagatuos**
Administration	**Pangasiwaan, Administrasyon**
Administrator	**Tagapangasiwa, Administrador**
Administrative Assistant	**Katulong Pampangasiwaan**
Assistant Administrator	**Pangalawang Tagapangasiwa, Katulong na Tagapangasiwa**
Assistant Chief	**Pangalawang Puno, Katulong na Puno**
Assistant Director	**Pangalawang Patnugot**
Executive Assistant	**Katulong Tagapagpaganap**
Library Assistant	**Katulong sa Aklatan**
Special Assistant	**Tanging Katulong**
Technical Assistant	**Katulong na Tekniko**
Auditor	**Auditor**
Supervisory Auditor	**Auditor Tagamasid**
Board	**Lupon**
Board of Directors	**Lupong Patnugutan, Lupon ng mga Patnugot**
Board of Examiners	**Lupong Tagasulit, Lupon ng mga Tagasulit**
Board of Governors	**Lupon ng mga Gobernador**
Board of Regents	**Lupon ng mga Rehente**
Board of Trustees	**Lupong Tiwalaan**
Cashier	**Kahero (-a)**
Chairman	**Tagapangulo**
Vice Chairman	**Pangalawang Tagapangulo**
Commissioner	**Komisyonado**
Deputy Commissioner	**Puli Komisyonado**
Consultant	**Kasangguni**
Property Custodian	**Taga-ingat ng Ari-arian**
Forest Products Research Institute	**Surian ng Pananaliksik sa Produktong Gubat**
Director	**Patnugot, Direktor**
Executive Director	**Patnugot Tagapagpaganap**
Regional Director	**Patnugot Pampurok**
Editor	**Editor**
Information Editor	**Editor Pangkabatiran**
Foreman	**Kapatas, Porman**
Associate Judge	**Kasanggguning Hukom, Kagawad na Hukom**

Executive Judge	**Hukom Tagapagpaganap**
Presiding Judge	**Nangungulong Hukom, Tagapagpangulong Hukom**
Associate Justice	**Kasangguning (o Kagawad na) Mahistrado**
Chief Justice	**Punong Mahistrado**
Librarian	**Katiwala ng Aklatan, Tagaingat-Aklatan**
Manager	**Tagapamahala**
Branch Manager	**Tagapamahalang Pansangay**
General Manager	**Pangkalahatang Tagapamahala**
Operations Manager	**Tagapamahala ng Pagpapakilos**
Production Manager	**Tagapamahala ng Produksiyon**
Sales Manager	**Tagapamahala ng Pagbibili**
Traffic Manager	**Tagapamahala ng Trapiko**
Officer	**Pinuno**
Accounting Officer	**Pinunong Tagatuos**
Administrative Officer	**Pinunong Pampangasiwaan**
Budget Officer	**Pinuno ng Badyet**
Collecting and Disbursing Officer	**Pinunong Tagalikom at Tagapagbayad**
Executive Officer	**Pinunong Tagapagpaganap**
Hearing Officer	**Pinunong Tagadinig (o Tagalitis), Pinuno sa Pagdinig (o Paglilitis)**
Information Officer	**Pinuno sa Impormasyon; Pinunong Pangkabatiran**
Legal Officer	**Pinunong Pambatas**
Liaison Officer	**Pinunong Tagalakad**
Officer in Charge	**Pinunong Namamahala**
Personnel Officer	**Pinunong Pantauhan**
Press Relations Officer	**Pinuno sa mga Pabalita, Pinuno sa Ugnayang Balita**
Procurement Officer	**Pinuno sa Pamimili**
Public Relations Officer	**Pinuno sa Ugnayang Madla**
Records Officer	**Pinuno sa mga Kasulatan**
Supply Officer	**Pinuno sa Panustos**
Training Officer	**Pinuno sa Pagsasanay**

Register of Deeds	**Tagatala ng mga Kasulatan**
Registrar	**Tagatala**
Secretariat	**Kalihiman**
Secretary	**Kalihim**
Appointment Secretary	**Kalihim Pantipanan**
Board Secretary	**Kalihim ng Lupon**
Confidential Secretary	**Katiwalang Kalihim**
Private Secretary	**Kalihim Pansarili**
Secretary of the . . .	**Kalihim ng . . .**
Social Secretary	**Kalihim Panlipunan**
Building Superintendent	**Tagapamahala (o Superintendente) ng Gusali**
Shop Superintendent	**Tagamasid Pampurok, Superbisor ng Talyer**
Supervisor	**Tagamasid Pampurok; Superbisor**
Sales Supervisor	**Superbisor sa Pagbibili**
Regional Supervisor	**Tagamasid, Superbisor**
Shop Supervisor	**Superbisor ng Talyer**
Trial Attorney	**Abogado sa Paglilitis**
Treasurer	**Ingatyaman, Tesorero (-a)**
Undersecretary	**Pangalawang Kalihim**

KATAWAGAN SA DIPLOMA
(Diploma Terms)

ENGLISH	PILIPINO
Associate in	Asosyado sa
Bachelor of Science in	Batsilyer sa Agham ng Dalubhasa sa Agham ng
Master of Arts in	Master sa mga Sining ng Pantas sa mga Sining ng
Doctor of Philosophy in	Doktor sa Pilosopiya ng Paham sa Pilosopiya ng
Actuarial Mathematics	Matematikang Aktuwaryal
Mathematics	Matematika
Agriculture	Pagsasaka
Agricultural Engineering	Inhinyeryang Pampagsasaka
Agricultural Education	Edukasyon sa Pagsasaka
Architecture	Arkitektura
Arts	Mga Sining
Business Administration	Pangangasiwang Pangnegosyo
Chemical Research	Pananaliksik Kimikal
Chemistry	Kimika
Commerce	Komersiyo
Community Development	Kaunlarang Pampamayanan
Dental Medicine	Panggagamot ng Ngipin
Diplomacy	Diplomasya
Divinity	Dibinidad
Economics	Kabuhayan
Education	Edukasyon
Agricultural Education	Edukasyon sa Pagsasaka
Christian Education	Edukasyong Kristiyano
Elementary Education	Edukasyong Pang-Elementarya
Industrial Education	Edukasyong Industriyal
Physical Education	Edukasyong Pangkatawan
Commercial Education	Edukasyong Pangkomersiyo
Engineering	Inhinyerya
Electrical Engineering	Inhinyerya Elektrika
Agricultural Engineering	Inhinyeryang Pampagsasaka

Aeronautical Engineering	**Inhinyerya Aeronautika**
Chemical Engineering	**Inhinyerya Kimika**
Civil Engineering	**Inhinyerya Sibil**
Structural Engineering	**Inhinyerya Istruktural**
Industrial Engineering	**Inhinyerya Industriyal**
Marine Engineering	**Inhinyerya Marina**
Metallurgical Engineering	**Inhinyerya Metalurhika**
Mechanical Engineering	**Inhinyerya Mekanika**
Mining Engineering	**Inhinyerya sa Pagmimina**
Radio & Electronics Engineering	**Inhinyerya sa Radyo at Elektronika**
Radio & Electrical Engineering	**Inhinyerya sa Radyo at Elektrika**
Textile Engineering	**Inhinyerya sa Tela**
Aircraft Maintenance Engineering	**Inhinyerya sa Pangangalaga ng Eruplano**
Geodetic Engineering	**Inhinyerya Heodetika**
Public Health Engineering	**Inhinyerya ng Kalusugang Pambayan**
Arts	**Mga Sining**
Fine Arts	**Magagandang Sining**
Industrial Arts	**Mga Sining sa Industriya**
Fisheries	**Pangingisda**
Food Technology	**Teknolohiya sa Pagkain**
Foreign Service	**Lingkurang Panlabas**
Forestry	**Panggugubat**
Geology	**Heolohiya**
Home Economics	**Karunungang Pantahanan**
Hygiene	**Ihiyene**
Home Technology	**Teknolohiyang Pantahanan**
Sugar Technology	**Teknolohiya sa Asukal**
Hospital Administration	**Pangangasiwa sa Ospital**
Industrial Chemistry	**Kimika Industriyal**
Industrial Education	**Edukasyong Industriyal**
Industrial Engineering	**Inhinyerya Industriyal**
Industrial Pharmacy	**Parmasyang Industriyal**
Journalism	**Pamamahayag**
Laws	**Batas**
Management	**Pamamahala**
Mathematics	**Matematika**
Actuarial Mathematics	**Matematikang Aktuwaryal**

Pure Mathematics	**Dalisay na Matematika**
Medicine	**Panggagamot**
Music	**Musika**
Nursing	**Pagnanars**
Occupational Therapy	**Terapeutikang Panghanap-buhay**
Office Management	**Pangangasiwang Pangtang-gapan**
Pharmacy	**Parmasya**
Philosophy	**Pilosopiya**
Physical Therapy	**Terapeutikang Pangkata-wan**
Physics	**Pisika.**
Psychology	**Sikolohiya**
Political Science	**Agham Pampulitika**
Public Administration	**Pangangasiwang Pamba-yan**
Science	**Agham, Siyensiya**
Secretarial Science	**Agham Pangkalihim**
Social Work	**Gawaing Panlipunan**
Statistics	**Istadistika**
Surveying	**Pagsukat-Lupa**
Teaching	**Pagtuturo**
Veterinary Medicine	**Panggagamot sa Hayop**
Primary School	**Paaralang Primarya**
Elementary School	**Paaralang Elementarya** **Mababang Paaralan**
High School	**Mataas na Paaralan**
Aeronautical High School	**Mataas na Paaralang Ae-ronautika**
Vocational High School	**Mataas na Paaralang Bo-kasyonal**
Agricultural High School	**Mataas na Paaralan ng Pagsasaka**
College	**Dalubhasaan** **Kolehiyo**
University	**Pamantasan** **Unibersidad**
Automotive Mechanic	**Mekaniko sa Auto**
Master Baker's Course	**Kurso ng Pagkadalubha-sang Panadero**
Collegiate Secretarial Course	**Pandalubhasaang Kursong Pangkalihim**
Commercial Arts	**Sining Pangkomersiyo**

Diesel Engine Mechanic	**Mekaniko sa Motor Disel**
General Secondary Course	**Pangkalahatang Kursong Sekundaryo**
Inter-Combustion Engine Technician	**Tekniko sa Makinang Panloob-Kombustiyon**
Liberal Arts	**Malayang Sining**
Machine Shop Technician	**Tekniko sa Talyer ng Makina**
Medical Technician Course	**Kurso ng Tekniko sa Panggamot**
Radio Mechanic	**Radyo Mekaniko**
Radio Technician	**Radyo Tekniko**
Radio Telegram Operator	**Operator ng Radyo Telegrapo**
Radio Telephone Operator	**Operator ng Radyo Telepono**
Refrigeration Technician	**Tekniko sa Reprihirasyon**
Secondary Course	**Kursong Sekundaryo**
Sheet Metal Technician	**Tekniko sa Plantsang Metal**
Sportsman Pilot	**Pilotong Isportman**
Commercial Pilot	**Pilotong Pangkomersiyo**
Stenography & Typing	**Takigrapiya at Pagmamakinilya**
Television Technical Course	**Kursong Tekniko sa Telebisyon**

PHYSICS—CHEMISTRY—BIOLOGY
SOCIAL SCIENCES

I. LIKNAYAN — PHYSICS

	English	Filipino
1.	physics, the physical sciences	liknayan (pisika)
2.	physical (adj., 1)	liknayin
3.	physical (adj., 2)	liknayanin
4.	physicist	
5.	physics worker, asst. physicist	manliliknay
6.	natural	likas
7.	unnatural	dilikas
8.	supernatural	higlikas
9.	metaphysics	higliknayan
10.	strength	lakas
11.	intensity	tindi
12.	force (vector quantity)	isig (mat. Tag.)
13.	energy (capacity to do work)	kusog (Bis. at Bkl.)
14.	work (product of force & dist.)	himo (Bis.)
15.	power (rate of doing work)	isog (Bis. at Bkl.)
16.	Matter	butang (Bis.)
17.	body (of inorganic things)	lawas (Eusebio T. Daluz, 1913)
18.	body (of organic things)	katawan
19.	weight	bigat
20.	mass	bugat (Bis.)
21.	specific weight	hambinging bigat
22.	weight density	kasiksikan
23.	mass density	bugating kasiksikan
24.	inert	matigal
25.	inertia	tigal
26.	isostasy	katigalan, katiglan
27.	impulse	dantay
28.	momentum	dagsa
29.	torgue	habyog
30.	moment	sigwat
31.	stress	dagil
32	strain	banat
33	motion (pure movement independent of force	

	force)	kilos
35.	displacement (linear)	galaw
36.	vibration	kinig
37.	speed	bilis
38.	velocity	tulin
39.	acceleration	darasig
40.	accelerate	darasigin
41.	decelaration	balidarasig
42.	decelerate	balidarasigin
43.	rest	tigil
44.	stop	hinto
45.	distance	agwat
46.	time	oras
47.	duration	lawig
48.	instant of time	takna
49.	period of time	takda
50.	space (physical)	lawak
51.	field	kalawakan
52.	equilibrium	larang
53.	space (mathematical)	katiningan lawak
54.	centripetal force	gitisig (pagitnang isig)
55.	centrifugal force	basisig (palabas na isig)
56.	kinetic energy	galaw-kusog
57.	potential energy	binit-kusog
58.	friction	kiskis
59.	gravity	dagsin (Ilk.)
60.	gravitation	karagsinan
61.	gravitational	dagasinin
62.	application of a force	tuon ng isig
63.	action	bisa
64.	reaction	gantimbisa
65.	thrust	sikad
66.	recoil	gantinsikad
67.	uniform	maligo (mat. Tag.)
68.	uniform motion	maligong kilos, maligong lihok
69.	uniform velocity	maligong tulin
70.	uniform acceleration	maligong darasig
71.	expansion (phys. & math.)	buklad
72.	contraction	daginsin, saginsin
73.	compression	tipil, kipil
74.	pressure	diin
75.	position	katayuan
76.	condition	kalagayan
77.	state	himtang, kahimtangan (Hlg.)
78.	place, position	lunan
79.	property	angkin, kaangkinan
80.	quality	uri, kaurian

81.	characteristics	katangian
82.	peculiarity	kakanyahan
83.	flexible	hutukin
84.	inflexible	dihutukin
85.	flexibility	pagkahutukin
86.	elastic	igkasin
87.	inelastic	diigkasin
88.	elasticity	pagkaigkasin
89.	rigid	tigambay
90.	plastic	makalaw
91.	fluid	malapuyot
92.	solid	siksin
93.	liquid	danum
94.	gas	buhog
95.	plasma (phys.)	dinagipik
96.	porous	malabuga
97.	porosity	kabugaan
98.	malleable	pukpukin
99.	quantity	dami
100.	amount	daghan
101.	value	halga (halaga)
102.	magnitude	dakil (Ilk.)
103.	direction	tungo
104.	vector	tugano
105.	vector quantity	daming tugano
106.	scalar	bilangin
107.	scalar quantity	dawing bilangin
108.	measurement	sukat
109.	dimention	sukod (Hlg.)
110.	length	haba
111.	width	lapad
112.	area	dawak
113.	height	taas
114.	altitude	tayog
115.	volume	buok
116.	cube (geom. solid)	binuok
117.	cubic	buukin
118.	cubit (a measure of length)	kubit
119.	fathom	dipa
120.	inch.	dali
121.	yard	yarda
122.	meter	metro
123.	milli-	mili-
124.	centi-	senti-
125.	deci-	desi-
126.	kilo-	kilo-
127.	micro-	mik-
128.	mile	milya
129.	gram	gramo
130.	pound	libra

131. poundal — librahin
132. newton — nyuton
133 dyne — dina
134. foot-pound — talampakan-libra
135. foot-pound-second — talibsog (tal.-libra/seg.)
136. joule — dyul
137. erg — ergi
138. erg per second — ergi bawat saglit
139. watt — wat
140. technics, technique — aghimo (agham himo)
141. technical — aghimuin
142. contrivance, deviced — sigmo **(isig himo)**
143. machine — makina
144. lever — dalawit
145. screw — balukay
146. wedge — singkal
147. pulley — kalo
148. inclined plane — dahilig
149. wheel & axle — gulong a't gargaran
150. spring — paigkas, balintang
151. gyroscope — halintigal
152. efficiency (of a machine) — katalban (katalaban)
153. (efficient) — (matalab)
154. electricity — dagitab (elektrisidad)
155. electric current — saloy-dagitab
156. current — saloy (karen)
157. electron — dagisik (mat. Tag.)
158. galvanic electricity — dagitab galbanhin
159. galvanic current — saloy galbahin
160. static electricity — dagitab tigil
161. static (in a radio circuit) — saloy tabluwas
162. electric charge — tablay (dagitab na taglay)
163. positive charge — tahas na tablay
164. negative charge — baling na tablay
165. charge (v.) — tablayan
166. discharge (n.) — tabluwas (dagitab na luwas)
167. discharge (v.) — tabluwasin, tabluwasan
168. static **discharge** — tigaling tabluwas
169. spark — titis
170. arc — bantok
171. bypass — lulos
172. electrical connection — dagitabing kabit
173. series connection — sunurang kabit
174. parallel connection — agapayang kabit
175. series circuit — sunurang salikop
176. parallel circuit — agapayang salikop
177. series-parallel con- — sunurang-agapayag

	nection	kabit
178.	across-the line	halang-sa-kawad
179.	the line	ang kakawaran
180.	interrupter	panggatol
181.	intermittent **current**	gatol na saloy
182.	direct current	tuwirang saloy
183.	alternating current	saliding saloy
184.	network	kabalagan
185.	closed circuit	pinid na salikop
186.	open circuit	bukas na salikop
187.	internal circuit	panloob na salikop
188.	make or close a circuit	ipinid ang salikop
189.	break a circuit	buksan ang salikop
190.	circuitry	kasalikupan
191.	resistance	sakwil
192.	resistor	panakwil
193.	resistivity	kasagwilan
194.	capacitance	lulan
195.	capacitor	panlulan
196.	induction	karawitan
197.	inductor (induction coil)	panawit (kidkidpanawit)
198.	inductance	dawit
199.	magnet	balani
200.	magnetic	**balaniin**
201.	magnetism (the property)	kabalanian—magnetismo
202.	magnetism (the science)	balniing isig
203.	magnetic force	balniing guhit
204.	magnetic lines of force	balniing larang
205.	magnetic field	balniing higom
206.	magnetic attraction	balniing taluktok
207.	magnetic poles	hilagang balniing taluktok
208.	north magnetic poles	timugang balniing taluktok
209	south magnetic poles	batubalani
210	lodestone	bakalbalani
211.	iron (bar) magnet	dagitabbalani
212.	electromagnet	kadagibalnian
213.	electromagnetism (science)	da gibalnian
214	permanent magnet	laging balani
215	temporary magnet	pansamantalang balani
216.	magnetic repulsion	balniing sikway
217.	electromagnetic waves	dagibalniing liboy
218.	magnetic shield	balniing dangga
219.	electrify	dagitabin

220.	electrification	pagdagitab
221.	electromotive force	dagikilusing isig
222.	electrostatics	dagitigalan
223.	electrostatic (adj.)	dagitigalin
224.	magnetohydrodynamics	balnidanum-isigan
225.	magnetic compass	balniing paraluman
226.	fuse	tunawin
227.	electrostatic generator	likhablay
228.	electric generator, dynamo	likhitab
229.	electric motor	dagisog
230.	charger	panablay
231.	electric storage battery	tinggalitab
232.	cell	silid
233.	battery	**baterya**
234.	electric transformer	palitab
235.	wave (mechanical)	alon
236.	wave (electromagnetic)	liboy
237.	electric wave	liboy dagitab
238.	electromagnetic waves	liboy dagitabbalani
239.	positive electricity	tahas na dagitab
240.	negative electricity	baling na dagitab
241.	conductor	saluyan
242.	non-conductor	disaluyan
243.	circuit	salikop
244.	insulation	hadlang
245.	insulator	panghadlang
246.	switch	kabtol (kabit putol)
247.	break (in circuit)	pugto
248.	cut (in circuit)	putol
249.	ground (in circuit)	sayad
250.	short circuit	laktod (Hlg.)
251.	coil	kidkid
252.	vacuum tube	awanging tubo
253.	oscillation	tugoy
254.	oscillator	panugoy
255.	oscilloscope	tugoysipat
256.	oscillogram	talantugoy
257.	oscillograph	talaantugoy
258.	detector	paniktik
259.	amplifier	pangibayo
260.	electrode	dagindas
261.	anode (positive electrode)	tahandas
		balindas
		duhandas
262.	diode	duhandas
263.	tunnel diode	talundas

264. triode	patandas
265. tetrode	limandas
266. pentode	antena
267. antenna	antenang likaw
268. loop antenna	alunig
269 **resonance**	aluniging kidkid
270 resonant coil	dalas
271. frequency	libuyhaba
272. wavelength	libuybigkis
273. waveband	libuyan
274. channel — (electro-magnetic)	alunan
275. channel (mechanical)	dagilap, karagilapan
276. radiation, radio-activity	diglap—(radyo)
277. radio (technical prefix)	siglap—(radar)
278. radar	hatidlap—(radyogram)
279. television	tanlap—(telebisyon)
280. radiogram	hatidwad
281. cablegram	pahatidkawad
282. telegram	talinig
283. microphone	miktinig—(mikropono)
284. earphone, headphone	
285. loudspeaker	daktinig—(loudespiker)
286. telephone	hatinig (telepono)
287. radiotelephone	hatinig-diglap
288. radio communications	pahatirang-diglap—
289. radio transmitter	pangalat-diglap radyo transmiter)
290. radio receiver	panagap-diglap—(radyc resiber)
291. home radio receiver	radyo
292. regenerative radio receiver	mulikhaing panagap-diglap
293. radiomagnetic indicator	diglapbalaning 'pamatlig
294. radio telescope	daksipat-diglap—(teleskopyo)
295. radio operator's room	padiglapang silid
296. semiconductor	malasaluyan
297. transistor	saligwil—(transistor)
transistor	diglap-saligwil, transistor
298. collector	panlikom
299. base	takad
donor atom	bigaying mulapik
300. acceptor atom	tanggaping mulapik
301. unbound electron	malayang dagisik
302 miniature circuit	miksalikop
303. electronic (adj.)	dagisikin—(elektronik
304. astronomy	dalubtalaan

305. astronomer	dalubtala
306. astronomical	dalubtalain
307. heavenly body, astronomical body	lawas na langitnin, lawas na dalubtalain
308. star (astron.)	tala
309 star (as a 5-pointed figure and in ord. sense)	bituin
310. planet	buntala
311. satellite	buntabay
312. astreroid	malatala
313. planetoid	malabuntala
314. comet	barikod
315. meteoroid	bulalayak
316. meteorite	bulalato
317. meteor	bulalakaw
318. constellation	talanyo
319. star group	talumpok
320. star cluster	talumpon
321. nebula	ulanag — (nebula)
322. zodiac	tahaklaw — (sodyak)
323. ecliptic	guhitlaw
324. magnitude (astron.)	kinang
325. horizon	ka giliran
326. zenith	ituktok
327. nafir	idalum
328. telescope	daksipat
329. Sun, Sol	adlaw
330. Moon, Luna, Selence	Bulan
331. New Moon	patay na Bulan — (bagong buwan)
332. First quarter Moon	Bulang Nagbibilog
333. Full Moon	Bulang Kabilugan
334. Last quarter Moon	Bulang Nagdudurog, Bulang Palba
335. Cresent Moon	Bulang Gasuklay
336. selenography	talabulanan
337. Earth, Tiera, Tellus	Duta
338. terrestial	dutain
339. terrestial magnetism	dutaing balani
340. the Whole world, worldwide	sandaigdigan sandaigdigan, pandaigdig
341. planetary system	kabuntalaan, kaayusang buntalain
342. planetary	buntalain
343. interplanetary	pangkabuntalaan, kabuntalaanin
344. Solar System	Kaayusang-Adlaw, kabuntalaang-adlaw (solar sistem)
345. solar flare	adlawing liyap
346. sun spot	batik-adlaw

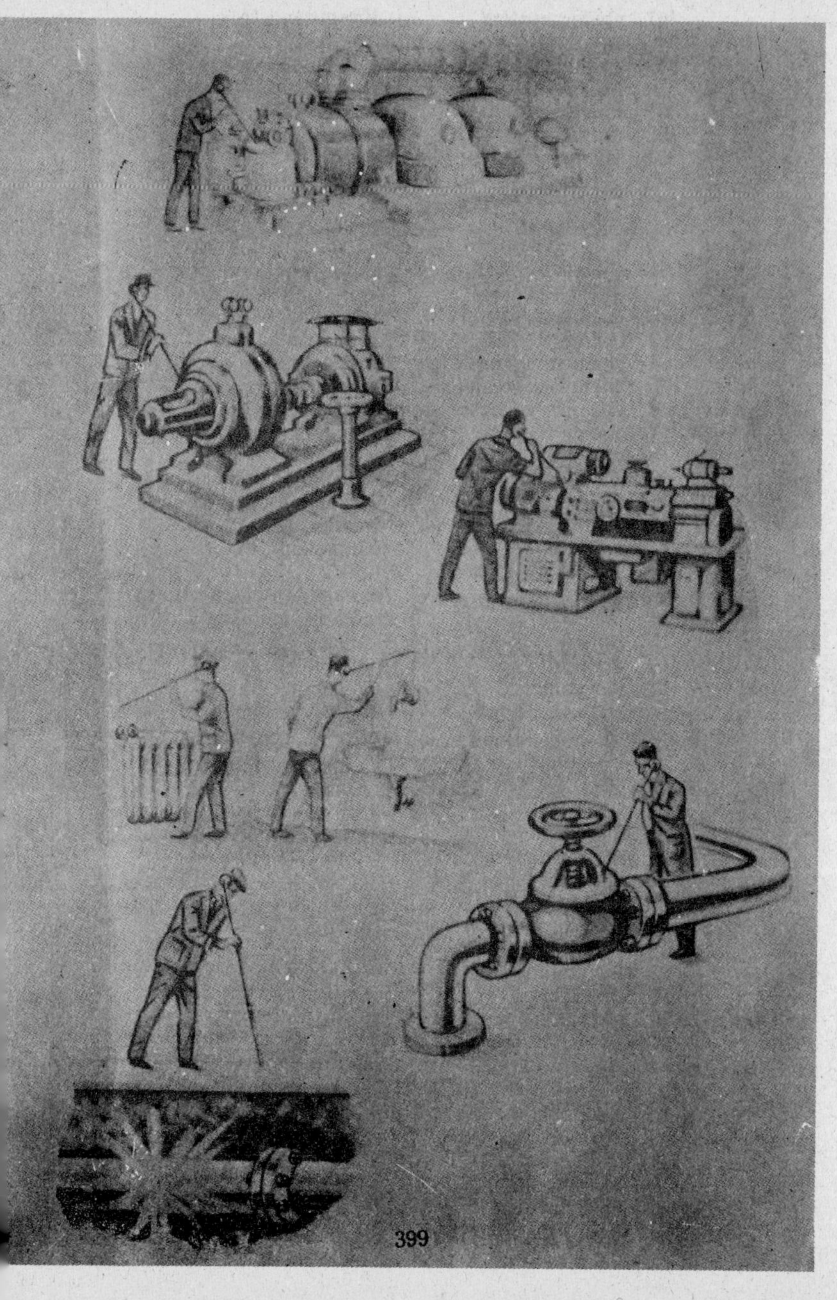

347. steller system	Kaayusang tala
348. galaxy	sanlibutan
349. galactic (adj.)	sanlibutnin
350. Milky Way	Daang Malagatas
351. universe	sansinukob
352. universal	sansinukbin
353. island universe (galaxy)	pulong sansinukob

II. KAPNAYAN — Chemistry

1. chemistry, the chemical sciences	kapnayan (kemistri)
2. chemical (adj.,)'	kapnayin
3. chemical (adj.,)²	kapnayanin
4. chemist (scientist)	kapnayanon
5. chemist (registered)	mangangapnay
6. chemistry graduate	tapos-kapbayan
7. chemical (n.)	sangkapin
8. material, substance	sangkap
9. chemical element	mulangkap (mulaang sangkap)
10. chemical compound	balangkap
11. mixture	halungkap
12. particle	tipik
13. atom	mulapik (mulaang tipik)
14. molecule	mulatil (mulaang butil)
15. isotope	kahasik
16. organic	buhayin, hayin
17. inorganic	dibuhayin, dihayin
18. chemical bond	kapnaying bigkis
19. Chemical Bond Approach	kapnaying Bigkisang Aral
20. CBA	KBA
21. ion	dagipik
22. ionic bond	dagipiking bigkis
23. ion exchange	palitang-dagipik
24. electron	dagisik
25. Hydrogen (H)	Haydrohen
26. Helium (He)	Helyum
27. Lithium (Li)	Lityum
28. Beryllium (Be)	Berilyum
29. Boron (B)	Boron
30. Carbon (C)	Karbon
31. Nitrogen (N)	Nitrohen
32. Oxygen (O)	Oksihen
33. Fluorine (F)	Plorin
34. Neon (Ne)	Neyon
35. Sodium (Na)	Sodyum (Natriyum)
36. Magnesium (Mg)	Magnisyum
37. Aluminum (Al)	Aluminum
38. Silicon (Si)	Silikon

39. Phosphorus (P) Posporus
40. Sulfur (S) Asupre. Malilang, Sulpur
41. Chlorin (Cl) Klorin
42. Argon (A) Argon
43. Potasium (K) Potasyum (Kalyum)
44. Calcium (Ca) Kalsyum
45. Scandium (Cc) Iskandiyum
46. Titanium (Ti) Titanyum
47. Vanadium (V) Bonandyum
48. Chromium (Cr) Kronyum
49. Maganese (Mn) Manganis
50. Iron (Fe) Bakal (Perum)
51. Cobalt (Co) Kobalt
52. Nickel (Ni) Nikel
53. Copper (Cu) Tanso (Kuprum)
54. Zinc (Zn) Sink
55. Gallium (Ga) Galyum
56. Germanium (Gr) Hermanyum
57. Arsenic (As) Arsenic
58. Selenium (Se) Selenyum
59. Bromine (Br) Bromin
60. Krypton (Kr) Kripton
61. Robidium (Rb) Rubudyum
62. Strontium (Sr) Istrontiyum
63. Yttrium (Y) Itriyum
64. Zirconium (Zr) Sirkonyum
65. Niobyum (Nb) Nayobyum
66. Molybdenum (Mo) Molibdenum
67. Technitium (Tc) Teknisyum
68. Ruthennium (Ru) Rutenyum
69. Rhodium (Rh) Rodyum
70. Palladium (Pd) Paladyum
71. Silver (eg) Pilak (Arhentum)
72. Cadmium (Cd) Kadmiyum
73. Indium (In) Indiyum
74. Tin (Sn) Tinggaputi (Istanum)
75. Antomony (Sb) Antimony (Istebin)
76. Tellurium (Te) Teleryum
77. Iodine (I) Yodin
78. Xenon (Xe) Senon
79. Cesium (Cs) Sesyum
80. Barium (Ba) Baryum
81. Hanthanum (Ha) Hantanum
82. Cerium (Ce) Seryum
83. Praseodymium (Pr) Praseyodimyum
84. Neodymium (Nd) Neodinyum
85. Promethium (Pm) Prometyum
86. Samarium (Sm) Samaryum
87. Europium (Eu) Yuropyum
88. Gadolinium (Gd) Gadolinyum
89. Terbium (Tb) Terbiyum
90. Dysprosium (Dy) Disprosyum

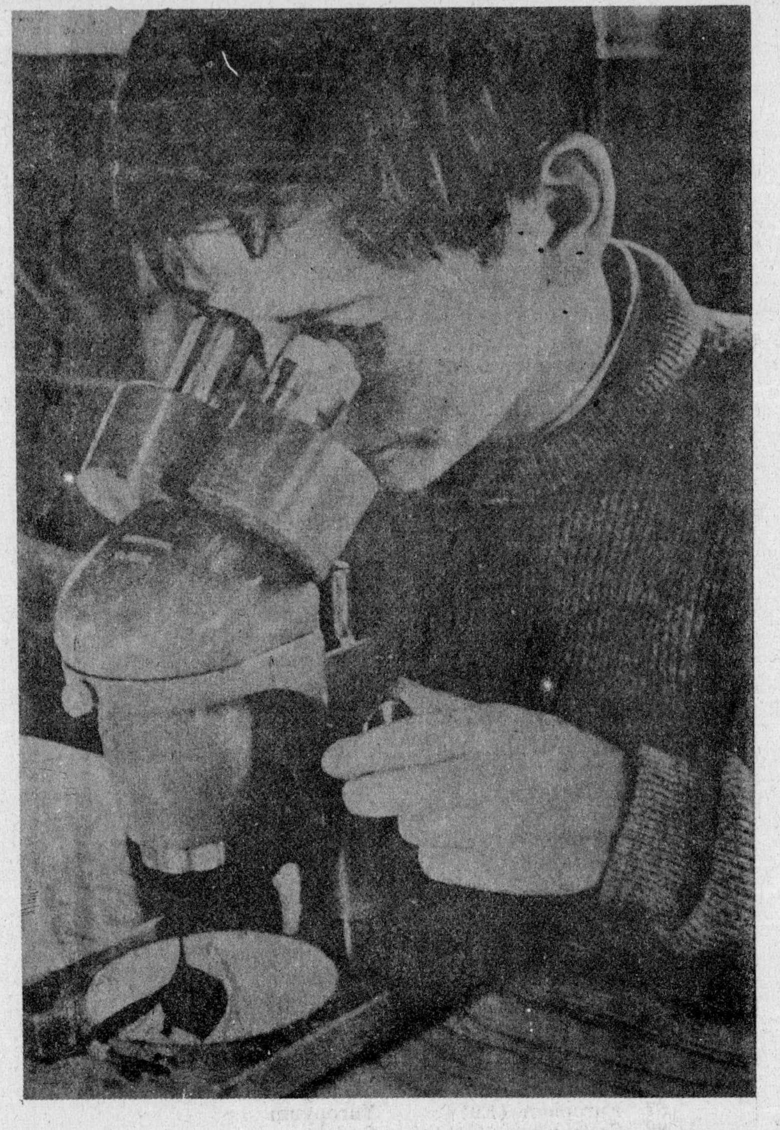

91. Holmium (Ho)	Holmiyum
92. Erbium (Er)	Erbiyum
93. Thulium Tm)	Tuluyum
94 Ytterbium (Yb)	Iterbiyum
95. Lutetium (Lu)	Lutesyum
96. Hafnium (Hf)	Hapniyum
97. Tantalum (Ta)	Tantalum
98. Tunsten (W)	Tungsten (Wolpram)
99. Rhenium (Re)	Renyum
100. Osmium (s)	Osmiyum
101. Iridum (Ir)	Iridyum
102. Platinum (Pt)	Platinum
103. Gold (Au)	Ginto (Awrum)
104. Mercury (Hg)	Asoge (Hidrargirum)
105. Thallium (Tl)	Talyum
106. Lead (Pb)	Tingga (Plubyum)
107. Bismuth (Bi)	Bismut
108. Polonium (Po)	Polonyum
109. Astatine (At)	Astatin
110. Radon (Rh)	Radon
111. Francium (Fr)	Pransyum
112. Radium (Ra)	Radyum
113. Actinium (Ac)	Aktinyum
114. Thorium (Th)	Toryum
115. Protactinium (Pa)	Protaktinyum
116. Uranium (U)	Uranyum
117. Neptunium (Np)	Neptunyum
118. Plutonium (Pu)	Plutonyum
119. Americium (Am)	Amerisyum
120. Curium (Cm)	Kuryum
121. Berkelium (Bk)	Berkelyum
122. Californium (Cf.)	Kalipornium
123. Einsteinnium (E)	Ensteinyum
124. Fermium (Fm)	Permyum
125. Mendelevium (Md)	Mendelegum
126. Nobelium (No)	Nobelyum
127. Lawrencium (Lw)	Lawrensyum

III. HAYNAYAN — Biology

1. biology, the biological sciences	haynayan—(bayologi)
2. biological (adj.., 1)	haynayin
3. biological (adj., 2)	haynayanin
4. biologist	haynayanon
5. biological worker	manghahanay
6. biochemical	haykapnayin
7. biochemist	haykapanayanon
8. organic	hayin, buhayin, taghayin
9. inorganic	dihayin, ditaghayin
10. living, being, living	

thing	katubaghay
11. organism	tataghay, mayuhay
12. microorganism	mikhay (mikmik o maliit na nilikhang maybuhay
13. protozoon (protozoa)	mulhay (mulaang buhay)
14. animalcule, microbe, germ	lithayop (maliit na hayop)
15. Bacterium, bacteria	ishay (isahang pulit ng buhay)
16. virus	haykap (malabuhay at malasangkap)
17. mite	kagaw
18. zoologist	dalubhayop
19. zoo	hayupan
20. garden, ordinary	halamanan
21. garden, botanical	halmanan
22. botanist	dalubhalman

V. ULNAYAN — Social Sciences

1. the sócial sciences	ulnayan
2. society, the social order	ulnong
3. society, the leisure class	lipunan
4. community	pamayanan
5. social (adj., gen. sense)	ulnungin
6. social (adj., lim. sense)	panlipunan
7. social (adj., part to studies)	ulnayanin
8. social study	ulnayaning pag-aaral
9. social scientist	ulnayanon
10. social science worker	mang-uulnay
11. social worker	manggagawang panlipunan
12. sociology	dalub-ulnong
13. sociologist	dalub-ulnong
14. sociological worker	mang-ulnong
15. sociological (adj.)	dalub-ulnungin
16. superorganic	highayin
17. social force	ulnunging isig
18. social development	ulnunging kaunlaran
19. social welfare	kagalingang panlipunan
20. culture	kalinangan
21. faith, worship	pananampalataya, panamamba
22. religion	agamahan; relihiyon
23. theology	bathalaan
24. linguistics	dalubwikaan

25.	philology	palawikaan
26.	anthropology	dalubtauhan
27.	technology	aghimuan
28.	livelihood	kabuhayan
29.	ecology	palamuhayan
30.	economics	agimatan—(ekonomiks)
31.	economy	kapamuhayan
32.	economist	dalub-agimat
33.	politics	pulitika
34.	politician	pulitiko
35.	political science	dalub-bayanan
36.	political scientist	dalub-bayan
37.	socioeconomic	ulnuagimatin
38.	sociopolitical	ulnubayanin
39.	sociocultural	ulnukalnangin
40.	socioreligious	ulnuagamahin
41.	sociability	pagkahalubilo
42.	section	pangkat
43.	co-member of a section	kapangkat
44.	group	lipon
45.	co-member of a group	kalipon
46.	committee	lupon
47.	co-member of a committee	kalupon
48.	subcommittee	kublupon
49.	co-member of a subcommittee	kakublupon
50.	association	kapisanan
51.	member (of an association)	kaanib
52.	member (of any org. in general)	kapisan
53.	(union—usually) of workers	kaisahan, unyon
54.	co-member of a union, unionist	kaisa, kaunyon
55.	member (of a katipunan)	katipon
56.	assembly, convention	kapulungan
57.	the body (in a meeting, assembly or convention)	kapulong
58.	participant in a meeting	kasali sa pulong.
59.	federation (of orgs.)	kalipunan
60.	proprietor, owner	may-ari
61.	share of a partnership	bakas
62.	partnership	bakasan
63.	partner	kabakas
64.	company (commer-	samahan, kompanya

cial)	(sa kalakal)
65. staff member of a com. company	kasama
66. corporation	sapian—(korporasyon)
67. shareholder of a corporation	kasapi
68. share (of stock)	sapi, sosyo
69. incorporated	isinasapian
70. inc. (abbr.)	isp. (daglat)
71. unit of organization	tatag
72. organize (v.)	magtatag
73. organization	katatagan
74. co-founder, charter member	katatag
75. institution (establishment)	tatagin
76. institution (established practice, custom, law, etc.	gawiin
77. institution (act of instituting	pagtatatag
78. constitution	saligang batas
79. articles of incorporation	mga batayan sa pagsasapian
80. charter (of an org.)	batayang kasulatan
81. bylaw	patakarambatas
82. policy	patakaran
83. policies and rules	mga patakaran at alituntunin
84. rules and regulations	mga alituntunin at panuto
85. practice	palakad
86. Guide rules	panuntunan
87. origins	kasimulan
88. precedent	kasumundan
89. tradition	kasumundan
90. civilization	kabihasnan
91. way	gawi
92. habit	ugali
93. custom	kaugalian
94. childhood environment	kamulatan, kinamulatan
95. behavior	asal
96. behavior pattern	kaasalan
97. morality	kasanlingan, kagandahang-asal
98. immorality	dikasanlingan, karumihang-asal
99. moral (adj.)	masanling, magandang-asal
100. morals (n.)	palasanlingan
101. dignity	kahanagan, dignidad

102. dignified	mahanag
103. undignified	dimahanag
104. integrity	katapatang-asal
105. chastity	puri, karangalan
106. honor	sanlingan—(onor)
107. background	sanligan
108. base	sandigan
109. support	kaligiran, kapaligiran
110. environment	kamanahan
111. heredity	mana, manahan
112. inheritance	pamana
113. legacy	katuruan, edukasyon
114. education	pagsasanay
115. training (act of)	pasanayan
116. training (formal course)	pasanayan
117. training (place or inst.)	nagsasanay
118. training (gerund)	kasanayan
119. training (experience)	pinagsanayan
120. training (social instruction)	
121. natural resources	likas na kayamanan
122. manpower	likas-tao
123. manpower service	lingkurang lakas-tao
124. project	panukala, pabalak
125. agent (abstract)	kinabisa
126. agent (concrete, as a person or institution acting in behalf of another	kinagawa
127. agency (abstract)	kabisaan
128. agency (concrete)	kagawaan
129. discipline	takdang-asal, disiplina
130. population	satauhan
131. human	tao, tauhan
132. humanity	sangkatauhan
133. nonhuman	ditao, ditauhan
134. humane	makatao
135. inhuman	dimakatao
136. humanities	katuruang-tao
137. humanism	palaturuang-tao
138. humanistic	makaturuang-tao
139. humanitarian	mapagkawanggawa
140. humanitarianism	palamakatauhan
141. natural (adj.)	likas
142. unnatural	dilikas
143. supernatural	higlikas (higit sa likas)
144. real	tunay
145. unreal	ditunay
146. realistic	tunayin, makatunay

147. unrealistic	ditunayin, dimakatunay
148. artificial	gawa-gawa, artipisyal
149. synthetic	lagumlalangin
150. synthesize (v.)	lagumlalangin
151. ethics	asalan, palaasalan
152. esthetics	santingan, palasantingan
153. rite	gali
154. ceremony	galian
155. ceremonial place	galian
156. history	kasaysayan
157. historical	makasaysayan
158. nation	bansa
159. state	banwa
160. United Nations	Nangagkakaisang Bansa
161. United States of America	Estados Unidos ng Amerika
162. sovereign (n.)	higpuno
163. sovereign states	higpunuan bansa
164. sovereign power	higpunong lakas
165. sovereignty	kahigpunuan
166. statesmanship	palabanwahan
167. statesman	palabanwa
168. land	lupa
169. territorial	lupainin
170. territory	lupain
171. territorial rights	lupaining karapatan
172. territorial limits	lupaining katakdaan
173. territorial waters	lupaining dagatan
174. territoriality	kalupainin
175. province	lalawigan
176. city	lunsod
177. capital city	ulunlunsod
178. metropolis	daklunsod
179. main city	pangunahing lunsod
180. chief city	punong lunsod
181. urban	panlunsod, lunsurin
182. rural	pangkabukiran, kabukiranin
183. village (barrio)	nayon
184. community	pamayanan
185. locality	pook
186. local	pampook
187. district	purok
188. hamlet	bahayan
189. civil (adj.)	bayanin
190. military (adj.)	hukbuhin
191. civil government	bayaning pamahalaan
192. military government	hukbuhing pamahalaan
193. civil service	lingkurang bayanin
194. civil service employee	kawaning bayanin
195. civil service eligible	nakasulit sa lingkurang

bayanin

196. military service — hukbuhing paglilingkod
197. civic (adj.) — pambayan
198. civics (br. of pol. science) — palamayanan
199. civilian (n.) — taumbayan
200. military (n.) — taunghukbo
201. citizen — mamamayan
202. citizenship — pagkamamamayan
203. natural-born citizen — mamamayang likas
204. naturalized citizen — isinamamamayan
205. naturalization — pagsasamamamayan
206. national (n.) — taumbansa
207. national (adj.) — pambansa, bansain
208. nationalization — sa bansa
209. nationalize — sabansain
210. nationality — katauhambansa
211. profession — panungkulan
212. position (in an org.) — katungkulan
213. professional (adj.) — panungkulin
214. professional service — panungkuling lingkod
215. professional fee — panungkuling bayad
216. professional training — panungkuling sanay
217. professional education — panungkuling katuruan
218. professional (n.) — manunungkulan
219. adult — nasagulang
220. adult education — pagtuturo sa nasagulang
221. percapita — bawat ulo
222. underdeveloped — digaunlad, malaunlad
223. developing — papaunlad
224. standard of living — pamantayan ng pamumuhay
225. income — kita
226. expenditure — gugulin
227. budget — talagugulin
228. appropriation — laanggugulin
229. shop (working place) — gawaan
230. factory works — pagawaan
231. laboratory — panaliksikan
232. work (abstract) — gawain
233. work (concrete, product) — gawa
234. public work — gawaing bayan
235. industry — kalalang
236. industrial — pangalalang kalalangin
237. industrial plant — kalalangin, plantang pangalalang
238. industrialize — kalalangin, isakalalang
239. industrialization — pagsasakalalang
240. industrial accident — sakunang kakalangin

241. commerce	kalakalan, pangangalakal
242. commercial	kalakalan
243. trade (n.)	baliwasan
244. trade (adj.)	baliwasin
245. exchange (n.)	palitan
246. exchange (adj.)	palitan
247. barter (n.)	tuwayan
248. barter (adj.)	tuwayin
249. commodity	kalakal
250. goods	bilihin
251. merchandise (n.)	baligyain
252. merchandise (v.)	ibaligya, ipamaligya
253. product	lalang, bunga
254. production	pangangalalang
255. distribution	pamamahagi
256. capital goods	puhunaning bilihin
257. gratuity	gantimpagal
258. tip	pabuya
259. revenue	katimbayan
260. agriculture	pagsasaka, sakahan
261. farm	sakahan
262. agricultural	sakahin

MGA KARANIWANG KATAGA UKOL SA KALIMITAN AT KALAYUAN	TERMS USED FOR FREQUENCY AND DISTANCE
Minsan	once
Paminsan-minsan	once in a while
Malimit	often
Malimit na malimit	very often
Madalang	seldom (infrequently)
Miminsan	only once
Malimit-limit	oftener than not
Madalang na madalang ..	very seldom
Makalawa. (Dalawang beses)	twice
Makatlo. (Tatlong beses)	thrice
Makaapat. (Apat na beses)	four times
Makalima (Limang beses)	five times
Makasampu (Sampung beses)	ten times
Malayo.	(It's) far.
Malayo rito.	Far from here.
Malayong-malayo.	Very far.
Malapit	(It's) near.
Malapit nang kaunti.	Quite near.
Malapit na malapit.	It's near.
Sa kabila.	(It's) on (at) the other side.
Sa kabilang silid.	In the next room.
Sa kabilang daán.	In the next street.
Sa ibayo.	On the opposite side of a waterway (as a river or lake).
Sa ibayo ng ilog.	On the other side of the river.
Sa ibayo ng dagat.	On the other side of the lake (sea, ocean).

MGA KATAWAGANG SIYENTIPIKO	SCIENTIFIC TERMS
aeronautics	eronautika
algebra	alhebra—aldyebra

anatomy	anatomiya—anatomi
anthropology	antropolohiya—antropologi
archaeology	arkeolohiya—arkelogi
arithmetic	aritmetika
astrology	astrolohiya—astrologi
astronomy	astronomiya—astronomi
biology	biyolohiya—bayologi
botany	botanika—botani
chemistry	kimika— kemestri
geography	heograpiya—giyograpi
geology	heolohiya—giyologi
geometry	heometriya—giyometri
linguistics	lingguwistika
logistics	lohistiko
mathematics	matematika
physics	pisika
psychology	sikolohiya—saykologi
rhetoric	retorika
semantics	semantika
statistics	estadistika
zoology	soolohiya—soology

Ama	Sr., Senior
Ling., Linggo	Sun., Sunday
Huweb., Huwebes	Thurs., Thursday
Mart., Martes	Tues., Tuesday
Miyer., Miyerkules	Wed., Wednesday
pd., pandiwa	v., verb
yd, yarda	yd., yard
tn., taon	yr., year

HALA HALAGA NG KUWALTA	**MONETARY UNITS**
isang pera, isang sentimo, walong kuwarta, (in Batangas, isang bagol; singko)	₱0.01, one centavo 0.05, five centavos, a nickel
diyes	0.10, ten centavos
kinse	0.15, fifteen centavos
isang piseta; beinte; (in Batangas, isang bilyon)	0.20, twenty centavos
beinte singko; kahati	0.25, twenty five centavos
singkuwenta; isang salapi	0.50, fifty centavos
sesenta; tatlong piseta	0.60, sixty centavos
setenta	0.70, seventy centavos
otsenta; apat na piseta	0.80, eighty centavos
piso	1.00, one peso

uno-diyes	1.10, one peso and ten centavos
uno singkuwenta	1.50, one peso and fifty centavos
dalawang piso	2.00, two pesos
dos singkuwenta; limang salapi	2.50, two pesos and fifty centavos
tatlong piso	3.00, three pesos
tres-singkuwenta	3.50, three pesos and fifty centavos
sampung piso	10.00, ten pesos
sandaang piso	100.00, one hundred pesos

TALAPANGKATAN NG MGA AGHAM

Ito ang pinakamaayos at pinakamaugnaying talapangkatan ng mga agham sa buong daigdig. Sa saklaw ng talaang ibaba ay maipaloloob, o dagling mahuhugot, ang ngalan ng anuman at alinmang pangkat o sangay ng agham na naisip na, o malilikha pa, ng kaisipan ng tao.

I. Sipnayan (sip hanayan) — mathematics, the mathematical science — (matematiks)

1. Palatangkasan (set algebra)
2. Bilnuran (arithmetic)
3. Sukgisan (geometry)
   a. Lapya (plane)
   b. Siksin (solid)
4. Panandaan (algebra)
5. Tatsihaan (trigonometry)
   a. Lapya (plane)
   b. Timbulog (spherical)
   c. Laumin (integral)
6. Palautatan (statistics)
7. Higsipnayan (higher mathematics)
8. (Dalub) wikaan (linguistics)
9. (Dalub)-isipan (psychology)
10. Palaasalan (ethics)
11. Palasantingan (esthetics)
12. Bathalaan (theology)
13. Ulnayaning Batnayan (social philosophy)

II. Liknayan (likas hanayan) — physics, the physical science — (pisiks)

1. Sigwasan (mechanics) danumsigwasan (hydraulics) buhagsigwasan (pneumatics)
   a. Tigilan (statics) Danumtigilan

hydrostatics)
buhagtigilan
(aerostatics)

b. Isigan (dynamics)
danum-isigan
(hydrodynamics)
buhag-isigan
(aerodynamics (1)
Lihukan (kinematics) (2)

LUPON SA AGHAM

I. SIPNAYAN — Mathematics

1.	mathematics, the mathematical sciences	sipnayan — matematika)
2.	mathematical (adj., 1)	sipnayin
3.	mathematical (adj., 2)	sipnayanin
4.	mathematician	sipnayanon
5.	mathematical worker	maninipnay
6.	quantity	dami
7.	standard quantity	pamantayang dami
8.	order	panunuran
9.	number	bilang
10.	numeral	pamilang
11.	digit	tambilang
12.	integer	buumbilang
13.	fraction	bahagimbilang
14.	zero	awan, sero
15.	the zero integer	ang awang buumbilang
16.	real number	bilang na tunay
17.	natural number (bilang)	bilang na likas
18.	counting number	bilang na panalatag
19.	imaginary number	bilang na guni, gunimbilang
20.	rational number	bilang na matwirin
21.	irrational number	bilang na dimatwirin
22.	abstract number	bilang na basal
23.	imperfect number	bilang na balhag
24.	prime number	bilang na lantay (balho)
25.	even number	bilang na tukol
26.	odd number	bilang na gansal
27.	cardinal number	bilang na paulat
28.	ordinal number	bilang na panunod
29.	composite number	bilang na pinaglakip
30.	rectangular number	bilang na paritadlungin
31.	triangular number	bilang na tatsihain

32. numbering	kabilangan, pagbibilang
33. numerology	palabilangan
34. positive integer	tahas na buumbilang
35. negative integer	bilang na buumbilang
36. consecutive integer	kasunod na buumbilang
37. consecutive integers	magkasunod na buumbilang
38. consecutive odd integers	magkakasunod na gansal na buumbilang
39. consecutive even integers	magkakasunod na tukol na buumbilang
40. similar fractions	hawig na bahagimbilang
41. numerator	panakda
42. denominator	pamahagi
43. proper fraction	bahagimbilang na angkop
44. improper fraction	bahagimbilang na di angkop
45. decimal	sampuan
46. decimal system	panampuan
47. decade	sinampu
48. decimal point	tuldok-sampuan, sampuing tuldok
49. decimal notation	sampuing pananda, sampuing halat
50. decimal (notation) fraction	sampuing bahagimbilang
51. terminating decimal	sampuang maytakda
52. repeating (periodic) decimal	sampuang ulitin
53. nonrepeating decimal	sampuang diulitin
54. addition	palaragdagan
55. subtraction	palabawasan
56. multiplication	palaramihan
57. division	palahatian
58. operation	sakilos
59. operator	pakilos
60. four fundamental operations	apat na batayang sakilos
61. sum	dagup (Ilk.), suma
62. total	kabuuan
63. deduct	awasin
64. minuend	bawasin
65. subtrahend	pabawas
66. difference	kaibhan
67. remainder	labi
68. multiplier	parami
69. multiplicand	damihin
70. product	bunga
71. result	kinalabasan
72. dividend	hatiin
73. divisor	pahati

74.	quotient	kinahatian
75.	unit	isahan
76.	unity	kaisahan
77.	equal	katumbas
78.	unequal	di katumbas
79.	identical	kasiya
80.	identity	kasiyangaan
81.	equality	katumbasan
82.	inequality	dikatumbas
83.	equivalent	kahalaga
84.	equivalence	kahalagahan
85.	set algebra, theory of sets	palatangkasan
86.	element	mulhagi
87.	member	kabilang
88.	pair	kapid (Bis.)
89.	ordered pair	kapid na ayos
90.	set	tangkas
91.	set notation	talihalat ng tangkas
92.	universal set	lahatang tangkas
93.	disjoint set	tangkas na diugnay
94.	unit set	isahing tangkas
95.	empty set	walang-lamang tangkas
96.	Venn Diagram	Guhiting Venn
97.	Associative Law	Ugnaying Batas
98.	Distributive Law	Bahagihing Batas
99.	Commutative Law	Paliting Batas
100.	set of number	tangkas ng mga bilang
101.	set of positive integers	tangkas ng mga tahas na buumbilang
102.	element of a set	mulhagi ng isang tangkas
103.	member of a set	kabilang ng isang tangkas
104.	closed	pinid
105.	closure property	katangiang pinid
106.	finite number of elements	hanggang bilang ng mga mulhagi
107.	finite set	hangganing tangkas
108.	infinite number of elements	awangganing bilang ng mga mulhagi
109.	infinite set	awangganing tangkas
110.	roster tabulation method	pamamaraang panalatag
111.	rule (defining property) method	pamamaraang paturing
112.	subset	kubtangkas
113.	complement of a set	kapunuan ng isang tangkas
114.	operation on sets	sakilos sa mga tangkas
115.	union of two sets	kaisahan ng dalawang tangkas
116.	intersect (v.)	bumagtas
117.	intersection	bagtas

118	intersection of two sets	bagtas ng dalawang tangkas
119.	reflexive property	katangiang pabalik
120.	symmetric property	katangiang patimbang
121.	transitive property	katangiang (paragdag) palipat
122.	addition property	katangiang paragdag
123.	multiplication property	katangiang parami
124.	equivalent set	katangiang tangkas
125.	a not equivalent set	di-kahalagang tangkas
126.	equation	tumbasan
127.	formula	sanyo
128.	equals, is equal to	tumbas, ay katumbas ng
129.	to satisfy an equation	lapatan ang isang tumbasan
130.	known	alam
131.	unknown	di-alam
132.	conditional equation	pasubaling tumbasan
133.	variable (n.)	aligin (Mat. Tag.)
134.	variable (adj.)	aligin
135.	constant (n.)	lagiin
136.	constant (adj.)	lagian
137.	(equals) independent variable	sarilining aligin
138.	dependent variable	di-sariling aligin
139.	solve	lutasin
140.	solution	kalutasan
141.	proof	patunay
142.	confirmation	patotoo
143.	test	sulit
144.	principle	simulain
145.	error	mali, kamalian
146.	fault	sala, bisala
147.	discrepancy	biso
148.	constant quantity	lagiang dami
149.	variable quantity	aligang dami
150.	complex variable	hugnayang aligin
151.	even	tukol
152.	odd	gansal
153.	exact	singkad
154.	inexact	disingkad
155.	complete	ganap
156.	incomplete	di-ganap
157.	approximate	madapit
158.	absolute	wagas
159.	perfect	himpit (Bis.)
160.	common	pambalana
161.	double	ibayo
162.	multiple (n.)	kalambal
163.	multiple (adj.)	lambalin

164. random	alisaga
165. random choice	alisagang pili
166. extreme (n.)	sukdulan
167. extreme (adj.)	sukdulin
168. maximum (n.)	higdulan
169. maximum (adj.)	higdulin
170. minimum (n.)	kubdulan
171. minimum (adj.)	kubdulin
172. finite (adj.)	hangganin
173. infinity	awanggan (awan Hanggan)
174. infinity (adj.)	awangganin
175. term	takay
176. lowest term	kababaang takay
177. simplest term	pinakapayak na takay
178. monomial	isakay
179. binomial	duhakay
180. trinomial	talukay
181. polynomial	damikay
182. algebraic expression	panandaing pahayag
183. least common multiple	kababaang lahatang kalambal
184. least common denominator	kababaang lahatang pamahagi
185. inverse	baligtad
186. invert (v.)	baligtarin
187. additive inverse	dagdaging baligtad
188. reciprocal (n.)	kabaligtaran
189. reverse (v.)	tumbalikan
190. reverse (adj.)	tumbalik
191. reverse (n.)	katumbalikan
192. reversible	tumbalikin
193. proportion	hagway
194. ratio	tagway
195. coefficient	katuwang
196. factor (n.)	kabuo
197. factor (v.)	bungkagin
198. factorial	bungkagin
199. function (math.)	bunin
200. domain of a function	kabisa
201. range of a function	saklaw ng isang kabisa
202. linear function	abot ng isang kabisa
203. function (mechs.)	tuwiring kabisa
204. purpose.	taan
205. score (rating)	laan
206. series (math.)	lubig
207. one-to-one correspondence	dalayray
208. distributive	sungkad
209. associative	bahagihin
	ugnayin

210. commutative	palitin
211. symbol, notation	halat
212. representation	talihalat
213. average	balasak
214. average cost	halagang balasak
215. average weight	bigat na balasak
216. median	gitnaan
217. mean	tamtaman
218. mean value	tamtamang halaga
219. percent	bahagdan
220. frame	bastagan
221. matrix	baskagan
222. graph	talangguhit (grap)
223. diagram	guhitin (dayagram)
224. chart	taltaguhit (tsart)
225. design	antangan (disenyo)
226. pattern	hulwaran
227. model	uliran
228. scale (of measure- ments	talasukan (iskala)
229. scale (of degrees)	talaantasan
230. scale (of sizes)	talasukatan
231. permutation	pamalitan
232. combination	palakipan
233. probability	kalagmitan
234. certainty	katiyakan
235. uncertainty	di-katiyakan
236. calculate	taya
237. calculator	pantaya
238. compute	tuos
239. computation	tuusan
240. computer	panuos
241. accounting	palatuusan
242. rounding off	pagbilog
243. clock arithmetic	bilnurang taknain
244. degree	antas
245. degree of a term	antas ng isang takay
246. degree of a polyno- mial	antas ng isang damikay
247. length	haba
248. width	lapad
249. height	taas
250. altitude	tayog
251. area	dawak (erya)
252. side	silid
253. circle	bilog
254. semicircle	hatimbilog
255. oval	habilog
256. ellipse	duyog
257. disc	dalipay

258.	circumference	tikop (sirkumperensiya)
259.	perimeter	gikop (gilid salikop)
260.	diameter	bantod
261.	radius	lihit (lihang guhit, radiyus)
262.	diagonal	hilis
263.	hypotenuse	gilis (gilid na hilis)
264.	vertex	tuktok
265.	base	takad
266.	tangent	dikit
267.	perpendicular	tadlong
268.	envelope	bilot
269.	shape	hugis
270.	form	anyo
271.	figure	laraw
272.	point	tuldok
273.	line	guhit
274.	slope	hilig
275.	curvature	kakiluan
276.	curve	kilo (kurba)
277.	surface	dayag
278.	surface as contrasted the reverse	karayagan
279.	surfaces	kubdayag
280.	plane	lapya
281.	plane figure	lapyang laraw
282.	plane closed figure	lapyang laraw na pinid
283.	angle	siha
284.	acute angle	sihang kipot
285.	obtuse angle	sihang bika
286.	straight angle	sihang ladlad
287.	right angle	sihang tadlong
288.	base angle	sihang takaran
289.	alternate angle	sihang magkasalisi
290.	adjacent angle	sihang magkatabi
291.	opposite angle	sihang magkatapat
292.	complementary angles	sihang magkapuno
293.	supplementary angles	sihang magkaladlad
294.	complement (of angles)	kapuno
295.	supplement (of angles)	kaladlad
296.	equilateral	parigilid
297.	equianggular	parisiha
298.	polygon	damiha
299.	triangle (trigon)	tatsiha (tatsulok)
300.	tetragon (quadrangle)	patsiha
301.	quadrilateral	patgilid

302. trapezoid	tagigapay
303. parallelogram	parigapay
304. rhomboid	tagihilis
305. rectangle	paritadlong
306. rhombus	tagisukat
307. square	parisukat
308. pentagon	limsiha
309. hexagon	nimsiha
310. heptagon	pitsiha
311. octagon	walsiha
312. nonagon	samsiha
313. decagon	pulsiha·
314. volume	buok
315. bulk	bikil
316. perspective (3-dim. effect)	sawang
317. sphere	timbulog
318. hemisphere	hatimbulog
319. globe	hilihid
320. hoop	bagway
321. cope	talulo
322. pyramid	tagilo
323. truncated	tinapyas
324. prism	binalimbing
325. cylinder	bumbong
326. cylindrical	binumbong
327. evolution (math.)	sultag (sulong latag)
328. involution	balisultag
329. power	lambal
330. exponent	paulit
331. root	ugat
332. radical	pang-ugat
333. radical sign	halat pang-ugat
334. radicand	ugatin
335. index of a radicand	kaugatan
336. exponential function	pauliting kabisa
337. repeating function	uliting kabisa
338. square root	pariugat
339. cube root	taluugat
340. extraction of roots	hiugat
341. raising to a power	paglalambal
342. extract the 6th root of 729	ugatin hanggang ika-6 ang 729
343. square (the 2nd power)	parirami
344. cube (the 3rd power)	talurami
345. perfect square	himpit na parirami
346. difference of two square	kaibhan ng dalawang parirami

IBA PANG URI NG KORESPONDENSIYA*
Assorted Correspondence
KORESPONDENSIYANG PANLOOB-TANGGAPAN

Ang Korespondensiyang panloob tanggapan ay sumasakop sa lahat ng nasusulat na komunikasyong nauukol sa gawain ng tanggapan na nagdaraan sa mga kamay ng mga kawani at mga pinuno. Ang mga tanggapang malalaki ay may magagaling na sistema ng korespondensiyang panloob. Upang makapagtipid sa maraming bagay, sila ay gumagamit ng mga makabagong pamamaraan gaya ng telepono, radyo, diktorgrap, atb. nguni't higit na pinahahalagahan at mapagkakatiwalaan ang nasusulat lalo na kung iyon ay ninanais gawing sanggunian sa hinaharap. Bukod sa mga nabanggit, ang ano mang bagay na nasusulat ay madaling natutunton ang pinanggalingan at sa gayon ay nakatutulong sa mabisang pagpapalakad ng tanggapan.

MGA HALIMBAWA NG KORESPONDENSIYA SA LOOB NG TANGGAPAN

1. Memorandum Panloob-Tanggapan. May mga memorandum na ukol lamang sa isa o iilang tao kaya ang memorandum ay kinokopya sa ibang papel at nilalagyan ng pangalan ng pinag-uukulan. Madalas namang ang memorandum ay ukol sa lahat ng kawani at/o pinuno kaya sa halip na maghanda ng maraming sipi para sa mga kinauukulan, isang sipi na lamang nito ang inilalakip sa minimyograp na pangalan ng mga kawani at pinuno. Maraming tanggapan ang lagi nang may minimyograp o nilimbag na pangalan ng lahat ng kawani para sa ganitong mga layunin. Narito ang isang halimbawa:

* Mula sa PATNUBAY SA KORRESPONDENSIYA OPISYAL NG SURIAN NG W-P-1970

Mga Pinuno at Tauhan ng
SURIAN NG WIKANG PAMBANSA

Patnugot:	PONCIANO B. P. PINEDA
Pangalawang Patnugot:	FE ALDAVE YAP

PANGALAN

1. ____________________
2. ____________________
3. ____________________
4. ____________________
5. ____________________
6. ____________________
7. ____________________
8. ____________________
9. ____________________
10. ____________________
11. ____________________
12. ____________________
13. ____________________
14. ____________________
15. ____________________
16. ____________________
17. ____________________
18. ____________________
19. ____________________
20. ____________________
21. ____________________
22. ____________________
23. ____________________
24. ____________________
25. ____________________
26. ____________________
27. ____________________
28. ____________________

29. ____________________

30. ____________________

31. ____________________

32. ____________________

33. ____________________

34. ____________________

35. ____________________

36. ____________________

37. ____________________

38. ____________________

39. ____________________

40. ____________________

41. ____________________

42. ____________________

43. ____________________

44. ____________________

45. ____________________

46. ____________________

47. ____________________

48. ____________________

49. ____________________

50. ____________________

____

____

____

Petsa:

____________ **LAYUNIN:**

____

May mga sulat na ipinadadala sa mga tao o tanggapang hindi siyang nararapat pag-ukulan. Mayroon namang sumusulat na hindi rin nakatitiyak kung kanino dapat sumulat, magtanong o humingi ng kaukulang impormasyon. Ito'y karaniwan lalo na sa malalaking tanggapan gaya ng kagawaran. Mayroon namang sulat na bagaman ipinadadala sa tumpak na patunguhan ay hindi karaka-rakang masagot sapagka't kailangang isangguni o itukoy muna sa iba. Ito ay kung saan-saan pang tao dumaraan sapagka't itinutukoy muna sa mga kinauukulan. Ito ang tinatawag na *paglilipat.* Maaari itong isang rekomendasyon o tagubilin, puna, sagot o pansin na idinadagdag sa sulat na ililipat sa kinauukulan.

Ang isang paglilipat ay maaaring isulat na lamang sa ibaba ng saligang liham kung ito ay may sapat na puwang. Ang mga bahagi nito ay binubuo lamang ng salitang paglilipat na pinangungunahan ng bilang na nagpapakilala kung ikailan na ang paglilipat. Sa ilalim ng paglilipat ay nakalagay kung saang tanggapan galing at sa ilalim ng tanggapan ay nakasulat naman ang petsa. Ang mga ito ay nakasentro sa papel gaya ng makikita sa ibaba

Unang Paglilipat
KAWANIHAN NG MGA PAARALANG BAYAN
Oktubre 22, 1969

Ang mga paglilipat ay inuukol sa mga taong maaaring may katungkulang higit na mataas na nagpapadala ng paglilipat, maaaring kapantay, at maaari namang mas mababa. Kaya sa simula ng mga paglilipat ay nakikita ang mga pariralang "Mapitagang itinutukoy..." kung ang paglilipat ay ukol sa isang nakabababa ang tungkulin kaysa nagpapadala ng paglilipat; kung ang paglilipat ay nauukol sa nakatataas, ginagamit ang pariralang "Mapitagang itinutuloy..." at kung magkapantay naman ang nagpapadala at pinadadalhan ng paglilipat, angkop nang gamitin ang "Mapitagang inililipat ..' bagaman bilang paggalang, ang iba ay gumagamit ng pariralang ukol sa nakatataas. Halimbawa, buhat sa isang direktor patungo sa kapwa direktor ay sapat na ang "Mapitagang inililipat..."

Ang paglilipat ay hindi na nilalagyan ng patunguhan gaya ng karaniwang liham. Nguni't iyon naman ay binabanggit sa katawan ng paglilipat at sumusunod sa mga salitang ginagamit sa pagtutukoy gaya ng makikita sa mga halimbawang sumusunod:

"Mapitagang itinutuloy sa Kagalang-galang, Ang Kalihim Tagapagpaganap, Tanggapan ng Pangulo, sa pamamagitan ng Kagalang-galang, Ang Komisyondo ng Badyet, Maynila . . . ."

"Mapitagang ibinabalik sa pamamagitan ng Kagalang-galang, Ang Komisyonado ng Badyet, sa Kagalang-galang, Ang Kalihim ng Edukasyon, Maynila . . . . ."

"Mapitagang ibinabalik, sa pamamagitan ng Kagalang-galang, Ang Auditor Heneral, sa Kagalang-galang, Ang Kalihim ng Edukasyon, Maynila . . . . ."

Ang paglilipat ay karaniwang maikli, madalas na bumabanggit na lamang sa nilalaman ng saligang liham na lagi nang kasama ng paglilipat at humihingi ng aksiyong kinakailangan. Kaya madalas, pormula ang ginagamit gaya ng sumusunod:

". . . upang pagpasiyahan."	(. . . for action)
". . . upang pag-ukulan ang kuru-kuro at ibalik pagkatapos."	(. . . for comment and return.)
". . . upang ihingi ng kuru-kuro at tagubilin."	(. . . for comment and recommendation.)
". . . lakip ang tagubiling pagtibayin."	(. . . recommending approval.)
". . . kalakip ang pagpapatibay."	(. . . approved.)

Ang paglilipat ay nilalagyan din ng lagda katulad ng isang karaniwang liham pampamahalaan. At katulad din ng karaniwang liham, ang paglilipat ay maaaring lagdaan ng ibang tao na hindi siyang tinutukoy sa paglilipat gaya ng mga halimbawa sa kabila:

FAUSTINO SY-CHANGCO
Komisyonado ng Badyet

Ni:

(LGD.) MARIA D. DELA CRUZ
Namamanihalang Tagasuri ng Badyet

ISMAEL MATHAY, AMA
Auditor Heneral

Ni:

(LGD.) MARCELO B. CONCEPCION
Auditor
Sangay ng mga Ulat Piskal
at Estadistika

Republika ng Pilipinas
Kagawaran ng Edukasyon
TANGGAPAN NG KALIHIM
Maynila

Unang Paglilipat
Setyembre 30, 1970

Mapitagang ibinabalik sa Patnugot ng Kawanihan ng Paaralang Bayan, Maynila. Nabatid na ng tanggapang ito ang nilalaman.

Para sa Kalihim ng Edukasyon:

(LGD.) JOSE J. LIM
Pinunong Pantauhan IV

Re: Bb. Fortunata D. Mendoza
J3/dcs

Republika ng Pilipinas
Kagawaran ng Kalakalan at Industriya
KOMISYON SA MGA PANAGOT AT PALITAN
Maynila

Unang Paglilipat
Enero 14 1970

Magalang na itinutukoy sa Puno, Tanggapan ng Katulong ng Pangulo sa Pagpapabahay at Paglilipat-Tahanan, Tanggapan ng Pangulo, Lungsod ng Quezon, hinihiling ang kanyang kuru-kuro at tagubilin sa kalakip na mga artikulo ng inkorporasyon sa binabalak ng DIVILACAN SETTLERS ASSOCIATION, INCORPORATED, dahil sa mga tadhana ng talataan (2), Artikulo II nito.

Lubos na pahahalagahan ang maagang pagbabalik ng mga papeles na ito lakip ang pagpapasiya.

ARCADIO E. YABYABIN
Puli Komisyonado ng mga Panagot at Palitan

Kal.: Gaya ng nasasaad.

MGA KOMUNIKASYON BUHAT SA MAYKAPANGYARIHAN

KAUTUSANG TAGAPAGPAGANAP
(Executive Order)

Ang mga ito ay aktang pampangasiwaan at kautusan ng Pangulo hinggil sa organisasyon o pamaraan ng pagpapakilos ng pamahalaan, ng muling pagsasaayos o muling pag-aakma ng alin mang distrito, dibisyon, bahagi o mga bahagi ng Pilipinas, at lahat ng akta o kautusang sumasakop sa pangkalahatang pagtupad sa tungkulin ng mga empleado ng bayan, ng pagpapasiya sa mga isyung may kahalagahang pangkalahatan.

Halimbawa:

MALAKANYANG
TAHANAN NG PANGULO NG PILIPINAS
MAYNILA

KAUTUSANG TAGAPAGPAGANAP BLG. 187

NAG-AATAS SA LAHAT NANG KAGAWARAN, KAWANIHAN, TANGGAPAN AT IBA PANG SANGAY NG PAMAHALAAN NA GAMITIN ANG WIKANG PILIPINO HANGGA'T MAAARI SA LINGGO NG WIKANG PAMBANSA AT PAGKARAAN NITO, SA LAHAT NANG OPISYAL NA KOMUNIKASYON AT TRANSAKSIYON NG PAMAHALAAN.

SAPAGKA'T ang pagpapaunlad at pagpapalaganap ng isang wikang pambansang Pilipino na itinatadhana ng Saligang-Batas at ng Batas Komonwelt Blg. 570 ay isa sa mga pangunahing layunin ng pangasiwaang ito; at

SAPAGKA'T ang ating wikang pambansa, na tinatanggap na at nakikilala ngayon ng lahat bilang "Pilipino" ay isa sa mga mahalagang sangkap ng nasyonalismo na makapagbubunsod sa ating bayan sa ibayong kaunlaran, katiwasayan at pagkakaisa;

DAHIL DITO, ako, FERDINAND E. MARCOS, Pangulo ng Pilipinas, sa bisa ng kapangyarihang ipinagkaloob sa akin ng batas at bilang pagbibigay-buhay sa layunin ng Saligang-Batas at ng Batas Komonwelt Blg. 570, ay nag-aatas at nagpapahayag na gamitin hangga't maaari, sa lahat nang kagawaran, kawanihan, tanggapan at iba pang sangay ng pamahalaan ang wikang Pilipino sa Linggo ng Wika at gayon din pagkaraan nito sa lahat nang komunikasyon at transaksyon ng pamahalaan.

NILAGDAAN sa Lunsod ng Maynila, ngayong ikaanim ng Agosto, sa taon ng Ating Panginoon, labinsiyam na raan at animnapu't siyam.

(LAGDA) FERDINAND E. MARCOS
Pangulo ng Pilipinas

Nilagdaan ng Pangulo:

(LAGDA) ERNESTO M. MACEDA
Kalihim Tagapagpaganap

KAUTUSANG PAMPANGASIWAAN
(Administrative Order)

Sa kalahatang ito ay binubuo ng mga akta o kautusan ng Pangulo na ang kahalagahan ay hindi panlahat at mahalaga lamang sa isang tiyak na sangay o tanggapan ng pamahalaan, gaya halimbawa ng pagtitiwalag o pagpipigil sa tungkulin ng mga hinihirang ng Pangulo at iba pang matataas na pinuno ng pamahalaan, paglikha ng mga komite at paglalapat ng mga kabawalan sa mga pinuno at kawani hinggil sa kanilang mga gawaing ekstra opisyal.

Ang kautusang pampangasiwaan ay nagpapaliwanag kung anu-ano ang magagawa o hindi dapat gawin ng isang administrador.

PROKLAMASYON O PAGPAPAHAYAG
(Proclamation)

Ito ay pagtatakda ng petsa kung kailan magkakabisa ang isang tanging batas, resolusyon, o kautusan, o ano mang impormasyon ng kahalagahang pambayan na itinakda ng batas, resolusyon o kautusang tagapagpaganap. Paglalaan ng lupang gobyerno para sa mga layuning pambayan. Paglalagay ng isang purok sa isang subdibisyong panghеograpika bilang nasa katayuang pangkagipitan. Pagpapahayag ng pagdaraos ng tanging eleksiyon, pagtawag sa kongreso para sa tangi ng pulong pagpapahayag ng pista opisyal. Pag-ukol ng alin mang linggo para sa mga tanging layuning pambayan, atb.

Narito ang ilang halimbawa ng memorandum sirkular memorandum pangkagawaran at memorandum pantanggapan.

TANGGAPAN NG PANGULO NG PILIPINAS
(OFFICE OF THE PRESIDENT OF THE PHILIPPINES)

MEMORANDUM SIRKULAR BLG. 384

PAGTATALAGA NG KAWANING MANGANGASIWA SA LAHAT NG KOMUNIKASYON SA WIKANG PILIPINO SA LAHAT NG KAGAWARAN, KAWANIHAN, TANGGAPAN, AT IBA PANG SANGAY NG PAMAHALAAN AT KORPORASYONG ARI O PINANGANGASIWAAN NG PAMAHALAAN.

Ang Kautusang Tagapagpaganap Blg. 187 na may petsang Agosto 6, 1969 ay naglalayong pag-ibayuhin ang pagpapalaganap ng wikang pambansa sa pamamagitan ng paggamit hangga't maaari ng wikang Pilipino sa lahat ng komunikasyon at transaksiyong pampamahalaan. Alinsunod sa isinasaad ng naturang kautusang tagapagpaganap, ay iniaatas sa lahat ng kagawaran, kawanihan, tanggapan, at iba pang sangay ng pamahalaan, at korporasyong ari o pinangangasiwaan ng pamahalaan ang pagtatalaga ng kaukulang kawani na mangangasiwa ng lahat ng komunikasyon at transaksiyon sa wikang Pilipino na tinatanggap at/o nagmumula sa kani-kanilang mga tanggapan.

Ang sirkular na ito ay magkakabisa agad.

Ayon sa Kapangyarihang gawad ng Pangulo:

(LAGDA) ALEJANDRO MELCHOR
Kalihim Tagapagpaganap

Maynila, Agosto 17, 1970

TANGGAPAN NG PANGULO NG PILIPINAS

MEMORANDUM SIRKULAR BLG. 400

PINAHIHINTULUTAN ANG LAHAT NG TAUHAN NG GOBYERNO NA LUMABAS SA OPISINA MULA SA 4:00 ng hapon, Okt. 13, 1970

Dahil sa ulat mula sa Kawanihan ng Panahon na ang bagyong "Sening" ay inaasahang daraan sa Gitnang Luson, kasama ang Maynila, anumang oras ngayong gabi, ang mga opisyales at kawani ng gobyerno na nag-uupisina sa purok ng Malawak na Maynila ay pinahihintulutang umuwi na ngayong hapon, simula sa alas-4:00.

Sa pahintulot ng Pangulo

(LGD) ROBERTO V. REYES
Pansamantalang Kalihim Tagapagpaganap

Maynila, Oktubre 13, 1970

Republika ng Pilipinas
KAGAWARAN NG EDUKASYON
Maynila

TANGGAPAN NG KALIHIM

Setyembre 1, 1970

KAUTUSANG PANGKAGAWARAN
Blg. , s. 1970

HUMIHILING NG PUSPUSANG
PAG-ALINSUNOD SA MEMORANDUM
SIRKULAR BLG. 348

Sa Lahat ng mga Direktor ng Kawanihan
at mga Puno ng Tanggapan:

Kalakip nito ang Memorandum Sirkular Blg. 384 ng Tanggapan ng Pangulo ng Pilipinas na may petsang Agosto 17, 1970, na pinamagatang PAGTATALAGA NG KAWANING MANGANGASIWA SA LAHAT NG KOMUNIKASYON SA WIKANG PILIPINO SA LAHAT NG KAGAWARAN, KAWANIHAN, TANGGAPAN, AT IBA PANG SANGAY NG PAMAHALAAN AT KORPORASYONG ARI O PINANGANGASIWAAN NG PAMAHALAAN. Hinihiling na ang pangalan ng mga itatalagang tauhang mamamahala sa disposisyon ng lahat ng korespondensiya opisyal sa Pilipino ay ipadala sa Tanggapang ito.

(LGD.) ONOFRE D. CORPUZ
Kalihim

Kal.: Gaya ng nasasaad.

Republika ng Pilipinas
Kagawaran ng Edukasyon
TANGGAPAN NG KALIHIM
Maynila

Enero 5, 1970

KAUTUSANG PANGKAGAWARAN
Blg. 1, s. 1970

PAGKAHIRANG SA PANGALAWANG KALIHIM ANDRES CLEMENTE

Sa Lahat ng mga Direktor ng Kawanihan
at mga Puno ng Tanggapan:

Simula ngayon, ang Kgg. Andres Clemente ay manunungkulan bilang Pangalawang Kalihim ng Edukasyon. Sana'y maging patnubay ninyo ito gaya nang nararapat.

(LGD.) ONOFRE D. CORPUZ
Kalihim

Republika ng Pilipinas
(Republic of the Philippines)
Kagawaran ng Edukasyon
(Department of Education)
KAWANIHAN NG PAARALANG BAYAN
(BUREAU OF PUBLIC SCHOOLS)
Maynila

Oktubre 19, 1970

MEMORANDUM NG TANGGAPAN

Sa Lahat ng Puno ng Sangay:

Kalakip ng Memorandum na ito ay sipi ng Memorandum Pangkagawaran Blg. 39, s. 1970 — "Seminar sa Korespondensiya sa Pilipino para sa mga Direktor ng Kawanihan at Puno ng mga Tanggapan."

Hinihiling na ang lahat ng puno ng mga sangay ay dumalo sa Seminar sa Pilipino na idaraos sa BPS Operations Center mula bukas, Oktubre 20 hanggang 22, 1970, sa pangangasiwa ng Surian ng Wikang Pambansa. Kalakip din nito ang palatuntunan ng Seminar.

(LGD.) LICERIA BRILLANTES SORIANO
Patnugot

Kalakip:
Gaya ng nabanggit

Kagawaran ng Edukasyon
SURIAN NG WIKANG PAMBANSA
Maynila

Oktubre 20, 1970

MEMORANDUM kina:

PAMFILO D. CATACATACA
ADELA M. QUIZON
LETICIA T. AUSTRIA
LAMBERTO C. MANUZON
MACEDONIO G. NECESITO
DOMINGO SM. DELA CRUZ

Sa kabutihan ng paglilingkod at bilang pagtupad sa Memorandum Sirkular Blg. 277 ng Pangulo ng Republika, kayo ay inaatasang dumalo na kasama ang nakalagda rito sa Seminar sa Pilipino na gaganapin sa Lungsod Quezon, simula sa Oktubre 21-23, 1970, upang magbigay ng panayam at magsagawa ng kailangang pakikipag-ugnay sa nasabing seminar.

Ang inyong pagdalo ay sa oras na opisyal at ano mang kaukulang gugol ay masisingil, sa pasubaling may pondo at sa ilalim ng mga pagsusuri at pagtutuos at pag-aaudit.

(LGD.) PONCIANO B. P. PINEDA
Direktor

Pormularyong S.S. Blg. 32

Republika ng Pilipinas
KOMISYON NG SERBISYO SIBIL

PANUNUMPA SA KATUNGKULAN

Ako, si .... ng

....

na (hinirang/itinalaga) sa katungkulan bilang ....

....

ay taimtim na nanunumpa na tutuparin kong buong husay at katapatan, sa abot ng aking kakayahan, ang mga tungkulin na aking kasalukuyang katungkulan at ng iba pa pagkaraan nito'y gagampanan ko sa ilalim ng Republika ng Pilipinas; na aking itataguyod at ipagtatanggol ang Saligang-batas ng Pilipinas; na ako'y tunay na mananalig at tatalima rito; na susundin ko ang mga batas, mga utos na ayon sa batas, at mga atas na pinaiiral ng mga sadyang itinakdang may-kapangyarihan ng Republika ng Pilipinas; at kusa kong babalikatin ang pananagutang ito, nang walang ano mang pasubali o hangaring umiwas.

KASIHAN NAWA AKO NG DIYOS.

....
(Hinirang/Itinalaga)

NILAGDAAN AT PINANUMPAAN sa harap ko ngayong ika- .... araw ng ...., sa .... Pilipinas. Nagharap ng kanyang Sedula Blg. A- ...., kinuha sa .... noong ika- ...., 19 ....

....
(Pinunong Tagapanumpa)

Dikitan ng isang 30 sentimong selyo dokumentaryo

....
(Katungkulan sa Pamahalaan)

Pormularyo Blg. 48 ng Serbisyo Sibil

TALAORASANG PANG-ARAW-ARAW

....

(Pangalan)

Para sa buwan ng .... 19 ....

Opisyal na oras ng pag-dating at pag-alis (Karaniwang mga araw ....
(
(
(Sabado ....

ARAW	UMAGA		HAPON		PAGPASOK NANG HULI PAGLABAS NANG MAAGA	
	Pagda-ting	Pag-alis	Pagda-ting	Pag-alis	Oras	Min-uto
1						
2						
3						
4						
5						
6						
7						
8						
9						
10						
11						
12						
13						
14						
15						
16						
17						
18						
19						
20						
21						

22
23
24
25
26
27
28
29
30
31

Kabuuan ....

....

Pinatutunayan ko na ang nasa itaas ay totoo at wastong ulat ng oras na aking ipinaglingkod, at ang pagtatala ay ginawa araw-araw pagdating at pag-alis sa tanggapan.

....

Napatunayan ayon sa takdang oras ng opisina.

....

Namamahala

(TINGNAN ANG PANUTO SA LIKOD)

18—28

MGA PANUTO

Ang Pormularyo Blg. 48 ng Serbisyo Sibil, matapos maisagawa, ay dapat tipunin sa kasulatan ng Kawanihan o Tanggapang naghaharap ng buwanang ulat ng Pormularyo Blg. 3 sa Komisyon ng Serbisyo Sibil.

Sa halip ng nasa itaas, ang mga interprete at takigrapo ng hukuman na sumasama sa mga hukom ng Hukumang Unang Dulugan ay susulat sa pang-araw-araw na ulat ng oras sa pormularyong ito nang triplikado, pagkatapos ay dapat pagtibayin ng hukom na kanilang pinaglilingkuran, o ng isang pinuno ng Kagawaran ng Katarungan na may kapangyarihang gumawa nito. Ang orihinal ay dapat ipadala nang madalian sa katapusan ng buwan sa Komisyon ng Serbisyo Sibil, sa pamamagitan ng Kagawaran ng Katarungan; ang ikalawang sipi ay iingatan ng Kagawaran ng Katarungan; at ang pangatlong sipi ay sa tanggapan ng Eskribano ng Hukuman na siyang pinaglilingkuran.

Sa puwang sa kabila na inilaan para sa layuning ito ay ipakikita ang kinakailangang oras ng opisina na dapat sundin ng isang kawani, gaya, halimbawa ng "Karaniwang araw, 8:00-12:00 at 1:00-4:00; Sabado, 8:00-1:00."

Tinatawagan ang pansin sa talataan 3, Kautusang Tagapagpaganap Blg. 5, serye ng 1969, ng alituntuning XI ng Serbisyo Sibil, na mababasa gaya ng sumusunod

"Kakailanganin ng bawat puno ng isang Kawanihan o Tanggapan ang isang pang-araw-araw na talaan ng pagpapasok ng lahat ng pinuno at kawaning sakop niya na may karapatan sa pagliban o bakasyon (kasama ang mga guro) na iingatan sa angkop na pormularyo at gayon din ang isang maayos na rekord ng tanggapan na nagpapakita sa bawat araw ng lahat ng pagliban sa tungkulin sa anumang dahilan. Sa simula ng bawat buwan siya ay mag-uulat sa Komisyonado sa angkop na pormularyo ng lahat ng pagliban, sa anumang dahilan, kasama ang tamang bilang ng oras ng pagpasok nang huli at pagkalabas nang maaga ng bawat tao sa bawat araw. Ang mga pinuno at kawaning naglilingkod sa larangan o sa tubig ay hindi na hihinging gumawa ng isang pang-araw-araw na talaan subali't lahat ng mga pagliban ng ganyang mga kawani ay dapat isama sa buwanang ulat ng mga pagbabago at pagliban. Ang panghuhuwad ng talaorasan ay pananagutan ng nagkasalang pinuno o kawani ng tuwirang pagkakatiwalag sa tungkulin at pag-uusig ng kriminal."

(PANSIN. — Ang isang talaang ginawa batay sa gunita sa pagkakataong sumusunod sa pagkaganap ng isang pangyayari ay hindi mapanghahawakan. Ang di-pagtalima sa mga oras ng opisina ay mag-aalis sa isang kawani ng karapatan sa bakasyon kahima't naglingkod nang obertaym. Kapag naglingkod sa labas ng tanggapan sa buong umaga o hapon, dapat itala ang gayon nang maliwanag.

KAHILINGAN SA PAGLIBAN
Pormularyo ng S.S. Blg. 6
Serye ng 1968

TANGGAPAN/AHENSIYA SURIAN NG WIKANG PAMBANSA	Pangalan (Huli, una, gitna) Katungkulan Suweldo (Buwanan)
(Bakasyong Hinihiling) ☐ Bakasyon ☐ Sakit (Mangyaring lagyan ng tsek) ☐ Panganganak ☐ Terminal	Sanhi (kung pagkakasakit, personal, pagbibitiw, atb.)
Blg. ng araw (*Mga Saklaw na Petsa*) Mula Hanggang	
Komutasyon ☐ hinihiling ☐ di-hinihiling Petsa ng Pagharap	LAGDA NG MAY- KAHILINGAN

Pasiya (ng Tanggapan o Ahensiya)	Petsa Lagda Opisyal na Titulo
Pasiya (ng Puno ng Kagawaran, kung kailangan)	Petsa Lagda Opisyal na Titulo

MGA PANUTO

1. Ang kahilingan sa libang-bakasyon o pagkakasakit para sa isang buong araw o higit pa ay dapat gawin sa pormularyong ito.
2. Ang kahilingan sa libang-bakasyon ay dapat iharap nang lalong maaga o hangga't maaari, limang (5) araw bago magbakasyon.
3. Ang kahilingan sa liban sa pagkakasakit na iniharap nang lalong maaga, o higit sa limang (5) araw ay dapat lakipan ng sertipiko medikal.

KAHILINGAN SA PANSAMANTALANG PAGTATALAGA
S.S. PORMULARYO BLG. 405

Republika ng Pilipinas
KOMISYON NG SERBISYO SIBIL
Maynila

(Dapat isagawa ng ahensiyang pinaghirangan sa empleado nang palagian. Kung ang pagtatalaga ay buhat sa isang tanggapan tungo sa iba, ang mga Aytem Blg. 1-7, 10-11 ay dapat na may patunay ng ahensiyang pinapasukan ng empleado at ang mga Aytem Blg. 8-9, 12-13 ng ahensiyang humihiling.)

1. Pangalan ng Empleadong Binabalak na Italaga	2. Katungkulan	3. Katayuan ng Paghirang (Palagian, probisyonal, temporaryo)	4. Pangkat at/o Sangay

5. Katungkulan (sa panahon ng pagtatalaga)	6. Saan	7. Panahon ng Pagtatalaga (Sabihin ang Saklaw na Petsa)

8. Uri ng mga gawaing isasagawa samantalang nakatalaga

9. Dahilan ng Pansamantalang Pagtatalaga	10. Kabuuan ng Tauhang Bumubuo ng Ahensiya	11. Bilang ng mga taong nakatalaga na nang iharap ang kahilingang ito

12. Ang kahilingan ba sa pagtatalaga ng nasa itaas na empleado ay ☐ Para sa unang pagkakataon ☐ Para sa pagpapatuloy ng pagtatalaga	13. Kung ang kahilingan ay para sa pagpapatuloy, sabihin ang petsa ng orihinal na pagtatalaga

PINATUNAYANG WASTO:

Lagda ng puno ng kagawaran ng humihiling na ahensiya

Lagda ng puno ng kagawaran ng humihiling na ahensiya empleado

PORMULARYONG PANLAHAT BLG. 15 (A)
(Binago noong Hulyo, 1947)

KAPANGYARIHAN NG KINATAWAN

ALAMIN NG TANANG MAKABABASA NITO:

Na ako, si ...., nagtatrabaho sa ...., Republika ng Pilipinas,
(*Kawanihan o Tanggapan*)
bilang ...., sa pama-
(*Ilahad ang uri ng katungkulan*)
magitan nito'y hinihirang si ....
ng .... na tunay at legal kong kinatawan, para sa akin at sa aking pangalan, katayuan, lugar, at sa halip ko upang sumingil sa nabanggit na Pamahalaan ng Republika ng Pilipinas ng halagang .... 100 piso ((P..................) ....
(*Ilahad ang dahilan ng halagang singilin*)
buhat sa alin mang bayad o mga gantimpala, o ano mang paghahabol o mga paghahabol ng ano mang uri na ngayon ay dapat bayaran o pagkatapos nito'y babayaran sa akin ng naturang Pamahalaan, at lumagda sa mga resibo para rito at mag-indoso sa mga "warrant" o tseke na kinuha sa Tesorero ng naturang Pamahalaan o alin mang lagakan ng Pamahalaan, at gumawa ng lahat ng bagay na kailangang isagawa at yaong magagawa ng aking sarili kung ako ay personal na kaharap, at sa pamamagitan nito'y aking pinatitibayan at pinatutunayan ang lahat ng legal na hakbang na isinagawa ng aking nabanggit na kinatawan sa bisa nito. Ang kapangyarihan ng kinatawang ito ay may bisa hanggang sa maipadala ko sa Tesorero ng Pilipinas at sa Auditor Heneral ang isang nakasulat na patalastas ng pagpapawalang-bisa.

BILANG KATUNAYAN NITO, ako ay lumagda ngayong ika .... araw ng ...., 19 ....

....
(*Lagda ng Nagtatalaga*)

G./Gng./Bb. .... ay lalagda:

....
(*Pangalan ng Nagtatalaga*)

Ni ....
(*Kinatawan*)

REPUBLIKA NG PILIPINAS)
LALAWIGAN NG ....)ss.
MUNISIPYO O LUNGSOD NG ....)

Sa Munisipyo o Lungsod ng ...., Lalawigan ng .... ngayong ika .... araw ng ...., 19 ...., ay personal na humarap sa akin si .... na kilala kong iyon ding taong nagsagawa ng naunang kapangyarihan ng kinatawan at nakilalang yaon ay kanyang malayang pasiya at gawa, nagharap sa akin ng kanyang Sedula Blg. ...., kinuha sa ...., noong ...., 19............

Iginawad sa pamamagitan ng aking lagda at tatak.

Dikitan ng isang
50-sentimong
Selyo Dokumentaryo

Dok. Blg. ....
Pahina Blg. ....
Aklat Blg. ....
Serye ng ....

....
Notaryo Publiko
Ang aking komisyon ay magwawakas sa

...., 19..............

TANDAAN. — Dapat tugunin ang lahat ng kahingian sa limang kopya, ang orihinal ay ipadadala sa Auditor Heneral, ang ikalawang kopya ay sa Tesorero ng Pilipinas, ang ikatlong kopya ay sa Puno ng Kawanihan o Tanggapang magbabayad, ang ikaapat na kopya ay sa notaryo publiko at ang ikalimang kopya ay sa nagtatalaga

O — 023524

TALANG DATOS NA PERSONAL
S.S. Pormularyo Blg. 212 (1965)

Republika ng Pilipinas
Kagawaran ng Edukasyon
SURIAN NG WIKANG PAMBANSA
Maynila

PANUNTUNAN

1. Gawin ang pormularyong ito at sa sariling sulat-kamay.
2. Kung kailangan ang higit na espasyo para sa mga kasagutan, maaaring gumamit ng malinis na papel pangmakinilyang 8-1/2 x 14. Sundin ang ayos na tulad ng sa aplikasyon at lagyan ng bilang gaya nang nararapat.

1. Pangalan (Huli) (Una) (Panggitna)

6. Katayuan sa Buhay
☐ Walang asawa
☐ Balo

. Petsa ng kapanganakan

7. Sekso
☐ Lalaki
☐ Babae

3. Pook na sinilangan

8. Kung may-asawa, itala ang pangalan ng asawa at mga pangalan at gulang ng buhay na anak

4. Tirahan sa Lungsod ....

....

5. Tirahan sa Lalawigan ....

....

9. Edukasyon

Paaralang Huling Pinasukan	Pinakamataas na Antas na Natapos o Tinanggap na titulo	Saklaw na Petsa ng Pagpasok	Karangalan o Katangiang Natamo
A. Paaralang Elementarya			

B. Mataas/Bokasyonal na Paaralan

K. Kolehiyo/ Pamantasan

D. Pag-aaral na Graduwado

---

10. Iba Pang Pagsasanay

Isama ang lahat na pagsasanay sa-gawain at dinaluhang seminar, tanging pag-aaral, at iskolarship na tinamo.

Uri-Pangalan	Saan	Kailan	Bilang ng Oras ng Pagsasanay

11. Karapatang Mahirang sa Serbisyyo Sibil

Isama ang pagsusulit sa *bar* o board. Gayundin, isunod matapos maisulat ang markang natamo sa pagsusulit kung (E) entrance o bago, (Q) qualifying o kalipikatibo, (P) promosyonal, (T) testimonyal o (VP) *veteran* preference o karapatan sa pagiging beterano.

Pangalan ng Pagsusulit	Saan	Markang Natamo	Petsa ng Pagsusulit

12. Natatanging Kasanayan: ....

....

13. Iba Pang Natatanging Kakayahan: (nalathalang aklat, isinulat na artikulo o mga gawad na tinanggap.

....

....

14. Para sa layunin ng Seksiyon 30,, Batas ng Republika Blg. 2260, ikaw ba ay may kaugnayan sa dugo o angkan ng humihirang o nagrerekomenda, na puno ng kawanihan o tanggapan o taong kagyat na mamamahala sa iyo? ☐ Oo ☐ Hindi. Kung "oo", ibigay ang sumusunod na impormasyon.

Pangalan ng Kamag-anak	Kaugnayan	Katungkulan	Tanggapan/ Sangay

15. Ikaw ba ay naparatangan, isinakdal o nilitis sa paglabag sa batas, kautusang bayan, o tuntunin sa alinmang hukuman o kapulungan? ☐ Oo ☐ Hindi. Ikaw ba ay pinaratangan o nilitis sa anumang paglabag sa disiplinang militar, pandagat, o konstabularya sa alinmang kapulungang militar, pandagat o konstabularya o nalapatan na nang disiplinang administratibo? ☐ Oo ☐ Hindi. Kung ang kasagutan sa alinmang katanungan ay "oo", ibigay ang mga partikular na bagay sa ibaba.

16. Talaan ng Paglilingkod — Isama ang karanasan sa paglilingkod sa pamahalaan at/o pribadong bahay kalakal.

Petsang Nasasaklaw ng Paglilingkod	Katungkulan	Taunang Sahod	Pangalan ng Tanggapan Bahay Kalakal	Uri ng Pagkakahirang

17. Ikaw ba ay itiniwalag na sa anumang paglilingkod? ☐ Oo ☐ Hindi o sapilitang pinagbitiw maliban sa kakulangan ng gawain o pondo? ☐ Oo ☐ Hindi o nagpahinga sa paglilingkod? ☐ Oo ☐ Hindi. Kung ang kasagutan ay "oo" sa alinmang katanungan, ipaliwanag sa ibaba.

18. Kasalukuyang kinaaanibang organisasyon, kapisanan, o lipunan:

19. Hilig at libangan

Pinatutunayan ko na ang inilahad kong kasagutan sa itaas ay totoo at pawang tama sa abot ng aking nalalaman at paniniwala.

(Lagda) ....
Bilang ng Sedula ....
Kinuha sa ....
noong ....

Nilagdaan at pinanumpaan sa harap ko

....
(Pinunong Tagapagtalaga)

....
Petsa ....

Republika ng Pilipinas
Kagawaran ng Edukasyon
TANGGAPAN NG KALIHIM

TALATUNTUNAN

SA	*UPANG*
——— Kalihim	——— Pagtibayin o Lagdaan
——— Pangalawang Kalihim	——— Pasiyahan
——— Pinunong Pampangasiwaan	——— Aksiyunan
——— Sangay ng Pagtutuos	——— Inisyalan
——— Pambansang Lupon sa Edukasyon	——— Pulong
——— Lupon sa Saligang-Aklat	——— Pansinin at Magtagubilin
——— Sangay ng Badyet at Pananalapi	——— Tupdin
——— Pangkat ng Kas at Ari-arian	——— Itala
——— Tagapag-ugnay ng mga Suliraning Kultural at Iskolarsip	——— Patunayan
——— Tagapag-ugnay ng mga Kolehiyong Pampamahalaan	——— Sagutin
——— Sangay ng Pagpapianong Pang-edukasyon	——— Sinupin
——— Sangay ng Kastila at Kultura	——— Impormasyon
——— Lingkuran sa Audit Panloob	———————
——— Pangkat ng Pagsisiyasat	———————
——— Pangkat Pantauhan	
——— Pangkat ng Kasulatan	
——— Kalupunang Teknikal	
——— G./Bb./Gng. ———	

Republika ng Pilipinas
Kagawaran ng Edukasyon
SURIAN NG WIKANG PAMBANSA

TALATUNTUNAN

SA	*UPANG*
——— Tanggapan ng Patnugot	——— Aklatin
——— Tanggapan ng Pang. Patnugot	——— Aksiyunan
——— Sangay ng Pananaliksik	——— Baguhin
——— Sangay Pampangasiwaan	——— Basahin ang pruweba
——— Pangkat ng Pagsusuring Aklat	——— Klipin
——— Pangkat ng Aghamwika	——— Editin
——— Aklatan	——— Hanapin
——— Kaha	——— Ikintal-Tinig
——— Pagtutuos	——— Igawa ng burador
——— Panustos	——— Inisyalan
——— Kasulatan	——— Ipadala
	——— Isalin
	——— Istensilin
	——— Itala
	——— Iwasto
	——— Lagdaan
	——— Mabatid
	——— Makipagkita sa akin
	——— Makinilyahin/Sipiin (.......... sipi)
	——— Mimeograpin
	——— Magtagubilin
	——— Pabalatan
	——— Padalhan ng lathala
	——— Pag-aralan
	——— Pagtibayin
	——— Pahalagahan
	——— Pansinin
	——— Pasiyahan.
	——— Sagutin
	——— Saliksikin
	——— Sinupin
	——— Sulatan
	——— Sumulat ng artikulo/balita
	——— Suriin at punahin
	——— Ulitin
	——— Gawin ang nararapat

PAKIUSAP

....

....

....

....

....

....

Mula kay ....

Petsa: .... 196 .....

——— Paglilipat
Kagawaran ng Edukasyon
TANGGAPAN NG KALIHIM

...., 19 ....

Magalang na Ibinabalik/itinutukoy sa:

—— Patnugot, KPB (BPS)	—— pinagtibay, maliban sa pasubali ng mga alituntuning umiiral.
—— Patnugot, KPP (BPrS)	—— pinagtibay, maliban sa mga aytem: ____________
—— Patnugot, KEP (BVE)	—— di-pinagtibay.
—— Patnugot. SWP (INL)	—— upang sundin.
—— Patnugot, PA (Nat'l. Library)	—— upang mabatid at maging patnubay.
—— Patnugot, PM (Nat'l. Museum)	—— upang isagawa.
—— Tagapangulo, PKP (NHC)	—— upang lapatan ng kaukulang hakbang.
	—— upang sundin na may kalakip ng hinihiling na impormasyon/kailangan/materyal.

Tungkol sa (T.s.): Kalihim

....

....

Republika ng Pilipinas
Kagawaran ng Pagtuturo
SURIAN NG WIKANG PAMBANSA
Maynila

SOBRE NG SAHOD

Pangalan ....

Panahong Saklaw ....

Sahod .... ₱..................

MGA BINAWAS:

Prima sa Retiro .... ₱..................

Prima sa Siguro ....

Utang sa sahod ....

Binawas na Buwis ....

Dagdag na Siguro ....

Utang sa Ari-ariang-
Di-Matitinag ....

Utang sa Polisa ....

IBA PANG BINAWAS::

....

....

KABUUANG BINAWAS .... ₱..................

HALAGANG
TATANGGAPIN .... ₱..................

Pagkatanggap ng sobreng ito'y suriin ang nilalaman at ipagbigay-alam ang ano mang kamalian, kung mayroon; ang pagkukulang sa hakbang na ito'y mangangahulugan ng kawalang-kapanagutan ng Kahero at Tagapagbayad.

050265